FOURTH EDITION

Fundamentals of Teaching English to Speakers of Other Languages

in K-12 Mainstream Classrooms

Eileen Whelan Ariza
Florida Atlantic University—Boca Raton

Noorchaya Yahya
King Saud University in Riyadh, Saudi Arabia

Hanizah Zainuddin
Florida Atlantic University—Boca Raton

Carmen A. Morales-Jones
Retired, Florida Atlantic University—Boca Raton

Ancillary Materials Provided by Linda M. Gerena

Kendall Hunt
publishing company

Cover image © Shutterstock, Inc. Used under license.

Kendall Hunt
publishing company

www.kendallhunt.com
Send all inquiries to:
4050 Westmark Drive
Dubuque, IA 52004-1840

DEDICATION

We wish to dedicate this book to all the children who, for many reasons, become English language learners in our schools. It is our strong belief that they deserve the most qualified teachers possible. This book is our contribution to the training of teachers who will make a positive difference in the lives of these children, who in turn will significantly influence the future of this great nation.

The Authors

CONTENTS

Foreword   ix
Preface   xi
Acknowledgments   xvi
About the Authors   xvii
About the Contributors   xviii

Part One: Multicultural Issues in Teaching English as a New or Second Language   1

1. Multicultural Education, *Susanne I. Lapp*   3
2. Culture in the Classroom, *Eileen N. Whelan Ariza*   13
3. Language Determines Culture, *Eileen N. Whelan Ariza*   17
4. Examining American Values, *Eileen N. Whelan Ariza*   21
5. Culture Shock: Reaction to an Unfamiliar Environment, *Eileen N. Whelan Ariza*   25
6. Differences in Verbal Communication, *Eileen N. Whelan Ariza*   31
7. Nonverbal Communication, *Eileen N. Whelan Ariza*   37
8. Teaching and Learning Styles: A Reflection of Cultural Backgrounds, *Eileen N. Whelan Ariza*   43
9. Cultural Implications for Refugees, Immigrants, and English Learners in the United States, *Eileen N. Whelan Ariza*   49
10. A Rainbow of Children: A Sampler of Cultural Characteristics, *Eileen N. Whelan Ariza*   55
11. Interesting Insights and Cultural Facts, *Eileen N. Whelan Ariza*   79

Part Two: Principles and Practices in Language Teaching   81

12. Teaching for Communication, *Carmen A. Morales-Jones*   83
13. Methods/Approaches of Teaching ESOL: A Historical Overview, *Caitlin McHugh and Eileen Whelan Ariza*   91
14. Principles of Communicative Language Teaching, *Hanizah Zainuddin and Caitlin McHugh*   107

Part Three: Organizing and Planning for New or Second Language Instruction 125

15. Integrating Language and Content, *Carmen A. Morales-Jones and Caitlin McHugh* 127

16. Curriculum Design and Day-to-Day English Language Instruction, *Carmen A. Morales-Jones and Eileen Whelan Ariza* 135

Part Four: Development and Instruction of Language Skills for English Language Learners (ELLs) 159

17. English Language Listening Development and Instruction, *Noorchaya Yahya* 161

18. English Language Oral Development and Instruction, *Noorchaya Yahya* 181

19. English Language Vocabulary Development and Instruction, *Noorchaya Yahya* 203

20. English Language Learners' Reading Development and Instruction, *Maria Coady and Eileen Whelan Ariza* 223

21. English Language Learners' Writing Development and Instruction, *Hanizah Zainuddin and Maria Coady* 261

22. Teaching Grammar to English Learners in the Mainstream Classroom, *Linda Gerena* 295

Part Five: Teaching ESOL through the Content Areas 305

23. New Standards and Teachers of Today, *Eileen Whelan Ariza and Katee Anderson* 307

24. Effective Strategies for Teaching Mathematics to English Language Learners (ELLs), *Joe Furner* 317

25. Teaching and Learning through the Arts: Strategies for English Language Learners (ELLs), *Susannah Brown* 343

26. Teaching Science to English Language Learners, *Joan Lindgren and Julie Lambert* 355

27. Social Studies from a Global Perspective: Effective Pedagogy for English Language Learners, *Toni Fuss Kirkwood-Tucker and E. Andy Brewer* 375

28. Special Education and the Linguistically Diverse Student, *Cynthia Wilson and Margarita Bianco* 385

29. Using Technology with English Learners, *Susanne I. Lapp, Sherrie Sacharow, and Renee Zelden* 405

Appendix A. Tying it All Together: Tools for the Teacher, *Agostina Mittone*   421
Appendix B. ESOL Instructional Strategies Matrix   449
Appendix C. Lesson Plan: The Water Cycle   453
Appendix D. Student Data Tracking and Graphing   471
Appendix E. *Charlie and the Chocolate Factory*   483
References   505
Index   547

FOREWORD

Every year I work with hundreds of dedicated and talented K–12 teachers who know their subject matter well—whether it be math, language arts, science, history, art, social studies, or physical education—but face classes that contain more and more English language learners (ELLs). The average native speaking teacher today is not equipped to teach math or social studies to non-native students. As a result, these teachers, as well as education majors training to be future teachers, need assistance to educate these learners.

The population of non-native speakers in K–12 classrooms is increasing, yet states are allocating fewer resources and staff to address the specific needs of this growing group. Most teachers are native speakers of English, so it is difficult for them to appreciate the true dimensions of the language plight of ELLs in their classes. To effectively work with these learners, teachers need specific ideas for making their subject content accessible to all students.

In this new edition of their *Fundamentals of Teaching English to Speakers of Other Languages in K–12 Mainstream Classrooms,* the talented authors admirably meet this goal. Their book provides theoretical frameworks for working with ELLs in content areas, but the bulk of their writing is directed at specific teaching strategies and methods. In fact, I would say the biggest strength of this book is that it gives solid information on real techniques teachers can use in their classrooms from the beginning stages of language acquisition. In sum, the information is *practical*.

Part One helps teachers understand and appreciate their own culture better so that they can then better recognize the differences between their culture and that of their students. I lived and taught outside the United States for eleven years in four countries. There were so many things about the United States that I had never contemplated at all until I was living abroad. Seeing life on a daily basis in Saudi Arabia, Malaysia, Japan, and Kuwait highlighted American values and nonverbal communication differences. By reading and studying Part One, teachers can empathize with their ELLs who are living in a new land.

Part Two discusses the various methods and approaches that our field has developed for teaching English to non-native speakers. By default, today's K–12 teachers are often the sole source of English input for our ELLs, so all teachers need to be aware of communicative language teaching techniques so that in-class activities in science or history classes actually serve as beneficial sources of English input.

Part Three deals with curriculum and lesson planning. New teachers will learn how to organize a lesson plan, and experienced teachers will gain ideas for how to incorporate accommodations for their ELLs.

In **Part Four**, these authors address specific language skills that are important for academic success, including listening, speaking, vocabulary, reading, writing, and grammar. One chapter in Part Four of this fourth edition deals specifically with teaching grammar. It is extremely important for all teachers to be aware of some of the unique grammatical errors that ELLs make. Teachers who are aware of these problems can know which problems are expected and which skills may take students longer to master. Furthermore, teachers who know that certain grammatical areas, such as prepositions, are naturally problematic to the very end, will perhaps then not be distracted by these errors when assessing ELLs' papers. This section is especially important for teachers because the chapters here explain how social studies and science teachers can teach their subjects while including work on English language skills.

Finally, **Part Five** addresses specific questions applying standards in teaching ELLs in different content areas, including math, music, drama, art, science, social studies, special education, and technology. I know teachers are most interested in information specific to their individual classroom subjects and will therefore greatly appreciate this last part of the book.

I commend the authors of this work for their ability to present such valuable information in accessible language. With their combined years of teaching experience in a variety of classroom settings, the authors have written a truly practical work that will benefit teachers and their students for years to come.

Keith Folse, PhD
Professor, TESOL
University of Central Florida

PREFACE

The ongoing feverish debates concerning education of English learners as well as native English speakers have taken the spotlight in many school districts and governmental chambers across the country. Currently, the most popular refrain we hear is that academic failure of the students is the fault of the teacher, who becomes the scapegoat for everything that contributes to the lack of academic success. These negative factors could be lack of English proficiency, or underdeveloped literacy skills, poor or inappropriate parenting skills at home, the students' lack of self-discipline, involvement with gang activity, drug use, poverty, learning disabilities, or any other social problem with which the student comes to school that might adversely affect academic success. In their quest to raise standardized test scores, legislators try to link poor academic performance with faculty pay reductions, penalization by dismissal, and loss of school funding, especially to those schools that need funding the most. The recent national sweep of better, more rigorous standards for all learners so they will be prepared for college and the work force has taken the country in a storm. For our part, we, as instructors, understand the profound issues relating to the English learner in the mainstream classroom, and have gathered collectively to make our books as pertinent and timely as possible for teachers to use as accurate resources in their everyday classroom routines. We know it is crucial to update our knowledge, research, skills, and instructional styles to keep abreast of the flow of constantly changing information in the field. In this book, we have tried to include the most pertinent and appropriate material to make the mainstream teachers' instructional delivery more current and applicable to the specifics needed for today's classroom.

Fundamentals of Teaching English to Speakers of Other Languages in K–12 Mainstream Classrooms, Fourth Edition, helps teachers effectively educate ELLs in their classrooms by providing appropriate methodology to improve English and academic content proficiency. In addition, we provide a vehicle for the understanding of ELLs' cultural background, so that teachers can provide more effective instruction and comprehension,.

Organization

Fundamentals of Teaching English to Speakers of Other Languages in K–12 Mainstream Classrooms is organized into five parts.

Part One defines the term *multicultural education* and provides ideas for modifying classroom instruction by incorporating multicultural components into the curriculum. This section also offers the reader valuable insights into how variations in cultures do not necessarily indicate deficiencies in the learners' experiences but provide the knowledge base for teachers to comprehend the multifaceted nature of culture in language learning and teaching.

Two additional sections provide valuable information about cultural characteristics of specific cultural groups, such as Spanish, Islamic, and Arabic speakers; Haitian students; Asian Americans; and Native Americans. We also provide "Interesting Insights" about beliefs that signify good and bad luck in specific cultures.

Part Two gives a brief overview of first and second/new language acquisition theories with specific examples to clarify each. The impact of Stephen Krashen's five hypotheses on the field of English language teaching is highlighted. In addition, this section exposes the reader to the historical development of methods of teaching English to speakers of other languages (TESOL) and how that applies to classrooms of today. The theoretical underpinnings of the communicative language teaching approach are discussed. Salient aspects in planning classroom tasks that are communicative in nature are emphasized. Specific ideas and examples for teaching English to speakers of other languages (ESOL) from a communicative perspective are described and discussed. This section ends with a discussion on the paradigm shift in grammar instruction and the benefits of teaching grammar with a communicative focus.

Part Three emphasizes the integration of language and content when planning for English language instruction. Capitalizing on the importance of teaching English from a communicative perspective, various integration approaches are described. In addition, this section provides a framework for planning interdisciplinary, content-based thematic units of instruction. Each step provides examples taken from actual units. Bloom's taxonomy, including helpful tables, is introduced and discussed in detail. Gardner's model of multiple intelligences is also discussed at length. A wealth of ideas for activities to employ in developing multiple intelligences using Gardner's model are provided.

Part Four explores research and its application for teaching listening, speaking, reading, and writing skills to English language learners (ELLs). Specific examples of activities to employ for teaching as well as ways to assess listening and speaking are described in respective chapters. One chapter is devoted to the teaching of vocabulary, complete with specific suggestions for teaching vocabulary for multiple levels of proficiency. Two chapters of this section give a description of the historical movements and perspectives on first and second/new language reading and writing research. These chapters also stress the close connection between reading and writing and offer a variety of instructional strategies for multiple-level learners that facilitate the development of various language arts skills and critical thinking in content-based learning. This section includes discussion of a variety of reading and writing assessments, including students' self-assessment of their attitudes and strategies for learning to read and write.

Part Five addresses teaching ESL/ENL through specific content areas. Beginning with a chapter on the Common Core State Standard and ELLs, this segment is written by content area experts and provides the reader with a rationale for teaching ESOL through the content area as well as a wealth of concrete ideas on how to do so.

These ideas are of significant value for teachers who are seeking specific ways to teach ESOL in content areas such as art, music, drama, science, social studies, and mathematics. In addition, Part Five contains a chapter on addressing the needs of the exceptional education English language learner with helpful insights for the exceptional student educator. A chapter devoted to using technology with English learners is included and we conclude with a chapter of authentic teacher-made materials and documents that teachers need to consider in the current educational climate.

New to this Edition

Throughout this fourth edition, we have made revisions to update knowledge and references, incorporate information concerning the Common Core State Standards, and include the latest information about today's concerns, such as climate change in science, math proficiency, and technological literacy. The cultural information formerly found in the appendix is now attached to the cultural section at the front of the book. Throughout the book, citations and charts have been updated, as well as information on proficiency standards for classroom instruction and assessment. More resources, topics, and strategies are included for teachers to utilize in their classes. The technology chapter has been updated to include the use of recent (albeit quickly changing) classroom technology for teachers and ELLs, and ways for teachers to align themselves with the phenomenon of social networking for use as instructional tools. Each chapter has suggested corresponding Internet sites, videos, and ancillary materials. To further help the reader, PowerPoint slides are available for each chapter, as well as test banks with multiple choice, true and false, and short essay questions, as well as interactive electronic material.

The beginning chapters have been updated with references, technology, and corresponding ancillary materials.

In Chapter 13, Caitlin McHugh added a section to each language learning method called **Main-**

stream Classroom Use. While it may be important to know the history of language learning methods for linguistics and language teachers, Caitlin thought it would be helpful for classroom teachers to read about ways to adapt these older and possibly outdated methods so they can be used in mainstream classes, according to the teacher's specific objective. By adding some examples of how these methods are/were used in language classrooms, she thought it would help to create a more friendly voice in the chapter and not just a history lesson.

Chapter 22, the grammar chapter by Linda Gerena, includes updated information on the Common Core State Standards (CCSS) and how they impact ELLs in mastering standard English language, grammar, and conventions. It includes updated references and a list of fifteen websites that will be of great use to teachers to make grammar teaching interactive, engaging, and enjoyable.

Chapter 23 is a new chapter devoted to understanding and implementing the Common Core State Standards while instructing ELLs and mainstream students in the same classroom. Eileen Whelan Ariza and Katee Anderson talk about approaches to planning for instruction using the CCSS. This new chapter is written from a teacher's perspective and describes how CCSS can be applied during instruction of English learners. It includes strategies and techniques that mainstream teachers can use for instruction of ELLs in the mainstream classroom.

Chapter 24 is teeming with updates that include visuals, manipulatives, and hands-on techniques to teach math to ELLs so that instruction meets the Common Core State Standards objectives. Joseph Furner is dedicated to making math comprehensible to all students, and believes that visuals and manipulatives are the key to helping ELLs understand math concepts.

In Chapter 25, Susannah Brown has written about teaching and learning through the arts. She offers solid evidence that the arts (dance, drama, music, visual art) encourage reading, writing, listening, and speaking proficiency. She shows us how a visual representation of skills plays an important role in language development. Susannah believes the arts encourage greater language proficiency and

that creativity reaches all specters of the multiple intelligences model.

Chapter 26 offers cutting edge knowledge in the business of science today. Lindgren and Lambert realize the great significance of climate change and other hot topics in science. They offer a myriad of information and techniques for teaching ELLs so that they can receive the most up-to-date instruction, and meet the objectives in science put forth by the Common Core State Standards.

In Chapter 27, Social Studies, Fuss Kirkwood-Tucker and Brewer have made substantial changes that simplify the text, update resources, create more efficient charts, streamline lessons, with revised reflections and points to consider.

In Chapter 28, Wilson and Bianco have made changes to their special education and the linguistically diverse student chapter which includes a discussion regarding the Individuals with Disabilities Education Act (IDEA) provision to allow states to discontinue use of discrepancy model for identifying individuals with LD, and instead, use response to intervention (RTI) criteria. References to new research are included as well as a discussion of the affective needs of culturally and linguistically diverse (CLD) gifted learners. They talk about how teachers can include differentiated instruction for CLD gifted learners. Additionally, two new tables illustrating interdisciplinary thematic units appropriate for CLD gifted learners are offered.

Chapter 29 is packed with ideas, aids, and strategies to use for elementary, middle, and high school students. Technology is a moving target and changes by the minute. Lapp, Sacharow, and Zelden talk about apps, mobile technology, social media, and other interesting and innovative ways to exploit the natural interest students show in technology for the purpose of furthering language learning gains.

The Appendix, *Tying it All Together: Tools for the Teacher,* is a new addition to the book. Agostina Mittone has compiled a number of materials that she has created that she uses in her classroom such as templates, organizational ideas, and differentiation charts that enhance and organize her teaching and classroom routines.

Pedagogy

The book's pedagogy is perhaps its best feature because it umbrellas several attractive features of the book that make it a reader-friendly text or a reference book.

❖ **Key Issues**

Each chapter opens with a list of important key issues, such as research, problems faced by ELLs, strategies and skills, and assessments that later are fully discussed in the chapter.

❖ **Classroom Vignettes**

The key issues are followed by a classroom vignette(s) that expose(s) readers to strategies and techniques of teaching language skills used by teachers. The narrative and illustrative features of the "real-life" scenarios allow readers to visualize the applications of important ideas used in classrooms.

❖ **Points to Remember**

They summarize and highlight the main ideas of the chapter, and conclude every chapter. This feature not only recycles, but also restates, the most important points in the chapter, making it easier for students to focus on the main issues in the chapter.

❖ **CD Workbook**

The CD contains a collection of challenge sheets. In every chapter, students are challenged to recall/research information from the text, apply their knowledge based on ideas given in the text, and to evaluate strategies and techniques presented in the text.

❖ **Applications and Activities**

The inclusion of instructional applications and/ or activities in each chapter offer preservice teachers specific ideas to incorporate in designing their own lessons.

❖ **Internet Resources**

Each chapter concludes with a list of Internet websites and videos that support the information in the chapter.

❖ **Ancillary Materials**

Each chapter offers PowerPoint slides and test banks of multiple choice, true/false, essay, and short answer questions.

Audience and Purpose

We wrote this book specifically for individuals who might not be trained to teach English learners, but would be de facto ESOL teachers in a mainstream classroom. The book offers a knowledge base to aid teacher effectiveness in today's classrooms, where students of multiple cultures and ethnic groups speak a variety of languages and learn through a range of styles. The general education teacher must know how to reach all students, regardless of the students' prior knowledge, home language, or cognitive capacity. Today's teachers are far more responsible for issues that were unheard of in earlier educational eras.

Teachers in our present society need to know how to teach critical content that is cognitively demanding yet modified to match the ability of the student's language proficiency. In addition to the multitude of tasks and traditional issues attended to by the classroom teacher, teachers must be skilled in offering alternative assessments as well as standardized assessments; know how to interpret the students' cultural background and prior educational and life experience; and offer affective comfort so that learning can take place in a nonthreatening environment. The responsibilities are immense.

In this book, we offer an inclusive overview of pertinent topics for teachers who are responsible for providing comprehensive instruction to all students. We discuss standards, culture, multicultural education, technology, exceptional education (both gifted and students with learning disabilities), art, music, drama, grammar that teachers need to know, and instructional strategies to present modified critical content.

The book covers the most salient aspects of teaching. It addresses multicultural education; cultural issues; language learning, and skills such as listening, speaking, reading, writing, and vocabulary; content area teaching such as math, social studies, art, science, technology, music, and drama; and the simultaneous teaching of subject matter content and language skills using scaffolding techniques.

Our primary goal for this book is to provide comprehensive information about English language learners for the purpose of helping all teachers, regardless of training, to acquire an in-depth knowledge of the issues vital to understanding and teaching English as a new or second language. Although we realize that ideas, instructional approaches, and technologies come and go at a rapid pace, in this fourth edition we seek to expose the readers to current practices and information in the field. We would love to hear the readers' comments.

Until the next edition, we wish you much success in your teaching journeys.

Sincerely,
The Authors

ACKNOWLEDGMENTS

The authors would like to thank all those involved in making this project come to fruition, especially those who have provided valuable comments on the earlier version of the manuscript.

ABOUT THE AUTHORS

EILEEN N. WHELAN ARIZA received her Ed.D. in Multilingual/Multicultural Education from the University of Massachusetts, Amherst, and M.A. in TESOL, M.A. in Spanish, and Bilingual/Multicultural Endorsement from the School for International Training in Brattleboro, Vermont. She spent several years as an award-winning teaching fellow at Harvard University's English Language Institute before transferring to Florida Atlantic University, where she also was honored with the Distinguished Teacher of the Year and Excellence in Undergraduate Teaching Awards. She is a professor of teaching and learning, and serves as the ESOL Coordinator for the College of Education. Her many publications include journals and bestselling books. From 2006–2009 she was the editor of TESOL International's member publication, *Essential Teacher*. A 2009 Fulbright Scholar to La Universidad de las Americas in Puebla, Mexico, Dr. Ariza was selected to be a Fulbright Alumni Ambassador and travels throughout the country to talk about her Fulbright experience. She just received her second Fulbright Award to the University of Costa Rica for Spring 2016. Frequently an invited speaker, she shares her lifetime experience in teaching and culture with ESOL teachers. She continues to travel, write, and appreciate the challenges of teaching how to teach ELLs.

NOORCHAYA YAHYA received her Ph.D. in Rhetoric and Linguistics from Indiana University of Pennsylvania. Currently, she is an Associate Professor at King Saud University in Riyadh, Saudi Arabia, where she teaches Linguistics. She has taught ESL for more than fifteen years at institutions of higher learning both inside and outside the United States. She was involved in the training of preservice teachers for ESOL endorsement and in-service teachers for ESOL certification in Florida. Her research interests lie in the areas of second language writing, teacher education, second language acquisition, and learners' motivation in second language learning.

HANIZAH ZAINUDDIN received her Ph.D. from Indiana University, Bloomington, Indiana, in 1995 and is currently an Associate Professor of TESOL at Florida Atlantic University, Boca Raton. Her areas of interest include second language writing, contrastive rhetoric, teacher education, assessment of English learners for special education services, and family literacy. She also has extensive experience teaching English as a second language to adults and adolescents inside and outside the United States. She currently supervises and offers ESOL endorsement training to teachers in the six counties served by FAU and has co-developed a Masters in TESOL and Bilingual Education at FAU with funds from Title III National Professional Development Program, U.S. Department of Education.

CARMEN A. MORALES-JONES received her Ph.D. in Curriculum and Integrative Studies from Florida State University, Tallahassee, Florida, in 1975. Her career encompasses the teaching of ESL and French at the Laboratory School of the University of Puerto Rico, as well as teacher training at Florida Atlantic University, Boca Raton, Florida. She has taught courses in the area of language acquisition such as methods of teaching language arts (for elementary education majors), methods of teaching foreign languages (for foreign language majors), and numerous courses in the field of teaching English as a new language. Currently, she is a retired professor from Florida Atlantic University, after a tenure of thirty-five years at this institution. Dr. Morales-Jones is a past president of Sunshine State TESOL (2004–2006). Also active in TESOL International, she served as co-chair for the poster sessions (TESOL /Tampa, 2006). In addition, she served as District V Director/Mu State (2004–2006) of Delta Kappa Gamma, a professional international organization for women educators.

ABOUT THE CONTRIBUTORS

KATEE ANDERSON received her Bachelors in Elementary Education at Florida Atlantic University and is currently working on her Masters in Elementary Education. For the last three years she has worked as a kindergarten dual language teacher in Palm Beach County, Florida. Her areas of interest include English as a second language in the mainstream classroom and specialized programs in public schools.

MARGARITA BIANCO, Ed.D., is an Associate Professor in the School of Education and Human Development at the University of Colorado Denver and Executive Director of Pathways2Teaching [http://www.Pathways2Teaching.com]. Her research interests include the underrepresentation of teachers of color and the underrepresentation of students of color and twice-exceptional learners in gifted programs. Professor Bianco is the recipient of several awards including the Outstanding Researcher Award from the Council for Learning Disabilities, University of Colorado Denver's Rosa Parks Diversity Award, the 2011 University of Colorado President's Diversity Award, and most recently the University of Colorado's 2012 Teaching Excellence Award.

SUSANNAH BROWN is an Associate Professor of Visual Art Education at Florida Atlantic University, College of Education, Department of Teaching and Learning. She has been teaching and inspiring students to discover their own creativity for twenty-four years. Prior to working at the university level for the last twelve years, she worked as the art educator at public elementary schools. Her areas of research include: arts integration, environmental art issues, and creative literacy development. She has published a book, articles in scholarly journals, and contributed book chapters on her research interests of the importance of the arts in education, professional development in the field of the arts and education, and arts integration. A professional visual artist in painting, printing, and ceramics, she exhibits her work in juried exhibitions throughout Florida.

E. ANDY BREWER is the Associate Director for Academic and Assessment Support for the Department of Teaching and Learning in Florida Atlantic University's College of Education. Prior to this position he served as Social Studies Education Program Coordinator at Florida Atlantic University from 2006 to 2007 and as Acting Social Studies Education Coordinator from 2007 to 2013. Formerly, Dr. Brewer taught fifth and sixth grades in Florida's public schools. He has co-authored one book and authored articles in scholarly journals on his research interests: the content knowledge of elementary social studies teachers, integration in the social studies, and character education.

MARIA COADY, Ph.D., is an Associate Professor of ESOL at the University of Florida. She began her career in Paris, France, as an EFL teacher, and has subsequently taught English and Spanish in the United States and abroad. Dr. Coady's research includes cross language transfer in writing of Spanish-speaking students; building home–school partnerships with immigrant families; and preservice ESOL teacher preparation. She is a Fulbright Specialist Scholar and English Language Fellow with the U.S. Department of State and an Associate Editor of the first TESOL Encyclopedia.

JOSEPH M. FURNER, Ph.D., is a Professor of Mathematics Education in the Department of Teaching and Learning at Florida Atlantic University in Jupiter, Florida. He received his Bachelor's degree in Education from the State University of New York at Oneonta and his Masters and Ph.D. in Curriculum and Instruction and Mathematics Education from the University of Alabama. His scholarly research relates to math anxiety, the implementation of the national and state standards, English language issues as they relate to math instruction, the use of technology in mathematics instruction, math manipulatives, family math, and children's literature in the teaching of mathematics. Dr. Furner is the founding editor of *Mathitudes Online* at: http://www.coe.fau.edu/centersandprograms/mathitudes/. He has worked as an educator in New York, Florida, Mexico, and Colombia. He is concerned with peace on earth and humans doing more to unite, live in Spirit, and to care for our Mother Earth and each other. He is the author of *Living Well: Caring Enough to Do What's Right*. Dr. Furner currently lives with his family in the city of Lake Worth, Florida. He enjoys his job, family, civic and church involvement, his beach, and his little city by the sea. Please feel free to write to him at: jfurner@fau.edu.

LINDA GERENA, Ph.D., is a Professor of Teacher Education at York College, City University of New York (CUNY), and a Fulbright Senior Scholar. Dr. Gerena received her Ph.D. in Educational Policy/Bilingual Education from San Diego State University, as well as an MATESOL degree from New York University (NYU), and an M.A. in Urban/Bilingual Education from California State University at Los Angeles. Her professional research interests include bilingualism, second language acquisition, dual immersion program development, effective practices in second language instruction, and Content and Language Integrated Learning (CLIL). She is dedicated to preparing highly qualified teachers who will provide effective instruction for linguistically and culturally diverse populations and who will be sensitive to issues related to social justice and providing culturally sensitive instruction for all students, especially linguistically and culturally diverse students.

In 2011, Dr. Gerena was awarded the prestigious Fulbright Senior Scholar Researcher Award, and was invited to the Autónoma University of Madrid in 2012 as a guest professor and researcher. As a Fulbright Senior Scholar and visiting professor at the Autónoma, Dr. Gerena was a guest lecturer on second language acquisition theory and practice, effective methodology in the CLIL classroom. In addition, as a Senior Fulbright Researcher, Dr. Gerena conducted research on bilingual program develop-

ment in Spain, and focused on bilingual program implementation in Madrid's public school system. In 2013, as a U.S. State Department English Language Specialist, Dr. Gerena developed and implemented bilingual teacher professional development training seminars in the Extremadura and Castilla-La Mancha provinces in Spain. Her background and research can be viewed at: https://www.york.cuny.edu/portal_college/lgerena

TONI FUSS KIRKWOOD-TUCKER, Ed.D., is Associate Professor Emerita in Social Studies and Global Education from Florida Atlantic University and Visiting Professor at Florida State University. Her primary scholarship includes seminal publications on the role of global education and pedagogy in teacher education programs and schools, criticality of teaching from a global perspective, and empirical research on the *worldmindedness* of graduating high school seniors and teacher candidates.

SUSANNE LAPP is an Associate Professor of Reading/Language Arts, and was the Director of Undergraduate Programs for Teacher Education—both at Florida Atlantic University. She holds a doctorate in Curriculum and Instruction from the University of Cincinnati in Cincinnati, Ohio. Prior to joining the faculty at Florida Atlantic, she taught reading and language arts at the University of Texas-Pan American. Her research interests include multicultural literacy, educational technology, and assessment.

JULIE LAMBERT, Ph.D., is Professor of Science and Environmental Education at Florida Atlantic University. Her Ph.D. is in science education, and her M.S. degree is in biological oceanography. She was an earth and space science teacher in Virginia, and authored a high school marine science textbook titled *Life on an Ocean Planet*. Lambert is Principal Investigator (PI) on a NASA-funded grant on climate change education programs to develop Climate Science Investigations (CSI): South Florida curriculum for high school and undergraduate students. Her objectives are to help students learn to analyze scientific data and address skeptics' questions and general misconceptions about climate change. She also is co-PI on another NASA-funded project to provide professional development for teachers in Ventura County, California. She is currently interested in evidence-based scientific argumentation to help ELLs develop a deeper understanding of climate science.

JOAN LINDGREN, currently retired, was Associate Professor at Florida Atlantic University in the Department of Teacher Education in Science Education. She received her Ph.D. from the University of Florida in 1993 in Curriculum and Instruction and then taught at Frostburg State University in Maryland from 1994 to 1998. She was a classroom teacher in Florida from 1977 to 1994 and had also worked as a bilingual teacher in Stockholm, Sweden, and in the Peace Corps, Philippines, in the early part of her career. Her research interests include the examination of self-efficacy beliefs of preservice teachers, gender issues in science education, and strategies for improving the learning of science for all students. She has a special interest in working with second language learners to determine how they learn and understand science. She also has a strong interest in climate change research and teaching about climate change.

CAITLIN MCHUGH has a Master's degree in Applied Linguistics from the Universidad de Las Americas Puebla where she focused on bilingual education and dual-language programs. She also has Bachelor's degrees in Elementary Education and Spanish from Saint Michael's College. She is currently teaching English as a Second Language at an American school in Mexico. Her research interests include bilingual educational theory and first/second language acquisition.

AGOSTINA CHIARA MITTONE received her Bachelor's degree in Political Science from Queens College, New York. She began her career by owning and operating a group family day care in Queens, New York. She relocated to Florida to teach, and will graduate in December 2014 with her Master's degree in Elementary Education. Currently she teaches second grade at Championship Academy of Distinction in Hollywood, Florida, and plans to pursue a second Master's degree in Leadership.

SHERRIE SACHAROW received her M.S. in TESOL from Nova Southeastern University and is currently a doctoral candidate in Curriculum and Instruction at Florida Atlantic University (ABD). She is an instructor at Broward College where she teaches grammar, writing, and conversation. Ms. Sacharow taught in the TESOL teacher education program for several years at FAU and her areas of interest include instructional technology, policy, and educational media for language learners.

CYNTHIA L. WILSON, Ph.D., received her Ph.D. from Florida State University in 1988 and is currently a Professor in the Department of Exceptional Student Education at Florida Atlantic University. Her research and instructional focus emphasizes the preparation of educators to implement research-based, effective practices to improve educational opportunities for special education students, exceptional learners from culturally and linguistically diverse backgrounds, and students at risk for academic failure. Dr. Wilson has been the Department Chair, the Director of the Genesis Teacher Education Project, and the recipient of the Florida Atlantic University Award for Excellence in Undergraduate Teaching. She is co-author of the book *Leadership from the Ground Up: Effective Schooling in Traditionally Low Performing Schools*; has authored/co-authored numerous book chapters and journal articles; served as principal/co-principal investigator of federal, state, and local grants; and has presented papers at international, national, regional, and state conferences.

RENEE ZELDEN was awarded an M.S. in TESOL from Nova Southeastern University and is an instructor at Miami-Dade College and Broward College where she teaches college English, grammar, writing, conversation, and TOEFL preparation. She is currently Academic Coordinator at FIU Global First Year. Her areas of interest include teacher training, reading, technology, study skills, and standardized test preparation.

Multicultural Issues in Teaching English as a New or Second Language

chapter 1

Multicultural Education, 3
SUSANNE I. LAPP

chapter 2

Culture in the Classroom, 13
EILEEN N. WHELAN ARIZA

chapter 3

Language Determines Culture, 17
EILEEN N. WHELAN ARIZA

chapter 4

Examining American Values, 21
EILEEN N. WHELAN ARIZA

chapter 5

Culture Shock: Reaction to an
Unfamiliar Environment, 25
EILEEN N. WHELAN ARIZA

chapter 6

Differences in Verbal
Communication, 31
EILEEN N. WHELAN ARIZA

chapter 7

Nonverbal Communication, 37
EILEEN N. WHELAN ARIZA

chapter 8

Teaching and Learning Styles:
A Reflection of Cultural
Backgrounds, 43
EILEEN N. WHELAN ARIZA

chapter 9

Cultural Implications for Refugees,
Immigrants, and English Learners in the
United States, 49
EILEEN N. WHELAN ARIZA

1

chapter 10

A Rainbow of Children: A Sampler
of Cultural Characteristics, 55

EILEEN N. WHELAN ARIZA

chapter 11

Interesting Insights and Cultural
Facts, 79

EILEEN N. WHELAN ARIZA

chapter 1

Multicultural Education

KEY ISSUES
- ❖ Multicultural education
- ❖ Goals of multicultural education
- ❖ Negative cultural diversity
- ❖ Multicultural curriculum

Student–student collaboration in multicultural setting

It's 5 p.m. on a Friday evening. Fall semester is over, and Alex and Gregory, two teacher education students, have just turned in their final language arts project to their professor. The halls of the university seem deserted except for the interesting sounds and unfamiliar chatter coming from the large reception room at the end of the hall. Rhythmic music, laughter, and the delicious smell of exotic food beckon Alex and Gregory to peer inside the room. To their surprise, they discover approximately twenty international students gathered in the room for an end-of-year party. Through the crowd of students, they identify a familiar face. Fan, a classmate from their statistics class, appears and invites them to come in and join the party. The university Multicultural Club is celebrating the end of finals and the beginning of the summer break. Although everyone appears very happy, Alex and Gregory are hesitant. Both Alex and Gregory's families have been in the United States for several generations, and therefore they have never identified themselves as being multicultural. Alex explains to Fan that neither of the young men feels like he could fit into the club. Fan laughs out loud and tells her friends that they would fit perfectly into the club, "If you two guys are going to be schoolteachers you better start learning as much as you can about multicultural issues!"

Defining Multicultural Education

The notion of multicultural education is to encourage individuals to become aware of themselves, their cultural group, and their place in the world at large, while at the same time acknowledging and appreciating other cultures. Banks and Banks (2009) define multicultural education as the:

1. Creation of equal educational opportunities for students from diverse racial, ethnic, social class, and cultural groups;
2. Acquisition of knowledge, attitudes, and skills needed to function effectively in a pluralistic democratic society; and
3. Interaction, negotiation, and communication with peoples from diverse groups to create a civic and moral community that works for the common good.

Multicultural individuals maintain an appreciation of their culture while developing an appreciation of other cultures. Becoming aware of oneself, one's culture, and/or other cultures provides an effective formula for functioning successfully within the larger society.

The two young men featured in the preceding vignette needed to understand that multicultural education and awareness are not merely associated with individuals from other countries, but are also integral to their own personal development and their relationships to other individuals and society as a whole. As future teachers, it is essential that Alex and Gregory develop greater multicultural sensitivity and awareness because their classrooms will increasingly reflect the multicultural, multilingual nature of our diverse society.

Background of Multicultural Education

Banks and Banks (2010) state that multicultural education embraces the notion that all Americans have come from many races and ethnic groups and that these individuals and groups have helped to create and establish the United States. As a result, their contributions must be welcomed and celebrated, and these individuals must feel represented in America.

Banks' philosophy on multicultural education rings true, as researchers predict that the minority population will continue to increase. Currently in U.S. public schools, Hispanics are the largest and fastest growing ethnic minority. By 2020, Hispanics are projected to represent 27 percent of the U.S. population under five years of age. English language learners (ELLs) are the fastest growing student population in the United States, 82 percent of which report Spanish as the language most often spoken at home.

The increased population of Hispanics in the United States has also affected educational institutions. Olszewski-Kubilius and Clarenbach (2014) found that children who come from cultural and linguistic minority backgrounds often flounder in school. Unfortunately, according to the 2011 National Assessment of Educational Progress, only 29 percent of eighth grade ELLs perform "at or above basic" in reading levels, compared with 78 percent of their non-ELL counterparts (Snyder & Dillow, 2012). This statistic follows students as they enter high school and as young adults, they are inadequately prepared for higher education or for all but unskilled employment. Despite these rather low numbers, more than 80 percent of Hispanics believe that it is crucial for immigrants to learn to speak English.

As the demographics of American society change and educators begin to instruct students from diverse language and literacy communities, they must also be prepared to handle any negative reaction to cultural diversity. Negative cultural diversity occurs when individuals and groups regard each other suspiciously. This negative reaction to cultural diversity creates an unhealthy social dynamic with both dominant and subordinate cultures competing for economic, social, and political power.

To guard against negative cultural diversity, teachers must encourage all students to understand that cultural diversity means that societal groups coexist in harmony. All people should feel that they have equal access to the resources of the nation (civil rights, political power) and they must feel that they are represented equally. Everyone regards the other person with tolerance and appreciation of individual differences.

Creating a Multicultural Curriculum

The classroom environment should strive to be a place where children learn to become more tolerant individuals and members of society. As a result, the American multicultural mosaic must be reflected appropriately in instructional materials and school life. Because of the changing demographics in American schools, teachers need to learn to appreciate and attend to the new voices, languages, and educational needs of their students.

Generally, classrooms in the United States have made attempts at exposing students to multicultural themes by setting aside special days, weeks, and months to celebrate a variety of holidays and customs. Noteworthy in their efforts, teachers and administrators must strive to go beyond exposing students to short-term multicultural celebrations and instead strive to integrate multicultural themes into their everyday school curriculum.

Creating and establishing a multicultural curriculum, in many cases, involves reshaping the social climate of the school. Teachers and administrators must find effective ways to instill a multicultural atmosphere in the school. Recognition of deep cultural values (such as family values, health issues, family structures, and male/female roles) instead of the typical surface cultural values (such as clothing, music, and food) must be explored.

Multicultural curriculum should

❖ Establish a nonthreatening atmosphere for learning so that students can explore creative activities and succeed in school.
❖ Encourage students to become more culturally literate.
❖ Create a classroom atmosphere of equal opportunity for all students.

❖ Create an atmosphere of cultural diversity and positive attitudes for people from all backgrounds and cultures.

Additionally, schools must open their doors and welcome the support of parents and the school community. Involving parents and the school community helps to extend the goals of multicultural education (Banks & Banks, 2010).

Involvement of Parents and the School Community

Involving parents in the school community is an excellent way to establish bridges of communication between immigrant families and the school. Parents who feel welcomed into the school community will become more involved and engaged in their child's academic growth and development. Several strategies for establishing parent–school communication include

❖ Use language that parents can understand. School professionals need to remain courteous and sincere and provide parents with time and opportunities to share concerns about their child.
❖ Support parents' confidence in actively participating in their child's school experiences and help them realize that school success is possible.
❖ Initiate cross-cultural interaction and encourage parents and community members to explore new educational and academic ground.
❖ Send messages home in the parents' native language. Use an appropriate reading level that parents can understand.
❖ Encourage parents to integrate new information into their child-rearing practices and incorporate new ideas about education into their family networks.

❖ Multicultural education encourages individuals to become aware of themselves, their cultural group, and their place in the world at large, while at the same time acknowledging and appreciating other cultures.

❖ Multicultural education (Banks & Banks, 2010) is the:

1. Creation of equal educational opportunities for students from diverse racial, ethnic, social class, and cultural groups;

2. Acquisition of knowledge, attitudes, and skills needed to function effectively in a pluralistic democratic society; and

3. Interaction, negotiation, and communication with peoples from diverse groups to create a civic and moral community that works for the common good.

❖ Negative cultural diversity occurs when individuals and groups regard each other suspiciously, which creates an unhealthy social dynamic with dominant and subordinate cultures competing for economic, social, and political power.

❖ To discourage negative cultural diversity, students must understand that cultural diversity means that societal groups coexist in harmony.

❖ Schools must welcome the support of parents and the school community.

❖ Involvement of parents and the school community

1. Motivates cross-cultural interaction and encourage parents and community members to explore new education and academic ground.

2. Supports parents' confidence in actively participating in their students' school experiences and helps them realize that school success is possible.

3. Encourages parents to integrate new information into their child-rearing practices and incorporate new ideas about education into their family networks.

Sample Activities for the Multicultural Curriculum

Activity 1

Topic:

Our unique histories: "Quilts: Weaving together the story of our lives"

Age Level:

Pre-service elementary education teacher candidates working with elementary-age students on a family lineage project

Activity:

Students in intermediate level elementary classes are frequently requested to write essays or complete projects based on their ethnic and cultural backgrounds as a way to understand the world around them and their place within a diverse, global society. In this assignment, the pre-service teacher asks students in the fifth grade to listen to the story *The Keeping Quilt* (1988) by Patricia Polacco.

1. Once the story is completed, the pre-service teacher distributes a piece of blank 8 x 10 paper to each student. The paper is referred to as a quilting sample and the teacher has specific guidelines as to how the sample should be completed.
2. In each corner of the paper, the student is asked to list and then draw an example of how they relate to each of the categories.
3. The categories are:

    a. Top left corner: My favorite food
    b. Top right corner: My favorite place to vacation with my family
    c. Bottom right corner: My favorite hobby
    d. Bottom left corner: My cultural background/Where is my family from?
    e. The center of the paper contains a drawing of the student's family.

4. Students complete their quilting sample, and the pre-service teacher collects the samples, attaches them together, and creates a classroom quilt based on the students' cultural backgrounds.

Activity 2

Topic:

Learning from each other

Age Level:

Pre-service elementary education teacher candidates

Activity:

The professional responsibilities and experiences of parents from multicultural backgrounds play a significant role in family discussions and interactions. These experiences often impact children, who in turn bring these topics to the classroom. It is imperative that teachers seek innovative ways to bridge the students' home and school cultures. Classroom activities that encourage teachers to address these differences will make academic material more relevant to students.

1. Pre-service teachers will arrange to visit the homes of students to gain an understanding of their students' cultural backgrounds. Pre-service teachers will inform parents that they are interested in learning more about the family interests, jobs, or hobbies as a means for making academic material more relevant to the students.
2. Parents who express interest in this activity will be visited in their homes by pre-service teachers, who will use an interview protocol to interview parents. The interview should last between five and ten minutes, and the interview should focus on family interests, jobs, or hobbies.
3. Questions should be open ended; however, pre-service teachers should try to shape their questions by asking parents

   a. What types of hobbies/interests does your family share?
   b. Can you describe these hobbies/interests?
   c. What type of professional responsibilities do you have in your career?
   d. What are some important tasks that you must be aware of to be effective in your career?
   e. Do you enjoy the career that you have chosen?

4. Pre-service teachers should briefly summarize their interviewees' responses and share their findings with other pre-service teachers.

During one sharing session, a pre-service teacher described an interview she conducted with a parent who worked as a fisherman on a small fishing vessel. The pre-service teacher learned about the importance of ocean currents and weather forecasts (including temperature and tidal patterns and marine life). The pre-service teacher drew on the expertise of this parent and created a thematic science unit based on weather forecasting and oceans. Another pre-service teacher interviewed a parent who worked in a local bakery and was able to create a meaningful mathematics lesson on measuring. The interviewing activity helped pre-service teachers devise effective instructional approaches that were directly meaningful for their students.

Activity 3

Topic:

Using instructional conversations to develop student-text relationships

Age Level:

Pre-service elementary education teacher candidates

Activity:

Keene and Zimmerman (1997) conclude that students comprehend more effectively when they make personal connections to the text. These connections relate the reader's own life experiences to that of the reading material. This relationship helps to set a purpose and need for reading. By carefully and effectively guiding students to think about their personal connection to text, teachers help to set the stage for effective comprehension of the text.

Instructional conversation (Tharp, 1997) is a teaching approach that allows teachers to guide and facilitate student learning by helping them actively connect to reading material. Teachers help students use their own ideas and prior knowledge to make connections, build mental schemata, and develop new concepts from previous understandings. Students are encouraged to express their own ideas as they develop increasingly sophisticated levels of comprehension.

Elements of the Instructional Conversation:

1. The teacher selects a theme or book to focus the discussion and has a general plan for how the theme will unfold.
2. The teacher provides students with pertinent background knowledge necessary for understanding the text, and then carefully weaves that information into the discussion.
3. The teacher is sensitive to students' needs and provides direct teaching of a skill or concept if students are confused or uncertain about information within the text.
4. When necessary, the teacher encourages students to extend their contributions by asking them to expand, question, and restate their ideas.
5. Students are encouraged to use text, pictures, and reasoning to support a statement.
6. The instructional conversation has multiple, interactive, connected turns that build on previous comments, thus increasing the students' overall understanding and comprehension of the material.

chapter 2

Culture in the Classroom

KEY ISSUES ❖ Learning styles
❖ Cultural styles

Effects of culture in the classroom

Ms. Whelan chats with her colleagues in the front doorway of the bilingual colegio in Mayaguez, Puerto Rico, where she is doing her internship. The bell rings, and children charge noisily through the halls, each clamoring to be the first in line to go home. Marco, in his hurry to be first, accidentally slams his full weight into Ms. Whelan, almost knocking her down. Angrily, she admonishes him, "Can't you say 'excuse me' when you bump into someone?" He ignores her and just stands there looking at the floor. Even angrier because he ignores her, Ms. Whelan repeats her words, "Don't you know you are being rude? Excuse yourself when you bump into someone! Look at me when I am talking to you!" But Marco still keeps his head down, ignoring her outburst. Ms. Whelan leaves the school with a very bad impression of Marco's manners.

Sang Li has recently arrived from Korea and is assigned to Mrs. Cannon's class. Mrs. Cannon explains the activity the students are to do, and then asks, "Does everyone understand the assignment?" The students answer in unison, "Yes, Mrs. Cannon," and begin to work diligently. After a few minutes, the teacher notices that Sang Li is looking over Peter's shoulder and copying what he has written. She quickly says, "Sang Li! Do your own work. Cheating is not allowed!" Sang Li hangs his head and turns red with shame.

In the previous scenarios, each child is from a different culture, and each culture has different values. Nowhere is this more evident than in the classroom. In the first scenario, Marco does not say, "excuse me," because in his culture, it is impolite to look at an adult in the eyes when being chastised, and he is too ashamed to answer. The typical American child is raised hearing, "Look at me when I am talking to you," and is encouraged to look directly into the adult's eyes when spoken to. In the Puerto Rican and Haitian cultures (as well as others), children are taught to never look at an adult in the eyes, as it is a sign of insubordination.

In the second scenario, Sang Li is looking over Peter's shoulder to see how to do the assignment. Not only does Sang Li not understand the directions, but in Korea, students are expected to work together cooperatively.

By learning about students' cultures, the classroom teacher can provide better instruction because learning styles are directly related to cultural values. If teachers are aware of the values that individual cultures hold dear, they will be better equipped to reach and teach the diverse children in today's multicultural classrooms.

A Historical Overview of Culture

When research on culture and the phenomenon of culture shock became prominent in the 1950s, renowned researchers such as Edward Hall, Kalvero Oberg, and others launched their landmark findings that are benchmarks still referred to by scholars today. A more recent definition of culture was coined by Saravia-Shore and Arvizu (1992), who refer to "culture" as a "dynamic, creative, and continuous process that includes behaviors, values, and substance shared by people that guides them in their struggle for survival and gives meaning to their lives" (p. xviii). Others describe culture as an unconscious or conscious pattern of behaviors that reflects the societal beliefs and values shared by the people who are members of the group (Goodenough, 1981; Kohls, 2001; Saville-Troike, 1978).

When references are made to the word *culture*, people often think of the arts, music, and theater. When speaking of a person being "cultured," this description might be used when an individual likes opera, has good manners, and is well read. However, in this book, the reference to *culture* implies the learned behavior patterns and attitudes of people in their societies.

Oberg (1960) first explained culture as the "environment, which consists of man-made physical objects, social institutions, and ideas and beliefs." He also said that parents are not consciously responsible for the culture they transmit to their young. By means of this culture, "the young learn to adapt themselves to the physical environment, and to the people with whom they associate" (p. 180). After individuals learn their culture, it becomes a sure, familiar way of life, and they function automatically within this cultural system, using the appropriate actions to get what is desired from the environment. This process manifests itself as a "value" of that particular system.

Ethnocentrism

The term *ethnicity* refers to the sense of belonging to a cultural group. Tiedt and Tiedt (1998) explained that ethnicity includes the national or linguistic background with which the individual is affiliated. At this point, it is important to mention the problem of "stereotyping" individuals instead of "sociotyping" (Bennett, 1990; Bennett, 1993). According to Bennett (1993), stereotyping can happen when false and exaggerated characteristics of a group are attributed to the individual, but sociotyping involves an accurate generalization about cultural groups as a whole.

Oberg (1960) further explained that people accept their culture as the best and only way of doing things and that this attitude, called ethnocentrism, is normal and understandable. Being ethnocentric is presuming that one's culture, race, ways of life, and nations form the center of the world. Typically, individuals of any cultural entity identify strongly with the rest of the group, and when a negative comment is made against the group (or country, or family, and so on), the individual is indignant and takes the affront personally. It is this attitude that begets stereotypes, which is the tendency to attribute all individual peculiarities as national characteristics.

People from the United States can be described as nationalistic, patriotic, and even ethnocentric. Picture it this way: Most Americans are raised hearing how lucky they are to be Americans, that the United States is the greatest nation in the world, the best country in the world, and so forth. If the United States is the superior country, doesn't that imply that every other country is inferior? This is, by definition, ethnocentrism.

Each individual's cultural viewpoint is based on meaningful context from internalized patterns buried in the unconscious. The blueprints for social existence control thought and speech patterns, conceptual and motor habits, and emotional responses (Condon, 1974). These behavioral traits are accepted as common, normal behavior, and any behavior outside the norm is considered somewhat deviant. This unconscious ethnocentrism stems from an individual's inability to see beyond their own perception of reality.

Condon further explained that different cultural groups inhabit different orders of reality, each determined by a specific cultural heritage. Those who are not conscious of differing world perceptions, or that perceptions are shaped in different ways by different societies, are bound to be engaged in misunderstandings with members of other societies, even when speaking the same language.

It is unlikely that an individual is fully cognizant of the depth and strength of his or her own cultural patterns until that person has the opportunity to experience a cross-cultural interaction that threatens, challenges, or violates the person's cultural values. As the saying goes, "You can't ask a fish to describe water."

Members of a cultural group are aware of the obvious cultural values and assumptions, but often are ignorant of their own cultural values until they are challenged. Culture is an integral part of language (Kramsch, 1993). Edward Sapir (Whorf, 1956) believed that culture determines the contents of human actions and thoughts, while language formulates them (p. 178). Today, proponents of multicultural education believe that language and culture are intertwined, and practices that build on students' language skills and cultural backgrounds should be reflected in the school curriculum.

The Role of Culture

Culture plays the role of ensuring that members conform to socially acceptable actions, and cultural groups use laws as external restrictions to enforce appropriate behavior. However, within this framework, an allowance for diversity and a certain amount of freedom of individual choice exist.

An individual's culture provides a safe haven because common behaviors and familiar surroundings allow automatic responses and a relaxed state. The world is predictable, and the individual is firmly oriented. Words and actions do not need to be translated, and the appropriate response to almost every encounter is internally ingrained. Within one's own culture, a common frame of reference exists for acceptable behavior.

In their own cultures, people have learned what to do and do not need to make radical decisions as to what type of behavior is expected of them. When individuals come into contact with other cultures, they undergo an acculturation process, and the original patterns of behavior and language are interchanged (Miranda, Bilot, Peluso, Berman, & Van Meek, 2006; Padilla, 1980).

Points to Remember

❖ Each society has its own set of values and belief system.

❖ Cultural values often influence learning styles.

❖ By learning about students' cultures, teachers can better provide instruction.

❖ *Culture* refers to a loosely unified set of beliefs, customs, values, and ideals belonging to a society. Within the society, there is individuality and a continuum of behaviors.

❖ Ethnocentrism is the belief that one's culture, people, nation, society, or ways are the best. Your way is the only way.

Language Determines Culture

KEY ISSUES

- ❖ The relationship between language and culture
- ❖ Cultural misunderstandings
- ❖ Deep culture and surface culture
- ❖ Assumptions about culture

Señora Salazar, the director of a growing school in a fairly large city in Colombia, decided that her new "bilingual" school needed to offer a more authentic experience if the students were to become bilingual. The current teachers of the colegio were native-born Colombians with excellent English skills; however, parents were complaining that none of the teachers were native English speakers. To look for teachers willing to teach overseas, Señora Salazar began advertising in the United States for teachers to direct and teach in her bilingual program. Three young women with master's degrees and a collective total of 12 years living abroad and teaching ESOL accepted the challenge and decided to go to work in Colombia. After eight months at the position, the director of the colegio became rude and intolerant of the North American teachers, continuously made nasty remarks, and decided that she hated Americans. One teacher quit under threat of arrest, and the other two shortly began to think of ways to get out of their situation. After the North American teachers left, the director hired British teachers, with the same disastrous results.

What had gone wrong? The young women were experienced language teachers, familiar with culture shock, and knowledgeable about adapting to other cultures. They applied their skills to their working situation, and nothing seemed to be appropriate. When they left, it was under volatile auspices.

Language and culture are inseparable. The director of the school wanted the English language taught without any American culture traits. However, language is a mirror of its speakers' attitudes and ideas (Chaika, 1989; Kramsch, 1993), and it is impossible to teach the language in a vacuum. Speakers of different languages have different perceptions of the world (Whorf, 1956) according to their own cultural perceptions.

The North American teachers who went overseas to teach took their American values with them. By only seeing through their "American" cultural lenses, problems rapidly arose.

In the vignette, the first North American teacher to leave was the only one who had a working knowledge of Spanish. She was placed in the position of interpreting, from her perception, everything to her colleagues. If she misinterpreted, no one would know, so it was uncertain what, if any, misinterpretation had taken place.

The cross-cultural miscommunications mounted quickly, both in professional and personal areas. Señora Salazar did not understand why the American teachers had to make decisions collectively; she expected the American hired as director to make all the decisions and direct the other two teachers. Additionally, the American teachers were shocked when the director would not hire a fluent English speaker because she was not attractive enough. The director explained that the students would not accept the teacher if she was of a lesser status (which included beauty, dress, manners, and social class) than they.

Other cultural differences were soon evident to the North Americans. They could not accustom themselves to the attitude of unimportance of time. They would decide on time frames and deadlines to implement educational strategies, and these were totally disregarded. The North American teachers were more informal in their dress and manner in the classroom. They would sit on the desk, would talk to the maid who served them morning coffee, and would not hesitate to state their opinions if they disagreed with the director. To the director, all these behaviors denoted their lack of proper decorum and total lack of respect for tradition and ritual, resulting in daily discord. Inevitably, the teachers left believing that the director was a cruel person with a dictatorial style, and that she was abusive to the overworked Colombian teachers. The director, however, was left with the feelings that North Americans were rude, disrespectful to authority, and lazy.

It is easy to see what went wrong after examining the typical cultural values that are being challenged on both sides. Egalitarianism, time values, and discomfort with being deferential are traits within the American value system, whereas the Colombians value more formality, respect for traditional roles, and less pressure on time and schedules. It is clear, then, that language learning cannot be successful without cultural learning. Conversely, when people from other cultures arrive in the United States, they bring their own cultural baggage that inevitably results in misunderstandings.

Deep Culture and Surface Culture

In school situations, teachers often decide to highlight different cultures in an effort to incorporate the mosaic of ethnic diversity. Hispanic Month or Black History Month will be declared, or perhaps a cultural festival will be held. Although these ideas may be entertaining, they only highlight the surface culture that is visible at first glance. These activities do not touch the roots of deep culture that are perceptible when serious challenges are made to the belief system of individuals.

Think of it in this simple way:

Surface culture consists of things or indicators that can be easily or obviously seen, such as dress, food, music, holiday celebrations, traditions, arts and crafts, history, music, and famous persons. These are the examples of the indicators that are highlighted in schools for the month long celebration of a culture mentioned above, such as Hispanic Month, or Black History Month, Multicultural Month, or Women in History Month.

Deep culture, on the other hand, may not be evident to us (and others) until cultural beliefs are suddenly, or unexpectedly challenged, threatened, or insulted. Deep culture consists of a set of beliefs within a culture or society that influences how people live, and what is acceptable or what is objectionable behavior. It controls and guides suitable practices, customs, and mores about how families function, political behavior, and the attitudes we hold about religion, health, life, death, courtship, marriage, and sexual practices. Conflicting or negative judgements are often made when we notice things like grooming (e.g., some people are fanatical about dental care, while others never even think about flossing teeth. Pulling a tooth may be the most logical option when dental care maintenance [e.g., for a cavity] is scant or nonexistent.). Bathing several times a day is a given for those who have plenty of water (usually hot) but may be sporadic for those who must preserve every precious drop. In the United States, we actually determine that someone's mental faculties are questionable if they don't bathe regularly. Washing clothes is easy when you have a machine, and dry cleaning is standard for those in more affluent countries. Yet people without access to these extravagances tend to have a higher tolerance for body and clothing scents, while others are more judgmental and critical.

Ethics is another arbitrary concept found in deep culture. For example, in the United States, citing references is mandatory, while in other countries (such as Korea) they might not cite someone's work because it is an honor to the author and most people already know who is being referenced. *Ethics* might be questioned in a country such as Mexico when it is quite customary to pay someone a little bribe (la mordida, or "little bite") for a service, or to protect a car when parked. Ideas about the roles of ethics in sexual situations are evident when people from other countries comment on American naiveté or provincialism when an unfaithful politician is shamed into resigning due to marital infidelity. A system of multiple "wives" is very common (and quietly tolerated) in certain countries.

Appropriate gestures are determined by cultural meaning. It is easy to make a mistake by unwittingly pointing the wrong finger or using a symbol that is insulting or suggestive, or threatening in another culture, but innocent or meaningless in yours. Deep cultural meaning is assigned to these symbols—it may mean nothing to the outsider, but highly significant to the cultural insider.

Deep culture taboos exist in every culture (e.g., men kissing, hugging or holding hands). Other points of deep cultural meaning are found in how individuals use eye contact (e.g., Americans must look you in the eye to show candor, but children in Haiti or Puerto Rico may not look adults in the eye because it is insolent); proxemics (e.g., how close you can comfortably stand next to a person); duties and rituals according to gender (e.g., only women do housework; only grandfather carves the turkey); and time values (e.g., "time is money;" it is rude or unacceptable to be late, or conversely, everyone knows the invited hour really means two hours later) are other values you might not be aware of until you are insulted or challenged.

A significant concept that you may find with your students is the notion of health practices or death rituals in other cultures. Attitudes differ within each culture with regard to who decides what treatment will be sought (often it is the male head of household) and by whom (a medical practitioner, doctor or traditional hospital within the host country, a Shaman, Santeria, Voodoo, Hoodoo, coining, cupping, mental or emotional health care [often vehemently rejected] or some other cultural remedy). People will seek attention by whomever they trust. Death rituals determine how to grieve, handle the deceased individual, the time, amount, and rituals of mourning, etc. All these factors are determined by deeply imbedded individual beliefs and cross cultural variations.

One's culture can determine what a word means, and what may be a negative connotation to one culture may be neutral to those in another culture. In Spanish, for example, terms of endearment such as "*Gordita*" or "*Mi Cielo*" sound silly or offensive when translated into English. Greeting someone as "*Little fat one*" or "*My Heaven*" just won't work in English. We are quite content to use euphemisms (such as being called a senior citizen, as opposed to being called "old").

The way we address elders may sound disrespectful to younger students. No matter how many times I give my English learners (adults) permission to call me Eileen, they still feel more comfortable calling me Dr. Ariza because it is a way for them to show me respect. I never offer my American undergraduate students the opportunity to call me by my first name because it feels disrespectful to me (my cultural value), and it somehow gives them an impression that we are on a more familiar basis than we really are. This is an example of a deep cultural value. As a child of the 1960s, I was taught to call my friends' parents by their last names (Mr. Kelleher or Mrs. Whelan). Today, my children's "American" friends call me "Eileen," yet their friends from Venezuela call me Senora.

We acquire our own deep culture by internalizing (spoken or unspoken) acceptable behaviors and attitudes of the culture in which we are born. We learn surface culture explicitly; manifestations of surface culture are easy to see or differentiate. To learn and understand the deep culture of other societies, we must make a concerted effort to discover the most profound, yet least visible attitudes and mindsets.

Points to Remember

- ❖ Language and culture are inseparable.

- ❖ Language determines culture.

- ❖ Cultural miscommunication occurs because people perceive concepts through their own cultural lens.

- ❖ Surface culture and deep culture are very different. Surface culture is the superficial outer layer of a culture and is noticed as the way people dress, talk, and look and the foods they eat.

- ❖ Deep culture is the underlying value and belief system of a society and may not be recognized until values are seriously challenged (Gonzalez, 1978).

- ❖ What seems logical, sensible, important, and reasonable to a person in one culture may seem irrational, stupid, and unimportant to an outsider.

- ❖ Feelings of apprehension, loneliness, and lack of confidence are common in persons who visit another culture.

- ❖ When people talk about other cultures, they tend to describe the differences but not the similarities.

- ❖ It requires experience as well as study to understand the many subtleties of another culture.

- ❖ Understanding another culture is a continuous and not a discrete process.

Examining American Values

- ❖ The term "American"
- ❖ Looking at "American" values

Four teachers from Massachusetts—Jane, Mary, Paula, and Cathy—decided to take a trip to explore the culture and history of Mexico and visit some local schools. Victor, the first teacher they met, asked the ladies where they were from. "We are American," they answered, to which Victor took great offense. He insisted he was American, too, which the teachers from Massachusetts did not understand. "Aren't you Mexican?" they asked. He insisted that Mexico was a part of the Americas, and therefore, he called himself American.

Tomoko, a new student from Japan, was very quiet in Mrs. Silva's fifth grade classroom. Mrs. Silva never knew if Tomoko understood what was being taught because she never raised her hand to answer questions, and when asked if she understood, she always smiled and said, "Yes, teacher." After the first formative assessment, Mrs. Silva was surprised to discover that Tomoko failed miserably. "Why didn't you tell me you did not understand?" she asked. Tomoko just smiled, which to the teacher was an inappropriate response.

Mrs. Silva happened to mention Tomoko's behavior to the ESOL specialist in the school. He explained that in Tomoko's culture, silence is a virtue. The student is not expected to question the teacher, and if the student does not understand, she will try to figure it out at home or ask a classmate later. A smile does not always indicate happiness; it can mean embarrassment or nervousness. The individual in Tomoko's culture is not supposed to stand out—that is negative behavior.

Mrs. Silva reflected on how these cultural expectations were contrary to what she expected in the American classroom. The other children clamored to answer the questions to show they were the smartest and knew the answer. If they did not understand a concept, they often interrupted the flow of the class to ask for further explanation. After learning a little about Tomoko's culture, Mrs. Silva was able to adjust her "American" expectations to understand the norms under which Tomoko was operating. Mrs. Silva also vowed to gently teach Tomoko about expectations in her new American classroom.

In this book, the word *American* is used to refer to the people of the United States only for its facility. No offense is intended to citizens of Central America, South America, Mexico, or Canada, as it is realized that they, too, are from "The Americas."

Before looking at other cultures, there is a need to take a critical look at the American system. By identifying characteristics of the United States, it will be easier to understand why Americans criticize others. The United States is a country with tremendous diversity as a result of the influx of immigrants from countries all over the world who bring their cultural traits and customs to their new country. Regional diversity is also very influential in lending to the flavor of the country. For example, the South is famous for its hospitality, charm, and southern cooking, whereas the Northeast is famous for its history, educational institutions, and seafood. However, despite the individuality, American mainstream values are pervasive; all regions of the country share the same government, educational, and economic system and receive the same mass media exposure. Over time, a sort of acculturation takes place, and a degree of "Americanization" occurs. Eventually, the traditional culture is less prominent, and segments of mainstream values are absorbed.

The irony of a value system is that often individuals are not aware of their values until they are challenged. Only when people compare and contrast themselves with people from another culture do they realize what their cultural values are.

Every group has individuals who do not conform and are therefore not "typical" representatives of their group. Although care must be taken not to stereotype cultural groups, each culture has a set of mainstream values by which the majority abides. Different societies are often recognized by their general overarching traits.

Many anthropologists have depicted a set of values pertaining to American culture, as observed by outsiders. Table 4-1 lists observable traits (according to Kohls, 1984; Kohls, 2001) attributed to the majority of Americans and a "contrasting value" that can be observed in non-Western cultures.

American values stem from historical, political, and religious beliefs throughout a long period of time. It can be a challenge to ascertain whether the values an individual displays result from the country, the ethnic group, the family, or the individual. Whatever the case, it is easy to see why cross-cultural clashes can occur. However, with prior knowledge of cultural characteristics, teachers can better understand the behavior of students and their parents.

Table 4-1 **Observable American Traits and Contrasting Values**

American Values	Contrasting Cultural Value
1. Personal control over the environment. Man can determine the direction of his life.	Fate: Life's plan is our destiny that cannot be altered by willpower.
2. Change and progressiveness are good. The past is something to learn from and improve on.	Tradition, rituals, customs, and the old tried-and-true ways are honored.
3. The importance of control over time. Time should not be wasted, but should be saved. Schedules are important. For example, invitations say 2:00 until 4:00, and the party will end at 4:00.	Time is unimportant. There is no rush. The "mañana" syndrome is present (i.e., "tomorrow" the work will be finished, but there is no specification of *which* tomorrow).
4. Egalitarianism: The ideal of equality. "All men are created equal," and all races and creeds must enjoy equal rights under the law.	Hierarchy, status, class differences, and rank determine importance in life. Someone is always superior or inferior to another.
5. Individualism and promotion of one's own benefit and needs. Individuality is more important. Privacy is honored.	Group orientation: The individual acts for the good of the family, to uphold the family, group, or the nation, and any acts that bring dishonor to the "group" disgrace everyone. One must "save face" at all cost.
6. Future orientation: Live for what is to come and live for today. (America is basically a very young, progressive country that looks toward future growth.)	Past orientation: Follow the path of your ancestors and traditional ways.
7. Self-help: Honoring the "self-made" man. One can create his own luck and fortune with hard work and can rise from poverty to riches.	Birthright inheritance: People are born into their place in life. Individuals may not have a penny, but if they are born into royalty, position and status are afforded.
8. Informality: Newcomers can become confused by the apparent lack of formality and "casual" attitude when dealing with Americans. Ritual and formality do exist, but are not easy to discern.	Formality: Addressing people by titles, last names, and observing formal rituals. Formal address is even included in language forms and functions (e.g., *tu* is informal, and *usted* is the formal way to say *you* in Spanish).
9. Directness, frankness, and candid honesty are valued. It is better not to "beat around the bush"; one should "get right to the point." This trait is reflected in writing as well.	Indirectness and "saving face" so as not to hurt or embarrass anyone is of prime importance.
10. Action and work orientation: As an example, look at the saying, "Idle time is the devil's workshop." It reflects the moral value placed on work. The employee must find something to do, even if the job is finished. Some kind of action must be taken, or the employee is seen as lazy.	"Being" orientation: One is not defined by a career or by what one does.
11. Materialism: The tangible items are more important than intangible ideals.	Spiritualism and intellectual pursuits are valued.

❖ Some people are offended because people from the United States use the word *American* to describe themselves. *American* can refer to Latin Americans, Central Americans, South Americans, Mexicans, and North Americans. The term is used because no easier or more appropriate word exists to describe people from the United States.

❖ Once people understand their own cultural values, they can understand why other cultures may be so "different"—not wrong, just different. Every culture functions well within its own system.

❖ Cultures have mainstream values, but stereotypes need to be avoided. Individuals are different within their own culture.

❖ American values, and values of every culture, stem from historical, political, and religious beliefs over a long period of time.

Culture Shock: Reaction to an Unfamiliar Environment

KEY ISSUES
- ❖ Culture shock
- ❖ Symptoms
- ❖ Acculturation and recovering from culture shock

Anne, an American student studying to be a teacher, realized the benefit of learning another language. She thought it would make her more marketable, and she would be able to understand children better by knowing what they were going through trying to learn in another language. She had studied Spanish I and II and felt she had a strong language foundation. She memorized vocabulary and grammar and felt ready to take the challenge of studying at a Mexican university. Upon arriving at the university, she was shocked to find that everyone spoke Spanish to her, and she didn't understand anything. She could not even use the telephone because the dialing system and money were different, and she was unable to understand the language without face-to-face contact.

In trying to register for classes, Anne was shocked to find that no one spoke English. She thought, "Don't they realize I am here to learn Spanish, and that I don't know it yet?" She was also surprised in class to learn that her instructors were going to teach her Spanish through Spanish. How could that be? She hadn't considered that because in the United States, her Spanish teachers taught her Spanish through English!

Anne suffered terribly. She had a horrible headache every evening from trying to think in Spanish all day long. Uncharacteristically, she cried at the least provocation, got angry when she got lost on the subway, and was horrified when men she didn't even know would pay for her bus fare. She quickly realized that there was no way she was going to transfer credits from the Mexican university to her home college as she had planned. She knew it would be impossible to get all As, and this would ruin her perfect grade point average. She longed for someone to speak English to, but became irrationally angry when men would try to practice their English by talking to her. What was wrong with her?

After several months, Anne finally became more adjusted to her situation. When she reentered the United States eight months later, she attended a seminar on *culture shock*. After discerning that culture shock was the reason for her discomfort, she understood what had happened to her and wished that she had known about this phenomenon before leaving the United States. She also knew this experience would make her a better teacher because she would have great compassion for any student new to the American culture.

In discussing culture shock, reference is again made to older research because it is the groundwork on which more recent literature is based. Because an individual's cultural patterns are so deeply ingrained, both consciously and unconsciously, an instinctive reaction toward the unfamiliar is likely to occur when he or she encounters a new culture. This adjustment process is not limited only to a move overseas, but can also happen during any geographic relocation, even within a person's own country. Moving from the familiar to the new, moving from the North to the South, from urban to rural, or from the East Coast to the West Coast can cause culture shock. The superficial environment might be the same, but any cross-cultural contact can be sufficient cause to provoke emotional discomfort.

The term *culture shock* refers to "a removal or distortion of many of the familiar cues a person encounters at home and the substitution of them for other cues which are strange" (Hall, 1959, p. 156). The individual reacts to cultural stimuli that possess no recognizable significance. Culture shock is described as an occupational disease, or silent sickness, which is precipitated by the anxiety that results from losing all our familiar signs or signals of social intercourse. These signs or cues include the thousands of ways in which we orient ourselves to the situation of daily life (Miranda, Bilot, Peluso et al., 2006; Furnham & Bochner, 1986; Gordon, 2001; Juffer, 1984; Oberg, 1960). Physical manifestations of culture shock are easy to see, especially in children. Thus, it is easy to understand why they may pass through a silent stage, refusing to speak or respond positively in new cultural situations. It is assumed that few people escape without experiencing culture shock altogether and that people do not realize that they are handicapped by culture shock until the phenomenon has passed because the symptoms are difficult to isolate. Adults, who can control and make rational sense of their environment, can suffer drastically from culture shock. Imagine the plight of a child who did not choose to leave the home country and now is in a strange classroom, listening to the babble of a foreign language. The prospect can be terrifying.

Familiar signs, symbols, and cultural rules that people learned as children are the internal blueprints used to decipher everyday cues that guide them to respond appropriately. Words, gestures, facial expressions, customs, and norms are the unconscious props that dictate their behavior. An unconscious level of comfort is maintained because there is no threat to their beliefs. However, when an individual is suddenly transplanted, no matter how exciting the situation may be, he or she can feel discomfort because, "No matter how broadminded or full of goodwill you may be, a series of props have been knocked from under you, followed by a feeling of frustration and anxiety" (Oberg, 1960, p. 177). People react to the frustration of a new culture in much the same way; only the degree to which culture shock affects individuals differs greatly.

Some classic reactions of culture shock in Oberg's model are:

- ❖ A feeling of helplessness
- ❖ A desire for dependence on long-term residents of one's own nationality
- ❖ Fits of anger and irritability over delays and minor frustrations
- ❖ Depression
- ❖ Loss of appetite
- ❖ Poor sleep
- ❖ Impatience or curtness with the nationals
- ❖ Delay and/or refusal to learn the host language
- ❖ Great concern over minor pains
- ❖ A terrible longing to be back home

Disgust with the host country, its food, its citizens, and its customs and a constant comparing of how bad the new place is compared with the home country may be displayed. These negative feelings impede and delay adjustment to the new environment. Students new to the classroom may manifest any number of negative reactions, and the problems are compounded by lack of expertise in English.

Another way to look at this uncomfortable phenomenon is to call it *language shock* (Agar, 1994; Smalley, 1963) and recognize the accompanying emotional distress (Bennett, 1993; Paige, 1993). In this framework, language is the primary determinant of culture shock, and the study of language itself may cause culture shock for some people. Until the cues of the new culture are learned, individuals remain culturally and linguistically disoriented as adults are reduced to the level of being a child again, stripped of their primary means of personal interaction—language. Language learners feel insecure about how to participate in language discourse, such as knowing when it is appropriate to interrupt in a conversation, or when to ask questions (Mauranen, 1994). Further, new language learners are subjected to making constant mistakes and being corrected. They find themselves responding to intelligent and educated people as if they were children because of their incapability of responding as educated, intelligent adults. The newcomer's education and intelligence are not recognized by the host country, which can be a blow to self-esteem and adult status.

Children who are developing their primary language as well as acquiring the new language are not subjected to the loss of status, but they suffer with the inability to express themselves in interpersonal relations. Additionally, where the adult might have the cognitive concepts and abilities that can transfer to the second language, the child may lack the prior knowledge to transfer to English, which can result in a tremendous cognitive burden. Not only does the child have to learn English to survive, but he or she then must learn academic concepts through the foreign language. It is much easier to acquire the decoding skills necessary in reading the native language first and then transfer that knowledge, than it is to learn to read in a foreign language with no previous reading skills (August & Hakuta, 1997, 1998; Chamot & O'Malley, 1996; Cummins, 1984).

Children may also manifest their cultural discomfort and anxiety with physical symptoms, such as upset stomachs, headaches, and malaise, as the body responds to cultural disorientation. Trying to function all day long through another language is physically and mentally exhausting, and as a result, students may be unable to resist an overwhelming desire to sleep. An exhausted head on the desk may irritate the teacher but would be better met with understanding and compassion.

Researchers have given different names to the stages of culture shock, but all agree on these basic four:

1. **Honeymoon stage.** This stage includes a euphoric feeling of fascination with novelty. Experiencing the country for the first time, feelings of enthusiasm, admiration, and enchantment are prominent while the individual experiences friendly and cordial yet superficial relationships with host nationals. The similarities of the new culture with those from home are salient because the individual has not had to deal with the realities of functioning in daily life. The newcomer may overly depend on another newcomer with good English skills who knows how to maneuver within the country. This stage can last for a few days or weeks to six months, depending on the circumstances.

2. **Hostile or aggressive stage as a reaction to crisis.** Immersion causes initial differences to become salient; daily activities become insurmountable problems. The individual struggles with a different language, concepts, and values he or she is unaware of or does not understand. Familiar cues, symbols, and signs no longer evoke the same responses, which may lead to feelings of inadequacy, frustration, anxiety, and anger. In an attempt to rationalize the adjustment problem, the individual is very critical of the new culture, its people, and its ways and may describe the people of the new country, as well as the country itself, in derogatory terms. At this point, the newcomer may seek solace in associating with others who reject the environment that is causing such discomfort—"the ways of the host country are bad because they make us feel bad" (Oberg, 1960, p. 77)—and the home country becomes "irrationally glorified." If individuals can make it through this dismal period, they can overcome culture shock. If this stage of crisis is not tolerable, individuals will often return to their home country before adaptation is possible.

3. **Recovery.** At this stage, the individual reconciles with the language and begins to understand the cues of the culture. Humor returns, and helping newly arrived people who are struggling may offer feelings of confidence, as the "old-timer" can speak and get around.

4. **Adjustment.** Finally, the host culture is accepted in a meaningful way, as the customs of the country are seen as just another way of living. Living and working in the new culture with a minimum of anxiety and moments of strain make life acceptable. Understanding of the new language is clearer, and the individual accepts and enjoys the food, drinks, customs, and habits of the new country.

Acculturation and Recovering from Culture Shock

The teacher plays a pivotal role in facilitating a child's adjustment to the new culture. Learning the new culture and understanding how it operates is one antidote to culture shock. A good way to get over culture shock is to try to get to know the people of the country, the customs, and the culture. Learn what culture shock is and realize that it will pass. Of course, this is difficult if one does not have facility with the language of the host country.

The key to success in the new culture entails the acquisition of behaviors, skills, and norms appropriate to function within the cultural paradigm. It is like trying to play a game where one player does not know the rules. Can you imagine the chaos and ambiguity he or she would feel while trying to interpret everyone else's actions? Eventually the player would become frustrated and probably ask himself/herself what the point in playing was, as it certainly was not fun.

How can the teacher help students overcome culture shock while respecting their native culture? Teachers wield a powerful influence on the attitudes of their students. They can deflect focus from the mainstream or more extroverted children in the class who often tend to monopolize classroom time by focusing attention on the English language learner. To highlight the favorable aspects of each child's culture, the teacher must express positive value in whatever appears "foreign" to the native English speakers. Demonstrating a positive attitude toward music, food, clothing, and other manifestations of the new culture is within the power of the classroom teacher. This attitude helps the children learn how to respond with an open mind. With a little imagination, teachers can plan instruction so that all students can integrate their cultural histories into reading, writing, art, social studies, or any other subject across the curriculum.

Music from a variety of heritages can be highlighted and appreciated. Food and traditional dress can be incorporated as superficial exhibitions of culture, but it is also more meaningful to make the students aware of the feelings, values, and belief systems of their classmates. Developing lessons that spark questions, discussions, and critical thinking will allow the mainstream students to experience a new cultural dimension, while highlighting the affective aspects of the multicultural children.

Alma Flor Ada (1993) recommended home–school interaction to validate the child's culture. Teachers who make visits to the homes of children gain valuable insight and information. Most parents from other countries have a deep respect for the teacher. By knowing the parents and the child's home situation, the teacher can further assist in the child's learning. Additionally, the teacher can aid the parents by explaining the important roles they play in the education of their children in the American school system. Paraprofessional teacher assistants, parent volunteers, and other bilingual personnel provided by the school system can lend support by interpreting for the teacher in these meetings. However, the child should not act as interpreter as it may disrupt familial hierarchy by usurping parental authority.

Classrooms that embrace and value multiculturalism by using dialogue journals, providing the children with buddies, engineering study groups, sharing cultures, and fostering feelings of being "at home" in the classroom will smooth the transition for the newcomers.

❖ Culture shock is a distortion of many of the familiar cues encountered at home and is substituted for other cues that are inexplicable.

❖ Learning another culture is like trying to play a game with the wrong set of rules. Children experiencing culture shock may manifest cultural discomfort with physical symptoms such as headaches, upset stomachs, and an overwhelming desire to sleep.

❖ Learning a foreign language is physically exhausting.

❖ Four basic stages of culture shock are:

1. Honeymoon stage: Euphoria with the idea of being in a new culture.
2. Hostile or aggressive stage: The honeymoon is over, and daily activities become insurmountable problems.
3. Recovery: The individual reconciles with the language and begins to understand the cues of the new culture.
4. Adjustment: Life is now acceptable, and the anxiety and strain of life in the new culture diminishes.

Teachers can help students overcome culture shock by understanding the symptoms, embracing multiculturalism, incorporating the home culture into daily lessons, reaching out to the families, and making positive parental contact.

Differences in Verbal Communication

KEY ISSUES
- ❖ Participation structures
- ❖ High involvement/high considerateness conversational patterns
- ❖ Directness/indirectness in speech
- ❖ Saving face
- ❖ High-context/low-context culture

"To know another's language and not his culture is a very good way to make a fluent fool of one's self."
—Winston Brembeck

Ms. Saidi's class consists of seven Koreans, two Japanese, one Italian, one Greek, one Arab, two Venezuelans, and two Spaniards. The Asians indicated in their preclass conferences with the teacher that they wished to improve their speaking skills. Ms. Saidi's instructional plans included much time for opportunities to practice meaningful conversations. She decided to start the class with a half-hour cooperative learning project wherein the students would be in mixed groups of four for maximum cross-cultural exposure. As the activity got under way, Ms. Saidi circled the classroom and listened in on the discussions. Although each student had a task to complete, the Asians were not conversing with the rest of the individuals in the groups. Ms. Saidi wondered what was wrong.

Cultural differences can interfere with student participation within classroom activities. Participation structures (Hancock, 1997; Jarvis & Robinson, 1997; Philips, 1983) describe the interactions of students in the classroom, and each culture has its own rules about when and how to speak and even what to speak about. Some students are only comfortable with whole-class activities, and others function better in small group or individual formats of instruction rules. Many cultures are based on cooperation for the good of the whole, and group instruction reflects this background. In other words, culture influences communication, which can (and often does) create misunderstandings. It is up to the teacher to notice which formats are best for individual students.

Individuals from some cultures appreciate heated discussions about politics and other potentially volatile topics, whereas other cultures participate in a more reserved style of conversing. Generally speaking, Americans shy away from controversial topics and may even "agree to disagree." Italians or Germans (for example), who like a lively discussion, might actually be angry that an American will not argue.

According to Deborah Tannen (1990), a sociolinguistic researcher who wrote a book called *You Just Don't Understand*, people from some cultures value *high-involvement* conversational patterns, whereas others might follow a *high-considerateness* pattern. She explains that typically, people from conversationally high-involvement cultures tend to talk and interrupt more, expect and are not bothered by people who interrupt them, and speak louder and quicker than those individuals from conversationally high-considerateness cultures. She names cultures such as Russian, Italian, Greek, Spanish, South American, Arab, and African (p. 207) as belonging to the high-involvement category. People from cultures that follow a high-considerateness conversational pattern speak one at a time, do not interrupt while others are speaking, listen politely to the speaker, nod, show interest, and make positive sounds that indicate they are paying attention. The conversational partners are more hesitant, and individuals are likely to avoid confrontational or heated discussions. Tannen characterized the Asian cultures (such as Chinese, Korean, and Japanese) as belonging to the high-considerateness profile of conversational style. American conversational patterns are also high considerateness; however, there is so much regional, ethnic, and environmental diversity that it is easy to see the differences along the cultural continuum.

The conversational clash can occur when Americans are speaking with people from other cultures and may not know how to interrupt or interject a comment. Additionally, American culture values small talk, whereas most Asians (and other cultures) value silence, which might lead them to believe that Americans talk too much. Although the American is not comfortable with long periods of silence in the conversation, the Asian will take more time to answer. This can carry over into the classroom, when more wait time is necessary, as the English learner may be slower to answer for a multitude of reasons (processing the questions, thinking of how to translate, cultural conversational style, etc.). It is imperative that the teacher allow more wait time and appear to be comfortable doing so. Teachers can set the tone of the class, and if they demonstrate patience, the students will learn patience as well.

Another consideration in verbal conversation is the directness or indirectness in speech. In "mainstream" American culture, directness is typically valued more than indirectness, yet there is a continuum within these qualities as well. The Californian may consider the New Yorker as too direct (or rude), whereas the New Yorker may consider the Southerner as too slow. The English language reflects a positive attitude toward directness by its expressions: "Get to the point." "Don't beat around the bush." "The bottom line is . . ." Yet people from other cultures may consider Americans rude because in their own cultures, they do not directly disagree. In Japanese, for example, there are many ways to say "no" or disagree without actually saying no. To disagree or point out a mistake would be very rude. Being direct is such an important value in the American culture that courses are offered to teach people (especially women) how to be assertive, to be direct, and to say "no."

If students from non-American cultures are in the classroom with a teacher who does not realize the implication of indirect communication, great misunderstandings can occur. Not embarrassing or shaming another person ("saving face") is an objective of indirect cultural conversation patterns cherished by many cultures (Asian, Latin American, Native American), without regard to high-involvement or high-considerateness styles.

By being aware of ingrained cultural conversational patterns, the teacher can better control classroom discussion and verbal interactions, as some students may monopolize conversations and discussions. The teacher can orchestrate the activities so that all students can have their turn sharing thoughts and opinions and answering questions. This is especially important when non-native English speakers are in the classroom with native English speakers. Although it might take more time for the language minority students to gather thoughts and decide what and how to say what is on their minds, the native English speaker does not have this linguistic hurdle and has blurted out the answer.

Although Americans may appear to value direct speech, English learners should be taught that this idea can be deceptive because we do have certain "rules" about being politically correct in an attempt to avoid insulting each other or minority groups. Again, euphemisms are frequently used to mask distasteful subjects. We try to be careful about how we refer to religions, skin colors, races, sexual preferences, and other names that can be disparaging.

The teacher can develop techniques to ensure that everyone has a chance to answer. Two simple ways to guarantee that everyone has participated are methods such as the following:

1. Write the names of all the students on slips of paper and put the slips into a bowl. One by one, randomly select a name and direct a question to the individual whose name was drawn. If the student cannot answer the question, put the slip of paper in a different bowl to be drawn later. Names of students chosen to answer go back into another bowl to be started over again.
2. Place an object (such as an eraser or stuffed animal) on the table where students are clustered. Before speaking, the student must pick up the object. No one can speak without picking up the object. This system also buys more time for the language minority speaker to prepare to speak.

High- and Low-Context Cultures

Anthropologist Edward Hall introduced the idea of high- and low-context cultures. He explained the difference by saying, "Words and sentences have different meanings depending on the context in which they are embedded" (1976, p. 91; 1983, p. 59). High-context (HC) communication or message is one in which most of the information is either in the physical context or internalized in the person—very little is in the coded, explicit, transmitted part of the message. Information about procedure is rarely communicated; members are supposed to know how to perform in various situations, but the rules of cultural performance are implicit.

A low-context (LC) communication is just the opposite: the mass of the information is vested in the explicit code. Information is abundant, procedures are explained clearly, results and expectation are discussed frequently, and instructions are followed as given. American culture, according to Hall, is in the middle of the scale that measures context, whereas Japanese are very high context, and Germans and Swiss are very low context. Simply put, in high-context cultures, people do not have to speak very much, and they know what others mean, think, and expect. The culture is static, and because customs are long-lived, the culture is unified. In low-context cultures, individuals need to be very specific, explain what is expected, and almost go overboard in training because the culture is fast changing. The low-context culture is unstable and is progressively changing over time, whereas the high-context culture might maintain its hold on its high-context position too long. These types of communication reflect thinking patterns as well, based on high- or low-context cultural modes.

Some researchers believe that cultural traits reflect the hemisphere in the brain that corresponds to the definition of high-context and low-context cultures. Based on this theory, Dr. Carmen Judith

Nine-Curt developed a chart of hemispheric traits that is interesting to compare:

Low-Context Left Hemisphere Societies

(Anglo)

1. Speech, verbal
2. Logical, mathematical
3. Linear, sequential ordering, monochronic
4. Emotionally controlled, detached, uninvolved
5. Task, work oriented
6. Worldly, active, dominant
7. Analytic, precise
8. Detailed, specific
9. Reading, writing, naming
10. Perception of significant order
11. Recognition of complex motor sequence

High-Context Right Hemisphere Societies

(Puerto Rican, Hispanic Caribbean)

1. Nonverbal, spatial, musical
2. Artistic, symbolic
3. Simultaneous, polychronic
4. Emotionally involved, empathetic
5. Family oriented
6. Spiritual, quiet, receptive
7. Synthetic, intuitive, imprecise
8. Holistic, gestalt
9. Creative, facial recognition
10. Perception of abstract figures
11. Recognition of complex figures

Taking a cue from these findings, teachers can begin to understand why some classroom behaviors may be reflections of cultural values. Students from a variety of cultures will behave according to how they are taught within their culture, and the home values can conflict with school values. However, if teachers are aware of the systems under which other cultures operate, they can adjust instruction to address the needs of their students more appropriately.

❖ Based on cultural norms, "participation structures" describe the interactions of students in the classroom, when and how to speak, and what to speak about.

❖ People from cultures with "high-involvement" conversational patterns talk and interrupt more, expect and are not bothered by people who interrupt them while speaking, and speak louder and quicker than those individuals from conversationally "high-considerateness" cultures. Cultures such as Russian, Italian, Greek, Spanish, South American, Arab, and African are examples of the high-involvement category.

❖ "High-considerateness" conversational patterns are found in the Chinese, Korean, Japanese, and even American cultures. Individuals from these cultures do not interrupt while others are speaking, listen politely to the speaker, nod, show interest, and make positive sounds that indicate they are paying attention to the speaker.

❖ Directness in speech is valued in the American cultures. "Don't beat around the bush," "Get to the point," and "The bottom line is . . ." are indicators of the values placed on direct speech.

❖ Indirect speech is an objective of cultural patterns held by Asians, Native Americans, and many Latin American cultural groups. It is important to "save face" by not embarrassing others or shaming another person.

❖ High-context cultures (such as Japanese) do not have to talk much because the members of the society communicate with intrinsic knowledge of how others think and feel and what they expect.

❖ Low-context cultures (such as Americans, Swiss, and Germans) must be very specific and explain everything—what is expected, what the rules are, and how things should be done. These cultural expectations are mirrored by how people think and act.

Nonverbal Communication

KEY ISSUES ❖ Proxemics

❖ Kinesics

❖ Paralinguistics

❖ Haptics

❖ Oculesics

❖ Monochronic time

❖ Polychronic time

Mariela was a first grader who recently arrived from Cuba. Her family settled in northern Florida, where there was a very small Hispanic community. Her father believed that his children would have a greater opportunity to learn English if they were immersed in a majority English-speaking community. When Mariela started school, her teacher spoke in a soft manner to Mariela, so that even though she did not understand what the teacher was saying, the teacher's voice sounded nice. But several times Mariela approached her teacher and the teacher kept backing away from her. Mariela left school that day broken-hearted and went home crying to her mother. "Mami, la maestra no me quiere!" (Mommy, the teacher doesn't love me.)

Atsama was a Chinese girl from Thailand, whose family was transferred to Vermont. When Atsama started school, she noticed that she was smaller than her classmates, and everyone kept saying what a "doll" she was. The teacher thought Atsama was so cute that she couldn't resist patting the little girl on her head. Atsama immediately recoiled from the teacher's touch. Later, when it was story time, all the children sat on rugs on the floor, while the teacher sat in a chair with her legs crossed, ready to read to the children. Atsama would not sit with the children and insisted on standing. The teacher could not help thinking the child had problems interacting with people, while the child was shocked and insulted at the teacher's behavior.

Mr. Omiya, a fifty-two-year-old gentleman from Japan, came to Boston to study English for the summer. The teacher, Ms. Whelan, a fun-loving young woman who had lived in many countries, was well aware of the cultural values of her students. In addition to presenting practice in reading, writing, listening, and speaking English, Ms. Whelan inundated the class with cross-cultural experiences and opportunities that would broaden their knowledge base of foreign cultures (especially that of the United States). The dialogue journals the students wrote revealed precious reflective sharing, and Ms. Whelan thought Mr. Omiya was stepping out of his cultural patterns when he allowed her to hug him at the end of the summer, during the graduation ceremonies. However, Ms. Whelan began to realize just how deeply ingrained his cultural patterns were when she read Mr. Omiya's last journal entry:

Dear Professor,

I wish to give thanks to you for all you have shown and taught us this summer. You are wonderful teacher I will never forget. I go now to meet my son at airport. I have not seen him for four years and I wish to embrace him. However I cannot. I must only bow because I am Japanese man.

Yours truly,

Mr. Tsuneyoshi Omiya

If nonverbal communication is akin to speaking without words, what were the nonverbal cultural misinterpretations in the preceding scenarios? In the first scene, Mariela is hurt because she tries to get close to her teacher, and it appears to her that her teacher shuns her. In reality, individuals unconsciously maintain a certain personal distance between themselves and others. This is referred to as *proxemics* (discussed further in this chapter), a term coined by Hall to describe the use of space as it relates to different cultures. People in Arab and Hispanic cultures are more comfortable standing closer to one another than are Americans, who typically stand farther apart from each other (from eighteen inches to four feet, according to Edward Hall in *The Hidden Dimension*, 1966). To "invade" the personal space of an American signifies a certain intimacy or aggression.

Little Mariela, being from a "warm" culture in which individuals touch one another frequently and stand closer together, wanted to be physically closer to her teacher, but she was making her American teacher uncomfortable. Teachers in the United States are often advised not to touch their students, and this teacher in particular was not a physically demonstrative person. Mariela did not understand the teacher's reluctance to embrace her and was hurt by her coldness and supposed rejection.

Atsama is from a spiritual Buddhist family, whose members believe that the head, which houses the soul, must not be touched. Additionally, when the children were sitting on the floor, the bottom of the teacher's shoe was facing them, which is an insult to Thais (and to people from Saudi Arabia, and

others). They consider the foot the dirtiest part of the body. Atsama was insulted by the teacher's body language, and the teacher was confused by Atsama's strange reaction.

Finally, Mr. Omiya, who is aware of his cultural constraints, longs to embrace his son, whom he has not seen for four years, but cannot because his life-long cultural patterning is stronger than the values he learned in the summer he spent learning English and American culture.

Kinesics (the study of body language) includes facial expressions, posture, gestures, body movements, eye contact, or any ritual that conveys messages or meaning for a culture. The Japanese bow is an example of kinesics. From the American standpoint, a bow is just a hello or good-bye gesture. However, to the Japanese (and some other Asian cultures), a bow can be quite complex because a deeper meaning can be conveyed by the bow. The lower status individual must begin the bow and must bow lower than the higher status person. When the individuals bowing are equals in society, the bow is simultaneous and of the same depth.

Body posture can convey different meanings. The American informality and friendliness stance can appear rude to more formal cultures. However, teachers should take care when judging body language; the message the teacher believes is being conveyed may not be the same truth as seen from the student's cultural context.

From the previous scenarios, we learn that it can be dangerous to attempt to read someone's behavior based on our own frames of reference. Although emotions such as happiness, sadness, anger, hatred, embarrassment, shame, and love are universal, the ways they are expressed are as individual as the culture itself. Take a smile, for example. In the American culture, a smile usually appears friendly, but it can signify affection or disguise feelings. Americans smile at strangers, and they are just being polite. People from Russia may think that is unusual, inappropriate, or even suspicious. If an American smiled at a Russian who did not return the smile, the American would probably think the Russian rude. In some Asian cultures, a smile can be used for completely inappropriate reasons, according to the American perception. A smile can cover pain, embarrassment, and sadness for Asians.

Sadness, grief, and pain are expressed openly in some cultures and are borne silently in others. Some individuals mourn openly (e.g., Arabs, Iranians, and Irish), whereas others are more stoic (Chinese, Japanese, and some individuals within any culture) and do not display their grief for the world to see.

Paralinguistics is the set of vocal, nonverbal utterances that carry and augment meaning. How people speak and use pitch, intonation, grunts, and so on help to clarify what they are trying to say. Intonation can infer sarcasm, humor, disbelief, emotion, and any other type of meaning.

Haptics is the art of how people use touch to communicate. Touching indicates different meanings in different societies. In the American, German, English, and other white Anglo-Saxon cultures, individuals are usually not touch-oriented. Arab, Jewish, Eastern European, and Mediterranean cultures have been characterized as cultures wherein individuals frequently touch each other.

Displays of friendship or feelings of love are expressed quite diversely as well. In the Philippines, girls walk hand-in-hand, and boys can embrace unself-consciously, but boys and girls will not be seen holding hands (unless they live close to the American military bases, ironically). Young Korean men are quite comfortable sitting with their arms innocently around one another (while only the American teacher will watch with discomfort).

In the United States, heterosexual males usually do not touch one another. Men will shake hands and maybe slap each other on the back, but even some male family members will not touch each other. Females are allowed to openly display affection and may kiss cheeks or hug on greeting or when saying good-bye. Males and females will show affection publicly (depending on the individuals). In certain cultures, such as in France, it is perfectly acceptable for men to kiss each other on the cheeks; in other cultures, it is acceptable for men to kiss on the lips.

Because facial expressiveness can mean different things to different cultures, people should not try to interpret the faces of others as they would interpret the faces of people from their own culture. Emotions are shown in different ways by every cultural group, and even by individual families within those cultural groups. There is no single standard of measurement for everyone.

More about Proxemics

Proxemics refers to how a person uses and perceives body space. For example, if you are angry and are close to someone, it is more intimidating than if the angry person is farther away. In the United States, we stand closer to each other only if we share intimacy. Each culture perceives this concept differently and behaves according to their own standards (Remland & Jones, 1995).

In his book *The Hidden Dimension* (1966), Edward T. Hall stated that people from all cultures have patterns of interaction between themselves and others. All individuals have a zone of personal space surrounding their bodies. American and Northern Europeans stand farther apart from each other and touch each other less than do people from cultures such as Greek, Latin American, Arab, Turk, and individuals from African countries. Americans touch one another more than do Japanese adults; however, Japanese have more tactile contact with babies and children than do Americans. The continuum is relative when comparing all cultures.

Gestures

Gestures are not universal. What is common and polite in one culture can be considered rude in another. Snapping fingers at a waiter can be considered appropriate in one culture and not acceptable in another. The "OK" symbol in the United States holds different meanings in other countries. It stands for money in Japan and in Brazil means something vulgar.

In the United States, people beckon others to come by putting the palm up and wiggling the fingers toward themselves, or they hold the palm up and wiggle the crooked pointer finger toward themselves. This is how animals are called in the Philippines, and the gesture is rude in Korea and in some parts of Latin America as well. People are called by cupping the fingers, palms facing toward the other person, and waving the hands downward.

In many Spanish-speaking countries, tapping the flexed elbow with the palm of the opposite hand means someone is cheap; wiggling the pointing finger (straight up) side-to-side in front of one's body means no; and animals are measured with the arm out to the side horizontally with the hand extended, palm parallel to the floor (the way people's height is measured in the United States).

Gestures considered vulgar or obscene in non-American cultures are the American hitchhiking (thumb out) signal in New Zealand and Australia and using two fingers to make "horns" on someone's head (which accuses someone's wife of cuckolding her husband) in Spanish-speaking countries.

Eye Contact

Oculesics is the study of eye movement and position. Eye contact is frequently misunderstood. Americans acknowledge each other's presence by making brief eye contact, although it is considered rude to stare. In more intimate settings (e.g., a classroom or at a friend's party), eye contact can be made and held longer, especially if the individual wants to get to know someone. In a store or an airport terminal where people are just passing through, people would be less likely to make eye contact. Too much eye contact makes Americans feel uncomfortable, and too little eye contact indicates untrustworthiness or a lack of attention or interest. Navaho Indians attribute eye contact as a severe indication of disapproval, and therefore, individuals do not look directly at each other.

Studies show that American babies are attracted to their mother's eyes, and the mother's gaze is often focused lovingly on her baby. Experiments demonstrate that babies respond by smiling when shown a pair of eyes (Hall, 1976). In Japan, however, babies are often carried on their mother's back, thereby providing less eye-to-eye interaction. As a result, Japanese adults are not prone to place emphasis on eye contact to gather conversational meaning from one another. One's gaze during a conversation in Japan might be on the neck of one's conversation partner. Compare this to the American, who shows interest in his conversation partner by the proper gaze, but feels distrust for the individual who does not look him in the eye. The classic misunderstanding of encoding or decoding cultural meaning incorrectly occurs when the Haitian or Puerto Rican child, who is taught that it is disrespectful to look at an adult's eyes, does not look at the American teacher's eyes and is accused of being rude.

For North Americans, winking the eyes can indicate teasing or flirting. Nigerians wink at their children when they want the children to leave the room, and a friendly wink in India may be perceived as an insult (Hall, 1982). A Colombian might wink one eye if he does not understand something or wants something explained, and a Filipino might raise the eyebrows to indicate "yes."

Polite American behavior includes looking at someone's eyes when engaged in conversation (Andersen, 1999). But in many cultures, widening the eyes construes meaning. Condon and Sato (1976) offer an illustration of the cultural significance of widening the eyes.

Significance	Intention	Culture
Really!	Surprise, wonder	Anglo
I resent this.	Anger	Chinese
I don't believe you.	Challenge	French
I don't understand.	Call for help	Hispanic
I'm innocent.	Persuasion	Black American

Chronemics is the way a person views and uses time (Hickson, Stacks, & Moore, 2004). Hall (1959) says the use and thought of time, chronemics, is a powerful element of culture. Polychronic time and monochronic time are expressions that describe cultural views of time, its importance, and how it is used. It appears that a continuum of time exists with monochronic time (doing one thing at a time) on one end of the spectrum and polychronic time (doing many things at once) on the other. Cultures are oriented in either direction. Individuals probably possess both inclinations depending on the situation, so it can be said the individuals have the overwhelming predisposition toward one tendency or another.

Monochronics (e.g., American, British, Canadian, and German individuals) think in terms of linear sequential, time-ordered patterns with a beginning, middle, and ending. For example, a party invitation will specify the beginning and ending of the event (e.g., from 2:00 to 4:00). The guests know the party will be over at 4:00 and are usually conscious not to linger. They arrive on time or a few minutes early. If they are late, they apologize. The individuals in the culture know when they are late and feel self-conscious because the pattern of being on time is ingrained. The need to have closure in all aspects of life is evident in work, school, relationships, and daily activities.

Polychronic individuals (largely Latin American, African, Middle Eastern, and Southern European cultures) tend to think about and involve themselves in a number of activities simultaneously. They may feel overloaded, which may result in pro-crastination because they are trying to do too much. Polychronics follow a time orientation not dictated by the clock or schedules. Everyone knows that an invitation to dinner at 7:00 does not really mean 7:00. Depending on the culture, it could mean 8:00, 9:00, or even 10:00. Problems arise only when the monochronic is in the polychronic culture (or vice versa) and does not know the rules. That is when people start labeling others as "lazy," "never on time," or "neurotic about arriving early."

The use of time tells a subliminal story. If the telephone rings in the middle of the night in the United States, it can signal an emergency. Being late for an appointment indicates lack of interest. In Latin America, a long wait for an appointment may not be unusual, but to a North American, being kept waiting is an insult. In other cultures such as those in some villages in Africa or in the culture of the Sioux Indians, time starts when everyone is ready, and there may not even be a word that indicates late or waiting (Porter & Samovar, 1988). Time can be informal (after a while, later, some time ago), or time can refer to exact points (at "2:00 p.m. today" or "yesterday at 6:30"). The misunderstanding occurs when individuals operate on different concepts of time.

❖ Every culture has its own way of depicting the following domains of nonlinguistic communication:

♦ Paralinguistics: Sounds that accompany language and vocalizations that replace speech.

♦ Kinesics: The study of body motion, gestures, and unconscious body movement.

♦ Oculesics: Eye contact and motion to indicate meaning.

♦ Haptics: Location, frequency, and contexts in which people touch.

♦ Proxemics: The unconscious use and organization of personal space.

♦ Chronemics: Perception and use of time.

♦ Monochronic time: Doing one thing at a time, in a linear fashion.

♦ Polychronic time: Doing many things at a time.

❖ All cultures operate on their own systems of communication, and these beliefs will be manifested within the everyday context of the classroom.

❖ Knowledge of nonverbal communication specific to other cultures will help teachers to understand the students they teach as well as students' parents.

❖ Educators must be careful not to make the mistake of judging people's emotions by using their own cultural indicators.

❖ Not everyone shows grief, anger, happiness, embarrassment, or other emotions in the same manner.

Teaching and Learning Styles: A Reflection of Cultural Backgrounds

KEY ISSUES

- ❖ Cultural learning and teaching styles
- ❖ Field-dependent/field-independent learners
- ❖ Curriculum that facilitates learning
- ❖ Teacher strategies for culturally diverse classrooms

Ms. Peters teaches a first grade bilingual class and adores the beautiful children she sees in front of her. She has spent many years learning Spanish, and this is her first bilingual class. Her thirty-four students are almost all from Puerto Rico, with the exception of one child, who is from Peru. She has no teacher's assistant yet, but she has invested a lot of time in organizing and planning for instruction, so she feels well prepared. She chooses an assignment to get to know her children. "Niños, vamos a hacer algo muy divertido. Hagan un dibujo que muestre lo que hicieron durante sus vacaciones este verano." ("Children, we are going to do something that is a lot of fun. Make a drawing that shows what you did during your vacation this summer.") The children began a barrage of questions, "Pero que hacemos? Usamos las crayolas o los marcadores? Teacher, usted me puede ayudar a dibujar un barco? No se' que hacer." ("But what do we do? Do we use the crayons or the markers? I don't know what to do. Teacher, can you help me draw a boat?") "Wow!" thought Ms. Peters. "So many questions for such an easy assignment."

All individuals have their own learning styles and approaches to educational experiences. Age, cultural environment, and the family's beliefs and training mold the child into a certain type of learner, which is reflected by his or her cognitive behavior in the classroom. When home beliefs are incongruent with those of the teacher and culture of the American classroom, misunderstandings occur. As a general rule, Americans cherish individuality, independence, and self-reliance. Consequently, children are raised in a corresponding manner. For example, American babies are usually expected to sleep in their own rooms, away from their mothers, at a very early age. (Imagine the disbelief a newcomer to this country might feel on learning Americans will let their dogs sleep in their beds, and yet the children are expected to sleep in their own rooms!)

In kindergarten, children are expected to know their telephone numbers, addresses, and how to call 911 and are taught how to care for themselves. They are encouraged to "be a big girl" while Mommy's gone, and not to cry. Role-play or videos might be used to teach children how to act appropriately in various hypothetical situations. For example, children learn how to ward off sexual predators and to distinguish inappropriate touch. The implication is that they will be alone, think for themselves, and make responsible decisions. Children in day-care situations, where independence is promoted, are encouraged to become self-reliant. Later, they often have more freedom of choice in matters such as choosing friends and making certain decisions at an earlier age.

On the other hand, parents of children from many other cultures (e.g., Hispanics, Asians) might be more inclined to "hover" over their children, doing things for them, which promotes more dependence on the family members. Family interaction often consists of greater contact with grandparents and extended families.

Children who come from cultures that promote independence are often "field-independent," which suggests that their learning styles may be more analytical and independent. Gollnick and Chin (1998) mentioned that children who are less assimilated into the dominant society (with the exception of Asian Americans) may have the tendency to be global or "field-sensitive" learners. Neither style is better; the point here is to highlight the comparisons, because if the teachers are from the typical "American" culture, those cultural values will be manifested in their classroom expectations. Teachers and students who understand each other's expectations can expect fewer cultural collisions that disturb the educational process. Students can become bored, unresponsive, discouraged, or test poorly if they are uncomfortable in class (Felder & Henriques, 1995). However, if teachers misinterpret learning style data because they have lumped all students into one category, and then make instructional decisions based on incorrect assumptions, students can be hurt or limited in their school experience. For example, a student deemed field-independent might not be expected to contribute to cooperative learning activities, or a child labeled as field-dependent might not be chosen for a leadership role.

Students who have teachers from their same culture have little problem understanding the cues provided by the teacher and the appropriate interactional behaviors expected in the classroom. Those children and teachers from differing cultures do not know the rules of each other's "games" and have difficulty interpreting correct teacher–student interactions. Although not the panacea to end all classroom problems, effective teaching is more apt to take place if both the teacher and student are aware of the benefits of integrating appropriate instructional materials that correspond with culturally congruent teaching and learning styles (Smalley & Hank, 1992).

Knowing that cultural patterns drive behavior, teachers who are aware that their children have differing cognitive styles are able to adapt their classrooms to include activities that incorporate all types of learning in their teaching. The teacher will begin to understand why some students experience problems when their natural learning styles are incompatible with the teaching style of the teacher. Various researchers have pointed out that Asian students tend to be highly visual learners (Ehrman & Oxford, 1995; Reid, 1995). Hispanics are generally auditory learners, and non-Westerners are more inclined to learn through tactile and kinesthetic modes.

Differences in cognitive styles also can be demonstrated by examining the impulsive/reflective dimension. Impulsive students are those who are the first to raise their hands to answer questions and the first to finish a test. Reflective learners may be slower, but often they make fewer errors. The teacher has the power to teach impulsive learners to be more reflective and to foster impulsive behaviors in the more reflective student (such as during a timed test).

Much research has been carried out about learning styles and patterns of behavior that students employ to help them learn. Teachers must understand that language learners from different cultures use diverse strategies that affect learning outcomes (Ehrman & Oxford, 1988, 1989; Oxford & Ehrman, 1988). Chapelle and Roberts (1986) wrote about field-independent learners and the positive effects of having a high tolerance for ambiguity as being helpful in learning another language.

Ramirez and Castañeda (1974) have determined characteristics of field-sensitive and field-independent learners. Individuals sensitive to their surroundings or to the social field may be more likely to choose careers such as teaching or social work, whereas the more field-independent learners might choose to work in more impersonal, abstract, or analytical professions, such as the hard sciences or mathematics. However, with the guidance of the teacher, students can learn to become bicognitive, which means that they are able to function appropriately in any given situation, whether it is formal testing or cooperative learning. Cognitive learning and teaching styles are derived from early socialization patterns, which can be changed and modified. Learning strategies are teachable (Park-Oh, 1994; Sano, 1999) and will result in greater student achievement, increased motivation, and less anxiety. Field-sensitive instruction includes group projects, cooperative learning activities, culturally and ethnically relevant topics, and close interaction with the teacher. Field-independent instruction involves charts, diagrams, individual work, minimal teacher interaction, and analytical endeavors.

Multicultural Education in a Pluralistic Society (Gollnick & Chin, 1998) offers the chart in Table 8-1, adapted from Ramirez and Castañeda (1974), that categorically depicts the differences in behavior between field-independent and field-sensitive students. Additional characteristics have added to the list.

Although it is tempting to categorize individuals according to their ethnic group's cultural characteristics, it is important to keep in mind that reliability of all the learner style preference tests is questionable, and often data are unsupported by research findings (Ariza, 2002). However, mismatches of teaching and learning styles in the classroom often occur, and it is up to the teacher to bridge the gap. Teachers often teach the way they were taught or teach in a way that reflects their own learning styles (Oxford, 1990). It is no surprise, then, that research shows a higher level of academic achievement when the teacher's instructional style is congruent with the student's learning style (Cornet, 1983; Dunn & Dunn, 1979; Dunn & Griggs, 1995; Oxford, Ehrman, & Lavine, 1991). Cornet (1983) and Marshall (1991) found that a teacher's instructional style can influence a student's learning style preference, as can factors such as prior knowledge, motivation, context, and age (Dunn & Dunn, 1979; Oxford & Ehrman, 1995; Reid, 1987).

Cheng and Banya (in Reid, 1995) offered several ways for teachers to mitigate teaching/learning mismatches:

❖ Teachers should be cognizant of their own teaching styles as well as their students' learning styles, provide varied opportunities for students to discover their own learning styles, and take risks by experimenting with a number of instructional styles.
❖ Students need to be cognizant of their own learning styles, become more tolerant of ambiguity in the foreign language learning environment, and help themselves become more autonomous learners.

Table 8-1 Field-Independent versus Field-Sensitive Behavior

Field-Independent Behavior	Field-Sensitive Behavior
Relationship to Peers	
Prefers to work independently	Likes to work with others to achieve a common goal
Likes to compete and gain individual recognition	Likes to assist others
Is task-oriented; is inattentive to social environment when working	Is sensitive to feelings and opinions of others
Social atmosphere is secondary	
Personal Relationship to Teacher	
Rarely seeks physical contact with teacher	Openly expresses positive feelings for teacher
Is formal; restricts interactions with teacher to tasks at hand	Asks questions about teacher's tastes and personal experiences; seeks to emulate the teacher
Instructional Relationship to Teacher	
Likes to try new tasks without help from the teacher	Seeks guidance and demonstration from the teacher
Impatient to begin tasks	Seeks rewards that strengthen relationship with the teacher
Likes to finish first	Is highly motivated when working individually with the teacher
Seeks nonsocial rewards	Teacher expresses approval
Teacher uses formulas, charts, and graphs to instruct	Teacher instructs primarily by modeling
Learners prefer trial and error	Teacher provides personal rewards
	Teacher holds informal discussions in class
	Teacher is sensitive to students' problems
Characteristics of Curriculum that Facilitate Learning	
Emphasizes details of concepts	Explains performance objectives and global aspects of curriculum carefully
Parts have meaning of their own	Presents concepts in humanized story format
Teaches math and science concepts based on the discovery approach	Relates concepts to personal interests and experience of students
Emphasizes facts and principles	Approaches learning in a global perspective
Focuses on instructional objectives	Personalizes curriculum based on human needs of the learner
Encourages competition and independent achievement, which are approached analytically	

Different Cultures; Clashing in the Classroom

Mr. Cooper is the new teacher on the reservation. He has great respect for Native American cultures and appreciates the opportunity to work with the children of this nation. He has carefully introduced the concept of his lesson, and feels sure that his students understand what is being taught. He decides to test comprehension and directs a question to Running Bear, who does not know the answer. In an effort to help him, Mr. Cooper asks Sara, his brightest student, to help Running Bear by giving him the answer. Sara just puts her head down and does not answer. Mr. Cooper calls on one child after another, but no one will answer the question. Mr. Cooper is confused by his students' behavior. They are deliberately refusing to answer the simple question.

In this situation, Mr. Cooper does not realize that Native Americans are more group oriented than are Anglos, and the children must "save face" for their friend. They will not embarrass Running Bear by answering the teacher's question, even if they know the correct answer. No one wants to be singled out above the others because, like their elders, no one really directs because the group is the most important entity.

Although knowing about cultural learning styles and applying this information in the classroom can make instruction more effective for diverse learners, care must be taken not to simplify issues that are really quite complex. Bennett (1990) admonished teachers to beware of thinking that merely understanding learning styles is a panacea for all the ills in the classrooms of today. Within the cultural paradigm, every family is unique, with its own set of traditions and values, and finally, individuals have their own idiosyncrasies. Taking all these factors into consideration, the teacher can then determine the most effective methods of reaching each child.

Ogbu (1988) explained that cultural differences of Anglo, mainstream teachers are often at odds with students from other cultures. Pajares (1992) found that teachers' cultural beliefs often clash with students' cultural beliefs, thus preventing learning. Conflicts can occur because the "way of life" of these students is discordant with the cultural values, beliefs, and norms of mainstream schools. As a result of research on culture and learning styles, advocates claim that the closer the congruence in the teacher's instructional styles and the student's learning style, the more academic success the student will have in the classroom. As an additional point of interest, Clarkson (1992) noted that women and minorities are more likely to be field-sensitive or field dependent.

Recommended Teacher Strategies

No matter what culture teachers are from, they can get to know their students' preferred learning styles by daily observation and sensing what works best. Cox and Ramirez (1981, pp. 64–65) suggested that daily instruction techniques take into account the culturally reflected learning styles of the individual and offered a six-point plan to follow:

❖ Observe student behavior and note the changes from situation to situation. From this assessment, it is easy to determine the students' preferred way of learning.
❖ Design your teaching methods, strategies, incentives, materials, and situations so they complement student preferences.
❖ Execute the learning experiences as planned.
❖ Evaluate the learning experiences by determining whether instructional objectives have been met, but also in terms of student behavior and task involvement.
❖ Throughout the year, gradually plan and implement learning experiences that require behaviors that the students have previously shunned. Include one aspect of the unfamiliar behavior during each learning episode, focusing on the reward, the materials, the situation, or the task requirements. In this manner, the students have a scaffold to support the new learning experience with prior experience.
❖ Continue the effort to provide familiar, comfortable, successful experiences while gradually presenting new ways for the children to learn.

❖ Teaching and learning styles reflect cultural backgrounds.

❖ Students who have teachers from their same culture have little problem understanding the cues provided by the teacher. Students will already be familiar with the appropriate interactional behaviors expected in the classroom.

❖ With proper instruction, field-dependent and field-independent students can learn to be bicognitive; that is, their learning styles can be expanded to function appropriately in any given situation.

❖ Teachers need to provide activities that incorporate all types of learning styles.

❖ Teachers need to be aware of their own cultural learning styles and preferences, as well as those of their students.

❖ Stereotyping can happen when false and exaggerated characteristics of a group are attributed to the individual, but sociotyping involves an accurate generalization about cultural groups as a whole. If teachers misinterpret the learning style data and make decisions based on incorrect assumptions, students can be hurt or limited in their school experience.

❖ Mainstream teachers are often at odds with their diverse students because they are unaware of the differing cultural values they bring to the classroom.

❖ Teachers need to plan curriculum and instruction to incorporate the learning styles of their students.

❖ If students are uncomfortable in class, they may become bored or unresponsive or test poorly (Felder & Henriques, 1995).

Cultural Implications for Refugees, Immigrants, and English Learners in the United States

KEY ISSUES
- ❖ Differences among English learners
- ❖ Refugee concerns
- ❖ Best practices for refugees
- ❖ Students with interrupted formal education (SIFE)

Bisa Haasan and her five-year-old daughter Anana, Somali refugees from a camp in Ethiopia, were relocated to a fairly small community in Maine. They lived alone and eked out a meager subsistence on welfare, food stamps, and Medicaid health benefits. Bisa and her husband, who she assumes is dead, lost contact with each other during a bombing in their homeland, so she raises Anana by herself in her new host society. She struggles with trying to fit into the American culture while maintaining her native cultural values. They are Muslims in a small city whose residents are primarily white Christians. Her English is limited as well. However, there is an ever-growing support system within the Somali refugee community. Anana is now in kindergarten and plays with American girls and boys, which greatly worries Bisa, who fears that without a proper genital circumcision (clitoral amputation) or infibulation (vaginal sutures that only allow a slit for urine or menstrual flow), her daughter may run wild and become impure before her wedding, especially in the more permissive American culture. Bisa decides to go to her caseworker for a referral to a doctor who accepts Medicaid to perform the circumcision in Maine. Bisa wants to do right by her daughter but has no money to go back to Africa for the highly private ritual to be performed. Caseworker Sherrie Jones, speaking through the interpreter, is not shocked at this request because she has much experience working with this particular ethnic group. She had received ongoing training and support from migrant and refugee program organizations and knows how to proceed. First Sherrie calls on a Muslim leader in the community to explain to Bisa that the Quran does not require this practice; instead, Bisa learns that it is a cultural custom and not a religious mandate. She also is taught about the health issues that could harm her daughter, and that this cultural practice is a criminal act in the United States.

English learners in United States public schools cannot all be classified as immigrants, because they come from a variety of backgrounds. Many people are surprised to learn that the majority of English learners in the public school system are born in the United States. Researchers note that 77 percent of English learners in prekindergarten to fifth grade are born in the United States, and over half of the English learners in grades 6 through 12 are U.S. born (Batalova, Mittelstadt, Mather, & Lee, 2008). This background information is significant because it helps the teacher to identify certain special needs of the student population. For example, if we know that the student was born in the United States but English is not the home language, it tells us that the parents speak a primary language other than English and the family may be second or third generation, may already be comfortable living in the United States, may have extended family in the area, and may possess a variety of language proficiency in English. The more the teacher is cognizant of the student's background, the better the teacher can meet the needs of the student.

An **immigrant** is one who is born outside of the United States and arrives in the country at any age. It is possible to be an immigrant and be a native English speaker, such as those individuals from Canada, Australia, England, etc. But for the purpose of this book, we are referring to immigrants who are nonnative speakers of English. Immigrants may arrive in the country at any age or stage in life. If the children are young, they enter the public school classroom and may start learning English even before they are fully proficient in the native language. Issues arise when the student is not literate in the native language but has to learn literacy skills in the foreign language, English, with no prior knowledge to draw from.

Throughout this book we have written about ELLs and the fundamentals of teaching English learners. This section will address refugee and other special populations of students in today's classrooms. It is crucial for teachers to be aware of the background conditions and prior lives that students are encumbered with so the schools can provide a comfortable and appropriate instructional setting for all.

What Is a Refugee?

A **refugee** is someone recognized by international law as one who flees his or her homeland and goes to live in another country to live freely and safely. The receiving country is determined by international laws and regulations, and through cooperating governments and agencies. Refugees are a protected population. The Office of Refugee Resettlement (http://www.acf.hhs.gov/programs/orr/press/office_refugee_factgsheet, 2010) describes refugees as those who must have a well founded fear of persecution in their native countries due to their race, religion, nationality, society group, or political beliefs. Refugee status is granted by the Bureau of Population, Refugees, and Migration in the U.S. Department of State, and by the Bureau of Citizenship and Immigrations Services at the U.S. Department of Homeland Security. Within this designation are further distinct populations that include **displaced persons** (although they may leave their locale or region but remain in the home country); **evacuees** (who flee manmade or natural disasters); **asylees** who flee their countries quickly without asylum status, and later apply for asylum in the host country; **unaccompanied minors** who arrive as refugees without families and need child protection services in the United States; persecuted **victims of torture** in the home country who have had insufficient time to apply for refugee status; and **victims of human trafficking** who go to other countries under the promise of employment but once in the country, their captors keep their passports, which makes the victims unable to prove their native citizenship. Individuals applying for official refugee status must show evidence of their claims before being officially granted refugee status.

For teachers who have students from unstable or traumatic environments, classroom issues can range far beyond the typical academic situations. Immigrant and refugee concerns can include limited English proficiency; interrupted formal education; illiteracy in the native language; physical, mental and emotional health issues; loss; genital circumcision; trauma symptoms (posttraumatic stress disorder); cultural and resettlement issues; services; interventions; and immigration procedures. The Refugee Act of 1980, P.L. No. 96-212, provided for the Office of Refugee Resettlement (ORR), which in turn created the Refugee Children School Impact Grant Program for students aged five to eighteen years. In school districts with large numbers of refugees, this grant provides financial assistance to school districts for refugees and special populations.

Refugees can be from many countries, such as Somalia, Liberia, Congo, Sierra Leone, Sudan, Afghanistan, Thailand, Laos, Burma (or Myanmar), Haiti, Iraq, Iran, Cuba, and Bhutan, just to name a few. Governmental agencies determine where the families will relocate. Usually the first place that people flee to is across their borders to the nearest country. When they get to the United States, it is often better for refugees to settle in the smaller towns and cities than the large, overcrowded, overburdened urban cities. Sometimes refugees settle in clusters, such as Somali refugees in Minneapolis, Minnesota; Somali and Sudanese refugees in Lewiston, Maine; Iraqis in Atlanta, Georgia, and Portland, Maine; Burmese in Western Kentucky; and Mon (from lower Burma) in Akron, Ohio, and Fort Wayne, Indiana. The first wave of refugees from Viet Nam and Cambodia settled in Lowell and Lawrence in Massachusetts. Some communities are more desirable than others due to available resources, volunteers, programs, and a welcoming attitude.

Teachers need to partner with refugee and migration agencies to create a support system to handle issues that arise. American teachers are mandated to report abuse, and it may be a great conflict to determine what cultural practices are ascribed to each different group, and how to handle any difficult situation that may arise. For example, refugees from Sudan, Ethiopia, and Kenya may suffer from parasites endemic to their homelands. With knowledge of these illnesses, teachers can be aware of what student health complaints may be. A simple test can screen for parasites, and then students can receive treatment and avoid severe organ damage.

Life Before the United States

Before entering the United States, refugees may have lived lives of horror, civil conflict, political terror, mass murders or amputations, or any other type of unimaginable brutality. They might have lived through years of a war that ravaged their lives, and then perhaps years of living in refugee camps. They have had no control over their lives or the trauma that was inflicted upon them. They might have had to flee abruptly, live in hiding, live in fear, escape stealthily from situations in which their lives were at stake, and suddenly bolt from their homes due to an unanticipated crisis. The constant disruptions; disturbance of daily routines; loss of family, friends, property, and possessions; loss of familiar homes; anxiety and worry over loved ones left behind; and the constant adaptation to new or ambiguous environments can wreak havoc on one's emotional, mental, and physical health.

School-aged refugees (and their parents) may come from extremely undeveloped countries, with little or no literacy or technology. If youngsters were born in refugee camps, they may know nothing outside of the camp and often have no or limited education or language training. Although they may receive some amount of predeparture orientation to Western life, it is impossible to prepare for the unimagined. When they arrive in the new society, they are extremely dependent on the school system, caseworkers, and teachers to provide guidance as the newcomers may not have any experience with formal education in the new or the home country.

Once in the new country, refugee parents are in an extremely complex situation because they cannot yet provide stability and normalcy for their children when they are struggling with their own culture shock. All aspects of the new country will be extremely different, and parents will lack the ability to help bridge the gap for their own children. Refugee parents will be struggling with the language, finding housing and employment, and providing basic needs. Because the parents are occupied with providing an adequate life for the family, the children may go unattended, which puts them at great risk for problems such as gang activity, victimization, and other trouble. Lack of knowledge about cultural expectations and behavior can jeopardize successful adjustment to the new culture.

Regardless of the degree of prior trauma, the abrupt changes and new culture will require adjustment in all areas: psychologically, emotionally, and mentally. The teachers, school administrators, counselors, school/community liaison, and perhaps caseworkers will play a large part in the successful adaption and adjustment of refugee students. Taking an individual interest and providing mentors for the newcomers will help with the transition to the new environment. It is vitally important that refugee students be understood, because they may not display their anxiety or maladjustment externally through body language or expression. They may internalize their stress and act out in inappropriate behaviors that may be detrimental to their health or that of others, such as fights, temper tantrums, debilitating shyness, depression, or symptoms of posttraumatic stress disorder (PTSD). Although the teachers may not be expected to play the role of a therapist, they must be aware that the students may not want to share their horrific stories for a very long time, or ever. Proper intervention at the appropriate level and time must be implemented in the school environment, the daily classroom, or individually, such as providing support for academic and personal success.

Teaching Culturally Appropriate Behavior

Refugee students will come into the country, the community, and the school system oblivious to the appropriate behaviors expected of them. American society, as well as American public school culture, are dictated by specific norms that may not be overtly evident to the newcomer. If refugee students have not attended formal schooling in their country, they will be unaware of any systematic classroom behaviors, regardless of culture. It is in this first school environment that students will become socialized into school and the American culture. The greatest service a teacher can offer a newcomer is to teach explicitly the most simple, rudimentary classroom rules and norm. This should be done by modeling appropriate behavior, using illustrations that are posted around the room, using visuals, and physically showing the students what to do at the appropriate time. Never assume they know what to do;

although posting written rules around the room is a good strategy for students, don't expect great literacy proficiency from the new students—they may not be able to read the rules for a long time. Have the new student watch another student model the expected behavior.

In American culture, we expect people to be independent and self-managed, but the refugee family will be expecting the teachers in the school to be acting as the monitors, using strict discipline or corporal punishment to keep their children in line behaviorally and academically. In this country, we promote self-regulation and reflective thinking and do not use corporal punishment in the classroom. In fact, child abuse is such a volatile topic in the United States, newcomers who are accustomed to spanking or other punitive physical measures to discipline their children feel totally disoriented to learn they can be arrested or have their children removed from the home by governmental authority if they touch their children in anger. This upsets the hierarchy of the family structure as the children then gain control of the parents, often with devastating results, because the parents fear police intervention, a child abuse charge, or losing their children.

Programs for Students with Interrupted Formal Education (SIFE)

Clearly, the SIFE student who matriculates in U.S. public schools will have difficulty if placed in the classroom without strong support and careful consideration. School administrators usually try to place children according to their age. However, a twelve-year-old student from a refugee camp who has never attended school will be misplaced if planted in an American middle school. Newcomer Programs or classrooms exist in some school districts which help SIFE students with the transition from the Newcomer Program into the mainstream classroom. These programs concentrate on intense acculturation training, intensive English development, vocabulary, and literacy training so that students can slowly evolve into becoming better prepared participants in the new school culture.

Schools that do not offer a Newcomer Program can still take steps to provide adequate resources for SIFE students. Following are some strategic measures recommended by the Office of English Language Learning and Migrant Education that schools can employ:

- ❖ Pull out models
- ❖ Push in models
- ❖ Sheltered content instruction
- ❖ Content-based ESL
- ❖ Standards-based learning
- ❖ Teaching social and academic language
- ❖ Teaching language content and objectives
- ❖ Organizing teacher schedules to include block programming for longer teaching time
- ❖ Creating flexible curriculum for SIFE students and modifying language and concepts to be taught
- ❖ Offering remedial courses on material that needs to be covered again
- ❖ Using a team teaching approach

- ❖ Offering after-school tutorials, evening classes, and Saturday programs
- ❖ Extending the high school experience so that students can have a longer time to process and become oriented to the American educational system
- ❖ Collaborating with each other
- ❖ Offering individualized instruction for struggling learners
- ❖ Recruiting native language tutors and community liaisons
- ❖ Offering a buddy system for students to spend time with
- ❖ Offering a mentoring system
- ❖ Inviting community members of the same cultural groups to interact with the students
- ❖ Ensuring access to same-language tutors for SIFE students
- ❖ Teaching through multidisciplinary thematic units
- ❖ Offering ongoing up-to-date training for teachers

Points to Remember

- ❖ Refugees are a protected population.

- ❖ Refugees come to the new country with many issues that need to be addressed, such as limited or interrupted schooling, inadequate nutrition, and trauma from previous experiences in the home country.

- ❖ Refugees will need many services that are available from refugee centers, psychologists, housing specialists, and so on. Seek assistance to meet their needs.

- ❖ Students who are refugees may have no experience or limited experience in classrooms, particularly Western style schooling. Take great care to acclimate your refugee students.

- ❖ Health issues may be problematic due to cultural beliefs. The teacher may have to probe to find the problem because the refugee student or family may be reluctant to discuss the issues (health practices based on superstition, genital circumcision, and illness may need to be treated).

- ❖ Be sensitive and aware of the issues your refugee students encounter but may be hesitant to discuss with anyone.

- ❖ Try to bridge the gap for your students and anticipate what problems they may encounter due to the abrupt move to the United States.

- ❖ Find community resources for your students from people who can speak the language or practice the same religion.

A Rainbow of Children: A Sampler of Cultural Characteristics

The following characteristics are not comprehensive, but are general, overarching tendencies and characteristics of individuals from Spanish-speaking, Muslim, Haitian, Asian, and Native American cultures. The purpose of highlighting these cultural groups is to demonstrate the differences and similarities teachers can expect to find in today's diverse classrooms. By understanding the cultural values of their students, teachers can plan more effective instruction while incorporating a variety of techniques to address the multitude of learning styles.

Culture Quiz 1: Test Your Cultural Knowledge

1. In Belarus, a republic of the Soviet Union, the language spoken is:
   A. Russian
   B. Belarusian
   C. Polish

2. To give a gift in India, the best color to wrap it in would be:
   A. Yellow
   B. White
   C. Green

3. Australians use the term "full bottle." It means:
   A. Fully clothed
   B. Completely naked
   C. Fully informed

4. Americans bathe, soak, wash, and rinse themselves in the same water. They do not use the same wash and rinse routine with dishes or clothes. Japanese use different water for bathing, soaking, and washing themselves because:
   A. They have more access to water
   B. They think it is dirty to use the same water to bathe and rinse in
   C. They are superstitious

5. Brazilians speak which language?
   A. Spanish
   B. Brazilero
   C. Portuguese

6. An Arab person is telling you to calm down. He will:
   A. Cross his arms and bend over slightly at the waist
   B. Put his finger in front of his mouth in a shushing motion
   C. Bring the tip of all his fingers and thumb together and move the hand up and down

7. Dutch people indicate people are miserly by:
   A. Running the forefinger down the nose
   B. Lightly slapping the side of one's neck
   C. Making a quick slapping noise with the hands

8. In China, one points to something:
   A. With an open hand
   B. By pointing to his nose
   C. With the thumb

9. In India, orthodox Hindus will eat with their own clean hands because:
   A. They don't have silverware
   B. Leaves are not big enough
   C. They believe knives, forks, and spoons are dirty

10. When giving a gift to an Indonesian, he or she will open it:
    A. After the gift giver has left
    B. In front of the gift giver
    C. When the family comes home

Culture Quiz 2: Spanish Speakers

1. To indicate someone is cheap in Colombia, one would:
   A. Point to the pocket and grimace
   B. Tap the left hand under the right elbow
   C. Make the "OK" sign

2. In Bolivia, a banana is eaten:
   A. With a knife and fork
   B. With one hand while the other hand peels it
   C. Only as dessert

3. The term used for Costa Ricans is:
   A. Costinos
   B. Ticos
   C. Ricanos

4. In Colombia, women greet each other:
   A. With a modified handshake, except they grab each other's wrists
   B. With a traditional handshake
   C. By hugging each other

5. When a person from Honduras puts his finger below his eye, it means:
   A. He is flirting with you
   B. He is telling you he has something in his eye
   C. Be careful

6. Seeing a black person in Bolivia is considered:
   A. Good luck
   B. Bad luck
   C. No difference

7. The majority of Mexicans speak:
   A. Mexican
   B. Spanish
   C. Azteca

8. What is the attitude toward punctuality in Spanish-speaking cultures?
   A. Casual
   B. Time is strictly adhered to
   C. If you have an appointment, the person you are visiting will not let you wait long because it is seen as very impolite

9. In Mexico, standing with your hands on your hips shows that you are:
   A. Sexy
   B. Angry
   C. Making a challenge

10. In Latin America, yawning is impolite. It may signify that:
    A. The person is poor
    B. The person does not know proper etiquette
    C. The person is hungry

Spanish-Speaking Cultures

Spanish-speaking cultures include people from many countries (including the United States) with unique characteristics. The common thread, of course, is the fact that they all speak Spanish, albeit with varying degrees of fluency, accents, intonation, and verb structures (i.e., *tú, usted,* and *vos*) and certainly different connotations for similar words. These societal variations can be likened to the differences among the United States, Great Britain, Australia, New Zealand, Canada, Jamaica, and South Africa. These countries are extremely different from one another, yet they all claim English as their native language.

Examine the following scenario and discuss the assumption made.

> Two young men are shopping in the local supermarket and are conversing in Spanish. Two American young ladies hear the gentlemen talking and say, "Those Spanish guys are handsome!"

The statement is not negative, and the young men are speaking Spanish, but they might not be from Spain. To say an individual is Spanish is equivalent to hearing someone speak English and calling them English (from England). A Spanish speaker is often called Hispanic (traditionally associated with the Iberian Peninsula), or Latino/a (usually referring to the population from the Americas). Much debate arises with regard to this kind of labeling, but it is safe to say that being called Latino/a versus Hispanic depends on the individual's preference. Non-Hispanics probably are more familiar with the term Hispanic in reference to all Spanish-speaking individuals.

Statistics show that Spanish speakers are the fastest growing population in the United States. The U.S. Bureau of the Census projected that by the year 2020, 15% of the population will be Hispanic, an increase from 9% in 1992. Many factors affect the academic and cognitive development of Spanish-speaking students, including the heritage of their families, the length of time residing in the United States, the educational level attained, and socioeconomic level reached. Carrasquillo (1991) noted that Hispanic students are diverse due to different backgrounds, but they may share general experiences through family structure, religious beliefs, and general customs. However, they are in a country that does not always value diversity, but rather appreciates uniformity through a common language, culture, and race.

The following charts are general characteristics of customs observed by Hispanic/Latinos (taken from the book *Culturegrams,* produced by Brigham Young University) as an "aid to the understanding of, feeling for, and communication with other people." Although distinct regions and countries have their own styles (e.g., in Colombia women will shake the wrist of another woman instead of shaking her hand), the general customs may be similar throughout most Spanish-speaking countries.

Answers to World Culture Quiz

1. B. Belarusian
2. C. Green
3. C. Fully informed
4. B. They think it is dirty to use the same water to bathe and rinse in.
5. C. Portuguese
6. C. Bring the tip of all his fingers and thumb together and move the hand up and down
7. A. Running the forefinger down the nose
8. A. With an open hand
9. C. They believe knives, forks, and spoons are dirty
10. A. After the gift giver has left

Answers to the Spanish Culture Quiz

1. B. Tap the left hand under the right elbow
2. A. With a knife and fork
3. B. Ticos
4. A. With a modified handshake, except they grab each other's wrists
5. C. Be careful
6. A. Good luck
7. B. Spanish
8. A. Casual
9. C. Making a challenge
10. C. The person is hungry

Greetings

❖ A handshake is shared at the very least; sometimes a full embrace. It is very important to greet everyone when meeting and say goodbye when leaving.

❖ Woman-to-woman and man-to-woman greetings are given with a kiss on the cheek, or both cheeks (Spain).

❖ People stand very close to each other while talking, sometimes touching a friend's clothing, hand, or arm.

❖ Family names and titles such as Señor (Mr.), Señora (Mrs.), or Señorita (Miss) are used to address elders or professionals. Don and Doña are used with first names to show respect.

Gestures

❖ The smile is an important gesture of goodwill.

❖ Much affection is displayed publicly.

❖ Hand, arm, and other gestures are often used in conversation.

❖ People say "salud" if someone sneezes.

❖ People are beckoned by waving the fingers or the whole hand, with the palm down.

❖ It is not impolite for men to stare and make flattering remarks to women they do not know.

❖ Yawning is impolite because it is a sign of hunger.

Some General Attitudes

❖ Individualism and personal pride are important in these societies.

❖ A person's appearance is extremely important.

❖ People strive to project an impression of affluence and social position. Styles and quality of clothing indicate status and respectability.

❖ People often feel it is their duty to correct or point out "errors" they see in others.

❖ Political power is often coveted.

Time

❖ The individual is more important than schedules. Punctuality is not expected in social affairs; it is not impolite to be late, and people usually arrive late.

❖ If a visitor arrives unexpectedly or someone suddenly needs help, people will drop everything, regardless of how long it takes or how long someone else is kept waiting.

❖ Time is fluid.

Family

❖ The family plays a role of utmost importance.

❖ Family members share good fortunes with each other.

❖ Although this custom is rapidly changing, the father traditionally provides for the family, while the mother is responsible for the home.

❖ Families often host members of the extended family for long periods.

❖ Traditionally, men enjoy more social freedom than do women.

❖ Family obligations are extremely strong.

Ramirez and Casteñeda (1974) found that Hispanic students respond well to classroom strategies using techniques such as:

❖ Cooperative learning

❖ Personalized rewards

❖ Modeling

❖ Informal class discussion

❖ Concepts presented globally, rather than detail oriented

❖ Explicit classroom rules

❖ Personal interaction such as hugs and pats

❖ Humanizing the curriculum using humor, fantasy, or drama

Other successful tactics include utilizing group projects, offering hugs and pats as personal rewards, standing closer to the students while teaching, and avoiding the use of debates (as an instructional method) and question-and-answer format. Short-term daily projects are more successful than long-term projects. To enhance interpersonal understanding, the teacher should stand closer to the children when teaching.

In many Hispanic cultures, religion and religious holidays pervade every segment of daily life and can even interfere with school attendance.

Frequently, religious observations are linked to education and usually accompany political events. Educational systems may be more authoritative, and children wear uniforms. Students might be separated by gender and find it difficult to study with students of the opposite sex. The idea of dressing in front of peers for physical education classes may be inappropriate and misunderstood, as Hispanic students tend to be modest.

Children may be accustomed to different desk configurations in the classroom. They might have worked with partners or groups or sat with students in a row of attached desks. Children can become confused with democratic classroom expectations if they are accustomed to more authoritarian teachers who quickly mete out corporal punishment for transgressions and improper behavior. Educational experiences with the Socratic method, the use of audiovisual aids and laboratories, and access to special education might be foreign concepts to some children. Teaching by rote memorization, with less emphasis on critical thinking, might be what the newcomers are familiar with, so American education might appear "easier" to Hispanic students from other countries.

As with some other cultural groups, Hispanic students might be expected to lower their eyes when communicating with elders, especially when they are being reprimanded.

The classroom teacher is the main contact for the student and will provide for the needs of the student in all educational capacities. In other countries, schools do not usually have guidance counselors, special education teachers, or the PTA. Classes involving special education might be seen as an insult or retribution for wrong behavior. Most importantly, the teacher is the ultimate authority, and parents are not expected to become involved other than to ensure that students complete their homework.

American teachers might be surprised to learn of the ethnocentric feelings that Hispanic groups feel for Hispanics outside their respective groups. For that reason it is important to identify individuals correctly. For example, just because someone is speaking Spanish in a place such as Miami, non-Spanish speakers should not assume they are all Cubans.

Culture Quiz 3: Islamic and Arab Culture

1. If you are a man greeting a Muslim woman, you should:
   A. Give her a hug
   B. Wait until she extends her hand
   C. Kiss both cheeks

2. What would be the worst day to do business with a Muslim company?
   A. Friday
   B. Saturday
   C. Monday

3. In the Arab culture, the people are:
   A. Individualistic
   B. Independent
   C. Close to one another, with much personal interaction

4. To do business with Muslims, you must:
   A. Get to know the family
   B. Establish trust
   C. Have someone be a mediator

5. Which is the most accurate statement?
   A. Women are forced to cover their heads (hijab) so men will not look at them.
   B. Women choose to cover their heads (hijab).
   C. Wearing hijab depends on the culture, the woman's choice, and her relationship with her husband.

6. With regard to Muslim males, which of the following is true?
   A. They are obligated to be covered from the navel to the knee.
   B. They must cover their heads.
   C. There are no restrictions.

7. You are in a business meeting in Saudi Arabia. During a break, you go to the restroom only to see a man washing his feet in the sink. Why?
   A. He is getting ready to go take a nap and wants his feet clean.
   B. Someone spilled sweet tea on his shoes.
   C. He is getting ready to pray.

8. The best gift for a Muslim businessman would be:
   A. Good perfume
   B. A silk scarf
   C. Flowers

9. On your travels, you go into a market with Muslim/Arab vendors. You are trying to buy a rug. You ask how much, and the price seems really high. What should you do?
   A. Walk away. You should forget about it.
   B. Look insulted.
   C. Haggle—offer another price.

10. Which statement is true?
    A. All Muslims are Arabs.
    B. Muslims and Arabs are interchangeable words.
    C. Followers of Islam are Muslims.

Islamic Cultures and Speakers of Arabic

Islam, reported to be one of the fastest-growing religions in the United States and around the world, is practiced by Muslims. Many Americans consider themselves Muslims, and they are native speakers of English. Muslim students can be from any racial or ethnic background. Students from Algeria, Djiboati, Egypt, Iraq, Jordan, Kuwait, Lebanon, Libya, Mauritania, Morocco, North and South Yemen, Palestine, United Arab Emirates, Oman, Qatar, Saudi Arabia, Somalia, Sudan, Syria, Chad, and Tunisia (and other African countries) are usually Arabic speakers. Arabic is used in the Koran (Qur'an, Islam's book of scripture). However, most Muslims are not Arabic. They come from diverse countries, such as Indonesia, Malaysia, Pakistan, China, Fiji, and Barbados, and do not necessarily speak Arabic.

No matter what the nationality, the Islamic follower is familiar with the Arabic language and can recite it and therefore is subject to Arabic influence. Although Muslim students are influenced greatly by their ethnic and cultural heritage, the practices of Islamic religion often supersede cultural traits. Those individuals who follow pure Islamic tradition will demonstrate the same religious practices and observances, which means the public schools must formulate and implement policies to create a culturally sensitive academic environment.

Educators should be familiar with fundamental beliefs of Muslims and make allowances for religious holidays, days of fasting, dietary requirements, prayer time and its accompanying rituals, expressions of personal modesty, and curriculum issues. The First Amendment of the U.S. Constitution protects the religious rights of individuals, which signifies that the classroom teacher should know as much as possible to foster understanding toward the Muslim student. The fundamental religious aspects of Islam are reflected in the classroom, just as cultural aspects are. Some practices the teacher can expect are addressed in this book. The Islamic perspectives highlighted are culled from the information disseminated from the Council on American-Islamic Relations in its publication, *An Educator's Guide to Islamic Religious Practices*. Also included are some general cultural characteristics as perceived by the Educational Service Staff of AFME (American Friends of the Middle East, or AMIDEAS), taken from its chapter "Cultural Clues to the Middle Eastern Student." Because of the fundamental teachings of the Koran, characteristics of different ethnic groups that practice Islam might be similar, although the cultures might be very different. For example, Muslims from Malaysia are distinct from Muslims from Saudi Arabia, although they practice the same religion.

Social Relationships

Manners reflect the formality of the culture, which is formal in social customs and daily routines. Respect for one another is of vital importance. Personal relationships, family, and friendship are central to life. The American ways of forming relationships quickly, but superficially, are seen as having little depth or significance. Male/female relationships are restricted and are governed by a rigid set of cultural rules. In some conservative countries, the roles of women are less prominent than those of men, as the culture is male-dominated. However, in more progressive Islamic countries, women are allowed to hold high positions in public office.

Answers to Quiz (Islam)

1. B. Wait until she extends her hand
2. A. Friday
3. C. Close to one another with much personal interaction
4. B. Establish trust
5. C. Wearing hijab depends on the culture, the woman's choice, and her relationship with her husband.
6. A. They are obligated to be covered from the navel to the knee
7. C. He is getting ready to pray
8. A. Good perfume
9. C. Haggle—offer a lower price.
10. C. Followers of Islam are Muslims

Food/Hospitality

Refreshments, even if only coffee or soft drinks, are always served when visiting. Not to offer refreshments is unthinkable.

Fatalistic Attitudes

Life events are designed by an omnipotent God and occur as a direct result of the will of God, without respect to the desires of man. The phrase *Inshallah* (God willing) is frequently uttered, which means the will of God will determine whatever occurs.

Emotional Displays

Arabs generally are conservative and are not comfortable with shows of affection in public. They will not display emotion outwardly, but will wait until they are home to laugh loudly, or argue in private.

Touch

Traditional Islamic countries like Saudi Arabia, Iraq, and Iran may find cross-gender touching inappropriate, whereas more liberal societies may be comfortable with some interaction between the sexes. Unless one is certain of the cultural mores, women are to be greeted with words, because it may be inappropriate to touch them. Most Muslims avoid body contact with the opposite sex; however, men may kiss and embrace men, and women may embrace and kiss women. Men may shake hands, but the handshake should not be pulled away too quickly. Individuals may stand close to one another, and "bathe the other person in one's breath," as a way of being deeply involved with one another (Hall, 1966, p. 49). Hall also says that "Arabs look each other in the eye when talking with an intensity that makes most Americans highly uncomfortable" (p. 161).

Dewariahs

Dewariahs are a place to gather to socialize and celebrate, as conversation is a tonic; however, men and women are separated from each other.

Gifts and Invitations

If an individual admires something an Arab has, it will be given to him or her. Arabs expect to pay for meals if they invite someone to dine. Gifts given are not to be opened in front of guests. Additionally, friendship implies that favors will be done for one another, and favors are expected to be repaid reciprocally.

Saving Face

Arabs are nonconfrontational and will avoid arguments at any cost. They act humbly, are sensitive to others' feelings, and will never disgrace or embarrass others. Politeness will be shown to individuals at all times, even to one's enemy, because the Koran dictates that "God loveth not the speaking ill of anyone in public." This includes writing about an individual.

Privacy

Arabs prefer to have close personal interaction with one another and therefore have large spaces inside the home instead of walls. Physical privacy as we know it is nonexistent, and to be alone, Arabs will simply stop talking. They are very private inside their homes, and outsiders will not be invited into the home until they are very close. One can assume that an invitation into an Arab home is an honor that indicates deep friendship.

Children and Family

The family is traditional in that the father is head of the household and the mother takes care of the children and home. Children are taught their roles early in life and are given responsibilities according to their age. The parents' word is final, and elders are greatly respected. Academic choices of children will often reflect the wishes of the parents instead of their individual choice. The culture is paternalistic, and this authoritative familial pattern is evident throughout societal patterns.

Guidelines for Educators

Because the Muslim population is growing rapidly in American public schools, teachers need to be knowledgeable about how to respect the rights and beliefs of these students. Learning about the rights of Islamic students can be accomplished by adhering to guidelines set forth by the Council of American-Islamic Relations.

Adolescence and Gender Relations

According to Islamic rule, certain parameters regarding personal modesty are prescribed for postpubescent boys and girls when dealing with the opposite sex. Shaking hands with the opposite sex, even if it is a teacher or administrator, for example, might be viewed as immodest, as well as coed physical education classes and school dances. No pressure to participate should be exhibited, nor should students be penalized for refusing to take part in these mixed gender activities.

Physical Education

Muslim children are prohibited from uncovering their bodies and are not allowed to participate in communal showers after sports. Private showers should be available, and if the class is scheduled late in the day, students should be allowed to skip the showers altogether and wait until they get home. Physical education clothing should be modified so that the girls wear full track suits, and the boys wear knee-length shorts.

Mixed-sex swimming classes are a problem for Muslim students. They should not be penalized for nonparticipation on religious grounds. Alternative outside certification can be an option if the school has mandatory certification.

Muslim Holidays

The major celebrations that all Muslims celebrate are the two Eid (holiday) days. The first Eid day is the day after the month of Ramadan (which is marked by a month of fasting), the ninth month of the Islamic lunar calendar. The second major celebration is observed on the tenth day of the twelfth Islamic month. Schools should note Muslim holidays on their calendars, as the students are obliged to take at least one day off from school, which should be without penalty. However, the exact date of the Eid depends on the sighting of the new moon, which is uncertain until the night before the celebrated day.

Dietary Requirements

Muslims are careful about food and how it is prepared because they follow Islam's Holy Scripture, which prescribes the Halal (permissible by Islamic law) consumption and preparation of foods. The Koran (or Qur'an) prohibits consumption of alcohol, pork (including byproducts or derivatives), shellfish, and other objectionable foods such as:

Fish without fins
Pepperoni, sausage, and pork hot dogs
Bacon, alone or in foods
Animal shortening (vegetable shortening is
    acceptable) in breads, puddings, cookies,
    cakes, donuts, pastries, etc.
Gelatin in Jell-O, desserts, candies, marshmallows,
    chocolates, etc.
Lard in any form or product
Ingredients containing alcohol (vanilla extract,
    Dijon mustard)

School cafeteria personnel can demonstrate respect for these religious observations by highlighting their menus with a visual clue when these food items are offered.

Personal Modesty for Men and Women

According to Islam, modesty in behavior and dress encourages value for wisdom, skills, and community contribution, rather than physical attributes. Modesty, chastity, and morality are emphasized, and individuals are responsible for their deeds by the time they reach puberty.

Males are obliged to be covered from the navel to the knee, and some students cover their heads with a kufki. In public, females cover their heads and wear loose-fitting, nonrevealing clothing called hijab, or khimar.

Wearing a head covering is a practice misunderstood by many and may cause problems in school settings. Teachers and administrators need to protect the student's personal and religious right to wear a scarf and should prohibit and reprimand classmates who pull or remove a Muslim girl's scarf.

Family Life/Sex Education

Because Islam has its own specific set of teachings about human development and related issues, parents need the option to remove their children from any family life programs offered by the school.

Daily Prayer

Islamic believers must pray five times every day. The prayer times that fall within school hours must be observed, and students will need about fifteen minutes to complete prayers. Muslims must wash their faces, hands, and feet with clean water (a restroom or any facility with running water will suffice) for about two minutes. According to the Qur'an, the individual will stand, bow, and touch the forehead to the ground and recite specific prayers. The worshiper needs a quiet, clean room where he or she will face toward Mecca (usually northeast in America). Although total silence is not necessary, others should not walk in front of or interrupt the person praying. Being considerate, the other students should not interrupt the person praying unless it is an emergency. The person praying is thoroughly engaged, so he or she would probably not respond anyway.

Fasting

In Islam, holy days and festivals are governed according to the lunar calendar, which, like the solar calendar, has twelve months. A lunar month (marked by the new crescent moon) may last only twenty-nine days, so the lunar year is about eleven days shorter than the solar year. Muslims are required to fast in the month of Ramadan, during the ninth month of the Islamic lunar calendar.

Islam has five "pillars," which include fasting, declarations of faith, daily prayer, offering regular charity, and pilgrimage to Mecca. Fasting is to re-

frain from eating and drinking from break of dawn to sunset. The exact dates that determine when followers should fast change throughout the full solar year. Students who are fasting can be excused from going to the cafeteria at lunch time and from participating in strenuous physical activity. In an effort to support multiculturalism in the community, the teacher can seize this teachable moment by inviting guest speakers to teach the other students about the rituals observed in a variety of religions.

Curriculum Issues

Muslims take issue with their portrayal as the enemy in outdated social studies texts. Negative depictions can contribute to suspicion, harassment, and violence toward followers of Islam. Textbooks should be reviewed for religious prejudice and selected under the guidance of Muslim educators to ensure that history, geography, and social studies texts offer reliable information about the tenets of Islam. One major falsehood is that "Allah" is a Muslim god, instead of the traditional Judeo-Christian God.

School Issues

Other issues that might conflict in the traditional school setting are not saluting the flag, or refusing to recite the Pledge of Allegiance. Muslim parents may teach their children to stand up, but perhaps not salute the flag when reciting the pledge because Islam discourages acts that are irreverent to God. This is not meant to be offensive or a symbol of disrespect to the symbol of the nation.

Finally, conscientious followers of Islam might be expected to be released at midday on Friday, the day for congregational worship. This is called Jum'ah, and it takes place at the mosque. Students might need to ask for an extended lunch period to fulfill this obligation. If many Muslim students attend the same school, the prayers can be held on school property, which is a right upheld by the Supreme Court in 1990 as the Equal Access Act.

Suggestions for the Teacher

To embrace and enjoy interactions with new beliefs, cultures, and ideas, the Council on Americanιslamic Relations offers the following suggestions for religious accommodations for Muslim students in public schools.

❖ To note pork and pork byproducts in lunches, mark items with a red dot or a picture of a pig.

Muslim holidays

❖ Schedule exams and other major events around holidays.
❖ Do not mark students absent.

Ramadan fast

❖ Allow students to study in the library or elsewhere during lunch.

Physical education

❖ Discuss clothing requirements with Muslim parents.
❖ Reschedule classes for students who prefer a same-gender exercise environment.

Gender relations

❖ Do not extend your hand first for a handshake with the opposite sex.

Family/sex education programs

❖ Allow parents reasonable time to review any material dealing with "sex education."
❖ Allow children to opt-out from all or part of the family life program.

Prayer

❖ Allow Muslim students to pray in unused rooms.

Fairness in classroom and text preparation

❖ Check textbooks for religious biases.
❖ Invite Muslim speakers to social studies and world religion classes.

Culture Quiz 4: Haitians

1. Many Haitians are misunderstood because:
   A. They practice voodoo
   B. They have a caste system
   C. They have a high literacy rate

2. Haitians are very proud because:
   A. They speak Haitian Kreyol
   B. They were the first independent black nation in the world
   C. They have many children

3. Haiti has a thriving market system primarily run by:
   A. The man of the family
   B. The children after they return from school
   C. Itinerant female traders

4. Usually you can determine social status by:
   A. The amount of French one speaks
   B. The amount of livestock one has
   C. The number of children one has

5. The wealthiest people in Haiti tend to be:
   A. Foreigners
   B. Farmers
   C. Lighter skinned

6. One of the most important things to Haitians is:
   A. Money
   B. Having many children
   C. Education

7. Fosterage or "restavek" is:
   A. A system in which children may be sent to other families to perform domestic service with the understanding that the children will be sent to school
   B. A system where the children leave the country to attend school
   C. A system where the children are expected to care for the parents

8. When entering a Haitian's yard, it is customary to shout out:
   A. "Honor," and the person being visited responds with "Respect"
   B. "Come out friend!" and the person being visited responds with "Welcome!"
   C. "Here we are!" and the person being visited responds with "Come in!"

9. Haitian literature is typically written in
   A. Kreyol
   B. French
   C. Dominican

10. Haiti shares an island with which other country?
    A. Dominica
    B. The Dominican Republic
    C. Cuba

Haitian Students

The Refugee Service Center at the Center for Applied Linguistics offers current information on ethnic groups so that educators can meet the needs of their students. The information contained in this section can be accessed on the center's website at http://www.cao.org/RSC.

Haitian communities are flourishing socially, economically, and culturally in places such as South Florida, Boston, and New York. Their historical backgrounds offer richness to the multicultural fiber of the United States. Miami's Little Haiti is often the first stop for recent Haitian immigrants as they climb the ladder to self-sufficiency and eventual participation as citizens in mainstream American life.

Recent immigrants often find that they do not relate to African-Americans because the two cultures are worlds apart. Unfortunately, Haitians have been the victims of inaccurate cultural misunderstandings and negative stereotypes that have inflicted great damage on youngsters from this culture, causing them to deny their heritage. The lack of ethnic self-pride is manifested in the phenomenon of young, more assimilated Haitians claiming to be African-American, Caribbean-American, West Indians, or Haitian-Americans. They often deny that they speak Creole or claim to speak French when they cannot. Later, Haitians may assume the identity, lifestyle, language variations, and mannerisms of African-American youth to gain acceptance by their peers; hence, the rejection of the native cultures and a denial of knowledge of the native language (Portes & Rumbaut, 1996; Portes & Zhou, 1993).

The Haitian school system was modeled on the French system, which offers fourteen years of education, seven at the elementary and seven at the secondary level, in the "elite" language of French. The system was restructured in 1978 to offer ten years of basic education and three years of secondary education. After much debate, and with much resistance, Haitian Creole became the language of instruction for the first four grades.

Education is highly valued, and schooling is technically "free," but many Haitians do not have access to it because the poverty level is too high to afford the uniforms, books, and supplies. Consequently, the majority of the population receives little or no formal education at all. Teachers who have Haitian students in their classes must ascertain the extent of their previous educational experience. Their educational backgrounds will depend on the socioeconomic status the students encountered in Haiti.

Students from the Haitian educational system are accustomed to different educational beliefs and will exhibit behaviors that mirror those distinct values and school behaviors. As a result of different teaching and learning styles, students in Haitian schools are expected to learn more subjects in greater detail through rote learning and memorization. Haitian students will be unfamiliar with the American penchant for analysis and synthesis of material, and they will be confused by the number of correct answers possible in testing situations. Students will have to be taught explicitly how to think and discover for themselves and exactly what is expected of them when being tested.

In Haiti, grading and testing are formal and follow strict procedures. It is more difficult to get good grades, and therefore, Haitian students will place importance on studying for quizzes, tests, and making high scores.

Answers to Haiti Quiz 4

1. A. They practice voodoo
2. B. They were the first independent black nation in the world
3. C. Itinerant female traders
4. A. The amount of French one speaks
5. C. Lighter skinned
6. C. Education
7. A. A system in which children may be sent to other families to perform domestic service with the understanding that the children will be sent to school
8. A. "Honor," and the person being visited responds with "Respect"
9. B. French
10. B. The Dominican Republic

Teacher–student relationships are formal in Haiti. The informality of teacher–student relationships in the U.S. school system may be perceived as a lack of respect for teachers. In the Haitian classroom, students are addressed by their last name. The student speaks only when asked a question and does not look the teacher in the eye. The teacher has total authority over the class. For Haitian newcomers to the American classroom, the idea of "democracy" in the classroom is foreign and is not understood. Haitians are used to having a teacher who is feared and respected. Corporal punishment by the teacher enforces discipline and is sanctioned by the parent.

In Haiti, parent–teacher communication is formal; the only time the parent will hear from the teacher is when the student is doing wrong. This communication will result in the parent inflicting corporal punishment on the child for committing the transgression. There is no PTA; parents are not encouraged to participate in school matters. Papers, letters, and notices are not sent home with the child; parents are expected to go to the school to pick up report cards and such. In the United States, papers are sent home from school with the child, but they might not be returned to the school because of this reason. Thus, parents who react negatively to the request for parental involvement need to be educated about what is expected of them in their new country.

In Haiti, the teacher is the absolute authority, always knows best, and is not to be questioned. Haitian children in the United States may be confused on seeing the apparent informality of the American classroom. In trying to learn the proper classroom etiquette from their American classmates, they may inadvertently overstep their bounds. Haitian students will be unaccustomed to the "democratic" atmosphere found in the United States and need to be gently reminded of expected behavior.

Because of the poverty level in Haiti, the literacy rate is extremely low in the countryside. However, Haitians possess a rich oral tradition that includes the art of storytelling, riddles, songs, and games. As a result, they may be stronger as auditory learners rather than as visual learners.

Other points that American teachers should be aware of are:

❖ In Haitian schools, desks are not individualized; they are attached in rows and students sit side by side. Students might feel isolated when seated individually.

❖ Many Haitian schools are segregated by gender, and students will feel uncomfortable being in mixed classes. Additionally, the concept of playing together during physical education might be disquieting. It is culturally inappropriate for Haitian students to dress and undress in front of others, even those of the same sex. Arrangements should be made to accommodate the needs of these students.

❖ Haitian students might be unaccustomed to owning their own textbooks. In Haiti, they probably had to borrow a book and copy it by hand. In Haiti, audiovisual aids might be nonexistent; experiential learning is not an instructional method used; most schools have no laboratories to practice in; and learning is traditionally by rote, memorization, and recitation. Finally, due to the type of learning Haitian students are accustomed to, they are uncomfortable with and initially will resist engaging in activities that demand critical independent thinking.

❖ Many Haitians are religious, maintain a strong work ethic, hold deep respect for authority, and revere education, because it is a means of social mobility. Parents demand obedience from children, and children are expected to help out by translating for them, shopping, taking care of siblings, and doing other household chores. Frequent absenteeism might result as a consequence of familial expectations.

Culture Quiz 5: Asian

1. Asian cultures:
   A. Are all the same
   B. Are often influenced by characteristics of Buddhism
   C. Are individual-oriented

2. Asian values include a:
   A. Respect for authority
   B. Respect for elders
   C. Both

3. Asians usually greet each other with a:
   A. Hug
   B. Kiss
   C. Bow

4. It is customary for Koreans to:
   A. Refuse a gift three times
   B. Accept a gift after two refusals
   C. Only give a gift to elders

5. Business cards should be accepted:
   A. And immediately placed in the back pocket
   B. With one hand
   C. With two hands

6. A gift to a Chinese person should be wrapped in:
   A. Red
   B. Yellow
   C. Black

7. You should avoid giving Chinese which gift?
   A. A cat
   B. Anything with the number nine
   C. A clock

8. The Japanese culture is influenced greatly by:
   A. Confucianism
   B. Buddhism
   C. Catholicism

9. While in a meeting with Japanese businessmen, it is usual to expect:
   A. Everyone to speak at the same time
   B. Some people to interrupt
   C. Long periods of silence

10. In Asian cultures, it is not appropriate to:
    A. Touch someone on the head
    B. Say goodbye
    C. Cough

Asian Americans

Asians are not a homogeneous group. They do, however, constitute a significant minority group in the United States. Asian Americans represent many distinct subgroups who speak different languages, worship through different religions, and practice different customs and beliefs. The main groups are East Asians (Chinese, Japanese, Korean), Pacific Islanders, Southeast Asians (Thai, Vietnamese, Cambodian, Laotian), and South Asian (Indian and Pakistani). Threads of similarities may run through the subgroups, but they all have distinct histories, origins, and cultural roots. Among these groups, differences also exist within national groups, families, and individuals themselves.

Some Asians were born in the United States, whereas others come from abroad. Some are affluent and come with highly developed skills, whereas others are barely literate (Brand, 1987b). Regardless of success or acculturation, many Asians are stereotyped as the "model minority" because the Asian student is often the one who is at the head of the class and is the valedictorian at graduation. Many people believe that the Confucian ideas that stress family ideals, respect for elders, deferred gratification, and discipline (Brand, 1987a) are the reason for high educational achievement. Studies show that Asian Americans are more likely to believe that success in life is connected to what has been studied in school.

American schooling may contradict the fundamental cultural beliefs of Asians because it emphasizes individualism and competition, whereas the ethnic identity of Asian children is often based on their relationship to the group and allegiance to family (Trueba & Cheng, 1993). Academic achievement and upward mobility are viewed as an obligation for the maintenance of the family, which is the responsibility of all family members (Pang, 1990).

Additionally, Asian parents teach their children to respect authority, feel responsibility for relatives, and show self-control. School failure is seen as a lack of will, and this failure can be alleviated by increasing parental restrictions. Baruth and Manning (2002) claim that Asian-American children need reinforcement from the teacher and work more efficiently in quiet, well-structured surroundings. These children appear to be more dependent, conforming, and obedient by placing the family's welfare before their own desires.

Like students from other cultures, Asians may be confused with the apparent teacher–student informality of the American classroom and function better with structure and organization (Baruth & Manning, 2002). Asian cultures also value the idea of humility and/or self-effacement. Children may not volunteer to participate in the classroom until specifically asked by the teacher. Drawing attention to oneself by virtue of misbehaving might cause great distress and result in "losing face" (Morrow & McBride, 1988), because children are taught to value silence, listen more than speak, speak softly, and be modest in dress and behavior (Feng, 1994).

The following suggestions are offered by Feng (1994) as a formula for teachers to address issues concerning the diversity of Asian-American cultures. It should be noted, however, that these suggestions could be implemented for any ethnic group.

❖ Get to know the customs, values, and traditions of various cultures, and learn the conditions under which students came to the United States. Try to visit the students' homes and get to know the families.
❖ Learn a few words of the students' native language to set the tone for communication.
❖ Encourage native language use at home. Use English-proficient interpreters with parents.
❖ Try to learn the children's names and pronounce them correctly.
❖ Be careful not to encourage discord between home values and school expectations. For example, if the home expectation is conformity, don't encourage the child to challenge the teacher.
❖ Academic expectation should be based on ability rather than stereotypical beliefs.
❖ Peer tutoring can be used for children who are not yet proficient in English.
❖ Know who makes decisions for the child and utilize the natural support system.
❖ Develop strong home–school links for communication.

- Avoid assumptions about children's prior knowledge and experience (e.g., not every child has experienced a birthday party).
- Discover what you can about Asian parent networks. The best way to remove a cultural barrier is to appear sincere.

Common Characteristics of Many Asian Cultures

(from *Culturegrams*)

Greetings
- Bow or nod.
- Individuals do not touch each other.
- Little or no public display of affection.
- Stand far apart (even farther than Americasns do).

Gestures
- Smiling and laughing often indicate embarrassment.
- Little or no affection is shown in public.
- It is impolite to speak loudly.
- Hand and arm gestures are not often used in conversation.
- People's sneezes are not usually acknowledged.
- People are beckoned by waving all the fingers with the palm of the hand facing down.
- Pointing is done with the entire hand.
- Japanese say no by shaking the hand from side to side with the palm forward and point to themselves with their pointer finger facing their nose.
- People must sit erect with both feet on the floor; it is impolite to put an ankle on the knee.
- Yawning is impolite.
- Vietnamese men do not offer to shake hands with women.

General attitudes
- Society is group oriented.
- Loyalty is to the group, the family, and to one's superiors, as opposed to personal feelings.

- Humility and self-effacing comments are normal.
- It is essential to act similar to or in harmony with the crowd.
- People strive to conform in appearance (even when wearing the latest Western styles, people must try to look like everyone else).
- Reserve and modesty must be observed at all times.
- It is important to save face at all times, for self and others.
- People will often allow others to escape potential embarrassment with dignity.
- Goals and decisions are made with the good of the group in mind, not for the personal benefit of any individual.

Time
- Being late is impolite.
- People are prompt or a little bit early (for social as well as business affairs).

Family
- The family is extremely important.
- The family has a strong tradition of respect and loyalty.
- There is a strong sense of family reputation and family obligation.
- Elders are highly respected.
- Many members of the extended family (particularly in-laws) live together.

Answers to Asian Culture Quiz
1. B. Are often influenced by characteristics of Buddhism
2. C. Both
3. C. Bow
4. A. Refuse a gift three times
5. C. With two hands
6. C. Black
7. C. A clock
8. A. Confucianism
9. C. Long periods of silence
10. A. Touch someone on the head

Culture Quiz 6: Native Americans

1. Native Americans speak:
   - A. The same languages
   - B. More than several dozen languages
   - C. More than 2,200 tribal languages

2. Native American students will:
   - A. Reflect their cultural values in the classroom
   - B. Take on the cultural values of their teachers
   - C. Take on the cultural values of the mainstream culture

3. The most effective instructional style for Native American students:
   - A. Includes holistic, mental instruction with nonverbal images
   - B. Includes competition
   - C. Includes highlighting individual success

4. Native Americans believe:
   - A. That one should own the land their ancestors lived on
   - B. That man cannot own the land
   - C. That because they are nomadic, they cannot own land

5. The pilgrims invented Thanksgiving.
   - A. True; this is the real story
   - B. False; Native Americans celebrate many occasions
   - C. No one knows for sure

6. All Native Americans wear buckskins, feathers, and beads:
   - A. True; this is traditional dress
   - B. False; traditional dress may be worn only for special ceremonies
   - C. There is no research to be sure

7. All Native Americans live on reservations.
   - A. True
   - B. False
   - C. There are no records to indicate

8. For Native Americans, Thanksgiving is:
   - A. A celebration of friendship
   - B. Another day off
   - C. A day of mourning for the havoc that the "pilgrims" caused

9. A neutral facial expression will indicate:
   - A. Anger
   - B. Sadness
   - C. Respect

10. Native Americans may use what part of the body to point?
    - A. The lips
    - B. The hand
    - C. The fingers

Native Americans

With more than 500 Native American tribal groups and about 2,200 different languages (Baruth & Manning, 1992), it is impossible to generalize the English language proficiency and acculturation of these populations. Language and cultural differences manifest themselves in the disparity of values found in the home and in the schools. Philips (1983) found that community norms and socialization practices influence the classroom behavior of children. By understanding the values of Native American populations, teachers can adjust classroom situations to provide optimum instructional settings.

Although many tribal groups exist, the shared characteristic of being indigenous allows for some similarities, despite differences in cultural styles. Some researchers have noted that many Native American students have the tendency to be field-dependent (Baruth & Manning, 1992; McShane & Plas, 1982; Swisher & Deyhle, 1989; Tharp, 1989a), whereas other researchers posit that Native American students can also tend to be field-independent (Tharp, 1989b). Ultimately, individual characters are the deciding factor regarding field-dependent and field-independent learning. The behavior of Native American children reflects the values of their culture. Diaz-Rico and Weed (1995) mentioned a research project that took place in several Sioux classrooms, where the students appeared withdrawn and silent. American teachers, who are unaccustomed to prolonged periods of silence in their verbal discourse patterns, were met with students who only gave monosyllabic or nonverbal responses when questioned. The teachers were dismayed to learn that the students were purposefully shutting them out to avoid the teacher–student learning exchange. Once they discovered that the silence was a control issue, the teachers began to involve themselves in the community and daily lives of the students. The students began to participate more when the context was changed (Dumont, 1972).

Socialization in the classroom is a direct reflection of life in the community. Teachers with typical Anglo values, expectations, and instructional methods will not be able to reach the child who prefers not to read aloud, speaks so softly that he is inaudi-ble, and feels more comfort with a lifestyle in which only one individual is directing and controlling all activity (Philips, 1972).

Answers to Native American Quiz

1. C. More than 2,200 tribal languages
2. A. Reflect their cultural values in the classroom
3. A. Includes holistic, mental instruction with nonverbal images
4. B. That man cannot own the land
5. B. False; Native Americans celebrate many occasions.
6. B. False; traditional dress may be worn only for special ceremonies.
7. B. False
8. C. A day of mourning for the havoc that the "pilgrims" caused
9. C. Respect
10. A. The lips

Navajo children pattern their discourse after the adults in their society. Students speak at length, one at a time, while the other students wait politely until the end of the statement before beginning to speak their thoughts. Ideas are developed completely and might not have any relation to the thoughts of the previous speaker. Discourse is related to peers instead of being teacher-dominated. In this manner, the students are not silent or resentful.

Writing styles also reflect cultural values. The American culture demands a linear writing form. The thesis statement is written, and the rest of the text must provide supporting facts. This trend reflects the American culture. In Native American discussions, topics are seldom addressed directly. The listener must make his own connections after points are made indirectly. This tendency is also reflected in students' writing. Writing styles that incorporate the ways of the people will produce more success than styles based on the "foreign" style of the teacher (Scafe & Kontas, 1982).

A compilation of findings suggest the following strategies be used for developing a successful classroom for American Indian learners (Boseker, 1991; Boseker & Gordon, 1983; Gordon & Boseker, 1984; Pepper, 1976):

- Small cooperative groups and peer learning are better than traditional large class grouping and oral questions and answers. Students need to feel as though they are part of the group.
- Use learning manipulatives and incorporate activities that allow students to feel and touch to enhance learning through use of the senses. Information gained by visual, motor, tactile, spatial, perceptual, or auditory tasks/games are highly recommended.
- Use mental, nonverbal images to teach concepts rather than depending on word associations.
- Freedom of movement within the classroom is encouraged; allow students to sit on the floor, arrange desks comfortably, and permit a range of motion.
- Avoid highlighting individual students' success, accept silence, and deemphasize competition.
- Don't use show-and-tell venues that require students to get up in front of the class and speak (Philips, 1972). Take time to let the child approach the teacher individually.
- Learning is best accomplished experientially, in natural settings, and by watching and doing instead of trial and error.
- Allow students to learn privately. Let them observe, listen, and take over parts of the task, in cooperation with and under the supervision of an adult. Then let the child test him- or herself (Diaz-Rico & Weed, 1995).
- Utilize holistic presentations, visual representations, and presentation of the whole picture before isolating skills into small segments.
- Conciseness of speech, slight variation of intonation, and limited vocal range are most valued. Silence is used for personal power and for creating and communicating rapport with others.
- Do not force individual competition, although students may enjoy competing in teams. Emphasis should be on the group. Native American children do not want to show themselves as superior, especially if it presents someone else in a poor light (Baruth & Manning, 1992). Harmony within the group is desirable.
- Child rearing may be done by the extended family.

- In class, allow more response time so students can feel comfortable after considering responses. Allow them to practice their skills before expecting them to answer. Allow time for delay in responding answering questions.
- Students may ask for help silently by looking up from their work without speaking.
- Native Americans are spiritual and live in harmony with nature and natural settings. Incorporate instruction with this knowledge in mind.
- Know your Native American cultural groups and their value systems. What is innocuous to the American teacher might have deep spiritual significance for the students.

Tips for Becoming Culturally Aware

1. Peruse the textbooks used in your classes. Note the depiction of females, males, people of color, and obvious ethnic minorities. Does it look fair to you? Be sure to make mention of inequities.
2. Be aware of the nonverbal communication you use (gestures, hand movements, body language, etc.) and focus on teaching your students what these types of communication mean.
3. Communicate respect (verbally and nonverbally) and sincere interest for your students and their cultures.
4. Look around your classroom. Make sure your class environment sends a positive, welcoming message.
5. Do all you can to encourage home–school interaction. Parents are your greatest allies and can help bridge the cultural gap. Attend cultural celebrations in your students' community. Communicate and involve parents.
6. Be vigilant about accurate assessment. Make sure you are assessing content and not mere language ability.
7. Avoid using children as interpreters for their parents. This upsets the natural familial harmony and parental hierarchy, robbing parents of their authority.
8. Understand the struggle of conflicting home and school values. Support the parents as they try to maintain their cultural roles, values, responsibilities, and forms of discipline.

9. Encourage parents to continue to speak to their children in their rich native languages. A complete home language is a good basis for transferring knowledge to the second language.

Cultural Activities and Strategies for the Classroom

It is important to build a positive and nonthreatening classroom environment. Activities and strategies that highlight the variety of cultures represented by your students can be incorporated in a multitude of ways. Following are some ideas to consider trying with your students. This opportunity to learn interactively about other cultures will validate the importance of the newcomer's culture and engage the mainstream student as well. (An additional note, you might want to offer your newcomers a private place, or a home space, where they can store their things or get away from the hustle and bustle of frenetic classroom activity. In the United States we are always on the go. Other cultures may have long moments of reflection, silence, and down time, which the newcomer might need and appreciate. Also, teach the newcomer to come to you if they are unsure about what to do when students ask them questions or make requests that may be inappropriate or embarrassing or that put them on the spot.)

❖ Assign buddies for your newcomers to escort them to lunch, specials, and the library; to help with computer time, sports activities, and games; to sit with in classes; and so on, so they can follow along if they don't understand what to do. The buddy can escort the newcomer to the office, to guidance, or to get a hall pass or a late slip, or any other school routines. Very often people from other cultures are never alone and they feel sorry for Americans who live alone.

❖ Set aside a daily designated time you and/or other teachers will be available for newcomers should they need to speak with you privately. Be observant about their behavior. Watch for signs of depression, sadness, loneliness, culture shock, confusion, fatigue, and so forth. Make a concerted effort to be sure the student is never alone and feeling lost. He or she may not be able to accurately express his or her feelings.

❖ Try to connect with people in the community who speak the language of your newcomers. Invite them to your class to get to know your students. In the community, look in ethnic markets, churches, temples, synagogues, mosques, etc. for people from your students' cultures who may be able to help ease the transition and make the student feel welcome.

❖ If there comes a time when the student is invited to write or make a presentation about the home culture, and they are able to, offer to help edit or review the product. If a student is not yet fluent enough to be able to do it alone, use the interpreter to help. Be sure the English is accurate.

❖ Be sure to guide the student in the library and computer room. Many countries do not have lending libraries, and technology may be nonexistent.

❖ Find out the students' birthdays, a saint's day, or a special day that is celebrated in the home country. Think of a simple way to honor your students with some type of remembrance of their special days.

❖ Be sure that you advise or prepare your students for any type of celebration that is coming up in the school. Make sure they understand what to expect and how to behave. Even a fire drill will throw an unknowing student off guard.

❖ Ask students from all cultures to collect artifacts that depict their own culture. City and country maps, tourist brochures, money, songs, newspapers, pictures, labels from products found in their countries, recipes, menus, postcards, and crafts are good artifacts to share with others. Show them how to find information on the Internet. Give them the tools, supplies, and instructions to prepare some type of representation of their home land or culture. Be ready to assist the student if he or she is going to present. When appropriate, have the student talk about the country, the family, the previous school (if it existed), and daily life. Perhaps the other students could ask questions. Be sensitive to the student's comfort zone. Lower proficiency English speakers can put together visuals with labels. Use both languages.

❖ When appropriate, and with sufficient proficiency, the student may want to investigate famous people from the home country. This may be the first time the student is learning about the home country, as sometimes one does not know much about the home country until he or she leaves.

❖ Have the newcomer teach the class common vocabulary in the native language. Pictures and visuals will be great tools, especially for lower level proficiency students. Pointing and saying the words will allow the learner to connect the written word with the sound of the word.

❖ Have students draw family trees with labels of who the person is. The level of language proficiency will determine the degree of explanation the student can engage in.

❖ Be aware of using slang or idioms. They will have to be explained, and unless they can be explained with the use of visuals, the meaning will be really abstract. Think about how you would explain "might as well" or "to take advantage of."

❖ Practice the art of giving and following directions in the class and in the school. Later this can be extended to the yard, the playground, the town, and the community.

❖ Read aloud, and tape your voice as you go through the book. Later the students can put on headphones and play the tape again and again. This will help them to internalize the sound of the language, and hear correct pronunciation. Make sure you point to the word as it is spoken so the students will know what sound accompanies the correct words.

❖ Once the students start reading, or verbalizing, tape their voices so they can hear themselves pronounce the words. Repeat the words to model the correct sounds. Physically show them how to make sounds and where the teeth and lips go to make a correct sound, and let them touch the vibration in their throats or lips. Use a mirror so they can see you and then themselves.

For example, they delight in seeing their tongues actually stick out when making the "th" sound.

❖ Simulate a virtual experience for your students using the Internet. This can be shopping or eating out at a restaurant. Include the things you would find in a real supermarket and restaurant. Practice shopping, looking at the menu, asking questions, etc. This activity can be extended to any place—the zoo, the hospital, the doctor or dentist's office, the aquarium, or the mall. *Note: your students may never have been to the mall, or used an escalator or elevator. Students from countries with traditional markets, such as Haiti, are accustomed to shopping at these markets and not in malls.* They will have no prior knowledge, and even when they are in the United States, they continue to shop at open markets, such as the flea markets and garage and yard sales as opposed to malls. Keep your mind open and ask yourself if there is a chance that your student may never have experienced what is being referred to. Housing, bathrooms, plumbing, bedding—virtually everything may be different. We may think it is rude to clean the nose by sniffing out to the street, but they may think it is disgusting to blow your nose into a piece of paper and carry the contents around in your pocket, and even use the tissue again. In many cultures, the bathroom is never near the kitchen, and in fact, they may think it is disgusting to defecate in a room inside the dwelling. Imagine the shock they feel when they discover that we keep out toothbrushes in the room where we leave our human waste. It is all a matter of perception.

❖ Try to use music from their culture and from the American culture as a way to study vocabulary and practice pronunciation. The songs you use can later be made into cloze tests, and using songs is a great way to learn vocabulary.

❖ Learn proverbs from the students' cultures and then teach proverbs from the American culture. See if students from each culture can guess the meanings from the words. Proverbs reflect the culture, and we can gain an insider perspective from understanding how others think.

❖ Teach colors by using colors, and numbers by using numbers. Explanations of many prepositions are easily made by modeling: the pencils are *in* the box, *on* top of the box, *beside* the box, *under* the box, and so on. Incorporate culture into this activity to make a connection.

❖ Create opportunities for your students to talk about their traditional foods, music, arts, and crafts, and then try to incorporate them into the classroom. Very often families will cook traditional dishes and share recipes with interested individuals. Every culture seems to have a certain way to prepare rice. Ask students to share how they prepare and eat rice.

Interesting Insights and Cultural Facts

All cultures have beliefs that signify good and bad luck. The following are some common beliefs interesting to know and demonstrate how easily misunderstandings can occur (Lip, 1985; Maple, 1971).

Colors

- Red ink is a death sign for Koreans. Teachers should refrain from correcting papers with red ink.
- In Afghanistan, white is a symbol of friendship for a bride and an omen of luck, harmony, and happiness for the wedding couple. In India, only an enemy would wear white to a wedding, as it can bring bad luck or death to the wedding couple. Red would be a better color to wear.
- At a Chinese wedding, black or white should not be worn because both colors are associated with death.
- In China, yellow is used to mark a defective product. Green is used to indicate a product has passed inspection.
- White products cannot be sold in Hong Kong because white is associated with death.
- Yellow can have negative connotations cross culturally:
- In American culture, yellow can mean cowardice.
- In France, yellow is associated with being a traitor.
  - Judas is often depicted wearing yellow.
  - Nazis made Jews wear yellow stars.
  - Spanish executioners wear yellow.
- To the Chinese, a green hat connotes infidelity, but the color green itself means health, prosperity, and harmony.
- Yellow flowers mean "I miss you" to Armenians, but they mean "I hate you" to Iranians. Peruvians also feel negatively about yellow flowers, as do Mexicans.
- White flowers indicate mourning for the Chinese (and other Asians), especially gladioli. Bringing white gladioli to a Chinese family would indicate a death wish for them. A little red envelope with a coin in it would mean good luck is wished.

Numbers

- In Mandarin and Cantonese, the word for the number 4 sounds like the word for death. Japanese and Koreans feel the same way. To have this number in an address is bad.
- For the Chinese, numbers have positive and negative values. For example, 7 is related to the idea that ghosts return 7 days after someone dies. Positive meanings also abound: 1 for guaranteed, 2 for easy, 3 for life, 6 for happiness, 8 for prosperity, and 9 for long life. Combinations have significance also. By itself, 5 is neutral, but if it is in front of an 8, the good effect of the 8 is negated. In the Chinese culture, the fourth floor is often eliminated. Some Asian airports eliminate Gate 4.
- Many traditional Chinese people refuse to be photographed with an uneven number of people. To have three people in a photo is the worst: it is an indicator that the person in the middle will die.
- Phone numbers can be lucky or unlucky. Many Chinese companies moved into the San Gabriel Valley in California, which has the telephone area code 818. This combination of numbers means "prosperity guaranteed prosperity."
- Armenians believe that an even number of flowers is unlucky. Numbers involved in funeral or death rituals are usually even in number; therefore, on happy occasions an uneven number of flowers is presented.
- In many English-speaking cultures, the number 13 is negative. Buildings may not have a 13th floor. Many Americans will refuse to stay in a room on the 13th floor. Friday the 13th is a dreaded day.
- Students from the Middle East, Korea, Africa, Mexico, and perhaps other countries might bring a gift to the teacher expecting the teacher to inflate the student's grade.

PART TWO

Principles and Practices in Language Teaching

chapter 12

Teaching for Communication, 83
CARMEN A. MORALES-JONES

chapter 13

Methods/Approaches of Teaching
ESOL: A Historical Overview, 91
CAITLIN MCHUGH AND EILEEN N. WHELAN ARIZA

chapter 14

Principles of Communicative Language
Teaching, 107
HANIZAH ZAINUDDIN AND CAITLIN MCHUGH

Teaching for Communication

KEY ISSUES

- ❖ Language as a complex system
- ❖ Native language acquisition theories
  - ◆ Behaviorist
  - ◆ Innatist
  - ◆ Interactionist
- ❖ Principles in second/new language acquisition
- ❖ Krashen's monitor model
- ❖ Implications of Krashen's monitor model for the ELL teacher

What Is Language?

Language is the vehicle humans employ to express and communicate emotions and/or ideas by means of speech and hearing. Speech denotes the power to articulate utterances. Although animals can be said to have a "language" of their own, they do not have speech. However, language encompasses more than simply being able to communicate ideas and emotions orally. Thus, developing communicative competence requires mastery of all four language processes: listening, speaking, reading, and writing.

Table 12-1 illustrates the complexity of language.

First Language Acquisition Theories

How do people acquire their native language? Through the years there have been numerous attempts to explain the phenomenon of language acquisition.

Behaviorist Theory

B. F. Skinner (1957) based his explanation of acquisition of language on behaviorist principles. The basic elements in the behaviorist theory are stimulus, response, and reinforcement. Behaviorists hypothesized that children learned their first language through the same process of stimulus, response, and reinforcement. They also gave much importance to the processes of imitation and association. This theory made much sense because in observing the interactions of parents/caregivers and young children, it seemed apparent that children acquired their language as a result of this interaction.

Stimulus: Parents/caregivers talked to the young child using gesturing, demonstrating, showing, and telling.

Response: The child produced some form of utterance/speech.

Reinforcement: The parent/caregiver praised or demonstrated understanding. This reinforcement encouraged continuation of the behavior.

Table 12-1 **Comparison of Behaviorist, Innatist, and Interactionist Theories of Language Acquisition**

Acquisition	Behaviorist Perspective	Innatist Perspective	Interactionist Aspects
Linguistic Focus	Verbal behaviors (not analyzed per se); words, utterances of child and people in social environment	Child's syntax	Conversations between child and caregiver; focus on caregiver speech
Process of Acquisition	Modeling, imitation, practice, and selective reinforcement of correct form	Hypothesis testing and creative construction of acts Syntactic rules using LAD	Acquisition emerges from communication; scaffolded by caregivers
Role of Child	Secondary role: imitator and responder to environmental shaping	Primary role: equipped with biological LAD, child plays major role in acquisition	Important role in interaction, taking more control as language acquisition advances
Role of Social Environment	Primary role: parental modeling and reinforcement are major factors promoting language acquisition	Minor role: language used by others merely triggers LAD	Important role in interaction, especially in early years when caregivers modify input and carry much of conversational load

LAD, language acquisition device
Source: Peregoy and Boyle (2008)

While this process is taking place, the child is imitating what he or she hears and associates meaning to the concrete examples to which he or she is exposed in everyday interactions. Behaviorists employed the term *tabula rasa* to describe the child's mind as a blank mental slate. Thus, children's language development comes as a result of imitating and associating the stimulus to which they are exposed and as it is reinforced by their parents/caregivers.

Scenario

Mother: The kitty is saying meow.

Child: Kitty meow.

Mother: Yes! The kitty is saying meow.

This scenario is repeated numerous times, and eventually the child will say: "The kitty is saying meow."

There was a major flaw with the behaviorist theory because it could not explain how children would come up with novel (new) utterances (i.e., language [words] they had never heard before).

Scenario

Mother: Where did the ball go?

Child: It *goed* under the table.

Mother: You are right! It *went* under the table.

The child has never heard the word *goed*, yet spoke it. However, if this sentence is analyzed, it makes perfect sense; the mother asked a question that requires the use of the past tense in the response; the child responded by using the past tense ending (-ed) of a regular verb (such as jump*ed* or laugh*ed*), thus forming the past tense. This process would not make sense if the child were strictly responding following the behaviorist principles. In addition, in this example, the mother did not correct the child's grammatical error but simply reinforced the meaning of the response: "You are right." These and other concerns led to the realization that there had to be more to explaining language acquisition.

Innatist Theory

Linguist Noam Chomsky (1957), engaged in a heated debate with Skinner, claimed the behaviorist theory was inadequate to explain observations of children's language development.

Chomsky was a linguist with a genius mind for analyzing syntax. His early work on syntax and transformational grammar revolutionized the field of linguistics. As Chomsky studied the complexities of children's applications of grammatical principles and rules, he concluded that the only way to explain these was by assuming the possession of an "innate" ability to do so. He hypothesized that infants were born with a biological language acquisition device (LAD), or a system that equipped them for linguistic analysis. Chomsky concluded that infants universally possess an innate "grammar template" or universal grammar that allows them to select out the many grammatical rules of the language they hear spoken around them, as they gradually construct the grammar of their own native language (Peregoy & Boyle, 2008). According to Chomsky (1957, 1959), children construct grammar through a process of hypothesis testing. For example, a child may hypothesize the rule that all past tenses of verbs are formed by adding -*ed*. Thus, when they are faced with the verb "to go" and the need to use it in the past tense, they say "goed" instead of "went." Gradually, children revise their hypothesis to accommodate exceptions or the past tense of irregular verbs. Thus, Chomsky contended that children create sentences by using rules rather than by merely repeating what they have heard, as the behaviorists assumed. This is how the innatists explained the production of novel utterances.

Scenario

The scene takes place in a home in Puerto Rico. The mother is American (native born and raised in the United States) and has always spoken to her daughter, Ana, in English. Ana is three years old and has always spoken to her mom in Spanish.

Mom: Ana, did you hang up your clothes?

Ana: Si, Mami. Ya yo *la jangué*. (Yes, Mom. I already hung it.)

Analysis

Ana's response, though incorrect Spanish (novel utterance "jangué"), makes sense and is grammatically correct. She has applied the rule for the past tense of regular "*ar*" verbs in Spanish: drop "ar" and add an accented "é." She has also employed the correct ending for first person singular ("yo"; "I"). In addition, Ana employed the appropriate feminine pronoun, "la," because "clothes" in Spanish is "ropa," and it is a feminine noun. She used the singular for "la" because the noun "ropa" in Spanish is a singular noun whether it refers to one piece of clothing or more than one. What Ana did was apply the rules for Spanish grammar, but she created a novel utterance for a verb (to hang), which she did not know in Spanish. Ana's mother had never used the word *jangué*; thus, Ana had never heard this word.

This is the kind of analysis that Chomsky and his followers did. They concluded that children acquired language with little help from their parents/caregivers. They diminished the role of the parents/caregivers to such an extent that their theory was unable to explain why people who are deprived of linguistic interactions are not able to fully develop language; those born deaf or who develop a hearing loss at a very young age are limited in their language development or are void of oral language. These observations, which were not fully explicable, led to further study of the complex process of language development.

Interactionist Theory

Rooted in the cognitive psychology, with such proponents as Jean Piaget, Lois Bloom, and Dan Slobin, the interactionist theory embraces the view that language is directly related to cognitive development. In addition, cognitivists/interactionists place great importance on social interactions in the development of language. The interaction between nature (innate ability to acquire language) and nurture (the role of the social environment) is what allows language to develop.

Children's language develops over time, with many instances of the same or similar interactions. It would be nearly impossible for young children to produce language to which they have been exposed only once or twice. How many times do infants hear the words *bottle* or *daddy* before they actually produce those words? Thus, their ability to acquire the words, plus the numerous encounters with those words, account for the fact that eventually, after many approximations to those words (e.g., ba; baba; da; dada) the child, one day, says "bottle" and "daddy." It is not known, though, which factor in language development plays a greater role (i.e., is nature the most important factor or does nurture play the greater role?). More research is needed on both the biological and social factors. However, it is important to acknowledge the importance of both factors. Language cannot develop fully without the child's innate ability and the sociolinguistic interactions that occur as the child grows and develops.

Second/New Language Acquisition

Very few parents/caregivers are linguists, yet all normal children develop language. If first languages are acquired so naturally, what implications does this have for second language teaching? Should the same conditions present in first language acquisition be replicated for second language teaching? Would second language acquisition occur as naturally if the same conditions were present in the second language learner's classroom?

Stephen Krashen (1982) developed five hypotheses that have greatly impacted the teaching of foreign languages in the United States, as well as the field of teaching English to speakers of other languages (TESOL): (1) the acquisition versus learning hypothesis, (2) the natural order hypothesis, (3) the monitor hypothesis, (4) the comprehension hypothesis (2002), and (5) the affective filter hypothesis. Each one will be discussed in the following section.

The Acquisition versus Learning Hypothesis

Krashen makes a distinction between acquiring language and learning language.

Acquisition	Learning
Informal process	Formal process
"Picking up"	"Knowing about"
Unconscious process	Conscious process
Implicit	Explicit

According to Krashen, for students to acquire a second/new language, teachers must focus on communication rather than on the rote memorization of rules (form).

For acquisition to occur, students must be immersed in meaningful and comprehensible contexts. It is not "knowing about" the language that helps develop communicative competency, it is using the language in meaningful interactions. Therefore, teachers must provide for these meaningful interactions to occur in the classroom.

Krashen contends that language that is simply "learned" is not the language that is spoken. Language "learning," or knowledge of grammatical rules, or use of much drill-and-pattern practice, does not account for spoken language (Krashen, 2004, 2009). For example, many students in the United States study foreign languages in high school. Years later, most are still able to conjugate a verb (in those languages) but are not able to speak the languages. The emphasis was placed on "learning about" the language and not in "using/speaking" the language in a natural way.

Krashen has been criticized for his claims that (1) only language that is acquired leads to fluent communication and (2) language that is "learned" cannot "turn into" spoken language. However, despite the criticisms, his insistence on the value of using the second/new language in meaningful communicative contexts has had a positive impact on the field of English language teaching.

In recent writings, Krashen (2009) has indicated that English language learners should be aware of how languages are acquired. He purports that this knowledge will be helpful to the ELLs in their continued language learning process.

The Natural Order Hypothesis

According to Krashen, second language acquisition models first language acquisition. This means that there is a natural progression in the process of acquiring a second language that is similar to that of acquiring the first language. There are four stages or periods in first/second language acquisition:

1. Preproduction, comprehension, or silent stage or period
2. Early production
3. Speech emergence
4. Intermediate fluency

Children progress from not speaking at all (infant) to acquiring full command of the first/second language. According to Krashen, second language acquisition follows these four stages, so it is then understandable why second language learners usually go through a period when they do not speak; they are simply listening, "taking-in," getting their ears acclimated to the new sounds that surround them.

Krashen also indicates that grammatical structures and certain language structures are acquired in a predictable order. For example, in the English language, the concept of plural and the rule for forming the present progressive by adding "-ing" are acquired earlier than the rule for forming the third person singular by adding an "s." Also, vocabulary/words are acquired in a natural order: from no words at all (silent period) to one- to two-word sentences (early production period), to three- to four-word sentences (speech emergence period), to more complex sentences (intermediate fluency period). According to Krashen, errors are developmental, and students will outgrow them as they are exposed to what is appropriate or correct.

The Monitor Hypothesis

Krashen states that people produce language that they have "acquired," not language that they have "learned." However, he does assert that language learning is helpful in monitoring output. When the learners know the rules of the language, they can employ them to correct what they are thinking about saying (self-correct) or to correct what they have said (self-repair). For the monitor to work (or for the monitoring to take place), three conditions need to be present: (1) the learners need to have time to think about what they are about to say or have said; (2) the learners need to focus on "form," "how do I say it so that it is correct?"; and (3) the learners must have knowledge and be able to apply the rules. English language learners who are literate in their first language and adult second language learners are more likely to use the monitor. In many instances, adult English language learners tend to overmonitor; therefore, it takes them longer to speak the second language.

The monitor is easier to employ in the written language because the learner has more time to go back, reread, and edit, processes that take additional time and are not "natural" when speaking at a normal pace.

The Comprehension Hypothesis

One of the most important elements in the acquisition of a second/new language is whether or not the input received by the learner is comprehensible. However, according to Krashen, the input not only needs to be "comprehensible input," but it also needs to be slightly beyond the students' current level of competency. This concept is represented as i + 1 (comprehensible input plus 1—slightly beyond the student's current level of proficiency). For the input to be comprehensible, teachers must present the material in ways that are not tied to language. That is, teachers must use visuals, objects, realia, manipulatives, gesturing, modeling, "parentese" (repeat, rephrase, slower speech), charts, graphs, and maps. In addition, teachers must give positive feedback to the students to encourage their risk taking in the second/new language acquisition process. According to Krashen, vocabulary and grammatical structures must take into account i + 1 and should always be presented in meaningful contexts, not in isolation.

The Affective Filter Hypothesis

Krashen's fifth hypothesis addresses affective or social-emotional variables related to second/new language acquisition. Citing a variety of studies, Krashen concludes that the most important affective variables favoring second/new language acquisition are a low-anxiety learning environment, student motivation to learn the language, self-confidence, and self-esteem. Students are able to acquire the second language if they are in an environment where they feel accepted, where they are free to take risks, and know that if they make mistakes, they will not be "ridiculed." When students feel uncomfortable, nervous, anxious, or afraid, their affective filter goes up as a defense mechanism, and acquisition of knowledge is interrupted or stifled. A nonthreatening teaching/learning atmosphere is indispensable for language acquisition to take place. Krashen claims that "people acquire second languages when they obtain comprehensible input and when their affective filters are low enough to allow the input in" (Krashen, 1981).

Implications of Krashen's Hypotheses for the Classroom Teacher

Hypothesis #1: Acquisition versus Learning

1. Employ thematic instruction: If students are totally immersed in a theme, they will have many opportunities to grasp the concepts and content. They will have numerous encounters with the same content/vocabulary/language structures, yet from different perspectives.

2. Avoid putting emphasis on rote memorization/drill for acquisition of learning to occur. For example, emphasis on rote memorization of spelling words should be avoided. Spelling words should be always taught in meaningful contexts and practiced in meaningful communicative activities.

3. Provide students numerous opportunities for employing/practicing the new concepts/language. Saying it once or writing it once will not allow for acquisition of knowledge.

4. Employ integrated curriculum: It also provides for numerous encounters with some of the same content because students not only learn about "mammals," for example, in science but they also learn about mammals in reading, as well as in social studies and mathematics. Thus, reinforcement of the acquired concepts and vocabulary will take place throughout the entire school day. Students would have many opportunities to acquire the knowledge and develop second language competence throughout the entire school day for as long as the integration is taking place.

5. Focus on the need to communicate; to create the "information gap" wherein students have a need to communicate with other students and/or the teacher. This provides for meaningful communication. Cooperative groups are a positive vehicle for creating the environment conducive to this meaningful interaction among students. One student in the group has information that the others in the group need to fulfill their task. This is what is known as the "information gap." ("I have some information you need, thus it is necessary for us to communicate, so together, we have the total information we need.") This technique takes into account the way language develops (i.e., based on need).

Hypothesis #2: Natural Order

1. Organize instruction from simple to complex taking into account the way language develops.
2. Respect the silent period. Teachers should not force students to speak until they are ready. In the meantime, teachers must engage students who are in the silent period in activities wherein they can respond nonverbally.
3. Allow mistakes because errors are developmental. One positive technique is to allow students to employ "invented spelling." If students know they will not be penalized for incorrect spelling, they will be more encouraged to write and will feel successful in their attempts.
4. Allow students to make mistakes in oral communication without the fear of being "corrected" each time they mispronounce a word or employ incorrect grammar/syntax. Teachers should simply make note of errors students are making and address these in lessons, thus providing for meaningful practice.

Hypothesis #3: Monitor Hypothesis

1. Allow "think time" so students can self-correct prior to speaking. Second/new language learners may need to "rehearse in their head" what they are going to say and how to say it before they can respond.
2. Provide numerous encounters with the same to allow students to grasp the concepts. If students develop the concept of how specific language "sounds," they will eventually produce accurate language.
3. Plan lessons employing the "discovery method," wherein students are provided many examples and much opportunity to be engaged in discovering the knowledge instead of being told and required to memorize a set of facts. Discovery learning takes more time to plan, but it is a much more effective teaching practice. If students are to employ the monitor, they must know how the output ought to be. By discovering the knowledge, it is more likely to be retained, and it will be easier to retrieve than if the students simply memorize something that they soon forget. If students discover grammar rules, for example, they are more likely able to apply them when trying to use the monitor.
4. Model appropriate language and provide numerous opportunities for students to be exposed to appropriate models. Students may not always know why an utterance is produced in the appropriate way, but if they have had much exposure to appropriate models, they will eventually be able to monitor their output effectively.

Hypothesis #4: Comprehension Hypothesis

1. Find ways to provide comprehensible input. One way is to employ means of presenting content that is not tied to language. Thus, the use of modeling, demonstrating, visuals (charts, graphs, gestures, pictures, models), and manipulatives is crucial.

2. Employing "parentese" (repeating, rephrasing, slowing down, simplifying language) is crucial.

Hypothesis #5: Affective Filter

1. Create a nonthreatening teaching/learning atmosphere in the classroom.
2. Create a risk-safe environment where students will feel free to take chances, to try although they are not sure, and to make mistakes when producing language.
3. Create a warm, accepting classroom climate where students will not be worried about being criticized or "put on the spot" for not being able to respond quickly and accurately.
4. Capitalize on what the students know rather than on what they do not know.
5. Create a teaching/learning environment where students encounter success rather than failure on a daily basis.
6. Provide positive feedback on a regular basis so students will be encouraged to engage in the lessons rather than remain disengaged due to fear of being criticized.
7. Provide many opportunities for cooperative learning and hands-on activities so students can interact with peers; this type of interaction is less threatening to them.
8. Self-reflect on attitudes toward certain groups of students/people so as to ensure that negative attitudes (either overtly with verbal comments, or nonverbally with gestures and body language such as facial expressions) toward students of certain cultural backgrounds are not being displayed.

Points to Remember

❖ Communicative competence requires mastery of all four language processes: listening, speaking, reading, and writing.

❖ Aspects of language encompass phonology (sound system of a language), morphology (rules of word formation), syntax (order of words in a sentence), discourse (rules for processing beyond the sentence level), and pragmatics (sociolinguistic rules governing language use in communicative contexts).

❖ Behaviorists explained first language acquisition as a process of imitation of the caregiver.

❖ Behaviorists could not explain novel utterances.

❖ Innatists claimed that first language acquisition resulted from an innate ability.

❖ Innatists hypothesized that infants were born with a biological language acquisition device (LAD) that equipped them for linguistic analysis.

❖ Innatists could not explain how children/adults who were not exposed to language could not develop language.

❖ Interactionists explain first language acquisition as a result of the interaction between nature (innate ability to acquire language) and nurture (the role of the social environment).

❖ Much research is needed in the field of first and second language acquisition.

❖ Stephen Krashen's monitor model for second/new language acquisition encompasses five hypotheses: acquisition versus learning, monitor, natural order, comprehension, and affective filter.

❖ Krashen's monitor model has impacted the field of second/new language teaching. It has tremendous implications for the English language teacher.

Methods/Approaches of Teaching ESOL: A Historical Overview

KEY ISSUES

- ❖ Historical overview of methods and approaches to teaching English as a foreign/second language
- ❖ The Grammar-Translation Method
- ❖ The Direct Method
- ❖ The Audio-Lingual Method
- ❖ Suggestopedia
- ❖ The Silent Way
- ❖ Total Physical Response
- ❖ The Natural Approach
- ❖ The Communicative Approach

For centuries, people have used formal education as a way to learn new languages. Over time, the methods and approaches have evolved to theories of language acquisition and educational theory. In addition to adjustments to the theories, changes to the populations of students and their objectives for learning new languages have also changed. More and more the students in mainstream classes are speakers of other languages. Language acquisition methods and strategies are no longer limited to the language-learning classroom. These techniques can be used in a variety of settings depending on the needs of the students.

The Grammar-Translation Method

The grammar-translation method (also known as the classical method) is a method of language teaching that emphasizes grammar rules and one-to-one vocabulary translation. Grammar rules are taught through presentation and explicit instruction. Instruction in this style of language teaching is in the students' native language. Student practice the grammatical rules through translation exercises between the native and target language. Vocabulary lists, dictionary definitions, and memorization strategies—which are frowned upon in other language teaching methods—are the main focus of this style of language teaching.

Grammar-translation first began based on a belief that different kinds of knowledge were stored in separate sections of the brain. Mathematic knowledge, for example, was thought to be located in one area, art in another, language in another, and so on. It was believed that studying different subjects was a good way of exercising the brain. Thus, learning another language provided the necessary mental exercise to develop the part of the brain believed to be reserved for languages.

At this time, the main goal for learning a language was not for speaking and/or communication. The driving force was to exercise the mind and at the same time to be able to read in that language. The languages taught in those early days were Latin and Greek, so another reason for studying foreign languages was to appreciate the classics in their original language.

When educators first started using this method, communicating in the language was not a goal. Therefore, classes were taught primarily in the students' native language and the teacher made no effort to emphasize correct pronunciation of the language. Grammar study was the focus of the lessons, with much rote memorization of grammatical aspects such as verb conjugations and recitation of rules that described language functions. Educators soon began to notice that because the primary emphasis was on reading and translating passages, the conjugation of verbs, and explanation and memorization of grammatical rules their students were not learning to use the language. Even after many years

of studying, the students were unable to speak the language. It became clear that using the grammar-translation method by itself is ineffective. The students needed to play a more active role in their language acquisition in order to actually use the language for communication purposes.

Although this method is unsuccessful when used in isolation, there are some opportunities to use pieces of the grammar-translation method with language learners in the mainstream classroom today. Often language learners develop a fossilization of errors when learning in an immersion setting. When chatting with their peers, students' errors often go uncorrected. Using the grammar-translation method, teachers can encourage the students to practice specific grammatical points that they have trouble with.

Mainstream Classroom Use

Emilio is having trouble understanding *present participle* verbs. He confuses his tenses, misuses the participles, and has trouble understanding this grammatical concept when he hears it or reads it. Since Emilio's teacher has some knowledge of his home language, Spanish, she is able to share comparisons between the two languages to help him to positively transfer this prior knowledge to his work in English.

Exercise: Translate the following sentences from Spanish to English.

❖ Mi abuela ha corrido tres maratones.— Translation: My grandmother has run three marathons.
❖ Pedro ha comido cinco rebanadas de pizza.— Translation: Pedro has eaten five slices of pizza.
❖ Ruth ha vivido en México seis años.— Translation: Ruth has lived in Mexico for six years.

This adaptation of the grammar-translation method can help to distinguish what elements positively or negatively transfer between Emilio's languages. While this method is not recommended as the sole approach for a language teacher, it is possible to use adapted versions of the grammar-translation method as a supplement for specific skills that need further practice.

The Direct Method

The direct method began as a complete departure from the grammar-translation method. Instead of focusing on reading and writing, this method focused on speaking and listening.

The emphasis is on the direct associations the student makes between objects and concepts and the corresponding words in the target language. The use of the native language is avoided; the use of the target language is emphasized at all times. In this method, the primary goals are for students to think and speak the language; thus, no use of the native language is allowed. Teachers use objects, visuals, and realia to provide the comprehensible input. Instruction revolves around specific topics. Aspects of grammar are taught inductively through the handling of the topic. The basic focus of this method of language instruction is that students learn their second language in a similar way to their first language. This method aims to prove that there is no need for a deep analysis of grammatical rules or spelling patterns. Instead, the students are taught that the sole purpose of language is communication.

The direct method uses a lot of repetition to encourage students to learn new vocabulary and language patterns. It follows a five-step process: Show, Say, Try, Mold, Repeat. Using real life objects, pictures, or flash cards, the teacher will present a vocabulary word or grammatical structure. For example, using pictures of a child doing different actions the teacher can present the *present progressive* structure. This use of cards can be modified for different verb tenses and different pronouns that will encourage the same vocabulary while slowly introducing more grammatical structures. The practiced structure could be "The boy is running." By switching the flash cards, the students can practice "The boy is sleeping," "The boy is eating," "The boy is dancing," "The boy is smiling." This can be practiced in a question/answer structure by demonstrating and asking: "The boy is sleeping. What are you doing?", "The boy is eating. What is Brooke doing?"

In addition, cultural aspects of the countries where the target language is spoken are also included in the lessons. For example, when studying Spanish, students would discuss the sports that are widely practiced in Spain or Latin America. This also allows for discussions regarding geography, climate, cultural traditions, and other elements that foster a richer conversation in the target language. Students recognize their new language as a tool with which they can communicate. Reading and writing are also taught from the beginning.

The most widely known application of the direct method is practiced at the Berlitz language schools located throughout the world. Berlitz classes are generally for highly motivated adults who need to speak a foreign language for business purposes. Although many of the techniques developed for the direct method have also been used in other methods, applying the direct method in noncommercial schools fell out of favor as early as 1920 (Richards & Rodgers, 1986). The grammar-translation method dominated public school and university language teaching in the United States until World War II.

Audio-Lingual Method

The United States involvement in World War II brought a significant change in the teaching of languages in U.S. schools. It quickly became apparent that the grammar-translation method had not produced people who were able to speak the foreign languages they had studied. The U.S. government asked the universities to develop foreign language programs that produced students who could communicate effectively in those languages.

Changes in the beliefs about how people learn impacted the teaching methodologies being developed. Based on theories of behaviorist psychology (refer to Chapter 1), the audio-lingual method (ALM) was developed.

In ALM, the emphasis was on the memorization of a series of dialogues and the rote practice of language structures. This method was based on the idea that language is speech, not writing, and language is a set of habits. It was believed that extended practice of the dialogues would develop oral language proficiency. The use of the native language was avoided.

The method became very popular in the 1960s. Language laboratories began to surge, and students were required to listen to audiotapes and repeat dialogues that captured aspects of daily living. In addition, specific structural patterns of the language studied were embedded in those dialogues. Students were required to participate in a number of practice drills designed to help them memorize the structures and be able to plug other words into the structure. For example, in a substitution drill, the structure might have been:

I am going to the *post office*.

Students were then required to substitute the word *post office* for other words, such as *supermarket, park, beach*, or *drugstore*.

The belief was that students, through much practice, would form a "habit" and be able to speak the language when needed. Although the intent was to develop fluent and proficient speakers by providing much oral practice of the dialogues and the use of numerous drills to help in this endeavor, the reality was that language proficiency was not the outcome. Years later, students who studied with the audiolingual method still remembered the dialogues but could not spontaneously speak the foreign language they had studied. Thus, the method was not successful at accomplishing the main goal. It was too prescriptive; there was no opportunity provided for true communication to take place in the ALM classroom. Students had been taught a script which is not the manner in which natural speech is produced.

Mainstream Classroom Use

Using scripts as the sole language exposure is not recommended, as described above, but there are opportunities to use this style of language instruction in the mainstream classroom with newcomers.

A daily routine in a classroom often has common instructions that are repeated frequently. Instructions in a typical classroom are given orally. In addition to verbally giving instructions, teachers with newcomers may choose to also write the instructions on the board and point to each step in the process while describing it. For a student who is a speaker of another language, seeing the instructions while hearing the instructions will help to emphasize the language being used. One way to help students to learn commands and steps in routines is to provide a smaller version of the same instructions that they can use to follow along and to review during their own time. The common phrases used in the classroom will vary between different grade levels, but some of these may include:

May I go to the restroom?
May I go to the nurse?
Could you repeat the instructions?
Please take out your notebooks.
Turn and talk to your partner about . . .
Raise your hand when you are ready.

This type of exercise does not require extensive planning or preparation by the classroom teacher. Instead, this exercise can be written quickly onto an index card that the student can keep on or in their desk. This type of exercise not only will be helpful for the student, but will also serve as a reminder to teachers to be mindful of our language when providing instructions to speakers of other languages.

Suggestopedia

Suggestopedia was developed by Bulgarian psychiatrist–educator Georgi Lozanov (1982), who wanted to eliminate the psychological barriers that people have to learning. This method uses drama, art, physical exercise, and desuggestive–suggestive communicative psychotherapy as well as the traditional modes of listening, speaking, reading, and writing to teach a second language. The influence of the science of suggestology is clear in this method that calls class meetings "sessions" (Freeman & Freeman, 1998).

In suggestopedia, the classroom atmosphere is crucial. Creating a relaxed, nonthreatening learning environment is essential for its success. The goal is that students will assimilate the content of the lessons without feeling any type of stress or fatigue.

Classrooms are equipped with comfortable seating arrangements and dim lighting in an effort to provide an inviting and appealing environment. Soothing music is employed to invite relaxation and allow students to feel comfortable in the language classroom. The use of the native language is also allowed, especially to give directions and to create that welcoming atmosphere. Based on the belief that how students feel about learning will make a difference in the learning process, suggestopedia takes into consideration the affective domain. It could be said that the philosophy of the little engine that could—"I think I can, I think I can, I know I can" (Piper, 1976)—is one of the basic underlying principles of suggestopedia. If the students feel they can learn, they will.

The use of drama, songs, and games provides for much practice, yet in a less threatening and more enjoyable fashion. As in the ALM, dialogues are employed, but they are presented in an enhanced fashion through creative dramatics. The rehearsing of roles provides the necessary practice, yet there is a purpose for practicing. When people are preparing for dramatic roles, they most likely spend much time rehearsing.

Despite the advancements over the audio-lingual method, suggestopedia has not been widely adopted in the United States. It is impractical for large classes. In addition, current textbooks do not embrace this methodology, thus making it difficult for teachers to apply the principles in regular classrooms. However, there are some basic principles of this method that can be adapted for mainstream classrooms.

Mainstream Classroom Use

A classroom teacher may be able to provide speakers of other languages with a comfortable space during the day. Lowering the sense of stress in the classroom by providing a less threatening environment will be helpful to developing a sense of confidence for the speakers of other languages. Calm, soothing music may be played during language arts lessons where the students are strictly focusing on language use. Also, using songs and role playing activities with not only encourage the use of the target language for the speakers of other languages, but also these activities encourage all speakers of English to be language models. In some classrooms the teachers is seen as the only language model. By hearing classmates using the target language, students are exposed to age-appropriate language and fluency that helps them to relate and join their peer groups more successfully.

The Silent Way

Developed by Caleb Gattegno, the silent way requires that the teachers remain silent much of the time, thus its name. In this method, students are responsible for their own learning. Based on the belief that students are initiators of learning and capable of independently acquiring language, the silent way provides a classroom environment in which this can take place. The teacher models once, and the students are then given the opportunity to work together to try to reproduce what has been modeled.

Beginners are initially taught the sounds of the new language from color-coded sound charts. Next, teachers focus on language structures, sometimes using colored, plastic rods to visually represent parts of words or sentences. As students begin to understand more of the language, they are taught stories using the rods as props. At all stages of the method, the teacher models as little as possible, and students try to repeat after careful listening with help from each other. The teacher leads them toward correct responses by nods or negative head shakes (Ibid).

The silent way is a fairly complex method that requires the teacher to receive extensive training in the use of the methodology. Students also need to be well versed in the use of the charts and the rods to participate effectively in the lessons. Because, according to research, teachers speak from sixty-five percent to ninety-five percent of the time in traditional classrooms, it is difficult to find teachers who are comfortable with the required "silence" of the silent way, thus limiting the number of teachers available to teach employing this method.

Mainstream Classroom Use

The silent way is a difficult method to use in a mainstream classroom. But, one element that teachers can adapt for the language learners is to encourage them to trust themselves and their classmates in developing language skills. One policy often employed in mainstream classrooms with language learners is the "three then me" policy. The idea behind this strategy is that the student must ask three classmates before asking for help from the teacher. This type of policy helps to remove the stereotype that the "teacher has all the answers." Instead, students are encouraged to use the language together in order to find the answer they were seeking.

Total Physical Response

The total physical response (TPR) method was developed by psychologist James Asher (1977). This method is based on the principle that people learn better when they are involved physically as well as mentally. In TPR, students are required to respond nonverbally (physically) to a series of commands. As the teacher gives a command and the students respond physically, the teacher ascertains students' comprehension of the command. Initially, the teacher begins with simple commands such as:

Teacher: Stand up! (teacher models)
Students: Respond by standing up. (physical response, not verbal)
Teacher: Walk to the front of the room.
Students: Respond by walking to the front of the room.
Teacher: Turn around and walk back to your seats.
Students: Respond by turning around and walking to their seats.
Teacher: Sit down.
Students: Respond by sitting down.

Once the students have practiced a number of times, the teacher simply gives the command and the students respond. Eventually the students will give the commands, thus developing oral proficiency.

In TPR, teachers can use pictures, objects, and realia for students to manipulate as they respond nonverbally. For example, the students are studying a unit on "emotions." The teacher can pass out pictures of people displaying different emotions. Then, the teacher can give the following commands:

Teacher: Raise the picture of the girl who seems sad.

Student: Raises picture of sad girl.
Teacher: Stand up if you have a picture of two boys who seem happy.
Student with the correct picture: Stands up.
Teacher: Place on the board the picture that shows a woman who seems surprised.
Student with the correct picture: Walks up to the board and places the picture on the magnetic board.

Commands become more complex as the students continue to develop listening comprehension and knowledge of subject matter. For example, with the assistance of pictures, students can be asked to categorize modes of transportation by land, water, or air, or they could be asked to rearrange pictures to show the life cycle of a butterfly.

Once students are able to respond to a series of commands and can give the commands themselves, the teacher can introduce the reading and the writing aspects of language. However, the emphasis in TPR is on listening comprehension until oral proficiency is developed.

TPR is an appropriate method to use with students who are in the preproduction/silent stage of language development. Students who are not yet speaking are able to be involved in lessons and respond nonverbally. Thus, these students begin to feel a sense of belonging and success as they participate in the lessons. Students benefit from the involvement in the lessons, and the teachers are able to determine whether or not the students are developing listening comprehension.

TPR is somewhat limited within the confines of a classroom; however, with the use of pictures, and other types of manipulatives, a resourceful teacher can bring the outside world into the classroom. For example, a teacher may prepare a transparency of a picture that shows many actions. Each student gets a copy of the picture (black and white is acceptable for this type of activity). The teacher uses the transparency to demonstrate the actions following the commands given. Students imitate and follow along. This is an excellent way to introduce verbs and new vocabulary using TPR.

Mainstream Classroom Use

Mainstream classroom teachers can demonstrate new words to language learners using the TPR method without much extensive planning.

Teacher: Class, for this activity we need to take out our science books. Please (demonstrating) **take out your science books.**

Students: Take out science books.

Teacher: Next, please open (demonstrating) to page 68 (write 68 on board).

Students: Open textbook to page 68.

Teacher: Who would like to raise their hand (demonstrating) to share (point to mouth) what the notice (point to eyes) on page 68.

Teacher: Thank you, Jimmy, for raising your hand (demonstrating). What did you notice (point to eyes)?

Jimmy: I see a big waterfall with trees all around it.

Teacher: Good, you're correct. Today we are going to discuss (point to mouth) three large waterfalls (place image on the board) here in our community (demonstrate community).

The lesson that this teacher is using is not a language lesson necessarily. However, the teacher is aware that this language may be difficult for a speaker of another language. She does not have to slow down or provide follow-up exercises for the student, but it is important that she is aware of her word choices and movements to help demonstrate new words for the newcomer.

TPR lessons are also fun and exciting for speakers of English. Many students will welcome the use of movement into their typical classroom activities. This type of lesson can easily be integrated into a mainstream classroom without pointing out that this activity is designed to support language learners.

Sample 1: Florida Waterbirds

List of Commands:

1. Look up at the clouds.
2. Show me the clouds.
3. Jump in the water.
4. Swim over to the blue heron.
5. Stand like the blue heron.
6. Flap your wings like a bird.
7. Let's count the birds in the picture
8. Wave to the pelican.
9. Squawk like a laughing gull.
10. Pet the flamingo.
11. Get out of the water.
12. Shake yourself off.
13. Wave "good-bye" to the birds.

Sample 2: In the Field

List of Commands:

1. Walk up to the scarecrow.
2. Walk around the scarecrow.
3. Wave "hello" to the scarecrow.
4. Touch the scarecrow's hat.
5. Wave "good-bye" to the scarecrow.
6. Walk up to the ball.
7. Pick up the ball.
8. Put down the ball.
9. Walk up to the pear tree.
10. Pick up two pears from the ground.
11. Place the pears in the basket.
12. Pick up one more pear.
13. Bite off a piece from the pear.
14. Chew the piece of pear.
15. Skip over to the other tree.
16. Get close to the trunk.
17. Step on and crush the leaves.
18. Look up!
19. Wave to the squirrel.
20. Peek in the hole in the trunk.
21. Walk past the scarecrow.
22. Wave "good-bye" as you leave the field.

Another way to use TPR is by the use of logical sequences of actions, also known as Gouin series, such as driving a car or taking a picture.

The following are two examples.

Driving a Car

I take my car key in my hand.
I walk to the car.
I unlock the car door or I use my remote to unlock the door.
I open the car door.
I get into the car.
I close the door.
I put on the seat belt.
I place the key in the ignition.
I start the car.
I take off.

Taking a Picture (Traditional)

I get the camera.
I open the film compartment of the camera.
I place the film in the camera.
I close the camera.
I check to see that the camera is ready.
I look through the lens of the camera.
I focus.
I take the picture.

Taking a Picture (Digital)

I get the camera.
I check to see that the camera is ready.
I take the picture.
I check the picture.
I save the picture (or I delete the picture).
I load the picture onto the computer.
I send the picture to my friend.

The Gouin series can be longer or shorter, depending on how much language the teacher wishes to use at one time. Initially, the teacher models the actions, and the students pantomime the actions. As soon as the teacher feels the students can respond without imitating the actions, the teacher simply describes the action, and the students respond by demonstrating the actions (Curtain & Dahlberg, 2004).

The following benefits of the Gouin series have been identified (Knop, in Curtain & Dahlberg, 2004):

1. It links language to action and visuals, leading to improved comprehension.
2. It teaches appropriate verbal and physical behavior, making it especially useful for teaching cultural behaviors.
3. It is easy to recall because it has multiple meaning reinforcers:
   - Physical actions
   - Visuals and props
   - Logical sequence
   - Appeal to several senses
   - Beginning, middle, and end

Gouin series are also a way of developing reading and writing skills. Once the students are able to say the series, the teacher can record the sentences on sentence strips. Students can then be introduced to the reading of the sentences. Students can illustrate the series and write the actions illustrated. Illustrations can be compiled in book form or can be displayed sequentially in the classroom.

Following is a sample Gouin series that has been illustrated and described in print.

I wake up at 6:00 a.m.

I get up and brush my teeth.

I get dressed.

I comb my hair.

I go to the kitchen.

I have breakfast.

I get my backpack.

I walk to the bus stop.

Other benefits of the Gouin series include:

1. It elicits students' interest and active participation;
2. It gives an authentic experience using the target language; and
3. It facilitates the natural emergence and development of oral communication (The State of New Jersey Curriculum Frameworks for World Languages, 2006).

The Natural Approach

Tracy Terrell (1977, 1981) developed the natural approach based on Krashen's monitor model (discussed in detail in Chapter 10). The main goal of this method is to develop immediate communicative competency. Therefore, most classroom activities are designed to encourage communication. Terrell (1977) suggested that the entire class period be devoted to communication activities rather than to explanation of grammatical aspects of language. The Natural Approach emphasizes providing the students with the opportunity to *acquire* language rather than forcing them to learn it. In this method, the key to comprehension and oral production is the acquisition of vocabulary. Thus, much opportunity for listening/speaking is given to students. Class time is not devoted to grammatical lectures or mechanical exercises. Any explanation and practice of linguistic forms should be done outside of class for the most part. Outside work is planned carefully and structured to provide the necessary practice with language forms. Although this was Terrell's position in his earlier writings, he seemed to amend his position in his latest writings (1991). He now suggests that there might be some benefit to providing form-focused instruction as a means of establishing form–meaning relationships in communicative activities. Teaching grammar for the sake of grammar instruction is not effective. However, clarifying it in context, using advanced organizers to tie it in with communicative activities, does have some value.

According to Terrell (1977), error correction is negative in terms of motivation and attitude; thus, he does not advocate the correction of speech errors in the process of oral language development. This position reflects Krashen's affective filter hypothesis, which says that when students experience an embarrassing situation, the affective filter goes up, interrupting the language acquisition process. Thus, error correction would have a negative effect on the process.

The natural approach bases language acquisition on the natural order of native language development. Because native language development follows a progression, during the silent period, students would be allowed to respond in their native language. The emphasis is on listening comprehension, so if students respond in their native language, they are demonstrating comprehension. At the same time, students can be exposed to a wide variety of topics and still be comfortable in the communication process.

Mainstream Classroom Use

In this method, teachers must provide comprehensible input at all times for their language learners. The use of visuals (graphs, charts, pictures, objects, realia), gestures, demonstrations, and motherese/parentese (slower speech, simpler language repetition, rephrasing, clear enunciation) is required. In addition, the use of yes/no type questions, either/or type questions, and questions that require short answers is strongly suggested in the beginning stages of language acquisition. The use of total physical response (TPR) is emphasized, particularly during the comprehension (silent/preproduction) stage.

Making simple adjustments to our instruction will help classroom teachers in a mainstream setting to provide their language learners with comprehensible input and opportunities for language practice.

For example:

Teacher: Sebastién, would you shut the window please?
Sebastién: I don't understand.
Teacher: Could you shut the window.
Sebastién: I don't understand.
Teacher: It is cold in our classroom (demonstrate). Please close the window (demonstrate).

In this example, the teacher has tried a few techniques to help Sebastién understand the instruction. Often as teachers we reuse the same vocabulary over and over again expecting different results. When working with language learners, it is important to share different ways to give the same instruction in order to help them to learn new vocabulary. In this example, Sebastién's teacher understood that he maybe didn't understand the modal verb "would" so she tried again using "could." When that didn't work, she tried to substitute "shut" with "close." An important follow-up with Sebastién would be to add "shut-close" to a personal word wall or student dictionary to show him that he has learned a new word. She could also use the instruction again with Sebastién in the future to help reinforce the new word that he learned.

The Communicative Approach

The communicative approach to language teaching is based on several theoretical premises.

1. The communication principle: Activities that involve communication promote the acquisition of language.
2. The task-principle: Activities that engage students in the completion of real world tasks promote language acquisition.
3. The meaningfulness principle: Learners are engaged in activities that promote authentic and meaningful use of language.

The main goal in this approach is for the learner to become communicatively competent. The learner develops competency in using the language appropriately in given social contexts. Emphasis is placed on activities that allow the second language learner to negotiate meaning in activities that require oral communication in the second language.

In the communicative approach, it is important to create an "information gap" between speakers. Thus, the need to communicate is authentic because communication must take place to narrow the gap and accomplish the task (i.e., "I/we have what you need, and you have what I/we need to complete our task"). The task cannot be completed individually; partners must work together to successfully complete the assigned task.

Classroom activities must be varied and must include interactive language games, information-sharing activities, social interactions, need for impromptu responses, and the use of authentic materials, such as the newspaper for oral discussions on current events.

Sauvignon (2002) suggests designing the curriculum to include language arts (or language analysis activities), language-for-a-purpose (content-based and immersion) activities, personalized language use, theatre arts (including simulations, role-plays, and social interaction games), and language use "beyond the classroom" (including planning activities that take the learners outside the classroom to engage in real-world encounters).

The communicative approach embraces the principle of "learning by doing," encouraging the use of English from the beginning of instruction. Thus, language acquisition takes place as a result of using the second language in meaningful communication from the onset in the process.

Kagan (1995), one of the greatest supporters of cooperative learning in the classroom, has described how this strategy is very effective in ESL classrooms, particularly when using the communicative approach. According to Kagan, language acquisition is fostered by input that is comprehensible, developmentally appropriate, redundant, and accurate. In cooperative groups, students need to be understood, so they naturally adjust their input to make it comprehensible. This is especially necessary in communicative settings. In cooperative groups, students receive repeated input from the members in the group, providing the necessary redundancy for language learning to move from short-term comprehension to long-term acquisition.

When analyzing the communicative approach, it could be said that peer output is less accurate than teacher output. However, Kagan stated that in cooperative groups, frequent output produces language acquisition far more readily than formal input. The same could be said of the communicative approach. Thus, the use of cooperative groups in a communicative approach environment should be strongly encouraged.

Mainstream Classroom Use

Group and partner activities are great ways to allow language learners the opportunity to produce language naturally and in a less stressful environment. The students will feel less pressure while working with only a few classmates, than they would if expected to volunteer or speak to the whole class. In addition to the lowered affective filter, the students will also have age appropriate models of language who exhibit language structures and forms that are common for children their age. Participation in small group or partner projects also encourages relationships with classmates that may not be fostered in the full class or independent work setting. Group and partner projects promote a comfortable and confident working space for new learners.

- In the grammar-translation method (also known as the classical method), the emphasis was on teaching grammar and employing translation to ascertain comprehension.

- The grammar-translation method did not produce speakers of the languages studied.

- In the grammar-translation method, much use of the native language was employed because the goal was not oral proficiency.

- In the grammar-translation method, teachers did not necessarily have to be fluent speakers of the target language because the focus was not on communication.

- The grammar-translation method dominated public schools and university language teaching in the United States until World War II.

- Today, unfortunately, there is still some evidence of the use of the grammar-translation method in some public schools.

- The direct method was a complete departure from the grammar-translation method.

- The direct method did not allow for the use of the native language in the classroom.

- The direct method required the use of visuals to convey meaning in an effort to eliminate translation.

- The emphasis in the direct method was on developing proficient thinkers and speakers in the target language.

- The direct method takes its name from the emphasis in the "direct" use of the target language.

- The most widely known application of the direct method is practiced at the Berlitz language schools.

- The audio-lingual method (based on behavioristic psychology) emphasized the use of habit forming as a way to develop language proficiency.

- The main goal of the audio-lingual method was to develop fluent speakers of the languages studied.

- In the audio-lingual method, the emphasis was on the rote memorization of dialogues.

- In the audio-lingual method, the belief was that much oral practice (dialogue memorization) would result in communicative competence.

- The audio-lingual method was unsuccessful because students could recite the dialogues but could not "communicate" in the target language.

- TPR stands for total physical response.

- In TPR, students are actively engaged in the language acquisition process by responding nonverbally (physically).

- TPR is an effective method to employ while second language learners are in the silent (comprehension/preproduction) period.

- The TPR method allows teachers to ascertain comprehension long before second language learners are able to respond verbally.

- TPR is an effective method of including second language learners in lessons while in the silent period.

- TPR helps second/new language learners develop a sense of belonging and accomplishment while still in the silent period.

- Pictures, objects, and realia are effective to enhance and expand the use of TPR in the classroom.

- ❖ The natural approach is based on Krashen's monitor model.

- ❖ The natural approach respects the ELL's silent period.

- ❖ Error correction is discouraged in the natural approach.

- ❖ In the natural approach, the emphasis is on developing oral language proficiency.

- ❖ In the natural approach, the teaching of grammar/language forms is discouraged.

- ❖ In the natural approach, TPR is widely employed.

- ❖ The communicative approach emphasizes meaningful communication in the ESOL classroom.

- ❖ The communicative approach requires the use of varied activities where authentic communication takes place.

- ❖ The communicative approach embraces the principle of "learning by doing."

- ❖ Cooperative groups provide a vehicle for language acquisition in the communicative approach.

- ❖ The communicative approach is based on the need for an "information gap" as a means to encourage meaningful communication.

- ❖ Although at times ineffective in isolation or difficult to apply to a classroom setting, mainstream classroom teachers can use elements of different language acquisition methods to help their language learners to be successful in their content classes.

Principles of Communicative Language Teaching

KEY ISSUES
- ❖ Principles underlying communicative language teaching
- ❖ Principles underlying communicative language teaching
- ❖ Differences between traditional and current practices of language teaching
- ❖ The roles of learning goals, nature of input, setting, and teachers and learners in communicative language teaching
- ❖ The changing views regarding grammar instruction

Ms. Williams, a monolingual English speaker, teaches a mainstream fourth grade class made up of ELLs and English-speaking students. Many of the ELLs speak Spanish or Vietnamese. Their English proficiency levels vary. In the past week, the students have been learning to use multiplication to solve real life problems and learning about the basic food groups and their nutritional values. Ms. Williams plans to incorporate the mathematical concepts in her language arts lesson, which centers on the topic of food and nutrition. The fourth graders will practice quantitative words such as more/the most, less/least during the next lesson.

Today the teacher brought in a diagram of the food pyramid, picture cards of food, and some food labels. She wants the students to figure out their daily food intake and to create a balanced food plan for one day.

Ms. Williams began the discussion by activating the students' prior knowledge asking them to log all of the food that they ate the day before. She asks them to look at their logs for the information they have recorded. As students reply, she lists their words on the board and sounds them out loud. She also pastes pictures of foods that are listed on the board. She then asks students to count the number of servings they ate for each food. She asks the students to find a partner and ask questions such as, "Did you eat more sweets than vegetables?" or "Did you eat less meat than fruit?" "What did you eat the most/least?" Students are asked to reply by saying: "I ate more X than Y," "I ate less X than Y," or "I ate X."

Next, she shows them the food pyramid chart and talks about the different food groups and the amount of servings for each group. The teacher says, "Last week, we learned that there are certain types of foods we should eat a lot of every day and foods we should eat less of. Can anyone tell me which food should we eat more of?" Isabelle answers, "Rice, we must eat more rice." Ms. Williams replies, "Yes, you're right, Isabelle." Felipe raises his hand tentatively, "Apple," and he points to pictures of fruits on the board. Ms. Williams sounds the words aloud for

Felipe. She then points to the food pyramid chart and asks, "What food group do apples and bananas belong to, Felipe?" Felipe answers, "Fruit." Next, Victor jumps in and says, "Meats." Ms. Williams retorts, "Do we need more meat than vegetables?" Victor responds, "No, more vegetables than meats. My father say meat is no good—they got many chemical inside their bodies and is no good for us." Ms. Williams responds, "Victor, I believe you are quite right. Yes, many farm animals are given hormones to make them grow faster and bigger. What do you think class?" Discussion continues and Ms. Williams provides positive feedback to the students for their answers.

Ms. Williams continues to ask students for the name of the food group of the items they mentioned and discusses why they need different amounts of each. Then Ms. Williams passes out food labels to each pair of students. She asks the pair to state the amount of servings they would have if they eat the food, and if it exceeds the recommended daily servings.

She asks, "Teng, if we need three to five servings of vegetables each day, how much should we eat each week?" Teng answers, "three times seven and five times seven, so we need about twenty-one to thirty-five servings each week." Ms. Williams says, "Nice job, Teng. You're a math whiz!" She then asks the class if there is another way to express the same idea. One student says, "We must eat twenty-one to thirty-five servings every week." "Yes," says the teacher. Ms. Williams gives similar math problems for other students to answer and asks students to rephrase their statements.

Next, Ms. Williams breaks the students into small groups with mixed levels of English proficiency. She asks them to create a balanced food plan for one day and gives each group a pyramid chart to fill in their information. Ms. Williams assigns roles to each student so that all students are participating in the project. She considers the students' English proficiency when assigning roles. For example, she may ask students with lower English proficiency to draw the pictures of food they select on their pyramid chart. She may also select the students with higher English proficiency to report orally to class the following information:

a. Foods they should eat more or less of

b. The number of servings of each food in their food plan

How would you characterize the classroom described in the vignette? Consider the following questions:

❖ What are the goals of language learning in this class?
❖ What areas of language are emphasized?
❖ What is the role of content in language learning?
❖ What are students expected to do?
❖ What types of materials are used?
❖ How did the teacher use the materials to teach the structures?
❖ Are the students learning real life language?
❖ What skills are they acquiring?
❖ How does the teacher respond to inaccuracies in language?

In the previous chapters, the lengthy description of language methods reveal the pendulum swing in our profession regarding the best way to teach and learn a second language. The early methods were strongly influenced by linguistic descriptions and contrastive analysis of languages, and hence, much of the teaching practices tend to emphasize linguistic analysis and overlearning of discrete linguistic rules. As educators gained more insights about how children acquire language naturally, they began to break away from drill and memorization to an emphasis on developing language learners' ability to communicate in the target language.

In the mid-1970s, educators questioned the best way to promote second language acquisition based on what they had amassed from research on second language teaching and learning. Researchers and educators realized that language learners who master and manipulate linguistic rules may not necessarily know how to use the language appropriately to perform the various linguistic functions typical of everyday social contexts. This distinction underscores a difference between linguistic competence and communicative competence. Linguistic competence refers to knowledge about language forms; communicative competence refers to knowledge that enables one to use language functionally and interactively. Hymes (1972) first introduced the term "communicative competence," which was later expanded by Canale and Swain (1980) and Bachman (1990). The term recognizes that social and cultural contexts of language use are just as important as the rules of language usage. Indeed, language learners must have communicative competence—knowing when to say what and how to adapt our language based on audience—to be successful at language learning. This principle of communicative competence provided impetus for the emphasis on communication as a goal for language learning. Canale (1983) identified four components that make up the communicative competence:

Grammatical Competence

Focuses on the skills necessary to speak and write accurately using vocabulary, grammar, pronunciation, spelling, phonology, etc.

Discourse Competence

Focuses on the skills to engage in conversations, which requires participants to connect sentences or stretches of discourse to form a series of meaningful, coherent discourse; also requires participants to become both sender and recipient of messages in spoken and written discourse.

Sociolinguistic Competence

Focuses on using socioculturally appropriate language and discourse patterns in a variety of social settings. It requires understanding of social conventions, roles of participants, and purpose of interaction, which determines the appropriateness of forms (register) and meaning. For example, knowing how to make introductions, expressing opinions, complimenting, or declining an invitation require sociolinguistic competence.

Strategic Competence

Focuses on manipulating language to achieve communication goals by utilizing verbal and nonverbal strategies. These strategies can be considered compensatory strategies that one can use to compensate for a breakdown in communication. Paraphrasing, repeating, avoidance, gesturing to convey a point, or modulating voice tone or volume to achieve effect are some examples.

Language learners must be taught the social, cultural, and pragmatic features of language and be given tools for generating unrehearsed language beyond the immediate classroom task. In this new paradigm shift, educators are no longer overly consumed with developing learners' accuracy only, but also help learners develop fluency. Many of the methods developed since the late 1970s reflect changing winds from a linguistic-structure approach to a communicative approach or communicative language teaching (Widdowson, 1990).

The term *approach* focuses on how our beliefs, assumptions, and theories about the nature of language and language learning are compatible with classroom techniques. In other words, it is an umbrella term for a number of methods that may fall within the same theoretical and philosophical framework. For example, the total physical response (TPR), language experience, and natural approach are considered communicative language teaching approaches because they all share fundamental ideas about the goal of language, which affects not only what is learned, but also what is expected of learners and what actually happens in the classroom. In essence, these methods stress that language is an instrument of communication, and hence, its primary emphasis is on meaning rather than knowing structural forms. Fluency rather than accuracy is sought, and thus, errors in learning are a natural developmental process. The learner negotiates and plays an active role in the process of learning. However, these methods may employ different techniques such as physical movements, personal experience, and natural language input through songs, poems, or stories to achieve the desired goal. Hence, the term *approach* implies a set of generalized beliefs, assumptions, and philosophical underpinnings instead of specific instructional procedures that reflect the approach. This position allows teachers to achieve some flexibility and, at the same time, maintain a principled approach in their teaching. Teachers do not slavishly adopt specific "methods" as a set of conventionalized procedures that fit all classroom contexts. Rather, effective teachers understand the value of undergirding their teaching with sound

principles that enable them to decide what, why, and how they will design their instruction, how they will monitor their teaching effectiveness, and how they will make necessary modifications. This kind of reflection allows teachers to gather new insights to make necessary modifications to their teaching plans.

Finocchario and Brumfit (1983) summarized major differences between language approaches that focus on form, namely the audio-lingual methodology, and the approach that focuses on meaning, in this case, the communicative approach, in Table 14-1.

Table 14-1 **A Comparison of the Audio-Lingual Method and Communicative Language Teaching**

Audio-Lingual Method	Communicative Language Teaching
Attends to structure and form more than meaning.	Meaning is paramount.
Demands more memorization of structure-based dialogs.	Dialogs, if used, center on communicative functions and are not normally memorized.
Language items are not necessarily contextualized.	Contextualization is a basic premise.
Language learning is learning structures, sounds, or words.	Language learning is learning to communicate.
Mastery or "overlearning" is sought.	Effective communication is sought.
Drilling is a central technique.	Drilling may occur, but peripherally.
Native-like speaker pronunciation is sought.	Comprehensible pronunciation is sought.
Grammatical explanation is avoided.	Any device that helps learners is accepted—varies according to their age, interest, experience, etc.
Communicative activities come only after plenty of rigid drills and controlled exercises.	Attempts to communicate may be encouraged from the very beginning.
The use of the student's native language is forbidden.	Judicious use of native language is accepted when feasible.
Translation is forbidden at early levels.	Translation is used when student needs it or benefits from it.
Reading and writing are deferred until speaking is mastered.	Reading and writing can start from the very first day, if desired.
The target linguistic system will be learned through the overt teaching of the patterns of the system.	The target linguistic system will be learned best through the process of struggling to communicate.
Linguistic competence is the desired goal.	Communicative competence is the desired goal.
Varieties of language are recognized but not emphasized.	Linguistic variation is a central concept in materials and methods.
The sequence of units is determined solely by linguistic complexity.	Sequencing is determined by any consideration of content function or meaning that maintains interest.

Audio-Lingual Method	Communicative Language Teaching
The teacher controls the learners and prevents them from doing anything that conflicts with theory.	Teachers help learners in any way that motivates them to work with the language.
"Language is habit," so error must be prevented at all costs.	Language is created often by the individual through trial and error.
Accuracy, in terms of formal correctness, is a primary goal.	Fluency and acceptable language are the primary goal: accuracy is judged not in the abstract but in context.
Students are expected to interact with the language system, embodied in machines and controlled materials found in language labs.	Students are expected to interact with other people, either in the flesh, through pair and group work, or in their writings.
The teacher is expected to specify the language that students are to use.	The teacher cannot know exactly what language the students will use.
Intrinsic motivation will spring from an interest in the structure of language.	Intrinsic motivation will spring from an interest in what is being communicated by the language.

Source: Finocchario and Brumfit (1983)

David Nunan (1991) has developed a list of key features of communicative language teaching. He describes them as the following:

❖ Focuses on meaning through interaction in the target language
❖ Uses materials or texts that reflect authentic or real world language
❖ Allows learners to rehearse language used outside the classroom by focusing on language forms or skills and the learning process
❖ Focuses on previous knowledge, experiences, or skills learners bring into the classroom as important contributors to language learning
❖ Plans a careful link between classroom language and real world language

From these lists, significant features that are central to communicative language teaching can be extrapolated. These features are categorized into the following broad areas as shown in Table 14-2.

What is abundantly clear in these lists is that there is an implicit agreement between them—the idea that language learning in the classroom can transfer to other uses of language in the real world. Hence, if the desired goal of a communicative ap-proach is to provide learners with the transfer of skills and knowledge developed inside the class-room to its use in the outside world, then learners need exposure to the types of language encountered in real life. This links directly with Nunan's (1991) concept of language authenticity, which is important within the communicative language teaching frame-work because it influences how teachers select ma-terials and design activities for interaction to achieve their learning or teaching objectives. The following discussion highlights the implications of authentic-ity, roles, and settings in language learning within a communicative language framework.

Language Authenticity

Nunan (1989) defined authenticity as "materials that have not been specifically produced for the purposes of language teaching." This definition implies that any oral and written texts that are used by native speakers for social or transactional purposes are considered authentic texts. The rationale for select-ing authentic materials includes: (1) they are much more interesting to learners; (2) they provide a "rich" source of input because they focus more on meaning than on form; (3) they have high face

Table 14-2 **Summary of Key Areas of Communicative Language Teaching**

Goals
Focus on meaning instead of discrete language forms; fluency and some level of accuracy are necessary in any interaction; emphasis on language use also implies that specific skills may be developed in the process of learning.

Inputs
Focus on language that is relevant to real-life use; has a strong, real-world focus reflected by choice of topics, language functions, use of relevant personal or real-world knowledge, and the way members of the target language use language to communicate in different settings.

Roles
Focus on learners having an active, negotiative role; learners are both senders and receivers of input.

Settings
Provides opportunities for learners to use language through oral and written interaction with other people inside and outside the classroom boundaries; cooperative learning structures in either pair or group work expose learners to a variety of language input and pragmatic skills in interactive discourse.

---

validity to learners because learners perceive these materials to be relevant, thereby increasing learners' intrinsic motivation; and (4) they expose learners to cultural concepts and skills through language use (Senior, 2005). Empirical research has also supported the use of authentic texts in language learning. Bacon and Finneman (1990) suggest that authentic materials can increase intrinsic motivation, which will result in successful acquisition. Duquette, Dunnett, and Papalia (1987) also found that authentic materials expose learners to cultural awareness besides language, a desirable goal if language learners wish to participate in the target culture effectively and appropriately.

The performance tasks that learners are asked to complete deserve careful consideration in the communicative approach. In the communicative approach, learners must be actively engaged in "comprehending, manipulating, producing, or interacting in the target language" (Nunan, 1989, p. 10); these tasks can help learners to use language for genuine communicative purposes, just as native speakers are "interested in meanings, and in getting things done" (Mitchell, 1994, p. 37). In other words, selecting materials that contain real life language use does not, in itself, make the task authentic; its authenticity

is also contingent on whether learners are asked to interact and become involved with the tasks in pursuit of a communicative outcome.

Nunan (1989) divided communicative tasks into two types: real world and pedagogic. Real world tasks resemble the type of interaction that occurs outside the classroom. Pedagogic tasks are those that are typically done in the classroom, but they enable learners to build necessary skills that are important for communication in the target language. In fact, the division between real world and pedagogic is not so distinct. For example, will the students in the opening vignette be required to describe their diet outside the classroom setting? The answer could be either yes or no. But will students find themselves using language structures such as "more . . . than . . ." or "less . . . than . . ." in making comparisons in the real world? These structures are likely to occur. Thus, it is important for teachers to examine whether classroom tasks will equip and empower students to produce language they would need in the real world. To determine whether language tasks are authentic or not, teachers must also make judicious use of appropriate, authentic texts and activities that will guide students through a developmental process and give students adequate exposure to the language they will eventually need to function autonomously.

Role of the Teacher

In many traditional classrooms, the teacher controls what goes on and what learners will say and do. In the communicative classroom, the teacher does not control in the same way that teachers do in traditional classrooms. Brown (1994) suggested that teachers play different roles to create an interactive classroom. Teachers must play the role of both a controller and a director. For interaction to take place, teachers must plan for interaction to take place. Specifically, they must know how to initiate an initial response from learners and how students will demonstrate performance skills. They must ensure the flow and direction of interaction and the production of desired responses. Teachers must also be the facilitators who advance the process of learning, helping students to overcome any "roadblocks" (Brown, 1994, p. 161). They must provide necessary motivation for students to take risks in discovering and using language pragmatically. Teachers must also be a resource, giving advice and proper counseling to students when they ask for guidance. Brown explains that a communicative language teacher must be able to assume these roles to assist students with varying levels of proficiency, to move from "total dependence to relatively total independence" (p. 162).

Role of the Learner

When teachers ask students to communicate in a language in which they have partial control, they are asking them to take risks. This implies that instructors need to encourage their students to experiment with language. Learners must also take responsibility for their own learning and develop autonomy and skills which help them to recognize how they learn. In a communicative classroom, learners may sometimes have to study and organize information on their own and become creative in experimenting with ways of creating and using language. They are also required to be active by completing performance tasks in class, interacting with fellow learners and the teacher, and listening, reading, and using language. They may also be asked to organize what they have learned by making notes and charts, displaying them, and using these materials to communicate. In other words, there are plenty of opportunities for students to rehearse language and for learning about how to learn.

Learners must also be taught to tolerate uncertainties and ambiguities. For example, learners may be encouraged to read or talk by comprehending the overall gist of the message as opposed to concentrating on every single word in the message. And if they do not understand, they should be encouraged to ask for help and error correction in order to ultimately learn from their errors. Learners must also be taught to live with errors and not let errors become an impediment to their understanding. In general, learners in a communicative paradigm must eventually take charge of their learning, with guided support.

To help learners become autonomous, teachers must create many opportunities for them to use language to express their ideas and opinions and to react to different ideas and opinions. Teachers must also encourage learners to accept mistakes as a part of their learning in order to improve their English and literacy skills. To achieve all these goals, teachers must create a classroom environment where students and teachers respect differences in opinions, and suspend judgments so that different perspectives can be heard and understood. This is especially important when students are learning historical events, concepts, and issues in their textbooks and curriculum units from the perspectives of the dominant group. For example, in concepts related to the discovery of America, the role of the pioneers often reflects views of European Americans and often ignores or marginalizes the feelings and experiences of different indigenous groups in America or those who were brought to America by slavery. Such a classroom climate can create stereotypes about racial and ethnic groups and also can cause nonmainstream students to feel left out of the American story. Teachers must also provide models and guidance for learning how to learn through various discussion and shared reading and writing activities so that new English learners will be able to apply and transfer skills they have learned.

Settings

According to Nunan (1989), "'settings' refer to two specific things: (i) the classroom arrangements specified or implied in the task," (p. 91), which he refers to as "learning mode," and (ii) the task that occurs in the classroom or outside the classroom, which he refers to as "environment." "Learning mode" refers to whether learners are working individually or in groups or working at a self- or teacher-directed pace. In contrast, "environment" refers to where the actual learning takes place.

Knerr and James (1991) advocate partner work and small group work to maximize the opportunity for students to practice grammar, vocabulary, and language strategies that are presented in a whole class situation. These types of cooperative learning have become increasingly popular in second language instruction; each group member is given a specific role or information that must be shared with other group members before the student can complete the final product and receive a group reward. The cooperative and noncompetitive atmosphere for learning not only improves group relations between learners in the classrooms, but also improves their academic achievement by lowering their affective filter or anxiety, which is often associated with learning something new, be it language or content information. Other benefits of cooperative learning include:

❖ Developing a greater sense of accountability and responsibility for students' learning as well as for their group if the task creates a necessity for each member in the group to contribute to the whole.

❖ Exposing learners to natural exchanges as students engage in extended discourses that are more realistic as learners try to decipher the message amid background noise, false starts, or listening to two people talking simultaneously.

❖ Encouraging learners to become communicators in a wide range of situations and to practice a full range of language strategies, such as hypothesizing, generalizing, disagreeing, summarizing, and clarifying (Long & Porter, 1985).

The following are several suggestions for grouping new English learners that would promote opportunities for interaction and language practice and form a basis for the multilevel class.

a. **Mixed groups of fully English proficient students and new English learners:** Grouping English speakers with new English learners on a specific task provides language modeling and encourages socialization of students and opportunities for newcomers to expand their circles of peers. In addition, fully English proficient students can help new English learners learn and practice basic English words and phrases through meaningful interactions; thus new English learners may benefit from the help of peers in a more relaxed setting. As fully English proficient students encounter English learners from different language and cultural backgrounds, they will learn to make adjustments as they expand their awareness and acceptance of students whose language and culture they know little about.

b. **Mixed groups of monolingual English learners and bilingual students:** Grouping the two types of students together validates the language and culture of the group and supports the maintenance of the bilingual students' language. New English learners entering a new culture often experience internal conflict as they begin to fit into the dominant culture and sometimes find themselves torn between accepting and learning the new culture and language and maintaining their home language and culture. Grouping bilingual students to work with the monolingual English learners is an excellent way to show that learning the ways of the new culture, its people, and language does not have to replace those of their home. Another advantage is the ability for bilingual students, who share one common language with the new English learners, to code-switch between two languages and thus provide additional support for new English learners to understand input in the new language.

c. **Monolingual groups of new English learners:** Grouping monolingual English learners (who speak a common first language) together provides a comfortable environment for sharing ideas and enables members to understand one another. Because learners in this group already share a common first language, and possibly the same culture, the stress of having to communicate in English all the time and the feelings of helplessness, embarrassment, and frustration of being misunderstood by other speakers are somewhat reduced. When new learners are socially and emotionally comfortable in their new environment, they are more likely to accept and learn the target language and culture. One possible setback of this type of grouping is the tendency for learners to rely heavily on their primary language and thereby reduce their exposure and use of the target language that is necessary for developing fluency and accuracy in the new language. For this reason, this grouping should be coupled with other grouping strategies already mentioned so that new English learners will not experience tremendous anxieties while learning a new language.

d. **Buddy system:** Pairing a newcomer with a "buddy," if possible with a bilingual buddy, will help the newcomer understand new routines and culturally specific rules of the classroom and school that may be foreign to the newcomer. This buddy will also help the newcomer to find important places on the school grounds such as the cafeteria, library, gymnasium, bathroom, parent pickup/drop-off area, and the bus stop. This buddy can be assigned to work with the newcomer for a specific term or throughout the year to allow sufficient time for the newcomer to bond with his/her personal buddy and alleviate initial anxieties commonly experienced by newcomers.

e. **Gender-based groups:** Extra care must be taken when grouping members from cultures where there are strong prescriptive role behaviors associated with each gender. In some Central and South American countries, Japan, Slovakia, and some countries in the Middle East, gender roles are clearly differentiated, and inequality between the sexes is more ac-

ceptable than in countries like Sweden, Yugoslavia, Norway, and South Africa that prefer gender equality. Men in the former cultures are typically expected to be competitive, visible, and achievement oriented, whereas women are expected to be nurturing. In contrast, the latter countries tend to accept men and women as equal partners working together for the survival of their cultures. These gender-based differences must be taken into consideration, especially when the group task requires members of different genders to assume equal responsibilities that are not congruent with the socialized norms of men and women in their group (Hofstede, 1991).

Knerr and James (1991, pp. 62–63) also provide other suggestions for grouping English learners on specific tasks:

a. **Interest groups:** Grouping English learners with other students based on their interests is particularly useful for longer and involved projects.

b. **Personality types:** Groups can be formed based on how well different personalities work together. Anyone who has been a classroom teacher can attest to the fact that there is a wide range of personalities that can influence classroom dynamics and learning. Some learners appear to be leaders; others are great motivators, listeners, focus setters, and so forth. For example, a group made up of students who tend to take charge and dominate others could actually restrict participation of linguistically less-proficient and quieter students. This type of grouping does not provide a low-anxiety environment for new language learners to feel safe in taking risks for fear of appearing foolish when they make mistakes. Likewise, a group of relatively shy and less-talkative students or those who come from cultures where it is improper to speak extensively in the classroom may not actively participate in group tasks that require high levels of oral interaction. Successful group work often depends on how well members are able to focus on their task. It is instrumental to have a member who can guide all members to remain in focus and direct other members to keep the same pace until their task is completed. In addition, it is also important to remember that communication often requires a degree of empathy or the ability to understand the other person's feelings and thinking, or communication will suffer. If empathy is predictive of success in language learning, it is important to train or prepare learners to develop empathy and understand how different cultures express it. An unbalanced composition of students may not maximize opportunities for engagement of learners with diverse personality styles.

c. **Student selected groups:** At times as teachers, we try to think of everything ahead of time in order to best plan for student learning. However, sometimes, leaving the decision up to the students themselves can be enlightening to teachers. Students should be reminded of their learning goals, rights, and responsibilities before selecting with whom they would like to work. They may surprise you with their selections and the products that they complete may be really exciting.

In many classrooms today, much of what students are learning goes beyond the confines of the classroom walls. In other words, teaching and learning can occur in natural settings found in individual communities. Many teachers who believe in the importance of teaching communicative language have included the use of resources in the wider community, where learners can collect information on specific themes or topics that are being learned in class, adopt communicative roles that have relevance to their real life, and interact with native speakers. For example, trips to a zoo, a library, a fire station, or a health facility can provide real life language and situations that learners will find useful in helping them to learn, to become more interested in what they are learning, and to become more confident about their interpersonal social skills.

The Changing Role of Grammar in Communicative Language Teaching

Since the advent of communicative language teaching, the role of grammar in language learning, particularly in the classroom setting, has been challenged and has become the topic of many debates in the language teaching circles. Disagreements occur over whether grammar instruction is appropriate in a communicative classroom and what type of grammar instruction is appropriate. According to Larsen-Freeman (1997), the role of "grammar is often misunderstood in the teaching field" (p. 1). Even if grammar was not eliminated, it was certainly neglected in many communicative classrooms. Larsen-Freeman (1997) lists some commonly held misconceptions about grammar and challenges these views:

Misconceptions about the Role of Grammar Teaching

Misconception #1: Grammar is acquired naturally; it need not be taught.

Challenge to misconception #1: Although some learners are able to acquire second language grammar without any formal instruction in grammar, there are still learners who may not be able to acquire proficiency without direct instruction. One criticism against communicative language teaching is that although it focuses on the expression and comprehension of meaning through language, it sacrifices accuracy. The theory behind the emphasis on meaning through communicative language teaching is that English learners can develop greater communicative abilities in the new language through instruction that resembles the "natural" environment. The question, however, is not so much whether grammar explanation would benefit ELLs but rather when attention to form may be most useful to ELLs within a communicative language teaching context. Direct attention to form may be necessary when ELLs are unable to distinguish between formal and informal rules used by native speakers of English, have difficulty understanding exceptions to general rules (as in making English plurals or verbs), or the restrictions for transferring an L1 rule to English (e.g., in the use of adjectives in noun phrases in languages with a dominant SVO order). Equally important is the concern for what Selinker (1972) termed language fossilization—a phenomenon that describes nontarget forms becoming permanent in the ELLs' interlanguage grammar. Fossilization also implies that although ELLs may make progress in certain areas, they may continue to make errors, for example in using simple past and simple present tense. At this point, no amount of grammar instruction is going to have any effect. Whether the source of language fossilization is attributed to transfer of native language patterns to the second language or exposure to ineffective teaching and learning methods, there is a consensus in second language research that errors that remain uncorrected over time will remain permanent in the learners' interlanguage grammar.

As language teachers, we know that ELLs need to develop fluency and accuracy to become proficient in the new language. Although some learners can become proficient at a faster rate, it is not surprising that some learners may take longer than others to fully master the English grammatical system, just as native English speakers developed mastery over some structures of their language later in adolescent years (Chomsky, 1969). Unless more studies provide evidence for the effect of implicit teaching of grammar on language learning across age levels and different sociolinguistic contexts of learning, educators cannot simply rule out the potential benefits of teaching grammar on language proficiency for some groups of learners.

Misconception #2: Grammar is a collection of meaningless forms and arbitrary rules.

Challenge to misconception #2: When people think of grammar, they automatically think of meaningless rules of language. However, grammar is not simply formulaic sets of rules. Grammar consists of nonarbitrary rules that embody morphosyntactic, semantic, and pragmatic interaction. For instance, the passive construction can only be formed with transitive verbs (i.e., a verb that needs an object such as see, teach, or eat is composed of the *be* verb + the past participle and sometimes includes the agent

with *by* in a preposition phrase, which is often deleted if the information regarding the agent is unimportant or unknown). But passive construction has other meanings. It shifts the status of the receiver, and so the focus from I shifts to the book, as in "Janet gave him the book," and "The book was given to him by Janet." Are these rules arbitrary? Not really. Passives are used when the receiver is the theme; when the doer of the action is unknown; when the identity of the doer is obvious and, thus, unnecessary to mention; or when someone wishes to conceal the identity of the doer of the action. As such, the agent and object movement can be explained by the sense that the grammar conveys, which supports the view that grammar rules are not arbitrary. What does this mean to the English learner? To be a proficient language user, English learners must understand how to use the English passives accurately and appropriately.

Misconception #3: Grammar is boring.

Challenge to misconception #3: Many people have the impression that grammar can only be taught by repetition and memorization of rules. However, this does not mean that there are no benefits from drills on language learning. If drills are used in a meaningful and purposeful way, the drill will not be monotonous or without meaning. For example, by asking students to reflect on what they typically eat, students can learn to use the structures for comparisons—more, less, most, and least—in an engaging way and not just provide mechanical responses.

Misconception #4: Given that students have different learning styles, some students cannot learn grammar.

Challenge to misconception #4: There is no doubt that some students have a more analytical approach to learning and approach language learning tasks as "rule formers" (Larsen-Freeman, 1997, p. 3). However, these learners may not necessarily be fluent language users. To date, there has been no research that shows students are incapable of learning grammar. However, the fact that we can master our first language is a testimony of our ability to learn the grammar.

Misconception #5: Grammar structures are learned one at a time.

Challenge to misconception #5: Although some teachers believe that grammar can be taught one structure at a time, there is no reason why students cannot learn other structures before they master new ones that are taught. Thus, it is not surprising to hear English learners make errors in using the present progressive tense after they have acquired the simple present tense, just as it is common among children learning their first language to make errors such as "wented" even though they have acquired the past form of irregular verbs. This regression is considered a natural phenomenon in language learning. "Unless learners internalize the distinct uses of the two tenses, it is expected that they will backslide between correct and incorrect language use."

Misconception #6: Grammar has to do only with sentence-level and subsentence-level phenomena.

Challenge to misconception #6: Just as subject–verb agreement or word order determines the grammaticality at subsentence and sentence levels, respectively, there are grammar rules that are applied at the discourse level. The choice of using the definite article "the" after a noun phrase has been introduced the first time is discourse governed, just as switching between past and present tense in a narrative may be explained by the whole discourse context. Consequently, it is necessary to explain grammar at both the sentence and intrasentential and discourse levels.

Misconception #7: Grammar and vocabulary are areas of knowledge. Reading, writing, speaking, and listening are the four skills.

Challenge to misconception #7: Learning rules of the language does not always guarantee that learners are able to use the newly learned grammar and vocabulary for communicative purposes. Many who have had the experience of learning a second or foreign language know that becoming proficient in a new language is a developmental process that takes a lot of practice. The question, then, is what kind of practice would speed up language acquisition? Ellis

(1993) argued that grammar teaching within a communicative framework through listening, speaking, reading, and writing activities should aim at raising learners' awareness instead of practicing toward accurate productions. VanPatten and Cardierno (1993) support this view by arguing that students benefit more from the experience of processing linguistic input than by simply being given a grammatical explanation followed by practice in producing the target structures.

Misconception #8: Grammar provides the static rules/explanations for all the structures in a language.

Challenge to misconception #8: Just as words and their meanings change over time, grammatical rules are not static either. Numerous examples can be found that were once frowned on by language specialists and English teachers, such as nouns turning into verbs. These changes have now become commonplace in the English language today. Consider the following:

> We *bus* children to school, where the teachers *school* them. We *pig out* at the local eatery. We *horn* our way into difficult situations, and we *weasel* our way out of them.

These examples demonstrate that grammar is subject to changes, presenting additional problems for the new language learners. It is imperative that teachers bear in mind that learning grammar is a process that requires learners to attend to linguistic analysis and descriptions as well as how speakers use grammar to accomplish their communicative endeavor.

Misconception #9: I don't know enough to teach grammar.

Challenge to misconception #9: It is not uncommon to hear teachers admitting that they don't know enough about grammar, let alone be able to teach it to their students. This feeling is not unusual, considering that most native speakers know grammar unconsciously or have developed intuition for the meaningfulness and appropriateness of a grammar item in question as a result of having learned grammar unconsciously through repeated exposure and doing. But to describe or analyze the grammar structure per se requires focused attention to rules that must be learned formally. As teachers of ELLs, we must use both our unconscious and conscious knowledge of grammar to assist ELLs in connecting the form, meaning, and use of a particular grammatical structure for a given communicative purpose. Ultimately, an effective grammar instruction is one that teaches learners how to use their grammar rules to communicate specific meanings that are appropriate to the task at hand.

When Is Grammar Teaching Helpful?

Students can benefit from grammar instruction in the following ways:

1. By knowing grammar, some students may be able to notice "the gap" between their own productions and the input they receive.
2. Students can benefit from learning short, simple rules that they can easily recall and use for monitoring output. Simple rules may best be taught deductively, while more complex rules may best be taught inductively. According to Ellis (2008, p. 2), "an inductive approach to grammar teaching is designed to encourage learners to notice pre-selected forms in the input to which they are exposed; a deductive approach seeks to make learners aware of the explicit grammatical rule." Learners skilled in grammatical analysis are likely to fare better with an inductive approach than those who are less skilled (Ellis, 2006).
3. When students' attention is drawn to specific structures, they are also made aware of how things are said, which in turn serves as input for planning their future utterances.
4. Some students vary in their expectations of what good language instruction should be. Depending on their cultural and training backgrounds, some students expect grammar instruction and will become more receptive to try different activities if their grammar needs are met.
5. Older learners tend to benefit more from explicit grammar instruction because they have more experience and knowledge about language to analyze and break down language into smaller parts. Younger learners tend to prefer interactive activities from which they will get the opportunities to use particular grammatical structures.
6. Some grammatical forms in the target language are likely to be misunderstood by learners unless their meanings and uses are taught explicitly. For example, while the simple present tense and the present progressive forms of English verbs generally describe actions or events in the present time, their meanings and uses are quite different. For example, if Sorel says: "I live in Florida. I am living with my aunt, uncle, and two cousins," English speakers would interpret that living in Florida is a permanent situation for Sorel, but living with her relatives is only temporary. To ensure proper understanding and use of these forms by English learners, it is necessary to explain the meanings and uses of these two grammatical forms. Refer to Table 14-3 for distinguishing simple present from present progressive verbs in English.
7. English learners can benefit from teaching of forms in their second language that are not yet salient to them despite high frequency of exposure to those structures. Salience is defined as the speaker/hearer's perception of a form (e.g., the third person simple present –s) which stands out against a regular or typical form in the language (e.g., the base form of the simple present) (Andersen, 1989). Second language experts state that second language learners' exposure to linguistic input does not translate into intake on the learners' part unless they have paid attention to specific cues. Which cues learners will pay attention to or consider more important for meaning depends on several factors that include but are not limited to the following: differences between the rules in their L1 and the target language, their ability to process the target structure, the linguistic demand of the task, and frequency of exposure to specific structure. Explicit focus on form in the instruction can increase English learners' chances of noticing and attending to specific grammatical points in the target language.

Table 14-3 **Meaning/Use of Simple Present and Present Progressive Verbs in English**

Simple Present	Present Progressive
Descriptions:	*Descriptions:*
General routines or habits	Actions in progress at the time of speaking
◆ He always *eats* a slice of pizza for lunch.	◆ What *is* she *doing* right now? She *is sleeping*.
Permanent situations	Temporary situations
◆ The movers *store* the boxes of tools in the garage.	◆ The movers *are storing* some of the boxes containing breakable items on the floor.
Timeless facts	Actions in progress around the time of speaking
◆ She *dislikes* outdoor activities.	◆ I *am taking* five courses this semester.
States and conditions	Actions
◆ The cat's fur *feels* soft.	◆ Jean *is feeling* the cat's fur. (implies voluntary action)
◆ She *is* foolish. (implies how she behaves all the time)	◆ She *is being* foolish. (implies temporary states of personality)

Source: Thewlis (2000)

8. Intensive instruction on grammatical forms obliges new language learners to pay attention to the grammatical form(s) by allowing time for students to practice the structures. This is especially important because some structures cannot be mastered without repeated practice. In addition, learners will not avoid using structures they have learned, which in turn allows them to receive corrective feedback necessary for acquisition (Ellis, 2006).

Strategies for Teaching Communicative Grammar

A number of factors need to be considered in implementing a communicative grammar task. These factors are as follow:

1. Choose appropriate content and materials that will provide engaging and varied opportunities for students to learn specific forms as well as their meaning(s) and use.
2. Extract or select a specific grammatical structure of English from the content.
3. Decide whether to teach the grammar structure inductively or deductively.
4. Integrate speaking, listening, reading, and writing skills in the grammar lesson. Adapt grammar input according to students' proficiency in English.
5. Include individual and pair/group work.
6. Decide on the number of procedures involved in completing a task. The number of procedures in each task should be tailored to learner's proficiency and cognitive skills.

The following are some examples of communicative grammar activities that can help learners to bridge knowledge and practice of structures through meaningful content and situations. These activities can help students practice specific grammatical structures to develop communicative competence.

Role-play
Imperative structure (giving directions)

a. Create an emergency situation, and let the students work together in small groups or individually in giving instructions to the other students and teachers about what they should do. These situations can provide students practice for using language connected to routine school emergency activities such as how to prepare for a hurricane or a fire at the school.

Contracted *be* with impersonal pronoun *it*

a. Give students one unusual/odd gift, which they must accept graciously. These gifts can be household items such as a can opener, rubber bands, dental floss, paper clips, a screwdriver, and so on. Items can be used more than once. Model the target pattern such as "Oh! It's a (*noun*). How nice!" Teachers should also point out the nuances of stress, intonation, and facial expressions when responding.

Question/Answers
Present progressive

a. What . . . Now? This game requires teachers to set up a hypothetical situation in a sentence and then ask each student prompt question, for example:

It's 9 a.m. in Florida now. Jing-jing, what is your _____ (any family member) doing **now**?

It's about 8 in the morning in Madrid right now. Sabri, what is your brother doing **at this moment**?

The student responds by using any of the following correct forms: "He's eating breakfast," "She's sleeping."

Students can also begin their sentences with: "What do you think they are doing?" which would require them to begin their responses with "I think . . . is/are . . ." Teachers can use a map or hand-drawn clocks to illustrate the time zones around the world.

Future Tense

a. What do you want to be when you grow up? Students can begin to think about their hopes and dreams for the future. Ask the students to brainstorm ideas of how they envision their futures. In small groups, ask the students to share their plans for their future. Provide sentence starters to encourage the use of "will" and "be + going to." Ask a few students to share their responses to the class. Finally, if the student's writing in English is advanced enough, the teacher may ask them to complete a writing project to explain their future using the target grammar skills.

Integrated Grammar and Reading Activities

Present Perfect and Past Perfect Tenses

a. Select example sentences from a reading text that illustrate the use of present and past perfect tenses. An excerpt of a passage containing present and past perfect verbs is shown following (in Schifini, Short, & Tinajero, 2005, p. 298):

> *For centuries the peregrine was prized by kings and falconers who used it to hunt. Bird lovers too* have *always* admired *the peregrine. Yet a few years ago it was feared that soon there would be no more peregrines. Scientists* have found *that DDT, a pesticide that farmers use to kill insects that are harmful to crops, poisoned the food that smaller birds eat. Later, when the peregrines eat these smaller birds, they eat the poison too. This poison causes the peregrines to lay eggs with shells that are too thin. These thin-shelled eggs lose moisture faster than thick-shelled eggs. Often the chick growing inside dies because the egg dries out too much. In sum, the poison DDT* had interfered *with the bird's ability* to produce babies.

First, explain to students that a verb can show when an action happens. First, point to the present perfect verb in the passage, *have admired*. For example, we use present perfect tense to tell about an action that happened in the past and is still going on today. The verb *have admired* tells us that people's admiration for peregrines started in the past and continues on to today. Then explain that the past perfect verbs tell past actions that are completed before another action in the past, as in *had interfered*. To form the past perfect tense, one has to use *had + a past participle*.

b. Have students underline the other present and past perfect tenses found in the remaining passage and explain their meaning in the sentence.

c. For additional practice, students write sentences relating what they know about peregrines, how these animals are endangered, and what should be done to protect these animals using the present and past perfect verbs. They will write variations of the example sentences found in the passage.

d. For further practice, students are asked to complete the following sentence starters:

We have talked _____ .

We had talked _____ .

Next, they will discuss different situations or sets of circumstances in which each perfect tense would be used.

Singular and Plural Nouns

a. First explain what a count noun is and show examples of singular and plural nouns found in a passage or poem. Draw students' attention to the endings of these nouns. Again using examples found in the text, explain that uncountable nouns are nouns that cannot be counted. Next, show students how to use a count noun with an uncountable noun to show "more than one." For example: *Give me a bowl* (count noun) *of cereal* (uncountable noun) and *Give me two bowls* (count noun) *of cereal* (uncountable noun). Then, students point out the singular and plural nouns in the poem before identifying uncountable nouns.

b. Students can be asked to respond to a set of questions about the poem that will elicit the use of singular and plural nouns.

c. Students can write variations to their responses to earlier questions in b.

d. For further practice, students name items they would eat/drink daily to give them energy and distinguish which nouns are countable and uncountable.

Points to Remember

❖ The framework for understanding the communicative language teaching approach can be understood by conceptualizing four interacting aspects:

◆ What is the goal of language learning?

◆ In what does the goal interface with the types of input that will be used for teaching language?

◆ What are the roles of teachers and learners?

◆ How do these roles impact classroom organization and types of instructional activities?

❖ Communicative language competence requires learners to draw from four knowledge domains: grammatical, sociolinguistic, discourse, and strategic. Learners must have knowledge of grammar, pronunciation, spelling, and phonology and be able to use these forms of knowledge to transform a string of utterances into a coherent written or conversational discourse. Learners must also have knowledge of how speakers use language to express different things. At the same time, learners must develop effective strategies for problem solving and coping with difficulties in comprehension and communication so that they will maintain an interest and motivational levels in learning the language.

❖ Although grammar teaching has been largely ignored in language practices, there is a pedagogical rationale for including some level of explicit grammar instruction. When determining what type of grammatical instruction is most effective for each learner, teachers must bear in mind a few simple rules such as the brevity and simplicity of the rule, the age of the learners, the learner's previous language training and views about grammar instruction, and when to introduce grammar explanation.

PART THREE

Organizing and Planning for New or Second Language Instruction

chapter 15

Integrating Language and Content, 127
CARMEN A. MORALES-JONES AND CAITLIN MCHUGH

chapter 16

Curriculum Design and Day-to-Day English Language Instruction, 135
CARMEN A. MORALES-JONES AND EILEEN WHELAN ARIZA

Integrating Language and Content

KEY ISSUES

- ❖ Integrating language and content
- ❖ Models of integrated approaches
- ❖ Experiential learning
- ❖ Content-based language learning
- ❖ Sheltered English or specially designed academic instruction in English (SDAIE)
- ❖ The SIOP model
- ❖ Language experience approach

English and literacy development are complex processes, particularly as they relate to non-native speakers of English. The bridge from English language literacy to content area literacy is academic English. Academic English is narrowly defined as the language of a particular discipline. In addition to developing literacy skills, English language learners (ELLs) must acquire content knowledge and content area literacy. The task is further complicated by the fact that each content area has its own set of terminology/vocabulary, writing conventions, and critical thinking skills that must be acquired if the learner is to become fully proficient in English (Echevarria & Short, 2002, 2007).

In the United States, Krashen's theory (1982) of second language acquisition has influenced the development of integrated instruction at all levels. Krashen suggests that a second language is more successfully acquired when the conditions are similar to those present in first language acquisition; that is, when the focus of instruction is on meaning rather than on form, when language input is at or just above the proficiency of the learner; and when there is sufficient opportunity to engage in meaningful use of that language in a relatively anxiety-free environment. This suggests that the focus of the English language classroom should be on something meaningful, such as academic content, and that modification of the target language facilitates language acquisition and makes academic content accessible to second language learners (Krashen, 2009).

What Is Meant by "Integrating Language and Content"?

The language immersion program is one of the most effective innovations to emerge in second/new language education during the last four decades. In this method of second/new language instruction, the regular curriculum is taught through the use of the target language (L2). Thus, the new language is developed at the same time that the subject matter content is being taught. Although the primary focus of immersion programs is academic instruction, language development occurs because teachers are cognizant of the advantages of integrating both academic content and language. The first immersion programs were developed in Canada to provide English-speaking students with the opportunity to learn French. Since that time, immersion programs have been adopted in many parts of the United States.

There are numerous advantages in integrating new language instruction and academic content instruction. First, this mode of instruction is believed to be more effective than teaching the language in isolation. When the integration takes place, proficiency in the target language is not a prerequisite to academic development; rather, language acquisition

results from using the target language to perform authentic communication functions. As discussed in previous chapters, language is acquired most effectively when it is employed for communication in meaningful and significant social situations. The academic content of the school curriculum can provide a clear basis for second/new language learning, assuming that the academic content is of interest or value to the students.

Secondly, students are able to acquire new vocabulary and language structures or patterns as they are immersed in important and interesting academic content. The new language learners are able to interact in meaningful communicative contexts. In this model, the new language learners acquire language at the same time that they acquire scientific knowledge, historical perspectives, or other content skills. Authentic classroom communication provides a purposeful and motivating context for acquiring the communicative functions of the new language. In the absence of meaningful communication, language is only learned as rote memorization, devoid of conceptual or communicative substance.

A third advantage of an integrated approach is that it addresses the relationship between language and other aspects of human development. Language, cognition, and social awareness develop concurrently in young children. Integrated new language instruction seeks to keep these components of development together so that new language acquisition is an integral part of social-cognitive development in school settings. Finally, knowing how to use language in one social context or academic domain does not necessarily mean knowing how to use it in others (Gottlieb, 2005). For example, evidence indicates that the way language is used in particular academic domains, such as mathematics (Echevarria and Graves (2003), is not the same in other academic domains, such as science (Gibbons, 2003). For this reason, it is important for teachers to identify language concepts that are tied to the subject matter content. They must also provide opportunities for oral language practice, developing background knowledge, and content-related vocabulary (Himmel, Short, Richards, & Echevarria, 2009). Once these objectives are identified, teachers must introduce the vocabulary and concepts employing English language acquisition strategies. In this fashion, the ELL is not only acquiring the subject matter content but is also acquiring the language concepts so necessary for effective communication.

Models of Integrated Approaches

Experiential Learning

Experiential learning has been defined as the process whereby action is linked to knowledge creation (Harkins, 2004). Harkins adds that important dimensions involved in experiential learning include activity, reflection, and application. Experiential learning acknowledges that action must be a part of the learning process for the learners to be able to fully produce and use knowledge. The knowledge is developed through the transformation of the experience of the learner who is at the center of the learning process. The experiential base for learning requires that students take responsibility for deriving meaning from their experiences. The impact of experiential learning is affected by various factors, including the reality of the experience or the relevance to the student, the level of risk and uncertainty (how meaningful it is to the student), and student reflection, which derives the acquisition of knowledge from the experience. Experiential learning goes beyond having a common experience in the classroom and dictating a story (language experience approach). It goes beyond an isolated experience; it involves the students in adventurous learning. The regular classroom imposes limitations when teachers try to employ experiential learning. This approach can be employed in a classroom; however, it requires a creative and resourceful teacher who will set aside the traditional ways of teaching and transform the classroom into a "learning by living" type of environment. In this type of environment, students acquire knowledge instead of simply memorizing a set of facts.

Although the mainstream classroom is limiting in and of itself, teachers who experiment with this approach to teaching provide excellent experiences for their students, as students learn by experiencing. This is how language develops from the onset; thus, language develops naturally in the experiential learning classroom. It is an excellent way to provide the concrete knowledge so indispensable for English language learners. Incorporating well-planned field trips, in which students have an opportunity to interact with the environment, is one way of providing this type of "adventurous" learning. These field trips must go beyond simple exposure to be considered experiential learning.

Service learning is a kind of experiential learning in which students engage in activities that address human and community needs together with structured opportunities designed to promote learning as well as language development. Experiential and service learning draws on multiple learning theories, including those of Piaget, Vygotsky, Kolb, and Gardner. In general, experiential learning involves learners in being creators of learning as they produce knowledge in context (Harkins, 2004).

Content-based Language Learning

In content-based language learning, teachers use instructional materials, learning tasks, and classroom techniques from academic content areas as vehicles for developing language. The emphasis is on developing language while an academic subject area is employed. Language development takes precedence over the academic subject content, although the acquisition of science, social studies, and/or mathematics subject content takes place simultaneously. Language arts skills such as listening for details, oral reporting, comparing/contrasting and/or organizing information by using charts, diagrams, or tables are developed by means of the subject matter content. New vocabulary is acquired, and language interference problems are addressed because the input is chosen deliberately from the academic textual material to provide the appropriate context for this to happen. Oral language as well as reading and writing skills are emphasized in this type of approach. This approach is of much benefit for English language learners because language development is stressed at the same time that students are acquiring knowledge in academic subjects. For this method to be successful, second/new language acquisition strategies must simultaneously be employed while content is being presented. The following strategies are essential: "parentese/caregiver speech" (slowing down, rephrasing, repeating, simplifying language), making input comprehensible (through use of concrete objects, realia, pictures, demonstration, gesturing, use of charts, graphs, diagrams), organizing instruction from simple to complex, and scaffolding (building on prior knowledge, connecting knowledge). For a wealth of ideas on how to apply this approach, refer to Part V of this book.

Sheltered English, or Specially Designed Academic Instruction in English

In the sheltered English, or specially designed academic instruction in English (SDAIE) approach, English language learners are taught subject matter content entirely in English. The emphasis is on teaching subject matter content skills and concepts such as those specific to mathematics, science, social studies, and history. Students develop language skills while being engaged in cognitively demanding and grade level–appropriate material. Teachers must utilize second/new language acquisition techniques to ensure comprehension. The name "sheltered English" is given because the teachers use sheltering techniques such as simplifying the language employed, adapting the textual material, and introducing and reinforcing new vocabulary throughout the units of instruction.

Sheltered instruction is most effective for students who have already achieved intermediate English language proficiency. This type of program is found mostly in secondary schools. The English language learners may still receive English language support in an ESL pullout program. This varies from school district to school district depending on district resources and student need.

The Sheltered Instruction Observation Protocol Model

Research shows that among in-school factors that contribute to student achievement, teachers have the highest impact (Himmel, Short, Richards, & Echevarria, 2009). It is imperative, therefore, that all teachers are able to make academic content comprehensible for English language learners.

When the sheltered instruction observation protocol (SIOP) model was introduced in 2000, it was met with much resistance, particularly from secondary teachers. They would comment: "I am a [science, math, social studies, etc] teacher, not a language teacher." Presently, there seems to be a much wider acceptance of the fact that all teachers must also be language teachers for the language needs of all ELLs to be met.

For this reason, the SIOP model is also having a much wider acceptance; thus, it has been included in this section as a model for sheltered English instruction.

The SIOP model has eight major components. *Lesson preparation*, the first component, requires that teachers identify language as well as content objectives. The second component is *building background*, which requires that teachers find connections with what the ELLs bring to the lesson from their own previous experiences. At the same time, the teachers must develop the necessary vocabulary using ESOL strategies to make the lesson/concepts comprehensible. A third component of the SIOP model is *providing comprehensible input*. This component must be familiar to the readers and includes effective ESL strategies such as use of visuals, gesturing, adapting content, use of motherese/parentese, etc. The fourth component is *strategies*. *Strategies* refers to teaching the ELLs those techniques that would help them acquire knowledge, such as identifying main ideas, re-reading, highlighting important passages, taking notes, summarizing, outlining, etc. Teachers must also emphasize *practice* and *application* of the new vocabulary and concepts. These components are crucial for academic success. Students not only need numerous opportunities to practice the new knowledge, but they must also have opportunities to apply the new knowledge. The last two components are *review* and *assessment*. Reviewing the major points of the lesson and assessing the knowledge are effective ways to end lessons in general as well as when employing the SIOP model.

The SIOP model provides teachers with specific lesson features that, when implemented consistently and to a high degree, lead to improved academic outcomes for English language learners (Echevarria,

Short, & Powers, 2006; Short, Fidelman, & Louguit, 2009).

Language Experience Approach

In the language experience approach (LEA), the students can develop their own reading materials, which the teacher later uses to teach reading skills. It is an excellent approach to teaching reading, not only for English language learners but for native speakers of English as well.

The teacher becomes a facilitator of knowledge. Students are engaged in a common experience, and afterward they dictate a story. The teacher records the story on the board, experience chart paper, or a transparency.

The following scenario illustrates the approach:

On a table in front of her class, Ms. Ramirez has an electric skillet, a bottle of cooking oil, some plastic knives, and four ripe plantains, called "amarillos" in Puerto Rico. Today she is going to teach the children how to make "amarillo frito" (fried ripe plantain), or "maduros," as the Cubans call them.

Ms. Ramirez asks the students, "What do you think we are going to do today?" The students give various responses, including cooking. Then, Ms. Ramirez reiterates that they will be cooking, adding that they will be cooking "amarillos" and tasting them. She also explains that afterward they will be dictating a story to her about what they did and she will be writing it down.

The lesson continues as Ms. Ramirez pours some oil in the skillet as she describes what she is doing. While the oil gets hot, she demonstrates how to peel and cut the amarillos. Ms. Ramirez fries the amarillos and serves all the students a piece for them to taste. The students willingly participate in the lesson, taste the amarillos/maduros, and share their impressions with each other.

After the students have finished tasting the amarillos, the paper plates and napkins are thrown away, the cooking utensils are put away, and the second part of the lesson begins.

Ms. Ramirez engages the students in dictating a story based on the common experience they just had. The students eagerly participate in dictating their sentences.

The students recall the event as follows:

Making and Tasting "Amarillos"

Today, Ms. Ramirez teached us to make "amarillos." (Pedro) We peel the "amarillos" and we cut them in pieces. (Juana) Then, we fried the "amarillos." (Brian) The "amarillos" are soft after you fry them. (Steven)

After we fried the "amarillos," we ate them. (Janet) I like the "amarillos." (Mary) They are sweet. (Ricardo) I no like dem, dey are mushy! But many like the "amarillos." We sink yummy. (Margarita) We cook more tomorrow! (Maria).

Ms. Ramirez wrote down exactly what the students dictated. She also wrote the name of the student who dictated the particular sentence. This helps the students in developing positive self-concepts because they are proud to see their names on the chart paper, board, or overhead. In addition, when reading the story out loud, students have no difficulty reading the sentences because they remember what they dictated. This type of reading requires minimal decoding skills because they already know the content.

Ms. Ramirez continues by saying, "Now we are going to read our 'sloppy copy' and make any necessary revisions." As the students read their sentences, she encourages other students to help decide whether or not some minor changes need to be made. Thus corrections are made.

The group-edited story reads as follows:

Today Ms. Ramirez taught us to make "amarillos." (Pedro) We peeled the "amarillos" and we cut them in pieces. (Juana) Then, we fried the "amarillos." (Brian) The "amarillos" are soft after you fry them. (Steven) After we fried the "amarillos," we ate them. (Janet) I like "amarillos." They are sweet. (Mary) I don't like them, they are mushy! (Ricardo) But many of us like the "amarillos." We think they are yummy.

(Margarita) We will cook more tomorrow! (Maria)

In the upcoming days, Ms. Ramirez will use the story created by the students as the text for reading instruction. This dictated story provides the textual material that will serve as a basis for teaching such skills as capitalization; punctuation, including quotation marks and exclamation marks; relational words; vocabulary development; and even aspects of grammar (such as past tense of verbs). In addition, Ms. Ramirez will address some language interferences that her Hispanic children are having (such as the "th" sound, which they are substituting for "d" voiced and "s" voiceless and the use of "no" instead of "do not" or contraction "don't" to indicate negation).

LEA is based on the premise that reading is facilitated when it stems from what the students' background knowledge.

In the language acquisition sequence of listening, speaking, reading, and writing, students who can "speak" or "dictate" stories are likely to have much more success in trying to read those stories, because the vocabulary is already in their background knowledge. As soon as they see what they have dictated, they are able to read it because they already can speak the words. Thus, all the teacher has done is demonstrate the process by which the students' own meanings, expressed orally, are put into print form. When students can read their own stories, they are able to experience the success of independent reading. This is reinforcing and helps to develop an interest in further reading.

To illustrate the point just discussed, try reading the following passage:

La casita de campo estaba rodeada de muchos árboles frondosos los cuales le deban una sombra *exquisita*. La pareja de enamorados, senta- dos en el balcón, escuchaban el riachuelo que atraviesa el *terreno*. Pájaros de todos *colores* y tamaños, llenaban la *atmósfera* de cánticos placenteros.*

How did it feel to try to read something in a language you do not know? Probably, very frustrated, to say the least. However, if you had dictated the passage, you would already know the vocabulary, therefore making it so much easier for you to read.

If you know any Spanish, you may have identified some of the words. You may have been able to attain some meaning of the passage by using the context surrounding the words you knew. However, if you do not know any Spanish at all, the only words you may have been able to "guess" would be the four in italics: *exquisita* (for "exquisite"), *terreno* (for "terrain"), *colores* (for "colors"), and *atmósfera* (for "atmosphere"). These words, called cognates, might have made you think that the paragraph relates to some type of atmosphere that is exquisite and something regarding some type of terrain and colors, but that is about all. These four words did not help you in gaining the meaning of what you read. This is exactly what your ELLs' experience is.

The beauty of LEA is that it builds on the linguistic, social, and cultural strengths of the students; it captures in print a common experience the students have had employing language. It can also be employed for students, individually or in small groups, to dictate their own stories based on their own social/cultural background.

---

*English translation:
The small country home was surrounded by many thick trees that gave it a delightful shade. The very-much-in-love couple, sitting on the porch, could hear the sound of the flowing water from the creek that flows through the property. Birds of all sizes and colors filled the atmosphere with pleasant melodies.

❖ When integrating language and content, the second/new language is developed at the same time that subject matter content is being taught.

❖ There are numerous advantages of integrating language and content:

A. Language is not taught in isolation; it is taught in context.

B. English language learners acquire new vocabulary and language structures as they are immersed in interesting academic content.

C. The language acquisition process is an integral part of the social-cognitive development.

D. English language learners acquire language concepts that are tied to the subject content.

❖ There are numerous models of integrated approaches. The following are just a few:

A. Experiential learning

B. Content-based language learning

C. Sheltered English, or specially designed academic instruction in English (SDAIE)

D. The SIOP model

E. Language experience approach (LEA)

❖ In experiential learning, English language learners acquire English by "living" the experience; it is characterized by "adventurous" learning.

❖ In content-based language learning, the emphasis is on developing language while an academic subject area is employed.

❖ In SDAIE, subject matter is taught in the second language by employing sheltering techniques.

❖ In the language experience approach, the teacher employs the dictated story to develop lessons that address students' language deficiencies.

Curriculum Design and Day-to-Day English Language Instruction

KEY ISSUES
- ❖ Generic principles that promote high academic standards
- ❖ Steps in planning interdisciplinary content-based thematic units
- ❖ Bloom's taxonomy
- ❖ Gardner's eight intelligences
- ❖ Activities to develop multiple intelligences

Most teachers realize that today's students comprise a great diversity of individuals, with a full range of cultural, ethnic, and economic heritage and first languages. They realize that America's people are multi-everything—multilingual (features of languages), multiethnic, and multicultural (our features of customs, religion, traditions, history)—and that the students in their classrooms represent the changing demographics of our pluralistic nation (Roberts & Kellough, 2005).

Careful planning and preparation by a community and a school are the most important preliminary factors in the ultimate success of school language development programs. Developing curriculum and planning for each day's instruction are the most important components of the program once it is in place. Each day's lesson fits into a larger framework of planning that makes it a part of long-range goals and unified, sequenced objectives. A planning process organized around communicative principles will develop activities that enable students to function effectively in situations that require them to seek and provide information, to express ideas and opinions, and to control their environment in a variety of ways. Such a planning process will first attempt to give students control over their immediate environment and then become more outward, enabling them to discuss their interests, needs, and concerns in the school beyond their classrooms, in their families, and in their communities. At the same time, the English language learners will use the new language in contexts that are planned to be rich with cultural meanings and associations.

Planning in an immersion, content-based classroom will focus on and take its direction from the goals of the subject-content area. In this type of situation, there is an extra dimension of planning that focuses on language development and on subject-content goals at the same time. Although the organizing principle for instruction will be the subject matter content, the language skills necessary to progress in communication about the subject matter content must also be intentionally developed through the planning process. This suggests that it will, most of the time, be necessary to do language development activities in preparation for, or as a component of, a lesson directed toward subject-content goals. The teacher of subject content in a second/new language must always be aware of the language skills demanded by the concepts and the activities involved in the subject-content goals. The teacher must also plan carefully for the concrete experiences and the visual reinforcement that will make the academic language of instruction comprehensible to the students (Curtain & Dahlberg, 2004). This will help the English language learner develop the linguistic skills necessary for dealing with the subject-content material.

Five Generic Principles

A review of the literature on innovative programs of school reform for diverse students (Collier & Thomas, 1999/2000) uncovered a core list of principles that promote the achievement of high academic standards for English language learners. Today, these principles are still considered important.

Principle 1

Facilitate learning through joint, productive activity among teachers and students.

Learning takes place best through joint, productive activity. Students must be actively involved in the learning process. Research has shown that teachers talk from sixty-five percent to ninety-five percent of the time. For the English language learner, as well as the native speaker of English, to be actively involved in the daily lessons, teachers must allow students to communicate by giving them opportunities to converse/exchange ideas on a regular basis. Those students who are at the preproduction level must be engaged in interacting nonverbally but in activities through which the teachers are ascertaining comprehension of the concepts and vocabulary.

Principle 2

Develop students' competence in the language and literacy of instruction throughout all instructional activities.

Language proficiency in listening, speaking, reading, and writing is the road to high academic achievement. Thus, language development must be a part of every lesson, a part of the entire school day. Language and literacy development should be fostered through meaningful use and purposeful conversation between teacher and students, not through drills and decontextualized rules (Berman et al., 1995; Speidel, 1987). Reading and writing must be taught both as specific curricula and within subject matter. The teaching of language expression and comprehension should always be integrated into each content area (Collier & Thomas, 1999/2000).

Principle 3

Contextualize teaching and curriculum in the experiences and skills of home and community.

Lessons need to provide experiences that show how rules, abstractions, and verbal descriptions are drawn from and applied to the everyday world. The use of personal, community-based experiences as the foundation for developing school skills affords students opportunities to apply skills acquired in both home and school contexts.

Principle 4

Challenge students toward cognitive complexity.

Often, English language learners are excused from certain academic challenges on the assumption that they are of "limited" English proficiency, or they are forgiven any genuine assessment of progress because the assessment instruments are not adequate. As a result, both standards and feedback are weakened; thus, academic achievement for these students is handicapped. Although the motives for such actions have been benign, the effect is that the English language learner is thus denied the challenges for academic progress. The clear consensus among researchers in the field is that English language learners, just like native language speakers, require instruction that is cognitively challenging, instruction that requires thinking and analysis, not only rote, repetitive, detail level drills. Working with a cognitively challenging curriculum requires careful planning, so students are stretched to reach within their zones of proximal development (Vygotsky, 1962), where they can perform with teacher guidance. It does not mean drill-and-kill exercises, and it does not mean overwhelming challenges that discourage the students. It is very important that teachers keep in mind Krashen's comprehension hypothesis when planning for instruction. Small increments of knowledge are crucial to ensure academic success.

Principle 5

Engage students through dialogue, especially in instructional conversation.

In the United States the instructional conversation is rare. More often, teaching occurs through the recitation of a script in which the teacher assumes the major role; teachers assign a task, students complete the task, and the teacher assesses. True instructional conversation transforms the classroom into a "community of learners." Teaching must become "a warm, interpersonal, collaborative activity" (Dalton, 1989; Collier & Thomas, 1999/2000) if students are going to grow academically.

Planning Interdisciplinary, Content-based Thematic Units

Thematic teaching provides context for concepts and activities through their relationship to a thematic center. One significant function of the theme is to focus on meaningful and interesting information and experiences as reasons for the students to acquire subject-content knowledge as they develop language proficiency. It also helps to connect ideas and information, making them more comprehensible and easier to remember. Students are immersed in a theme and are exposed to numerous encounters of some of the same content, yet from different perspectives and in meaningful contexts. This intertwining of ideas, concepts, vocabulary, and language structures facilitates the acquisition of knowledge as well as the development of English language competence.

Choice of Theme

The first step in developing a thematic unit is to select a theme. In choosing a theme, teachers should always take into consideration students' interest as well as teacher interest, relationship to the curriculum goals/objectives for the grade level (curriculum frameworks, benchmarks, statewide standards, etc.) or age of the class, and the potential for the application and development of appropriate and useful language functions. Other factors influencing the choice and development of a theme might include schoolwide or across-the-curriculum emphases, holidays or special school or community events, and available materials and resources.

The curriculum for a school year might well consist of several themes, each related to the others by systematic reinforcement of the unit just completed and by careful preparation for and transition to the units that follow. Language functions and basic vocabulary are encountered and reinforced from unit to unit due to the spiral character of the general elementary school curriculum (Curtain & Dahl-berg, 2004). Building on prior knowledge and scaffolding are indispensable in thematic teaching.

Figures 16-1 and 16-2 provide samples of theme words and theme sentences. These are simply some

FIGURE 16-2   Sample Theme Phrases

acceptance of one's self and/or others
overcoming fear
overcoming prejudices
importance of families
importance of friendships
developing self-understanding
establishing positive relationships
global connections
relationship between science and technology
time, continuity, and change
journeying to freedom
nature and it's beauty
interdependence among people
interdependence among neighbors
interdependence among nations
living with diversity
living in a new environment

Roberts, Patricia L.; Kellough, Richard D., *Guide for Developing Interdisciplinary Thematic Units, A,* 4th Edition, © 2008. Reprinted by permission of Pearson Education, Inc., New York, New York.

FIGURE 16-1   Sample Theme Words

administrations	cycles	inspirations
adventures	decisions	interactions
adversaries	democracy	inventions
aeronautics	demonstrations	issues
agreements	departures	journeys
alterations	depths	justice
arbitrations	deprivations	modern society
aristocracies	determinations	nationalism
beginnings	dictators	nations
blockades	dignity	navigations
bonanza	dilemmas	needs
boundaries	diplomacy	neighbors
boycotts	disasters	nonviolence
bravery	discoveries	oppression
breakthroughs	diversity	ordeals
buildings	dynasties	patterns
business	emergencies	pollution
calamities	emigrations	power
campaigns	encounters	prejudices
caring	environments	relationships
cause/effect	exploitations	relativity
celebrations	explorations	resources
changes	extinctions	revolutions
citizenship	families	searches
civilization	fighters	segregation
communications	freedoms	self-awareness
communities	government	settlements
conflict	hardships	social groups
conservation	heritages	survival
contributions	inclusion	traditions
conversions	incubation	others suggested
cooperation	independence	by students
cultures	individuality	

Roberts, Patricia L.; Kellough, Richard D., *Guide for Developing Interdisciplinary Thematic Units, A,* 4th Edition, © 2008. Reprinted by permission of Pearson Education, Inc., New York, New York.

examples. Themes must stem from the subject content used as the "umbrella" for developing the content-based thematic units.

Once the theme has been determined in a thematic unit, a resourceful teacher finds ways to relate the theme to as many subjects as possible. For example, Figure 16-3 shows a web of a theme such as Immigration to America (from 1890–1924).

This theme could evolve as an interdisciplinary unit in the following fashion:

❖ Mathematics: Graphing skills (learn how to create a pictograph; develop a pictograph to show the number of immigrants that came to the United States during that period and from what countries; interpret data from a pictograph)
❖ Science: How people solve problems (study famous immigrant inventors and their contributions)
❖ Social Studies: Map skills (study where immigrants came from; countries and location; continents; neighboring countries; capitals; bodies of water)

FIGURE 16-3 Sample Web

- ❖ Art: Create two-dimensional works of art (study and make flags of countries where immigrants came from)
- ❖ Music: Recognize and describe romantic and 20th century music and composers (study famous composers whose music immigrated to United States between 1890 and 1924)
- ❖ Language Arts: Writing skills (recording thoughts; focus on a central idea; study letter writing and compose a letter expressing feelings to someone left behind)

These are examples of how a specific theme can develop into an interdisciplinary content-based unit. The length of the unit will depend on the depth and breadth given to it in each subject.

Choice of Topics

Once a theme has been identified, subthemes as well as specific topics to be studied can be identified.

Topics are areas of study under the theme or subthemes.

A thematic interdisciplinary unit on Living Things in the World could explore many topics; one could be tree frogs. Figure 16-4 illustrates a sample breakdown.

Formulation of Goals and Instructional Objectives

Formulating goals and instructional objectives for a particular unit allows the teacher to create a clear picture of what the unit is going to be about. Goals are general statements or the final destination—the level(s) students will need to achieve. Instructional objectives are teachable chunks that, in their accumulation, form the essence of the unit. Clear understanding of goals and objectives helps teachers determine what material to teach and when and how it

FIGURE 16-4 Sample Web

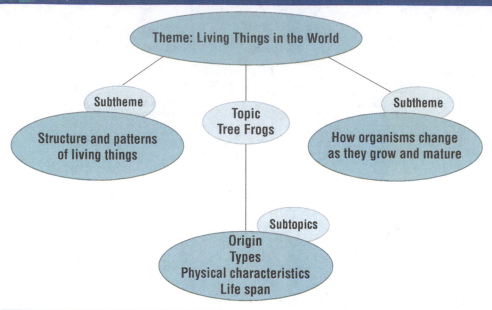

should be taught. Instructional objectives must be realistic and attainable within the time frame allocated. Instructional objectives drive the students' performance. Assessment of student achievement in learning should be an assessment of this performance. When the assessment procedure matches the instructional objectives, the assessment is referred to as aligned or authentic (more on assessment later in this chapter) (Roberts & Kellough, 2006). In Florida, as in other states, curriculum frameworks have been developed at the state department level.

Classifying Instructional Objectives

When planning instructional objectives, it is useful to consider Bloom's original taxonomy and his three domains of learning objectives: the cognitive domain, the affective domain, and the psychomotor domain.

The cognitive domain involves mental operations from the lowest level of simple recall of information to complex, high level evaluative processes. Bloom (1956) identified six levels of mental opera-

tions in the cognitive domain: knowledge, comprehension, application, analysis, synthesis, and evaluation. Whereas the intellectual needs are primarily within the cognitive domain and the physical needs are within the psychomotor domain, the other three areas of developmental needs (emotional/psychological, social, and moral/ethical) are mostly within the affective domain.

Specific verbs can be employed when writing instructional objectives for each domain. Figure 16-5 provides some appropriate examples for each of the six levels of mental operations identified within the cognitive domain.

The affective domain involves feelings, attitudes, and values and ranges from the lower levels of acquisition to the highest level of internalization and action. Bloom identified five levels within this domain: receiving, responding, valuing, organizing, and internalizing. Figure 16-6 provides some appropriate verbs that can be employed when writing objectives to address the affective domain.

The psychomotor domain originally dealt with gross to fine motor control. It ranges from simple

1. Remember

choose	complete	define	describe	identify	indicate
list	locate	match	name	outline	recall

2. Understand

change	classify	convert	defend	estimate	expand
explain	infer	interpret	predict	retell	summarize

3. Apply

compute	develop	discover	exhibit	modify	operate
perform	plan	predict	relate	show	simulate

4. Analyze

analyze	arrange	compare	contrast	debate	deduce
diagram	discover	identify	infer	inquire	outline

5. Evaluate

argue	assess	conclude	consider	criticize	decide
explain	interpret	judge	justify	rank	rate

6. Creating

arrange	combine	compile	create	design	develop
devise	document	explain	formulate	generate	modify

Verbs should be compatible with any nouns the teacher selects to represent knowledge types in cognitive domain objectives.

Roberts, Patricia L.; Kellough, Richard D., *Guide for Developing Interdisciplinary Thematic Units, A*, 4th Edition, © 2008. Reprinted by permission of Pearson Education,

manipulation of materials to the communication of ideas, and finally to the highest level of creative performance. Bloom identified four levels within this domain: moving (gross motor coordination), manipulating (fine motor coordination), communicating, and creating. Figure 16-7 provides some appropriate verbs that can be employed when writing objectives to address the psychomotor domain.

Revised Bloom's Taxonomy

During the 1990s, a former student of Bloom, Lorin Anderson, led an initiative to update Bloom's original taxonomy. Anderson, together with representatives from three groups (cognitive psychologists, curriculum theorists and instructional researchers, and testing and assessment specialists), spent six years finalizing their work. The revision includes changes in three broad categories: terminology, structure, and emphasis (Forhand, 2005). Figure 16-8 on page 143 provides a comparison of Bloom's original and revised taxonomy.

When developing/selecting the instructional objectives for designing interdisciplinary thematic content-based units, teachers must list subject-content objectives as well as language objectives. The language instructional objectives are those aspects of language that are indispensable for the English language learner to attain the subject-content objectives. The language objectives, thus, stem from the subject matter content to be taught. For example, the development of new vocabulary by having students recognize, identify, and use (if at the speech emergence level) new vocabulary is indispensable to ensure comprehension of the material in which this new vocabulary is embedded. In addition, aspects of language that may cause language interference problems or simply language problems for the English language students involved in the lessons must also be identified.

FIGURE 16-6 Verbs for Objectives for Bloom's Affective Domain

1. Receiving

ask	attend	choose	control	describe	differentiate
hear	hold	listen	locate	look	name
notice	recall	rely	select	share	use

2. Responding

assist	command	comply	discuss	greet	help
label	obey	perform	play	practice	read
recite	report	select	share	study	volunteer

3. Valuing

act	argue	complete	convince	debate	describe
form	help	initiate	invite	join	justify
read	report	select	share	study	support

4. Organizing

adhere	alter	arrange	balance	combine	compare
defend	define	discuss	explain	form	identify
modify	order	organize	prepare	relate	select

5. Internalizing (Characterizing)

act	complete	display	exhibit	influence	listen
perform	practice	propose	qualify	question	refute
resolve	revise	serve	solve	verify	resist

Source: Roberts, P. L. and Kellough, R. D. (2008). *A Guide for Developing Interdisciplinary Thematic Units* (4th ed.). Upper Saddle River, NJ: Pearson, Merrill-Prentice Hall. page 92. Reprinted by permission of Richard Overbaugh.

FIGURE 16-7 Examples of Verbs for Bloom's Psychomotor Domain

1. Moving (gross motor coordination)

adjust	clean	jump	obtain
carry	grasp	locate	walk

2. Manipulating (fine-motor coordination)

assemble	calibrate	play	turn
build	connect	thread	

3. Communicating (communication of ideas and feelings)

analyze	describe	explain
ask	draw	write

4. Creating (students' coordination of thinking, learning, and behaving in all three domains)

create	design	invent

Source: Created from: A. J. Horrow's *Taxonomy of the Psychomotor Domain*, 1977.

FIGURE16-8 Bloom's Taxonomy: Original and Revised

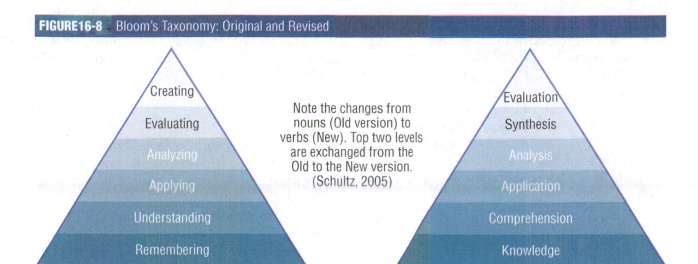

Note the changes from nouns (Old version) to verbs (New). Top two levels are exchanged from the Old to the New version. (Schultz, 2005)

NEW VERSION (top to bottom): Creating, Evaluating, Analyzing, Applying, Understanding, Remembering

OLD VERSION (top to bottom): Evaluation, Synthesis, Analysis, Application, Comprehension, Knowledge

Remembering: can the student recall or remember the information?

define, duplicate, list, memorize, recall, repeat, reproduce state

Understanding: can the student explain ideas or concepts?

classify, describe, discuss, explain, identify, locate, recognize, report, select, translate, paraphrase

Applying: can the student use the information in a new way?

choose, demonstrate, dramatize, employ, illustrate, interpret, operate, schedule, sketch, solve, use, write

Analyzing: can the student distinguish between the different parts?

appraise, compare, contrast, criticize, differentiate, discriminate, distinguish, examine, experiment, question, test

Evaluating: can the student justify a stand or decision?

appraise, argue, defend, judge, select, support, value, evaluate

Creating: can the student create new product or point of view?

assemble, construct, create, design, develop, formulate, write

Reprinted by permission of Richard Overbaugh

For example, a teacher has a number of Hispanic students in his/her class. Those students may have some specific language interference problems. Some of these are the use of the adjective in front of the noun (in Spanish it is used after the noun) and the use of *not* and the auxiliaries *does/do* to indicate negation (because in Spanish only *no* in front of the verb indicates negation). If this teacher is teaching a unit on living things around the world and the topic is frogs, these may be some aspects of language he/she could address in the social studies portion of the unit (refer to the section that follows on conceptualizing the content).

Conceptualizing the Content

The content is the body of knowledge/information/concepts to be taught. It is what the teacher expects the students to know at the end of the unit. It is the "what" that is going to be taught. When identifying the content, it is important to use resources available in the school (i.e., curricular materials, as well as children's literature fiction/nonfiction, and outside resources such as the Internet). Because the content is the body of knowledge students will be acquiring, it is important that teachers do research and expand their own knowledge of the particular content they will be teaching. Teachers must be well versed in the theme/topic to be taught to effectively teach it to students. For example, if a teacher is teaching a unit on living things in the world (Topic: Frogs) and one of the objectives is "use of simple maps, globes, and other three-dimensional models to identify and locate places" (Sunshine State Standard for Social Studies B1. 1.2), part of the content to be taught is the types of frogs that are found in different parts of the world. In teaching about tree frogs, the following content would be included:

Africa: red tree frog

Asia: flying tree frog

Australia: white tree frog

Madagascar: tomato tree frog

North America: tree frog

South America: red-eyed tree frog

Southeast Asia: barking tree frog

In this lesson, students would be learning map skills: locating places in the world where the different types of tree frogs exist. In addition, the English language learners would have a great opportunity to practice the use of an adjective in front of a noun (which could be a language interference for Hispanic students and even French-speaking students). The teacher could also address the use of *not* with the auxiliary *does/do* and the use of contractions in a yes/no–type question activity. For example:

Teacher: Does the red tree frog exist in Asia?

Student: No, the red tree frog does not exist in Asia. *or* No, it doesn't. (A Hispanic student may reply: "No, no exist.")

Teacher: Do flying tree frogs exist in Africa?

Student: No, flying tree frogs do not exist in Africa. *or* No, they don't.
A Hispanic student may respond: "No, no exist.")

Teacher: Do red-eyed tree frogs exist in Madagascar?

Student: No, they do not. *or* No, they don't.

The use of contractions would provide practice with what could be a language interference for Hispanic students, since contractions are nonexistent in the Spanish language.

Instructional Procedures

Once the content (what will be taught) has been determined, the next step is to decide "how" the content will be taught. There is a sequential order in which lessons should unfold. The teacher must decide what series of activities are necessary to develop the lesson and in what order to attain the specified objectives. The sequence in which the activities take place is crucial for a successful lesson and, therefore, for the attainment of the objectives. Teachers must always ask themselves, what is the best way to sequence the activities to ensure that they are "building on" and providing the scaffolding so necessary for the students' success in the attainment of the objectives? Teachers must also ask themselves what the students need to know/need to be able to do, for each activity. Identifying prerequisite knowledge and skills is crucial when deciding how to sequence the activities in each lesson.

The instructional procedures are the sequence of activities described in the lesson plan. There are numerous ways in which the instructional procedures can be clustered. It is important to note, however, that all lessons are developed in stages: beginning, middle, and end. Lessons usually begin with a warm-up and/or review activities, a way to connect the day's lesson to previous lessons and a way to motivate and interest students for the activities that will follow. Once the warm-up has taken place, the class is ready for the presentation and practice stages of the lesson (Jensen, 2001). These stages have been referred to with a variety of labels, such as engage, study, and activate (Harmer, 1998); lead-in, elicitation, explanation, accurate reproduction, and immediate creativity (Harmer, 1991); verbalization, automatization, and autonomy (Ur, 1996); initiating activity, core activities including guided practice, and closure activities (Florida Atlantic University adopted lesson plan format, 2009); and warm-up, introduction, lesson activities or procedures, options for recording student performance, and closure (Curtain & Dahlberg, 2004). All these labels describe stages in which (a) the content and/or language form is introduced and presented; (b) comprehension is checked before a form of guided practice is implemented; (c) there is some type of guided practice; (d) there is some type of application activity wherein students apply independently or in cooperative groups the knowledge/concepts they have just acquired; and (e) some type of closure activity, including an end-of-lesson review.

Materials

It is imperative for the teacher to decide what materials need to be developed to successfully deliver each lesson of the unit. Once this decision is made, materials need to be developed and listed in the section of the unit designated for this purpose. In addition, any other type of materials or resources that will be employed for the lessons must be listed.

In determining the materials to employ, it is imperative that the objectives for the lessons are kept foremost in the teachers' mind, because the materials are crucial for the attainment of the objectives.

In addition, in developing the materials, teachers must address the issue of providing comprehensible input for the second language students. The use of visuals, graphs, charts, objects, realia, and materials with which students can be involved physically to make learning as concrete as possible is indispensable. It is important to always remember that input is comprehensible when students can attach meaning to what is being presented. Thus, materials employed for the lessons are key to the success of the lessons.

Assessment

Why is it important to assess?

Assessment of student achievement is designed to serve in the following ways:

a. To assist in student learning
A teacher must determine how well the students are acquiring the knowledge, concepts, and skills being developed through the units. If students are not attaining the objectives, reteaching must take place to assist the students in their attainment of the objectives.

b. To identify students' strengths and weaknesses
When restructuring lessons for reteaching (if needed), teachers can build on the students' strengths and address their weaknesses identified through the assessment process.

c. To determine teaching effectiveness
When analyzing assessment results, competent teachers will determine how well they were able to reach the students and attain the objectives. In reflecting, teachers can determine which strategies were successful and which may need to be restructured, and which materials were effective and which ones need to be revised.

d. To determine teacher effectiveness in addressing the needs of English language learners
When reviewing the data resulting from students' performance, teachers can determine how well their English language learners are attaining the stated language and content objectives. Teachers could ask themselves: "Are the students progressing academically, or are they falling behind? If they are not progressing, what am I doing that needs to be modified? Am I making input comprehensible? Am I involving the students in the lessons, providing activities in which they can participate? Am I scaffolding and building on what they already know?"

e. To communicate and involve parents and guardians in their children's learning
Parents/guardians, communities, and school boards all share in the accountability of the children's academic success. Today, more than ever, schools are reaching out to engage parents/guardians and communities at large in their children's education. Teachers employ assessment results to communicate with parents/guardians and communities their important collaborative function in the education of their children.

The following eight principles guide an assessment program (Roberts & Kellough, 2006):

1. Teachers need to know how well they are doing.

2. Students need to know how well they are doing.
3. Assessment is a reciprocal process and includes assessment of teacher performance and student achievement.
4. Assessment results should aid teaching effectiveness and contribute to student growth.
5. Assessment results should be attained from a variety of sources and different types of data-collecting devices.
6. Assessment is an ongoing process.
7. Reflecting on assessment results is an ongoing process.
8. Teachers should be held accountable for facilitating student learning and for assessing student progress.

How Can Teachers Assess Students' Acquisition of Knowledge?

There are numerous ways in which teachers can assess acquisition of knowledge. Ordinarily, to assess unit objectives, teachers develop their own assessment instruments. The following are some types of items that teachers can develop/employ: arrangement type—students are asked to arrange or place in order of occurrence lists of events, such as historical, mathematical for problem solving, growth patterns of living things, events in a story, etc.; completion type—students are asked to complete a sentence given; correction type—students are asked to correct certain information given in context that is incorrect; essay type—students are asked to compare a response to a question or problem, in the form of sustained prose using their own words and ideas, based on what they learned in the unit of instruction; grouping type—students are asked to select and group several items presented that are related in some way; identification type—students are given unknown "specimens" to identify by name or some other criterion known to them; matching type—students are asked to connect/match items from two lists that are related in some way; multiple choice type—students are asked to select from a series of responses the response that best fits the statement (stem) presented; performance type—students are

asked to solve a problem or accomplish a task; short explanation type—students are asked to compose a short response to a given question or problem; true-false type—students are asked to respond to the accuracy of given statements by indicating if the statement is true or false (Roberts & Kellough, 2006).

This list is by no means exhaustive, nor does it represent on a continuum those types that are most effective to least effective. The effectiveness of the type of assessment will depend on what is being measured and for what purpose.

Providing Alternative Assessment

Well-designed assessment procedures are essential to meeting the needs of second language learners. Alternative assessment has become an umbrella term for any type of assessment other than standardized, multiple choice–type assessments. Examples include short answer response, extended response, observation, individual or group performance assessment, or portfolios. Performance assessment, a currently popular type of alternative assessment, requires the student to perform some type of task, which is then evaluated using some preestablished criteria.

Purpose and Definitions

Performance assessment and portfolios are complementary approaches for recording students' academic progress and language development. Both represent authentic assessment and are considered forms of alternative assessment. Valdez-Pierce (2003) clarifies these terms as follows:

Alternative assessment

❖ Is any method of finding out what a student knows or can do that is intended to show growth and inform instruction and is not a standardized traditional test;
❖ Is by definition criterion-referenced;
❖ Is authentic because it is based on activities that represent actual progress toward instructional goals and objectives and reflects tasks typical of classroom and real-life settings;

- ❖ Requires integration of language skills; and
- ❖ May include teacher observation, performance assessment, and student self-assessment.

Performance assessment

- ❖ Is a type of alternative assessment;
- ❖ Is an exercise in which students demonstrate specific skills and competencies in relation to a continuum of agreed-upon standards of proficiency or excellence; and
- ❖ Reflects student performance on instructional tasks and relies on professional rater judgment in its design and interpretation.

Portfolio assessment

- ❖ Is the use of records of a student's work over time and in a variety of modes to show depth, breadth, and development of the student's abilities;
- ❖ Is the purposeful and systematic collection of student work that reflects accomplishments relative to specific instructional objectives and goals;
- ❖ Can be used as an approach for combining the information from both alternative and standardized assessments; and
- ❖ Has as key elements student reflection and self-monitoring.

Teacher Reflection

Once a unit is completed and daily lessons have begun, teachers reflect on the individual lessons. Notes should be made and kept for future reference and for making necessary modifications to the original plan(s). Teachers must reflect on their delivery of instruction and on students' response to the lesson. The following are some questions that teachers can ask themselves (responses must be logged in the reflective journals):

1. Did I capture the students' attention with my initiating activity? If not, what would I have done differently?
2. Were the activities sequenced effectively? If not, how would I sequence them differently the next time I teach this lesson?
3. Were my materials appropriate for the lesson? If not, how would I modify them? What would I add/delete?
4. Did I make input comprehensible? How? Were my strategies effective for my English language learners?
5. Were students actively involved in the lesson?
6. Did I make learning concrete?
7. Was my pacing adequate to accomplish my objectives? If not, what changes would I make?
8. Did I attain my objectives?

Providing for Multiple Intelligences/ Learning Styles When Planning for Instruction

The theory of multiple intelligences (Gardner, 1983) has made an impact in most school curricula today. Gardner defines intelligences as "the capacity to solve problems or to fashion products that are values in one or more cultural settings" (Gardner & Hatch, 1989). In his own theory, based on biological and cultural research, which expands the traditional view, he argues that all eight intelligences are needed to function productively in society and must be considered to be of equal importance (Gardner, 2005; Blaz, 2002).

Teachers must be aware of the fact that students come into their classrooms with different sets of developed intelligences. Thus, teachers need to develop a variety of activities on a regular basis to provide for the differences in students' learning

FIGURE 16-9 Gardner's Eight Intelligences

- Linguistic: Involves the ability to use listening, speaking, reading, and writing to express and appreciate complex meanings; to remember information.

- Logical-Mathematical: Involves using deduction, induction, patterning, interpreting graphs, numbers, and sequencing of ideas to express and appreciate complex meaning; to remember information.

- Visual/Spatial: Involves using three-dimensional ways to perceive imagery, navigate, produce, and decode information.

- Kinesthetic: Involves using the mind to control bodily movements and manipulate objects; to remember information, to give output.

- Musical: Involves using rhythm, tone, melody, and pitch to recall information and give output.

- Interpersonal: Involves communicating and collaborating with others to recall information and produce output.

- Intrapersonal: Involves maintaining self-esteem, setting goals for oneself, and acquiring values in the learning process; looking inward to acquire information and to give output.

- Naturalist: Involves sensing patterns in and making connections with elements of nature to acquire knowledge and remember information.

Source: Adapted from Blaz, D. (1999). Foreign language teacher's guide to active learning. New York: Eye on Education.

styles. Figure 16-9 provides a list of Gardner's eight intelligences and a brief description of each.

Planning Activities That Appeal to Multiple Intelligences

Linguistic Intelligence

Linguistic intelligence encompasses listening, speaking, reading, and writing to acquire knowledge. It is the intelligence that has been addressed most in the delivery of instruction and in testing in the Western educational system (Lazear, 2000).

According to research, listening is the first activity in which second language learners must be engaged, particularly in the beginning stages of language acquisition. However, listening activities should always be purposeful and meaningful. Thus, when students are engaged in listening, they should be actively involved. Other types of listening activities are the use of audiotapes or videotapes (videotapes are more effective), CDs, satellite broadcasts, films on video, music on audio/visual tapes, poems on audiotapes, and so forth for more advanced learners.

When employing these audio materials, teachers must develop some type of interactive activity so students are listening for specific purposes. For example, if listening to an audio conversation, students could have a sheet to fill in information as it becomes available: Who is/are the speaker(s)? Where are they? What is/are the topic(s) of conversation? Is there a problem? Was the problem resolved? Have you ever had that same problem? How did you resolve it? What did you learn about the personality/character of the speaker(s)? and any other appropriate questions. Another way to keep students actively listening is to have students listen for idiomatic expressions they recognize, known vocabulary, and questions asked by the speaker(s). As students listen, they jot these down. Then they share with a partner what they "heard." In these activities, students are employing at least three aspects of the linguistic intelligence: listening, speaking, and writing.

Other activities for developing linguistic intelligence would be having students engage in meaningful conversations—topics of interest, discussions of material studied, sharing descriptions, memorizing speeches, giving oral reports, conducting interviews, and games. A fun game for students to play is "Who am I?" For a history/social studies class, students are asked to pick a historical character. One student comes to the front, and the rest of the students have to "guess" by asking yes/no questions about who the historical figure is that this student selected. If students are doing a unit on animals, the same game can be played by asking the students to pick an animal.

To stimulate conversation, teachers can engage students in creating a "Conversation Necklace": the teacher passes around different types of colored raw pasta that can be strung on yarn or twine (e.g., penne pasta, rigatoni, etc.). Students select a few pieces. Once they all have their pieces, they have to say a sentence for every piece chosen. As students say a sentence related to the topic/theme being studied, the pasta is strung in the yarn or twine. At the end of the activity, the necklace is placed on display. A jar of marbles could also be employed. Students pick marbles from a basket. As they say their sentences, the marbles get placed in a jar. When the jar is full, they have a popcorn party. Cooperative groups are also excellent for stimulating listening and speaking.

For developing the reading and writing aspects of the linguistic intelligence there are so many activities that only a few will be mentioned. The sky is the limit! Using the textbook is an obvious activity; however, before the students read the material, they should be familiar with the vocabulary they will encounter. Teachers must always employ listening and speaking activities prior to having students read. After they read, they should be engaged in some type of activity where they are reviewing and applying what they read. Newspapers and magazines (censored) are excellent reading materials, as well as role-playing and dramatization. Role-playing and dramatization require much practice, thus the practice becomes meaningful because the students are preparing for an audience. Students do not necessarily have to be the characters themselves. They can use different types of puppets such as string, finger, and stick puppets. They can draw their characters on transparencies or story rolls/scrolls and narrate/dramatize using the transparencies or story rolls.

Teaching students how to write poetry and then have "an afternoon of poetry sharing" is an excellent way to motivate students to write; or students can be encouraged to select favorite poems from poetry books, to share.

Logical-Mathematical Intelligence

The students who have strong logical-mathematical abilities are able to detect patterns, reason deductively, and think logically. This "scientific reasoning" is most often associated with the sciences or mathematics, but it may be quite effectively developed and applied through the teaching of language arts.

Students can read stories that later they can graph (Blaz, 1999). For example, after reading the following story, students can be asked to graph the favorite animals for each child in the story.

There were six children. They all went to the zoo. As they walked, they discovered their favorite animals. Maria thought her favorite animal was the parrot, but when she saw the giraffe, she exclaimed: Now I know what my favorite animal is! John and Shantel were most impressed by the roaring lion. That was their favorite. Pedro and Jose each had a different favorite. Pedro liked the zebra, while Jose preferred the Florida bobcat.

Favorite Animals

Name	Giraffe	Lion	Zebra	Bobcat	Billy Goat
Maria	X				
John		X			
Shantel		X			
Pedro			X		
Jose				X	
Evelyn					X

Evelyn was walking along when she saw her most favorite animal of all: the billy goat. They all had a grand time at the zoo.

Students can also develop their own graphs based on topics of interest: their own favorite cars, authors, characters, books, foods, clothing, people, or their views on specific issues discussed in lessons. Another way to appeal to the mathematical logical intelligence is by having students compare/contrast what they have learned. An excellent tool to do this is the Venn diagram. Other recommended activities include engaging students in finding connections/relationships between objects. The "odd-one-out" (Wright, 1999) is a great game to play to engage students in this type of activity. Students are given a series of pictures. They must decide which one does not belong in the group and state why. Another activity could be to give students a series of pictures and have them connect them (establish a relationship) among them and say or write how they connected the pictures. These activities are very effective in pairs or cooperative groups.

Visual-Spatial Intelligence

This is the ability to visualize, manipulate, and create mental images to solve problems. Students/people with visual-spatial intelligence think in three-dimensional ways and are able to re-create, transform, or modify these thoughts/perceptions and to navigate, and both produce and decode, graphic information (Blaz, 1999).

Creating a "visual rich environment" in the classroom is one way to develop and appeal to the visual-spatial intelligence. Encouraging students to interact with the displays by noticing changes/new displays, students' work displayed, and as Blaz (1999) suggests even giving extra credit questions on tests based on displayed material are excellent ways to help develop this intelligence. Changing the seating arrangement on a regular basis will benefit the visual-spatial oriented students because they "see" everything from a different perspective.

The visual-spatial learners have the ability to visualize in their mind; thus, activities such as pantomiming, imitating, and mental imagery are excellent for them. Having the students close their eyes and imagine themselves in a setting the teacher is describing is another way to reach the visual-spatial learner. Once they have completed the mental imagery activity, they can describe their scene either orally or in writing. Any type of visual arts activities are also recommended, for example, drawing, assembling, building, crafts, and illustrating in three-dimensional projects are effective for these students; flow charts and story maps are just as effective.

Musical Intelligence

This intelligence is defined as the ability to recognize and compose musical pitches, tones, and rhythms. Unfortunately, every time there is need to streamline curricular offerings in the schools, the music program is one of the ones to suffer cuts. Thus, elementary school students in general are not exposed to a wide variety of musical experiences unless the regular classroom teacher incorporates music into the daily lessons. Regular elementary school teachers do not need to be musicians to bring music into their daily activities. The use of tapes or CDs is an excellent way to incorporate music into units of instruction. Having children listen to songs for specific purposes is an excellent way to acquire new vocabulary. For example, children listen for words they recognize, they tell the teacher the words, and the teacher writes the words on the board/word strips. Later, these words are employed to re-create the song. Teachers can also use tunes to traditional children's songs to create songs that relate to the content of a unit of study. Even aspects of grammar, if they can be tied in to music, help the musical student acquire the concepts with more facility. The following very old song illustrates this idea:

Found a Peanut
Found a peanut
Found a peanut
Found a peanut, just now
I just now found a peanut
Found a peanut, just now.

Broke* it open
Broke it open
Broke it open, just now
I just now broke it open
Broke it open, just now

Found it rotten . . .
Ate it anyway . . .
Got sick . . .
Saw the doctor . . .
Gave me medicine . . .
Died anyway . . .

There are eight irregular verbs in the past tense of this song. There are two more verses that can be added in a Christian religious environment. Those are: went to heaven . . ., saw an angel. . . . If the teachers are in this type of environment, they would have a total of ten irregular verbs.

---

*changed from cracked to broke to use an irregular verb

Popular music is also an excellent tool to employ. Students not only acquire language but also are exposed to cultural aspects. Students can listen and circle phrases they hear or orally answer questions regarding the theme or some aspect of culture depicted in the song.

There are other ways to bring rhythm activities into the curriculum. Dancing is a great way to teach culture as well as enriching the vocabulary to which your ELLs are exposed. Popular dances as well as folklore are fun as well as educational. Choral reading (prose) and choral poetry are other ways to employ rhythm in classroom activities. For students to read prose or poetry in unison, they must learn to read together, to pause together, where to accent syllables, and what sounds the vowels make, which are very important aspects of language. Students begin to feel the beat, rhymes, and mood of the piece they are reading in an effort to read well. (Refer to Chapter 25 for more ideas on how to incorporate music into the curriculum.)

Bodily-Kinesthetic Intelligence

Kinesthetically talented people use their mental ability to coordinate their bodily movements and to manipulate objects (Blaz, 2001).

Kinesthetic learners need to have an opportunity to "move." A variety of activities that take children from one area of the room to another provide this opportunity. Employing the exact seating arrangement for the entire school day is counterproductive for the kinesthetic learner. In addition to providing opportunities to physically move, students also need to be involved in movement activities. Allowing students to respond physically, such as in TPR, also appeals to the kinesthetic intelligence. The use of manipulative games that involve physical movement, cooking, and field trips are excellent activities for the kinesthetic learner. Drama and simulations are additional activities to appeal to the kinesthetic intelligence. (Chapter 25 provides more ideas on how to include drama in the curriculum.)

Interpersonal Intelligence

The ability to communicate personal feelings to others and to understand others' feelings and intentions are characteristic of this intelligence. Interaction with others will appeal to and develop this intelligence, which relies on all the other intelligences. To strengthen this intelligence, students should be taught relational skills. Opportunities to practice listening, encouraging others, and reaching consensus are effective strategies to enhance the interpersonal intelligence. Because communication is both verbal and nonverbal, activities in which students focus on the nonverbal language such as gestures, facial expressions, and movements are an excellent way to begin teaching how to express emotions and convey meaning. A fun activity would be to survey students, including the English language learners, to find out gestures employed in different cultures and their meanings. Then have students teach these to each other and engage in using them to convey meaning. Emphasis should be given to gestures/facial expressions employed to convey emotions. For example, in Puerto Rico, a "wink" with the left eye is a sign of approval, while in the United States, a "thumbs-up" is a sign of approval; in Puerto Rico, an upward movement of the nose and holding it in that position for a few seconds means confusion or lack of understanding. This activity is an excellent way to involve ELLs and make them feel they have something to contribute to the lessons, even if they are still at the preproduction stage or at the early speech emergence stage.

Another way to develop the interpersonal intelligence is by having students share "All about me." Students can share about their hobbies; they can make collages using magazine or computer clip art pictures capturing their likes/dislikes, their favorite activities, or people. Once students have shared, engaging the class in a discussion of what was shared is essential. Show-and-tell is also an excellent activity to encourage interpersonal listening. Those students who are listening to the presenter are required to ask questions for clarification as the speaker presents, not interrupting but waiting for pauses from the presenter.

Cooperative groups are another effective teaching strategy to employ to appeal and develop interpersonal intelligence. Students are required to interact with each other to complete an assignment. In addition, interacting with other adults provides an opportunity for meaningful communication. Teachers should encourage volunteers to come into their classrooms: parents, retirees, college students. This is an excellent way to involve the community and at the same time provide opportunities for the students to interact with adults. Students can read a book to the adults and then discuss feelings about character or discuss their position/point of view or issues that came up in the story. The adults can share their life experiences with the students, and the students can engage in a conversation expressing their feelings, common interests, and any unusual experiences the adult may have had.

Intrapersonal Intelligence

The seventh intelligence is the ability some people have to understand their own feelings and motivations and to use this self-perception to plan and direct their own life. For students to develop this intelligence, teachers must engage students in activities that help them to get to know themselves. Students need to have an opportunity to explore "deep within" their inner thoughts. Blaz (1999) suggested the following questions as prompts for journal writing:

❖ Who is your hero/heroine?
❖ If you had three wishes, what would they be?
❖ What is one of your fears?
❖ If you could change anything about yourself, what would it be?
❖ What is your life motto?
❖ When I am in school/at a dance/at home, I am . . .
❖ Ideal parents are . . .
❖ Teachers seldom are . . .
❖ Agree or disagree: Sports are very important.

English language learners who may not be able to respond in English could use their native language (if teacher can translate it or has access to a translator) or they could draw/use magazine pictures to respond. Helping students explore human values is another way to develop self-knowledge, so important for intrapersonal intelligence to be strengthened. Children's literature, human interest stories from the newspaper, current events, and videos of movies where human values are evident are excellent resources to employ.

Naturalist Intelligence

The ability to notice changes in the environment and to express concern about environmental issues are what form naturalist intelligence. Students who have strong naturalist intelligence are those who notice and remember patterns and things from nature. They have keen sensory skills—sight, smell, sound, taste, and touch. These are the students who love animals, camping, hiking, and being outdoors. Units about animals, endangered species, and ornamental/medicinal plants are excellent to develop this naturalist intelligence. Experiential learning (as discussed in Chapter 13) would also provide ample opportunities for developing this intelligence. Taking students on walks to notice specific aspects of nature and then having students either discuss/write, or draw what they saw and how it made them feel are also effective activities to appeal to the naturalist intelligence. Today, teachers can use the internet to visit websites that show nature and outdoor activities in a way that could not be done years ago. Students do not have to be deprived of these activities today, if these are not within physical access to them.

The following multiple intelligence inventory, developed by Christison (1996), can be employed by preservice as well as inservice teachers to determine their strongest intelligences.

Multiple Intelligence Inventory

(Developed by Renee Zelden and Eileen N. Whelan Ariza)

Directions: Rank each statement below as 0, 1, or 2. Write 0 in the blank if the statement is not true. Write 2 in the blank if you strongly agree with the statement. A score of 1 places you somewhere in between. Compare your scores in different intelligences. Not everything in each category may apply to you. What is your multiple intelligence profile? Where did you score highest? Lowest?

Linguistic/Verbal Intelligence

Question   Score

1. Do you find it easy to learn other languages?   _____
2. Do you recognize or understand accents easily?   _____
3. Do you like word games such as crossword puzzles and Scrabble?   _____
4. Is writing is easy for you?   _____
5. Do you have a better than average vocabulary?   _____
6. Do you like to read and write?   _____
7. Could you see yourself in the field of education, journalism, writing, or law?   _____
8. Do you like to debate, or could you see yourself as a politician?   _____
9. Are you good at spelling?   _____
10. Do you have a good memory for words, text, or scripts?   _____

Musical Intelligence

Question   Score

1. Do you find a musical pattern when you listen to raindrops?   _____
2. Do you keep melodies in your head?   _____
3. Can you distinguish when people sing or play off key?   _____
4. When you listen to a musical group, can you hear individual sounds of instruments?   _____
5. Do you find yourself whistling or singing?   _____
6. Can you remember melodies?   _____
7. Can you play a musical instrument?   _____
8. Can you sing on key?   _____
9. Can you recognize musical tones or patterns?   _____
10. Do you pick up songs, rhythms, or tunes quickly?   _____

Logical/Mathematical Intelligence

Question   Score

1. Can you conceive numerical patterns?
2. Can you determine patterns or connections between one thing and another?   _____
3. Do you tend to organize things by category?   _____
4. Are you skilled at strategy games such as chess?   _____
5. Can you do calculations in your head?   _____
6. Are you a logical thinker?   _____
7. Are you a good puzzle solver?   _____
8. Can you think sequentially?   _____
9. Do you like math?   _____
10. Can you recognize abstract patterns?   _____

Visual/Spatial Intelligence

Question   Score

1. Are you good in the arts (drawing, sculpting, painting, photography, etc.)? _____
2. Are you good with directions (map skills)?   _____
3. Do you think in pictures or images as a studying strategy?   _____
4. Do you use video, or other technological aids for teaching, learning, or pleasure? _____
5. Did find geometry easier than algebra?   _____
6. Do colors and shapes intrigue you (clothing, art, architecture, etc.)?   _____
7. Are you good at doing 3D puzzles?   _____
8. Do you prefer books with illustrations?   _____
9. Would you prefer to visit an art gallery over dancing?   _____
10. Do you brainstorm by using mind maps (concept maps, or graphic organizers)? _____

Bodily/Kinesthetic Intelligence

Question   Score

1. Are you good at physical activities such as dancing or sports?   _____
2. Are you someone who cannot sit still and must be in motion?   _____
3. Are you good at playing pool, bowling, basketball (body/eye/hand coordination)? _____
4. Do you enjoy creating things with your hands?   _____
5. Do you learn better by doing?   _____
6. Would you rather touch something to see how things work?   _____
7. Is your sense of timing better than most other people?   _____
8. Can you imitate actions, movements, such as pantomime?   _____
9. Are you good at using your body for communication?   _____
10. Are you skilled in theatre arts, stage movement, or other physically artistic demonstration (that require precision, timing, and/or balance)? _____

Intrapersonal Intelligence

1. Are you self-reflective? _____
2. Do you analyze your own behaviors and emotions? _____
3. Are you aware of your own role within your relationships with others? _____
4. Are you able to plan your own life? _____
5. Do you find yourself making appropriate choices? _____
6. Are you able to determine when you have made an inappropriate choice and why? _____
7. Are you aware of your own feelings? _____
8. Are you aware of your own strengths and weaknesses, and as a result, those of others? _____
9. Are you able to sense your inner feelings? _____
10. Are you a person who is sensitive to justice and fairness? _____

Interpersonal Intelligence

Question   Score

1. Are you good at verbal and nonverbal communication with others? _____
2. Do you try to understand the point of view and feelings of others? _____
3. Do you find yourself extremely sensitive to group harmony and often become the mediator? _____
4. Are you "people smart"? _____
5. Do you frequently communicate with people through social media and technology in a positive manner? _____
6. Do you sometimes find yourself being somewhat manipulative with others? _____
7. Are you able to be socially sensitive and have a real concern for others? _____
8. Do you find yourself being able to persuade people to think differently, or see things your way? _____
9. Do you like to play noncompetitive games with family, friends, or others? _____
10. Do you enjoy collaborative work with others? _____

Naturalistic Intelligence

1. Do you find yourself attuned to nature and the environment? _____
2. Do you enjoy camping, hiking, and being in natural settings? _____
3. Do you have a green thumb and have the ability to make plants bloom? _____
4. Do you know a lot about plant life? _____
5. Can you classify trees, leaves, plants, fruits, vegetables, etc.? _____
6. Do you enjoy gardening? _____
7. Do you thrive in naturalistic? _____
8. Are you nature appreciative (e.g., cooking, stargazing, bug/rock/ shell collecting, bird watching)? _____
9. Are you offended or worried about littering, pollution, climate change, soil erosion, whale fishing, fur hunting, animal extinction, etc.? _____
10. Would you belong to an organization such at PETA (People for the Ethical Treatment of Animals) or Greenpeace? _____

Existential Intelligence

Question   Score

1. Do you find yourself ask questions like: "What does it all mean?" _____
2. Do you question life, death, our reason for being, etc.? _____
3. Do you wonder about life on other planets, and if we are the only living beings in the universe? _____
4. Are you reflective and deep thinking? _____
5. Do you seek or believe in spiritual understanding, guidance, mysticism, divine power, transcendentalism, or sacred rituals? _____
6. Do you wonder why there is good and evil in the world? _____
7. Do you ask or wonder about the fate of humanity and the universe? _____
8. Do you wonder if animals have feelings and if they can understand human beings? _____
9. Do you think ghosts really exist? _____
10. Do you wonder about heaven, and if souls reach out to us after they die? _____

Scoring: Add your total score in each area. The higher your total score, the stronger that intelligence.* _____

*For permission to use this questionnaire, contact the author by e-mail (eariza@fau.edu)

❖ Planning for ESL instruction must be organized around communicative principles.

❖ Language development and subject content goals must go hand in hand.

❖ Interdisciplinary, content-based thematic teaching allows students to develop language proficiency as they acquire subject matter content.

❖ Interdisciplinary, content-based thematic teaching takes into account students' interests and teacher interests, as well as curricular demands.

❖ Interdisciplinary, content-based thematic teaching provides for numerous meaningful encounters with the same content from different perspectives.

❖ Elements of interdisciplinary thematic content-based unit planning include identifying a theme, formulating goals and instructional objectives, conceptualizing the content, developing the instructional procedures, developing assessment procedures, and reflecting on each individual lesson.

❖ Bloom's taxonomy includes three domains of learning: cognitive, affective, and psychomotor.

❖ Bloom's cognitive domain includes six levels of learning: knowledge, comprehension, application, analysis, synthesis, and evaluation.

❖ Bloom's affective domain includes five levels of learning: receiving, responding, valuing, organizing, and internalizing.

❖ Bloom's psychomotor domain includes four levels of learning: moving, manipulating, communicating, and creating.

❖ Gardner has identified eight multiple intelligences: linguistic, logical-mathematical, visual/spatial, kinesthetic, musical, interpersonal, intrapersonal, and naturalist.

❖ Teachers must incorporate activities in daily planning and in units of instruction to appeal to multiple intelligences.

PART FOUR

Development and Instruction of Language Skills for English Language Learners (ELLs)

chapter 17

English Language Listening
Development and Instruction, 161
NOORCHAYA YAHYA

chapter 18

English Language Oral Development
and Instruction, 181
NOORCHAYA YAHYA

chapter 19

English Language Vocabulary
Development and Instruction, 203
NOORCHAYA YAHYA

chapter 20

English Language Learners' Reading
Development and Instruction, 223
MARIA COADY AND EILEEN WHELAN ARIZA

chapter 21

English Language Learners' Writing
Development and Instruction, 261
MARIA COADY AND EILEEN WHELAN ARIZA

chapter 22

Teaching Grammar to English Learners
in the Mainstream Classroom, 295
LINDA GERENA

English Language Listening Development and Instruction

KEY ISSUES

- ❖ Research on teaching listening to English language learners
- ❖ Types of spoken language and listening tasks
- ❖ Listening difficulties faced by English language learners
- ❖ Some strategies/skills for effective listening skills
- ❖ Some techniques for teaching listening skills for multiple levels of language proficiency skills
- ❖ Alternative assessments for listening comprehension

There are three English language learners (ELLs) in Ms. Santos's class of fifteen native English speakers. One student is in the preproduction stage, and two are in the speech emergence stage of language acquisition. The theme for today's language arts class is "bugs." Ms. Santos reads a poem on bugs and asks students to circle words as they hear them. Instead of words, the English language learners are asked to circle pictures. The words are given in minimal pairs—for instance, the students will hear the phrase "Bugs, bugs on a tree." On their paper, they are given the words tree v. three and are asked to circle what they heard. The ELLs are given a picture of a tree and a picture of the number 3. They are to circle the words they heard.

Another activity Ms. Santos often uses in her class is a game called "Chinese Whispers." Alma is chosen to think of a short sentence that she whispers into Jose's ear. This continues until everyone in class has heard Alma's sentence. Then Ms. Santos asks the last student to repeat the sentence back to the class. Students check to see if the sentence was the original sentence. This game presents a low-anxiety environment for students who would have a lot of fun with this listening activity.

How will these listening activities help ELLs with listening skills in English?

Introduction

"Ni hao ma?" "Apa khabar?" "Assalamualaikum." "Hola." "Bonjour."

These are greetings in Chinese, Malay, Arabic, Spanish, and French, respectively. To respond to these greetings, one must first listen to the sounds of the language before deciphering any meanings. It is important to understand that although listening skills are given the least attention among the other skills, they are crucial elements in the language acquisition process. Human beings have to be exposed to the sounds of the language before they can acquire the language. The classic case of a wild child such as Genie, a little girl who was kept in a dark closet by her father from the time she was a baby and was later discovered at the age of thirteen, reinforces the significance of listening in the language acquisition process. Genie's father barked at her and prevented her mother or brother from talking to her. Because she never heard the human language from the time she was born, Genie's native language was never fully developed, even though she went through speech therapy during her young adult and adult years. The story of Genie reinforces the social interactionist view of language acquisition, which forwards the idea that input from the environment that is usually received through listening is necessary and crucial for language to develop in humans.

David Nunan calls listening comprehension the "Cinderella skill" in second language learning; it is often overlooked by its older sister: speaking (Nunan & Miller, 1995). For a long time in the area of language learning, learners' competence in a language was measured by their ability to speak and write. However, for learners to respond in the forms of speech and written notes, they have to use listening or reading skills. Therefore, listening skills are crucial elements in the performance of a second language learner. Through listening, children and adults obtain their learning and understanding about the world and human affairs. In real life, learners use all language skills to communicate, so listening, speaking, reading, and writing skills should be taught as integrated skills. However, to give readers an in-depth look at listening, this chapter focuses exclusively on listening in a second language. It explores research reports on teaching listening skills; types of oracy (spoken and listening) tasks; the use of strategies, skills, and techniques for effective listening skills at multiple language proficiency levels; and the type of assessments for listening comprehension.

Listening is the ability to identify and understand what others are saying.

According to researchers Howatt and Dakin, listening is the ability to identify and understand what others are saying. An able listener is capable of simultaneously understanding a speaker's accent or pronunciation, grammar and vocabulary, and grasping meaning. A list of microskills of listening, which Willis (1981, p. 134) calls enabling skills, include:

❖ Predicting what people are going to talk about.
❖ Guessing at unknown words or phrases without panic.
❖ Using one's own knowledge of the subject to gain understanding.
❖ Identifying relevant points; rejecting irrelevant information.
❖ Retaining relevant points (note-taking, summarizing).
❖ Recognizing discourse markers (e.g., well; oh, another thing is; now; finally).
❖ Recognizing cohesive devices (e.g., such as and which).
❖ Understanding different intonation patterns and uses of stress, etc., that give clues to meaning and social setting.
❖ Understanding inferred information (e.g., speaker's attitude or intentions).

The array of microskills in listening shows that listening is not a passive skill. The microskills are used simultaneously to enable a person to receive and respond to messages. Recapitulate a conversation you had with someone yesterday. What did you hear first? During the conversation, did you have to predict the speaker's message? Was there information in the conversation that you found relevant? Was there any information that you did not focus on? Did you hear intonation patterns that made you understand the speaker's meaning better? Discuss your experience with the class.

Listening is a complex process that involves the listener, the speaker, the content of the message, and any visual support that accompanies the message (Brown & Yule, 1983). Several factors that influence a listener's listening skills are interest in the topic, the listener's background knowledge that facilitates understanding of the topic, and the ability to use negotiation skills such as asking for clarification, repetition, or definition of points not understood, all of which make the incoming message more understandable.

Five major factors affect listening comprehension (Rubin, 1994):

1. Text characteristics (listening passage/text or visual supplements)
2. Interlocutor characteristics (speaker's persona; character)
3. Task characteristics (purpose and associated)
4. Listener characteristics (listener's personal response)
5. Process characteristics (listener's cognitive activities and the nature of interaction between speaker and listener)

The research section in this chapter will address these major factors that affect listening. In using the listening skills, listeners have to deal with the speaker. If a speaker uses colloquial language and reduced forms, listening comprehension is more difficult. The rate at which speakers deliver their speech—whether it is too fast or too slow—also influences the listener's understanding of the message. The more the listener is exposed to the speaker's speech habits, the easier it is for the listener because he or she will use these speech habits as clues to decipher meaning. Another factor that influences listening is the content of the message. Content that is familiar to a listener is easier to understand than content for which a listener has no background knowledge. In addition, visual support such as pictures, graphs, diagrams, gestures, and facial expressions can increase listening comprehension if employed appropriately and the listener is able to interpret them correctly.

What Happens When We Listen?

Contrary to some people's belief that listening is a passive skill, it is an active skill that is gaining researchers' attention. Like the other skills, most of what is known about listening comes from research in native language development; however, there's a greater focus on inquiry into second language listening as the importance of teaching listening increases (Rubin, 1994). From the psycholinguistics standpoint, the ability to understand a spoken language is widely recognized as a complex and active skill that involves many different mental processes. According to Byrnes (1984, p. 318), listening comprehension can be regarded as a "highly-complex problem-solving activity" that is comprised of a set of distinct subskills. Those subskills are roughly categorized into the following two parts (Rivers, 1981): (1) the recognition of component parts of the language (i.e., words, verb groups, or simple phrases) and (2) memory for these linguistic elements, which is essential to the process of listening comprehension. It does not necessarily guarantee the comprehension of what is heard, because the utterance, which contains a lot of linguistic information, needs to be retained in the listeners' short-term memory for a while, so that the utterance can be processed for further semantic interpretation.

Listeners are not usually conscious of the steps they take in the listening process. These steps can occur simultaneously, sequentially, in rapid succession, or move backward and forward as needed. The listener:

❖ Determines a reason for listening (e.g., getting direction to the Kravis Center)
❖ Takes the raw speech and deposits an image of it in the short-term memory (remembering the right and left turns to the Kravis Center)
❖ Attempts to organize the information by identifying the type of speech event (conversation, lecture, radio ad) and the function of the message (persuade, inform, request)

- Predicts information expected to be included in the message
- Recalls background information (schemata) to help interpret the message
- Assigns a meaning to the message
- Checks that the message has been understood
- Determines the information to be held in long-term memory
- Deletes the original form of the message that had been received into short-term memory (Brown & Bailey, 1984; Dunkel, 1986)

Other processes at work are the two types of cognitive processing: bottom-up and top-down processing.

Top-Down Processing

Top-down processing refers to listeners understanding the big picture of the message. Here, listeners utilize the schemata or background knowledge they have of the subject in interpreting the message. For instance, students listen to the teacher's lecture on the many uses of lemons. The teacher shows students a map of India and explains that lemons probably come to us from India and were first planted in the United States during the California gold rush as a means to fight scurvy. The teacher proceeds to show how lemon juice can remove rust or mildew stains. She also demonstrates another use of lemon by squeezing lemon juice into a container, dipping a swab into the juice, and using it to write a message on a white paper. When the paper dries, the message appears on the page. She then says that lemon juice contains a compound that is colorless when dissolved in water. When heated, the compound breaks down and produces carbon, which is black. Students process the teacher's lecture by looking at the map and observing the experiment, primarily focusing on the uses of lemon that they can relate to. In this activity, students use top-down processing in listening to the lecture. Because students are already familiar with the subject matter, they raise questions only on issues that need further clarification. This example also underscores the significance of advanced organizers, content visuals, and realia as aids to listening.

Bottom-Up Processing

In bottom-up processing, the meaning of the message is interpreted based on the incoming data—from sounds, to words, to grammatical relationships, to meaning. Stress, rhythm, and intonation also play a role in bottom-up processing. Anderson and Lynch (1988) call this the "listener as a tape-recorder" view of listening because it assumes that the listener takes in and stores messages sequentially, similar to a tape-recorder—one sound, one phrase, and one utterance at a time. Beginning English language learners would focus on sounds of individual words and the intonation pattern to help them understand a statement or a question. They repeat these words several times in an attempt to understand the meaning of the sentence or question.

All the steps and processes mentioned influence the techniques and activities teachers choose in their lessons to assist learners to learn to listen as well as listening to learn.

Why Is Listening Difficult for English Language Learners?

Part of successful listening is the ability to concentrate on the message and maintain attention in listening to the message. One of the difficulties that English language learners face is the lack of attention they give to the speaker due to their limited understanding of the message. When students do not comprehend instruction or can only understand bits and pieces of the message, it is inevitable that they will have a shorter attention span. Another difficulty results in the continuous flow of speech in "real time" that may not be "played back" for the English language learners. English language learners also have to distinguish all the sounds, intonation patterns, and voice qualities in the English language and to discriminate between them and similar sounds in their native tongue. Unlike the reading comprehension task, where English language learners can revert to earlier parts of the reading passage, during listening comprehension tasks, where words and phrases are chopped off in a fleeting second, L2 listeners cannot look back at the beginning of each word or sentence that they have failed to understand (Ohata, 2006). According to Larry Vandergrift (2004), listening is probably the least explicit of the four language skills, making it the most difficult skill to learn. It involves physiological and cognitive process (Field, 2002; Lynch, 2002; Rost, 2002), as well as attention to contextual and "socially coded acoustic clues" (Swaffar & Bacon, 1993). Yet, another reason why listening is difficult for English language learners is the difference in the sound system of English to the sound system of the other languages. Unlike Spanish and many other languages that are syllable-timed languages, English is a stress-timed language. This characteristic in the sound system of the English language causes the unstressed syllables to be contracted or reduced and articulated more rapidly. Examples of contractions are (a) Who'd do that? (Who would do that?); and (b) We've been there. (We have been there). Examples of "dropping" of sounds are (a) Eat 'em. (Eat them); and (b) She's changin' her clothes. (changing). Another difficulty for nonnative speakers of English when listening to English speech is when the change of sounds occurs. The final sound of one word and the beginning sound of the following word combine to yield another sound. Examples are: (a) Did you do it? (the d sound becomes j sound); and (b) Is your brother home? (the s sound becomes z sound). In addition, there are sound contrasts that do not exist in Spanish and other languages, for example, the contrast between *sheep* and *ship*, *bait* and *bet*, *fool* and *full*. The preceding factors contribute to making listening in English a more difficult task for non-English speakers. Teachers who are aware of these factors would be able to use specific listening strategies that focus on these characteristics of the English sound system to teach listening skills to their English Language Learners.

What Does Research Say about Listening and Listening Instruction?

Research on Listening

Nunan traces the comings and goings of the attention given to listening comprehension skills. In the 1960s, the emphasis on oral language skills gave the teaching of listening skills a boost. Teaching listening became fashionable again in the 1980s, when Krashen's (1982) ideas about comprehensible input

gained prominence. Then James Asher's work on total physical response (TPR) reinforced the notion that a second language is learned most effectively in the beginning stages if the pressure to produce utterances is taken away from the learners. In the 1980s, work in the first language field also encouraged proponents of listening in a second language. The works of scholars such as Gillian Brown (1984, 1990) made a breakthrough in emphasizing the importance of developing oracy (the ability to listen and speak) as well as literacy in school. Listening is now recognized as an active activity, not a passive one, which is critical to L2 acquisition and a skill in its own right that deserves systematic study (Morley, 1999). Prior to this, reading and writing were the only skills considered important and that warranted instruction, whereas listening and speaking skills were taken for granted because native speakers were considered to be born with these skills.

From the viewpoint of cognitive psychology, listening is primarily "conceptualized as an act of information processing" (Imhof, 2010, p. 98). According to Lynch (2009), information processing is one of the main theories of listening that was developed during the computer revolution of the 1970s and 1980s. The driving force behind this theory, Lynch says, was "research into artificial intelligence" (Ibid, p. 10–11). It has been "a dominant theory of learning and memory" ever since (Slavin et al, 2009, p. 158). Information processing is defined as "a cognitive theory that describes the processing, storage, and retrieval of knowledge in the mind" (Ibid). It is performance, rather than behavior, that functions as the key word in this theory (Ortega, 2009).

The information processing view of listening "claimed that comprehension of a given message only occurred when it was internally reproduced in the listeners' mind" (Lynch, 2006, p. 33). Anderson's three-stage comprehension model comes under this view of listening (Ibid), which in itself is a model that has influenced the understanding of learner listening comprehension (Goh, 2002). Language comprehension, according to Anderson (2010), involves three stages: perceptual processing, parsing, and utilization. It is during the first stage, perception, that the acoustic message is originally encoded. This stage of listening involves bottom-up processing (see following section), and becomes gradually automatic via practice (Vandergrift & Goh, 2012). In the parsing stage, the message that is carried by words and retained in working memory is transformed into mental representations that include the combination of meanings of initial words. The first two stages, perception and parsing, "continue to inform each other within the available time, until a plausible mental representation emerges" (Ibid, p. 42). The final stage is utilization during which a listener, or reader, uses the mental representations of the sentence's meaning. During utilization, listeners use top-down processes by using information that is not part of the linguistic input, and which is stored in long-term memory, to interpret the parsed speech (Ibid). Although these three stages are partially ordered in time, in reality they do also partially overlap (Anderson, 2010). According to O'Malley et al. (1989), the three stages "overlap with and are consistent with listening comprehension processes identified elsewhere" (p. 419). One major problem listeners may face in the perception stage is the segmentation of the stream of words, since speech is not broken into distinct units the way written text is. This explains one of the main sources of difficulty for listeners, particularly those listening to a foreign language. Listeners rarely record meanings passively after having mapped a sentence into a representation of its meaning. Some form of utilization takes place as the final stage. Making sense of a sentence more often than not requires making connections and inferences. To understand a particular sentence, the listeners must make quite a few inferences. An inference compels the listener to go beyond the text to what is implied in the meaning (Anderson, 2010).

Controlled processing, according to Vandergrift and Goh (2012), "involves conscious attention to and processing of elements in the speech stream" (p.19). The limited linguistic knowledge L2 learners have does not allow for automatic processing of everything they hear. In fact, as Badger and Yan (2009) state, students learning to listen in a second/foreign language "are at least partially at the controlled stage" (p.73). However, controlled processing is not enough and comprehension will most likely suffer in such a case. Depending on what actions learners take, comprehension will either break down or the listeners will resort to whatever strategies at their disposal to compensate for missing information (Vandergrift & Goh, 2012).

Current research and theory once again point to the benefit of allowing beginners in a second language to go through a silent, or preproduction, period (Dunkel, 1991). An experimental group was deliberately kept from oral production in a study that involved beginning students of Russian at the Defense Language Institute (Rubin, 1994). The group was required instead to respond only in writing. They were then merged with students in the regular Russian program. After twelve weeks of instruction, it was found that the experimental group performed significantly better in listening comprehension than the control group. In addition, the experimental group outperformed the control group on the other three skills (speaking, reading, and writing).

Learners are given the opportunity to store information in their memories when they are not expected to produce speech immediately. This will also spare them the trauma of task overload and speaking before they are ready. The silent period can be long or short, depending on each individual learner's readiness for speech production. The silent period may be comprised of several class periods of listening activities that foster vocabulary and build comprehension, such as TPR. In TPR, the teacher gives a series of commands, and students demonstrate their understanding of the message by acting out the commands. For instance, the teacher says, "Walk to the door," and the student walks to the door. When the learner feels comfortable enough to speak, he or she will begin to give the commands. A listening period containing productive tasks enhances rather than inhibits language acquisition for both beginners and advanced-level learners.

Griffiths (2003) suggested that different languages have different "normal" rates, and the rates defined in studies using English cannot be applied exactly to students of other languages. Tauroza and Allison (1990) also noted that normal rates vary among text types and that the range of what is considered normal may vary from language to language. However, there are conflicting findings about speech rate on comprehension. Griffiths (1995) found that speech faster than 200 words per minute (w.p.m.) is hard for lower-intermediate learners to understand. He found that this level of student performed best at 127 w.p.m. Working with intermediate-level students, Kelch (1985) found significant comprehension effects for slowed speech (124 w.p.m). On the other hand, Blau (1990) found that speech ranging from 145 to 185 w.p.m. did not significantly affect comprehension of intermediate- and advanced-level students.

Another measuring impact of the rate is the kind of listening required. King and Behnke (1989) studied the interaction of the task with listening type for native speakers. They found that comprehensive listening performance deteriorated significantly as speech comprehension levels increased (i.e., faster speech), whereas interpretive and short-term listening comprehension remained stable until a high degree of time compression (sixty percent) was reached. Voss (1979) studied repeats, false starts, filled pauses, and unfilled pauses in spontaneous speech. He found that all types of hesitation phenomena cause perceptual problems and, thus, comprehension errors for nonnative speakers (NNs). NNs get stuck in bottom-up processing of phonetic utterances that do not affect comprehension, whereas native speakers (NSs) discard these utterances in favor of top-down processing. Fishman (1980) compared NSs of English with NNs who were at a fairly high level of ESL competence. He identified ten categories of error (largely phonological) and found that although native speakers made 2.5 times fewer errors than nonnatives, the same error categories turned up in L1 and L2 listeners. He concluded that in principle, the perception strategies used in the L1 and L2 follow similar lines. Markham (1988), in his study on the interlocutor characteristics, stated, "Gender bias is a pervasive factor that exerts an influence on ESL students' recall of orally presented material." For example, he found that both groups recalled more from the nonexpert female speakers than from the male experts. Shohamy and Inbar (1991) considered how different types of questions influence success in L2 listening tasks. They found that subjects performed better on questions referring to local cues in the text than on those referring to

global cues. Low-level test takers can respond to the local cues in the text. Students who respond to global cues can also respond to local cues, but not vice versa.

Studies in second language listening have increasingly shifted focus from examining product to process in listening comprehension tasks. Ohata (2006) succinctly underscored the significant role auditory short-term memory plays in L2 listening comprehension process. The three questions he raised in his research are (1) What processes are involved in L2 listening comprehension?; (2) What roles does memory play in L1 and L2 listening comprehension processes?; and (3) What are the relationships between short-term memory (STM) and L2 learning? In his research findings, he argued that L2 listening comprehension is initially constrained by the limited capacity of auditory STM available, but its development can be enhanced through L2 syntactic exercises that focus on structures. One of the implications of his study is that teachers' awareness of the role that memory plays in L2 listening comprehension processes will influence their choice of more effective teaching activities in the classroom.

Ohata's conclusion about the L2 listening process shares similar lines of arguments made by Vandergrift (2004). Vandergrift stated that beginning level L2 listeners have limited language knowledge, and therefore little of what they hear can be automatically processed. He further stated that these L2 beginners have to focus on details of what they hear, and due to the limitations of their working memory and the speed of speech, their comprehension suffers.

In his recent L2 listening comprehension study, Vandergrift (2006) developed his hypotheses from the reading hypotheses: (1) poor reading in L2 is due to poor ability in the L1—therefore, poor L1 readers will read poorly in L2 and good L1 readers will read well in the L2; and (2) poor reading in the L2 is due to inadequate knowledge of the L2, the linguistic threshold hypothesis (LTH), and the linguistic independence hypothesis (LIH). The LTH posits that to read or listen in an L2, one must first achieve a level of L2 linguistic ability (Cziko, 1980). The LTH posits that L2 knowledge is the key factor in success or failure in L2 listening or reading. The LIH implies that reading/listening performance in the L2 is largely shared with reading/listening ability in the L1. The LIH is similar to Cummins's (1979) notion of common underlying proficiency (CUP), and Alderson's (1984) LIH assumes that previously learned language processes such as reading or listening, once learned, can transfer across languages. The questions in Vandergrift's (2006) study are (1) To what degree does L2 proficiency contribute to L2 listening comprehension ability?; (2) Does L1 listening comprehension ability also contribute to L2 listening comprehension ability? If so, to what degree?; (3) Assuming that both L1 listening ability and L2 language proficiency are significant predictors of L2 listening comprehension ability, what is the relative importance of each with respect to one's ability to answer questions demanding different levels of comprehension, that is, inference questions and literal questions? From his findings, Vandergrift argued that both L2 proficiency and L1 listening ability contribute substantially to L2 listening comprehension ability. He goes on to say that given the statistically significant influence of L1 listening comprehension ability on L2 listening comprehension ability, there appears to be some support for the linguistic interdependence hypothesis (LIH). Vandergrift's study has several pedagogical implications, including (1) it is important to develop vocabulary knowledge in the L2 listening proficiency using both top-down and bottom-up skills, and (2) students may benefit from strategy instruction to reduce the gap in transfer of L1 inferencing skills to L2 inferencing tasks.

Research on Listening Instruction

1. A Strategy-based Approach

Mendelson (1995, p. 134) defines a strategy-based approach as follows:

> A strategy-based approach is a methodology that is rooted in strategy instruction. It sees the objective as being to teach students how to listen. This is done, first, by making learners aware of how the language functions and second, by making them aware of the strategies that they use—i.e., developing "metastrategic aware-

ness." Then, the task of the teacher becomes to instruct the learners in the use of additional strategies that will assist them in tackling the listening task.

Mendelson (1995, pp. 139–140) offered the following principles for the structure of a unit in a strategy-based listening course:

1. Attend to awareness and consciousness-raising. Both teachers and students need to be aware of the power and value of strategies.
2. Use prelistening activities. Here background knowledge is activated.
3. Focus on the listening. Students need to know what they are going to be listening to and why.
4. Provide guided activities. These are specially designed activities that provide students with ample amount of practice in using a particular strategy.
5. Practice with real data. Students should be exposed to a lot of listening practice using authentic data after having been trained in strategy use.
6. Use what has been comprehended. Make use of what has been heard: notes from talk, filling in a form, etc.
7. Foster self-evaluation strategies. This is an important addition to Mendelson's principles advocated by Vandergrift.

However, recent work has in fact, found that listening strategy instruction which aimed at bringing about improvements in learners' listening ability has led to mixed results (Graham & Macaro, 2008). Further, Goh and Hu (2013) state that "there are even calls to abandon a strategy approach in preference for more listening practice" (p. 15).

In fact, Field (2008) states that "in order to train learners more successfully in second language listening, we need to treat the skill as a form of expert behavior" (p.3).

This is a major area for the success of L2 listeners, for as Goh (2005) states, "a finding that has emerged quite consistently is that expert listeners make use of metacognitive strategies more frequently" (p.74). Also, Macaro (2010) makes clear that it was L2 listening studies that involved a strong metacognitive element in the instruction, by encouraging learners to reflect and evaluate their strategic behavior in listening, which obtained more positive results (p. 295).

Thus, some studies have revived the concept of "L2 listening expertise" and add an essential element of deliberate practice.

2. Using Advanced Organizers

Advanced organizers are found to be crucial in facilitating comprehension (Herron, Cole, York, & Linden, 1998). Visuals, content, and context are also found to be important aids to listening. Of the two, advanced organizers that are not directly related to the information (e.g., context visuals) are not helpful to the listener. Vandergrift (2004) summarized his research on advanced organizers by stating that beginning-level listeners are limited by working memory constraints. Advanced organizers that help listeners focus directly on the desired information are most useful for efficient processing. They free attentional capacity for focusing on desired details, which requires bottom-up processing skills.

3. Using DVDs with Captions

Vandergrift (2004) compiled studies that have been conducted on the widespread use of DVD video with multilingual soundtracks and captions. These DVD videos provide opportunities for written support to enhance listening comprehension. Studies have been conducted by Markham, Peter, and McCarthy (2001) and research done by Jones and Plass (2002). In the earlier study, the researchers argued that students would benefit from a cycle of repeated viewing, progressing from L1 captions to L2 captions, and finally to no captions, particularly using challenging video material. In the later study, the researchers found that students acquired more vocabulary and recalled the passage better with the help of both pictorial and written annotations instead of pictures only or written annotations only. For both vocabulary retention and listening comprehension, pictorial annotations are found to have a stronger and longer-lasting effect than written annotations. Vandergrift (2004) warned practitioners against

these listening supports provided in the aforementioned studies. Although they may be helpful for developing word recognition skills and learning vocabulary, they do not foster compensatory strategies development where listeners fill gaps in comprehension through the use of real life contextual information and limited word recognition skills.

4. Using Bottom-up Skills

There are mixed findings on research studies that examine the use of bottom-up skills. Although Segalowitz and Segalowitz (1993) maintained that automatization of word recognition skills (i.e., fluent bottom-up processing) is critical for successful listening comprehension, Poelmans (2003), in comparing a bottom-up processing group to a top-down processing group in her listening comprehension study, had found no significant differences between the two groups. However, Osada (2001) found that an overemphasis on bottom-up processing contributes to a lack of success in listening.

5. Using Metacognitive Strategies

Researchers such as Goh (2000, 2002), Hasan (2000), Mareschal (2002), Peters (1999), and Vandergrift (2003) highlight the importance of the effective use of metacognitive strategies for successful listening comprehension. Vandergrift (2003) found that the successful listener used an effective combination of metacognitive and cognitive strategies. His findings concur with Goh (2002) and Mareschal (2002).

Types of Spoken Language

English language learners should be exposed to as many types of spoken language as possible. Types of spoken language include:

- ❖ Formal lectures
- ❖ Casual chats
- ❖ Face-to-face interactions
- ❖ Telephone messages
- ❖ Radio and TV presentations
- ❖ Native speakers' speech in all kinds of situations

Listening Difficulties Faced by English Language Learners

Part of successful listening is the ability to concentrate on the message and maintain attention in listening to the message. One of the difficulties that English language learners face is the lack of attention they give to the speaker due to their limited understanding of the message. When students do not comprehend instruction or can only understand bits and pieces of the message, it is inevitable that they will have a shorter attention span. Another difficulty results in the continuous flow of speech in "real time" that may not be "played back" for the English language learners. English language learners also have to distinguish all the sounds, intonation patterns, and voice qualities in English and to discriminate between them and similar sounds in their native tongue. According to Cook (1991, p. 71), L2 learners have a sort of "cognitive deficit." This means that their mental processes work less efficiently in the L2 than in the L1. In other words, the memory span of L2 learners might be more restricted in the L2 than in the L1 (Brown & Hulme, 1992; Glicksberg, 1963). When L2 learners listen to utterances that are at a fast speed, their processing load might naturally be increased, which will result in the difficulty of understanding the meaning of the utterances. As Rivers and Temperly (1978) stated, L2 short-term memory is often overloaded, causing words to be purged before they can be organized in L2 patterns and then interpreted. Furthermore, Joiner (1986) explained that even though L2 learners can recognize each word of the sentence as it is spoken, they may not be able to retain all pieces of information long enough to interpret them—resulting in L2 learners' failure in listening. Therefore, Ohata (2006) argued that memory can contribute significantly to the difficulties second language learners face when listening to L2.

What Constitutes Successful Listening?

Nunan (1989) listed the following characteristics of successful listening:

❖ Meaningful words and phrases derived from segmenting the stream of speech
❖ Recognition of word classes
❖ Use of one's own background knowledge to relate to the incoming message
❖ Utterances and parts of the aural text identified for their rhetorical and functional intent
❖ Identification of information focus and emotional attitudinal tone through rhythm, stress, and intonation
❖ Ability to extract gist from a longer aural text without having understood every word

Tips on Selecting Listening Techniques and Activities

When selecting materials and activities for English language learners, teachers should have these considerations:

❖ Listening should be purposeful and interesting. Tasks such as following instructions to classroom routines provide purposeful listening, and listening to taped stories is an interesting listening activity. This activity uses the top-down processing in listening.
❖ Materials should be authentic. Examples include children's programs such as *Magic School Bus, Sesame Street,* and *Blues Clues.* Opportunities to develop both top-down and bottom-up processing skills should be offered. A top-down approach would involve students giving the title of a taped story that they listen to, and the bottom-up approach would be to involve students in answering specific questions on the taped story that they listened to, such as, "Who is Andy talking to on the phone?" Another bottom-up approach would be to have students distinguish pairs of words that contain sounds that are distinct in English, e.g., *sheep* vs. *ship, bait* vs. *bet, fool* vs. *full.*
❖ The development of listening strategies should be encouraged. Playing video with the sound turned off will elicit students' prediction of the script of the video, and playing it with the sound

turned on will confirm or modify students' predictions.

❖ Activities should teach, not test. Students should not only provide a one-word answer to listening tasks, but they should also be able to provide main ideas and details of what they have heard. The prelistening activity can involve students in using language to predict. Postlistening activities can help students assess their accuracy in their prediction. This task will help them develop listening skills that are beneficial beyond the classroom.

Some Strategies/Skills for Effective Listening Skills Using the TESOL Standards

In preparing a lesson that focuses on listening skills, TESOL standards for K–12 students should be included.

The English language proficiency standards (WIDA Consortium, 2006) are as follows.

The standards publication presents five language proficiency standards. They include both social and academic uses of the language students must acquire for success in and beyond the classroom.

Standard 1:

English language learners *communicate* for *social, intercultural,* and *instructional* purposes within the school setting.

Standard 2:

English language learners *communicate* information, ideas, and concepts necessary for academic success in the area of *language arts*.

Standard 3:

English language learners *communicate* information, ideas, and concepts necessary for academic success in the area of *mathematics*.

Standard 4:

English language learners *communicate* information, ideas, and concepts necessary for academic success in the area of *science*.

Standard 5:

English language learners *communicate* information, ideas, and concepts necessary for academic success in the area of *social studies*.

A Listening Lesson

The teacher can facilitate the development of a listening activity by creating listening lessons that guide the learner through three stages: prelistening, the listening task, and the postlistening task. In an activity that involves a student listening to a telephone conversation, students are asked to predict the content of discussion between the speakers. In the actual listening task, students can fill out answers to specific questions while identifying the pictures of words they heard in the conversation. In the postlistening activity, students are asked to verbally recall the information they heard or write a brief summary of the information they gathered after listening to the taped conversation.

Using Standards 1–5 (Grade Level 1–3)

Refer to Tables 17-1 through 17-5 for use of Standards 1–5.

To use English to communicate in social settings, students will use English to participate in social interactions. Some descriptors for listening lessons are engaging in conversations, using nonverbal communication in social interactions, and sharing and requesting information. Some of the sample progress indicators include using the telephone, engaging a listener's attention verbally or nonverbally, or describing feelings and emotions after watching a movie or listening to a recorded radio program.

Table 17-1   Standard 1*

Domain	Topic	Level 1	Level 2	Level 3	Level 4	Level 5
Listening	Directions–Instructions	Mimic responses to one-step oral commands supported by gestures, songs, or realia.	Follow one- to two-step oral commands supported by gestures, songs, or realia.	Follow a series of oral commands within oral discourse supported by gestures or realia.	Follow multistep commands within oral discourse supported by gestures or realia.	Follow multistep commands within oral discourse in various contexts.

*English language learners *communicate* for *social*, *intercultural*, and *instructional* purposes within the school setting.

From *Prek–12 English Language Proficiency Standards*. Copyright © 2006 by Teachers of English to Speakers of Other Languages. Reprinted by permission.

Table 17-2   Standard 2*

Domain	Topic	Level 1	Level 2	Level 3	Level 4	Level 5
Listening	Phonics–Phonemic awareness	Identify sounds, syllables, or compound words nonverbally (e.g., by clapping) in small groups.	Discriminate between regular and irregular words (e.g., count nouns or past tense) through gestures in oral sentences with a partner.	Identify affixes, root words, and derivational endings through gestures in oral discourse with a partner.	Replicate through gestures, stress, and intonation patterns or rhymes, prose, or poetry with a partner.	Identify the musical elements of literary languages (e.g., rhymes, repeated sounds, or onomatopoeia through simulation.

*English language learners *communicate* information, ideas, and concepts necessary for academic success in the area of *language arts*.

From *Prek–12 English Language Proficiency Standards*. Copyright © 2006 by Teachers of English to Speakers of Other Languages. Reprinted by permission.

Table 17-3   Standard 3*

Domain	Topic	Level 1	Level 2	Level 3	Level 4	Level 5
Listening	Time (digital–and analog)	Draw or show on clocks in response to oral directions (e.g., "Put the big hand on the 5.").	Role-play activities associated with different times of day in response to oral statements (e.g., "I go to bed at half past 8.").	Illustrate by drawing or using clocks in response to oral questions or statements (e.g., "Show me a time between 6 and 9 o'clock" or "When do we eat lunch?").	Estimate elasped amount of time from oral word problems using visual or graphic support.	Make inferences from oral grade-level story problems or classroom narratives.

*English language learners *communicate* information, ideas, and concepts necessary for academic success in the area of *mathematics*.

From *Prek–12 English Language Proficiency Standards*. Copyright © 2006 by Teachers of English to Speakers of Other Languages. Reprinted by permission.

Table 17-4 Standard 4*

Domain	Topic	Level 1	Level 2	Level 3	Level 4	Level 5
Listening	Astronomy	Draw or identify objects in the sky from models and pictures according to oral directions (e.g., "The sun is a round yellow ball.").	Draw and position objects in the sky from models or maps according to oral directions (e.g., "Draw the sun in the middle of the page.").	Locate objects in the sky from videos or maps according to oral descriptions (e.g., "Pluto looks small because it is the farthest planet from the sun.").	Differentiate among objects in the sky (e.g., constellations, meteors, comets) from videos or maps according to oral descriptions.	Define relationships among objects in the sky (e.g., eclipse or equinox) from oral descriptions.

*English language learners *communicate* information, ideas, and concepts necessary for academic success in the area of *science*.

From *Prek–12 English Language Proficiency Standards.* Copyright © 2006 by Teachers of English to Speakers of Other Languages. Reprinted by permission.

Table 17-5 Standard 5*

Domain	Topic	Level 1	Level 2	Level 3	Level 4	Level 5
Listening	Land forms–Globes–Maps	Make or point to major physical features according to color or other attributes from oral commands (e.g., "Find the oceans; they are blue.").	Visualize and point to physical features or places from different perspectives, following oral commands (e.g., "Find your state on the map and globe.").	Follow directions to locate places described orally using legends, icons, or the compass rose.	Interpret representations of major physical features from oral statements (e.g., "Show me the most mountainous region.").	Build models from examples based on a set of oral directions.

*English language learners *communicate* information, ideas, and concepts necessary for academic success in the area of *social studies*.

From *Prek––2 English Language Proficiency Standards.* Copyright © 2006 by Teachers of English to Speakers of Other Languages. Reprinted by permission.

For other grade levels, please refer to *PreK–12 English Language Proficiency Standards.* (2006). Teachers of English or Other Languages, Inc. Alexandria, Virginia.

Source: *PreK–12 English Language Proficiency Standards.* (2006). Teachers of English or Other Languages, Inc. Alexandria, Virginia.

Listening Activities for Students at Multiple Levels of Language Proficiency

Lund (1990) offers teachers numerous activities for developing English language learners' listening skills and ways to check their comprehension:

❖ Taking action: Listeners respond through TPR.

❖ Making choices: Listeners select from alternatives such as pictures, objects, texts, or actions.

❖ Transferring: Listeners transform the message they heard in the form of drawing pictures to fill in a chart.

❖ Answering: Listeners answer questions about the text.

- ❖ Condensing: Listeners take notes or make outlines of text heard.
- ❖ Extending: Listeners go beyond the text by continuing the story or solving a problem.
- ❖ Modeling: Listeners perform a similar task.
- ❖ Duplicating: Listeners simply repeat or translate the message.
- ❖ Conversing: Listeners are active participants in face-to-face conversations.

Listening Activities Using TESOL Standards

Teachers' daily class routine (calendar activity, class lining up, or a restroom break) can be a useful resource for listening tasks. The expressions used daily by teachers to accomplish the morning work or class work act as a source of repeated, patterned expressions that English learners will hear and understand. The actions performed as a result of these expressions will help students to participate in social settings. The language they hear in the classroom from the teacher or from other students will assist them in learning how and when to use the appropriate expressions to fulfill their needs in the social setting. For instance, when English learners hear others in class asking the teacher, "May I go to the restroom?" they will be able to utter those words themselves when they need to go to the restroom. Other examples include asking to borrow items from

others in class—"May I borrow your eraser, please?"

Listening to messages that are comprehensible to nonnative speakers of English is crucial. For learners in preproduction stage, actions, gestures, and visuals are important accompaniments to the messages they hear. Key words and phrases need to be emphasized and repeated. Daily routines in class, such as the expression, "Hand in your work," should be acted out so that English language learners can match what they hear to what needs to be done. While giving instructions, teachers should be specific in their directions—students at this stage need a lot of guidance to understand directions. For instance, if the task requires that students circle the correct answer, teachers should demonstrate what "circle" means. Also at this stage, giving action-related commands (TPR) will help learners with their language. A game such as "Simon Says" will help students learn common verbs like sit, stand, walk, and run. In a game called "Detecting Mistakes," students have a picture in front of them and they listen to a description of that picture. When the teacher mentions items that are not in the picture, students are to call out, "That's a mistake." Frequent activities at the listening center where students listen to taped storybooks will help them immensely in getting used to the sounds of the new language.

Students at the early production and speech emergence levels of language acquisition can be challenged with listening activities that expect them

Language Proficiency Stages Tasks

Level 1 (starting)	❖ Students listen to commands and act out commands.
	❖ Students select/point to a picture that shows the word they hear.
Level 2 (emerging)	❖ Students listen to a dialogue and provide one- or two-word responses. Listeners use duplicating strategy; they repeat or translate the message.
Level 3 (developing)	❖ Students check off items—this usually involves a list of words that the learners listen to and check off as they hear them (e.g., picture bingo).
	❖ Picture dictation—students draw pictures from verbal dictation.
Level 4 (expanding)	❖ Students highlight key points of the lecture they listen to.
	❖ Students model a similar task (e.g., retelling a story read to them).
Level 5 (bridging)	❖ Conversing—students listen and appropriately respond to a face-to-face conversation.

to produce short verbal responses. One such activity is the guessing game in which students listen to a short description of an item and then have to guess what it is. Teachers can use tasks and texts that are at different levels of difficulty. For the intermediate-fluency students, teachers can provide a taped story for them to listen to and later ask them to retell the story briefly.

Listening skills should be an integral part of all lessons in the class. Using some listening strategies such as focusing on key items and carrying out tasks requested after listening to important information are crucial in preparing students to function in their new language. Teachers should not force beginning students to respond. They should also understand that students need this silent stage to mull over what they hear and make sense of what they hear. For this reason it is hard to measure comprehension without any proof of performance from students. Nevertheless, the preproduction stage, or the silent period, is a crucial period in which students listen attentively to the new language around them.

What listening skills should students be taught at this stage? What listening tasks are they expected to do? How can teachers incorporate these basic listening skills and tasks in their daily classroom instructions?

Imagine you are teaching a new student from Mexico who does not know one word of English.

What is the first thing you will do to help him with his "listening" of the English language?

Listening Activities in a Multiple-Leveled Group: Language Arts (Grades K–3)

A Lesson on Phonics/Phonemic Awareness

Starting: Level 1

The teacher chooses a grade-appropriate storybook that contains words that contain consonant clusters such as /spr/, /str/, /sch/, etc., then instructs the students to clap their hands when they hear these sounds.

Emerging: Level 2

The teacher distributes pictures of, for example, nouns contained in the book such as sheep, ship, string, and school and instructs the students to show the pictures when they hear these words.

Developing: Level 3

The teacher selects students to act out verbs using present continuous tense found in the story (i.e., those that end with *ing*, such as sleeping, drinking, jumping, strolling, etc.).

Expanding: Level 4

The teacher selects students to repeat key words in the story after him or her, such as golden, goose, chicken, etc.

Bridging: Level 5

The teacher divides the class into three groups; each group echo-reads selected dialogues in the story.

Listening Activities in a Multiple-Leveled Group: Language Arts (Grades 6–8)

A Lesson on Synonyms, Antonyms, Metaphors, and Similes

Starting: Level 1

Students read a grade-appropriate multicultural book. They are asked to locate illustrations that depict words that are similar (synonyms) or different (antonyms) than the ones in the book. For instance, the highlighted words are big, tall, and happy.

Emerging: Level 2

Students are asked to match oral phrases involving figures of speech or idioms with visual representation of the meanings of these phrases, such as "as sweet as honey," "sitting on top of the world," "hit the hay," and "pulling my leg."

Developing: Level 3

Students listen to figures of speech in an oral discourse (e.g., poetry) and identify them or demonstrate comprehension through illustration (e.g., "sweet as a rose," "warm as a toast," "soft as silk").

Expanding: Level 4

Students role-play scenes that they hear in oral discourse involving figures of speech, such as "dead as a doornail," "busy as a bee," and "happy as a king."

Bridging: Level 5

Students provide other examples of figures of speech that have the same meaning as the ones they hear embedded in the oral discourse (e.g., for "You are my sunshine," the response may be, "You light up my life").

Listening Activities in a Multiple-Leveled Group: Language Arts (Grades 9–12)

A Lesson on Bias, Author's Perspective, and Points of View

Starting: Level 1

Students listen to a TV interview of a celebrity and identify and check off topics discussed in the interview.

Emerging: Level 2

Students listen to a brief talk about a celebrity containing false and true statements. With a partner, students identify and circle the true statements.

Developing: Level 3

Students view and listen to several TV commentators talking about a celebrity, such as Tiger Woods. With partners, students compare and contrast points of view presented by these commentators and state their own points of view.

Expanding: Level 4

Students work in groups to put together their own visually supported conclusions that concur with or refute other people's perspectives on news of a particular celebrity.

Bridging: Level 5

In groups, students conduct an impromptu rebuttal on a deduced stance based on the integration of information they heard from speakers in another group (e.g., topic of debate: Tiger Woods' doomed career).

In designing tasks, teachers should provide learners with opportunities to employ a flexible range of listening strategies. Teachers can have students listen to the same text several times, but each time students are asked to perform different tasks. For instance, in using the weather forecast, the first task may be to ask students to give the gist of the weather report. The second task may be to ask students to match the places that experience heavy rainfall. Finally, students might be required to listen for details, for example, the temperature in certain places and the expected percentage of possible rain in certain areas. Students should also be expected to be involved in reciprocal listening. This means that listeners are asked to take part in the interaction. Examples of such tasks may be to ask students to role-play a situation that will involve listening skills in the real world—answering the telephone, getting directions, or listening to classroom instructions.

Many books and articles address the techniques of teaching listening. An example is *New Ways of Teaching Listening*, a book edited by David Nunan and Lindsay Miller (1995), published by TESOL publishers. This text contains a series of classroom techniques that have been tried by teachers. Another good source for listening activities is the *Internet Journal*, which lists examples of activities and lesson plans.

Listening Comprehension Assessment

Besides formal tests, teachers can get a broad picture of their students' listening abilities by collecting data from other sources, such as self-assessment and student portfolios. Students can assess their own listening skills by responding to a self-assessment sheet that teachers create according to certain criteria. The following table is an example of a self-assessment sheet:

	☺	☺	☹
1. I understand most of what I hear.			
2. I understand some of what I hear.			
3. I understand very little of what I hear.			

Teachers can develop a portfolio system in which students' work based on listening tasks can be included. Over a period of nine weeks in which students have completed many listening tasks, teachers can request students to put their best work in their portfolio. An example of a listening task can be as simple as an activity called Blind Drawing. Teachers can describe a simple picture to the students while they draw what they hear. Students can also be paired up to do this activity, each taking turns to give the description. A little more complex activity is "What's this segment about?" After deciding on certain language objectives, such as the use of adjectives or nouns, teachers show the first three minutes of a movie, television commercial, or cartoons, without any visuals, just the sound (cover the monitor screen with a cloth). Then students are asked to define or list the items they heard. They play the segment again, this time with sound and images. The students are asked to compare their answers to the items they saw in the segment.

Douglas (1988) called for listening tests that are integrative and integrated, that are conceptualized, and that challenge learners to deal with a variety of listening tasks and conditions. Some forms of listening comprehension assessment are checklists that teachers can create to assess specific listening skills. For instance, students are assessed for their comprehension of phoneme change in minimal pairs such as /pin/ and /bin/; rising and falling intonation (He's gone out); or stress on words that signal a change in meaning of the same statement (She scolded him). Another form of listening comprehension is through the use of anecdotal reports in which teachers observe students' behaviors when they have a face-to-face conversation. By observing students' facial expressions, gestures, and one- or two-word responses, teachers are able to assess their listening skills.

Several prominent professional ESOL organizations offer interpretations of what English language learners should be able to do at each language proficiency level. Teachers can plan for differentiated instruction and appropriately leveled assessments by logging into the sites that offer descriptors and vetted Common Cores Standards. Recently, the World-class Instructional Design and Assessment (WIDA) consortium has developed *Can Do*

Descriptors which ESL teachers can use to assist general education (mainstream) teachers about differentiated instruction for English language learners (ELLs). These descriptors can be used for guiding lesson planning or determining students' language progress.

The WIDA English Language Learner Can Do Booklets for PreK–Kindergarten, Grades 1–2, 3–5, 6–8, and 9–12 are available for free download or for purchase.

https://www.wida.us/standards/CAN_DOs/

Another resource for classroom instruction, assessment, and theoretical frameworks for ELLs in the classroom can be found at the TESOL (Teachers of English to Speakers of Other Languages) International organization.

http://www.tesol.org/advance-the-field/standards/prek–12-english-language-proficiency-standards

TESOL was first established in 1964 and has been a great international resource for teachers of English learners.

Considerations in selecting suitable passages for listening comprehension tests are just as important as the task. Teachers should evaluate the level of the materials to the desired difficulty, interest, and relevance. Difficulty also resides in text, interaction of text variables with tasks, background knowledge, memory, and inferencing ability. When using authentic, unedited passages for lower-ability examinees, teachers should look for passages that are more "listener friendly"—those closer to the spoken language than to the written language.

Points to Remember

- ❖ Listening is the ability to identify and understand what others are saying.

- ❖ An able listener is capable of understanding a speaker's accent or pronunciation, grammar, and vocabulary and meaning.

- ❖ Factors that influence a listener's listening skills are interest in topic, listener's background knowledge of topic, and the ability to use negotiation skills.

- ❖ Listening skills involve two types of cognitive processing: top-down and bottom-up. Top-down processing refers to a listener's global understanding of the message, whereas bottom-up processing involves the interpretation of the message through analysis of the smaller components of the language, such as sounds and words.

- ❖ Teachers should be aware that students' knowledge of phonology, syntax, morphology, and semantics in L2 are activated through listening to produce speech.

- ❖ One of the many problems faced by English language learners is their lack of attention span. Because they cannot understand the message, it is inevitable that their attention to the speaker is rather short.

- ❖ Listening skills should be an integral part of all lessons in the class.

- ❖ Alternative assessments for listening comprehension, such as a student portfolio, should be used in addition to formal standardized tests.

English Language Oral Development and Instruction

KEY ISSUES

❖ Research on oral communication skills

❖ English language learners' difficulties in speaking

❖ Strategies/skills for speaking

❖ Techniques for teaching speaking at multiple levels

❖ Techniques for correcting errors

Ms. Santos, a third grade teacher, begins her lesson every morning by using a "hook"—an activity that piques her students' curiosity about the lesson. She uses these activities in rotation: poetry reading, songs, riddles, choral reading of multicultural literature books, picture-file activity, TPR overhead transparency, and games. Several of her students are English language learners. When she introduces her lesson with a song, she first pronounces all the words in the song slowly and clearly. Then her students echo-read the song's script with her. After they have read the song's script, Ms. Santos plays the song, and the students will sing along. She then discusses the meaning of some of the words in the song using pictures, TPR, and realia. She then focuses on the concepts and lexical items in the song that correspond to the lesson. For instance, in the rainforest lesson, she uses the "Rainforest Song," and the children sing this song to the tune of "If You're Happy and You Know It." She highlights concepts and vocabulary from the lesson such as *emergent, canopy, understory,* and **forest floor**. Students enunciate the words in the song, give word definitions, match pictures to vocabulary, and then reflect on their learning process by writing and illustrating in their journal. At the end of the thematic lesson, students take their journals home to share with their families.

Ms. Santos likes to use games as a culminating activity in her lessons. Today she uses a game called "Passing a Parcel" for a lesson on adjectives. Ms. Santos puts her students in a circle and asks them to describe a picture that she shows them. The first student who starts the game describes what she sees in the picture and then passes the picture to the student sitting next to her. The next student repeats the earlier student's statement and adds her or his own statement to it. So, Cathy looks at the picture in front of her and says, "I see a red ball on the beach," and passes the picture to Tim, who then says, "Cathy sees a red ball on the beach, and I see the blue ocean." Kim Huh continues with "Cathy sees a red ball on the beach, Tim sees the blue ocean, and I see the golden sand." This activity is completed when every student has a chance to come up with a statement that describes the given picture and also repeats the prior statements made by the other students.

How do these activities promote English language learners' oral language development?

These activities are great oral language development activities for English language learners (ELL) at various language proficiency levels because they give them the opportunities to not only use spoken English with their teachers and peers, but also to use English at their ability level to describe the pictures in the picture file activity; when singing songs, they also gain the opportunity to listen to and repeat words and phrases made by their teachers and peers. In addition to working with English sounds, rhythms, and stress patterns, teachers can also use these fun yet informative activities to help ELLs overcome the phonological and grammatical interference problems they may have.

Introduction

English language learners (ELLs) may come from homes that have provided them with a rich oral language environment, and certainly a firm background in the home language is a strong indicator of eventual success in learning another language (Collier & Thomas, 1999/2000; Cummins, 1980, 1981). However, at times these students do not bring a well-developed language background from their first or second language to school; therefore, teachers should offer students a rich and meaningful classroom environment with ample opportunities to develop their oral language. Students' presence within the classroom for more than eight hours a day should predispose them with the opportunities to develop their oral language. How, then, should a classroom that promotes oral language development look? To answer this question, teachers first have to understand and believe that oral language provides the foundation for literacy development (Cummins, 1981). ELLs who lack oral language skills are not only at a disadvantage among their peers, but this is also an obstacle to their future literary learning efforts (Wells, 1986). So, what are the important skills in oral language development? Speaking and listening skills. This chapter focuses only on speaking skills. Speaking is an interactive process of constructing meaning that involves producing, receiving, and processing information (Brown, 1994; Burns & Joyce, 1997). Speaking requires that learners not only know how to produce specific points of language such as grammar, pronunciation, or vocabulary (linguistic competence), but also that they

understand when, why, and in what ways to produce language (sociolinguistic competence). Speech has its own skills, structures, and conventions that are different from written language (Burns & Joyce, 1997; Carter & McCarthy, 1995; Cohen, 1996). To succeed in a given speech, a speaker synthesizes both the linguistic and sociolinguistic competence skills.

Research on Oral Communication Skills

Rivers (1981) reported that outside the classroom, listening is used twice as often as speaking, which is used twice as much as reading and writing. Inside the classroom, speaking and listening are the most often-used skills (Brown, 1994). Although they are recognized both by teachers and students as critical for functioning in an English language context, the teaching of speaking and listening has often been described as "the Cinderella of language teaching" (i.e., she never got to the ball) (Nunan & Miller, 1995). The teaching of speaking and listening has always taken a back seat in the teaching of the four language skills (listening, speaking, reading, and writing).

Spoken language has two main functions: transactional and interactional. The primary goal of the transactional function of oral language is transference of information, and it is message oriented (Brown & Yule, 1983). The speaker's purpose is to convey his message. Primarily, transactional spoken language is used to get work done in the real world: for instance, an employer giving instructions to employees, a teacher explaining math concepts to students, a patient discussing her symptoms with a doctor, or a child telling Santa Claus what she wants for Christmas. In all these situations, the speaker's purpose in communicating to listeners is to make their message clear so that they will not be misunderstood, which causes both speakers and listeners to be frustrated. When the message is the reason for speaking, the message must be understood. So, speakers usually (painstakingly) make themselves understood through repetition or rephrasing of their message.

The primary goal of interactional spoken language is to maintain social relationships, and therefore, it is listener oriented. Many social interactions seem to contain interactional content where the purpose of communication is to be nice to the listener. Most people spend a great deal of time chatting, and interactional chats are frequently characterized by shifting topics and a great deal of agreement on them. Two speakers conducting interactional speech should end up feeling comfortable with each other and friendly. We find speakers in these exchanges do not usually disagree with each other and do not argue, so the exchange does not require repetition of what was said. The listener might nod his head even if he does not hear what the speaker is saying. Interactional spoken language usually contains more generalized vocabulary and sparse information-packing. Most interactional chats contain greetings and farewells and a great deal of expression of opinion. Participants take turns leading the conversation.

Within spoken language, it is also important to understand "short turns" and "long turns" (Brown & Yule, 1983). A short turn consists of one or two utterances; a long turn consists of a string of utterances that may be as long as an hour's lecture. Short turns obviously demand much less of a speaker in the way of producing structures.

Consider the following conversation as an example of short turn:

Mario: Pokemon and Power Rangers + did you +

Jim: Pokemon + Power Rangers?

Mario: Do you like—

Jim: They are all right

Mario: My favorite is Pokemon + but I like the Power Rangers too + it's fun!

Jim: Do you like SpongeBob? + I love to watch SpongeBob—it's the best!

Mario: Yeah, SpongeBob is funny, that's one of my favorite cartoon shows too.

The primary interactional conversation among the two third grade boys consists of swapping turns. The longest of these short turns consists only of statements that contain additional information: Yeah, SpongeBob is funny, that's one of my favorite cartoon shows too. Compare this to what is needed to summarize the content of a book or your medical history to your doctor—it is obvious that what is needed in long turns is considerably more demanding than what is required of a speaker in a short turn. When a speaker takes the floor for a long turn, she or he takes responsibility for constructing a structured sequence of utterances to help listeners construct a coherent mental representation of what she or he is trying to say (Brown & Yule, 1983). What the speaker says must be structured coherently. She or he must speak clearly and specify any relevant properties before moving on to saying what happened. If the speaker is retelling a story, he or she must specify the main characters in the story and clearly recount the sequence of events in the correct order.

Consider the following long turn in the retelling of *Three Little Pigs and the Big Bad Wolf* by Maria, a third grade ELL:

Maria: Once upon a time, there were /tree/ little pigs and one big wolf. Eh . . . They lived in the eh . . . lot of trees, bosque, forest? First pig live in a /estraw/ house and the wolf came and blow his house down. The wolf said, huff and a puff and blow the house down. Then, the wolf go to the second pig house. He live in a wood house and the wolf huff and puff and blow his house down too. And then, the wolf go to the third pig house . . . and this pig live in /estone/ house, eh a more better house. The big bad wolf huffed and puffed but the house did not blow off because it was a more strong house. The pig came down the tube in the house? and the wolf died in eh . . . hot, aqua ebullicion, eh water hot? The End.

Models of Spoken Language

It is obviously easier to provide models of good written language than to do so with spoken language. Even though we oftentimes see teachers who expect students to provide complete sentences, we find that native spoken language obviously reflects the "performance" end of the competence-performance distinction. It reveals so many slips of tongue, errors, incomplete utterances, speaking in the here-and-now under pressure of time, and comparing what the speaker is saying now to what he just said to what he is trying to say later. Therefore, students should not be overly corrected when they produce partial sentences or incomplete phrases of the sort produced by native speakers. When nonnative speakers listen to native speakers, they hear language that is produced spontaneously, and they then realize that the speakers in this foreign language talk like human beings, and it is similar to talk in their native language. Native speakers do not produce ideal strings of complete, perfectly formed sentences; they use language manipulatively, explanatorily, to communicate with and make up what they say as they go along. Native speakers of English are perceived to speak perfect English when they address a public audience. Although nonnative speakers often simulate this type of perfect English, it is not appropriate when conducting a conversation.

Examine the following scenario in which an English learner communicates:

> Tan can walk into a shop that sells jeans, ask for a pair of jeans in excruciating English, and get rewarded; he walks out of the store with the jeans he wants. His same performance in his English class results in some sort of punishment—a low grade, a frown from his teacher and peers, and sometimes even a reprimand. It is of no surprise that some English language learners remain silent! Students realize that their teacher is not interested in what they have to say, but in how they say it.

By age three or four, children can communicate most of what they want to say. However, it is not until age eight that the majority of children achieve the ability to produce all the sounds of adult speech. Furthermore, it is not until around age ten that the speech of the majority of children reaches the syntactical level of adult speech. It is almost certain that English language learners will not reach the native level in their second language, at least not in class. A more realistic goal is to expect a functional ability to make themselves understood.

Why Is Speaking Difficult for English Language Learners?

Speech is somewhat like an iceberg: Most of the act of speaking is not directly observable. What we hear is the culmination of a series of five internal processes: (1) People's thoughts are an outgrowth of their feelings, desires, and needs. They have something to say and are motivated to communicate their thoughts to others. (2) Speech involves the conversion of thoughts to language. (3) The sounds, words, and forms used are stored in internal cognitive networks. (4) The speakers' competence is brought into play as they begin the conversion of thought to speech. (5) The listeners can hear the result, the performance skill, in action. In short, the speaker's cognitive networks contain the motivating force behind the thoughts, the content of speech, and the knowledge of the language system by means of which thoughts are converted into speech. All except the overt oral message itself are internal processes.

Learning to speak is obviously more difficult than learning to understand the spoken language. More effort is required on the part of the student. The entire process covers a greater period of time to develop than does listening comprehension and is more taxing on the students' energies. For English language learners, the act of speaking is a display of their competence of the second language, and not all their competence can be seen through their performance. One of the difficulties that English language learners face is the actual pronunciation of the sounds of the language. Lenneberg (1967), in his statement on the critical period hypothesis, forwarded the idea that at puberty the wiring of the brain is complete, and the muscles surrounding the vocal cord harden, both of which result in nonnative speakers' difficulty in pronouncing sounds with a nativelike accent. Second language learners who started learning a second language after puberty may not be able to produce nativelike pronunciation. A newborn has the ability to recognize all the universal sounds in any language, but the wiring of the brain for native language sounds occurs in the language environment in which that person grows up. When sounds from other languages are not reinforced, they will wilt away. This explains why some English language learners experience difficulty in producing sounds that are not present in their native language: examples are the /th/ and /sh/ sounds for Spanish speakers learning English and the rolling /r / sound in Spanish that English speakers may find difficult to produce. Spanish speakers of English will experience interference problems in producing English vowels because Spanish has only five vowels while English has fourteen vowel sounds and five diphthongs. For instance, /A/ sound in English yields two sounds: /e/ as in ate and /a/ as in after, whereas in Spanish /A/ is pronounced as /a/ as in *pluma*. Due to this difference, Spanish speakers of English may not produce the English vowels accurately, as they will use their L1 knowledge to pronounce these English vowel sounds.

Even though pronunciation is one of the many problems faced by English language learners, it is by far the least significant, because as long as speakers can communicate their meanings, some flaws in pronunciation will not prevent them from being understood. In fact, some speakers choose to retain their L1 accent when speaking English because of solidarity and identity issues. Perhaps the real difficulty faced by nonnative speakers of English is in the application of the grammatical rules they have learned. This is more apparent in adult learners of English, as they typically have the procedural knowledge of the target language (i.e., the "what" of the language but a limited opportunity to apply the knowledge in the actual performance of communicating in the language—the "how" of the language).

Many foreign students who come to the United States to further their studies perform better in reading and writing skills than they do in speaking and listening because they learned to read and write in English in their home countries, but lack oral communication skills due to limited opportunities to communicate in English. This lends to the discussion of accuracy versus fluency in oral communication. English language learners may attain a high level of accuracy in the production of the English language in situations in which they have enough time and knowledge to apply the rules they have learned. However, they may lack the natural flow to communicate in English because they have not attained the automaticity to communicate spontaneously in English, thereby disabling them from attaining fluency.

Krashen (1981) believes that when a learner acquires a language, he will attain fluency in the language, whereas a learner who learns a language may not attain the same level of fluency. Bialystok (1992) looked at fluency from the point of both a novice and an expert learner. The expert learner who knows how to juggle the constraints of a new language will be more fluent than the novice learner who is struggling to bring his new knowledge to bear. The concern to teachers in this issue of accuracy versus fluency is which is the more significant criteria to expect of learners. Teachers have to be aware of several factors that may influence students' fluency or accuracy in oral production. Some factors are students' personality and motivation. Extrovert learners will display fluency over accuracy because they are not inhibited about speaking, even though their oral production may not be accurate. Introvert learners may take their time about speaking in English for fear of being embarrassed by their ungrammatical English or mispronunciation of English words.

These language learners will overuse the language editor that Krashen (1981) described in his monitor model. Learners who are instrumentally motivated to learn English may only practice the use of the language in limited environments, perhaps only in the workplace or school, whereas learners who are integratively motivated to learn the language will practice using the target language more frequently and in wider dimensions—they want to learn English to integrate and feel they belong in the

English-speaking community. Teachers should not sacrifice students' attainment of fluency over accuracy; rather, they should allow students to develop both accuracy and fluency over time. They can help students to achieve the fluency goal by not overly correcting students' mistakes, and more importantly, they have to be mindful of the way they correct errors. Modeling correct language structures and rephrasing students' utterances in grammatically correct English will enable students to learn their mistakes in a less-threatening manner. By the same token, teachers can help students achieve the accuracy goal by not allowing students to continuously speak English with mistakes uncorrected; errors that are not corrected can be fossilized and become a part of learners' spoken and written English. In the next section, we will look at tools for developing oral language skills, but first let us examine the characteristics of learners at various levels of oral language proficiency.

English language learners progress in their acquisition of the target language in stages. As soon as they are in the target environment, they will be subjected to the forms and function of the language. Although at the beginning, or preproduction, level they are silent, they are still interacting with the target language. They are making sense of the new language by comprehending and internalizing what they see and hear around them. At this stage, they should not be forced to speak; however, they should be included in classroom instruction by doing tasks that are manageable and easily accomplished.

Teachers should be aware that newcomers vary in the duration of the silent period stage—some stay in this stage for about a week while others may take a few months. Teachers can make this transition into the new language less frustrating for learners by pairing them up with more proficient learners who can help them get around the class and school and also be successful in accomplishing their school work. Teachers should choose materials and design activities that meet students' language proficiency level. In the preproduction stage, teachers can put students in computer stations to utilize computer software, such as Rosetta Stone, that allows them to see and hear English spoken in a meaningful way.

By listening to English sounds and repeating them, students will move along in their acquisition stage—from the preproduction to the early production stage. At this stage, students begin to produce one or more words in English. Teachers should also paraphrase and use gestures, repetition, visuals, and acting out as means of communicating with students in a comprehensible way. Students can be included in class instruction and be made to feel that they belong by doing tasks such as drawing murals or by being a class helper or by helping teachers with chores around the class: distributing papers, cleaning the board, or compiling papers. When teachers engage students in these tasks, students will feel they are a part of the classroom and become motivated to interact and communicate in a meaningful way. Also, teachers should be mindful of the questioning techniques they use. Students at the preproduction stage can be asked to point at an object, nod their head, clap their hands—to do something to show their comprehension. They also can answer yes/no questions or questions for which they can provide a one- or two-word answer.

Students who have exited the silent stage and the early production stage will be able to produce multiple words in a more coherent structure. They are able to understand and speak English in face-to-face interactions, and they are less hesitant to speak. These students are at another stage of language proficiency: the speech emergence and the intermediate levels. At these levels, students are still developing their English language, and therefore, teachers will find students making grammatical errors, such as the third-person singular verb *he like* instead of *he likes*, and the nonuse of possessive form, such as *Mary bag* instead of *Mary's bag*. At this stage, teachers are cautioned not to jump on students' mistakes. Instead, they should celebrate students' accomplishments at producing the sounds of a new language and experimenting with the new language rules they are still juggling. Sometimes teachers' good intentions and overzealous manner in correcting students' mistakes may cause more harm than good. Students should not be corrected mid conversation because they will not be able to internalize the correction—these spoken mistakes are not concrete in nature. Rephrasing or modeling and repeating students' utterances with correct grammar will peripherally expose students to the correct form of the spoken language, and this is a better way of addressing students' developmental errors. Consequently, teachers should focus on correcting errors in a more concrete manner (i.e., through the written form). For example, students can be alerted to their errors of verb conjugation through their readings of stories that contain verb conjugations, or they can be asked to write sentences using verb conjugations.

At the speech emergence and intermediate stages, English language learners can produce phrases and short sentences. Students at the speech emergence stage will produce utterances that are telegraphic, whereas intermediate students will be able to engage in conversations more fluently, and they begin to develop more academic language. At both of these stages, teachers can present English language learners with more linguistically demanding tasks. They can be put in collaborative groups to solve problems, assume a speaking role in a class play, retell a story, and verbally share their native culture with the rest of the class. They can also be assigned to more challenging responsibilities such as being a buddy to a newly arrived student or running simple errands for teachers such as handing in papers to the office. Teachers may find students developing their English skills rather rapidly at this stage. Although students are displaying near native language abilities, teachers should continue using sheltering techniques and provide instructions that are comprehensible. Even though intermediate-level students are capable of understanding streams of verbal language, teachers should use graphic organizers, such as charts, visuals, diagrams, and realia to make learning more meaningful to students. Teaching strategies that match student learning styles by providing multiple representations of delivering content are helpful to learners. Teachers can engage learners in concrete experiences—learning by doing. Visual and kinesthetic learners will benefit by experiencing instructions that use pictures and diagrams, by role-play, and by creating a product. At this stage, teachers should also be aware of the different questioning techniques that they can use:

Students can be asked to read their journal entries that give their opinions about certain issues in a story, to tell a different ending to a story, to share their reasons for liking or disliking certain characters within a story, and so on.

In presenting the abilities of these English language learners who are in varying levels of language proficiency, the activity and task guidelines are by no means carved in stone or set in a rigid mold. Teachers should exercise their discretion on tasks and materials selection through their observation of their students' abilities. Some teachers may want to give students who are at the early production stage more challenging tasks than those prescribed as what they can do at their level of proficiency. For instance, instead of merely asking students to respond with yes or no, teachers ask them to respond with a simple sentence structure such as, "Yes, it is a dog." This is an acceptable initiative, as it puts into practice Krashen's input hypothesis—providing students with instruction that is I + 1—input that is a bit beyond their current level of proficiency.

Tools for Promoting Oral Language Development

Although oral language development is treated as a self-contained chapter in this book, it is important to note that all language skills—listening, speaking, reading, and writing—should be incorporated into English language learners' experience in the process of learning the new language. Although there are criticisms made about Krashen's (1981) acquisition versus learning hypothesis, in which he posits that learners who acquire the language will master the language better than the learners who learn the language, the practical application of his hypothesis is valuable. Teachers are encouraged to provide a natural environment in the classroom where English will be acquired. Teachers can achieve this goal by focusing on the most important elements in oral language development: comprehensible input and social interaction. By maintaining a routine classroom schedule, teachers are adding to the natural environment by providing a simulation of a real world workplace. Designating certain activities at a certain time, such as snack, lunch, journal response, and DEAR (drop everything and read), students are taught how to tell and manage time. In addition, by designing problem solving tasks that involve students working in collaboration, teachers provide real opportunities for English language learners to communicate and to practice using their newly learned language. Teachers who avoid using collaborative groups in their class because they have a low tolerance for noise may not realize that they have deprived English language learners of their only chance to communicate in English—many of these students go home to a non-English-speaking environment.

English language learners will have a better chance of learning English more rapidly when teachers incorporate new and innovative techniques that use English as a vehicle of communication. All learners, especially English language learners, will benefit from instruction that is fun and exciting and in a nonthreatening atmosphere. The next section discusses several ways to promote English language learners' oral language development. By no means is the following list exhaustive.

Explicit Teaching of Pronunciation Skills

Based on research findings on specific sounds that English language learners may have problems in producing, teachers can explicitly teach the production of these interference sounds. For example, Spanish speakers of English have difficulties in producing /th/ sound, /sh/ sound, and /u/ sound. They will substitute these sounds with their Spanish approximates such as /d/, /ch/, and /oo/. Teachers can use the knowledge of place of articulation, manner of articulation, and voicing for consonants. For example, the first sound in *think,* the /th/ sound, requires the tongue to be placed between the upper and lower teeth (interdental). For vowels, students can be made aware of the tongue and lip position. For instance, the vowel in *food* requires lip rounding, whereas, the vowel in *feet* does not. Pronunciation instruction is useful when it is used in meaningful and structured classroom communication.

Peer Tutoring

Peer tutoring, or a buddy system, is an effective tool that teachers can use. How is peer tutoring effective in teaching English to English language learners? In a peer tutoring setup, students receive individual attention. They also receive undivided attention as they read, spell, ask questions, and provide answers. Students are given sustained time to read and share their viewpoints. English language learners can practice conversational English while discussing academic English. They may find the buddy system structure less inhibiting and, thus, become more comfortable speaking up as compared with speaking up in front of the whole class.

Poetry

Poetry is yet another tool to help English language learners in developing their oral language skills. The benefits of poetry are obvious. Poetry is less intimidating because the short stanzas are easier and more manageable to memorize. The nature of reading poetry, which begs for reading and rereading, provides English language learners with ample opportunity to practice enunciating the words, and repetition promotes fluency. The rhythm, repetition, and rhyme of poetry facilitate students' comprehension of the meanings. The very nature of reciting poetry, first collectively and later individually, builds students' confidence in experimenting with their new language. Teachers can employ several strategies in using poetry in class. Teachers can model reading the poems aloud and then ask students to read the poem in unison. Some students who are at the early production stage can participate by repeating only certain stanzas. Teachers can divide the class up into two groups for "call and response method." In the "Sh, sh baby's sleeping" poem, one group can recite the first two lines while the other group can follow suit with the other lines. Singing poems that use music make the words more memorable. Poems can also be acted out in a form of a play. Many poems are easy to act out, and they do not require extensive preparation. This affords learners who have a kinesthetic learning style to maximize learning through acting out the poem. English language learners at the preproduction and early production stages can participate in this class activity because they can act out the poem.

Games

Games can be incorporated as a tool to help English language learners develop their oral language skills. Games, too, have obvious benefits for English language learners. They allow learners to practice what is taught in a fun way. Games allow learners to experiment with the English language in a nonthreatening way. Students learn what is taught in a hands-on way, and games will motivate learners with varying levels of proficiency to learn the new language without the burden of having been forced to learn language structures. Examples of games are card games, board games, simulation, and party-type games. An example of card games, "Happy Families," is inexpensive and is comprised of sets of four cards depicting various families. When all the cards are distributed, each student has to guess who has a member of the family he or she wants. Students then take turns asking for the particular family member they want. This game can be adapted to address any language feature, such as the reinforcement of question forms like "do, does, did," or it can be used for practicing telephone skills. Students are asked to role-play the act of answering the telephone. A student will ask for a particular member of the family by asking, "Is Phil home?" and the person answering the phone will have to say, "Sorry, Phil is not home," or, "Hold on, please." For ELLs at the preproduction stage, a concentration game can be utilized. Teachers gather a set of ten 8 × 10 picture pairs (fruits, animals, objects). Placing magnet strips behind these pictures will allow teachers to place them on the whiteboard. These pictures are scrambled and placed randomly on the board, and students are asked to pick one picture and guess where the pair is. This reinforces the recognition skill of the concept, and students can be taught to verbalize the sounds of these words (e.g., apple, orange, cat, dog, desk, book).

For intermediate learners, simulation games such as "Who Wants to Be a Millionaire?" or "Jeopardy" can be adapted for collaborative participation.

Students can be put in groups to make up questions, and the teacher chooses the questions to be used in the game. Students can take turns being the game host. Points are awarded to groups that answer the questions correctly. Small tokens can be given to the winning team. A very important point to note in using games is that they should be linked to syllabus concepts to be learned and must have a definite and purposeful place in lesson plans. Games that are effectively used in lessons reinforce students' learning of linguistic features and content area learning and are not just fillers of classroom time.

Songs

Songs are not meant for kindergartners and first graders only; songs should be used in higher grade levels, too. Teachers should make a point to allow students to sing at least one song a day. Songs should be used every day because songs make everyone feel alive and happy, and they usually bring laughter to learners. The repetitive and rhythmic nature of songs will reinforce learning of grammatical structures that may be difficult for learners. Teachers should choose songs that relate to students' interests. Today's younger students like hip-hop music—teachers can use the beat but should modify the lyrics to the linguistic or content features they are teaching. For example, learners have proven to be able to learn the names of the fifty states and their capitals by rapping them out.

Show-and-Tell

Children at all grade levels perform show-and-tell in different forms. Show-and-tell has been used by teachers for a long time to recognize students' individuality in the classroom. Students are asked to bring in their favorite toy or their favorite personal item to share with the class. Students welcome the notion of talking, sharing, and describing what they know best; therefore, motivation for oral language skills is high. This is an excellent way to open up pathways for newcomers to feel secure in their new environment as their identity and culture are being recognized. Younger English language learners and those at the preproduction and early production levels can be asked to give a one- or two-word description of the objects they bring in to share with the class. The adaptation of show-and-tell for these learners can be in the form of a game of twenty questions, wherein the learners answer questions raised by their peers. All they have to say is "yes" or "no" or provide a one-word answer. If students forget to bring items from home or may not have items to share, teachers can have them draw a picture to share with the class. The objective of show-and-tell is realized when students stand in front of the class communicating verbally with their peers. The oral language development in this form of communication is meaningful because learners receive immediate feedback verbally and nonverbally from their audience. The negotiation of meaning that takes place in such an activity presents real experience for English language learners to learn and develop their social, academic, and linguistic skills.

For intermediate learners, a variation of show-and-tell can be in the form of a poster display. Students can describe their posters on "how to save manatees," for instance. Students can work in pairs or groups to come up with slogans on how to save the manatees. Their posters can include artwork as well. Each team member is given time to explain the team's ideas to the class. Oral language development in such a task is seen at two levels: occurring when students work in their own group, brainstorming ideas and conversing with each other about an academic topic, and then taking it to another level in which they have to perform individually for a wider audience—the whole class. Therefore, show-and-tell is indeed a tool that works for students at various language proficiency levels because it draws on students' motivation to share with others what they know best—themselves, their possessions, or their creations. One of the most effective ways to promote oral language development, show-and-tell scaffolds learners' early speaking skills that start from their own comfort zone—their own world.

Recording Studio

Teachers can designate a small area in their class as a center for a recording studio where students take turns working on their oral language skills as they record their own voices. English language learners at preproduction or early production levels can be paired with learners at intermediate levels. Teachers can assign specific tasks for them to work on; for example, learners can recreate their own stories from looking at wordless books or cartoon strips. More advanced learners can work on retelling of stories from their favorite books and providing a different plot or ending to the stories. Here, the purpose of the activity is clear: Learners are expected to complete a task that piques their interest and motivation. As the pair works on meeting a common resolution to put on tape, both students are communicating with each other meaningfully as they examine the task at hand. The bonus point of this activity is when teachers can take the audiotape home to hear and evaluate their students' oral language skills. They can also use it in class for a listening comprehension activity. Children welcome and enjoy different ways of learning that involve anything other than filling in worksheets, so this activity can also serve as a reward for good behavior.

Riddles and Jokes

Riddles and jokes can be a lot of fun for learners. Riddles can be used in a closure activity within a lesson in which students are asked to find answers for riddles that involve their new knowledge on the subject they have just learned. Florida Atlantic University student teachers were observed using a book that exclusively contains riddles about spiders. It was a wonderful culminating activity of their thematic unit in which riddles were used as a form of assessment. Children were encouraged to discuss in their groups the answers to the riddles.

Similarly, jokes give students and teachers a break from the monotony of a routine day's work. Teachers must consider their students' ages and cultural backgrounds when sharing jokes. More proficient learners can be asked to share their own jokes with the class. Riddles and jokes help promote English language learners' oral language development in a fun and nonthreatening way, enhancing learners' use of the spoken English language at varying functional levels.

Choral Reading

Just as the term suggests, choral reading involves participation from everybody. Remember when you were asked to sing the chorus of a song? Wasn't it fun to hear the booming sound of everyone's voices? Of course, the best part of choral reading is even if you do not know the words of the song or the passage, you can fake it by following the words a split second after the other people have spoken them out loud. Choral reading is a valuable tool for oral language development, especially for beginning English language learners. They are placed in a non-threatening situation where they are not forced to perform before they are ready for an individual performance. This activity allows them to hear the pronunciation and intonation of the English language spoken by their peers as they repeat after them. Research indicates that choral reading helps children learn the intonation of English stories and improves their diction and fluency (Bradley & Thalgott, 1987). Choral reading also raises the enthusiasm and builds confidence of early readers (Stewig, 1981) and helps expand their vocabulary (Samson, Allen, & Sampson, 1990). Choral reading can be made more interesting by having students act out certain parts of the reading. Teachers can divide the class into different groups; each group assumes different responsibilities. Some groups can narrate the story by choral reading while others pantomime parts of the narrated story. This activity can be suitable for themes such as "Thanksgiving." Levels and complexity of the activity can be increased by using props and costumes in the dramatization of the choral-read story.

Television, Videotapes, and CD-ROMs

The use of technology such as television, videotape recorders, and computers in most classrooms is no longer a luxury but a necessity. With the advent of technology, television and videotape recorders and computers are easily accessible to teachers in classrooms. From time to time, teachers show students a movie as a means of a reward for good behavior. Teachers can incorporate oral language development activities into their lesson objective by showing students snippets of the movie without the sound. Students work in pairs or groups to create the dialogue of the scenes they have just seen. This activity enables students to interact with what they see in addition to watching the movie. Low-proficiency level learners can be paired up with more-proficient learners or they can be asked to identify the characters or story line by circling pictures and words. Learners can take part in choosing the movies they want to watch. An extension of this activity would be a script-writing task and dramatization of scenes of a homemade class movie; teachers can videotape their own class staging a play. Adaptations of using television and videotape or CDs are numerous. Teachers can explore current affairs by letting students watch news or documentary programs and engaging students in discussions of current happenings around the world. Activities using this technology provide English language learners with ample opportunities to develop and enhance their oral language skills. Picture a class busy at work. Students are talking and doing meaningful tasks that interest them. They are involved in a fun activity without even realizing that they are actually learning! Teachers have motivated their students to learn!

Oral Language Development in Language Arts and Content Area Instruction

Content area teachers in middle and high schools and elementary school teachers should include language skill objectives in their content area lessons. These teachers should teach to two objectives: content and language. Let us examine the development of English learners' oral language development in the following instructions: language arts, math, science, and social studies.

Language Arts

Cluster 1: Comprehension and Collaboration

Standard Code	Standard
LAFS.1.SL.1.1	Participate in collaborative conversations with diverse partners about grade 1 topics and texts with peers and adults in small and larger groups.
	a. Follow agreed-upon rules for discussions (e.g., listening to others with care, speaking one at a time about the topics and texts under discussion).
	b. Build on others' talk in conversations by responding to the comments of others through multiple exchanges.
	c. Ask questions to clear up any confusion about the topics and texts under discussion.
	Cognitive Complexity: Level 2: Basic Application of Skills & Concepts
LAFS.1.SL.1.2	Ask and answer questions about key details in a text read aloud or information presented orally or through other media.
	Cognitive Complexity: Level 2: Basic Application of Skills & Concepts
LAFS.1.SL.1.3	Ask and answer questions about what a speaker says in order to gather additional information or clarify something that is not understood.
	Cognitive Complexity: Level 2: Basic Application of Skills & Concepts

Cluster 2: Presentation of Knowledge and Ideas

Standard Code	Standard
LAFS.1.SL.2.4	Describe people, places, things, and events with relevant details, expressing ideas, and feelings clearly.
	Cognitive Complexity: Level 2: Basic Application of Skills & Concepts
LAFS.1.SL.2.5	Add drawings or other visual displays to descriptions when appropriate to clarify ideas, thoughts, and feelings.
	Cognitive Complexity: Level 2: Basic Application of Skills & Concepts
LAFS.1.SL.2.6	Produce complete sentences when appropriate to task and situation.
	Cognitive Complexity: Level 2: Basic Application of Skills & Concepts

Courtesy of Florida Department of Education accessed through www.cpalms.org.

The above are speaking and listening standards for first grade. The following are example activities for linking and incorporating speaking skills in language arts lessons. This particular example is geared toward developing English language skills in first grade. These sample activities correlate with the above-mentioned Florida Sunshine State Standards.

Beginning Speaking Activities: Recognition and pronunciation of key words

Objective: Auditory discrimination and oral production of intonation/stress patterns in spoken English.

Procedure: Choose students' favorite story books to do this activity. Select ten to fifteen key words (depending on your class level). Draw the pictures of these words and cut them out. Place a popsicle stick on each picture cut-out. Distribute them to selected students (beginners, intermediate, advanced). The teacher will read the book and when she pronounces these ten to fifteen selected key words, students with the picture cut-outs will raise them and show the class. Make the student with the picture cut-out pronounce the key word first and then the rest of the class will echo. Do a couple rereadings and distribute the picture cut outs to the other students. Teachers may want to repeat this activity until all students get a chance to participate. This activity also helps teachers to observe and assess ELLs' ability to recognize and pronounce challenging English words.

Intermediate Speaking Activities: Charades/hidden items

Objective: Oral production to describe individual items or actions.

Charade Procedure: Team members guess who/what the teacher (or another student) is silently role-playing (e.g., a bird, playing soccer, eating noodles, etc). The team that guesses correctly gets a point.

Hidden items: Ten to fifteen items are placed in a closed bag. Choose a student to pick one item from the bag, at a time. The student may also be blindfolded for this activity. First, the student should provide a description of the item, e.g. soft, hard, round, sharp, etc. Then he/she will give the answer by saying the name of the item, such as an apple, a pencil, a teddy bear, etc. For advanced level students, ask them to generate a sentence using the word, e.g., I eat an apple every day.

Advanced Speaking Activity: Ten Questions

Objective: Ask oral questions about a photo or picture, or what students are thinking.

Procedure: A student from one team selects a specific item in a picture without showing it to the members of the teams. For instance, in a picture of a farm house with animals, hay, barn, farmer, tress, etc., the student chooses one item from the picture, e.g., a horse. Teams take turns asking yes/no questions. The picture holder can only answer yes or no. Points are awarded based on the number of guesses

that the team makes. For example, if the team guess correctly on the first try, it will get ten points; if the team guesses correctly after six tries, it will receives four points (ten to six), etc.

Although the picture holder only answers yes or no, the other team members use complex questioning techniques that ELLs at an advanced level are able to accomplish. The teacher can model and then expect students to use specific questioning format, focusing on particular grammar and vocabulary items in the lesson.

Math

Although math is considered a universal language, ELLs can experience difficulties in learning mathematical language in English, which includes unique vocabulary, sentence structure, semantic properties, and text structures, both oral and written. For instance, ELLs who are familiar with the concepts of addition, subtraction, and multiplication will be able to do the numerical problems but may not understand the different terminology used to describe the addition and subtraction operations. Even though learners who have developed these math concepts in their native language transfer their academic skills from L1 to English, they must still relabel these concepts using English words. For example, several words can be used for the addition operation, such as add, plus, increase by, the sum of, or more than, which English language learners may not realize are synonyms. Therefore, content area teachers should help learners expand their vocabulary and understand the English language structure to enable them to solve word problems. In achieving this objective, the language objective teachers can engage students in collaborative groups to solve word problems—teachers can put students in pairs and use a cooperative learning structure of think-pair-share to solve word problems. Students can create their own word problems by discussing their ideas and writing them down so other students can solve the word problems they have created. Competitive games can be played in teams; the teacher creates word problems, and students compete to solve them. Teachers can model think-aloud protocol by showing students how to think through math problems by verbalizing their thoughts while solving their math problems. There are many activities (some of which were mentioned earlier) that teachers can incorporate into their math lessons, including concrete objects, the use of manipulatives, diagrams, charts, and tables, as well as activities that involve students in the act of speaking out and using their spoken English to communicate with peers and solve the math problems.

Science

Science is another content area that contains cognitively demanding oral language uses. As in teaching math, teachers should have two lesson objectives for teaching science: content objectives and language objectives. The process-oriented inquiry approach (Kessler & Quinn, 1987) is one of the teaching strategies that teachers can use to teach science. In this approach, students work in pairs or groups to define a problem, state a hypothesis, gather data, record observations, draw conclusions relating data to hypothesis, and explain and summarize findings. Academic language is used to convey the thinking involved in observing, classifying, comparing, measuring and inferring, predicting, and synthesizing and summarizing. English learners' motivation to learn science is high as they investigate real science problems that engage their natural curiosity. They are involved in hands-on activities in solving their science problems, and most importantly for oral language development, they talk to other students when carrying out the investigation. Look into this class where Ms. Evans is teaching a science lesson on the basic needs of all living things, using the scientific inquiry:

Ms. Evans teaches the concept of the eating habits of two types of whales: baleen and toothed. Students use combs and chopsticks to simulate the eating habits of these two types of whales. Students also make their own whale and act out a poem using their whale. Students listen to a story called "The Whale Song" and engage in a class discussion on whales' basic needs. Ms. Evans' science lesson, which is rich in oral language activities, is conducive to oral language development.

Figure 18-1 displays the framework for Classroom Instruction and Assessment for English Language Proficiency Standard 4: English language learners communicate information, ideas, and concepts necessary for academic success in the content area of science.

Social Studies

Opportunities for oral language development in social science studies are abundant. Usually the main mode of information delivery is aural–oral—teachers lecture and students listen and take notes from the lecture. This is perhaps the most difficult way of comprehending instruction for ELLs, because understanding academic lectures, according to Cummins (1981), is a cognitively demanding task in which context is highly reduced. Visual aids such as pictures, graphs, time lines, flowcharts, and gestures are crucial in the presentation of highly academic discourse to ELLs. There are ample oral language development activities that teachers can utilize when presenting social studies subjects such as historical or political events. Reenactments or simulations and

FIGURE 18-1	Classroom Instruction and Assessment for English Language Proficiency Standard 4				
Domain	Level 1 Entering	Level 2 Beginning	Level 3 Developing	Level 4 Expanding	Level 5 Bridging
Speaking	Create and present collages or depictions of **scientific** issues.	Brainstorm ideas based on illustrations of **scientific** issues that affect everyday life (e.g., "What are some examples of pollution?").	Describe ways in which **scientific** issues can be resolved (e.g., "How can we reduce pollution?").	Discuss pros and cons of **scientific** issues using graphic organizers.	Engage in debates on **scientific** issues (such as genetic engineering, nuclear energy).

Source: Peregoy and Boyle (1990)

debates can be incorporated easily into social science lessons. Students can role-play important historic and political leaders and discuss issues pertaining to the topics they are studying. Social science inquiry should be encouraged; students can survey, interview, and observe their own communities and families when researching key concepts such as racism and prejudice in the 1950s.

Teachers need to find ways to present the content through the use of visuals, dramatizations, and other multimedia. They also should use some innovative ways of increasing students' oral language performance using the academic language.

Look into Ms. Wagner's first grade class, which is studying how individuals, ideas, and events can influence history:

The class is learning about the space program (NASA) and the people who have influenced it. Students learn what a space shuttle is and describe what happens when it is launched. They will be able to explain the notable figures in the space program. Students work at computer stations in pairs doing research on notable astronauts using preselected sites. Students discuss their findings with each other. They are then asked to compile a fact sheet about these astronauts to use in a game of "twenty questions" played at the end of this activity. The class will ask each team about its own astronaut.

This lesson is lively and interesting, with plenty of speaking opportunities for ELLs.

Oral Language Assessment

There are several ways to assess ELLs' oral language in the classroom. Teachers can use the Student Oral Language Observation Matrix (SOLOM) (Peregoy & Boyle, 2008), observation checklists, and anecdotal observations. The five focused language traits within SOLOM are comprehension, fluency, vocabulary, grammar, and pronunciation. In using observation checklists, teachers can develop their own lists of oral language behaviors to focus on, such as conversational interactions, presentational skills, vocabulary, and particular grammatical structures. Anecdotal observations contain on-the-spot assessment of students' oral language performance during classroom activities. These assessment techniques allow teachers to evaluate ELLs' use of spoken English in the social contexts of the classroom. The next section explores each of the three assessments in greater detail.

Student Oral Language Observation Matrix

The use of student oral language observation matrix (SOLOM) is more personal than using standardized and commercialized tests such as the Language Assessment Scales (LAS) in assessing students' progress. SOLOM can be used intermittently over a period of time to chart students' progress in their oral language. It gives teachers a much closer look at their students' improvements in specific areas of the spoken language. Although the evaluation made by teachers using SOLOM is subjective, its frequent use sensitizes teachers to analytical linguistic dimensions, making evaluations of students' progress accurate and meaningful. The beauty of using SOLOM lies in its function. SOLOM allows teachers to observe students communicating in real life contexts. Teachers should use SOLOM to observe students' participation in classroom presentations, students' discussions of ideas with peers in collaborative groups, students' conferences with teachers, and students' performance of routine classroom activities. As a result, teachers are able to truly evaluate their ELLs' oral language progress in authentic contexts within the classroom, which makes oral language assessment more meaningful.

Refer to Figure 18-2 for an explanation of how to use SOLOM. Each trait (i.e., comprehension, fluency, vocabulary, pronunciation, grammar) receives a rating from one to five, according to the descriptors. After placing a check on the appropriate descriptors, the scorer tallies the ratings of all five traits. Once the numeric score is obtained, it is matched to the phases of English language proficiency: Phase I, 5–11, non-English proficient; Phase II, 12–18, limited English proficient; Phase III, 19–24, limited English proficient; and Phase IV, 25, fully English proficient. Teachers should record their conversation with an ELL, and then listen and analyze the taped conversation using SOLOM to evaluate and comment on the student's oral language skill.

FIGURE 18-2 SOLOM: Student Oral Language Observation Matrix

A Comprehension	1 Cannot be said to understand even simple conversation.	2 Has great difficulty following what is said. Can comprehend only "social conversation" spoken slowly and with frequent repetitions.	3 Understands most of what is said at slower-than-normal speed with repetitions.	4 Understands nearly everything at normal speed, although occasional repetition may be necessary.	5 Understands everyday conversation and normal classroom discussions without difficulty.
B Fluency	Speech is so halting and fragmentary as to make conversation virtually impossible.	Usually hesitant; often forced into silence by language limitations.	Speech in everyday conversation and classroom discussion frequently disrupted by the student's search for the correct manner of expression.	Speech in everyday conversation and classroom discussions generally fluent, with occasional lapses while the student searches for the correct manner of expression.	Speech in everyday conversation and classroom discussions fluent and effortless, approximating that of a native speaker.
C Vocabulary	Vocabulary limitations so extreme as to make conversation virtually impossible.	Misuse of words and very limited vocabulary; comprehension quite difficult.	Student frequently uses the wrong words; conversation somewhat limited because of inadequate vocabulary.	Student occasionally uses inappropriate terms and/or must rephrase ideas because of lexical inadequacies.	Use of vocabulary and idioms approximates that of a native speaker.
D Pronunciation	Pronunciation problems so severe as to make speech virtually unintelligible.	Very hard to understand because of pronunciation problems. Must frequently repeat to make himself or herself understood.	Pronunciation problems necessitate concentration on the part of the listener and occasionally lead to misunderstanding.	Always intelligible, though one is conscious of a definite accent and occasional inappropriate intonation patterns.	Pronunciation and intonation approximate that of a native speaker.
E Grammar	Errors in grammar and word order so severe as to make speech virtually unintelligible.	Grammar and word-order errors make comprehension difficult. Must often rephrase and/or restrict himself or herself to basic patterns.	Makes frequent errors of grammar and word order that occasionally obscure meaning.	Occasionally makes grammatical and/or word-order errors that do not obscure meaning.	Grammatical usage and word order approximate that of a native speaker.

SOLOM PHASES: Phase I: Score 5–11 = non-English proficient; Phase II: Score 12–18 = limited English proficient; Phase III: Score 19–24 = limited English proficient; Phase IV: Score 25 = fully English proficient.

Based on your observation of the student, indicate with an "X" across the block in each category that best describes the student's abilities. The SOLOM should only be administered by persons who themselves score at level "4" or above in all categories in the language being assessed. Students scoring at level "1" in all categories can be said to have no proficiency in the language.

Source: Courtesy of California State Department of Education.

Anecdotal Observations and Checklists

Anecdotal observations and checklists are more open-ended forms of evaluating students' oral language performance. Refer to Figure 18-3 for an example of a checklist and Figure 18-4 for an example of an anecdotal observation. Teachers can include their own specific evaluation needs in these assessment tools. They can adapt and modify the checklist and anecdotal models to suit their own goals and the objectives of their programs. These two assessment tools present teachers with a blank page that will take practice and training to fill. Nevertheless, teachers have the advantage of expounding on their observations of students' on-the-spot oral language skills without being constrained to other people's criteria. Both of these forms focus on the participant structures or interaction patterns; therefore, these forms are best used during group work or observations of students' daily classroom routine of getting their work done. Each form contains language functions such as informal talk, reporting, discussing, debating, and reflecting, which allow teachers to look for appropriate use of language. They also contain linguistic elements that display ELLs' progress in English phonology, morphology, syntax, and semantics. The checklist form is used in a slightly different way. Teachers jot down their observations of students who are at these levels of language proficiency: beginning, intermediate, and advanced. The anecdotal form is more of a running record of the entire interaction.

In all the oral language assessment mentioned, the key point for teachers to note is that the use of a task-based approach should possess some constancy of elicitation input. Every student is assessed on the same learned concepts. Teachers can use the following task types to elicit spoken English:

1. Static relationships
   a. Describing an object or photograph
   b. Instructing someone to draw a diagram
   c. Instructing someone on how to assemble a piece of equipment
   d. Describing/instructing how a number of objects are to be arranged
   e. Giving route directions
2. Dynamic relationships
   a. Storytelling
   b. Giving an eyewitness account
3. Abstract relationships
   a. Opinion-expressing
   b. Justifying a course of action

FIGURE 18-3 Informal Chart to Follow the Oral Language Development of Your Students

Classroom Involvement	Beginning Level		Intermediate Level	Advanced Level

Functions
   Informal talk
   Reporting
   Discussing
   Describing
   Explaining
   Questioning
   Debating
   Evaluating
   Persuading				

Interaction patterns
   Partners
   Small groups
   Large groups				

Linguistic elements
   Vocabulary
   Syntax
   Organization
   Ideas
   Audience sensitivity				

Other comments:

Student Name _____ Date _____

Source: Based on *Oral Language Guidelines,* by M. H. Buckley, 1981. Unpublished.

Examples of these task-based approaches can be incorporated easily in simulation and games used by teachers in their classroom. The show-and-tell activity allows students to use the spoken language to describe objects or photographs they bring to the class. Teachers can use the game "One Sees and One Doesn't" to assess students' spoken language in following instructions in drawing a diagram. Students take turns describing a picture or an object for their partner to draw. The person who is drawing the picture can ask clarifying questions to help draw the described object/picture. In this activity, a lot of spoken language can be generated to enable teachers to assess their ELLs' oral language development.

FIGURE 18-4   Oral Language Observation Chart

Participation structure

Formal presentation — individual / group

Structured cooperative group work
Informal group work
Pair work

Language functions
    Heuristic
        Hypothesizes
        Predicts
        Infers
        Considers
        Asks
        Reports
    Informative
        Describes
        Explains
        Synthesizes
        Summarizes
        Clarifies
        Responds
        Retells
    Instrumental
        Requests
        Asks for
    Regulatory
        Directs
        Commands
        Convinces
        Persuades
Personal and interactional
Divertive and imaginative

Language forms
    Vocabulary: particular to domain
    Vocabulary: general vocabulary
    Sentence structures:
        declarative
        question
        command
        exclamation
        grammatical correctness
Morphology
Phonology
Discourse

Overall Evaluation

Source: Based on *Learning How to Mean: Exploration in the Development of Language,* by M. A. K. Halliday, 1975, London: Arnold.

Hands-on activities such as the use of clay, Lego pieces, or even matchsticks for students to make objects can be used to elicit spoken language. Students are instructed to assemble objects like a toy car, a miniature bridge, or a dinosaur. This enables teachers to listen in on students' spoken language and make the necessary assessment.

The dynamic relationship tasks, such as storytelling and giving an eyewitness account, can be accomplished easily within lesson instructions. Students can retell stories they have read to the whole class or to their partner. Learners can perform a short skit on events that range from witnessing an accident to witnessing a bank robbery, bringing forth spoken language that meets the function of an eyewitness account.

Activities involving abstract relations such as expressing an opinion and justifying a course of action are more cognitively demanding—specific language structures are needed to do the job of convincing the audience. For older learners, teachers can present a controversial issue that students can debate. A more authentic task in the classroom can be election of a class president. Teachers ask students to give a speech to express their opinion on who is the best candidate for the position. These tasks are enjoyable and motivating, and at the same time, enable teachers to assess students' oral language development.

Techniques for Correcting Speech Errors

Research has shown that correcting speech errors has very limited benefit to students. Many experienced teachers can testify that correcting students' errors is a frustrating and futile task. Montrul (2011) conducted a study in which he examined grammatical and morphological errors in the speech of children learning Spanish in an immersion program in the United States. He reported the following:

> The third grade teacher has tried to call the children's attention to these errors by correcting them and having them repeat the correction; the fourth grade teacher has attempted to teach these grammar points more formally, giving the class

explanations at the blackboard and then having children do oral drills and written follow-up exercises. However, although the students seem to grasp the concepts, both teachers admit there has been little improvement in the children's speech (Plann, 1977, p. 222).

Although it has been reported that correcting errors has very little impact on learners, teachers do have the responsibility to correct them. To prevent fossilization of learner errors, error correction does assume a small place in language learning. A more important discussion on error correction involves the manner or techniques that teachers need to know about. Before teachers examine the "how" of speech error correction, it is important to be aware of the priority they attach to the errors they correct. Errors made by L1 and L2 children are called developmental errors, which will gradually disappear when the children become more proficient in the language. In choosing the errors to correct, teachers should also be aware of global and local errors. Global errors affect overall sentence organization and significantly hinder communication (Dulay, Burt, & Krashen, 1982). Global errors include wrong order of major constituents (e.g., Chinese language use many people; missing, wrong, or misplaced sentence connectors; e.g., not take this train; we late for work or she will be rich until she marry; missing cues to signal obligatory exceptions to pervasive syntactic rules—the employee's work looked into the boss; and regularization of pervasive syntactic rules to exception—we amused that play very much).

Local errors are errors that affect single elements (constituents) in a sentence and do not usually hinder communication significantly. Local errors include errors in noun and verb inflections, articles, auxiliaries, and the formation of quantifiers. The distinction of global/local error can be seen in these examples:

Why love we each other? vs. Why we love each other?

The first is more "un-English" than the second. The first violates the SVO word order in English and therefore is a global error. The second does not; the auxiliary "do" is missing in the second, making it a local error.

Teachers, if compelled to correct, should focus on correcting more global errors than local. There are several techniques in speech error correction that may have some impact on learner errors. Here are some dos and don'ts of speech error correction.

Dos

1. Model or rephrase students' utterances using the correct form. Speech is learned through listening to speakers, so modeling speech gives the students a chance to listen to correct speech.
2. Make note of students' speech errors and incorporate the correct form in instruction.
3. Use a nonthreatening form of correcting errors by using a nonintrusive signal code such as "thumbs-down" when students make errors. This will give them a chance to self-correct.
4. Ask students to record their own oral language and listen to these tapes on your own time. Discuss the errors during student–teacher conferences.
5. Have students compare their own taped oral reading to a model tape or a tape produced by a more proficient peer. ELLs can imitate the correct pronunciation.
6. Make speech error corrections in written form to enable students to grasp and concretize the corrections.
7. Errors should always be corrected in context and not in isolation.
8. Create a learning environment that consists of a community of learners who will help each other in correcting their mistakes.
9. Engage students in a speech-rich environment. This enables them to listen to speech and practice their own speech. Meaningful speech experiences can help reduce speech errors.
10. If fluency is the goal of oral language development, design meaningful tasks that allow students to speak freely and keep correction of grammatical errors to a minimum.

Don'ts

1. Do not correct errors made in conversations because the likelihood of learners' remembering these corrections is almost nonexistent.
2. Do not overly correct students' speech errors. This will result in students' reluctance to participate in class.
3. Do not do correction in the form of oral drills. This may not impact students' learning of the correct form.
4. Do not overwhelm students by correcting the different forms of errors that they make all at once.
5. Do not let students continue making the same error without some form of intervention.
6. Do not correct form over meaning, especially in speech errors made by beginners.
7. Try not to correct students' speech errors in front of the whole class. This may embarrass them and hinder them from speaking up.
8. Do not correct accent if learners' speech is intelligible. This can be an identity issue.

Speaking is the key to communication. Teachers can help learners improve their speaking and overall oral language competency by examining what good speakers do, by examining the kinds of speaking tasks used in the class, and by recognizing learners' specific needs in learning spoken English.

❖ Teachers should provide English language learners with classrooms that are rich in oral language.

❖ Speaking, an interactive process of constructing meaning, involves producing, receiving, and processing information and requires learners not only to know how to produce specific points of language such as grammar, pronunciation, or vocabulary (linguistic competence), but also to understand when, why, and in what ways to produce language (sociolinguistic competence).

❖ Spoken language has two main functions: transactional and interactional. The primary goal of the transactional function of oral language is transference of information, and it is message oriented. The primary goal of interactional spoken language is to maintain social relationships and, therefore, is listener oriented.

❖ Second language learners display their competence of the second language through speaking. Unfortunately, not all of their competence can be seen through their performance. One of the difficulties that second language learners face is the actual pronunciation of the sounds of the language.

❖ Spoken language has "short turns" and "long turns." A short turn consists of one or two utterances, whereas a long turn consists of a string of utterances that may be as long as an hour's lecture. Short turns demand much less of a speaker in the way of producing structures.

❖ Comprehensible input and social interaction are important elements in a classroom that provide a natural environment for oral language development.

❖ Strategies for oral language development include use of games, songs, poetry, and a recording studio; technologies such as television, VCR, audiotape recorder, and computers; and show-and-tell and choral reading.

❖ Oral language assessment includes SOLOM, observation checklists, and anecdotal records.

❖ Oral language development should be an important part of teaching content area lessons such as math, science, and social studies.

❖ There are two types of error: global and local. Teachers should spend more time correcting global errors because they impede meaning. Local errors do not hinder communication.

English Language Vocabulary Development and Instruction

KEY ISSUES

❖ Research on teaching vocabulary to English language learners

❖ Difficulties faced by English language learners in learning vocabulary

❖ Some strategies/skills of teaching/learning vocabulary for English language learners

❖ Techniques of teaching vocabulary for multiple levels of language proficiency

❖ Alternative assessments for vocabulary learning

> The mind remembers what the mind does.
> —Rivers, 1981

Mr. Olson is a first grade teacher. He uses thematic units in his class. This week, his class is learning about ocean life. He incorporates content area centers such as social studies, science, and math into his lessons. All these centers consist of tasks that contain literacy skills. As Mr. Olson teaches the math, social studies, and science concepts, he also teaches to the language objectives. Today, his class is learning new words such as *hermit crab, symbiosis, camouflage,* and *schools of fish,* and they are introduced through total physical response and the use of realia. Mr. Olson shows his students a real hermit crab. For the phrase "schools of fish," he asks students to act out the movement of schools of fish by moving as a group. He then asks students to write sentences using these new words in their discovery journal. Mr. Olson always ends his lesson by reviewing the vocabulary words as a means of assessing his students' level of comprehension of the concepts.

Introduction

Many second language learners can attest that when they are faced with an unfamiliar text in a nonnative language, their first challenge seems to be its vocabulary. When texts have many new words, students quickly despair and are discouraged. A key component of reading ability is vocabulary. Therefore, there is no doubt that there is a close connection between vocabulary knowledge and success in reading comprehension tests, as shown in many studies. Researchers (Alderson, 1984; James, 1996; Laufer, 2003) have reported the relationship between L2 vocabulary knowledge and L2 reading ability. Huckin and Bloch (1993), when discussing the cognitive model of strategies that L2 learners make use of when they attempt to infer an unknown word's meaning, stated, "Research has shown that second language readers rely heavily on vocabulary knowledge, and that a lack of vocabulary knowledge is the largest obstacle for second-language readers to overcome" (p. 154). Laufer (2003) found that vocabulary is most important, syntax least important. Folse (2004b) stated, "While correlation does not necessarily imply causality, the fact is that empirical studies have shown that good L2 readers, writers, speakers, and listeners have a more extensive vocabulary under their control" (p. 28).

What Is Vocabulary Learning?

Vocabulary learning is more than the study of individual words. Nattinger and DeCarrico (1992) observed that a significant amount of the English language is made up of lexical phrasal verbs (two or three words) to longer institutionalized expressions (Lewis, 1997). Lexical phrases can often be learned as single units, so the principles of learning them are similar to those for learning individual words. Keith Folse (2004b) categorized vocabulary for second language learners as single words, set phrases, variable phrases, phrasal verbs, and idioms. Examples of single words are animals: alligator, lions; countries: Malaysia, Iran, Brunei; actions in the past: slept, ate, played football; descriptions: excited, sad, lazy. This group also contains multiword vocabulary such as blackbird, teapot, table

scraps, etc. Examples of set phrases are *in other words,* not *in other terms; the bottom line,* not *the lowest line; all of a sudden,* not *most of a sudden.* A good example that Keith Folse (2004b) used for a variable phrase is, *It has come to my attention that . . .* If one receives a letter that starts out this way, it usually does not contain a good message. Therefore, this is an example that the learner needs to know that the whole phrase is a single phrase or single vocabulary item. Native speakers use phrasal verbs all the time and do not understand why they are difficult for L2 learners. A phrasal verb consists of two or three words. The first word is always a verb and the second is a preposition or particle/adverb. If there's a third word, it is usually a preposition. Examples of phrasal verbs are: put away, put on, put off, come back, come off, come up, come down with. Examples of idioms are feeling blue, selling like hotcakes, break a leg, etc.

Why Is Vocabulary Difficult for English Language Learners?

English language learners experience difficulties in learning L2 vocabulary because they have to relabel familiar concepts with foreign terminologies. These new vocabulary items have to be learned and stored in their long-term memory, and their retrieval initially may not be easy.

Jiang (2004) explains the difference between L1 children's vocabulary acquisition and adult L2 vocabulary acquisition as follows:

> Adult L2 learners often do not have as much contextualized input as children, which makes the extraction and integration of lexical meanings difficult. More important, adults already possess a well-established conceptual and lexical system, and most L2 words have a correspondent concept and translation in the adult learner's first language (L1). Thus there's little need for them to learn new concepts or meanings while learning L2 words, at least at the early stages of L2 acquisition. The lack of contextualized input and the presence of an existing conceptual and L1 system make adult L2 acquisition fundamentally different from vocabulary acquisition in the L1. When children learn new

words in their L1, they learn words and concepts at the same time. As a result, word form and meaning are often inseparable. Thus, when children or adults see a word in their L1, its meaning becomes available automatically. When people speak in their L1, the retrieval of lexical forms is usually spontaneous and effortless. In contrast, adult L2 vocabulary acquisition is accompanied by little conceptual or semantic development. Instead, the existing L1 linguistic and conceptual systems are actively involved in the L2 learning process (p. 417).

Four other factors contribute to the difficulties ELLs experience while learning English vocabulary. One is confusion over synonyms, resulting in the use of inappropriate synonyms. For example, English language learners may say, "My brother is long and thin" instead of "tall and thin." This may be due to the fact that in ELLs' L1, a distinction is not made between the synonyms *long* and *tall*. In English, the expression that the tea is strong is used, whereas in Chinese the collocation is "thick tea." Another factor is using circumlocution in place of an exact word as a result of a lack of one-to-one correspondence between the words in L1 and English. For example, English language learners may say, "A lady who is carrying a baby" instead of saying the word "pregnant." A third issue is false cognates, words such as *embrassa* (which does not mean *embarrassed*; it means pregnant in Spanish), may be used. Idiomatic expressions by far are the most difficult domain of vocabulary learning for English language learners. For instance, ELLs will take these idiomatic expressions literally. Expressions like *break a leg, lost his marbles*, and *green with envy* may all be confusing for ELLs.

With learning strategies and practice, English language learners will be able to acquire the new vocabulary and expressions.

Research on Vocabulary Teaching

Hunt and Beglar (1998) proposed a systematic framework for instruction of vocabulary development through the use of three approaches: incidental learning, explicit instruction, and independent strategy. Incidental learning of vocabulary is defined as

an approach that requires teachers to provide opportunities for extensive reading and listening. Explicit instruction involves diagnosing the words learners need to know, presenting words for the first time, elaborating word knowledge, and developing fluency with known words. Hunt and Beglar (1998) defined independent strategy as an approach that involves practicing guessing from context and training learners to use dictionaries. They also caution teachers that students' level of language proficiency has to be considered when choosing each approach. They propose that, in general, explicit instruction is best used with students who are at the beginning and intermediate levels, because at these levels, students' vocabularies are limited. For intermediate and advanced learners, vocabulary learning is suggested through the use of extensive reading and listening, and it is best to train students to use the dictionary earlier in the curriculum.

Incidental Learning

Nagy, Herman, and Anderson (1985) stated that most words in first and second languages are probably learned incidentally through extensive reading and listening. In their study, they found that for native speakers of English, learning vocabulary from context is a gradual process. They estimated that, given a single exposure to an unfamiliar word, there was about a ten percent chance of learning its meaning from context. Likewise, L2 learners can be expected to require many exposures to a word in context before understanding its meaning. Several recent studies have corroborated their statement confirming that incidental L2 vocabulary learning through reading does occur (Chun & Plass, 1996; Day, Omura, & Hiramatsu, 1991; Hulstijn, Hollander, & Greidanus, 1996; Zimmerman, 1997). Extensive listening is also found to increase vocabulary learning (Elley, 1989).

Explicit Instruction

For second language learners entering a university, Laufer (1992) found that knowing a minimum of about 3,000 words was required for effective reading at the university level, whereas knowing 5,000 words indicated likely academic success. Coady

(1997) proposed that beginners should supplement their extensive reading with study of the 3,000 most frequently used words until the words' form and meaning become automatically recognized (i.e., "sight vocabulary").

Independent Strategy Development

One of the principles of independent strategy development is guessing from context. Studies have shown that guessing from context is a complex and often difficult strategy to carry out successfully. To guess successfully from context, learners need to know about nineteen out of twenty words (ninety-five percent) of a text, which requires knowing the 3,000 most common words. In addition, learners need to know the same part of speech as the unknown word. They should also break down the unknown word into parts ("rewrite" becomes "re + write") and determine if the meaning of the parts matches the meaning of the unknown word. Another principle within the independent strategy development is to teach students how to use dictionaries. Use of bilingual dictionaries has been found to result in vocabulary learning (Knight, 1994; Luppescu & Day, 1993). Hulstijn, Hollander, and Greidanus (1996) showed that compared with incidental learning, repeated exposure to words combined with marginal glosses or bilingual dictionary use led to increased learning for advanced learners. Luppescu and Day's (1993) study on Japanese students reports that use of bilingual dictionaries resulted in vocabulary learning unless the unfamiliar word had numerous entries, in which case the dictionaries may have confused learners. Knight (1994) found that use of a bilingual dictionary may be much more likely to help lower-proficiency learners in reading comprehension because their lack of vocabulary can be a significant factor in their ability to read. Laufer and Hadar (1997) found that students who use bilingualized dictionaries that contain L2 definitions, L2 sentence examples, as well as L1 synonyms had better comprehension of new words than students who used either bilingual or monolingual dictionaries.

Sanaoui (1995) conducted one of the most important studies on vocabulary learning strategies (VLSs). In vocabulary learning, she found two distinct approaches among learners: structured and unstructured. Learners who use the structured approach do something and do it consistently; they engage in independent study, initiate learning activities and opportunities, record the lexical items being learned, review vocabulary notes, and practice the vocabulary outside class. Learners who use the unstructured approach either do not use any of these strategies or do not use them consistently. Sanaoui (1995) made a strong case for VLSs teaching. She suggested that class time be spent on assisting students to become autonomous learners who can work on vocabulary development independently inside or outside the classroom.

Kojic-Sabo and Lightbown (1999) surveyed ninety students on their use of strategies in learning English vocabulary. They found that students with higher levels of achievement had more frequent and elaborate strategy use. In addition, they found that two factors that contribute to these learners' success of vocabulary learning are the time they spent on task and learner independence. Students who spent more time on the task—by studying, initiating opportunities for practicing vocabulary, and being exposed to the target items—and those who can learn independently seem to be the ones who are more successful at vocabulary learning (cited in Folse, 2004b).

The effect of metacognitive strategy training was studied by Rasekh and Ranjbary (2003). Fifty-three Iranian college-age ELL students participated in their study. The students were randomly assigned into the control and experimental groups. Both classes were subjected to the same variables: textbook, instructor, and instruction time. The only difference between the two groups was that the experimental group received explicit instruction in metacognitive strategies; for ten weeks, the students in this group were reminded of strategy use; appropriate strategies for various words were discussed. Both groups took the vocabulary posttest at the end of the course. The researchers found that the experimental group had higher vocabulary scores than the control group.

Rasekh and Ranjbary (2003) concluded as follows:

The explicit instruction and practice the experimental group received about how to plan their vocabulary learning, set specific goals within a time frame, select the most appropriate vocabulary learning strategy, monitor strategy use, use a combination of strategies, self-testing degree of mastery of the new vocabulary items after meeting the words for the first time, managing their time by devoting some time during their study hours to vocabulary practice, and finally evaluating the whole process, contributed to this improved and expanded lexical knowledge (p. 12).

All the preceding studies underscore the significance of teaching English language learners vocabulary learning strategies (VLSs). The use of incidental learning alone is not sufficient for English language learners to acquire English vocabulary; it is highly recommended that teachers use a more direct vocabulary teaching approach of new vocabulary items and VLSs training.

Strategies and Skills in Vocabulary Learning

Robb (1999) developed a basic vocabulary strategy that can be used with any grade level. There are three steps to this strategy:

1. Identify the vocabulary words that students will need to comprehend the reading.
2. Preteach only three to five words. More than five words will confuse or bore students.
3. Connect the new words to concepts that students already know. For example, to help students grasp the meaning of the word *perplexed*, link it to the word *confused*.

In using this approach, the teacher can first identify the key concepts in the unit on simple machines: tools such as levers, pulleys, and wedges. The teacher then preteaches a few new words (e.g., lever, fulcrum, and effort or load). The teacher can also draw pictures on chart paper of such simple machines such as a shovel, a wheelbarrow, and a bottle opener and label them with the different elements of

a lever. Then the teacher connects the new words to ones that were familiar to the students. The result is the following:

Lever—A crowbar used to loosen a large stone or tree stump from the ground; a bottle opener used to pry off a cap

Fulcrum—A seesaw and a balance scale and the point at which they balance

Effort or load—The resistance of a bottle cap or the weight of children on a seesaw, of dirt in a wheelbarrow, and of a stone or tree stump

Teachers can use many methods to teach vocabulary or to encourage vocabulary self-learning by their students. Hulstijn (1992) and Hulstijn, Hollander, and Greidanus (1996) distinguished between incidental and intentional vocabulary learning. They claimed that both approaches are present in second language learning—students learn vocabulary intentionally as part of course requirements but also gain knowledge of words incidentally through reading. Their study shows that intentional vocabulary learning is more effective for retention. In other words, words learned intentionally through reading are better retained than words learned incidentally. They suggested that learning words through incidental learning is inefficient because of these reasons:

1. The readers' false belief that they know the words
2. The readers' decision to ignore the words
3. The readers' ignorance of the connection between the form of a new word and the meaning contained in the context
4. The readers' inability to infer a word from context
5. The nonrecurrence of new words (i.e., a single encounter of words)

Paribakht and Wesche (1999) claimed that systematic vocabulary instruction, in addition to learning through reading, is a more successful approach. Even a new and exciting computer program that enables incidental learning will not make students retain vocabulary efficiently without further offline effort by the learners. Her study supports the literature that incidental vocabulary learning is not particularly efficient; therefore, intentional learning should be encouraged.

One way to promote vocabulary development is through sustained silent reading (SSR) that teachers can use in class. Once students develop the ability to read in a sustained fashion, then most of the reading should be done outside class. Another strategy for vocabulary development is through the learning of word pair translation; vocabulary cards should be used because learners can control the order in which they study the words. Moreover, additional information can be added to the cards. When teaching unfamiliar vocabulary, teachers need to consider the following:

1. Students need to hear the pronunciation and practice saying the word aloud in addition to just seeing the form, because the stress patterns of the words are important. Words are stored in the memory in both ways.

2. Students should start learning vocabulary by learning semantically unrelated words. They should avoid learning words with similar forms and closely related meanings at the same time. For example, "affect" and "effect" have similar forms and are likely to cause confusion. Likewise, words with similar, opposite, or closely associated meanings may interfere with one another if studied at the same time.

3. Students should be encouraged to study words regularly over several short sessions instead of studying them for one or two longer sessions. Repetition and review should take place almost immediately after studying a word for the first time.

4. Students should study five to seven words at a time, dividing larger numbers of words into smaller groups. As learners review these five to seven vocabulary cards, they will more quickly get repeated exposure to the words than when larger numbers of words (twenty to thirty) are studied.

5. To promote deeper mental processing and better retention, teachers can use activities like the key word technique. Learners remember words bet-

ter when a word is associated with a visual image.

6. Teachers can add various L2 information to the cards for further elaboration. Learners can consciously associate newly met words with other L2 words that they know and add these words to the card. In addition, they can add sentence examples, parts of speech, definitions, and key word images.

In teaching vocabulary, teachers should also be aware of receptive and productive knowledge. Receptive knowledge means being able to recognize one of the aspects of knowledge through reading and listening, and productive knowledge means being able to use it in speaking and writing. Therefore, teachers should be selective when deciding which words deserve deeper receptive and/or productive practice as well as which types of knowledge will be most useful for their students.

Students can be taught to elaborate word knowledge through expanding the connections between learners' knowledge and new information. Students can choose L2 words from the surrounding context and then explain the connections to the recently learned word (Prince, 1996). Nation (1994) suggested that teachers should create opportunities to meet these useful, recently learned words in new contexts that provide new collocations and associations. Exercises that can deepen students' knowledge of words include sorting lists of words and deciding on the categories; making semantic maps with lists either provided by the teacher or generated by the learners; generating derivatives, inflections, synonyms, and antonyms of a word; making the trees that show the relationships among superordinates, coordinates, and specific examples; identifying or generating associated words; combining phrases from several columns; matching parts of collocations using two columns; completing collocations as a cloze activity; and playing collocation crossword puzzles or bingo.

Teachers should provide students with opportunities that build fluency. An activity that promotes fluency includes the recycling of already known words in familiar grammatical and organizational patterns so that students can focus on recognizing or using words without hesitation. Other activities that promote fluency include the development of sight vocabulary through extensive reading and studying high-frequency vocabulary. Fluency exercises include timed and paced readings. In timed reading, learners can increase their speed by sliding a 3 × 5-inch piece of paper down the page while attempting to understand eighty percent of a passage. Learners' practice should be looking up groups of words rather than individual words when reading. Students can practice timed reading on passages that have already been read. In paced readings, the teacher determines the time and pushes the learners to read faster. One type of paced reading is a "reading sprint," in which learners read their pleasure reading book for five minutes and count the number of pages they have read. Then they try to read the same number of pages as the time decreases from five minutes, to four, to three, to two for each sprint. Finally, they read for five minutes again at a relaxed pace and count the number of pages they have finished.

Students should be trained to use dictionaries. Unfortunately, in most classrooms, very little time is provided for training in dictionary use. Students may need extra practice to locate words with many entries. Furthermore, learners need to be taught to use all the information in an entry before making conclusions about the meaning of a word. Learners should be alerted to the value of good sentence examples that provide collocational, grammatical, and pragmatic information about words. Teachers should also emphasize the importance of checking a word's original context carefully and comparing this to the entry chosen, because context determines which sense of a word is being used. Teachers should also explore electronic dictionaries with multimedia annotations, which offer a further option for teachers and learners. Teachers may want to investigate the CD dictionaries published by Collins CO-BUILD, Longman, and Oxford. However, these CD dictionaries do not link most of their entries to a visual image. The one exception is The New Oxford Picture Dictionary CD (1997), which includes 2,400 illustrated words (mainly concrete nouns) and is available in a bilingual version.

Techniques of Teaching Vocabulary for Multiple Levels

Beginning Level

English language learners who are at the beginning level stage of English proficiency either may have no word recognition at all or may possess a very limited amount of word recognition—spoken or written. Students at this level may frequently misuse words, making communicating with others difficult because of limited vocabulary. Teachers can use several strategies to help these learners develop word recognition at this level. Word families help these learners to handle learning new words in a manageable way because students can be taught to separate onset and rimes in a word. For instance, the teacher can introduce the rime -en, and students and teachers can collectively brainstorm for words that they can form using this rime with different onsets, such as p, h, d, t, m. "Word family flaps" is an activity that uses word families. Each student will have a specific word family to work with. Each student will get a premade flap card—a piece of paper folded in half, lengthwise, and then cut so that there is one empty space and three flaps. On the empty space, the child will write the word family (e.g., -ake). On the underside of each flap, the child will draw a picture of a word made from that word family (cake, lake, rake). On the top of the flap "cake," the child will write the letter "C" to indicate what letter was added to the word family to make the word. All the children's flaps will be bound together and posted in the classroom for practice saying words.

Another enjoyable activity for these students is the creation of a word wheel, wherein the rimes match with the onsets to form words as they turn the wheel. Another strategy that teachers can use is to provide these learners with words that have root words that originate from their native language. For instance, Spanish learners may recognize the word *denture* from the Spanish word *dentadura*. Teachers can then explain that *diente* means "teeth" in English. This will not only help students to bridge new knowledge to old, but helps them later in searching for and recognizing words with root meaning (e.g., dentist, dental, orthodontist). For other languages that may not have the same root words as English, such as the Asian languages, teachers can teach students to look up etymologies of words in the dictionary. Likewise, students can learn about cognates.

Teachers should also adapt vocabulary lists for students by choosing between five and eight words that have root meanings that come from their native language.

At this level, teachers can utilize fun activities to reinforce the already taught vocabulary by having the students play a word grab-with-song activity. This is a simple activity that does not require a lot of preparation. For this activity, the teacher needs a song that students know most of the words from and a stack of word cards. The word cards are placed on the board using putty (blue tack) or magnetic strips. The teacher lines students up in two rows, and she plays the song. As the song is playing, each student in each row will walk up and grab the word he or she heard in the song. This is a great word recognition activity for beginning learners.

A gamelike activity that teachers can use to teach word association is called "What's the Word?" On an index card, the teacher writes a word, for example, *school*, and writes four or five key words that cannot be used to describe that particular word (e.g., teachers, blackboards, students, desks, tests). Any other words can be used except for the words written on the index card. Students then guess the word on the index card. Another recognition activity that is suitable for beginning students is the "Chime-In" poster. Students are invited to repeat a word and write its beginning letter on an index card. For instance, when a student sees the word *man*, the student says the word and then says the first letter of the word, which is /mmm/.

Using Mnemonic Associations

Learners can learn and remember words through mnemonic links. Cohen (1990) suggested nine types of mnemonic associations:

1. Linking the word to the sound of an L1 word, to the sound of an L2 word, or to a sound of a word in another language

2. Attending to the meaning of a part or several parts of a word
3. Noting the structure of part or all of the word
4. Placing the word in the topic group to which it belongs
5. Visualizing the word in isolation or in a written context
6. Linking the word to the situation in which it appeared
7. Creating a mental image of the word
8. Associating some physical sensation to the word
9. Associating the word to a key word

In applying this list and assuming that the native language is English and we are learning Malay as our second language, the following would be appropriate:

1. Linking the word to the sound of an L1 word, the sound of an L2 word, or a sound of a word in another language. Suppose a student wants to learn the Malay word *bendara* ("flag"), for example. In remembering the word *bendara*, he/she could think of the English word *banner*, because it has a similar sound.
2. Attending to the meaning of a part or several parts of a word. To remember the Malay word *perjalanan* ("journey"), a student may associate with part of the word, *jalan* ("road").
3. Noting the structure of part or all of the word. A student may learn the Malay word *terbang* ("fly") from the already learned word *kapal terbang* ("airplane").
4. Placing the word in the topic group to which it belongs. These Malay words can be categorized in the category for greetings: *Selamat pagi* ("Good morning"), *Selamat tengahari* ("Good afternoon"), *Selamat malam* ("Good night").
5. Visualizing the word in isolation or in a written context. Visualizing the word in isolation involves remembering of the configuration of the word; for instance, the student can memorize the Malay word *makan* ("eat") by remembering that it has two *a*'s or it has a *k* in the middle of the word.

6. Linking the word to the situation in which it appeared. A student first heard the Malay word *tidur* ("sleep") when someone said that Alan sleeps in class. He/she could remember it by remembering the situation in which it was heard and, in this case, the situation of Alan sleeping in class.

7. Creating a mental image. A student can learn the Malay word *senyum* ("smile") by picturing the image of his/her mom smiling at him/her.

8. Associating some physical sensation to the word. A student may remember how faces scrunch up when people eat a sour mango, which then reminds the learner of the Malay word *masam* ("sour").

9. Associating the word to a keyword. The Malay word *hujan* can be learned by first thinking of the English word "hurricane" as the key word and then have the mental image of the downpour. To retrieve the meaning of *hujan*, evoke the word "hurricane," which in turn will reevoke the image of the downpour. This strategy combines strategies 1 and 7.

Flash Cards

Picture Flash Cards

Beginning learners can prepare words on small flash cards. Individual words are written on the front of the flash cards, and students can draw pictures on the back. Flash cards should be made small so that learners can transport them easily from one place to another so that they can study the words.

Native Language Flash Cards

Learners can also make flash cards that contain native language meanings of words on the back of the cards or native language mnemonics that will remind them of the target language words that they are learning.

Teachers can monitor students' learning of new vocabularies by giving bonus points to students who create their own flash cards and an inventory of flash cards. Students can exchange an inventory of flash cards with their peers in the classroom.

Beep It, Write It, and Frame It

This strategy is best used with new English language learners. Students are asked to sound the words out, write them out in the air, and use imagery to frame them in their mind. Students tend to learn the vocabulary words better when they learn and remember the words in many different ways: pronouncing them out, kinesthetically writing the words out in the air, and then visualizing the words in their head.

Enrichment Packets

Along with teaching vocabulary items using pictures, teachers can—on their own or with the help of students—create vocabulary packages by using department store catalogues. Using these catalogues offers teachers and students a natural categorization of vocabulary words, especially nouns. The categories range from furniture to sports to clothing. For instance, under the category of clothing, teachers can cut and mount the pictures of different types of clothing on index cards. Words that describe the items are listed on the back of the cards. Students can work individually using these enrichment packages, or they can work in groups to sort the picture cards out and learn the new vocabulary items. Students can create their own dictionary based on the words that they want to learn.

Semantic Maps or Word Webs

Semantic maps or word webs can work both ways: convergent or divergent. In the convergent approach, teachers draw a circle with arrows pointing inward. Each arrow is linked to another smaller circle. For instance, the teacher fills in six smaller circles with words/pictures such as *glove, bat, ball, bases, umpire*, and *players*. Students then guess the word in the larger circle that is in the middle—*baseball*. For the divergent approach, the teacher draws a circle with arrows pointing outward. At the tip of each arrow is a word that contains similar meanings to the word in the big circle. For instance, the teacher writes the word *happy* in the big circle. Students can fill in the smaller circles surrounding the big circle with *pleased, glad, joyful, delighted*, or *thrilled*.

Songs

Teachers who use songs in the classroom allow their beginning English language learners to "hide behind the music" (McDonald, 1975). McDonald stated:

> . . . avoids the heat of a spotlight landing on a timid student. It also warps the students' perceptions of how difficult it is to use the new language. The result is . . . a loss of certain inhibitions, a new respect for one's own voice and the learning of whatever vocabulary, grammar and punctuation the song has to offer (p. 43).

The repetitive nature of words in the chorus part of songs makes learning words for beginning learners easier as well as enjoyable. These students can chime in only on the chorus parts of the songs, which will make learning the words manageable. Because they will be singing the song alongside the other students, they will be less intimidated by the task of producing the sounds of the target language. A catchy tune rings in these learners' ears and makes them want to repeat the words of the song over and over. This repetition reinforces their learning of new words and grammatical structure. The use of songs offers a variety to the classroom structure and takes away the monotony of a classroom routine in which students only read and write. Singing will lower students' affective filter and make them want to learn because of the gaiety and fun-filled atmosphere.

Activities that utilize songs can offer practice with similes, metaphors, and vocabulary learning. The words and combination of words in similes and metaphors are some of the more difficult features of the language for nonnative speakers. Certain songs contain a lot of similes or metaphors. Songs such as "The Traveler" have phrases such as "riding like the wind" and "like a crazy fool." The song "The Green, Green Grass of Home" contains expressions such as "lips like cherries." Bette Midler's song "Wind Beneath My Wings" is rich with similes and metaphors that English language learners can learn from in a fun way. Many songs contain words that deal with a particular theme or emotion. Students can be asked to identify various words, and then they can form clusters of words. By teaching vocabulary words for literal and nonliteral meanings using the song "Wind Beneath My Wings," for instance, teachers can ask following questions:

> What does the phrase *wind beneath my wings* mean?
>
> What does the phrase *flying higher than an eagle* connote?
>
> What does the phrase *content to let me shine* mean?
>
> List words that describe the admiration the singer has for her hero.

Games

Teachers can use commercially made games such as Pictionary, Scrabble, Password, Hangman, and Jeopardy, or students can create their own games while learning new words. The famous game show "Who Wants to Be a Millionaire?" can be adapted to search for meanings of words students have learned from literature reading or content areas. In the more competitive and kinesthetic game Fly Swatter, teachers write words on the board or a poster board and put students in two teams. Each team has a fly swatter. When the teacher reads the definitions of the words, one student from each team walks up to the board and swats the word that fits the definition. The student who swats the correct word first gets a point for his or her team. This game is a lot of fun, and students learn vocabulary words without realizing that they are learning.

A crossword puzzle is a common game that students enjoy as they are challenged to link meanings with vocabulary terms. Software programs are available that allow teachers to construct their own crossword puzzles or games that they can use to teach different sets of words to students. When students encounter words, new and old, and discuss these words in terms of meanings, origin, and analysis, they will incorporate them into their daily use in speech as well as writing.

Teaching Vocabulary through TPR

Asher (1972) first reported the field testing of teaching language using commands. He called the method total physical response (TPR). Teachers can teach beginning learners using commands or mime—children like to imitate and love to role-play. Action words like *cry, laugh, tremble, eat, run*, and *hop* can all be acted out easily by newcomers to the target language without having to produce the sounds of these words. The beginners may find this strategy of learning vocabulary less intimidating and fun to do. Teachers can easily use short poems from Silverstein's collection of poems for students to act out. Jazz chants are other examples of materials that students can use in a TPR activity when learning new vocabulary.

Intermediate Learners

English language learners who are at the intermediate level frequently use wrong words, and their vocabularies are inadequate for a smooth conversation. Terms may be used inappropriately due to constraints in lexical usage. They may be able to use some idiomatic expressions that approximate those of the native speakers. Vocabulary teaching strategies that teachers can use with these learners include structural analysis, semantic feature analysis, categorization, and dictionary use.

Structural Analysis

In structural analysis, students are taught a simple technique of using word parts to determine meaning. Because there are many affixes in the English language, teachers can teach students to locate word meanings by showing them prefixes and suffixes in words that can determine part of the meaning of the words. For instance, the words *bimonthly, rephrase*, and *semicircle* are words that can be taught using the structural analysis—parts of the words such as *bi* ("two"), *re* ("again") and *semi* ("half") give students clues to the meanings of the words.

Intermediate learners possess a little more of the language and are able to learn new vocabulary through a semantic feature analysis technique in which they have to categorize and recognize the relationship of interrelated terms. This technique is best used at the end of a unit of study. Teachers create a matrix of columns and rows. For instance, in teaching vocabulary words from a literature book, *Red Riding Hood*, teachers can set up the table shown in Figure 19-1.

FIGURE 19-1 Semantic Feature Analysis for *Red Riding Hood*				
	Human	**Animal**	**Small, Vulnerable**	**Big, Uses Deceit**
Wolf				
Red Riding Hood				
Hunter				

Semantic Feature Analysis for *Red Riding Hood*

First, a grid of rows and columns is created. The topic or concept is placed above the grid as a title (characteristics of characters in *Red Riding Hood*). Down the first column on the left, members of the topic or concept or word (wolf) are listed. Across the top row, the features or attributes of the members of the topic or concept or word (e.g., human, animal, uses deceit) are placed. Spaces can be added to enable students to add their own attributes of the word or concept. Students then determine which characteristics belong to each member of the concepts under study, and place Xs in those boxes. A follow-up discussion of these words or concepts will help students have a better comprehension of the usage of these words or concepts in context.

Dictionary Use

Dictionaries are usually used to find out the meaning of unknown words. However, a lot of information is contained in dictionaries that learners can access to use vocabulary productively.

The following activities are examples of how teachers can teach vocabulary through the use of a dictionary. Teachers can write an unfamiliar word on the board and tell the learners to form groups. Then learners are asked to follow these steps to gather information about the word that will help them write an original sentence containing the word (Nation, 1994):

1. Find the meaning of the word.
2. Use the grammar notes and an example in the dictionary to find out about the grammar of the word.

- ◆ What part of speech is it?
- ◆ If it is a noun, is it countable or uncountable?
- ◆ If it is a verb, does it take an object?
- ◆ Look at the example and note the similarity in their sentence patterns.
- ◆ Copy these patterns to write a new sentence.
- ◆ Have each group write its sentence on the board and discuss the results.

Another activity that teachers can use is the following (Rutledge, 1994).

Introduce students to a dictionary of synonyms. Give students a short passage in which several words are identified as key words. Have the students supply synonyms for the key words by looking them up from the dictionary of synonyms. Students can also attempt to write sentences using the words they found in the dictionary that are synonymous to the key words the teachers identified.

A strategy that teachers can implement with the use of a dictionary is to teach students how to deal with polysemous words (Folse, 2004b). Many English words have multiple meanings. When learners look up the unknown words in their monolingual or bilingual dictionary, they often have to decide which meaning they should select. Teachers should teach this skill explicitly and have students practice it. Teachers should find high-frequency words for this dictionary activity. Look at the following example from *Intermediate Reading Practices*, 3rd edition (Folse, 2004a):

Dictionary Usage: Definitions and Contexts

Exercise: Read this entry, and answer the questions by placing a check (✔) by the correct answer.

Form (form) n. 1. The shape or structure of something. 2. A variety or kind of: form of ocean life. 3. A paper or application with blanks of information. 4. Condition, especially about health or fitness. 5. A change in a word, vt 1. Make or shape. 2. Organize. Vi Take shape; develop [Middle English forme, Fourme, from Old French, from Latin forma, form, shape]

Choose the meaning or context that form has in each sentence

4. Please complete this form.
    _____n.1   _____n.2   _____n.3   _____n.4   _____n.5

5. He won because he was in excellent form.
    _____n.1   _____n.2   _____n.3   _____n.4   _____n.5

6. Did you learn those irregular verb forms?
    _____n.1   _____n.2   _____n.3   _____n.4   _____n.5

Of course, in addition to these strategies, songs, games, and TPR can also be used to teach vocabulary to intermediate learners. The level of difficulty for these learners will have to be varied from that of the beginners.

ELLs can create their own personal dictionaries by selecting their own organizing principle: subject specific, alphabetical, general/technical, or social/academic (Reiss, 2008). Students can include their native language in the dictionary. An example of a personal dictionary is shown in Figure 19-2.

Another variation of the personal dictionary is vocabulary figures. Students can choose to draw any figure they want. They then divide the figure into four parts (refer to Figure 19-3). Other items that can be included in the figure are synonyms, antonyms, context clues, and words/phrases that go with the selected words.

FIGURE 19-2	Personal Dictionary Theme: Classroom	
English	**Portugese**	**Picture**
pencil sharpener	o apontador de lapis	
student	a aluna	
whiteboard	o quadro branco	
desk	a carteira	

FIGURE 19-3 Vocabulary Figures

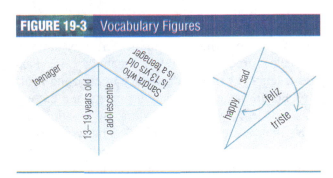

Another strategy that teachers can use to teach vocabulary items is through the use of a text analysis website that can help you narrow down the words that you really need to teach. One such site is The Compleat Lexical Tutor developed by the Universite de Quebec a Montreal. The Web address is http://www.lextutor.ca/vp/eng. There is a space on this site that you can either type or paste your text and submit it. Within seconds, a color-coded vocabulary profile of the text will appear. This color-coded profile represents four different frequency types (Reiss, 2008):

❖ The most frequent 1,000 word families
❖ The second 1,000 most frequent word families
❖ Academic word list, or words that are common across all subject domains
❖ Off-list words: topic specific, technical, and/or infrequently used words; also dates, place names, and names of people

Based on the result of the text that teachers input, they can prioritize the words that they want students to learn.

Vocabulary Teaching in Content Areas

Content areas teachers must teach to two objectives: language and content. Besides teaching concepts within math, science, and social studies, teachers must make a point to teach key content vocabulary as well as elements of language structure and functional language use. Language objectives should be identified in lesson plans, introduced to students at the beginning of the lesson, and reviewed throughout the lesson (Echevarria, Vogt, & Short, 2004). Analogy, the process of linking newly learned words to other words with the same structure or pattern, can help learners develop key vocabulary. Teachers can teach and review vocabulary items using analogy. For instance, in a seventh grade world culture class, students learn that Muslims are monotheistic (i.e., they believe in one God). The word *mono* (meaning one) in this lesson is emphasized. Students then are referred to other words with the same morpheme (e.g., *monopoly, monogyny, monologue*). Teachers can review and recycle words drawing students' attention to tense, parts of speech, and sentence structure. Students become familiar with the newly learned words and English structure as teachers repeat and reinforce language patterns. Let us examine a teaching scenario of a social studies unit on Egypt in which students' second language acquisition, especially the learning of vocabulary, is supported. In this unit, students are to (a) describe how

archeologists learned about the building of pyramids, (b) describe five discoveries made by archeologists during the exploration of the pyramids, and (c) define and correctly use the following vocabulary: pyramids, evidence, excavation, architecture, and sepulchral chambers. In the first lesson plan on this unit, teachers can include the following activities:

1. Brainstorm words about pyramids that students already know.
2. Create an interactive "Word Wall" using the brainstormed words.
3. Group the reading of the first five pages of the chapter.
4. Invite students to select words from their reading to add to the Word Wall.
5. Complete the first section of the graphic organizer listing initial steps used by the archeologists.
6. Include in the graphic organizer words from the Word Wall (pyramid, evidence, excavation, architecture, and sepulchral chambers).

The subsequent lesson plans in this unit will contain the review of key words taught in the first unit. Students will continue to extend the Word Wall to include other words they learn throughout the unit, and they will be challenged to articulate the key vocabulary orally and in writing. During this unit of study on pyramids, many terms and phrases related to pyramids are introduced, discussed in the text, and included on the Word Wall, graphic organizer, and worksheet. However, teachers can still limit the number of words students are expected to master to five or six. This is one way in which teachers use scaffolding techniques in helping English language learners learn English vocabulary through content area study. A note on using a Word Wall: Words should be organized around a theme and placed in categories to facilitate and speed up the learning of new words. For real beginners, however, some of these vocabulary words can be explained through the use of picture files or a bilingual dictionary. The *Oxford Picture Dictionary for the Content Areas* (Figure 19-4) is a great resource for content area teachers in their class. Examples of topics in this volume are The U.S. and the World, World History, U.S. History, etc. There are clear pictures that match the content area key vocabulary items in the unit, and they are theme-based.

FIGURE 19-4 Example from the *Oxford Picture Dictionary for the Content Areas (Adapted)*

Asia, Africa, and Australia
Religions and Important Features

1. Buddhism   2. Christianity   3. Confucianism   4. Great Barrier Reef

5. Great Pyramid   6. Hinduism   7. Islam   8. Judaism

9. Mount Everest   10. Nile River   11. Sahara   12. Sikhism

13. Shinto   14. Taoism   15. Uluru   16. Victoria Falls

Ask About the Past
Ask *Where did . . . start*? to find out where something started.
Where <u>did</u> Islam <u>start</u>?

Use . . . *started* to answer the question.
Islam <u>started</u> in Saudi Arabia.

Look at the maps. Ask and answer questions about where religions started.
A: Where did Buddhism start?
B: Buddhism started in _____.
B: Where did _____ start?
A: _____

Source: Adapted from *Oxford Picture Dictionary for the Content Areas*, 2nd Edition Monolingual Dictionary. Oxford University Press: 2010.

(continued)

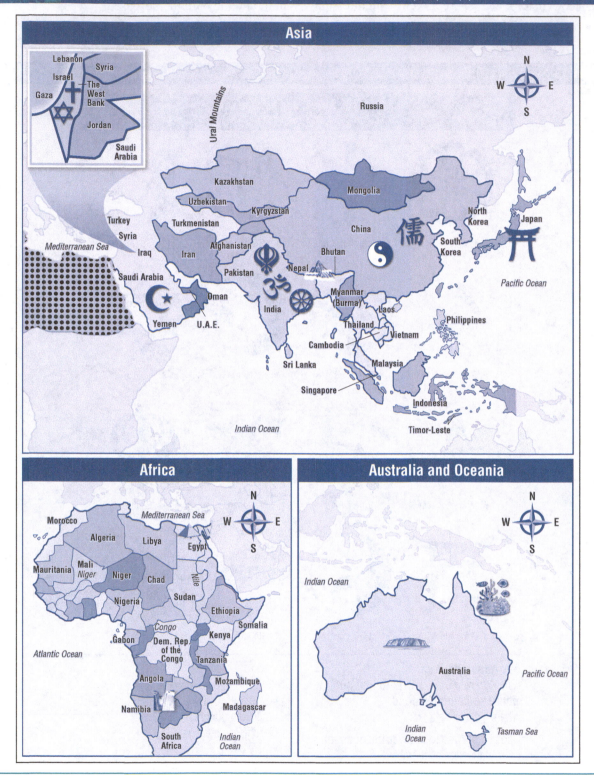

Asia

Lebanon, Syria, Israel, Gaza, The West Bank, Jordan, Saudi Arabia

Ural Mountains, Russia, Kazakhstan, Mongolia, North Korea, Japan, Uzbekistan, Kyrgyzstan, China, South Korea, Turkey, Turkmenistan, Syria, Afghanistan, Bhutan, Mediterranean Sea, Iraq, Iran, Pakistan, Nepal, Saudi Arabia, Oman, India, Myanmar (Burma), Laos, Pacific Ocean, Yemen, U.A.E., Thailand, Vietnam, Philippines, Cambodia, Sri Lanka, Malaysia, Singapore, Indonesia, Indian Ocean, Timor-Leste

Africa

Morocco, Mediterranean Sea, Algeria, Libya, Egypt, Mauritania, Mali, Niger, Niger, Chad, Nile, Nigeria, Sudan, Ethiopia, Congo, Somalia, Gabon, Dem. Rep. of the Congo, Kenya, Atlantic Ocean, Tanzania, Angola, Mozambique, Madagascar, Namibia, South Africa, Indian Ocean

Australia and Oceania

Indian Ocean, Pacific Ocean, Australia, Indian Ocean, Tasman Sea

Adapted from *Oxford Picture Dictionary for the Content Areas*, 2nd Edition Monolingual Dictionary. Oxford University Press: 2010.

The multiple modalities of introducing vocabularies will facilitate learners in learning the new vocabulary items.

Students then can incorporate the ongoing vocabulary study in this unit in their individual word study books. A student-made personal notebook that includes frequently used words and concepts is an individual word study book. Ariza (2009) recommend that vocabulary in word study books be organized by English language structure, such as listing together all the words studied so far that end in -ion, -sion, and -tation. This may prove to be a useful framework. Another way to use the word study book is to group words according to topic (e.g., pollution-related words).

Folse (2004b) suggested a strategy that put Sanaoui's research findings on "structured approach" into practice. He recommended that teachers teach students to keep a vocabulary notebook that promotes student retrieval practice. Folse (2004b, p. 103) stated that "one of the most important factors in learning a word is the number of times that the learner retrieves it." One way of keeping a vocabulary notebook that allows multiple ways of retrieving words should contain four important pieces of information: a target word, a translation, a synonym or antonym or key connecting word, and a brief example that does not have to be a whole sentence, just a good collocation. "Vertical pairings" is one of the four retrieval possibilities that Folse (2004b) suggested that allow the following question/prompt-to-answer pairings: (1) word–synonym, (2) synonym–word, (3) translation–collocation, (4) collocation–translation. Learners are asked to fold the page vertically so that the only one column (i.e., the entire left column for #1 and #2 or the entire right column for #3 or #4) is visible. Learners should then cover the entire column with another piece of paper or large card. Students should fold the right column under the left column if they want to retrieve an English synonym or definition of the vocabulary. When this is done, only half of the page (vertically) is visible (i.e., the left half). Everything in the column should be covered up except the very top word, and then students work their way down the page exposing only the vocabulary word at first, pausing to recall/retrieve the synonym, and then the cover is pulled down to uncover the correct answer. For the retrieval of the target word from the synonym, learners start with the last vocabulary item on the page and reverse the process moving upward on the page.

Vocabulary Teaching in Elementary Grades

Beginning Vocabulary Activity

Teaching Vocabulary through TPR (Total Physical Response)

Grades: Elementary

Objective: Identify vocabulary words and their meanings

Preparation: Put several fruits such as apples, oranges, bananas, mangoes, etc. in a basket. Label these fruits and write down three to five expressions (low to high level of difficulty) such as pick up the apple, put down the orange, give me the banana, take the mango out of the basket, etc.

Procedure:

Model the action as the teacher says the statement aloud. For instance, the teacher says, "Pick up the apple" and she picks up the apple from the basket. Ask one of the students to do the same. Each statement will be demonstrated by an action.

This group activity is a visual and fun way of teaching vocabulary to ELLs who are beginners. Some vocabulary items that may not be presented using real objects or realia can be substituted with pictures. Teachers can use this activity to teach other concepts such as shapes and colors to lower grades and even a more complex concept such as the digestive system to the higher grades.

Assessment

How do teachers assess their ELLs' competence and production of vocabulary? There are many standardized tests that focus on vocabulary testing; however, classroom teachers can use nonverbal assessments to gauge their students' proficiency of the English vocabulary. Teachers can observe students' acquisition of vocabulary through their performance in a TPR lesson. When teachers give commands using action words, students' response through doing the action words—such as walk to the door, jump up and down—will inform the teacher that the students understand the vocabulary. This assessment can take the form of a game of "Simon Says." Another alternative assessment is by using recognition tasks. Beginning students, especially, can be given pictures of vocabulary items to identify and categorize. Another type of assessment that tests students' vocabulary knowledge is through the cloze test. To construct the cloze test, teachers can choose an unfamiliar passage of 250 to 300 words and delete every fifth word in the passage, leaving the first sentence intact. Students' ability to fill these blanks will indicate whether they can handle materials independently or need some assistance. Another observation teachers can make is when students work on the list-group-label method. Students, in groups or individually, engage in a brainstorming session of putting words in their correct category. Teachers list a topic such as mammals, and students brainstorm for words that are associated with the topic (warm-blooded, give birth to their young). Students then label these words as belonging to a certain category (physical attributes). Students can discuss why these words belong to one category and not the other. In moving away from the traditional assessment, teachers can also use games to assess students' comprehension of vocabulary. For instance, a game called "One Looks, One Doesn't" tests students' ability to produce final products based on their understanding of key vocabularies. Students are given a picture or an object to describe for their partner. The partner's ability to reproduce the object demonstrates that he or she recognized these key terms. Teachers then can use these products as evidence of students' comprehension of learned vocabulary or concepts. Riddles can also be used to assess students' comprehension of vocabulary items within a unit of study. For instance, after studying a unit on insects, teachers can put students in two teams. The teams compete in solving the riddles that are either made by the teacher or by their own peers. Through observation, teachers can find out which students need assistance and which students have mastered the vocabulary items within the unit. Of course, the true measure of vocabulary acquisition is through its use. Teachers can ask students to write sentences using the given vocabulary words. Students' appropriate usage of the vocabulary words in their writing is another means of assessing their mastery of new vocabulary. A more common way of assessing students' acquisition of vocabulary is guessing meaning from a context clue. Students are given a passage that contains words that they have to find definitions or synonyms for through the other words in the passage. They are given multiple-choice questions from which they can choose the correct answer.

In summary, there are many creative ways for teachers to assess their students' proficiency skills in vocabulary. Teachers can observe beginning students' comprehension of word meanings through nonverbal gestures such as TPR and picture drawings. For intermediate learners, teachers can use semantic feature analysis, the list-group-label method, multiple choice questions, riddles, cloze tests, and sentence making to test students' recognition of word meanings. Teachers measure students' mastery of vocabulary through observation, anecdotal records, and charts.

❖ Vocabulary learning involves more than learning individual words in a word list.

❖ Second language learners experience difficulties in learning L2 vocabularies because the relabeling of concepts they have acquired in the native language with foreign terminologies makes it difficult for them to retrieve the newly learned words in the target language.

❖ The three approaches to vocabulary development are incidental, explicit, and independent strategies.

Incidental learning of vocabulary is an approach that requires extensive reading and listening. Explicit instruction involves diagnosing the words learners need to know, presenting words for the first time, elaborating word knowledge, and developing fluency with known words. Independent strategy is an approach that involves practicing guessing from context and training learners to use dictionaries. There are three steps to this strategy:

1. Identify the vocabulary words that students will need to comprehend the reading.
2. Preteach only three to five words (more than five words will confuse or bore students).
3. Connect the new words to concepts that students already know.

❖ Explicit instruction is best for beginning and low-intermediate students, whereas high-intermediate and advanced students can learn vocabulary through the use of extensive reading and listening. Training students to use the dictionary earlier in the curriculum is highly encouraged.

❖ Vocabulary development is promoted through sustained silent reading (SSR) and word-pair translation.

❖ Teachers should also consider receptive and productive knowledge when teaching vocabulary. Students with receptive knowledge recognize new vocabulary words through reading and listening, and students with productive knowledge can use the vocabulary words through speaking and writing.

❖ Students can be taught to elaborate word knowledge by expanding the connections between learners' knowledge and new information. Exercises that can deepen students' knowledge of words include sorting lists of words and deciding on the categories; making semantic maps; and generating derivatives, inflections, synonyms, and antonyms of a word.

❖ Beginning level students may either have no recognition or a very limited amount of word recognition, spoken or written; they also often misuse words, making communicating with others difficult. To promote word recognition at this level, teachers can use word families, cognates, and words that have root meaning from students' L1 and adapt the amount of words students learn at a time.

❖ Teachers can be creative in teaching students to use the mnemonic associations to develop their vocabulary.

❖ Techniques that teachers can use to teach vocabulary include picture flash cards; "beep it, write it, and frame it"; enrichment packets, semantic maps, or webs; and songs, games, and teaching vocabulary through TPR.

❖ Intermediate learners frequently use wrong words, and their vocabularies are inadequate for a smooth conversation. Strategies to be used with this group include structural analysis, semantic feature analysis, categorization, and dictionary use.

❖ Content area teachers should teach to two objectives: language and content.

❖ Teachers should use both standardized and alternative assessments to evaluate students' vocabulary development.

English Language Learners' Reading Development and Instruction

KEY ISSUES
- ❖ Overview of research on reading
- ❖ Reading as a social and interactive process
- ❖ Critical thinking and higher order thinking skills
- ❖ Role of oral language in developing second language reading competence
- ❖ Cognates, effective strategies, and sheltered English
- ❖ Strategies for beginning and intermediate ELL readers
- ❖ Characteristics of beginning and intermediate ELL readers
- ❖ Selecting appropriate literature for ELLs
- ❖ Alternative assessments for ELLs

The following vignette describes a regular third grade class in an urban school district. ESOL and non-ESL students make up the class, which is taught by a monolingual English teacher. Most of the students are Spanish speakers, and the students' English proficiency levels vary. The first vignette describes a science lesson.

Science Lesson

The class has been studying concepts about planets and the solar system. Today, students will be discussing how day and night are created. The teacher, Ms. Lopez, starts the discussion by asking the students to respond to her questions by raising their hands. She asks, "How many have seen the sun rising in the morning?" and waits for a response. She asks students what the word for "sun" is in their first language. She then asks another question, "How many of you have seen the sun set?" and mentally notes their responses. She then proceeds by asking the class, "Now, can anyone tell me in which direction the sun rises and the sun sets?" After listening to their answers, Ms. Lopez then asks, "Do you think the sun is moving?" Students volunteer their predictions individually.

Then Ms. Lopez tells the students that they are going to visualize what really happens when the sun rises in the morning. She tells the students that she needs a knitting needle, an orange, and an unshaded lamp for this experiment and shows them each item as she lists it on the board. She then begins to demonstrate the concept by

223

pushing the knitting needle through the center of the orange, which represents the earth. Next, Ms. Lopez places the unshaded lamp near the center of the room. She then dims the light in the room and announces to the class that the lamp represents the sun. Then she turns on the lamp. She asks a student to volunteer to hold the orange by the needle and turn it counterclockwise like a top and walk around the room. Ms. Lopez then asks a few beginning students of English to share their observations by asking yes/no questions such as the following: "Is this part (pointing to the ball) dark or light?" She extends the language by asking, "Is it darker or lighter?"and then simple questions such as, "Which part of the orange is bright? Which part is dark? Was the sun (lamp) moving?" She poses the same type of questions to the whole class, and the students share their observations. Ms. Lopez then introduces other concepts such as the earth's rotation, revolution, and axis into the discussion by asking the students to spin and walk around the lamp in a circle. She notes the cognates for rotación and revolución. After the demonstration, she draws a diagram to explain the concept and labels the diagram using the words she introduced earlier. They then read a text on the topic, and highlight the vocabulary they previously learned through their science experiment. Ms. Lopez creates mixed ability groups so that the more proficient students can write the instructions for the experiment, whereas the less proficient students will listen to the instructions read to them and carry out the experiment. They will also be given very specific roles in their groups, such as "asking for clarification." In this way, Ms. Lopez can ensure that her ELLs are actively listening. Her goal is have students participate in engaging, academic conversations, which will build a foundation for the ELLs' academic reading and writing.

After reading the vignette, what can you say about how the lesson was organized and delivered? How did the teacher make sure that (1) ELLs were actively participating and (2) were developing the literacy skills they needed? Finally, (3) how was instruction differentiated for language ability level?

What Does Research Tell Us About Reading?

Recent research in education has honed in on the importance of literacy development for all children, in particular for English language learners (ELLs). Over the past two decades research on reading development for ELLs has identified several key aspects of reading that have a direct impact on teachers and that can facilitate their work with ELLs. In this chapter, we review recent research on reading for ELLs. We associate reading development with theories undergirding second language acquisition processes, questioning techniques, and higher order thinking skills. Finally, we identify several useful materials and strategies that teachers can use to support ELLs' reading development in English.

Brief Overview of Research on Reading

Think about how many times each day you read text, symbols, or other media. We tend to do this repeatedly throughout the day without awareness of the quantity of materials we actually read. In fact, reading is a *receptive* skill that all students must develop to high degrees for academic success in the twenty-first century. Some scholars view reading to be a psycholinguistic process that "starts with a linguistic surface representation encoded by a writer and that ends with meaning which the reader constructs" (Goodman, 1998, p. 127). We discuss this process in greater detail below.

Though it may seem to be a straightforward process, reading development for ELLs is quite complex. In fact there are many areas in which the reading process can "go wrong" for English leaners. For example, if an ELL has limited recognition (or experience) with symbols of the English language, or if she lacks prior knowledge related to the topic, then she cannot make sense of the text. Teachers of ELLs must be aware of how the reading process works, how the process is related to ELLs' first language and literacy development, and how to build literacy and reading skills in English for ELLs.

Research on reading for ELLs has been quite controversial over the past two decades. The controversy lies, in part, due to various approaches to reading that have developed in the late twentieth century. Those camps are the "top down" approach to reading, or reading development as a holistic process that occurs and is enhanced when students have access to engaging reading materials (Krashen, 2011). Teachers who subscribe to this camp would ensure that learners have access to highly engaging text, significant free reading time, and utilize strategies to ensure that students comprehend and make sense of text as a whole.

A second, opposing view considers reading development as a set of component subskills, such as decoding, encoding, vocabulary-building, and structural knowledge of language and text. A teacher who subscribes to this view may provide students with opportunities to learn the grammatical rules of language, build vocabulary through practice activities, and develop rapid word recognition skills in written text. This camp is evident in schools or school districts, where the five components of reading, or "fab five," subskills associated with reading processes are taught and assessed directly. The five reading components include: phonemic awareness (the ability to hear and manipulate different sounds or phonemes); phonics (associating sounds with letters or graphemes sometimes referred to as the alphabetic principle); vocabulary (the ability to understand and use words in English); fluency (the ability to read text quickly and accurately with stress and intonation; and comprehension or understanding text.

In 2000, a meta-analysis of research on reading was published by the National Reading Panel (NPR, 2000). The work was convened with the expressed purpose of identifying effective approaches to teaching reading, and work consisted of analyzing more than 100,000 studies related to reading. The NPR findings ultimate supported the direct teaching of the subcomponent skills of reading, in particular:

❖ Explicit instruction in phonemic awareness;
❖ Systematic phonics instruction;
❖ Teaching methods that will improve fluency; and
❖ Identifying ways to enhance comprehension.

The Panel's work influenced subsequent research on the process and component skills of reading, and it continues to do so today.

Reading as a Social and Interactive Process

A third view of reading considers the process as social and interactive (see Grabe, 2009; Grabe & Stoller, 2013). The term "interaction" has historically referred to two distinct reading concepts. The first concept refers to the simultaneous use of higher order (or top-down) and lower order (or bottom-up) procedures. The idea that reading as an interactive process between top-down and bottom-up skills was first associated with Rumelhart in 1977. A second association to the concept of "interactive reading" likens the reading process to a dialogue between reader and text (Carrell and Eisterhold, 1983). This position views the process of reading as one in which the text, as it is read and comprehended, activates knowledge in the reader's mind (Grabe, 2000). Hence, there is an interactive process that occurs between the reader and the text itself.

The reality of reading for ELLs is that learners need to learn the grammatical and lexical rules of written language, sometimes through direct instruction, in addition to interact with rich, engaging text that connects to their backgrounds and life experiences. In addition, ELLs bring with them a wealth of prior knowledge related to first language (and sometimes first literacy) development, background knowledge, and cultural knowledge that are essential to reading comprehension. In other words, reading for ELLs means not only acquiring English language subcomponent skills such as phonology, syntax, and vocabulary, but also the ability to activate prior knowledge and to connect the written word to the world.

Theories of Reading as an Interactive Approach

The interactive reading approach draws heavily on cognitive, psycholinguistic, and sociolinguistic models of reading. This research is extremely important because it views reading as an active and constructive process instead of a passive one (Anderson & Pearson, 1988; Carrell & Eisterhold, 1983; Eskey, 1973; Goodman, 1988; Harste, Woodward, & Burke, 1984; Rosenblatt, 1994; Samuels & Kamil, 1988; Smith, 1988; Widdowson, 1983). The research also takes into account the critical contributions of both automatic processing skills and high comprehension and reasoning skills that are necessary to reading. In the remaining discussion, several perspectives on reading as an interactive process and their influences on reading instruction are discussed.

Psycholinguistic Perspective

During the early 1960s and 1970s, Goodman developed a model of reading known as the psycholinguistic perspective. This model set the stage for viewing reading as an interactive and active process. In this model, readers do not just extract meaning from written texts. Instead, they construct meaning from written texts by using three cueing systems: syntactic, semantic, and graphophonic. We use syntactic knowledge by relying on what we know about the way language works to process what we read or hear. We use semantic cues by drawing on our past experiences and background knowledge to a story or an expository text. We use graphophonic cues by sounding out words and to recognize words holistically. Goodman's model also highlights that reading operates within a sociolinguistic context that includes readers and writers. Because language is social, people have used it to convey meaning. Likewise, efficient readers are not only efficient, but also are effective in using strategies that will help them to assimilate and accommodate the writers' thoughts rather than rely solely on the printed message.

Goodman (1994) stated that "readers use their selection strategies to choose only the most useful information from all that is available" (p. 1125). For instance, when a reader reads the sentence, "Jupiter is the fifth planet from the sun," he or she may use real world knowledge of Jupiter and the sun and other context clues, or sound out the words fifth and planet, to construct meaning. In other words, readers will select from any of these three cueing systems and confirm their predictions by relating to past ex-

periences and knowledge about language to construct and minimize uncertainty in making meaning. According to Goodman, a reader does not have to process all or most of the letters in the words fifth and planet to arrive at the meaning unless these words occur in isolation. In his model, little emphasis is placed on teaching phonics or subskills, which could fragment the process of reading or make reading more abstract and difficult. Although this model may not be able to capture the more detailed processes of reading, it has certainly initiated a holistic perspective of reading as being meaning driven rather than being fragmented subskills.

Other reading experts (Anderson, 1994; Stanovich, 1980) have characterized Goodman's model as concept driven, in which top-down procedures (a holistic approach) interact with bottom-up procedures (subskills approach). Top-down procedures include using appropriate background knowledge, text mapping strategies, text previewing, and introduction and discussion of key vocabulary to obtain overall comprehension of text. The emphasis on deriving meaning is not far from what early readers do when they begin to read or are read to. Early readers often memorize the whole story before they focus on individual words in the story. In contrast, bottom-up procedures include identifying letters and words, matching sounds and letters, phrase identification, or "reading in meaningful groups of words or sense groups" (Nutall, 1982). Bottom-up procedures make learning easier by breaking the complex task of reading into smaller component skills. Hence, instruction proceeds from the simple to the more complex tasks. Although readers must be able to process letters and words to comprehend what they read, Samuels (1994) asserted that more experienced readers tend to process words holistically or break them down into components, whereas novice readers may focus on processing every letter or word.

Similar findings have also been found in second language reading. Researchers in second language reading have found that the process of reading in the first language is similar to reading in the second language (Carrell, Devine, & Eskey, 1988; Eskey & Grabe, 1995; Grabe, 2009). Second language readers must use all their knowledge of print, sound, discourse, semantics, and grammar to construct meaning from text. In addition, the reading process is affected by readers' background knowledge on text topics and text types or structures and by their use of appropriate strategies such as inferencing, skimming, guessing the meaning of words in context, and interpreting what they read to achieve their reading purpose. Because readers are expected to put their personal response and interpretation at the center of the reading process, it is no longer important that readers stick close to the author's message.

Schema Theory of Reading

Influenced by Goodman's earlier model of reading as a "psycholinguistic guessing game," schema research theory revealed the importance of background knowledge, which is often neglected in earlier psycholinguistic model of reading. Anderson, Reynolds, Schallert, and Goetz (1977, p. 369) eloquently expressed, "Every act of comprehension involves one's knowledge of the world as well."

Schema theory is a reader-centered model of second language reading that explains that oral and written texts can only provide directions for interpretation, but meaning is constructed by the background knowledge that the reader brings into the process of reading (Carrell & Eisterhold, 1983). These previously acquired background knowledge structures are called schemata. To understand how background knowledge affects comprehension, it is useful to distinguish between formal and content schemata. "Formal schemata" refers to background knowledge of text structures and genres, whereas "content schemata" refers to knowledge of the content of a text. For example, we can recognize that there are different types of writing, each serving a different purpose. Our schema of writing genres may include stories, scientific reports, newspaper articles, recipes, poetry, drama, advertisements, and so on. We also recognize that ideas can be organized differently, commonly referred to as text structures. Emergent readers who have had stories read to them almost invariably begin with "once upon a time" when asked to tell a story. Early on, children have demonstrated their knowledge of story grammars. Story grammar refers to the principal components of a story: main character, problem, action, and outcome.

Research has also supported the view that awareness of text structures can assist readers to form expectations about the text that will enable them to locate, summarize, store, and recall information easily (Carrell, 1992). Knowledge of text structures facilitates comprehension by serving as templates from which readers can make predictions of ideas that might be expected in text. Generally speaking, students may find narrative text much easier to comprehend than expository texts. There are two reasons for this: First, the content of the narrative text is usually more familiar than the factual information found in an expository text. Second, expository texts tend to include more complex and varied structures, which require students to master several different text structures. In some expository texts, ideas follow an attributive or enumerative pattern, in which the main idea is stated first, followed by supporting details. This pattern is signaled by the use of cohesive ties such as first, second, in addition, moreover, and so on. These cohesive ties serve as signposts that indicate how ideas are related within and across paragraphs and, thus, enable readers to read and remember information more efficiently.

Table 20-1 Cohesive Ties

Relationship	Words
Addition	also, in addition, too, moreover, besides, then
Example	for example, thus, for instance, namely, specifically
Contrast	but, yet, however, on the other hand, in contrast, conversely
Comparison	similarly, likewise, in the same way
Concession	of course, to be sure, certainly, granted
Summary	hence, in short, in brief, in summary, in conclusion, finally
Time sequence	first, second, third, next, finally, before, soon, later, meanwhile
Place	in the front, in the back, at the side, adjacent, nearby, in the distance, here, there

Other types of text structures found commonly in expository texts include comparison–contrast, cause–effect, problem–solution (Peregoy & Boyle, 2012), and pro–con. Sometimes more than one structure can be found in a single text, making it difficult for less proficient readers to find and comprehend information efficiently. Finally, expository writing often includes complicated verb structures and embedded clauses, which are not often heard or are used infrequently in social, informal discourses, for example, "can be misused if not implemented properly" and "need no longer fear."

Awareness of text structure can facilitate comprehension, so it is important that teachers are aware of how to teach these strategies to students in a flexible, opportunistic manner that will lead to student reading achievement. Teachers can use concept maps to graphically illustrate the relationship between key ideas in a text. Figure 20-2 demonstrates different types of graphic organizers that could be used to teach text structures. Many additional graphic organizers may be found online and used interactively by teachers and students. Another aspect of text structure that students can use to facilitate comprehension and memory is the use of headings and subheadings in text. Students can use subheadings and headings to preview and make predictions about the content. This strategy enables readers to establish a purpose/goal for reading and monitor how well they have achieved their goals in reading.

Rosenblatt's Transactional Theory of Reading

Rosenblatt's (1994) transactional theory defined reading transaction as an event in which the text is conditioned by the reader, and the reader is conditioned by the text. In other words, "meaning does not reside ready-made 'in' the text or 'in' the reader but happens or comes into being during the transaction between reader and text" (p. 1063). This reading transaction can be affected by two different approaches or attitudes that readers take, which are referred to as the efferent or the aesthetic stance. "Efferent" is taken from Latin to mean "carry away." When solving a math or science problem or reading instructions, readers may take the efferent stance, as the focus is on obtaining information. When readers take an aesthetic stance, they focus on how words can evoke feelings, attitudes, associations, and ideas. In other words, readers focus on "experiencing the piece" (Rosenblatt, 1978, p. 10). This is particularly useful when reading and experiencing literature. Because literature often makes greater demands on the reader's careful reading and reflection, Rosenblatt (1991) explained that aesthetic reading should then result in a deeper level of involvement for students. For instance, in reading Kenzo's, *A Mother for Choco*, a young reader may feel sad for Choco, who is desperately looking for a mother figure, and might be able to relate the feelings of sadness to a similar experience. To promote aesthetic reading, teachers should find ways to encourage readers to focus on the personal experience by using pictures and having students imagine while reading or viewing, identifying themselves with the characters in the story, making connections with other stories and their personal experiences (Cox & Many, 1992), and encouraging reflection and discussion of personal feelings, attitudes, and values that relate to the story (Rosenblatt, 1991).

To foster children's imaginative and creative responses, teachers should allow children to choose their preferred form of responses, which may include writing a poem, a letter, or a journal log; an oral response; dramatizing; drawing; and so on. Teachers should also give ample wait time for students to respond, share, discuss, and reflect on their ideas. Typically, ESL students need more than one second wait time to respond to teacher questions; this wait time could be even longer, depending on the student's English proficiency. If the questions being asked call for simple recall of information, elaboration, or explanation, English learners should be given more than a three-second wait time to construct a response to the teacher's questions; sometimes it is helpful to pose the questions before calling on students to answer so that they have time to reflect and compose their answers.

It is important to remember that readers may not take an either/or stance to reading literature. In fact, readers may take both stances or move closer to a particular stance depending on their expectations and focus. For instance, when a young reader reads the story *The Magic School Bus: Lost in the Solar System* and responds to the exhilaration, surprise, and fear felt by the children in the bus when their bus blasts off into space, the reader's stance becomes aesthetic. At the same time, the reader may also take away information about the moon, the sun, and the various planets, and thus, the stance becomes efferent.

The Importance of the Interactive Perspective

There are several reasons why ESL researchers and classroom practitioners should be interested in the interactive models of reading. First, these models try to account for an array of processing that distinguishes good and poor readers. It is consistently found that good readers recognize letters and words rapidly, which frees their cognitive space for thinking about the meaning of what they read. In other words, good readers automatically recognize words and do not rely heavily on context-guessing to arrive at an interpretation of the text. Not only can experienced readers process words rapidly, but they also have a large reservoir of vocabulary that is a prerequisite to fluent reading skills. Second, the interactive models assume that bottom-up and top-down skills are used for text comprehension and interpretation. Good readers can read fast because their eyes can quickly process good-sized chunks of text in building up the overall meaning for the text. In contrast, many beginning English readers try to read word by word, placing an intolerable amount of strain on their memory system and, ultimately, lessening their chances of comprehending the text (Klingner et al., 2012). They may spend more time processing word meaning or are afraid to use context, even though they have used this skill effectively in reading texts in their primary language. These models imply that many lower level processing skills, as well as higher level skills, are basic to good reading.

Although vocabulary knowledge is vital to good reading, it is only a part of the reading process. Inexperienced English language readers who rely heavily on this single strategy may have difficulty comprehending text accurately and fluently. In other words, a beginning reading approach that encourages the use of multiple strategies for identifying words and understanding meaning would be beneficial to beginning readers. Low level readers can benefit from "phonics" instruction and basic recognition exercises to improve their speed and accuracy of reading, and at the same time, learn to use their background knowledge of text structures or stories and relevant experiences to compensate for their lack of syntactic knowledge to comprehend text. Students can still benefit from a reading program that adopts an "as-needed approach," in which a teacher identifies the skills the students require and teaches these skills within meaningful reading activities that emphasize communication and meaning. Finally, these interactive models highlight that the reading process is not simply a linguistic analysis; rather, it requires readers' skillful use of appropriate comprehension strategies. As students are increasingly expected to read and write longer and more complex texts in higher grades, it is important that they learn how to use effective strategies employed by good readers and writers.

Social Interactionist Perspective of Reading

As noted earlier, children learn to read not only by actively engaging in the act of reading itself, but are also often facilitated by the quantity and quality of interactions in which adults discuss matters that are of interest to them. In short, children learn language and progress from one stage to another by interacting with others. L. S. Vygotsky (1978), a Russian psychologist and a leading developmental theorist, stressed the social nature of language and learning and how adults play an important role in both. In his theory, Vygotsky explained that through interaction, children will move from their zone of actual development to their zone of potential development through adults' expert guidance. This progression is known as the zone of proximal development. Actual development refers to the current level of the student, whereas potential development refers to what the child might be capable of achieving with assistance. For example, if a student cannot comprehend an unfamiliar word in a passage, the teacher or parent might prompt the student by asking, "Are there other words that you know that look like this word?" "What do you think it means?" "Can you guess its meaning by looking at other words in the sentence?" Through constant guidance and stimulation, children's knowledge and skills will be fostered.

In a longitudinal study of children, Dickinson and Tabors (2001) found that young children who are actively involved in conversations with their parents later achieve a higher level of language and literacy development. What exactly, then, is the role that parents play in the language development of children? Parents and other adults help children by extending their children's responses and providing relevant and pertinent knowledge of the world and vocabulary that will raise children's thinking to higher levels.

Critical Reading and Thinking in Literacy Instruction in Content Areas

The link between critical thinking and literacy instruction in content areas is especially important when dealing with English language learners who are still developing their English language proficiency. Some teachers may feel that English language learners cannot handle challenging content and tasks because they do not have adequate English proficiency to express and understand complex concepts in the new language. Although success in academic learning hinges on a threshold of linguistic proficiency, it is important for teachers to prepare English language learners for the type of cognitively demanding academic work required beyond the primary levels so that they can achieve academic parity with their fully proficient, English-speaking peers. This means that complex academic information to be learned must be broken down into simple components using simplified language and a variety of scaffolding strategies that make content understandable to the new language learner, as seen in the vignettes at the beginning of the chapter.

Scaffolding strategies are used as a metaphor to reflect the instructional supporting structures that are employed on a temporary basis until the student has mastered the content. For example, to assist learners in understanding bird migration and the effects of urban development on wildlife in the wetlands, teachers can set up a simulated activity in which students can "experience" the effect of destroying wetlands. This activity requires squares of vinyl that represent rest and feeding areas in wetlands. The squares are set up around the classroom or in an outdoor, open space. Students can "fly" (jump) south, stopping at their favorite wetlands. As they travel, these wetlands will be replaced with a mall, a gas station, or other structures, and students will have to stop at other rest and feeding areas. Teachers can prompt the discussion by asking how students feel about urban development and its effect on the wildlife. By using a variety of scaffolding strategies, beginning learners of English can participate in the experience and obtain access to content that has depth and breadth in scope that more proficient students are often privileged to and interesting instruction that deemphasizes rote memorization.

To achieve academic success, new English learners must learn the academic language, which differs in many ways from the social language used in every day speech (Chamot, 2001; Schleppegrell, 2001, 2004). Academic language requires sophisticated knowledge of complex language structures and vocabulary, has fewer context cues, and expresses content that is more cognitively demanding. It is also used for very specific purposes that are particular to academic learning; these purposes include ability to explain, inform, justify, compare and contrast, describe, prove, debate, and persuade and to evaluate facts, concepts, ideas, and opinions. English learners must learn how to use both lower and higher level thinking processes to fully understand difficult, unfamiliar, and new ideas. This calls for greater use of content area reading as a vehicle for developing academic language functions and skills (Schleppegrell, 2004; Fang and Schleppegrell, 2008).

Table 20-2 illustrates a hierarchy of cognitive levels of thinking based on Bloom's (1956) taxonomy, and their corresponding learning process and products (Anderson & Krathwohl, 2001). These cognitive skills can be divided into two levels: lower and higher order thinking. Lower order thinking skills are cognitive operations that require recall, comprehension, and application of information to tasks that are similar to the learning. Tasks that call on these levels of thinking include memorizing, listing, recording, describing, restating, showing/demonstrating, dramatizing, applying, and other such skills. Higher order thinking requires breaking down information into its components, composing, inventing, predicting, synthesizing, and evaluating information.

Although it is important to sequence instruction that begins with lower level skills, it is also important to include a substantial portion of higher order thinking skills in each lesson. Many statewide and national performance assessments across the United States measure high levels of cognitive thinking at higher grade levels. In fact, the proportion of higher-order thinking questions increases by ten percent at eighth grade and twenty percent at tenth

grade (Region V Academic Center for Educational Excellence, 2000). This demonstrates the importance of building high degrees of academic language across all content areas for ELLs while they are developing their English language proficiency. Teachers must prepare all learners to function in an increasingly complex technological world where the demand for literacy is high. This means that readers must be challenged to be critical of what they read, be selective and efficient in choosing information that is important, and evaluate what they read or hear and use insights from varying perspectives to make a judgment. To read critically, readers must be able to suspend their judgment and consider viewpoints other than their own or the more popular views. They must also feel free to offer divergent viewpoints and support controversial opinions. In short, teachers who value these principles view teaching and learning as an inquiry process in which students formulate and reformulate their own thoughts as well as those of others, through experimentation, testing, and evaluation. Higher order thinking and problem solving abilities are important skills for students to learn. Teachers can utilize scaffolding strategies such as graphic organizers and cooperative learning structures to stimulate critical thinking.

Higher Order Thinking Skills, Questioning Techniques, and Learning Objectives

Teachers frequently use questions in the classroom for several reasons: to probe into what learners already know; to help students develop concepts; to build students' background knowledge; to expand students' thinking by analyzing, synthesizing, and evaluating; and to increase students' retention of information. The questions asked by teachers also shape students' comprehension and how they understand a concept or its significance in a text. Because of their importance, teachers must take great care in planning their questions, and this is especially true for teachers of ELLs who have varying language proficiency levels in English. Early work by Benjamin Bloom (1956) identified, classified, and associated various behaviors with increasingly difficult levels of cognitive function. Blooms early work was intended to facilitate language learning objectives for teachers. This work was considered foundational to teachers' instructional planning and assessment. A more recent iteration of the taxonomy, which moves from lower to higher order functioning across six levels, was created in 2000 (Anderson & Krathwohl, 2001) (see Table 20-2).

Table 20-2 Bloom's Taxonomy of Cognitive Levels Revised (Anderson & Krathwohl 2001)

	Cue Words		Products	
Remembering: Retrieving, recognizing and recalling previously learned material.	observe repeat label/name cluster list record match	memorize recall recount outline define read	labels list fact recitation	names definition test knowledge
Understanding: Determining the meaning of communication (oral, written, instructional), includes interpreting, exemplifying, classifying, summarizing, inferring, comparing, and explaining.	recognize express locate identify restate paraphrase tell describe	report explain review cite support summarize reproduce, sort	reproduction summary description	retelling report
Applying: Carry out or follow a procedure, includes executing or implementing.	select manipulate organize show how to dramatize test out	use sequence imitate frame apply illustrate	illustration diagram collection puzzle report	lesson diorama map diary
Analyzing: Breaking down material into its component pieces, identify how parts are (inter)related, includes differentiating, organizing, and attributing.	examine distinguish map characterize compare–contrast	classify outline relate to	questionnaire report chart diagram list summary	survey graph outline conclusion plan category
Evaluating: Involves making evidence-based judgements using criteria and standards, includes checking and critiquing.	compare: pro/con prioritize/rank judge rate criticize justify persuade value	decide evaluate argue convince assess predict	judgment opinion scale value evaluation investigation editorial recommendation	panel verdict conclusion report survey
Creating: Involves putting different elements together in a novel way, making an original product, includes generating and producing.	propose compose design emulate speculate invent	plan formulate construct imagine create	art products media, new games, advertisements	invention prediction story solution project machine

Let's take an example of a multicultural text, *Cinder Edna* (Jackson, 1994), which parallels plot of the traditional, common story of Cinderella. In Cinder Edna, the main character, Edna, faces some of the same challenges as Cinderella, who is also included in the story, but Edna is a self-sufficient and sprightly young woman. Edna enjoys a good joke and working in the garden. She meets the prince's brother, Rupert, who is equally down-to-earth, and the two fall in love. The reader is given an opportunity to contrast the two Cinders and determine which was more likely to live happily ever after. Let's apply Blooms revised taxonomy and teachers' questioning techniques to the story of Cinder Edna. Note that the story of Cinderella is also found across many cultures, such as Domitila from Mexico or Yeh-Shen from China. Some of the questions that could be adapted to ELLs are shown in Table 20-3. Notice that even higher level questions (create, evaluate) may be used with ELLs with lower language proficiency levels, as long as the language (both input and response) is adapted to the students' levels.

Several factors must be considered when developing questions for new English language learners: (a) Ask questions that suit the ability levels of the students. Students with more literacy experience may be able to handle complex concepts, although their English skills may be lagging behind, whereas some students may have difficulty in both areas. It's important not to assume that just because ELLs are limited in English proficiency that they cannot answer higher order thinking questions. Questions can be structured in such a ways that ELLs can continue to evaluate content by pointing or using simplified responses. Teachers must be able to strike a balance in the amount of low level and high level questions they ask students and, at the same time, be able to adjust the levels of linguistic demand placed on how students should respond to their questions. In other words, students can respond to a high level question such as, "What similarities do you see between the two planets or characters?" in several ways, depending on their English proficiency. They can draw a Venn diagram to highlight similarities and differences using limited phrases and words or compose an extended response orally or in writing. (b) Focus on important concepts and not trivial facts. (c) Ask clear questions using simple and clear language that students can understand, and use scaffolding strategies to facilitate comprehension. (d) Sequence questions starting from the least demanding to those that require higher mental analysis. Start with a simple yes/no question and recall questions requiring a one-word response such as, "What is this?" or "Who is this person?" before asking open-ended questions requiring longer utterances such as, "What did the character do?" or "What is solar energy?" (e) Ask factual questions that require knowledge recall and application as well as productive and evaluative questions that invite a range of plausible responses to stimulate thinking.

Table 20-3 Bloom's (rev) Taxonomy Level and ELL Questioning Technique for Cinderella

Sample Taxonomy Level	Questioning Technique
Understanding	Name the main character(s) in the story.
Apply	What was the turning point in the story?
Evaluate	Did the story have a good outcome for the stepmother? For Cinderella? For Cinder Edna?
	Would you prefer to wear Cinder Edna's comfortable shoe or the Cinderella's glass slipper?
Create	What might have happened if the glass slipper fit one of Cinderella's stepsisters? Or if the comfortable shoe had fit Cinderella?

The Role of L1 in Developing L2 Reading Competence

There is considerable research that supports the idea of transferability of language skills across bilinguals' first and second languages. Cummins' (2001) work on linguistic interdependence and the common underlying proficiency (CUP) model claims that cognitive skills in the first language can facilitate the development of second language competence if bilingual learners have adequate motivation and exposure to both languages in school or the wider environment. The CUP model claims that there are underlying cognitive or academic proficiency skills that are common across languages. Bilinguals with cognitive skills, implicit metalinguistic skills, and conceptual knowledge in one language can use those skills when learning another language. For example, bilingual learners may understand broad literacy concepts such as the text-to-meaning principle (alphabetic principle) and directionality of print. However, they may not have the precise knowledge of English, such as in which direction English is read.

Most longitudinal data of bilingual children's performance in bilingual immersion programs for majority and minority language groups suggest that first language fluency facilitates progress and competence in the second language. This body of research points out that learners in additive bilingual situations (e.g., English-speaking children in Canada's French-English immersion programs whose first language is promoted alongside their second language; Finnish immigrant children in Finnish-Swedish bilingual programs) can achieve competence in two languages necessary to make accelerated cognitive growth in both languages (Cummins, 2001; Skutnabb-Kangas & Toukomaa, 1976). There are also cognitive benefits of engaging in academic work in two languages; proficient bilinguals have better problem-solving skills and higher levels of creativity and divergent thinking than monolinguals (Baker, 2011; Bialystok, 1991, 2001). On the contrary, learners in subtractive situations (e.g., U.S. Spanish-speaking children in structured English immersion programs that are exclusively focused on English language development) not only lost their Spanish skills but showed no improvement in English (Ramirez & Politzer, 1976). Learners who stopped learning their L1 before they begin conceptual thinking may have difficulty with higher cognitive development in the L2 (Collier & Thomas, 2009).

The research on models of bilingual education, such as two way immersion, highlights two important factors that are linked to bilinguals' academic achievement: (1) the value of first language maintenance in academic language development; and (2) the importance of literacy development. The difference in academic achievement between majority and minority learners in immersion settings is linked to whether the first language (L1) is valued and promoted. The majority language learners who are learning a second (minority) language are presumably exposed to their first language outside of school settings, which aids their ongoing development of L1. However, bilinguals from minority language groups are often expected to focus exclusively on English at the cost of losing their first language. Such programs are referred to as monolingual outcome with assimilationist goals. This means that minority language students are not only expected to use a language they know poorly for learning new academic concepts but are also prevented from using what they already know in their first language to make input in the new language comprehensible. What English learners in U.S. public schools need is the same opportunity to develop their first language when second language exposure begins, just as their English-speaking peers have developed their first language upon entering school. Early intensive exposure to the second language when the first language is underdeveloped can hinder development of the second language.

There is a minimum threshold of first and second language competence before bilinguals get optimal benefit from their bilingualism. The threshold level varies based on where learners are at different cognitive stages and the academic demands in each grade. Research has abundantly provided evidence that older learners with developed academic language in the first language will acquire academic language in English more rapidly than younger learners (Cummins, 2001; 2007; Krashen, Long, & Scarcella, 1979). However, no research trend has shown that older learners have an advantage in acquiring social language skills (basic interpersonal communication skills [BICS]) over younger learners. In addition, there is a lower threshold of L1 competence needed in the lower grades; children can survive in the lower primary grades if they have communicative language skills and some skills for low level comprehension. On the contrary, academic survival in the upper grades demands high levels of academic language proficiency, less use of contextual clues for meaning, and knowledge that is conceptually more demanding. Because academic language in the L1 and L2 are interdependent, bilingual learners' ability to handle academic instruction in two languages depends more on measures of academic language than measures of BICS, although L1 or L2 BICS may increase students' motivation and interpersonal contacts in the L2. For example, if we compare two bilinguals, Student A who scores in the seventieth percentile on L1 academic language proficiency and twentieth percentile on L2 academic language proficiency and Student B who scores in the fortieth percentile on L1 academic language proficiency and thirtieth percentile on L2 academic language proficiency, which bilingual is more likely to survive in an English-only program? Student A, with a more developed L1 academic language is more likely to survive in an English-only program even though he/she has a lower L2 academic language than Student B. In other words, L1 development (academic language) is a stronger determinant of L2 academic language than is BICS in L1 or L2 (Cummins, in Baker & Hornberger, 2001).

What aspects of literacy in the first language will aid the development of second language? Evidence of linguistic interdependence highlights overlapping skills for fluent reading comprehension in both languages:

a. *Vocabulary concept knowledge:* A child's understanding of concepts or meanings of words can significantly influence his/her reading comprehension. Second language readers may be able to produce or decode L2 words, but may not be able to interpret their meanings. This difficulty may be due to a lack of experience with developing conceptual knowledge of words in L1 and unsystematic exposure to both languages prior to school. Second language learners can improve in this area through their L1 easier than in the L2.

b. *Learner's metalinguistic awareness:* Learning to read involves recognizing that print has meaning and is different from speech. Children who do not recognize these differences may not be motivated to learn to read or make accurate predictions about text meanings.

c. *Processing decontextualized language:* Literacy learning involves the ability to explore, interpret, and extend the meaning of written symbols from an interpersonal to an ideational/ functional level. Highly literate learners develop this ability by using their own abstract form of L1 and being read to frequently.

ELLs in unilingual situations and from the low SES group may not have developed knowledge in some of these aspects of language due to a lack of quality L1 reading materials and adequate exposure to and use of L1 outside of the home. These learners depend more on schools and teachers to provide L1 support necessary for acquisition of literacy in the L2.

Why Is Reading Difficult for English Language Learners?

Although research has demonstrated that readers use the same processes in both first and second language reading, some second language readers still find reading in the second language to be more difficult. There are a few reasons for this apparent difficulty. First, second language readers do not have second language proficiency and relevant background knowledge or experience that may be pertinent to the text. The following expository passage is excerpted from work conducted by Clair, Snow, and Fillmore (2001). Consider how second language readers may process this passage:

Icebergs and Glaciers by Seymour Simon
The thicker the glacier the faster it moves. That's because the greater weight of the glacier

causes the crystals of ice to creep more rapidly. Also, a steep glacier will flow much more quickly than one on level land.

Temperature is a third factor that affects the speed of a glacier. The warmer the glacier the faster the ice moves because there is a greater amount of meltwater beneath the ice. In fact, scientists sometimes group glaciers together depending upon whether they are cold or warm. But even "warm" glaciers are still freezing.

What lexical items might not be familiar to an ELL reader? First and foremost, vocabulary words like steep, creep, greater, and meltwater. Even what seems like "less academic" words (e.g., creep) is very likely to be unknown to an ELL. Importantly, there is a significant amount of background knowledge that ELLs need to have in order to understand the passage. They need to know ice, movement, areas of land that are glacial, and so on, in addition to the relationship between temperature and states of matter. Finally, notice the opening sentence, "The thicker the glacier the faster it moves." This less common syntactic structure, where "thicker" takes a mock, first position as the subject, is confusing to even native English speakers (Clair, Snow, & Fillmore, 2001). In short, just being able to read the words does not mean ELLs will comprehend what they read. And teachers cannot assume that ELLs will have appropriate background and knowledge of English to comprehend the text.

In addition, ELL readers may lack a sound foundation of grammar and vocabulary in the language, unlike first language learners, before they begin formal reading instruction in school. Transfer effects from the home language may also cause difficulties for the English language learner. For example, the transfer of L1 syntactic knowledge and false cognates into English can cause interference in vocabulary recognition and comprehension for beginning readers.

False cognates are words that look similar but are, in fact, very different. These words can only sometimes be translated by the similar word in the other language. Examples of false cognates in English and Spanish are as follows:

- ❖ *Exito* vs. exit (*Exito* means "It's a hit or a success." If you're looking for the way out, look for una *salida*).
- ❖ *Nombre* vs. number (*Nombre* means "name or noun." Number is un *número*).
- ❖ *Asistir* vs. assist (*Asistir* means "to attend." To get help in Spanish, ask for *ayuda*.)

Despite these differences in knowledge of language, ELL students may have certain advantages. More academically oriented ELL readers typically have a large vocabulary in their first language, and thus, learning vocabulary in English is just a matter of finding a label for a concept that is already well understood. They also tend to be quite motivated to learn English for instrumental (desire to learn English to get a good education, job, salary, social recognition, etc.) or integrative (desire to integrate into the new country), reasons which can greatly improve their academic learning (Gardner & Lambert, 1972). Teachers can assist students' comprehension by providing the necessary background knowledge associated with the words they must know. It is also important for teachers to make texts readable by ensuring that they do not contain too many difficult structures and unfamiliar vocabulary and concepts for students to understand. This strategy can offset some difficulties that ELL readers may have because of their lack of English proficiency.

Another difficulty that ELLs may have in L2 reading lies in the differences between orthographic systems (Hornberger, 2003). Writing systems differ greatly in terms of the symbols they utilize. Chinese language uses a logographic system (derived from the Greek word logos, meaning "word") in which each character represents a morpheme. Although any student of Chinese language must be able to recognize an enormous number of symbols (at least 5,000 characters to read a newspaper article written in Chinese), it is not necessary for Chinese speakers to pronounce the word to read the written language. Contrarily, English readers rely on graphophonic cues, in addition to context, to distinguish between nouns and verbs, compound words and adjective–noun phrases, and homonyms. For example, English speakers use stress placement to distinguish between a noun and a verb in words like conduct and permit and between compound nouns and adjective–noun phrases in words like blackboard versus black board and greenhouse versus green house, respectively. Although these words appear to be the same or similar in spelling, their distinct pronunciations result in different meaning. ELLs may have difficulties with English homonyms because these words have the same spelling and pronunciation but different meanings. For example, the word pool can be used to refer to a pool table or a swimming pool, each with different meaning entirely. Unless ELLs have some vocabulary, knowledge of language structures, and background knowledge of topics, they may not be able to interpret these types of expressions and structures easily.

In syllabic languages like Japanese, each symbol represents a syllable used in composing words, whereas English uses letters to compose mono- or polysyllabic words. Unlike English words, a Japanese word may constitute more than one syllable. English, Hebrew, Arabic, and Russian use alphabetic writing systems; however, they differ in terms of letter symbols and directionality for reading. Arabic reads from right to left, whereas English and Russian read from left to right. In addition, Hebrew writing requires that only consonants be written down, and to read Hebrew, readers must "fill in" the vowels by inferring the overall context of the sentence. This is contrary to Russian and English, in which both consonants and vowels are available. These writing differences may have some effect on word recognition and comprehension, especially for beginning readers of English.

Table 20-4 provides some examples of logographic, syllabic, and alphabetic writing systems.

To be fluent readers of English, readers must be able to recognize letters and words and must possess the eye–motor coordination necessary for rapid reading. It is no surprise, then, that new English language learners with different writing systems in their primary language may not be able to do rapid reading as well as their fully proficient peers. However, teachers should not see this as a sign that warrants a "phonics instruction" and/or basic writing skills approach. These basic skills must be embedded in meaning-focused activities to help ELL readers achieve comprehension and communication.

Another significant difficulty that English language learners may have with reading is attributed to the "social contexts of literacy use in students' first language" (Grabe, 1991, p. 388). In some cultures, written texts represent "truth," and as such, students from such cultures are not encouraged to "challenge" or "reinterpret" the text in light of other texts. This factor can be compounded further by limited access to libraries and print information available in more literate societies. In such a situation, students may prefer rote memorization of knowledge to challenging or reinterpreting texts. Their differences in expectations about literacy use may lead them to see little value in doing extensive reading; consequently, this can have a profound impact on their academic reading skills in English.

Table 20-4 **Logographic, Syllabic, and Alphabetic Writing Systems**

Basic Types of Writing	Symbols
Logographic	Chinese 他是中國人 He be center country person
Syllabic	Japanese これは本です。 Ko re wa hon de su
Alphabetic	Some examples of Russian Cyrillic Alphabet Б б **b** В в **v** Г г **g** З з **z** С с **s** Hebrew חספ "psx" (Passover) שמש "sms" (sun)

Characteristics of Beginning Readers

As discussed earlier, beginning English readers are unfamiliar with the English alphabet and thus must be taught that English texts must be read from left to right. They must also learn the correspondence between sound and symbol in English before they can read text independently. They also recognize a few sight words and may not be able to process beyond sentence level text. At this stage, they are beginning to comprehend short, simple texts with predictable text structure and language patterns, but they still need to develop a larger sight vocabulary. Some may not have read in their first language and consequently will need extensive reading and writing op-portunities in and beyond the classroom. They must also become familiar with the various purposes we use reading and writing for, such as communication and personal enjoyment. Because of these reasons, these students need more contextualized lessons that are supported by a variety of visuals and scaffolds.

Characteristics of Intermediate Readers

Intermediate readers can read with greater fluency than their beginner counterparts because they have a larger sight vocabulary and are more familiar with reading a variety of different texts, such as stories, news articles, and letters. However, they still have difficulty reading texts containing new vocabulary and unfamiliar topics independently and can benefit from instruction that employs a variety of scaffolding techniques. They can generally speak with some degree of fluency and thus are able to participate in discussions with peers in literature circles. The following section describes some unique and shared features between effective and sheltered instruction that teachers need to know in order to plan and implement the instructional strategies recommended for beginning and intermediate readers of English.

Contrasts Between Effective and Sheltered Instruction

Before you read about specific reading strategies or sheltered strategies for producing good ELL readers, it is important for you to understand how effective instruction for mainstream students who are already proficient in English differs from sheltered instruction for English learners with limited English skills. Effective instruction is what many people refer to when they speak of good teaching. As you might already know, effective instruction is characterized by well-planned lessons and high levels of academic engagement. On the other hand, sheltered instruction, also known as specially designed academic instruction in English (SDAIE), refers to an approach for making grade level content such as science, math, and social studies more accessible for English learners while simultaneously promoting their English language development (Wright, 2010).

Figure 20-1 lists some shared and unique features between effective and sheltered instruction. While sheltered instruction shares a number of features with effective instruction, there are unique features which make sheltered instruction more than just good teaching. What this figure highlights is a difference in the intensity and range of instructional strategies that teachers of English learners ought to use with their second language students. The degree of strategies to be used with English learners must also be based on knowledge of their students (i.e., their first and second language competence, content knowledge and academic skills in L1, whether students' primary language is highly valued by society, the extent in which their primary language and literacy development is maintained at home and/or school, and how these social and cultural experiences might influence their responses to specific instructional interventions). While many of the unique features in Figure 20-1 can benefit all students, these features are critical and should be applied to a higher degree in sheltered instruction for English learners.

FIGURE 20-1   Unique and Shared Features of Sheltered and Effective Instruction

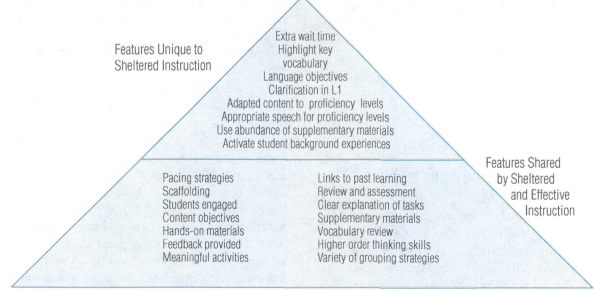

Features Unique to Sheltered Instruction

Extra wait time
Highlight key vocabulary
Language objectives
Clarification in L1
Adapted content to proficiency levels
Appropriate speech for proficiency levels
Use abundance of supplementary materials
Activate student background experiences

Features Shared by Sheltered and Effective Instruction

Pacing strategies
Scaffolding
Students engaged
Content objectives
Hands-on materials
Feedback provided
Meaningful activities

Links to past learning
Review and assessment
Clear explanation of tasks
Supplementary materials
Vocabulary review
Higher order thinking skills
Variety of grouping strategies

Source: Echevarria, J., and Graves, A. (2007). Sheltered content instruction: teaching English learners with diverse abilities (p. 57). Boston: Allyn and Bacon.

Unique and Shared Features of Sheltered and Effective Instruction

ELL readers who are already literate in their first language may be able to handle academic reading in English with fewer sheltered strategies than English learners with limited linguistic skills and conceptual knowledge in their first and second language. For example, ELL readers who are literate in their L1 can make reasonable progress in English reading when content and oral explanations are adapted according to their English proficiency levels and themes are explored through meaningful activities centered on meaning. However, English language learners with less developed academic skills and knowledge in their first language and limited knowledge in English cannot handle academic reading in a new language unless teachers also bring students' background experiences to the text, preteach new vocabulary that students will encounter in their reading so that they can make better predictions of text meanings, use a variety of supplementary materials that have been appropriately adapted to the students' proficiency levels and contain visual information that make input comprehensible, and provide additional time for students to provide meaningful responses. In other words, differentiated reading instruction is necessary for all English learners at any level, but some learners will require more intensive instructional support than others. The following section describes some effective language arts strategies that can be applied to content area teaching for beginning and intermediate readers of English.

Strategies for Teaching Beginning Readers

Language Experience Approach

The language experience approach, as discussed in Chapter 19, has been noted to present fewer difficulties for beginning readers who are developing their English language proficiency (Herrell & Jordan, 2011). This approach allows children to dictate their stories based on their personal experience. The teacher/teacher aide and/or parents write the story and use it as reading material to instruct the students. This approach integrates listening, speaking, reading, writing, and thinking through teacher-led discussion that helps students organize and reflect on their experiences. There are two different approaches to recording students' oral dictated stories. One approach entails recording of students' exact words, with minimal rephrasing of the student's language to show acceptance of the student's language and to prevent any difficulty in reading materials that do not contain language that is familiar to the reader. However, in the second approach, the teacher corrects any words that are mispronounced to reinforce graphophonic awareness. This approach also draws on students' culture, and thus, they read texts containing familiar and high-interest content that serve as a foundation for developing second literacy. This approach is not confined to narratives only; in fact, it can be used for content area learning in which group experience stories can be used to summarize key topics, concepts, or events.

The following steps are recommended for implementing this approach successfully: (1) The teacher starts with a group story by having the class share and discuss experiences related to a field trip, a literature selection, or other personal experiences. (2) The teacher encourages students to dictate how the story is written by asking them to contribute words, phrases, or sentences. (3) The students read and discuss their story. Teachers can model how to make revisions to their story and then involve students through the thinking process of revising their story. For example, if a student reads, "my brother and me goed to the park," the teacher can model the standard form and ask students how their ideas should be written. (4) The teacher encourages students to read their story through choral reading, followed by echo reading, where every student gets a chance to read different portions of the text. (5) The teacher uses the story to help students discover different aspects of print by doing different types of activities such as creating a big book version of their story, illustrating their story, matching words from the story to another set of words written on cards, and identifying letters, words, and punctuation (Walter, 1996). This group activity can help learners build a sense of community among students with varied backgrounds. Another advantage is that this approach is simple enough for parents or caregivers to adopt as one of many home literacy activities.

Read Alouds

Many students of all ages and abilities can benefit from a read aloud activity. When teachers read aloud to students, they make reading fun and, at the same time, assist students in developing print concepts, phonics knowledge, sight vocabulary, and comprehension. Books selected for reading aloud should be age appropriate in terms of language, length, and plot complexity. For beginning readers, choose a text that has a predictable structure and supporting illustrations. This text could be connected to a theme study in which students have learned key concepts and vocabulary (see text sets, below).

It is important to remember that listening to a story is not an easy task for beginning readers. Teachers can make this listening task easier by doing a few things. Teachers can ask several prereading questions such as, "What do you think this story is about?" "What picture tells the story?" "Can you point to the title?" "Who wrote the book?" or "What is the author's name?" while holding the book for students to see the cover. At the same time, some children with little or no experience with books can learn how to hold a book. As teachers read the book, they can point to the text so that students can see the direction of the print. To facilitate comprehension, teachers can stop at certain places in the text and ask students to predict what they think will happen next, how they think the story will end, and what they like about the story so far. Teachers can discuss different parts of the story by asking "What is happening here?" "What is the character doing?" and so forth. Taped recordings of books can also be used in learning centers to reinforce language patterns. As students listen, they can also look at the illustrations in the book to understand concepts.

Another way to reinforce comprehension and listening during oral reading is to have learners spot the mistake made by the teacher during oral reading. To do this, teachers must select several words in the text that can be substituted with other words that carry different meanings. For example, the sentence, "He bought a fish at the store" could become, "He sold a fish at the store." Students are given a copy of the text and underline the words that are different from what is read. Higher level readers can try to catch or write the exact words spoken by the teacher (Herrell & Jordan, 2011). Once students understand the procedure, they can be divided into pairs. Each student can make a change in different paragraphs or parts of a text and read his or her part to the other students and catch each other's mistakes. This strategy can also be applied to content reading by having students read aloud certain passages containing key concepts they have learned, listen to their peers' or teacher's oral reading, and spot any difference between the text and the oral reading.

Choral Speaking

This strategy encourages learners to participate in dramatic activities as they enjoy reading literature selections such as poems, songs, and pattern books. They can create props and add sound effects, gestures, and movements to make a story come alive. This is a fun and interesting way to introduce oral language patterns, vocabulary words, and sentence patterns. It also helps build students' confidence by making them feel that learning English is easy and fun. For example, teachers can select a poem such as the following free poems found at

> http://www.funny-poems-for-free.com/
> onomatopoeia-poems.html
> http://www.mywordwizard.com/onomatopoeia-poems.html

Or they can use a song such as "The Old Trolley" from 1944 with lyrics that use onomatopoeia:

> *Clang, clang, clang went the trolley*
> *Ding, ding, ding went the bell*
> *Zing, zing, zing went my heartstrings*
> *For the moment I saw him I fell*

Using appropriate props, the teacher can sing the song and show the students how to make clanging sounds, dinging bells, a heart shape (or hands folded by the heart), and they can act out the song.

Using a poem about fall and leaves (such as "When the Day is Cloudy," by Ada, Harris, and Hopkins, 1993), the teacher can show students how to act out the words. This strategy can be used for younger or older students.

First, the teacher recites the poem and the students can make sound effects such as rubbing their hands together in a circular motion to evoke the rustling leaves before the storm; snapping their fingers one at a time, lightly at first followed by faster and harder rhythms to suggest the patter of the first tiny raindrops; and clapping their hands to indicate the rain is pouring and slapping their hands on a desk as the rain pounds on the roof. These movements can be reversed to indicate the end of the storm. Teachers can then recite individual lines and have the students repeat in unison; this strategy is referred to as echo reading. Teachers can also have students fill in any missing words when they read a portion of the sentence. This encourages students to listen and works best with brief selections. If students do not want to participate in the choral-speaking activities at the beginning, they can be encouraged to do the body movements instead.

Another way to involve students in their reading is to have them read a selection aloud together; this is choral reading. Choral reading works best if the stories, poems, and songs have repeated structures, for example, selections such as *Brown Bear, Brown Bear What Do You See?* (Eric Carle), *The Napping House* (Audrey Wood), and *Bear's Walk: A Never-Ending Story* (Alma Flor Ada). After students have read such a book and heard the story many times, they can easily predict what the story will say and become familiar with predictable structures or refrains from the book, such as, "Ooh! What's that I see? It's just a cat/a fox/some bunnies." When selecting books with predictable structures, Peterson (1992) recommends books containing language patterns that relate to the content, are supported by illustrations found in the text, and relate to the background experiences of the learners. Texts that introduce nonsense refrains such as those that are found in the familiar story of *The Three Little Pigs* (Ziefert, 1995) may actually interfere with the beginning reader's comprehension. This is one reason why incorporating strategies such as encoding (reading) nonsensical words may interfere rather than support ELLs reading and comprehension-building skills.

Similar strategies could also be used to facilitate comprehension. When reading content that contains difficult words and concepts, teachers can model and/or invite students to use nonverbal means such as gestures, body movement, and sounds that they can understand. Teachers can also use visual forms of input such as maps and diagrams to provide additional means for comprehending difficult content. For example, teachers can model how to read a poem with stanzas by reading each stanza and stopping at the end of each to discuss its meaning. Students can work individually and/or in groups to record their ideas in a blank chart (Schifini, Short, & Tinajero, 2005). After students have completed the chart, ask, "Why is it important to read each stanza carefully?"

Choral reading is also beneficial for highlighting poetic features such as alliteration and assonance. Poets choose words for the way they sound together. Sometimes they use words that begin with the same sound, which are boldfaced in this sentence: I've sailed upon the seven seas. This is called alliteration. Sometimes poets choose words with the same vowel sound, which are boldfaced in this sentence: Some of us are serious. This is called assonance. Working in groups, students can recite one stanza in Maya Angelou's poem titled "Human Family" (2004) and then be asked to locate other examples of assonance and alliteration they hear. In addition, each group can read aloud one stanza, discuss the poet's message in each stanza, and then reflect on the overall meaning of the poem. Students can record their ideas on a chart.

Literature Circles

A literature circle is a type of discussion group that incorporates cooperative learning principles and provides students with materials based on student choices. This type of discussion group allows students to discuss their responses and engage in the same type of talk used when discussing literature or content area books with peers. This approach is well suited for ELLs who are still struggling with reading and works better in cooperative learning groups. Essentially, five to six students read the same book from a selection of texts with varying difficulty levels and interests.

Groups of five to six students are formed based on their choices of book selections. Teachers can try to match the book with the ability level of the students. Then each student is assigned a role by the teacher, or the group can decide who will fulfill each role. The roles reflect the things that students should be doing when they read. A discussion leader develops questions and leads group discussion. The summarizer summarizes the text; the literacy reporter finds passages/lines that stand out because they contain memorable language patterns or key ideas, and describes events that are funny, sad, and/or mysterious. When reading content books, the reporter can locate passages that use different and interesting language patterns to mean the same concept or different concepts. The reporter reads passages out loud and directs the group to read the selection silently or dramatizes them. The illustrator illustrates the main idea of the text by using a graphic organizer or drawing. The word chief searches for and defines difficult words or expressions found in the text with the aid of a dictionary. The connector finds links between books that the group has read or links the book(s) with other real events or situations. By playing these roles, readers become aware of the importance of questioning, making connections, summarizing, visualizing, and coping with difficult words that underlie the reading process. Each of the roles can be modeled, discussed, and practiced by the students. Job sheets can be handed out to assist students in carrying out the assigned role (Gunning, 2001). Figure 20-2 shows a sample job sheet for the literacy reporter.

Shared Reading with Big Books

Shared reading is a process in which students read a big book along with a teacher. Big books are oversized versions with colorful and supportive illustrations and have one to three sentences per page. They present predictable story structures and language patterns that students can follow very easily. Big books can be produced commercially; students can also select a familiar text and make their own big

---

FIGURE 20-2 Literacy Reporter Sheet

The literacy reporter's job is to locate and discuss passages that contain colorful language, figures of speech, or special techniques the author has used to tell the story. Write the page and paragraph number of these passages. Explain why you think they stand out.
Book Title: _River Ran Wild_

Quotes

P. 5
Long ago a wild river ran wild through
a land of towering forests. Bears, moose,
and herds of deer, hawks, and owls all made
their homes in the peaceful river . . .
One day a group of native people . . . came
upon the river valley. From atop the
mountain . . . they saw the river nestled
in its valley, a silver sliver in the sun.

My Reasons

I like the way the
writer describes the
beauty of the place.
The river was beautiful.
It is home to many
animals in the forests.

Groups are given about a week or two to complete a selection and schedules for how much and when reading can be done in school or at home. Then each group shares its book with the whole class.

---

book. They can copy the exact story into their personal big book, write the author's name on the cover, and after drawing their own illustrations, add their name to the cover as the illustrator (Peregoy & Boyle, 2012). They can also dictate and write their own versions of the story. Big books help students develop new vocabulary and a sense of the rhythm and syntax in the language while learning about the reading and writing process in an enjoyable and enriching way.

Thematic Units

A thematic unit is a way of organizing instruction around a central idea or topic. This central idea can be a theme such as "endangered animals," and can explore other unifying ideas such as "What does 'endangered' mean?" "What animals are considered endangered species and where are they located?" "Why are some animals in danger?" "What efforts is the world making to combat this problem?" "Is there a better solution to combat this problem? If so, what is it and why is it better than the existing solution?" A thematic unit has several advantages: (1) It integrates content from different areas of learning and thus helps students to make connections between areas of knowledge and stimulate deeper level thinking. (2) It helps students to make connections among listening, speaking, reading, and writing as they listen, talk, and write about what they have read or heard. (3) It helps teachers to integrate language arts and content lessons in a flexible way, thereby reinforcing both language and content, which are vital to students' academic success. The following suggestions are ways to create and implement a thematic unit instruction. (1) Students can collaborate with the teacher in identifying a topic or theme they wish to explore; teachers match themes or topics to students' age level (i.e., their interests) and a variety of content and skills from language arts, social science, art, and math. (2) The teacher helps students to identify inquiry questions they wish to explore and decides on materials and activities that will help students to find answers to their inquiries. Before students can explore the topic or theme related to endangered species, they are asked to imagine how they might feel if someone destroyed their homes to

build another building or parking lot. (3) The teacher conducts a holistic evaluation that must include a variety of information that reflects students' understanding of major concepts, skills, and strategies. Students' written notes, journal logs, diagrams, tests, oral retelling or summaries, essays, and illustrations are examples of authentic assessment that can be collected.

Strategies for Intermediate Learners

Intermediate readers generally have a larger sight vocabulary and demonstrate more automatic processing skills that help them to read more fluently than their beginning counterparts. They generally have little problem understanding texts such as stories, letters, and simple magazine and news articles. However, they may find expository texts and some stories difficult to read because of unfamiliar vocabulary, complicated syntax, and text structures that do not permit them to focus on conceptual aspects of the text. These students need further assistance in processing texts for comprehension and higher level thinking. The following section describes various strategies that are effective in fostering comprehension and higher level thinking of intermediate learners of English. Bear in mind that all the strategies that were recommended for beginning readers could also be used effectively with intermediate learners by using texts with higher difficulty with respect to language and concepts.

Directed Reading-Thinking Activity (DR-TA)

Directed reading-thinking activity (DR-TA) is an approach that coaches students to make explicit connections between print and meaning by responding to questions as they read segments of the text. This strategy replicates how the mind works and helps students to develop strategies that facilitate comprehension. This strategy can be used with narrative as well as expository texts. The process can be modeled by reading segments of the text or having students read independently or with a partner. The procedures for DR-TA are as follows:

- Divide the text into segments that will promote deep level reflection.
- Build students' background knowledge of the text prior to reading by pointing to the book cover and the title, headings, and subheadings and asking predicting questions such as, "What kinds of information do you expect to read from the text?" "Why do you think this?"
- Have students read the first segment of the text and then compare it with the original text. They must verify their predictions or identify which predictions were inaccurate or still unknown.
- Have students continue to read the next segment and respond to more predicting and verifying questions based on their reading.
- After reading the whole text, have students discuss their predictions and overall reactions and reread the whole text again.

Graphic Organizers

Intermediate readers can use graphic organizers to help them to understand stories as well as difficult content and vocabulary they are likely to encounter in expository texts. They can be used in pre-, during, and postreading activities. These visual maps allow students to "see" the interrelationship between ideas by organizing major and subordinate concepts in a text and discovering the underlying text structure. They are also effective in assisting learners to elaborate on their ideas and relate new information to old knowledge, as shown in Figure 20-3 (Herrell & Jordan, 2011; McTighe, 1992). Graphic organizers can also be used to help students monitor their comprehension of word meanings by having them search for ways to confirm their predictions as shown in Figure 20-4 (Schifini, Short, & Tinajero, 2005). Once students understand the words, they reread the whole passage and make inferences about the characters. They can talk about their ideas with a partner or in small groups.

Students can also use any of the graphic organizers in Figure 20-3 as a prewriting strategy for generating a plan for their writing or as a focal point for group discussions that becomes the final tangible product. In a cooperative learning group, graphic organizers can become a means for expanding students' own thinking as they consider facts, details, abstract ideas, and different points of view. In other words, graphic organizers are effective tools for enhancing thinking and learning.

FIGURE 20-3 Graphic Organizers

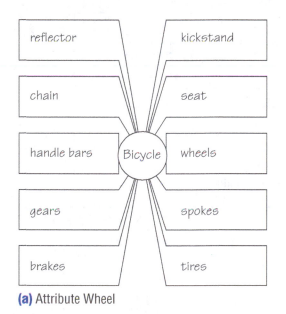

(a) Attribute Wheel

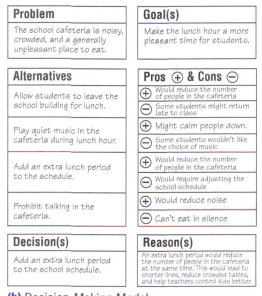

(b) Decision-Making Model

FIGURE 20-3 Graphic Organizers *(continurd)*

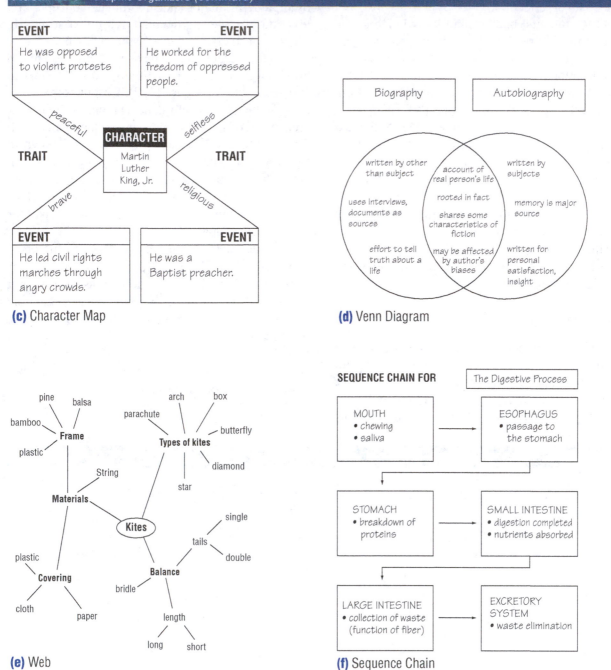

(c) Character Map

(d) Venn Diagram

(e) Web

(f) Sequence Chain

FIGURE 20-3　Graphic Organizers *(continurd)*

Title: ____A Christmas Present____

Setting: Time: Christmas Day – Christmas Day five years later
Place: Sara Smith's house

Characters: Sara Smith, 5 yrs old　　GiGi, a pet monkey
Jelly Bean, a teddy bear
Spot, a dog

Problem: Jelly Bean is Sara's favorite toy until she gets a new dog for Christmas. Then she doesn't pay any attention to Jelly Bean and he is upset.

Event 1: Sara gets Jelly Bean for Christmas and loves him very much.

Event 2: Five years later Sara gets a dog for Christmas

Event 3: Jelly Bean cries every night and complains to GiGi

Event 4: GiGi tries to calm him down

Event 5: Spot runs away. Sara takes Jelly Bean on a picnic instead.

Solution: Jelly Bean is happy because Sara learns that old things are just as good as new things.

(g) Story Map

main idea: The oceans and the waters of the world surround us.

facts & details:

Three-fourths of surface covered	Ponds lakes rivers	Most in oceans which join other oceans (1 giant)	Water vapor, snow

source:

pictures from outer space paragraph 1	p. 32	Pacific Atlantic Indian others?	(check water cycle)

(h) Main Idea Table

FIGURE 20-4　Confirming Meanings and Making Inference

Story Passage	How I Confirmed Meaning	Inference
Out back is a small <u>garage</u> for the car we don't own yet.	Context	They cannot afford to buy a car. But there is a small area for the car.
And so she <u>trudged</u> up the wooden stairs, her sad brown shoes taking her to the house she never liked.	Dictionary	Esperanza was sad because she didn't like the house. She dreaded being in the house.
But she doesn't know which subway train to take to get <u>downtown</u>.	Word parts	Her mother isn't good at getting her around town on her own.

Learning Logs/Journals

Learning logs, commonly known as journals, are excellent tools for getting students to discover their thoughts and write about what they read. Students can use journal logs to react to the text they have read, discuss specific elements or techniques that writers use to convey their points, identify difficulties in their reading that need further clarification, discuss real-world issues that are addressed in the text, and/or propose or evaluate a solution to a problem-solving task that is related to the book. There are several ways in which teachers can use journals to further their students' learning. Students can use logs in literature response groups in which they read and discuss each other's informal comments and reactions about the book or use them as means to reflect and discuss difficult concepts related to a body of knowledge. Teachers can allow students to write whatever they wish in their journal or they can provide some structure by posing several questions that allow students to discuss key points and concepts covered in a content lesson. Figure 20-5 illustrates a journal log that allows students to write sentences that reflect the author's point of view and purpose (Schifini, Short, & Tinajero, 2005). Beginners can be given a key point summary of the original passage and work in small groups to create sentences that tell the author's purpose. Intermediate readers can read or listen to an audiotaped reading of the passage and fill in the information on the journal log as a group, whereas advanced readers work in pairs to complete the journal log and then share their information with another pair.

The following book provides a plethora of instructional reading activities that aim at teaching pronunciation, vocabulary, and concept development in diverse and creative ways:

> Tomkins, G. (2013). *Literacy for the 21st Century: A Balanced Approach* (6th Ed.). Upper Sadde River, NJ: Pearson.

Selecting Appropriate Literature for English Language Learners

Few students, whether they are native speakers of English or learners of English, are fully proficient in academic language before entering school. This gap is even bigger if the students lack literacy experiences such as having books read to them in any language or even having books in their homes to read. To facilitate this learning, teachers must provide instructional support that will make input to be learned understandable and use authentic materials that draw attention to how language is used for academic purposes so that learners stay motivated to learn. Using authentic children's literature is one source of input for academic language.

FIGURE 20-5 Journal Log

A Celebration of the Everglades

What are some facts?	What words show the author's feelings?
The Everglades National Park was created in 1947.	*The landscape is green and lush.*
It is the most endangered national park.	*Nowhere else . . .*
Canals drain the water away.	*—one of America's wild and wondrous pageants.*
The water is polluted by runoff from fields.	*Water is the very soul of the Everglades.*

What is the author's point of view?	What is the author's purpose?
The author cares deeply about the Everglades.	*The author wants me to care about the Everglades.*

- Introduce vocabulary, grammar, and discourse conventions in the language they are learning.
- Introduce stories with a predictable structure, repetitive language, and discourse patterns that support children's understanding.
- Use multicultural texts that present topics that are interesting and relevant to students. These books typically reflect the multicultural groups in the students' communities.
- Use international texts and books written by authors outside the students' country and that reflect daily concerns, history, social life, art, and customs of various cultures outside the student's country. These texts can provide students a window to the world and may be published in multiple languages. Some folktales or fables from around the world have been translated into English from different languages.
- Introduce materials that contain simple language and concepts before moving to books with more complex language and words that are conceptually abstract.
- Offer a variety of writing genres.
- Use multilevel books/texts to make provision for individual learner differences.
- Encourage children to choose their own book to read.
- Take into account children's background knowledge.
- Use "real world" materials/print to help students discover the values and functions of written language.
- Use content area textbooks to support curricular areas like science, math, and social studies.
- Use materials with plenty of illustrations.

The following section provides a sample of materials that are suitable for all levels because they provide the necessary literacy scaffolds that ELLs need to make learning meaningful and use language in a communicative manner. However, teachers must remember that texts do not often reveal how language works or provide clues to how words are used and the meanings they carry. These materials will become usable input if teachers: (1) provide support and discuss difficult words and structures to help learners understand, (2) direct learners' attention to how a particular language or word is used in a text as well as in other texts, and (3) explain how grammatical cues indicate relationships between ideas such as cause–effect, consequence, comparison–contrast, sequential order, and so on (Clair, Snow & Fillmore, 2001).

Materials that Support Language Acquisition

"Real World" Materials

In today's academic environment of common standards and emphasis on student learning outcomes, teachers and educators are being asked to use increasingly complex academic text that is authentic and based on "real world" materials. Moreover, emergent literacy studies have shown that children's early literacy experiences begin with their ability to read environmental print that is readily available to them. Through their experiences with environmental print, children learn about the function and features of written language. Second language learners also exhibit similar literacy experiences. As such, it is important that instruction provides a rich input of written language from newspapers, food cartons, menus, letters, catalogs, brochures, book jackets, and so on. Children can look at the editorial section of a newspaper or magazine and compose a letter to the editor raising an issue of concern. They can also look at menus and compare prices of different foods, categorize different types of foods, discuss the nutritional value of particular foods, or suggest a different menu that is more nutritional and reasonably priced.

To get a deeper level of understanding from a literature text, students can use real world materials such as reproductions of historical letters, dramatic photographs, and excerpts from movies or critical reviews to engage readers emotionally and intellectually. These materials can also be used to develop genuine writing activities with interdisciplinary connections. For example, when students are asked to read the war novel *The Red Badge of Courage*, they can research and read reproductions of Civil War letters and newspaper articles. They can view dramatic photographs or paintings of notable people, troops, ships, artillery, and battles and then write responses to the letters. Students can also write a response to a critical review of a book in which they have to use various sources to locate incidents or moments that affirm the authenticity of the author's work.

Other authentic writing activities could include a composition comparing how a movie based on a novel effectively "echoes" the sentiments of the characters in a book or a reflective paper in which students write the lessons about war they could use today (Paulenich, 1992). After discussing the book, students can also examine the illustration on the book jacket and re-create a new book jacket complete with illustrations and a synopsis of the story. Real world materials provide an excellent opportunity for students to become more active in reading by responding to whatever is pertinent to them rather than merely pursuing the writer's meaning. These materials also provide an excellent opportunity for exploring critical reading and thinking, as readers actively examine and analyze facts and opinions. They search for evidence and logical fallacies by having a "dialogue" with the text or writing to the text and reading each other's writing. In this way, the interactive process takes on a transactional nature of reading, as students develop their personal voice and purpose that influence what and how they read and write.

Concept Books

One of the tasks that English language learners encounter in acquiring a new language is the development of new vocabulary to express knowledge and experiences that they have acquired in their primary language. Concept books can help new English learners to acquire vocabulary by describing different dimensions of an object, a class of objects, or an abstract idea. Some concept books have texts that come in varying lengths that are appropriate for different levels of English learners. For example, Byron Barton's *Machines at Work* offers clear and simple pictures of what machines can do, such as bulldoze a tree, knock down a building, dig up a road, load a truck, and so on. This book introduces a simple, imperative structure (used typically in giving instructions or commands) to describe each picture and, thus, is appropriate for beginning English language learners. Other concept books like John Malam's *Highest, Longest, and Deepest* introduces the concept of dimensions by illustrating and comparing various geological elements of the earth such as mountains, glaciers, lakes, deserts, rivers, coral reefs, volcanoes, caves, oceans, and waterfalls. Each illustration is labeled and accompanied by a short description of several sentences or paragraphs. This concept book is suitable for older ESL learners who have more experience and knowledge about language.

Concept books can also help students learn ways to organize new information. Christopher Maynard's colorful book *Incredible Mini-Beasts* helps students learn about different types of small insects and their habitat, anatomy, diet, and self-defense mechanisms. Concept books can also help learners to link old and new experiences. Marc Brown and Stephen Krensky's *Dinosaurs, Beware! A Safety Guide* teaches children about safety rules using colorful pictures that illustrate many safety tips and actions of dinosaurs undergoing the consequences of their actions as understood by people around the world.

For example, the book describes and illustrates some safety tips for traveling, such as using bicycle reflectors, warning others of your approach with a bell or horn, or obeying road signs and traffic lights. These illustrations and explanations invite students to share experiences that are similar or different in their cultures and country of origin. Concept books can also teach word recognition and grammar. For example, Betsy Maestro's *Taxi: A Book of City Words* is an excellent book for teaching word concepts and prepositions. Each picture in this book is large and colorful and has one or two sentences such as "A busy yellow taxi takes passengers to a railroad station/zoo/office building." The text highlights one- or two-word concepts like taxi and railroad station, respectively, as well as prepositions such as, ". . . drives over a bridge and through a tunnel."

The following books are excellent resources that provide annotated bibliographies of books suitable for different age and grade levels. Brown categorizes books by text types or genres such as picture books, legends, fables, folktales, fiction, and nonfiction for primary and secondary grades. It also provides a cross-reference list of these books based on topic and ethnicity/culture. Gunning's book provides a list categorized by author, title, theme, subject, skills, and language structures.

> Gunning, T. (2012). *Creating Literacy Instruction for All Students* (8th Ed.) Upper Saddle River, NJ: Pearson.

Pattern Books and Poems

Pattern books and poems are texts that have predictable story and/or language structures and frequently contain pictures that help students to understand the text. For example, *Birds Can't Fly* makes use of repeated phrases such as, "birds can fly but they can't swim," and, "birds have feathers but they don't have hard shells" to compare and contrast birds with other animals. This book introduces students to characteristics of birds such as ostriches and other animals, including alligators, turtles, and fishes. Students can elaborate by using their newly acquired vocabulary in a familiar pattern such as, "Birds can but they can't." Beginning readers can create their own phrases by using this predictable language pattern to create their own versions of big books, complete with illustrations. The following pattern books and poems can be used with old and young English language learners:

> Brown, M. W. (1947). *Goodnight moon.* New York: HarperCollins.
>
> Bryan, A. (1985). *Turtle know your name.* New York: Macmillan.
>
> Ginsburg, M. (1992). *Asleep, asleep.* New York: Greenwillow.

Text Sets

Text sets are related books that allow students to make connections between texts, which consequently enhances involvement in and thinking about what they read. Sets may cover the same theme or topic, such as chili pepper festivals, their history, and growth cycle. They may also be from the same genre—for example, bibliographies, fiction, and collections of poems, fairy tales, and so forth. A text set can also have collections of books written by the same author. Text sets can offer different versions of the same tale or present cultural versions of the same tale or story such as the traditional Cinderella tale and Louie's (1982) *Yeh-Shen: A Cinderella Story from China*. Text sets should represent a range of interests and difficulty levels that are appropriate for mixed ability groups. Text sets can be used to promote oral discussion. Students can read all the books or select some in the text set and discuss them in a literature circle group. They can compare and contrast the books they have read. If they have not read the same books, they can share the contents of the books they have read and then compare and contrast them. The Reading and Writing Project at Teachers College in New York compiles digital text sets for student use. See http://readingandwritingproject.com/resources/book-lists-classroom-libraries-and-text-sets-for-students/text-sets.html

Other categories of text sets include books:

- ❖ Of the same story or content with different illustrators
- ❖ About the same set of characters such as Amelia Bedelia and Frog and Toad

Reading Assessments

Current views on reading research reveal that reading is a developmental process consisting of holistic reading and writing processes as well as integration of language arts. (O'Malley & Pierce, 1996). Keeping this in mind, a single, norm-referenced test simply cannot capture all the complexities involved in reading. Instead, we recommend that teachers develop alternative forms of assessment by collecting a variety of information to learn about students' abilities, gains and achievement in reading, as well as their attitudes toward reading and knowledge about reading. Alternative forms of assessment are also known as authentic assessments to reflect the actual learning and instructional activities that can measure what students know and can do. Assessment information can also help teachers to evaluate the effectiveness of current instruction and plan future instructional activities to address students' needs. Authentic assessment can take various forms.

Anecdotal Records of Classroom Observation

Teachers can systematically document their students' literacy development by using anecdotal records or checklists with clearly defined sets of traits or behaviors. Teachers can organize anecdotal records by jotting down any spontaneous observations about the student behavior on index cards, sticky notes, or address labels. For example, a teacher may note that Latifa was able to capture the gist of a passage by recognizing familiar root words, even though she skipped several unfamiliar words, or Ravi had difficulty understanding the text on tornados because he does not know what a tornado is. The teacher can follow these initial notes by recording additional, related events such as the students' work habits and strategy use on specific tasks. With anecdotal records, teachers can record useful information that may not show up on a test, in retelling, or in students' written work. Teachers can observe the quality of their students' comprehension and the strategies they seem to be using, find out what difficulties they have that hinders comprehension, or observe what they do when they read different types of texts.

A checklist is a useful tool to document students' literacy development because it can be tailored to teachers' specific evaluation needs. Teachers can also minimize their time recording by simply checking off the observed behaviors. The list of behaviors can be modified or added to accurately reflect the progress the student is making throughout the year. Figure 20-6 provides an example of a story retelling checklist, and Figure 20-7 provides an ex-

---

FIGURE 20-6 Story Retelling Checklist

Name _____   Date _____

Title _____   Author _____

Quarter: 1st   2nd   3rd   4th

Text Difficulty: High predictability   Moderate predictability   Advanced

Response: Drawing/pictures   Oral response   Written response

Performance Tasks	Initiates	Responds to Prompt	Comments
Names main characters			
Describes setting			
Starts retelling at the beginning			
Identifies problem or issues			
Identifies major events			
Reports events in chronological order			
Describes resolution			

Adapted from a format developed by ESL teacher K. Harrison (1994), Fairfax County Public Schools, and based on National Education Association (1993)

FIGURE 20-7 Think-Aloud Checklist

Student _____   Date _____

Story/Text _____   Grade/Teacher _____

Place a check (✔) or write examples in the spaces.

Reading Strategy	Frequently	Sometimes	Rarely
1. Uses prior knowledge			
2. Self-corrects words and sentences			
3. Rereads			
4. Makes predictions			
5. Forms opinions			
6. Paraphrases			
7. Summarizes			
8. Adds ideas			
9. Other:			

Adapted from Glazer, S. M., and Brown, C. S. (1993). Portfolios and beyond: collaborative assessment in reading and writing. Norwood, MA: Christophers Gordon.

ample of a think aloud checklist that can be used when a reader explains his or her thought processes while reading a text.

Informal Reading Inventory

An informal reading inventory (IRI) is an assessment tool that records errors in oral reading and comprehension to determine students' reading levels. It is generally given at the beginning of a school year to obtain placement information for new students. To determine placement levels, students are asked to read books at the easiest level first and continue at the next level until the reading becomes obviously difficult for them. Like a directed reading activity, the students are told that they are going to read some stories and answer some questions about their reading. Before reading, students are asked to read the title and predict what the story will be about. This helps to set a purpose for the reader and determine his or her background knowledge. Typically, as students read the story orally, their reading errors, such as omissions, insertions, substitutions, and mispronunciations, are recorded. Any hesitations, repetitions, and self-corrections are not considered errors.

However, developing English learners are bound to mispronounce unfamiliar words, especially those that contain sounds that are difficult for them to produce. Hence, they may substitute a new word to replace the difficult word. Although it is easier to count all mispronunciations or substitutions as errors, it is important to interpret these errors in light of what students comprehend. After the students have read aloud, they are asked to answer comprehension questions about the text or construct an oral retelling. The same procedure is repeated for the silent reading portion. Using texts of the same level, students are asked to read a selection silently and then answer comprehension questions. The percentage score for word recognition is computed by dividing the total number of correct words by the number of words in the selection. Comprehension is calculated by averaging the scores for the oral and the silent sections. Table 20-5 shows placement levels of IRI.

Miscue Analysis

Miscue analysis is another assessment device to determine oral reading errors that reflect deviations from the print. Miscues provide information about readers' attempts at making sense of the text. The following are procedures for doing a miscue analysis (Gunning, 2001; Peregoy & Boyle, 2012):

1. Ask students to read a text that they have not read previously. Choose a selection that is grade level appropriate. If the selection is short, take a running record of the whole piece. If the selection is lengthy, take a sample of 100 to 200 words from the text.
2. Make one copy of the reading selection for the student and another copy for the teacher to write on. A sample of the coding system is shown in

Figure 20-8. Get a tape recorder and a blank tape to record the oral reading.
3. Prepare the student by giving the following instruction: "This is a passage that I want you to read aloud. If you come across a word that you don't know, try to figure it out on your own and then continue to read. After you have finished reading, I will ask you to tell me what you remember about the passage." After the student has finished reading, ask probing questions to find out what the student remembers about the text and ask additional questions to assess comprehension level.
4. The student can listen to the taped oral reading for fun.
5. Teachers can analyze the tape recording for any miscues.

Interpreting Miscues

Miscues can tell us about students' reading competencies and help us make decisions about how to assist them. Figure 20-9 provides an example of a reader's reading miscue (Peregoy & Boyle, 2012). These miscues reveal the reader's reading competencies in the following areas:

1. The reader shows a persistent difficulty with -ed endings of words and diagraphs, such as th- in thousand and sh- in shining (a sound made up of two letters), and blends (a blended sound made up of two letters) such as bl- in blanket, sp- in spoke, and st- in stopped.
2. The reader has difficulty with sight words such as from.

Table 20-5 Placement Levels for IRI		
	Word Recognition Comprehension (%)	Average Level in Context (%)
Independent	99	90–100
Instructional	95–98	75–89
Frustration	90	50
Listening capacity		75

Source: Gunning (2001)

FIGURE 20-8 Marking Miscues

1. **Insertion:** the child inserts a word not in the text; place a caret where the insertion is made and write the inserted word above it.

   also

   Example: The cat was ʌ in the kitchen.

2. **Omission:** the child leaves a word out; circle the word the child omits.

   Example: Many people find it (difficult) to concentrate.

3. **Substitution:** the child replaces one word with another; place the child's substitution over the replaced word.

   dog

   Example: The doll was in the little girl's room.

4. **Word Supplied by Tester:** child can't get word and tester supplies it; put supplied word in parentheses.

   (school)

   Example: Joe ran to school.

5. **Word Missed then Corrected by Reader:** child says word wrong then immediately corrects it; place missed word above word and place a check by it.

   rat ✓

   Example: The cat is sleeping.

FIGURE 20-9 Candy's Miscues on the Guadalupe Passage

John

Long ago in Mexico, there lived an Indian farmer named Juan

misión

Diego. Juan Diego went to Mass every Sunday at the Spanish mission.

en the   *cage*

Then one day, something happened that would change the entire

story

history of Mexico.

down

On December 9, (1531) Juan Diego rose at dawn to go to church.

wit

He put on his best white pants and shirt, covered himself with his

and   *misión*

blanket, and began the long walk to the mission. He followed the rocky

dree

dirt road over the dry desert hills. When Juan Diego got to the hill

on   *skee*

named Tepeyac, he heard a beautiful song coming from the sky. On the

shine

hill (op) Juan Diego saw a large white cloud with gold light shining from

sop   *apok*

it. Juan Diego stopped and looked. Suddenly a lovely voice spoke:

"Juan Diego! Juan Diego!"

sashen

Before him stood a beautiful lady dressed in a blue satin robe that

tousan

was covered with a thousand (glimmering) stars. Her skin was smooth

aroun

and brown, and her long black hair was crowned with a (shimmering)

halo.

3. The reader chooses to use John instead of Juan at first but then switches back to Juan the second time the name appears and uses the Spanish cognate *mision* for mission. These miscues, however, do not affect the reader's comprehension.

These miscues are then analyzed and interpreted in light of the student's responses to comprehension questions to determine if they affect comprehension. Although the reader made digraph errors and mispronounced Juan and mission, these errors do not seem to interfere with the student's comprehension. Moreover, these errors may reflect the learner's developmental level in oral English. Because meaning is unimpeded, these errors were ignored. However, the reader's difficulty with blends could result in confusion, and thus, additional instruction in this area may be appropriate.

Self-Assessment

Although current views in reading have stressed the importance of metacognitive knowledge and self-monitoring skills in fluent reading, these components have largely been neglected in classroom assessment. Research has indicated that students who are actively involved in self-assessment become more responsible for their own learning (Nilson & Zimmerman, 2013). Students who are new to self-assessment need teachers to show them how to evaluate their own progress and, thus, will be learning a new skill. Teachers can help students remember their goals for each task by having them jot their goals on an index card. Students can refer to these cards from time to time or they can discuss their goals in small groups or individual conferences. Some questions that might be asked to help students self-assess their reading are as follows (O'Malley & Pierce, 1996, p. 100):

❖ What have you learned about reading in this class?
❖ How do you feel about reading?
❖ What three things do good readers do?
❖ What do you need to improve in reading?
❖ What do you do when you come to words you don't know?

Students' self-assessment can also take other forms: checklists, scoring rubrics, sentence completion, and learning and reflection logs. Figure 20-10 shows a sample of self-assessment that contains short sentences and pictorial responses that are ap-

---

FIGURE 20-10   Self-Assessment of Emergent Reading

Name _____   Date _____

How do you read? Circle one of the faces.

	Usually	Sometimes	Not much
1. I read every day for 30 minutes.	☺	☐	☹
2. I read many different types of books.	☺	☐	☹
3. I look at the pictures for new words.	☺	☐	☹
4. I pay attention when the teacher reads a story.	☺	☐	☹
5. I read during free time.	☺	☐	☹
6. I like to read.	☺	☐	☹
7. I tell others about books I read.	☺	☐	☹

Adapted from a form developed by elementary ESL teacher J. Eury (1994), Fairfax County Public Schools, Virginia.

FIGURE 20-11 ESL Reading Rubric

Prereader

- ❖ Listens to read-alouds
- ❖ Repeats words and phrases
- ❖ Uses pictures to comprehend text
- ❖ May recognize some sound/symbol relationships

Emerging Reader

- ❖ Participates in choral reading
- ❖ Begins to retell familiar, predictable text
- ❖ Uses visuals to facilitate meaning
- ❖ Uses phonics and word structure to decode

Developing Reader

- ❖ Begins to make predictions
- ❖ Retells beginning, middle, and end of story
- ❖ Recognizes plot, characters, and events
- ❖ Begins to rely more on print than illustrations
- ❖ May need assistance in choosing appropriate texts

Expanding Reader

- ❖ Begins to read independently
- ❖ Responds to literature
- ❖ Begins to use a variety of reading strategies
- ❖ Usually chooses appropriate texts

Proficient Reader

- ❖ Reads independently
- ❖ Relates reading to personal experience
- ❖ Uses a wide variety of reading strategies
- ❖ Recognizes literary elements and genres
- ❖ Usually chooses appropriate texts

Independent Reader

- ❖ Reads for enjoyment
- ❖ Reads and completes a wide variety of texts
- ❖ Responds personally and critically to texts
- ❖ Matches a wide variety of reading strategies to purpose
- ❖ Chooses appropriate or challenging texts

Adapted from a draft compiled by ESL Portfolio Teachers Group, Fairfax County Public Schools, Virginia (1995).

propriate for young learners and those who have low literacy skills. When dealing with prereaders, teachers can read the questions aloud and jot down student responses. Figure 20-11 is an example of a developmental reading rubric developed by elementary and secondary school teachers that assesses reading behaviors at different levels. Figure 20-12 is an example of a reading log that can be used to assess the number and types of books students have read and their reaction to each selection. This log can help students discover the types of books and content that have high appeal to them and may explain their ability to read various texts in the classroom.

Running Records

A running record is an informal reading assessment that records student oral reading errors to determine students' word recognition skill, the strategies readers use when they read, and whether the material is at the appropriate level. To get a better sense of students' reading ability, teachers can assess students' comprehension by asking them to retell a story orally. Teachers typically use passages of about 100 to 200 words at different grade levels to determine students' strengths and weaknesses. Teachers can select passages from books currently used in their program, or students can make their personal selection. Unlike the IRI, teachers do not have a copy of the text to mark, and hence, they must write notes quickly. Despite this limitation, many teachers use this assessment because it can be used informally in classroom instruction to evaluate students' reading competencies. Figure 20-13 shows an example of a running record (Clay, 1979, in Peregoy and Boyle, 2012).

FIGURE 20-12   Reading Logs: Books I Have Read

My Name _____   Grade_____   Date _____

Title	Author	Date I Began Reading:	Date I Finished Reading:	How I Feel About It:
Gorilla		4/16/95	4/18/95	this book is abat a litto gile that wats to se a rel garela then her Fader bot her a toy garila That he gu and gu and gu an to a ril gorila o wel I lob the store
Matthew's Dream	Leo Leone	6/8/95	6/9/95	I likd the part wen Matthews was in hes drean I lik ol of the ameizen pekchers and Matthews paiten in to. Thes book is abat a moos tha waders what he wat to be and he does no want he wats to be. a paiter

Adapted from a reading log developed by elementary ESL teacher J. Eury (1994) and a sample from first/second grade ESL teacher L. Morse (1995), Fairfax County Public Schools, Virginia.

FIGURE 20-13   Some Guidelines Used for Recording Running Records

1. Check each word that is read correctly. In the example below there are five checks because all words were read correctly.

   Joe went to the store.   ✓ ✓ ✓ ✓ ✓

2. When a student gives an incorrect response, place the original text under it.

   Student: sale
   Text: store

3. If a student tries to read a word several times, record all the attempts.

   Student: stare | st- | story
   Text: store

4. If a student makes an error and then successfully corrects it, write SC.

   Student: stare | st- | story | ("store") SC
   Text: store

5. When the student gives no response to a word, use a dash to record it. If a student inserts a word, the word is recorded over a dash. If a student can't proceed unless you give a word use a T to record that you told the word to the student.

   a. doesn't give response: Student: –
   b. inserts a word: Student: star
   c. student told word: Student: T

Source: Clay, M. (1979). Based on the early detection of reading difficulties. New Zealand: Heinemann.

❖ Reading is an interactive process consisting of various subskills: automatic recognition skills, vocabulary and structural knowledge, formal discourse structure, content/world knowledge, synthesis and evaluation skills, and metacognitive knowledge and skill monitoring. Reading for ELLs may differ from native speakers in that ELLs have a developed first language on which they rely, and they likely have different world experiences and knowledge on which reading is based.

❖ Research has identified some characteristics of fluent readers: They have greater automatic skills in word recognition and knowledge of text structures that allow them to read at a rapid rate, freeing them to focus on conceptual ideas at the deeper level. On the contrary, less fluent readers do not have a sound foundation of automatic skills and tend to focus on word level, which limits their ability to use their content or previous knowledge to facilitate comprehension.

❖ ESL students may have different expectations of text structures in their primary language that would influence what they do in reading and what they understand. As such, these students could benefit from instruction that highlights and enhances their awareness of text features such as cohesive ties and text organization. Awareness of text structures, building metalinguistic awareness, can help readers to develop a purpose for reading and match their strategies to their purpose. Consequently, readers become actively involved in their reading.

❖ Readers interact with texts in different ways. They may take an aesthetic and efferent stance, both of which can influence the strategies they use during reading and their comprehension.

❖ ELL readers who are already literate in their first language may still encounter the following difficulties with reading in English:

1. Lack of familiarity with the sound/symbol system in English
2. Limited cultural or background knowledge of the topic or subject
3. Lack of vocabulary knowledge in English and inability to recognize or use cognates
4. Lack of cultural knowledge for ELLs to make appropriate inferences or to draw conclusions
5. Lack of critical thinking skills to develop conceptual knowledge associated with learning academic language and content
6. Lack of experience with evaluating information within texts or critiquing authors, because such activity might not be encouraged in some cultures
7. Lack of knowledge of text structures used for organizing ideas in written texts

❖ Sheltered instruction shares a number of features with effective instruction, but it also has a number of unique features which make sheltered instruction more than just good teaching. These unique features include: providing extra wait time; highlighting key vocabulary; including vocabulary that may seem "common" but could be unfamiliar to ELLs; incorporating language objectives; providing clarification in students' L1; adapting content and adjusting speech to students' proficiency levels; grouping for language learning with clear roles and tasks for ELLs; using abundant supplementary materials; and activating student background experiences.

❖ Scaffolding strategies are sheltering techniques that support students' language and academic learning. These strategies serve to help learners acquire content knowledge by varying the levels of linguistic and cognitive demands. When students are given challenging content, instructional delivery and materials must be adjusted for linguistic difficulty so that students can understand. Teachers must employ effective strategies such as visual organizers and cooperative learning structures.

❖ Reading assessments must come from a variety of sources that afford information about the strategies students use in reading, their attitudes about their reading, and their comprehension. To do this, authentic or alternative assessments should reflect instructional activities that students are doing so that the desired learning behaviors can be observed directly and measured. Students' self-assessment should be used to help them develop good metacognitive and monitoring skills, which are vital to helping them become independent readers.

English Language Learners' Writing Development and Instruction

KEY ISSUES
- ❖ English language writing research and practices
- ❖ Difficulties in English language writing
- ❖ Characteristics of beginning and intermediate second language writers
- ❖ Strategies to promote early literacy development and academic writing
- ❖ Developing appropriate writing tasks for ELLs
- ❖ Home literacy events
- ❖ Linguistic error or language transfer?
- ❖ Biliteracy development and assessment

The following vignette describes the process writing events in a fourth grade classroom in Florida.

Mrs. Brown's fourth grade classroom includes English language learners (ELLs) who are beginning, intermediate, and fully proficient writers of English. The class has been studying living organisms and the interrelationship between living things, such as cells, how cells grow, and what they require to thrive. Near the end of the unit, the students summarize and synthesize the facts they have learned and work together to publish a class book; students work together in mixed language ability groups and use both their first language and English to complete that task.

The book takes several steps to create. First, Mrs. Brown records the information shared by the students onto large sheets of paper. This list becomes the "draft copy" of the students' writing project. When all of the ideas are written down, the students cut their sheets into separate sentence strips. Mrs. Brown instructs the students to sequence the sentences by putting them in the order that they believe best describes their thoughts about living things. Then, the students paste, tape, and rewrite each sentence onto another sheet of paper. These sheets become their first writing draft. All of the ELLs can participate in this sequencing event, with varying levels of support.

Next, Mrs. Brown then carefully divides the students into groups based on her knowledge of the students' strengths and language ability levels. For example, specific groups are responsible for editing different aspects of the writing, such as checking for spelling errors; correct use of prepositions and transitional phrases to make ideas between sentences and paragraphs flow; verb tenses; and pronouns. In this way, Mrs. Brown believes that students of any level can become "experts" in some aspect of the unit and can make meaningful contributions to their own learning. Each group is then assigned a page of the final product to illustrate. Once all of the pages are illustrated, the students brainstorm some possible titles for their book and then vote on the best title. Mrs. Brown asks the students if they would like to include anything else in the book. Some students ask how they should write the authors' names on the cover of the book because all of the students in the class are authors. Mrs. Brown suggests that they could create a separate page called the "Authors' Page" in which all students could sign their names. They similarly create an "Illustrators' Page." She also has the students include a page for "readers' comments" so that anyone who reads the book can write comments on the page. Finally, some of the biliterate students create a bilingual glossary of key vocabulary to add to the book. The students then laminate their book and bind it using plastic rings.

When the book is ready, Mrs. Brown assigns students to different nights of the week when they can take the book home and read it together with their parents. A note attached to the book asks parents for their encouraging feedback and compliments about the book.

Now that the students have published their class book, they are working on creating their own individual books. Students allow other classmates to take their books home to share and read with their parents and thus get positive feedback from their fellow classmates and their parents.

- ◆ In what way do the writing activities in Mrs. Brown's classroom help students to develop writing skills?
- ◆ How does Mrs. Brown use students' first language as a resource for this writing activity?
- ◆ What do you consider to be important components of writing instruction for all learners?

English Language Writing Research

The following sections will describe various perspectives of first and second language writing research, beginning with earlier paradigms to more current research trends. These sections will discuss the paradigm shifts in writing research and how they affect classroom writing.

Traditional Perspective of Writing

Research on second language writing has been influenced and shaped by research in first language writing and best practices for writing development. Historically, first language (L1) composition teachers emphasized the written product in terms of grammatical accuracy and stylistic quality. Similarly, early research and work in second language (L2) writing emphasized grammatical correctness. This paradigm was influenced by the behaviorist work of psychologist B. F. Skinner. That position underscores teachers' beliefs that the best way for students to learn a language was to teach them a series of incremental steps and to provide positive reinforcements in the form of a reward or praise. In addition, to ensure students' success in language learning,

teachers had to first practice simple sentence structures and gradually move to learning more complex structures. Teachers also corrected student errors to develop writing fluency in the language. The focus on grammar and controlled writing tasks characterized and dominated most second language and English as a second language (ESL) writing classes until the 1970s.

Process Writing Movement

The traditional view of writing was challenged when researchers such as Emig (1977) and Elbow (1973) began to look at what good writers do when they write. In their seminal work, the researchers found that writers not only focus on grammar, but they also actively engage in thinking as they write and discover ideas through activities such as free-writing and brainstorming. This research initiated a movement known as process writing, which is a major influence in how teachers approach writing in their classrooms today. The focus of most writing instruction today has moved away from error correction and emphasis on the final product to thinking and discovering ideas using free-writing techniques, such as keeping a notebook, or using dialogue journals or graphic organizers in the initial stages of composing. Today, the English language composition classroom concentrates on helping student writers develop an authentic voice and construct complex essays across multiple genres, including narrative, persuasive, and expository text. Teachers work with students across the various phases of the writing process, resulting in a final product.

Social Nature of Writing

In the 1980s, research in writing began to examine the social nature of and purpose of writing. In this perspective, writing knowledge and behaviors are conditioned by social and historic situations in which writing processes are performed. In other words, individuals' conceptions of writing are always developed relative to their previous situations and experiences with writing, as well as previous encounters with text and the context of writing.

For example, a writer who has just returned from a cultural exchange program abroad would describe his or her experiences differently for distinct writing situations: (1) in a letter to his or her family or (2) in an essay for a social studies or composition teacher. The writer must make different rhetorical choices for each different audience, because these readers may construct meaning derived from the writing differently. Hence, to communicate successfully, the writer must have an awareness of the cultural, social, and rhetorical expectations of the discourse communities. Discourse community refers to a group of people with similar values, aims, aspirations, and expectations (Reid, 1993). Bartholomae (1985) expressed this notion eloquently in his article, "Inventing the University": "The [university] student has to learn how to speak our [academic community] language, to speak as we do, to try on the peculiar ways of knowing, selecting, evaluating, reporting, concluding, and arguing that define the discourse of our community" (p. 34). Although the ability to write grammatically correct sentences is a prerequisite to proficiency in writing, it alone is not a sufficient condition for generating text. Many composition teachers have encountered students who can write perfectly accurate sentences but can-

not generate text that accurately and appropriately communicates meaning to the reader. This apparent difficulty may stem from unfamiliarity with the multiple rhetorical conventions for different discourse communities.

Teachers can help student writers develop this awareness by guiding students to write beyond their own, limited present experience and knowledge. Dialogue journals, peer journals, and personal journals are effective tools for helping students develop an awareness of audience expectations and of themselves as writers. Teachers can also provide good sources of literature and essays written by a variety of writers and on a variety of topics for students to read, respond to, and recast their interpretation to increase awareness of the dialectal activity among the reader, the writer, and the text. Importantly, teachers can choose among sources that reflect the ethnic, racial, and linguistic backgrounds of the students in the classroom. Nathenson-Mejia and Escamilla (2003) have suggested guidelines for teachers of Spanish-speaking ELLs to use in selecting high quality children's literature for the classroom. They suggest that teachers analyze the author's purpose; cultural background; use of two languages; and positive identity affirmation of Latinos, including images portrayed in the books.

Early studies in composition (Flower, 1979; Kirsch, 1990; Kroll, 1985; Piche & Roen, 1987; Rubin, 1994; Rosenblatt, 1994, 2005) underscore that writing processes are also influenced by the circumstances in which writers write and their attempt to balance their purpose as authors of with the readers' purpose for reading. These studies strongly suggest that increased audience awareness and knowledge of textual conventions are characteristics of mature or proficient writers. This "to-and-fro" interplay between the reader and the text (Rosenblatt, 1988) is also echoed in L2 writing research (Mangelsdorf, Roen, & Taylor, 1990).

Research in contrastive rhetoric has underscored the influences of oral culture and social values on how individuals from different cultures choose to write (Anderson, 1991; Connor, 1987; Kaplan, 1988). Though some of this research (e.g., Kaplan, 1988) has been challenged as generalizations across cultural groups, different cultural thought patterns can reveal writers' preferences for organizing written texts in different languages. Rhetorically, English is generally considered to have a linear structure exemplified by the introduction of a general idea or topic followed by supporting statements or ideas. Writers of Thai and Arabic language can exhibit different organizational patterns that allow for higher degrees of digressions, repetitions, and use of narrative structures that are deemed less suitable to academic writing. Similarly, Spanish speakers sometimes use digressions in writing to provide detail and context.

In addition, writers may have different views about what is important in a subject or the appropriate way of communicating with someone who is older or an authority figure. These views will affect the way a writer writes. Because writing is a very complex skill that most students will find difficult to master without formal instruction, it is sometimes necessary to highlight these differences explicitly to second language writers by providing many good models of writing in English and opportunities to use writing extensively in learning other skill areas so that students can see the various forms, uses, and value of learning to write.

Emergent Literacy Perspective

Many researchers of first and second language writing have found similarities between L1 and L2 writers. Harste, Woodward, and Burke (1984), in their study of preschool literacy learning, revealed that children have already had some experience with language and opportunities to use language in a wide variety of settings before they start school. By observing and analyzing individual three-, four-, five- and six-year-olds, they challenged earlier readiness assumptions about children's reading and writing as a product of maturational processes by showing how children's knowledge about the reading and writing process reflects the kinds of literacy opportunities they have encountered and experienced before coming to school. Children at very early ages have shown their understanding about the concept of print and print conventions in English. These concepts of print include the following:

❖ Printed words represent spoken words.
❖ Letters are strung together to form words, and sentences are made up of words. This is the alphabetic principle.
❖ Writing has an organized structure, moving from left-to-right or right-to-left.
❖ Conventions for writing are different for oral and written language. Written conventions such as periods, question marks, exclamation marks, capital and small letters, and text features signify different functions. The context of children's written language parallels what adults do with written texts. Identifiable surface text features reflect knowledge of different genres such as notes, stories, letters, grocery or birthday lists, maps, and so on.
❖ There are many exceptions of sound–letter correspondences in English.

Samples of Writing

Reading Rockets is an excellent website for reading materials, resources, and authentic writing samples. (See www.ReadingRockets.org).

Table 21-1 **Reading Readiness Subskills and Sample Objectives**

Subskills	Sample Objectives
Auditory discrimination	Identify and differentiate familiar sounds (car, horn, dog barking, siren) Identify rhyming words Identify sounds of letters
Visual discrimination	Recognize colors Recognize shapes Identify letters by name
Visual motor skills	Cut on a straight line with scissors Color inside the lines of a picture Hop on one foot
Large motor skills	Skip Walk on a straight line

Early research in second language writing (Hudelson, 1991) has also demonstrated how young second language writers begin to experiment using written symbols and drawing as a means of supporting their written texts, similar to first language writers (Clay, 1975; Harste, Woodward, & Burke, 1984). Beginning writer samples show that the writing has no meaning without the accompanying picture. It is clear that the writer did not yet grasp the specific relationship among print, meaning, and language. However, the writer does understand that writing should convey a message and uses letters and visual cues to represent the spoken message.

Writing Samples of English-Speaking Children

To understand the complex processes involved in understanding written language, teachers must ask this question: What must beginning writers of English know to reconstruct the alphabetic principle that they see being used around them? If we consider that speech streams are made up of individual sounds strung together to form words, and a combination of words forms sentences, we will know that sounds can be represented by a letter or a combination of letters. For example, when saying the word *cake*, we do not say /k/ /ey/ /k/, but rather produce a blend of sounds. Further, we do not coarticulate the final letter *e*. However, young children may find it difficult to discern individual words because what they hear is simply one continuous sound. This task is further compounded by their effort to pay attention to the meaning conveyed by spoken language. They also have difficulty in detecting sounds because the skill requires learners to reflect on language on an abstract level. Despite this apparent difficulty, young children display a remarkable ability in understanding the concept of rhyming words like *bat, cat, sat*, and *pat*. This demonstrates that children understand the concept of speech sounds by replacing the initial consonant sound to create a new word. This concept of speech sounds, or phonemic awareness, has been shown to be an important skill in early reading development and spelling and is a strong predictor of success in reading (Adams, 1990).

Research on emergent literacy in English as a nonnative language has demonstrated that ELLs follow a pattern similar to that exhibited by native speakers of English (Heald-Taylor, 1991; Hudelson, 1984, 1986). However, ELLs may come from different L1 backgrounds and vary considerably in their English proficiency and literacy experiences. Chinese writers, for example, use characters that represent ideographs (ideas in symbol form) rather than letters, as in English, Spanish, or Portuguese. Because of these reasons, ELL writers may benefit from instruction that emphasizes skill building at the word and sentence levels as well as comprehension by engaging in meaningful activities, such as reading and talking about predictable stories, poems, public signs, advertisement clips, and songs. These activities will help them explore the purpose and nature of reading, use writing as a means to express what they have learned, and use appropriate strategies to meet their purpose for writing.

Development of Alphabetic Writing

Several studies revealed an understanding of how children attempt to connect symbols and sounds in creating their own texts (Peregoy & Boyle, 2012; Sulzby, 1985). Using students' journal entries, Peregoy and Boyle identified similar categories between Mexican-American children's writing strategies in Spanish and those of English-speaking kindergartners' studied in Sulzby's research. Figure 21-1 presents seven developmental scripting strategies from Peregoy and Boyle's (1990) emergent writing research.

The categories shown in Figure 21-1 represent developmental sequences from the least to the most advanced. They are not discrete developmental sequences but rather are distributed along a continuum. In other words, some children in these studies used several scripting strategies in a single written text.

FIGURE 21-1 A Continuum of Developmental Scripting Strategies

Writing Type	Definition	Example
1. Scribble writing	wavy lines or forms that don't look like letters, but look a little like writing	 *(handwritten scribble)*
2. Pseudo letters	forms that look like letters, but aren't	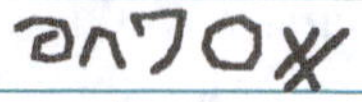 ꓛꓥ⨂Oⵝ
3. Letters	recognizable letters from the alphabet: often seen in long rows	edmch
4. Pseudo words	letter or pseudo letters that are spaced so they appear to be words	eracmn a onA
5. Copied words	words that have been copied from displays in the classroom	JOSE Verde
6. Self-generated words	words students created that are close enough to conventional spelling to be recognized	mesa sol
7. Self-generated sentences	conventional or nearly conventional sentences that communicate ideas	lo tengo 6 años

Source: Peregoy and Boyle (1990)

A Continuum of Developmental Scripting Strategies

Initially, young children use drawing to help develop their ideas for writing; they use wavy lines and forms that look like writing to represent ideas and write on topics that are familiar to them. As children begin to use print in the classroom, they develop early signs of letter formation that eventually become recognizable letters, representing sounds, and words strung together to form sentences. In experimenting with written language, children gradually reconstruct the spelling system to convey their meaning. Accuracy in conventional spelling does not develop until children have had much exposure and opportunities to use written language in formal instruction, and true accuracy in writing conventions typically occurs over multiple years of formal instruction and ongoing experience and exposure.

Children's writing samples reveal their spelling/scripting strategies. Figure 21-2 illustrates some interesting spelling strategies used by Linh, who was born in Vietnam and did not attend kindergarten when she first arrived in Canada. When she wrote the first sample, she was a first grader and was able to speak only a few words and simple phrases in English.

In Figure 21-2a, we see evidence of Linh's use of scribbling to symbolically represent the stories she wrote. Upon close examination, it appears that her scribbles have a strong resemblance to Chinese characters. A month later (in Figure 21-2b), she began using horizontal scribble that moved from left to right, indicating her awareness of the direction of English print. After two months (in Figure 21-2c), Linh used both conventional alphabet letters and scribble to symbolically represent her story about Halloween. In Figure 21-2d, she used scribble to represent her text except for the word *rain-day*, which she copied from a group chart. By December, she was well aware of the sound–symbol relationships, as revealed by her use of initial consonant spellings in words like *made* and *cookie*, as shown in Figure 21-2e. Although her subsequent texts contained decipherable words, complete thoughts about a single topic, and some correct spellings, she still relied on scribble as placeholders for parts of words she could not spell. Gradually, she could spell words

FIGURE 21-2 Linh's Writing Samples

Linh: Sept. 12, 1983. Age 5.9

(a)

I walking with my friend
to play with her.
I play the teacher.
It fun to play.
and my friend, I'm
the teacher. My friend
is a kid.

Linh Oct. 6, 1983. Age 5.10

(b)

Brian

Obc de fghÜKLMno P q r
stuv wx yz—ABC DE

My friend went out
trick or treating. She give
me candy. Her name is
Binh. I give her a candy.
Then I go home and give my
sister one candy or two. My
mom came home and said
I can't go out.

Linh Nov. 1, 1983. Age: 5.11

(c)

rain—day

I went outside with my
cousin. My cousin's name
Kien. My and my friend
is coming and we go inside
and we had hot water.

Linh Nov. 15, 1983. Age: 5.11

(d)

my mom m
a c r me a
a c my mom
I am m f
m C

My mom make me a cookie.

Linh: Dec. 1983. Age: 6.0

(e)

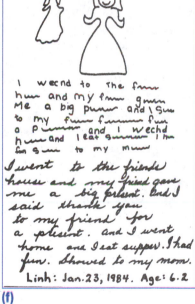

I wecnd to the f
h and my f g
Me a big p and I g
to my f f f
a P and I wechd
h and I eat 1 m
g to my m

I went to the friends
house and my friend gave
me a big present. And I
said thank you
to my friend for
a present. and I went
home and I eat supper. I had
fun. Showed to my mom.

Linh: Jan. 23, 1984. Age: 6.2

(f)

I am a rain drop.
and I'm droping
down. And I'm.
geting cold.
        The End.

Linh May 8, 1984 Age: 6.8

(g)

by sounding out the word (*wechd*, as shown in Figure 21-2f, and *dropping*, *getting*, as shown in Figure 21-2g) and use grammar and punctuation appropriately. These samples clearly demonstrate the nonlinear sequence of an emergent writer's scripting strategies. These texts also reveal an emerging writer's understanding that writing has meaning and purpose. It is also apparent that as Linh learned how to spell and included familiar sight vocabulary, she was gradually learning other aspects of literacy development like punctuation and writing sentences that convey complete, topically related thoughts. As Linh became more confident in her writing, her texts became longer and reflected her ability to integrate all conventions of writing: the symbolic representation, spelling, and composition.

How Do Home Environments Promote Early Literacy?

Children in many literate societies develop literacy skills well before they enter school. This evidence strongly suggests that children are exposed to language and literacy functions they see and use around them through environmental print in the form of magazines, billboards, food labels, road signs, television ads, labels on clothing and items, the Internet, text messaging, and different uses of literacy at home. Literate children also come from homes where printed text is readily available. One prevailing misconception commonly held by teachers to explain differential school achievement of language minority students and those from low income families is to attribute it to their deficient home environments, undeveloped language and values, and low self-esteem. However, a body of research refutes this commonly held assumption by demonstrating that children learn different functions of literacy that are used in their homes, regardless of their poverty and educational levels (Coady, 2009; Coady & Moore, 2010; Harste, Woodward, & Burke, 1984; Taylor & Dorsey-Gaines, 1988). For example, in her study of Spanish-speaking migrant families in north Florida, Coady (2009) found that home literacy practices included a variety of text and oral rhetorical structures that mainstream teachers may not be aware of when making home–school text connections. She noted that recipe sharing and reading of religious texts were important literacy events in the homes of the families.

One barrier to school success is attributed to how teachers' expectations of students from non-English cultures can influence their behaviors toward students and student achievement. Teachers who have high expectations for their students tend to spend more time interacting with students, give them more praise, and teach them valued and challenging curricula, all of which can increase student learning (Elliot, 1985). However, teachers who unconsciously form lower expectations for students may not spend as much time interacting with students and assign less challenging content and work in and outside the classroom, which will reduce learning opportunities and result in a wider gap between mainstream and ELLs. Although differences in cultural and social class differences may affect the speed at which students learn certain things, it is important for teachers to recognize and understand ways to use children's home language and literacy experiences as a means of facilitating their language and literacy in development in English.

Families can become more involved in their children's education and literacy development in several ways. For a start, parents can model the value of literacy to their children through literate behaviors such as reading newspapers, stories, or any available print material in their homes. Parents can also offer literacy opportunities in their everyday activities by making up a grocery list, reading and writing messages, looking for coupon ads in the newspapers, or reading public signs at the stores and on the road. These activities expose children to the value, function, and structures of written language that are instrumental to early literacy development. It is important that teachers of ELLs explore, recognize, and support the various, often non-mainstream literacy events of ELLs' families (Moll et al., 1992).

Too often, we hear arguments that low income and linguistically diverse parents are apathetic about their children's education or are unable to contribute to their children's school success. This popular view can be proven wrong if schools arrest the problem by responding in ways that are socially and academically promising for parents and their children to succeed. Schools can provide many ways in which parents can become involved in their children's literacy development. The vignette at the beginning of the chapter describes how teachers can encourage parents to read their children's publications and provide feedback to their children. And developing materials and products in both the first language and in English affirms' ELLs' bilingual and biliterate identities (Cummins, 2001c). Not only will children feel a sense of pride for their work and experience purposeful writing for a real audience from whom they will get feedback, but they are also able to see the growth that their children are making in school.

Parents who do not speak, read, or write in English can provide feedback in their home language or illustrate their reactions through drawings that can be translated. Even parents who lack high educational levels and English proficiency can appreciate the value of literacy in their everyday life and "know" when their children are making learning gains. As noted above, some ESL students may come from families with a strong oral tradition of sharing family stories and experiences. These families can be an excellent source of information for their respective cultures. Parents can share personal stories and pictures with their children, be invited to share books and cultural items, or demonstrate how to create something in their culture that could culminate in a writing activity for the whole class. These kinds of writing activities are usually fun and engage learners in deeper levels of thinking processes.

Differences between Oral and Written Language

The emergent literacy perspective has provided ample evidence that children use their oral language as a foundation for developing early literacy. Although written language is an extension of oral language, they are not exactly reflections of each other. One difference between oral and written language lies in their conventions. Some ELLs need explicit instruction in making sentences and paragraphs connect to each other; in spelling words, especially those with irregular patterns; or in introducing and organizing ideas in writing for an imagined or a real audience. Unlike writing, oral language provides more opportunities for the listener to ask questions for clarification, to use both verbal and nonverbal context cues, and to learn about the speaker to interpret the speaker's message. However, writers must learn to organize and express their thoughts clearly using precise and accurate language, without the benefit of elaboration to the prospective reader. This is often a major struggle for many second language writers in their early development of writing in English. Some ELLs who have a strong oral language tradition in their primary language may benefit from explicit instruction in writing. These students need models of good writing behaviors and exposure to different types of texts and functions of literacy uses. Table 21-2 lists various types of classroom writing and their functions (adapted from Peregoy & Boyle, 2012).

Teachers need to be familiar with what writing is all about: why people write, what kinds of things they write and for what purposes, and what writers of different kinds of writing need to write successfully. At the elementary levels, students should get ample opportunities to read and write different types of narrative and descriptive texts that emphasize telling, retelling, and descriptions. Students in secondary schools must, however, get more training and practice to compose texts beyond telling and retelling. Once students enter middle and secondary schools, they are expected to learn to compose with the ability to transform information (Grabe & Kaplan, 1996). This type of ability is often demanded in creative writing and in expository and argumentative texts that emphasize high levels of reasoning and thinking. These types of writing often require a number of critical thinking skills such as collecting and organizing information, analyzing and presenting evidence to support a claim or a position, synthesizing information, and evaluating evidence from different and sometimes opposing positions. Collaborative writing projects, in which students conduct research on their topic of choice within a cooperative structure, can help them develop both

Table 21-2 **Types of Classroom Writing and their Functions**

Forms of Print Used in Class	Sample Functions of Print Used in the Classroom
Lists	For organizing and remembering information
Order forms	For purchasing items for classroom activities
Checks	To pay for classroom book orders
Ledgers	To keep account of classroom responsibilities
Labels and captions	To explain pictures on bulletin boards or other displays
Personal journals	To generate ideas on a project, etc.
Buddy journals	To develop or promote a personal relationship
Record-keeping journal	To keep track of a project or experiment
Interactive journal	To converse in writing; to promote a personal friendship
Notes	To take information down so it will be remembered
Personal letters	To share news with a companion or friend
Business letters	To apply for a job; to complain about a product; to recommend a procedure
Narratives	To relate stories to others; to share tales about other persons or to illustrate themes or ideas
Scripts (e.g., reader's theater)	To entertain the class by acting out stories
Essay forms:	
Enumeration	To list information either by numbering or chronologically
Comparison/contrast	To show how two or more things are different or alike
Problem/solution	To discuss a problem and suggest solutions
Cause/effect	To show cause/effect relationships
Thesis/proof	To present an idea and persuade readers of its validity

thinking and language proficiency. (Specific strategies such as structured controversies and case studies that emphasize higher-order thinking will be discussed later in this chapter.)

Teachers must also be cognizant of the various stages of writing development to evaluate whether students are making normal progress in their writing development and plan reinforcement activities based on the students' needs. In addition, teachers must provide opportunities for learners to read good literature and opportunities to respond to them through social and intellectual exchanges with others. This process will help learners view writing and reading as a thinking activity, wherein students have to apply their knowledge of combining sentences into a coherent discourse to solve a problem for both the author and the intended audience.

Why Is Writing Difficult for ELL Writers?

Although there are similarities between first and second language writers, specific factors are unique to ELLs that may make writing in English quite difficult. One difficulty is that written language requires a greater degree of formality and lexical (vocabulary) range and longer and more complex sentences that are not often used in oral language. Fraser Gupta (2012) notes, for example, that oral language is far less rule-governed than written forms of the language. With respect to second language writing, she notes that "learning from speech presents even more problems than learning from reading. Speakers have greater freedom than do writers" (p. 251). Written language generally follows more conventions and stricter rules than does oral language production. Although second language writers frequently attempt to use their knowledge of oral English in writing, this results in poor writing outcomes.

For example, new ELLs may recognize and understand expressions like "cool it" (to become calm), "he lost a cool million" (entire or full amount), or "cool one's heels" (to be calm or to be kept waiting for a long time) easily because of their frequent use in everyday oral conversations, but they may not realize that these informal forms are less acceptable in written discourse. ELLs essentially use their emerging knowledge of (informal) oral expressions and structures in English to write (formal) structured text. Hence, their development of writing reflects, to some extent, the oral language they have acquired, so it is not surprising to see occurrences of informal vocabulary use in their academic papers that could affect writing quality. Moreover, the same word can carry multiple meanings in different contexts, which is confusing to new language learners. In other words, having a wide vocabulary is not always a sufficient condition for good writing; writers must have knowledge of different levels of formality (audience) and context-based meanings with respect to vocabulary use.

Similarly, knowledge of grammar is essential to good writing, and teachers know that they must pay some attention to grammar when responding to students' work. However, ELLs may not realize that there are levels of formal and informal grammar used by native speakers of English. For example, we often hear native English speakers utter statements such as, "Kim and me went to the store," and, "Who do you give the book to?" ELLs may pick up these forms and use them in academic writing when, in fact, the standard form is, "Kim and I went to the store," and, "To whom do you give the book?" In addition, there is a mismatch between form and function in learning English grammar that many new English learners will find confusing and complicated. For example, the English present progressive tense -ing is used to describe actions in progress, as in "She is reading a book." However, the same -ing form can be used to describe action in the future ("You are throwing a party this Friday") or to describe a habitual action ("The earth's temperature is rising"). In fact, future action can be expressed using any of the following forms: "I will study tomorrow; I am going to study tomorrow; I will be studying tomorrow." In other words, students must learn a variety of forms that express a similar function that they will hear and are expected to use in real life communication.

In addition to structural difficulties, ELL writers must also learn the conventions of written English. They have to learn how to initiate a discussion in written language, explain, elaborate, and present opposing views, and refute them, all of which require some attention to audience and purpose for writing. These highly complex skills can be an enormously daunting task for new English learners, who are unfamiliar with the expectations of a new discourse community because they have to confront changes in thinking and behavior that they ordinarily are not required to do. Teachers can help students to develop necessary skills for successful communication by focusing students' attention on audience expectations and explaining how rhetorical conventions of academic prose meet the expectations of the academic audience.

Another difficulty is evident in the way culture affects communication patterns. Studies in writing across cultures reveal cultural patterns of prose structure that are quite distinct from English prose. To communicate effectively within another culture, English language learners must learn the social processes and conventions for that culture. In addition, differences in attitudes and values about what constitutes cheating and plagiarism in academic writing may vary from culture to culture. For example, students who come from some Asian cultures emphasize respect for authority and expert knowledge of authors. The cultural view maintains that those authors must be preserved, and any changes made to those authors' work (e.g., through paraphrasing) would jeopardize the integrity of the author. Those practices are interpreted as plagiarism in U.S. classrooms (Yamada, 2003).

Moreover, in many Latin and Arabic cultures, cooperation rather than competition is emphasized;

hence, students sometimes expect cooperation from their peers in writing assignments that they may be required to do independently. Teachers can help ELLs become linguistically and culturally proficient in the expectations of the English-speaking academic community by encouraging them to discuss linguistic and cultural reasons for their writing errors in English. In this respect, students' self-assessment of writing can become a valuable tool for raising such awareness. It is also necessary for teachers to demonstrate that these errors are not necessarily "incorrect forms," but rather a set of unique conventions that fulfill the expectations of the target audience.

Linguistic Error or Language Transfer?

What teachers often misinterpreted as errors in writing may more accurately reflect a transfer of linguistic knowledge from the student's first language into English. ELLs, particularly those who have acquired literacy in the L1, tend to use that knowledge to inform their writing in English. The writing sample below of Diego, an eleventh grade ELL from Bolivia who had been in the United States for eight months at the time of his writing, is one example. In their analysis of Diego's writing, Coady and Ariza (2010) note that the linguistic "errors" are actually examples of language transfer from Spanish into English. One example in the writing is orthography or spelling of certain words. Diego uses sounds or phonemes from Spanish to write in English, such as the "cu" construction to write the word "quality."

In addition, Diego attempts to use idiomatic expressions in English, an advanced linguistic feature for ELLs, but he does so inaccurately. For example, he writes, "if I wake up on the president bush's pants," for which he intends to write, "if I were in the President's shoes." Although this "error" may give readers a chuckle, Diego's intention of using this complex writing feature is quite impressive and courageous, particularly as he had only been in the United States for a number of months at the time of the writing sample.

Upon closer analysis, we see that Diego's writing reflects a complex and sophisticated worldview, one that takes into consideration the audience of his writing, in addition to his knowledge of complex international political and economic systems. For example, note how Diego writes "America (continent)," in order to carefully clarify for the reader the difference between America (as in the United States) and the larger continents of North and South America. As noted earlier, one key characteristic of advanced writers is knowledge of audience and purpose for writing. So while Diego's writing may be viewed from an "error" perspective, a different analysis reveals very advanced features of language transfer (knowledge of two language systems), context (sociopolitical), and audience, namely his understanding that the audience may consist of monolingual and monocultural readers.

Characteristics of the Beginning Writer

Beginning writers demonstrate minimal writing skills because they lack familiarity with the language and the writing process. They generally lack a wide knowledge of vocabulary and sentence patterns and thus must first become acquainted with the English alphabet and simple sentence structures. They also need to acquaint themselves with English spelling and the sound–symbol relationships in written language. As such, beginning writers may write using phonetic spelling, a common strategy in which they write out the words based on how they sound them out. Although these phonetic spellings are incorrect, they can offer valuable information to teachers about what learners already know about letters and the sounds they represent. This information can then be used to design appropriate phonics lessons for students based on their need. Teachers must also bear in mind that much of the language produced by the beginning writer will closely mirror oral language. As such, the language experience approach, described in the chapter on reading and in the following section on shared writing, is effective because it encourages students to practice writing early

FIGURE 21-3 Diego's Writing Sample (Coady & Ariza, 2010)

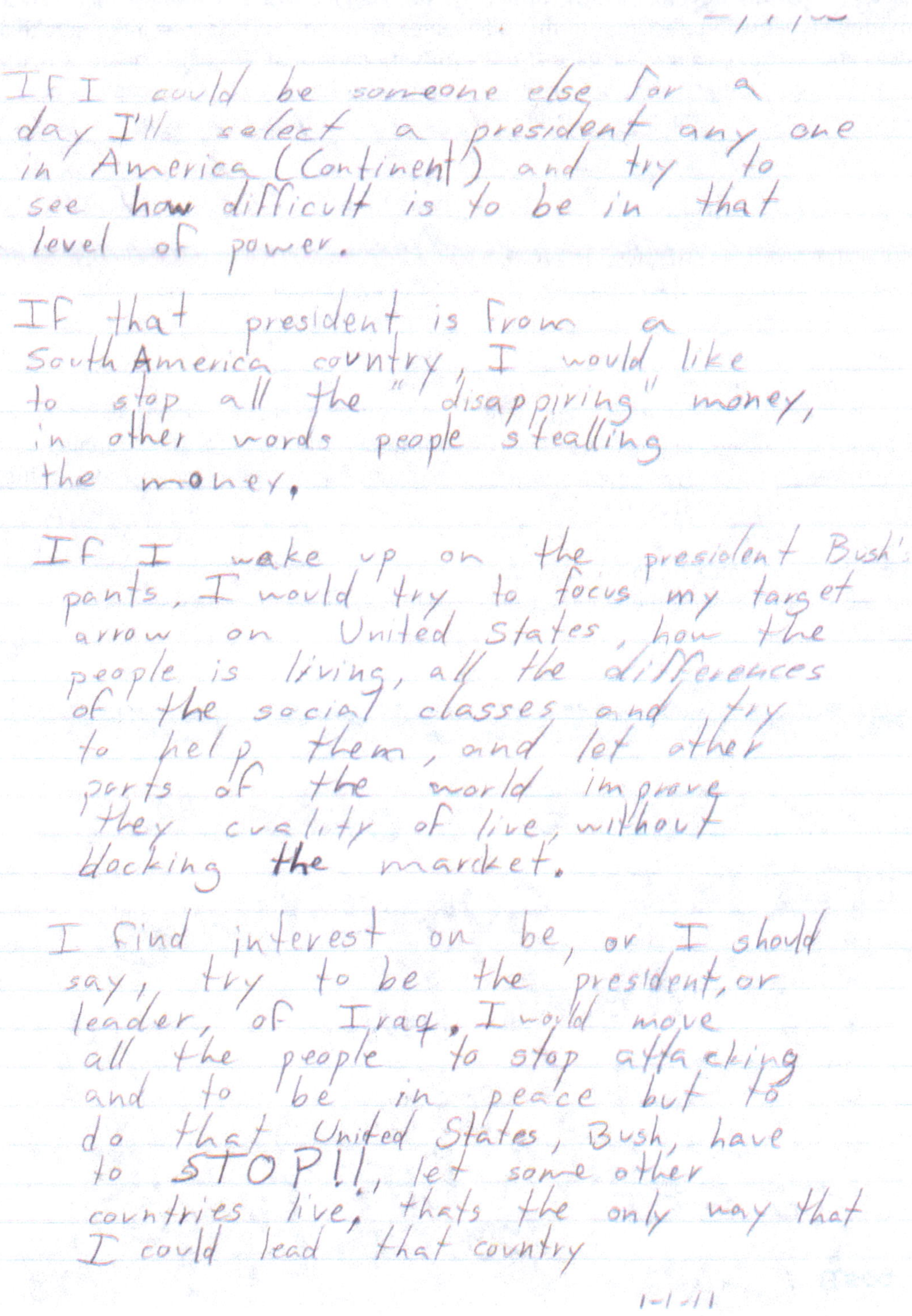

IF I could be someone else for a day I'll select a president any one in America (Continent) and try to see how difficult is to be in that level of power.

IF that president is from a South America country, I would like to stop all the "disappiring" money, in other words people stealling the money.

IF I wake up on the president Bush's pants, I would try to focus my target arrow on United States, how the people is living, all the differences of the social classes and try to help them, and let other parts of the world improve they cuality of live, without blocking the market.

I find interest on be, or I should say, try to be the president, or leader, of Iraq, I would move all the people to stop attacking and to be in peace but to do that United States, Bush, have to STOP!!, let some other countries live, thats the only way that I could lead that country

1-1-11

on by getting them to read, copy, and transcribe their own familiar texts. Writing development is further honed by inviting students to talk, brainstorm, and map their ideas and to use repeated language structures to expand their vocabulary and language use. Figure 21-4 demonstrates an example of beginning level writing.

Beginning Level Writing Sample

Although the writer wrote a fairly short text and used relatively few words to describe his little brother, he was able to convey his feelings about his younger brother quite clearly. It is evident that the writer already knows contracted forms (*don't* and *can't*). The writer also demonstrated early attempts at combining sentences using conjunctions such as *and* and *but* that seemed to mirror how the writer would speak orally. The text also used invented spellings that reflect sounding-out strategy ("youst" for *used*; "hier" for *hair*) and a visual strategy that indicates that the writer has seen the word but did

not get the sequence correct ("abuot" for *about*). Although the writer did not use many invented spellings in this text, it is important to note that he wrote a very short text. It is also obvious that the writer may need further practice in capitalization and punctuation as well as guidance in developing ideas.

Characteristics of the Intermediate Writer

Although intermediate writers have a more developed knowledge of simple sentences, mechanics, and conventional spellings than their beginner counterparts, they still need to master a variety of simple and complex sentence structures and develop organizational strategies for paragraphing and ordering their ideas in written composition. In higher grade levels, students may be introduced to more advanced vocabulary in their academic content, which can make their spelling skills appear less conventional initially. Thus, they need constant, repeated expo-

---

FIGURE 21-4   Beginning Level Writing Sample

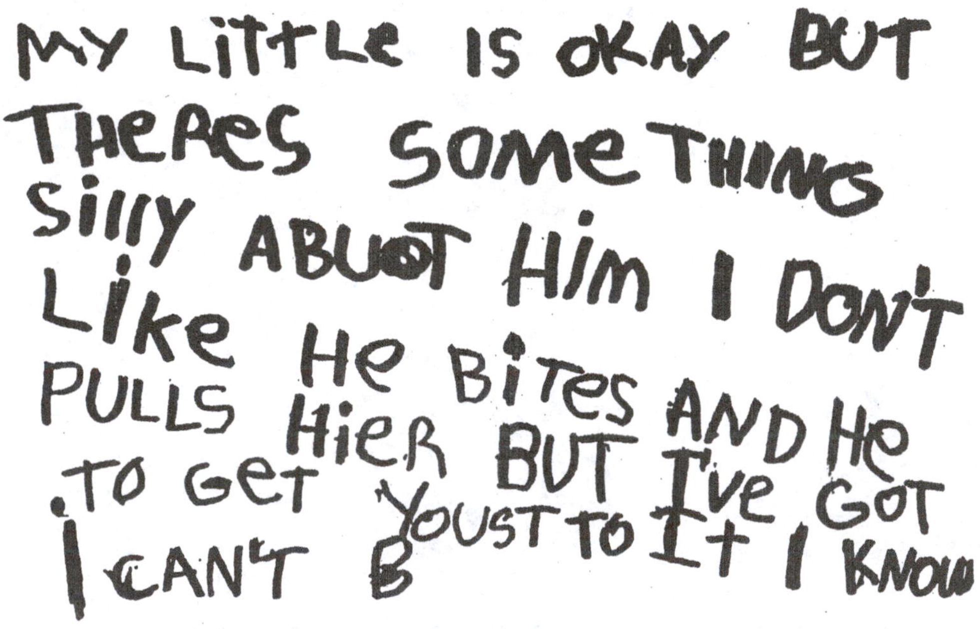

MY LITTLE IS OKAY BUT THERES SOMETHING SILLY ABUOT HIM I DON'T LIKE HE BITES AND HE PULLS HIER BUT I'VE GOT TO GET YOUST TO IT I KNOW I CAN'T B

Source: Broward County Public School K–3 Literacy Folder

sure and multiple passes to difficult content, and they need to become familiar with the spellings of complex words. Intermediate writers may still rely heavily on using a few sentence patterns while developing their English language skills as a conservative strategy to avoid errors. Because of this, teachers must encourage student writers to view error making as an active part of learning by responding to students' writing and providing opportunities for students to focus on different aspects of composing such as accuracy, quality of ideas, and organization of ideas. Although intermediate writers may write longer texts than those written by beginners, they may still make frequent and obvious errors in punctuation, grammar, and usage as they juggle other composing constraints. The essay shown in Figure 21-5 demonstrates an example of intermediate ELL writing.

From this example, it is clear that the writer had quite a good vocabulary to express different ideas about his parents. The writer also wrote a longer text than that written by the beginner shown in Figure 21-4. He has a good grasp of sentence structures in English and knowledge of present forms for ex-

pressing future ("My daddy is going to take me to Racha this summer") and frequent and habitual action ("Cyoba is so hot so my mommy likes hot") as well as past forms ("My mom came from Cyoba . . ."). The writer also attempted, quite successfully, to use subordinate clauses in complex sentences such as "My mom is going to take me to Cyoba when she feels safe," "My mom was varey rich intil the Bad prasadint in Cyoba tock thar money away," and, "Now thay are powr but daddy gives Mommy money." The writer also shows the ability to develop a topic using relevant supporting details. However, he used invented spellings and tended to use a few simple structures consistently throughout the paper (e.g., clauses beginning with *so*, as in "Racha is clod so my daddy likes cold" and "Cyoba is hot so my mommy likes hot") to express cause–effect relationships. The writer also used capitalization correctly most of the time except for some words. This can be reinforced through a series of reading and writing activities. This writer also needs further practice in developing different types of sentences and organizing ideas to improve his writing.

FIGURE 21-5 Intermediate Level Sample Writing

My Mom came from Cyoba and my dad came from Racha. My Daddy is going to take me to Racha this summr. My Mom is going to take me to Cyoba when she feels safe. Racha is clod so my daddy likes cold. Cyoba is hot so my mommy likes hot. My mom shows me lots of magasens about Cyoba.

My dad tels me about racha. My Dad's Dad was ararond in the time Anastasha was alive. My mom was varey rich intil the Bad Prasadint in Cyoba tock thar money away. Now thay are powr but Daddy givs Mommy Money.

Source: Broward County Public School K–3 Literacy Folder

Strategies for Assisting All ELL Writers

Process Writing

Process writing is a teaching approach that breaks down writing into manageable chunks or stages (Murray, 2004). It is a way of getting students to experience what most writers think and do when they write. These stages are not intended to be sequentially linear; rather, they are evolving processes that cause the writer to move back and forth between stages. These stages are broken down into five components: prewriting/brainstorming, drafting, revising, editing, and publishing.

Stage 1: Prewriting

In the first stage, writers are expected to think and plan for what they will write. A few techniques can be used to assist students in generating ideas. They are as follows:

❖ Brainstorm: Students call out ideas, words, or phrases. The teacher accepts all ideas from students and writes them down on the board. This activity helps students to generate many ideas that they may not be able to produce alone.

❖ List: Students list every idea that they can link with the topic without using complete sentences. This will help students to focus on the important and interesting ideas they have instead of struggling to find the correct form for those ideas.

❖ Freewrite: Students write very quickly in two to three minutes, any ideas they have that are associated with the topic. They have to write continuously until the time is up. If they run out of ideas, they write *"what shall I write next"* until the next idea comes along.

❖ Visual map: The teacher constructs a visual map, starting with a central idea in the middle circle, and asks students to generate as many ideas as they can. This map can be used to help students organize or classify ideas into categories or subcategories and to help them decide which ideas are important enough to include and which should be excluded. Figure 21-6 shows an example of a visual map commonly referred to as clustering (see examples of graphic organizers in the chapter on reading). Essentially, this is the initial plan of their writing.

❖ Question dial: Students generate many ideas using questions that journalists routinely ask themselves when gathering material for a story: Who? What? Where? When? Why? How? Figure 21-7 shows an example of this technique.

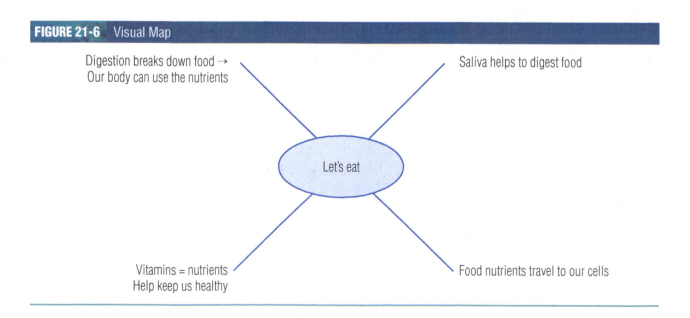

FIGURE 21-6 Visual Map

Digestion breaks down food →
Our body can use the nutrients

Saliva helps to digest food

Let's eat

Vitamins = nutrients
Help keep us healthy

Food nutrients travel to our cells

FIGURE 21-7   Question Dial

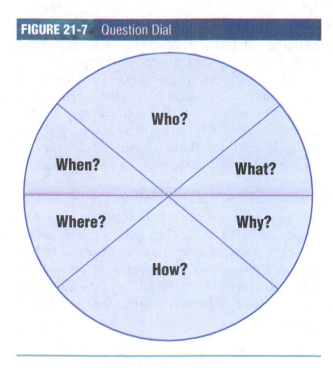

Stage 2: Drafting

Based on the plan students have created, they write their first draft, paying attention to their purpose and audience as they write. The significant part of this stage is to get students to focus on selecting words, sentence structures, and style that make sense to the author and convey meaning to the reader. Teachers can provide feedback to developing writers through conferencing to help students focus on content and meaning. Some questions that can be asked during conferencing may include, but are not limited to, the following:

❖ What is the essay about?
❖ Why are you writing it?
❖ Whom are you writing for?
❖ What is your favorite part? Why?
❖ What ideas did you leave out? Why?

These questions encourage students to elaborate and think about their topic at a deeper level of meaning, which makes a difference in students' thought processes and development of mature writing skills.

Stage 3: Revising

Students exchange their texts with their classmates to get new insights from their peers about what they have written. In this stage, students are encouraged to think as they rewrite and incorporate feedback to make writing clearer and more interesting. Because some students may not be accustomed to reading their peers' writing, much less give feedback to their peers about the writing pieces, these students may need additional help on how to give constructive feedback. Figures 21-8, 21-9, and 21-10 illustrate structured worksheets that teachers can give students for peer review (Reid, 1993). These questions can help students learn how to provide feedback to one

---

FIGURE 21-8   Worksheet: Reader-Writer Response

1. Writer: What one question would you like your reader to answer or what one problem did you need a second opinion about?

2. Reader: Answer the question. Be specific. Then complete the following statements:

    a. The best part of this paper was _____ .

    b. When I finished the essay I thought/felt _____ .

    c. One place I disagreed was where you said _____ .

    d. One experience or idea I had that was similar to this was _____ .

    e. When you said _____ , I thought about _____ .

    f. One suggestion I want to make to improve the paper is _____ .

Instructions: The writer provides draft copies for the readers.

1. Readers: Ask the writer: "How can we help you?"

2. Writer (who comes to class with notes that anticipate the question): Indicate specific areas in which you need help.

3. Readers: Listen and take notes, then offer verbal and written feedback and suggestions.

4. Writer: Listen and take notes. (Writer retains full authority to evaluate the advice and make the final decisions.)

FIGURE 21-10 Worksheet: Audience Analysis

1. What do you think influenced the writer to write this essay or paragraph? In other words, why did the writer choose this topic?

2. Who is the audience the writer is trying to change or influence?

3. What does the writer know about the audience? What doesn't the writer know about the audience?

4. What do you think is the writer's purpose in writing this paper?

5. What change or action does the writer think the audience will make?

6. What does the writer use to influence the readers?

7. Does the essay work? Does it answer questions that the readers will need?

another. Teachers can also model the use of these questions when discussing a shared writing piece produced by the class.

Stage 4: Editing

In this stage, students proofread their papers for accuracy in grammar, sentence structure, spelling, and organization. Many students find this a challenging task because error correction requires tacit knowledge of language that many beginning writers do not

yet possess. Hence, these writers may not be able to edit their own texts effectively to result in improved quality of writing. At the same time, some teachers are reluctant to correct student errors in writing because such an approach prevents students from learning to analyze their texts for accuracy and becoming aware of errors as a natural process of developing their writing skills. To help learners understand errors as part of the learning process, teachers must develop a means of providing error correction feedback that would lead students to correct independently. One suggestion to facilitate students' self-correction is to provide them with a marking code that lists different symbols to represent different types of writing errors. For example, SP for spelling, T for tense, and so forth. Table 21-3 shows a sample marking code (Chitravelu, Sithamparam, & The, 1995).

Table 21-3 Sample Marking Code

Symbol	Type of error
SP	Spelling
T	Tense
P	Punctuation
WC	Word choice
WO	Word order
WF	Word form
SV	Subject–verb agreement
C	Capitalization
?	Unclear
^	Add a word
X	Omit this
//	New paragraph needed

Another way to facilitate students' self-correction is to utilize students as experts in some areas of language. For example, in the vignette at the beginning of this chapter, the classroom teacher, Mrs. Brown assigned specific tasks to different individuals based on what she believed to be the students' areas of strength, including their first languages and home cultures. This strategy helps students build their self-esteem as they are recognized to be "experts" in a specific area and build a sense of community. It also reverts the responsibility on the learners to become editors of their own texts.

Teachers of ELLs might refer to both Herrera (2010) and Cummins (2007), who have studied the outcomes of using biographical and autobiographical writing as methods for affirming students' multiple linguistic and cultural identities. The Multiliteracies Project (www.multiliteracies.ca, Cummins, 2007) is one example of how multilingual students engage in literacy tasks that reflect multiple forms of writing (print, images, and digital contexts) that represent their knowledge and skills. In that project, multilingual students' identities are affirmed through the use of their (and other) language(s) to produce autobiographies that reveal their cultural and linguistic backgrounds.

Stage 5: Publishing

Publishing students' works that are produced collaboratively or individually is important because it supports and celebrates the writing success of ELLs. Students can publish their favorite poems or stories, their own alphabet or rhyming books, or a class newspaper in which different students are assigned to write different sections such as the editorial, feature articles, advertisements, and news stories. Newspapers can also be an excellent outlet for students to better inform their parents of class announcements and other upcoming projects and provide information about students' writing; however, these outreach materials must reflect the first languages of the families, and teachers must know which families can read printed materials. A bilingual newsletter can be published and sent out to parents on a monthly basis to keep parents informed about classroom accomplishments, activities, and upcoming events. Illustrations can also be published with a foreword written by the students in both English and the various first languages.

In addition to publishing stories and poems, students can write essays to gain additional practice in writing that is related to the content information they have learned. To expose students to a variety of writing purposes and tasks, they can publish a book containing letters that were used as a means for carrying out "written conversations" on a topic or issue related to specific content information. This publication invites students to articulate, examine, compare, synthesize, and evaluate their thoughts in light of the input they receive from other peers in the expressive form of writing that is most familiar to them. Other publishing activities include case studies that discuss a dilemma about an issue they have researched. Students can then read individual or group case studies and offer two written responses to the dilemma, each from a different point of view. These responses do not necessarily have to convey opposing viewpoints. This activity will help students develop a sense of the value and function of their own writing. Finally, Coady, Nelson, and Coady (2014, in press) created culturally and linguistically responsive *fotonovelas*, or graphic novels, to communicate with parents in a rural, north Florida school district. Students can discuss, create, and disseminate these types of materials to underscore home–school linkages and partnerships that support student learning.

Shared Writing

Shared writing, also known as interactive writing, is often utilized in the language experience approach. In shared writing, students and teachers are involved in the process of composing a text. Through discussion, teachers guide students in selecting topics and building ideas; provide a model for vocabulary, language structures, and text organization; introduce basic concepts of print; and emphasize reading and writing for meaning. The following is a sample dialogue that illustrates how shared writing works to teach phonemic awareness and mechanics:

Teacher:	What are some of the things that the click beetle does?
Cheng:	It go for a walk in the morning.
Teacher:	How shall we write this in our story?
Ravi:	The click beetle go for a walk.
Teacher:	How many words are there in the sentence?
Ravi:	Six.
Teacher:	To begin our sentence, do we use a small or capital T?
Jack:	Capital t.
Teacher:	How do we spell "the"?
Felipe:	T-h-e.
Teacher:	You're right. What words did you learn from the story that have the /th/ sound?
Jason:	Three.
Maria:	Then. The beetle say "thank you" to the old beetle.
Teacher:	Yes, then and thank have the /th/ sound. Are there other words?
Katya:	Earthworm.
Teacher:	How many sounds does earthworm have?
Cheng:	Six.
Teacher:	What comes after the /th/ sound?
Maria:	Weh-weh . . . worm.
Teacher:	What is the first sound in click?
Patrice:	kl-kl.
Teacher:	How many letters are there for the /kl/ sound?
Patrice:	Two . . . k and l

Another sample dialogue illustrates how shared writing can be used to highlight other aspects of composition. The teacher reads the following short passage the class had initially written:

Teacher:	*One day a girl was walking on the road. There were a lot of people and cars on the road. She dropped her book on the road. A woman tapped her shoulder. The woman gave her the book. The girl thanked the woman.*
	What can we add to make the story more interesting?
Cheng:	We can say it is a busy road in downtown Delray Beach. Can we give her a name too?
Teacher:	I like that, Cheng. What shall we call her?
Teresa:	We can call her "Jenny," like my grandmother.
Teacher:	That is a beautiful name. Okay we shall call her "Jenny." What else can we add so that the reader can see what the day was like?
Thomas:	The day was hot. And so people are wearing hats. They are walking very fast.
Teacher:	Can anyone say the first sentence in our story?
Gloria:	It was a very hot day. There were a lot of people walking on the road.

Tina:	Many people are wearing hats because it was very hot. There are many cars on the road, too.
Teacher:	Great. Now what else can we add to make us understand Jenny's feelings?
Krista:	She dropped the book which was a gift from her grandmother. It is her favorite book.
Teacher:	(She writes the students' dictated sentences.) Can we combine these two sentences? How should we write it?
Leo:	She dropped her favorite book which was a gift from her grandmother.
Teacher:	Great sentence, Leo. Now, do you think Jenny knows that her book was missing?

The students in the class unanimously agreed that Jenny did not know she dropped the book until the woman tapped on her shoulder. The teacher continued to write the students' sentences on the board until they completed a new story. The students were then asked to compare any differences in the way the events were told in the two versions.

Because students' shared-writing products are written collaboratively, the final product is written in standard spelling. These products can be placed on the wall so that the class can read the pieces over and over again. Students can use these stories to help them write other stories independently. Teachers can also ask students to point to the words as they read to ensure that they are not reading solely from memory.

Pattern Writing

Pattern writing, sometimes known as parallel writing, provides opportunities for students to experiment with new words and grammatical structures within a sentence frame that is already familiar to the student. At the simplest level, students are required to substitute words or phrases; this task can be more challenging by requiring students to use more complex vocabulary and sentence level structures. An example of a simple parallel writing task would require students to replace a noun found in a pattern structure such as "I paint my _____ (smile/hair/eyes) just like this" with new words encountered in other story readings and discussions. This is particularly helpful for beginning writers because it allows students to review previously learned structures while using newly acquired words or phrases. This type of scaffolding allows learners

to link new and old information and get additional practice in using new structures and words.

Journal Writing

Writing is essentially a thinking, social activity. Students can benefit from using various forms of journal writing to engage in "conversations" with themselves and with others. Different types of journal writing that are commonly adopted in classroom instruction include personal journals, dialogue journals, and buddy journals. In personal journals, students are encouraged to assess their own writing practices and the effectiveness of their language use and strategies for communicating meaning and understanding about themselves as writers. Students can keep a diary to record their concerns or issues related to their writing three or four times a week in class. Dialogue and buddy journals provide a platform for students to hold "written conversations" about a writing piece with teachers and fellow students who have varied interests and knowledge of a topic. Dialogue journals encourage writers to use freewriting as a way to discover their thoughts and anticipate how their audience might react to their ideas, and match strategy use to meet the purpose of the audience and the author.

Strategies for Assisting Intermediate Writers

Because intermediate learners need further training in developing and organizing ideas and in mastering a variety of sentence structures and styles, several strategies are recommended: pattern writing, structured controversies, case studies, and paragraph organization.

Pattern Writing

Pattern writing is an effective way to help intermediate ELL writers expand their language proficiency beyond sentence levels. Different types of pattern poems known as diamante and tanka provide opportunities for students to use creative expressions and a variety of grammatical structures and organize sentences into coherent discourse within a specific pattern. Figure 21-11 illustrates an example of a diamante, which was contributed by Rashid Moore, an instructor in the teacher education department at Nova Southeastern University. Figure 21-12 illustrates an example of a tanka.

FIGURE 21-11	An Example of Diamante

Jupiter

Gigantic   Gaseous

Crushing   Freezing   Burning   Floating

Tiny   Rocky

Mercury

FIGURE 21-12	An Example of Tanka

Drifting in the sky

Clouds come and go in patterns

I look to the sun

The darkness hovers around

Slowly rain begins to fall.

A diamante is a five-line poem whose subject gradually changes into its opposite. Students can use the following pattern to write a diamante poem on topics that relate to their curriculum units:

Line 1: A person, animal, place, or thing

Line 2: Two adjectives (or a phrase) that describe line 1

Line 3: A total of four verbs: two describe the action in line 1; two describe the action in line 5

Line 4: Two adjectives (or a phrase) that describe line 5

Line 5: The opposite of line 1

In terms of content, the diamante example in Figure 21-11 compares and contrasts features of Jupiter and Mercury. In a few well-chosen words, the writer has touched on the gravity levels on each planet (crushing, floating), their relative temperatures (freezing, burning), their surface structures (gaseous, rocky), and their sizes (gigantic, tiny).

Tanka (Figure 21-12) is a traditional Japanese poem that is arranged in thirty-one syllables with a structure of five, seven, five, seven, and seven syllable lines. This form is considered to naturally suit the breathing rhythms of the Japanese people. This pattern poem encourages students to explore the delicate shades of meaning conveyed by words and sentence rhythms and "experience" the feelings invoked by words. Its structure is as follows:

First line: five syllables

Second line: seven syllables

Third line: five syllables

Fourth line: seven syllables

Fifth line: seven syllables

Structured Controversies

In structured controversies, students are expected to research and prepare a paper in which they advocate a position, analyze and critically evaluate information, synthesize and integrate information, take the perspective of others, and use logical reasoning to reach the highest quality decision possible based on both perspectives of the controversy. Although its analytical and turn-taking perspective is similar to a debate format, it is quite different in terms of how the controversy is resolved. In debates, two opposing sides maintain the position they advocated originally, whereas in structured controversy participants achieve resolutions by arriving at conclusions that take multiple perspectives into consideration. In debates, a judge determines the winner of the best argument. Conversely, in structured controversy, participants are encouraged to create an original response to the controversy by introducing perspectives and facts that have not been originally introduced. This activity deepens students' understanding of their positions and helps them discover higher level reasoning strategies. An example of a structured controversy on environmental education and regulation pertaining to hazardous waste management could require students to advocate one of the opposing positions: "more regulations needed" or "fewer regulations needed." Other topics that are controversial include the following: Should nuclear energy be used? What caused the dinosaurs' extinction? Should the Florida panthers be a protected species (Johnson & Johnson, 1992)?

Organizing a structured controversy involves the following procedures:

1. Structure the academic controversy by selecting a topic that presents pro and con positions.
2. Assign students to groups of four. Then assign each pair of students to a pro or con position. Preferably, each pair should consist of high proficient and lower proficient students.
3. Provide necessary materials and references to help students gather information.
4. Have students share and master their information on both positions and then write a report in which they argue for a position that they feel is the most compelling based on the facts and perspectives they have learned.

Structured Controversial Dialogues or Case Studies

Utilizing the format of a structured controversy, students research different positions on a topic and write a controversial dialogue or case study. To simplify linguistic demands, the case study can be modified to take the form of a dialogue in which two perspectives are expressed in the everyday language familiar to the students. Teachers can assign students in heterogeneous groups, with high and low readers/writers. Students can be given supporting materials to read and study and a bibliography of further sources of information to research at the library. Teachers can assign two students to investigate the pro and con positions. Each pair must share and master all relevant information for both positions and write a case study that is then read by other groups. Each group then writes a response in the form of a resolution after having read and discussed various perspectives.

Procedures for Using Structured Controversial Dialogues

1. Students form groups of four and divide into two pairs.
2. Each pair is assigned an advocacy position.
3. Student pairs from different groups with the same positions can compare ideas after becoming familiar with the positions. Student pairs highlight the main arguments for their position.
4. Student pairs return to their original group and present their position to the other student pair. Pairs then reverse perspectives and present the best case for the opposing position. Encourage students to see the issue from both perspectives.
5. Groups now prepare a short dialogue discussing the two positions and provide supporting evidence. They may choose several characters to present different points of view. Each group must present a dilemma for the other groups to solve by posing a question that advocates two positions. Each dialogue must be given a short title that captures the controversial problem.
6. Groups exchange their dialogues and prepare a response to the dilemma. Students should drop their advocacy role and prepare a consensus report addressing the question posed (Zainuddin & Moore, 2003, p. 3).

Following is an example of a case study that intermediate and secondary level students can generate.

"To download or not to download, that is the question . . ."

(by Rashid Moore)

Many teenagers have been downloading songs for free from the Internet instead of paying for the music from stores for a number of years. Many rationalize this illegal activity as a crime only against wealthy record companies. Let's listen in on a conversation between two teenagers on this issue:

Carlos: I just downloaded an MP3 file of "What Does It Take to Be a Fly" by my favorite rapper, Melly. You ought to hear the quality of the file!

Lay Ping: How much did you pay for it?

Carlos: Pay? Are you kidding? I downloaded it for free off the 'net. Why pay money when you can get it for free?

Lay Ping: Don't you think that the musicians like Melly should get paid for their work?

Carlos: Melly? He's a millionaire already! Didn't you see his latest music video? Don't you remember his diamond bracelets and watches?

Lay Ping: Yes, I remember what he was wearing. But doesn't he deserve to wear those things with the money he has earned? After all, he wrote the music and had to pay for the costs of recording it.

Carlos: His music company picked up the costs for recording his music, and the costs of promoting the music. Anyway, musicians like Melly probably only get a few pennies for every CD the record companies sell. So, I'm only taking money away from greedy record companies!

Lay Ping: I know the record companies are rich, but don't they deserve the money they make, too? After all, the record companies take a big risk in signing musicians to contracts and paying for the costs of recording and promoting the musicians. Not every singer sells as well as Melly, you know, and sometimes the record companies take big losses when they back unpopular musicians. . . .

Carlos: Well, I'm not going to lose any sleep over a billion-dollar company losing a few dollars here and there because some of us want to download some music for free. Don't the record companies realize that we aren't all rich like they are? We can't afford to pay $20 for a CD when we only like a few songs off of it.

Lay Ping: You say Melly is already rich from selling his music to people who do pay for his CDs. What about new musicians who have not made it big yet? What if every fan of theirs was like you and downloaded their music for free instead of paying them and their record companies for it? Why would they want to record music anymore?

Carlos: Not everybody downloads music, you know. Some fans will still buy their CDs. Some download a few of their favorite songs just to see if they really like them before buying the CD.

Lay Ping: What about you personally, Carlos? You play the guitar so well. What if you join a band that gets signed to a record deal? Wouldn't you want to receive all the money you deserve from your CD sales?

Carlos: That would be different. . . .

Carefully consider the arguments of both Carlos and Lay Ping. Construct an argument that reflects your position on the issue while taking both opinions into consideration.

Paragraph Organization

As discussed earlier, the organization of written discourse in English is culturally determined and, thus, may not be familiar to English learners who have limited exposure to English writing. Students of English not only have to learn about how sentences are formed, but also how paragraphs and longer compositions are constructed. Outlining is one way to help students learn about the organization of English texts. Outlines can be used for two purposes: as a prewriting tool and as a tool for revision. An outline that is created before writing helps writers to

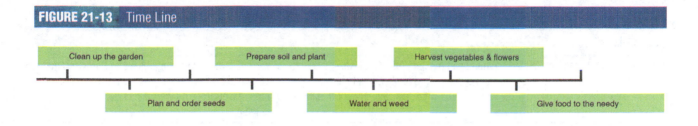

FIGURE 21-13 Time Line

Clean up the garden

Prepare soil and plant

Harvest vegetables & flowers

Plan and order seeds

Water and weed

Give food to the needy

organize their thoughts. When students make an outline after they have written a text, they will be able to see clearly what they have done and what they could do to make their writing clearer. A time line and a story staircase are graphic organizers that allow writers to organize events in sequence and, thus, help writers to remember when the events in the story happened. An example of a time line shown in Figure 21-13. Additionally, graphic organizers can be found for use at https://www.teachervi-sion.com/reading/graphic-organizers/55667.html.

To write good paragraphs in English, ELLs must understand that a paragraph is a group of sentences that work in concert to develop a unit of thought or topic. The sentence that contains the main idea of a paragraph is called the topic sentence, which is followed by statements that provide specific, logical support for the main idea. In other words, a paragraph generally moves from general to specific ideas. Paragraphing is also signaled by indentation and smooth progression from one sentence to the next by using transitional words and phrases. Figures 21-14 and 21-15 can be used to help students check whether their paragraphs have a main idea supported by more specific ideas or details. Figure 21-15 can be used to encourage students to draft a paragraph and have a partner check that it tells about just one topic and includes details to support the main idea in the topic sentence (Schifini, Short, & Tinajero, 2005c).

Paragraph Pyramid

There are other ways to organize paragraphs. Some paragraphs are organized by sequence signaled by the use of time words such as *first, after, then,* and *finally*. Comparison paragraphs tell how things are similar or different, often signaled by using comparison words such as *like, both, unlike,* and *however*. These paragraphs can be structured in two ways: point-by-point structure and a block structure. The point-by-point structure allows the writer to move back and forth between the two items being compared. The block structure allows a writer to discuss one item completely before discussing the other. Some paragraphs use space order to tell what you see often signaled by the use of directional words and phrases such as *left to right, near to far, top to bottom, along,* and *from a distance*. Cause-and-effect paragraphs tell the cause or why something happens, whereas detail sentences tell the effects or what happens as a result. Opinion paragraphs introduce an opinion about something in the topic sentence followed by sentences that explain

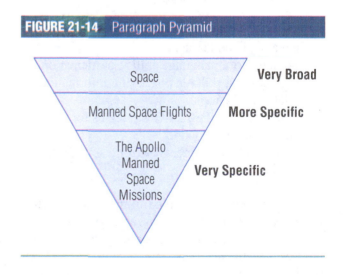

FIGURE 21-14 Paragraph Pyramid

Space — **Very Broad**

Manned Space Flights — **More Specific**

The Apollo Manned Space Missions — **Very Specific**

FIGURE 21-15   Paragraph Structure

Writing Tips	Not OK	OK
Make sure each paragraph tells about only one topic.	When I came to Los Angeles, I was surprised that no one played cricket. I liked to eat hamburgers. My sister got some new jeans.	When I came to Los Angeles, I was surprised that no one played cricket. It was my favorite game in India. I wondered if I would ever get to play it again.
Make sure your details support the main idea in your topic.	I was amazed by the freeways in Los Angeles. They are bigger than any roads I had ever seen. My mother drives me to the movies.	I am amazed at how enormous the freeways in Los Angeles are! Some are twelve lanes wide! Though there is a lot of traffic in India, the roads there do not take up nearly as much room as the LA freeways.

reasons for the opinion. Like the opinion paragraphs, persuasive paragraphs introduce an opinion or a main idea, which must be supported by facts, reasons, and/or statistics.

Writing Assessment

Integrated Language Assessment

In process writing, teachers have the opportunity to observe and assess integrated language skills such as reading, writing, listening, and speaking. The vignette at the beginning of this chapter illustrates how teachers can get different assessment information such as the following:

❖ Students' comprehension of the material they have read and learned
❖ Students' oral language ability, participation, and thinking skills in discussing information related to the topic
❖ Students' use of effective strategies for revising and editing their work
❖ Students' developmental writing skills through teacher observation

The instruction described in the vignette offers teachers a way of combining assessment and instruction. By giving a variety of instructional opportunities for students to use language in different settings, teachers are able to assess all four language skills without giving students a test that takes away valuable instructional time. In addition, process writing also gives students a chance to edit and revise their papers; this is particularly helpful to the new ELL writers.

Creating Suitable Writing Tasks

Writing performance is influenced by the writing tasks and the conditions in which students write, so teachers must take special care in developing appropriate writing tasks for ESL learners. Writing tasks used for assessment purposes should have the following criteria (Coombe, Folse, & Hubley, 2007; O'Malley & Pierce, 1996):

❖ Reflect the content, language functions, and genre types that students have learned and must know. This type of assessment will reinforce students' learning of knowledge and enable teachers to estimate the effectiveness of their instruction in achieving instructional goals. In other words, students' writing assessment should include writing different types of genre such as letter writing, writing a report of a class experiment or writing instructions for conducting an experiment, or writing a class newsletter on issues of concern to the students.
❖ Engage students in thinking and composing processes. In other words, students in the upper primary and secondary levels would not benefit from tasks such as, "Write about your favorite toy," that call upon a narration and/or descrip-

tion alone. Their tasks should closely reflect the kinds of thinking and skills in writing that they are expected to learn and know at their respective grade. To improve on the earlier task prompt, students may be asked to write about how today's toys reflect the tastes and interests of today's youth. For this task, students are required to use prior knowledge and experience about toys as a basis for analyzing the topic from different points, such as their technological capabilities and visual, interactive, and imaginative appeal to a younger audience.

❖ Allow writers to choose their own topic. Typically, students write better if they can choose a topic that interests them and on which they have background knowledge. When students choose their own topics, they are likely to produce more interesting compositions. Writing topics should also invite students to demonstrate knowledge that they have already learned in their subject areas.

❖ Provide a context that defines the writers' purpose and audience for writing. Instead of asking students to write about someone they consider a hero, the writing task could be worded in the following manner: "Many people in this class have someone whom they respect and admire for different reasons. Explain and describe the qualities you admire in a person you consider to be a hero to your fellow classmates and teacher."

Types of Scoring

There are three different ways of scoring students' writing products: holistic, primary trait, and analytical.

Holistic Scoring

Holistic scoring assesses the overall quality of a written product based on a set of criteria or dimensions. Figure 21-16 shows an example of a holistic scoring rubric to assess developmental writing levels of ELL students (O'Malley & Pierce, 1996). The rubric has six levels. Appropriate criteria such as idea development, fluency/structure, word choice, and mechanics are assigned to each level, reflecting the developmental nature of writing. For example, students at level one exhibit early literacy skills characterized by drawing, copying, and using limited phrases. Students at level six demonstrate the ability to use clear language and grammar and convey ideas in a coherent and organized fashion. When using holistic scoring, the student's paper may not meet all criteria in each level. Instead, it shows evidence that a paper has met overall conditions at each level.

Primary Trait Scoring

Primary trait scoring focuses on specific traits of writing that are being emphasized in instruction at the time the writing assignment is given. These traits can be any one or a combination of some listed in the holistic scoring rubric. Teachers may find primary trait scoring helpful when they want students to focus and demonstrate their ability on specific aspects of writing that need further improvement or are emphasized in the instruction. For example, in a writing task that asks students to write how machines simplify our lives, a teacher can evaluate students' papers on selected criteria such as: (1) if a paper shows accurate and sufficient content on machines used in daily work, and (2) if a paper shows coherent presentation of ideas supported by evidence. Primary trait scoring evaluates students' writing on selected criteria and ignores other traits related to composing.

Analytical Scoring

In analytical scoring, each component or writing trait is separated and assigned different weights. For example, students can be scored from one to four on each component. This type of scoring reflects the degree of control the student demonstrates on each component. This type of feedback is useful to students because they know in which areas they are doing well and which areas need further work. A score on each component is computed to get a total score. One limitation of analytical scoring is that it is more time consuming than holistic scoring. An example of analytical scoring is shown in Figure 21-17. Teachers can also assign different weights to various components based on what is emphasized in

Level 6
- Conveys meaning clearly and effectively
- Presents multiparagraph organization, with clear introductions, development of ideas, and conclusion
- Show evidence of smooth transitions
- Uses varied, vivid, precise vocabulary consistently
- Writes with few grammatical/mechanical errors

Level 5
- Conveys meaning clearly
- Presents multiparagraph organization logically, though some parts may not be fully developed
- Shows some evidence of effective transitions
- Uses varied and vivid vocabulary appropriate for audience and purpose
- Writes with some grammatical/mechanical errors without affecting meaning

Level 4
- Expresses ideas coherently most of the time
- Develops a logical paragraph
- Writes with a variety of sentence structures with a limited use of transitions
- Chooses vocabulary that is (often) adequate to purpose
- Writes with grammatical/mechanical errors that seldom diminish communication

Level 3
- Attempts to express ideas coherently
- Begins to write a paragraph by organizing ideas
- Writes primarily simple sentences
- Uses high-frequency vocabulary
- Writes with grammatical/mechanical errors that sometimes diminish communication

Level 2
- Begins to convey meaning
- Writes simple sentences/phrases
- Uses limited or repetitious vocabulary
- Spells inventively
- Uses little or no mechanics, which often diminishes meaning

Level 1
- Draws pictures to convey meaning
- Uses single words, phrases
- Copies from a model

---

the instruction. For example, more weight could be assigned to composing, style, and sentence formation instead of usage and mechanics. Teachers can create an analytical scoring format that fits with their program objectives.

Self-Assessment

To begin self-assessment, students must be able to see samples of exemplary and nonexemplary work (work based on benchmarks) and understand the standards by which the work is judged. Students can

FIGURE 21-17 Analytical Scoring Rubric for Writing

Domain	Formation	Usage	Sentence Score* Mechanics	Composing	Style
4	Composing: Focuses on central ideas with an organized and elaborated text	Style: Purposefully chosen vocabulary, sentence variety, information, and voice to affect reader	Sentence formation: Standard word order, no enjambment (run-on sentences), completeness (no sentence fragments), standard modifiers and coordinators, and effective transitions	Usage: Standard inflections (e.g., plurals, possessives, -ed, -ing with verbs, and -ly with adverbs), subject–verb agreement (we were vs. we was), standard word meaning	Mechanics: Effective use of capitalization, punctuation, spelling, and formatting (paragraphs noted by indenting)
3	Central idea, but not as evenly elaborated and some digressions	Vocabulary less precise and information chosen less purposefully	Mostly standard word order, some enjambment or sentence fragments	Mostly standard inflections, agreement, and word meaning	Mostly effective use of mechanics; errors do not detract from meaning
2	Not a focused idea or more than one idea, sketchy elaboration, and many digressions	Vocabulary basic and not purposefully selected; tone flat or inconsistent	Some nonstandard word order, enjambment, and word omissions (e.g., verbs)	Some errors with inflections, agreement, and word meaning	Some errors with spelling and punctuation that detract from meaning
1	No clear idea, little or no elaboration, many digressions	Not controlled, tone flat, sentences halted or choppy	Frequent nonstandard word order, enjambment, and word omissions	Shifts from one tense to another; errors in conventions (them/those, good/well, double negatives, etc.)	Misspells even simple words; little formatting evident

*4 = Consistent control
3 = Reasonable control
2 = Inconsistent control
1 = Little or no control

be required to keep samples of their work from a certain grading period and be asked to identify the characteristics of exemplary work. If students did not identify important characteristics initially, teachers can ask probing questions that will guide students to look at other aspects of performance. By doing this, students will get a clear idea of how their work will be evaluated. Students can also apply their assessment skill by evaluating their peers' work samples; this training will eventually help students to begin identifying their strengths and weaknesses and learn to set personal improvement goals based

on their weaknesses. Figures 21-18, 21-19, and 21-20 show different types of self-assessments that students can use to monitor their progress and strategy use for effective writing (O'Malley & Pierce, 1996).

Biliteracy Development and Assessment

Finally, it is important for teachers of ELLs to learn how biliterate students' writing differs from that of monoliterate students and to understand students' writing conveys content in ways that may appear

FIGURE 21-18 Self-Assessment Example #1

Author's Name _____ Date _____

Title of Work _____

Genre: Fiction   Nonfiction   Biography   Autobiography

Purpose and Organization	Yes	No
1. I stated my purpose clearly.	❑	❑
2. I organized my thoughts.	❑	❑
3. My work has a beginning, middle, and end.	❑	❑
4. I chose words that helped me make my point.	❑	❑

Word/Sentence Use

5. I used some new vocabulary.	❑	❑
6. I wrote complete sentences.	❑	❑
7. I used correct subject–verb agreement.	❑	❑
8. I used the past tense correctly.	❑	❑

Mechanics/Format

9. I spelled words correctly.	❑	❑
10. I used capitals to start sentences.	❑	❑
11. I used periods and question marks correctly.	❑	❑
12. I indented paragraphs.	❑	❑

Editing

13. I read my paper aloud to a partner.	❑	❑
14. I asked a partner to read my paper.	❑	❑

Genre: Poetry

1. I used descriptive language in the poem.	❑	❑
2. I used the required format (e.g., quatrain).	❑	❑
3. I illustrated the poem.	❑	❑
4. I used nouns, verbs, and adjectives.	❑	❑
5. I presented the poem to the class.	❑	❑

Adapted from Claire Waller, ESL Middle School Teacher, Fairfax County Public Schools, Virginia.

limited, due to the second language learning process and students' proficiency levels in English. For example, in their research on English language learners at a Colorado elementary school, Coady and Escamilla (2005) found that Spanish-literate students wrote highly complex text with dense, sophisticated, and internationally focused content. The authors found that when teachers assessed the bilingual students' writing using a monolingual scoring rubric, the writing was deemed to be of low quality. Teachers tended to focus on linguistic errors rather than content.

In contrast to using a monolingual scoring rubric to assess bilingual and biliterate students' writing, Escamilla, Hopewell, and Butvilofsky (2013) developed an informative and more appropriate (bi-

FIGURE 21-19 Self-Assessment Example #2

Name _____ Date _____

Check one box for each statement.

	A Lot	Some	A Little	Not at All
1. I like to write stories.	❑	❑	❑	❑
2. I am a good writer.	❑	❑	❑	❑
3. Writing stories is easy for me.	❑	❑	❑	❑
4. Writing to friends is fun.	❑	❑	❑	❑
5. Writing helps me in school.	❑	❑	❑	❑
6. I like to share my writing with others.	❑	❑	❑	❑
7. I write at home.	❑	❑	❑	❑

8. What kinds of things do you like to write about?

_____

_____

_____

9. How have you improved as a writer? What can you do well?

_____

_____

_____

10. What else do you want to improve in your writing?

_____

_____

_____

Adapted from materials developed by the Georgetown University Evaluation Assistance Center (EAC) East (1990), Washington, D.C.

lingual) assessment known as "literacy squared." Literacy squared refers to a comprehensive biliteracy program designed to accelerate English-Spanish biliteracy. The model includes supporting students' metalinguistic awareness of languages and cross language transfer skills, underscoring the concept that bilinguals' two language development is interconnected, rather than separate linguistic systems.

FIGURE 21-20 Self-Assessment Example #3

Name _____ Date _____

Check one box for each statement.

	Yes	No
Before writing:		
1. I talked to a friend or partner about the topic.	❏	❏
2. I made a list of ideas on the topic.	❏	❏
3. I made an outline or semantic map.	❏	❏
During writing:		
4. I skipped words I don't know and went back to them later.	❏	❏
5. I substituted a word from my own language.	❏	❏
6. I used drawings or pictures in my writing.	❏	❏
After writing:		
7. I checked to see if the writing met my purpose.	❏	❏
8. I reread to see if it made sense.	❏	❏
9. I added information or took out information.	❏	❏
10. I edited for spelling, punctuation, capitals, and grammar.	❏	❏

Other strategies I used:

Adapted from materials developed by the Georgetown University Evaluation Assistance Center (EAC) East (1990), Washington, D.C.

❖ Second language writing research has largely been influenced by L1 writing research, although more recent research emphasizes the biliteracy skill development of second language learners. Research in both L1 and L2 writing suggests a shift in the development of writing from an expressive activity in which the product is emphasized to a more balanced writing approach that encompasses both the product and the process.

❖ Writing research in L1 and L2 has identified similar findings about writing:

A. Writing is a recursive and not a linear process; the stages of prewriting, drafting, revising, and editing overlap and intertwine.

B. Writing is viewed as a social activity; in other words, writers' approach to writing is influenced by their previous situations and the experiences in which writing is performed.

C. Writing is seen as an invention and discovery process; teachers must assist learners in generating and discovering content and purpose for writing and attending to audience.

D. Beginning ELL writers exhibit characteristics similar to those of English-speaking children who are first learning to write. They generally do not have a wide knowledge of vocabulary and sentence patterns; they also use invented spellings and demonstrate developmental scripting strategies similar to those of first language writers. Their written language also resembles their oral language.

E. Intermediate ELL writers have a more developed knowledge of simple sentences and mechanics and use more conventional spellings. They may still make errors in grammar, spelling, and vocabulary when expressing difficult content. They do need further practice in using complex sentences and organizing and developing ideas when writing in English.

F. Process writing is an effective approach for teaching writing to all learners because it breaks down the process into small, manageable components. These components, or stages, allow developing writers to focus on specific aspects of composing, one at a time, and thus make it easier for writers to juggle with the constraints of writing in a new language.

❖ Because text organization is culturally determined, ELL writers must learn the organizational scheme of English rhetoric. Students can learn about English rhetorical organization by reading and analyzing models of English texts and outlining their texts before and after they write.

❖ Children develop literacy in first and second language writing before they enter school. Their early literacy products show their understanding about the concept of print and print conventions, which are similar in both first and second language writing. Children with a strong literacy experience in their first language are more likely to become successful at reading and writing in the second language than their counterparts with limited first language literacy experience.

❖ Second language writing is difficult for ELL writers because:

A. Students have not grasped the formality levels of structures and vocabulary expected in academic writing.

B. There may be a mismatch between form and function in learning English grammar, making English writing quite difficult and confusing.

C. Students must learn the conventions of English rhetoric (structure), which may be different from those in their first language. These conventions include the structural forms as well as the social attitudes, values, and roles of writing in English and other cultures.

Teaching Grammar to English Learners in the Mainstream Classroom

chapter 22

KEY ISSUES

- ❖ Typical errors of English language learners
- ❖ Teacher awareness of typical errors
- ❖ Strategies for teachers to scaffold English language learners who demonstrate predictable error difficulties
- ❖ Ways for teachers to make grammar lessons student centered, participatory, and enjoyable
- ❖ How to include oral and written language activities through thematic instruction and cooperative learning
- ❖ Specific games that teachers can use in their grammar classrooms

Mrs. Cruz teaches fourth grade in a school with many ESOL students who speak a variety of languages. The ESL curriculum requires her to teach English grammar as part of the language arts block. Despite many weeks of instruction and practice the students still are not demonstrating competence on many grammatical areas: verbs and tenses, prepositions, idioms, count/noncount nouns, etc. She decides that the students need more grammar exercises and so she increases direct instruction in grammar ten minutes daily. After several more weeks the students are still making the same errors, only now, they are starting to "act up" during the lessons. They seem bored and uninterested, and they begin to groan when Mrs. Cruz announces the grammar lesson. During this time, Mrs. Cruz agrees to allow a college student, Lin, who is studying to be an ESL teacher, to observe and volunteer in her class. After observing a couple of days and becoming familiar with the class, Lin asks Mrs. Cruz if she can analyze the areas that the students are having difficulty with and devise some activities that might engage them and keep their interests. Mrs. Cruz agrees and Lin decides the students need the most work on verb tenses and verb forms. She devises a series of simple interactive activities and games that get the students using verbs and talking to each other. Interest is growing and the students begin to look forward to the daily grammar lesson. Mrs. Cruz is keeping track of the students' progress, and after a couple of weeks, she begins to notice a remarkable improvement in the students' spoken and written work. One day the principal visits the classroom unannounced and sees the children in small groups speaking animatedly and playing a game. The principal calls Mrs. Cruz over and demands to know why there seems to be such disorder in the class. Mrs. Cruz responds, "The students are studying and learning grammar!"

Grammar in the ESL Classroom: What Should Mainstream Teachers Know?

Teaching grammar to English learners can be problematic for mainstream teachers who are not accustomed to teaching grammar to English language learners (ELLs). Teaching English to native speakers is very different from teaching students who are learning English as a new language. The issue of grammatical errors is very complex and particularly troublesome for teachers new to teaching students who may appear to be fluent in English yet struggle with the written and oral language grammatical conventions they are expected to know.

The adoption of the Common Core State Standards (CCSS), which are an attempt to improve instruction, impacts ELLs. Closing the Expectations Gap 2013 Annual Report on the Alignment of State K–12 Policies and Practice with the Demands of College and Careers (source: Achieve) can be reviewed at the following website: http://www.core standards.org/standards-in-your-state/. The expectation is that ELLs will be fully integrated into the learning environment, and there are direct implications as a result of this educational shift. The English Language Arts Standards include a section on specific language expectations and mastery that include conventions of Standard English grammar and usage when writing or speaking. ELLs are expected to master these grammar and usage conventions and standards and will need additional scaffolding and teacher support. It will be incumbent upon teachers to prepare carefully prepare and design instruction that will prove to be effective (CCSS, 2014).

With this in mind it is recommended that ELLs be involved in their own learning through hands on, student-centered environments. Cooperative groups, peer tutoring, and discovery learning are ways to engage ELLs to develop the skills and content knowledge they need to be successful in their future education and careers (Lafond, 2012).

An examination of the most common grammatical errors can help prepare mainstream teachers to understand the kinds of errors they might expect to encounter in their students' oral written communication skills. Knowledge of errors that students will make can help teachers to anticipate what problems to expect from their English learners, especially by knowing information about the language their English learners speak. Fawcett (2007) compiled a list of the most "common and annoying ELL errors" teachers might notice in their students' writing. These included grammatical, syntactical (word order), lexical (vocabulary), and stylistic errors. Among the most common mistakes made are ones with: verb tense, prepositions, articles, count/noncount nouns, subject–verb agreement, word choice, word forms, word endings, idiomatic usage, and sentence combining. Some examples of these common and annoying errors are:

❖ Verb tense: Yesterday, I <u>walk</u> to the park.
❖ Preposition: He got <u>off</u> the car (out of)
❖ Articles: She ate <u>a</u> apple.
❖ Count/noncount: I drink a lot of waters
❖ Subject/verb agreement: he/she and present tense 's': He <u>run</u> to school everyday
❖ Word choice: "fathers" for "parents"
❖ Word endings: The flowers are very <u>beautifully</u>
❖ Idiomatic usage: A driver see the sign "Do Not Pass" and stops the car, refusing to continue on down the road
❖ Sentence combining: she goes to Lakeside high school. She goes to school on the bus. Instead of "She goes to Lakeside high school on the bus."

Knowledge of the key areas of grammatical difficulty is the focus of Folse's (2009a) keys to ELL grammar issues. He lists key areas that present second language learners the most difficulty: the verb be, verb tenses to express time (future, past and present), count and noncount nouns (flowers, which can be counted vs. air, which cannot be counted), prepositions (at, on, in, etc.), adjective and adverb clauses and reductions (e,g., a person who types is a secretary), word choice (hard, hardly, hardship; sad, sadly, sadness), infinitives and gerunds (to write vs. writing), phrasal verbs (make up, run into), modals (can, could, would, should, etc.), passive voice (was painted by Sue vs. Sue painted), and conditions (if only, wish clauses).

The initial reaction of teachers who are unfamiliar with these areas of difficulty might be to immediately judge students' grammatical competency as critically flawed and ignore the content of the written work or spoken participation. At the same time, grammatical errors in writing may reduce the readability of a written work or hinder the reader's comprehension of the writing. Grammatical errors in spoken speech may limit the listener's understanding of what the speaker is trying to communicate. ELLs can make mechanical errors but still produce content that can be understood. A teacher who has background understanding about why this occurs will be able to help the student improve while maintaining the ability to accurately assess his or her academic performance holistically.

Folse (2009b) states that when teachers do not know how to explain grammatical errors when assessing student writing, it can have negative consequences. If a teacher writes "Pay attention to your writing," "Awkward sentence structure," or "These are errors" or simply circles mistakes, it leaves students wondering what they did wrong and without a clear understanding of how to correct the error. Or, if a teacher continually stops to correct oral communication because of grammatical errors, the learner will shut down and become nonparticipatory. This is counterproductive to language and gram-

matical acquisition. Clearly, it is incumbent upon all those who work with English learners, speakers, and writers to understand these errors and to make positive inroads into supporting learner's improvement of the spoken and written task.

In his analysis of multiple areas of difficulty, Folse (2009a) points out the interference between English grammatical rules and those of seven other languages (Arabic, Chinese, French, Japanese, Korean, Russian, and Spanish). In examining grammatical competency it seems that there are consistent patterns of errors. The areas were most errors are found are: the verb "to be" verb tenses (present past and future), verb forms, word choice, clause reduction, use of prepositions, and sentence construction. A secondary level of errors include such grammatical forms as count/noncount nouns, determiners and qualifiers (a, an, the/quantifiers, such as many, each/possessive adjectives such as my, his, their, etc.), verbs followed by a gerund (-ing) or an infinitive (to), and phrasal verbs (verbs paired with a preposition). The following chart contains selected examples that Folse (2009a) offers as examples of the kinds of errors that are commonly found across the eight languages.

FIGURE 22-1

Error	Language	Example
Verb "to be"	Chinese: only nouns can follow "to be" Korean: "To be" can NOT be followed by a noun	The dog very big She student
Verbs: Present Tense	Arabic: fourteen inflections based on subject Chinese: no verb tenses	"He likes cheese" is not the same as "She likes cheese" He live in Beijing last year
Verbs: Past Tense	French: simple past tense construction is with auxiliary Have/has	"Jean wrote a history essay" will be stated as "Jean has written a history essay"
Verbs: Future Tense	Japanese: no future tense Spanish: no specific work for "will" Verb is inflected (infinitive + ending) according to the subject	They go to school next week They to go to school next week
Word choice	False cognates: ♦ English: embarrassed ♦ English: realize	Spanish: *embarazada* (pregnant) Spanish: *realizar* (to accomplish)
Adjective clauses and reduction	French: "qui" and "que" are specific to the noun as subject or object and changes the meaning	The table who is red Dinner is on the table which is red

(continued)

FIGURE 22-1 *(continued)*

Error	Language	Example
Prepositions	Most speakers of other languages will have difficulty with prepositions since there are various ways they are used in English:	
	◆ Single word prepositions	in, on, by, down
	◆ Two word prepositions	because of, far from, next to
	◆ Three word prepositions	in place of, on top of
	◆ In/on/at	in fifth grade, in July, on the avenue, on the fourth of July, at school, at 10 o'clock
	◆ Adjectives + prepositions	good at, sick of
	◆ Nouns + prepositions	example of, interest in
	◆ Preposition + noun	for dinner
		on sale
	◆ Idiomatic expressions	in the nick of time
		on the fence
	◆ Verb + Preposition	belong to, agree with, count on
Count/noncount nouns	Japanese and Chinese have no plural forms; previous counter words are used	Two glass of water
Determiners and qualifiers (a, an, the)	Chinese, Korean, Russian, and Japanese have no articles	They eat apple and banana
	Arabic uses the definite article "the" with abstract nouns, and group nouns	The liberty, the tennis
Verbs followed by a gerund (-ing) or an infinitive (to)	Japanese, Arabic, Chinese, Korean, and Russian use a series of verbs	They like go see movies
Phrasal verbs (verbs paired with a preposition)	Phrasal verbs in English are difficult for many other languages: Separable phrasal verbs:	
	◆ Fill in	Fill in the blank or fill the blank in
	◆ Pick up	Pick up the laundry or pick the laundry up
	Inseparable phrasal verbs:	
	◆ Hurry up	Hurry up and get going
	◆ Keep on	Keep on trying until you get it

Source: Adapted from Folse (2009a)

In order to understand the kinds of errors ELLs are likely to make, it is useful to compare the native language with English. These comparisons prove very useful to understand what errors the teacher can expect to see. For example, if a teacher is aware that Arabic does not use the verb "to be" in the present tense, the sentence "my dog very small" it may be logical to understand why the student would make this mistake and error correction could focus on providing an explicit explanation of the use of the verb *to be* in English. If this occurs, the writer's intent and desired message would be better understood. Also, if teachers are working with French speaking children, they should be aware that the definite article "*the*" is used with whole concept nouns in French. For example:

❖ My favorite sport is golf
❖ Mon sport préféré est **le** golf

Yet, there are no indefinite articles (a, an) for professions

- ❖ My mother is **a** professor
- ❖ Ma mère est professeur

However, in English, we do not use the indefinite article with concept nouns:

- ❖ Friendship requires honesty and trust
  But in French they do:
- ❖ L'amitié nécessite **la** confiance et **l'**honnêteté

In examining grammatical points, teachers may notice a pattern among different speakers of native languages. Consider the following grammatical errors of Spanish speakers (Gerena, 2009a):

- ❖ Verb tenses
  - ◆ "My father never worry (worried) about us when we went to school"
  - ◆ "I always feel (felt) like my work was not good enough"

- ❖ Verb forms
  - ◆ "Things were become worse after we move to New York"
  - ◆ "They putting me in English class and I didn't understand nothing"

- ❖ Word choice
  - ◆ "Fathers" for "parents"
  - ◆ "Cloths" for "clothes"; "girth" for "weight"
  - ◆ "We procreated children" for "we had children"
  - ◆ "They remember my childhood" for "they remind me of my childhood"
  - ◆ "She worked strong" for "she worked hard"
  - ◆ "Small fingernails" (short)

- ❖ Clause reduction
  - ◆ "My social experiences were around my friends, most of which lived with both parents, therefore did not have any of the responsibilities I had"

- ◆ "I felt angry at her, but seemed that my opinions or my problems didn't count"

- ❖ Prepositions
  - ◆ "In that day I became the first daughter"
  - ◆ "I used to dream with new clothes"

- ❖ Sentence construction
  - ◆ "Even though my experiences as a girl in my development were different"
  - ◆ "My uncles made business" ("My uncles were businessmen")

- ❖ Count/noncount nouns
  - ◆ ". . . to talk in the front of a lot of people"
  - ◆ " He was very responsible and excellent father"

- ❖ Determiners and qualifiers
  - ◆ "I know teacher is always there . . ."
  - ◆ "House was huge and beautiful"

- ❖ Verbs followed by a gerund
  - ◆ "I didn't feel good to ask her for paying me a college" instead of "to pay for my college"

- ❖ Verbs followed by an infinitive
  - ◆ "She always went to school to meetings and see if everything there was fine"
  - ◆ "I was always told gain not to lose"

- ❖ Phrasal verbs
  - ◆ "But my dream was coming down"

It appears that there are certain errors that teachers should expect and anticipate in ELL grammar. Raising teachers' awareness levels can help address the ways these typical errors are handled in ways that help students. Researchers have investigated grammatical errors to substantiate whether errors have been consistent over time (Ferris, 2012; Hinkel, 2010). Ferris (2011) brings to the educational community questions such as the types of errors should teachers respond to and when should we respond to them. She discusses the most efficacious ways of responding to them and the role should error treatment should play in the teaching of the process of writing. It is suggested that teacher education programs prepare teachers to be aware of and treat student errors. Some Questions teachers may want to consider are:

- Given that teachers can somewhat predict and understand grammatical errors, how can they go beyond teaching isolated grammatical structures?
- What are some best practices that teachers can use to help students develop more accomplished grammatical skills?

Although it seems very simplistic to state that there is a set methodology or specific techniques to follow, there are student-centered qualities can greatly increase student interest in the second language classroom. Sheltering techniques can facilitate student language development, grammar, and content knowledge (Goldenberg, 2013; Saunders, Goldenberg, & Marcelletti, 2013). The following principles can be used successfully in the second language classroom to teach grammar:

- Instruction should be explicit and should include grammatical usage
- Students must be engaged
- Students must participate actively and not passively
- Students like activities that are fun
- Students want to work with peers
- Teachers should become facilitators of learning

Some effective practices that can be used to help students acquire grammar without being boring or raising anxiety levels are:

- Careful planning of interactive and participatory activities
- Student-centered instruction
- Student to student verbal interaction
- Asking higher order questions
- Providing for ample "wait time" for students to process information and organize tier thoughts

- Student self-assessment, allowing students to think about their own learning and self-assess areas of strength and weakness
- Hands on participatory activities
  - Graphic organizers
  - Comprehension activities

Students must be given the opportunity to communicate in oral and written form, interpret oral and written messages, show understanding when they communicate, and present oral and written information to various audiences for a variety of purposes. In examining effective teaching strategies, there are ways to develop communication and connection in language teaching. Teachers are encouraged to include communicative activities in their lessons, such as:

- Cooperative groups activities
- Pairs or triads
- Student to student interactions
- Opportunities for peer feedback
- Peer or cross age interactions
- Round robin
- Music, songs
- Venn diagrams, and other graphic organizers (word maps, concept definition maps, concept webs, cluster diagrams, spider maps, compare/contrast maps, fishbone maps)

Let's consider other ways to develop grammatical competence in a second language:

- Communicative activities and social interaction
- Cooperative learning, peer groups, student to student interaction
- Interaction with native populations
- Content and thematic instruction
- Analytical comparisons/contrasts between native and target language
- Accessing members of the target language to interact with students
- Using the language in real life contexts; not just "knowing the language" but really being able to use it in variety of contexts

Some specific techniques to improve grammatical competence and performance can be incorporated to provide students with the opportunity to write on a daily basis. In written language, grammar should be presented by immersing students in language-based interactive writing activities (Atkinson, 2003; Frodesen & Holten, 2003; Grabe, 2003):

❖ Make time every day to use English in authentic, meaningful ways
❖ Listen to music to teach grammar and semantics through songs
❖ Establish book clubs
❖ Round robin writing
❖ Write dialogue to picture frames
❖ Collaborative story writing
❖ Interviews and newspaper/newsletter articles
❖ Write invitations
❖ Have more advanced or older English speakers work with younger or less competent peers to edit and revise written work.
❖ Literature response journals: personal responses to text
❖ Develop scripts for readers theater
❖ Adapt text into various formats
   ◆ Text to dialogue
   ◆ Dialogue to text
   ◆ First person to third person
   ◆ Different endings
   ◆ Text to cartoon format
❖ Journals
   ◆ Dialogue journals
   ◆ Personal journals
   ◆ Literature response journals
   ◆ Buddy journals
❖ Free writing opportunities
❖ Relate writing to students lives, backgrounds, and experiences
❖ Contextualize it in real life activities and uses
❖ Review and recycle written discourse patterns
❖ Use songs, rap, chants, newspaper comics as sources of writing
❖ Chunk material; focus on one variable at a time
❖ Break complex concepts into simpler parts
❖ Teach gimmicks, mnemonics, writing strategies
❖ Use guided grammar writing activities

Over the past years, online resources for teachers that promote participatory, interactive, and enjoyable activities have rapidly become user friendly and accessible. The following websites have ample and abundant resources for teachers to make grammar instruction instructionally sound and student centered. They offer a wide array of downloadable activities, charts, puzzles, topics, themes, lesson plans, and exercises; multimedia and video-based learning platforms; and professional tips and suggestions. Also included are websites that offer reference resources such as an on line dictionary and thesaurus, and one dedicated to idioms, idiomatic expressions, phrasal verbs, and other grammatical irregularities.

1. 5 New Fun Ways to Teach Grammar to ESL Students
   http://busyteacher.org/2873-5-new-fun-ways-to-teach-grammar-to-esl-students.html
2. Teaching Grammar in an ESL/EFL Setting
   http://esl.about.com/cs/teachingtechnique/a/a_teachgrammar.htm
3. Teaching Grammar
   http://writing.colostate.edu/guides/teaching/esl/grammar.cfm
4. ESL Teacher Handouts, Grammar Worksheets & Printables
   http://www.usingenglish.com/handouts/
5. Teaching Grammar-ESL Partyland
   http://www.eslpartyland.com/teachers/nov/grammar.htm
6. Anglo maniac Grammar for Kids
   http://www.anglomaniacy.pl/grammar.htm
7. Teaching English Games
   http://www.teachingenglishgames.com
8. Fun English Games: Grammar
   http://www.funenglishgames.com/topics/grammar.html
9. Dave's ESL Cafe
   http://www.eslcafe.com/grammar.html
10. The English Club
    http://www.englishclub.com/grammar/
11. English Grammar
    http://www.englishgrammar.org

12. Conversation Questions for the ESL/EFL Classroom
    http://iteslj.org/questions/
13. English as a Second Language Teachers Creating ESL Video Quizzes for ESL Students
    http://www.eslvideo.com/index.php
14. Dictionary/Thesaurus/Word Dynamo
    http://dictionary.reference.com
15. English Idioms and Idiomatic Expressions
    http://www.usingenglish.com

Perhaps the most overlooked and underutilized strategy for providing student centered instruction and lowering the affective filter is simply: **Make it fun!!!!!!! Play Games!!!!!** Games are an indispensable strategy for incorporating grammatical structures into second language learning. Why use games in the language classroom? Evidence has proved that practical application through the use of games in the second language classroom can promote language learning. These games facilitate all the student centered and effective teaching practices and strategies listed above (Gerena, 2010a, 2010b; Gerena, 2009a, 2009b; Wright, Betteridge, & Buckby, 2006; Nguyen & Khuat, 2003; Ersoz, 2000; Yin-Young & Jang, 2000; Lewis & Bedson, 1999; Lee, 1995).

❖ Games help and encourage many learners to maintain their interest and work.
❖ Games give students a break from the usual routine and at the same time allow students to practice various skills—speaking, writing, listening, and reading.
❖ Games are highly motivating and amusing yet they can be challenging.
❖ Games are meaningful and provide useful language practice in real life contexts.
❖ Games encourage and increase interaction, communication, active participation, and cooperation.
❖ Games provide relaxation and fun for students, and help them learn and retain vocabulary and grammar more easily.
❖ Games bring real world context into the classroom, and improve students' use of English in a flexible, communicative way.

❖ General benefits of games (Lengeling & Malarcher, 1997)
  ◆ Affective: lowers the affective filter so learning can take place; encourages creative and spontaneous use of language; promotes communicative competence; provides motivation and fun
  ◆ Cognitive: reinforces what is learned; reviews and extends learning; focuses on grammar communicatively
  ◆ Class dynamics: student centered; teacher acts only as facilitator; builds class cohesion; fosters whole class participation promotes healthy competition
  ◆ Adaptability: easily adjusted for age; level, and interests utilize all four skills; requires minimum preparation after development

Here are some games that can be played to develop grammatical competence in both written and spoken form. They are all simple games that require little or no materials or resources. They have been used in many ESL settings and have been shown to increase student participation (Gerena, 2010b).

Game #1: Questions, Questions, Questions

❖ Make groups of three to five students. Choose a group leader and a scorekeeper.
❖ You will see a question to answer.
❖ You will have ten seconds to decide on an answer.
❖ The first leader to stand up and answer earns five points for your team.
❖ Next leader to answer (but must be a different answer) gets four points, next one three, etc.
❖ Examples of questions to ask
  ◆ Future tense
    • What will you do this weekend?
  ◆ Past tense
    • What did you do last weekend?
  ◆ Conditional
    • What would you like for your birthday?

- Modals
  - What should we do to help the Haiti earthquake victims?
- Present progressive
  - Where are you going to spend your spring break?
  - What are you going to do over spring break?

Game #2: Fantastic Fiction

- ❖ Divide into groups of six.
- ❖ Each group gets one sheet of paper.
- ❖ The first student writes the first part and folds the paper so as to cover what she/he has written.
- ❖ After writing, pass the paper onto the next person.
- ❖ As each person writes, only look at your own fold.
- ❖ When all team members have written, one student from each group will read the fantastic fiction they have created.

Who (two people)	Where were they at first	Where were they going	What did he say	What did she say	What did they do

Game #3: Grammar Round Up

- ❖ Divide into pairs or small groups of three to four.
- ❖ Each pair or group will get a page with a grammar exercise.
- ❖ Members of the pair/group will work together to answer as many questions as they can within three minutes.
- ❖ Students write their answers on the question sheet and answer the questions in any order they wish. If they can think of more than one answer for a particular question, they should write this also. (If correct, these extra answers are included in their score.)
- ❖ Each group will have five minutes. After time is up, a reporter reads out the questions and answers.
- ❖ The class will decide if the answers are correct.
- ❖ For each correct answer, the group will earn a point. The group/pair with the most points wins.

Game #4: Shiritori (Traditional Japanese Word Game)

- ❖ Each group will try to write as many verbs using the last letter of the last word. This works best with present and past tenses. It is also a good vocabulary building exercise.
- ❖ The word must start with a letter that is the same letter as the last letter of the previous word *and be in the same verb tense*
- ❖ For example, if the first word is *went*, then the next word might be *took*. The list goes on: went, took, kayaked, drove, ended, dried, etc.
- ❖ Each student takes a turn and each group tries to make the longest list
- ❖ Words cannot appear twice on the list
- ❖ Extension activity: Have several four- to five-minute game rounds. In the first round, all team members participate; in the second round, both teams choose their best member and those two students square off in a one-on-one match with teams providing support by shouting out words. In the third round, two of the best from each team square off, etc.

Sample Shiritori Verbs

- ◆ Grew
- ◆ Said
- ◆ Paint
- ◆ Play
- ◆ Climb

Game #5: Twenty Questions (Traditional Game)

- ❖ The question champ chooses a topic and writes an "answer."
- ❖ Audience asks "yes" or "no" questions. If the question is grammatically correct, the question champs ears a point and the question champ answers it. If the question is not grammatically correct, another player tries to ask the same question correctly. If correct, this player earns a point. (If it is still not correct, ask the teacher or group leader to ask the question.)
- ❖ If a student guesser thinks he/she knows the answer, say it.
- ❖ If it is not correct, the question champ earns one point and play continues as before. If it is correct, the guesser earns three points and you become the next question master.
- ❖ Play continues as before.
- ❖ If no one has guessed what the question champ is thinking of after twenty questions, the question champ states what it is and earns one point. Another student then volunteers to be the next question champ.

Sample Twenty Question Topics:

- ◆ Sports
- ◆ Geography
- ◆ The ocean
- ◆ Europe
- ◆ Holidays
- ◆ Singers
- ◆ Bands
- ◆ Countries
- ◆ Football
- ◆ Famous
- ◆ People today
- ◆ Clothing
- ◆ Actors
- ◆ Jobs
- ◆ Animals
- ◆ Landmarks
- ◆ Actresses
- ◆ TV shows
- ◆ The Americas
- ◆ Asia
- ◆ Movie monsters
- ◆ Science fiction
- ◆ Movies
- ◆ Famous people in history
- ◆ World capitals
- ◆ Books
- ◆ Fairy tales
- ◆ Current events
- ◆ Africa
- ◆ Foods
- ◆ Hobbies

Game #6: Team Topple

- ❖ Divide the class into two teams and then decide with the class how many points are needed to win (six to ten points works best).
- ❖ To begin, read the first question or show it on an index card. If a member of either team thinks they can answer, they raise their hand and must give their answer immediately. If it is correct, their team earns a point. If it is not correct, the other team has ten seconds to try to answer the question correctly. If they answer correctly, they earn a point. If neither team answers correctly, the teacher should give the correct answer(s).
- ❖ Continue play by asking one question from each category in turn. The game is over when a team reaches the target number of points.

Grammatical competence in both written and spoken structures is undeniably necessary for second language learners at all levels of education. However, teachers must be aware of the reasons learners make predictable errors and how they can intervene in nonthreatening and anxiety reduced environments. If teachers take the time to prepare lessons that are student centered, communicatively based, and stress free, they will undoubtedly see improvements in their students' grammatical competency and performance.

PART FIVE

Teaching ESOL through the Content Areas

chapter 23

New Standards and Teachers
of Today, 307
EILEEN WHELAN ARIZA AND KATEE ANDERSON

chapter 24

Effective Strategies for Teaching
Mathematics to English Language
Learners (ELLs), 317
JOSEPH FURNER

chapter 25

Teaching and Learning through the Arts:
Strategies for English Language
Learners, 343
SUSANNAH BROWN

chapter 26

Teaching Science to English Language
Learners, 355
JOAN LINDGREN AND JULIE LAMBERT

chapter 27

Social Studies from a Global
Perspective: Effective Pedagogy for
English Language Learners, 375
TONI FUSS KIRKWOOD-TUCKER
AND E. ANDY BREWER

chapter 28

Special Education and the Linguistically
Diverse Student, 385
CYNTHIA WILSON AND MARGARITA BIANCO

chapter 29

Using Technology with English
Learners, 405
SUSANNE I. LAPP, SHERRIE SACHAROW,
AND RENEE ZELDEN

New Standards and Teachers of Today

State Standards and the Mainstream Teacher
What should we know to provide effective instruction for English learners?

Ms. Wilson, a first year teacher, is conferring with her mentor teacher at her first teaching position. Having learned a little about the Common Core State Standards in her college teacher education program, Ms. Wilson asks her mentor teacher, "How do I use the higher standards and still be able to connect with my English language learners? Aren't these standards too difficult for them?" The mentor simply replied, "No standard is too difficult for an ELL to learn as long as you present the standard in digestible chunks for them to understand with lots of examples."

This scenario reflects the common misconception that English language learners (ELLs) will not understand the higher standards that the Common Core State Standards describe. This chapter will discuss the challenges mainstream teachers face when teaching ELLs through the new CCSS and provide simple strategies that will allow an easier transition inside the classroom.

ELLs are a heterogeneous group with differences in ethnic background, first language, socioeconomic status, quality of prior schooling, and levels of English language proficiency. Effectively educating English learners ideally requires diagnostic testing in the native language, the target language, and instructional planning according to the student's prior knowledge (NGA Center for Best Practices and the Council of Chief State School Officers, 2010). Some students come into the classroom with no English experience at all and others enter with a mix of low level proficiency in spoken English, and Spanish (or any other native language) being spoken in the home. These are two completely separate groups of students that teachers need to assess, and apply different strategies inside the classroom. Understanding what kind of background and home support a child has is the most important knowledge a teacher can possess. In my experience, I have found that a child with little to no support at home develops the English language at a much slower rate, but understanding this circumstance will help facilitate ideas which can be used to help the language development for children of this background. This chapter will describe typical English language students, their needs, and how to best use the Common Core State Standards while including ELL strategies in the mainstream classroom to provide educational support.

Key Issues

Today there is more complexity than one would think with respect to being a mainstream classroom teacher. Not only is the teacher responsible for the learning gains for the "typical " student, but the classroom population now consists of many ELL and ESE students for whom mainstream teachers

need to provide the best education and support. Over the past forty years, the population of non-native English speaking students has steadily grown in the public school systems and many different viewpoints of the best way to teach English learners exist. In the past, English learners were placed into a separate classroom such as an ESOL (English for Speakers of Other Languages) class, or they were placed in a "sink or swim" situation where their native language was not factored into their learning capabilities. This controversy sparked a lawsuit in San Francisco Unified School District in 1974. The 1974 Supreme Court case *Lau v. Nichols* resulted in perhaps the most important court decision regarding the education of language-minority students. This case was brought forward by Chinese American students in the San Francisco Unified School District who were placed in mainstream classrooms despite their lack of proficiency in English, and left to "sink or swim." The district argued that it had done nothing wrong, and that the Chinese American students received treatment equal to that of other students. In writing the court's opinion, Justice William Douglass strongly disagreed and argued that there was no equality of treatment if students were only provided the same facilities, textbooks, teachers, and curriculum. He pointed out that students who do not fully understand English are effectively excluded from meaningful education and will find their classroom experiences incomprehensible and meaningless (Wright, 2010).

The Lau case made a substantial impact on bilingual education reform and although there is no national law mandating bilingual education, the Supreme Court ruling required a complete overhaul on the U.S. Department of Education's equality policies in the public school systems. This case is only one of many that were necessary to pave the way toward the information and strategies we have today to help English learners succeed through comprehensible input in the mainstream classroom.

English language strategies and programs are readily available for teachers to use on a daily basis inside the mainstream classroom. Examples of different program requirements are: English language facilitators, English language learner pullout/push-in instruction, dual-language programs, and strategies to be used by a mainstream classroom teacher. The issue with providing English learners with the proper education they deserve is the lack of knowledge and training strategies provided for educators. This is why many universities have addressed English language instruction by offering or mandating courses for teacher candidates as a requirement for graduation. I believe that the college/university level is where a beginning teacher needs to learn who an English learner is, and how to provide the best instruction inside the mainstream classroom. Many states also now require school district and higher education teacher programs to offer ESOL endorsement or training for teachers in areas with high ELL populations.

What Are Standards and How Are they Used to Help English Language Learners in the Mainstream Classroom?

Standards are a list of skills that a student needs to acquire by the end of each grade. This knowledge allows students to be prepared for the following school year. Standards only tell teachers what skills need to be mastered by the end of the year. They do not tell a teacher how or what to teach inside the classroom. Standards are better viewed as the ending goal around which the teacher can plan curriculum. This allows the teacher to have the students in mind when preparing lessons or units to teach.

The Common Core State Standards were created to emphasize required achievements. While the majority of states have adapted CCSS, some states have withdrawn their initial alliance, while others have tweaked the standards to blend with their own state standards. Examples of states that have chosen combined standards are: Florida Standards, Alabama and Arizona College and Career Ready Standards, Iowa Core Standards, Kentucky Core Academic Standards, and, finally, the state of Nebraska has kept its own original state standards believing they are already as rigorous as CCSS. Other major issues pertain to decisions about which assessment instruments will be used, such as the (PAARC) *Partnership for Assessment of Readiness for College and*

Careers, or the other popular option, the *Smarter Balanced Assessments* in English and mathematics that are tied to Common Core Standards. Finally, states are divided yet again with much disagreement about the final assessment, so they might have accepted the CCSS, but reject these two tests.

Whatever is decided, CCSS leaves room for teachers, curriculum developers, and states to determine how those stated curricular goals should be reached and what additional topics should be addressed. The Standards do not mandate such things as a particular writing process or the full range of metacognitive strategies that students may need to monitor and direct their thinking and learning. Teachers are thus free to provide students with whatever tools and knowledge their professional judgment and experience identify as most helpful for meeting the goals set out in the Standards. In relation to English learners, the Common Core State Standards for English language arts (ELA) articulate rigorous grade-level expectations in the areas of speaking, listening, reading, and writing to prepare all students to be college and career ready, including English language learners. Second-language learners also will benefit from instruction about how to negotiate situations outside of those settings so they are able to participate on equal footing with native speakers in all aspects of social, economic, and civic endeavors (NGA Center for Best Practices and the Council of Chief State School Officers, 2010).

English learners bring with them many resources that enhance their education and can serve as resources for the classroom. Many ELLs have literacy skills in their native language that can be transmitted to the subjects learned in English. Teachers can use this previous knowledge to help build language acquisition skills needed for English language learners to become proficient and literate in English. Like native English speaking students, ELLs require regular access to best teaching practices that are most effective for improving student achievement. Literacy and mathematical tasks should be kept at higher academic level for English language learners to ensure the same mastery of the standards as that of native English speaking students (NGA Center for Best Practices and the Council of

Chief State School Officers, 2010). It is the process of **how** the content is taught that should take English language learners into consideration.

The Common Core State Standards can be successful for all students. Although some of the standards may seem challenging, students are capable of learning anything we have faith in teaching them. I believe teaching an English language learner with strategies is similar to teaching a group of students whose native language is English. You can use similar teaching techniques with both sets of students and provide the extra help for the English language learner. However, using scaffolding techniques for the ELL also gives the native English speaking student another interpretation of how something is explained. By using supportive techniques for all students, you are engaging each student at all times. In my experience, a clever way to tackle the new Common Core State Standards without becoming overwhelmed is to take a look at what you taught the year before. Have the topics covered in a grid, then go through each set of standards and match them to what you already teach. This takes frontloading time, but the effort is worth the time because you do not have to "re-invent the wheel" to teach new standards. The Common Core State Standards website (http://www.corestandards.org/) is easy to use and navigate so that you can modify every lesson to include one of the standards.

The standards in the United States have changed over the past eight years. We now have the Common Core Curriculum, which has been adopted by most states' educational systems. Each state has tailored these standards to the needs of the students in their state. Contrary to popular belief, the Common Core State Standards have been developed to better the level of education in the United States, not to place unreachable goals on our students. Many states simply have decided it is time to provide an education that better prepares our students for higher education, as well as the workforce.

The CCSS have not been positively received by some educational systems in the United States. This is largely due to the lack of knowledge that the systems and educators have about the new standards, as well as funding issues. With proper knowledge about the standards, we can see what students need

to master by the end of each grade level, and these objectives are attainable with support. The standards allow for a deeper understanding of the content that is being taught, while creating a higher level of thinking. The idea of using CCSS to teach ELLs can be challenging for educators who are not experienced in teaching English learners in the mainstream classroom. They may mistakenly believe that the level of proficiency of English learners is not sufficient enough until the language is adequately mastered. This is a common misconception about the English learner. By using an *unpacking* method of the standards and having an understanding of where the students stand academically, it will be easier to tackle the challenges facing teachers.

Incorporating the Standards: The *Unpacking* Approach

The *unpacking method* consists of taking one standard and finding many different ways to teach it over the school year. Let's take the second grade standard *CCSS.ELA-LITERACY.SL.2.1.A: Follow agreed-upon rules for discussions (e.g., gaining the floor in respectful ways, listening to others with care, speaking one at a time about the topics and texts under discussion).* After reading the standard, it is easy to see that almost anything you teach in the classroom from classroom discussion, answering questions, and small presentations will help the student master the standard. In my classroom, every Friday I have the students bring in something related to a topic I am teaching in a core subject that week. Then we have "show and share" about the object brought in.

An sample lesson plan would be the following: I am teaching the standard *CCSS.ELA-LITERACY. RL.2.1: Ask and answer such questions as who, what, where, when, why, and how to demonstrate understanding of key details* in a text this week and I have asked the students to bring in a book to share with the class. While sitting on the carpet (if this is

---

acceptable to all students) I share my book *Cat in the Hat* by Dr. Seuss, and I model *sharing* by standing up and explaining the who, what, when, where, and why of my story. Then I ask each student to do the same, one at a time, and remind the students that when one person is sharing, everyone else is listening respectfully. Using a common activity like *show and share* to help a child master a standard is one easy way for the students to be involved in the task. This also provides me with an observation assessment of the reading standard I have been teaching for the past week.

Planning for Lessons

Without the introduction, the students are trying to understand a topic they know nothing about, and for ELLs, understanding what the teacher is about to do is very important so that students are mentally prepared to learn. ELLs will often tune out when they do not know what is going on. After the introduction of the standard, tell the students exactly how you are planning to teach the lesson and why. This explanation offers clarity and eliminates confusion.

As discussed in the previous section about teaching strategies and the Common Core State Standards for English language learners, start the lesson in a whole group setting, either on the carpet or in students' seats. During the whole group lesson use visuals, classroom discussion, and peer buddies to get the standard across to the students. Once the whole group lessons is complete, have the students complete an individual or group activity directly connected to the standard being taught to show that they have individual understanding, and are able to connect to the material.

Whether the subject being taught is reading, math, sciences, or social studies, provide the students time to explore the standards within the subject. Creating center activities directly related to the standards allows students the opportunity for independent study based on their academic level. During this time, centers that can be created should include small group instruction, buddy work, independent study, and integration of technology. At the end of the time block for the subject being taught, always provide the students with a closing activity. Bringing

their attention back to the standard being taught and how they applied it that day is what should be discussed. If the lesson is to be continued into the following day, give the students a segue into the next days' activities.

Working with the Common Care State Standards does not have to be a daunting task. By using activities that are already used by the teacher, and using explicit modeling of the standard, all students will be able to master what has been taught. As stated before, a wide variety of teaching strategies can help guide instruction for the daily learning of ELLs. This list includes small group instruction, pictures, explicit modeling, and peer buddies, just to name a few. Adding these strategies to the new Common Core State Standards will help ease the transition from a relaxed to a more rigorous curriculum. In my experience, modeling what you want your students to be able to do and building schema (background knowledge) about the standards you are teaching is very important when teaching all students, especially ELLs. Without modeling, the students do not fully understand what you are requesting them to do. This step is most important in the early proficiency stages of learning English. Showing some step-by-step examples promotes a deeper understanding of the lesson and allows for easier comprehension for English speaking students as well. Developing schema is important when dealing with the difficult standards, especially for students with no background knowledge. Schema can be developed by having simple conversations about what a child likes, and unpacking the standard to build up to what the students need to master. For example, in my classroom I am teaching the strategies needed for *close reading*, which is needed for most state exams. Close reading is being able to read and draw the information from the text. My ELL students do not have the background knowledge to be able to read a text previously unseen, and pull details from the text to answer questions. I am using the text *Charlie and the Chocolate Factory*, a story my students have seen in the movies, to learn the skills needed for close reading. Using a text that they have prior knowledge about allows for an easier understanding of characters, setting, and plot. While I am reading to my students, I ask simple questions about character traits and how they relate to the events of the story, why the setting of the story is important to what is happening in the text, and why the author is writing about certain things in the story. These types of questions are the building blocks needed to complete close reading activities for my students.

Below is a common scenario for a new teacher:

A new teacher is given a classroom, CCSS, and some sort of state curriculum to guide classroom instruction. Everything else is up to the teacher, from classroom supplies needed to better a student's education, to navigating the curriculum and CCSS to provide digestible chunks for the students to learn. Then the week before school starts, the new teacher will probably be given a class list of native English speaking students and nonnative English speaking students on a broad spectrum ranging from beginning speakers to almost proficient. **How does a mainstream classroom teacher accommodate English language learners without slowing down the curriculum being taught to the entire population in the classroom?** This question can be answered simply by implementing ELL strategies into the day-to-day lesson planning.

Teaching Strategies and the Common Core State Standards for English Language Learners

Assessment is the most important tool an educator can use to help guide the learning process inside the classroom. If the teacher does not know what a student already knows about the subjects being taught, how will the teacher know how and what to teach? Assessments should be conducted on a regular basis, from simple observations, to standard based assessments. Simple observations, like the example lesson of show and share in the previous section, are a great way to have an idea of what knowledge students are taking away from the subjects being taught. Having a student discussion, one-on-one, or in a whole group setting, allows the English learners who may

not be able to show mastery of the standard on paper to have confidence in their explanation. A formal assessment permits students to demonstrate what they already know about the standard being taught, and allows the teacher to plan for that student's individual needs. Formal and informal assessments should be used to guide the lesson planning process for whole group and small group instruction.

Whole group instruction is the most common form of teaching. It should engage all students throughout the entire lesson and allow the students time to apply what is being taught. Let's take a look at the Common Core Standards for reading in the third grade. In the third grade, a student will describe characters in a story (e.g., their traits, motivations, or feelings) and explain how their actions contribute to the sequence of events. This concept can be taught in many different ways, but specifically looking at English language learners, introducing this standard should be done as a whole group. This standard should be introduced while the reading of a story is already taking place, so there is a sense of the character already in the story to pull student knowledge from. For example, reading the novel *Charlotte's Web* as a class is a great story to pull character traits from. The story includes Wilber, the brave pig. Through the help of his friend Charlotte, the spider, she devises a plan to foil the efforts of the farmer that is fattening up Wilber to eat him. In the end, their plan turns Wilber into a prize pig that no one wants to eat. The details of the story are not the important key for this lesson. The idea is to help the students understand what character traits lead to the great ending of the story.

While sitting in a whole group setting that your class is comfortable with, tell the students that they will be learning about character traits using *Charlotte's Web*. Explain that character traits are a way to describe how a character acts and feels throughout a story and affect the events that happen. Using a movie that the students already have seen, have the students turn and talk to each other about the main character of that movie. Help guide the discussion with examples of how you would describe the character, and make sure to write all answers clearly on the board. After the students' ideas are placed on the board, go through each idea and discuss why or why not it is a good way to describe the character. This makes the students feel confident in the answers they have given, because you are giving value to the students' answers by discussing them. Then turn to an anchor chart (see anchor chart below) with the character of Wilber placed in the middle of the page. Using adjectives that the students are familiar with (that are visibly posted for students to access and refer to) have the students describe Wilber in the same way they described the character from the movie. After the students' answers are written on the chart, engage conversation by asking why the author made Wilber the character he is, and how important his character is to the story. Having the students turn and talk to a partner is a great way for them to experience authentic interaction with their peers, while relating to the content.

FIGURE 23-1 Character Trait Chart

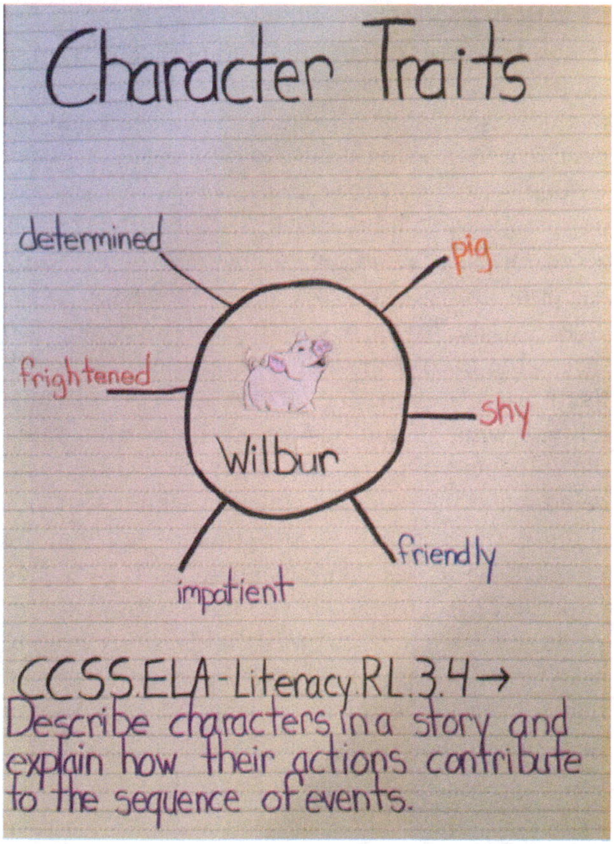

Created by: Katee Anderson

When an ELL needs more attention in one area, this is the time when the teacher should pull students into small groups based on reading/math levels. By pulling small groups, this allows for more one-on-one attention that all students need. Small group instruction is not for drilling skills, but for activities that give the students hands-on approaches to practice applying the knowledge the teacher is trying to teach; this technique allows for a deeper level of understanding of the material, rather than just service knowledge or memorization of facts. Small group instruction is an important strategy to use for an ELLs. In addition to more one-on-one learning experience with the teacher, it also provides the students with instruction at their academic level. Small group instruction includes between three and five students (based on classroom size) at the same academic level. Using the standards being taught during the week provides the group with activities that they can complete with the teacher and demonstrate an understanding at their level.

An example of a small group activity would be taking the standard of *CCSS.ELA-LITERACY. RL.3.3: Describe characters in a story (e.g., their traits, motivations, or feelings) and explain how their actions contribute to the sequence of events,** and creating differentiated activities for the students. For the lower language proficient students, use a worksheet with the same character from the anchor chart about *Charlotte's Web* (see example) and have lines going out from the character to the edge of the paper. As a group, look at the anchor created earlier as a whole group and recount the answers already written on the chart. After the short discussion, without using the anchor chart, have the students come up with the same answers as a group and write them down on the paper. For students who are on grade level, start with the anchor chart created in the whole group discussion and have the students create their own on a separate sheet of paper, including the picture. Then, for the students above grade level, use a completely different story for this activity. Using a set of guided reading books, read the story, and

FIGURE 23-2

Created by: Katee Anderson

using the anchor chart as a reference, have the students create a character chart from the characters in the new story. By using this strategy, the teacher will be able to reengage the students on their level with the standards being taught in the whole group lessons.

Using pictures at all grade levels allows ELLs (as well as all students) to relate the topic to the visual representation. The picture strategy includes actual pictures of the content and teacher-created anchor charts. Actual pictures are useful in making connections in subjects like reading, writing, science, and social studies. Having the picture of the content that is being discussed either on the board, document camera, or projector allows the instant connection and access of a student's prior knowledge. Providing these visuals during a test also allows for an English learner to understand vocabulary that might not be fully developed yet.

Anchor charts are a wonderful tool to create with the students, and they can be placed on the board to refer to while teaching content. When creat-

ing an anchor, the standard is introduced to the students, then the students brainstorm ways to apply the standard to the content being taught. These ideas are written on the anchor chart along with a visual representation to refer to during group or independent activities. Below is an example of a writing anchor chart I created for a dual-language kindergarten classroom labeling lesson that introduces basic skills needed to master the standard *CCSS.ELA-LITERACY.W.1.3*, which is about writing narratives. The lesson would be set in the beginning of the year and is based on the beginning steps of what writers do.

The standard used in this lesson was *CCSS. ELA-LITERACY.W.1.3: Write narratives in which they recount two or more appropriately sequenced events, include some details regarding what happened, use temporal words to signal event order, and provide some sense of closure.* Introducing the student to what standard the teacher is working on that day allows the student to see and keep the ending goal in mind. This should be the first step in any lesson because for complete comprehension, the students need an idea of what is going to be taught that day. Next, show the students the chart and explain that for a writer's story to be understood, when we don't know how to write the words, we can label our pictures for the reader to see what the story is about. Drawing about something the student already has prior knowledge about allows the lesson to become student driven. My students all loved dogs, so that is the thing I decided to draw and label with them. After drawing the picture, have the students tell you what should be labeled. Label everything the students point out and, once the picture is labeled, have the students come up with a sentence about the picture. When the students tell you the sentence, write it at their level (similar to Language Experience Approach). If you have a lower to on-grade level student, then explicitly show how to sound out the words, and write the letters they hear. If you have higher level students, make sure you spell the words correctly and explain the spelling

---

* © Copyright 2010. National Governors Association Center for Best Practices and Council of Chief State School Officers. All rights reserved.

FIGURE 23-3 Dual Language Class

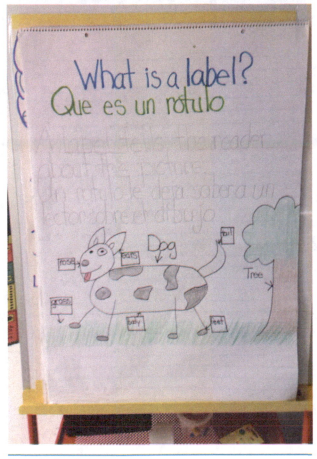

Created by: Katee Anderson

patterns to the students so they will understand why it is written that way. Again, this shows I am working more than one standard into my lessons.

Group work and *peer buddies* are two strategies that allow student interaction during the student application portion of a lesson. These strategies allow for students who understand the activity to show and explain it to their peers. Placing students in groups by varying learning levels is very important. If there are two students at the same academic level who do not understand what has been taught, neither student will be able to perform the task. If you have the opportunity, allow the English learners to speak in their native language to students who can provide the English translation. This can be a very important strategy when vocabulary is not at a level of understanding. A student's confidence level is the most important key to their success in learning. If they believe they can learn, then they will. On the other hand, if that confidence level is diminished because there is a lack of native language interaction, students may not perform to their full potential and can start to fall behind. If no other students speak the same language, create opportunities in the district or community to find speakers of these languages who may want to volunteer to help out in your classroom.

Points to Remember

❖ Understand the standards for your grade and subjects. Knowing how to use standards to help guide instruction is a very important skill to use for the English language learners in the mainstream classroom.

❖ Remember that integrating strategies for the English language learners in the classroom benefits all students, both native and nonnative English speakers.

❖ Always be very explicit in the way the lesson is introduced and how the standard will be addressed throughout the entire lesson.

❖ Finally, know that lowering the academic expectations for English language learners in the mainstream classroom is detrimental to their learning. Students will reach the goals set for them if the belief is that the goals need to be mastered.

Effective Strategies for Teaching Mathematics to English Language Learners (ELLs)

KEY ISSUES

- The Common Core State Standards (CCSS) for teaching mathematics have become state adopted standards and guidelines for teaching mathematics to all students, including the ELL population

- Math manipulatives and other concrete and visual representations of math concepts are critical to begin teaching mathematics

- Strategies that specifically address ELL needs

- Strategies/teaching methods for reaching more students, like cooperative learning, use of math manipulatives, children's literature, a problem-solving approach, technology, and active learning

- Special accommodations for assessing ELL students in mathematics

- Building on prior knowledge and cultural experiences to make mathematics meaningful

- The relationship between limited English proficiency and low mathematics ability

- Providing equal opportunities for all students to learn mathematics

- The importance of "differentiating instruction" in mathematics to reach each and every student in a class setting

- The need to prepare all students for a high-tech globally competitive world is critical in light of preparing more young people for STEM fields

Jung Lee is a new student in sixth grade. He and his family just moved from his native homeland of Korea. Jung is good at math and always excelled in school in Korea. Things are changing for him now because he has little grasp of the English language. Jung has become frustrated that he is not able to do many of his in-class and take-home word problems. Reading and speaking in English are difficult for Jung. Jung is quick to do any math that is a basic computational-type problem, but when any words are involved or the instructions are detailed, his confidence and ability to do math are hindered. Jung has always succeeded at math, and now his frustration with learning English while doing math in English has really devastated him. Jung has started copying his classmates' work from their worksheets and homework. The students think he is cheating and complain to the teacher. Jung only wants to succeed.

As a fourth grade teacher, "frustrated" is one word to describe how I feel about the diversity of my student population and how it relates to my success in reaching all students in my classroom. It is a challenge each day to teach to a classroom of students where as many as ten students' first language is not English. Nowadays, teachers not only need to know how to teach, but must teach students who speak a myriad of language. In one class alone, my students speak Spanish, English, Creole, and Samoan. Additionally, I have challenges such as large class size, and difficulties in communicating with the parents of my students. My quest is to reach all kids equally, regardless of the diverse cultural backgrounds and language barrier issues that may stand in our way.

The opening vignette demonstrates that language issues are critical in many schools across the country where there are large populations of predominantly non-English-speaking people. Teachers are frustrated and concerned with not being able to reach the students whose first language is not English. One math teacher says, "They speak little or no English. I would like to learn effective strategies that will help me as a teacher to instruct these children." Math is difficult for English language learners. Not only are ELL students learning in a new language, but they may also be learning new concepts in mathematics, which are oftentimes very abstract. This chapter focuses on strategies that teachers can use to address the teaching of mathematics to all students, but more specifically, the ELL students they may have in their classrooms.

Educators are striving to meet the increasingly diverse needs of students in the United States. The organization *Teachers of English to Speakers of Other Languages, Inc.,* and many states have responded to the challenge by working together to develop standards of performance for both teachers and students. The Common Core State Standards campaign is spearheaded by the National Governors Association Center for Best Practices (NGA Center) and the Council of Chief State School Officers (CCSSO), 2010 (Florida Department of Education, 1996; Secada, 2000; TESOL, 1991). These new *Common Core State Standards* (CCSS) promote strategies that build on and extend students' cultural background knowledge and experiences. Mathis (2010) contends that while there are still some kinks to work out and details to address, the CCSS in mathematics provide a good guideline and a tool for the U.S. math curriculum our teachers and students need for the twenty-first century. The new Common Core State Standards provide standards and goals for young people, whether going to college or directly into the workforce, so that they are better equipped for the current high-tech world we live in. Teaching mathematics effectively to all students, and particularly to those who are English learners, means making interdisciplinary and cultural connections. Today there is a big emphasis on better preparation of more young people for careers in STEM (science, technology, engineering, and mathematics) fields.

Holdren, Lander, and Varmus (2010) explain that standards are based on government input from the Obama Administration to better prepare and inspire more young people in K–12 education so they can enter into fields like science, technology, engineering, and math education for America's future, based on the President's Council of Advisors on Science and Technology, Office of Science and

Technology. The National Council of Teachers of Mathematics (2000) says that too often teachers have low expectations for nonnative speakers of English and that expectations must be raised because "mathematics can and must be learned by all students" (p. 13). Math teachers need to have high expectations for all students and work toward increasing honest effort and motivation among ESOL students; teachers should not shortchange ESOL students and need to emphasize all aspects of mathematical discourse among all populations (Flores, 1997; McCallum, 1999). Mathematical notations across the world may not share cultural uniformity and for children from diverse backgrounds, these differences can present obstacles to learning (Crandall, 1987; Dale & Cuevas, 1987; Diaz-Rico & Weed, 1995; Moore, 1994). Standards for teaching mathematics developed by NCTM (1989, 1995, 2000) and best practices suggested by Zemelman, Daniels, and Hyde (2012) are congruent with strategies that relate mathematics to prior knowledge, background, and real-life situations.

The National Council of Teachers of Mathematics (NCTM) has led the country in a standards-based movement to improve mathematics instructions for all students. In 1989, NCTM published its first standards document, paving the way by setting standards and guidelines. NCTM (2000) published its updated version of the mathematics standards. This education association contends such standards are needed to:

❖ Ensure quality
❖ Indicate goals
❖ Promote change

NCTM identified goals and stated that they are both a reflection of the needs of society and the needs of the students in our "Information Age." NCTM's new social goals for education are to promote:

1. Mathematically literate workers
2. Lifelong learners (who are flexible, adjustable, and problem solvers)
3. Opportunities for all
4. An informed electorate in a democratic country

The updated Principles and Standards for School Mathematics (NCTM, 2000) are outlined in the following principles and content standards as we begin a new millennium:

Principles for Teaching

❖ Equity—High expectations for ALL students
❖ Curriculum—Coherent and articulated K–12
❖ Teaching—What students know and what they need to learn; effective pedagogy
❖ Learning—For understanding and prior knowledge
❖ Assessment—Support learning and give information to teacher and learner
❖ Technology—What is taught and enhances learning

Standards for pre-K–12 in grade-level clusters (K–2, 3–5, 6–8, and 9–12):

Content Standards

❖ Numbers and operations
❖ Algebra
❖ Geometry
❖ Measurement
❖ Data analysis and probability

Process Standards

❖ Problem solving
❖ Reasoning and proof
❖ Communication
❖ Connections
❖ Representations

These process standards highlight ways of acquiring and using content knowledge. The new *Common Core State Standards for Mathematics* are a reflection of the *Curriculum Focal Points* (NCTM, 2006) which all were a reflection of the Third International Mathematics and Science Study (TIMSS) results in keeping with the idea of creating a more coherent and in depth math curriculum. The CCSSM and the *Curriculum Focal Points* were developed as an effort to get away from the inch-deep, mile-wide math curriculum in the United States, where teachers often were unable to cover all the material or to do so with much depth. The CCSSM and *Curriculum Focal Points* are a reflection of the most important mathematical topics for each grade level, pre-K through grade 8. They encompass related ideas, concepts, skills, and procedures that form the foundation for understanding and using mathematics and lasting learning. The *Curriculum Focal Points* have been integral in the revision of many state math standards throughout the United States now, giving more depth and breadth to the math curriculum. Each grade focuses on specific developmental and deep understanding/mastery of particular math concepts. Today, the new *Common Core State Standards in Mathematics* (CCSSM) now used in almost all fifty states follow this model of a deeper and richer curriculum based on the international research of a deeper and richer coherent and focus curriculum. According to the CCSSM, they want the mathematical understanding and procedural skills to be equally important and assessable using mathematical tasks of sufficient richness in math classrooms. The CCSSM Standards set grade-specific standards but do not define the intervention methods or materials necessary to support students who are well below or well above grade level expectations. It is also says it is beyond the scope of the standards to define the full range of supports appropriate for English language learners and for students with special needs. However, the CCSSM standards espouse that all students must have the opportunity to learn and meet the same high standards if they are to access the knowledge and skills necessary in their post-school lives. The CCSSM should allow for the widest possible range of students to participate fully from the outset, along with appropriate accommodations to ensure maximum participation of students with special education needs, language issues, and other types of accommodations for all students to achieve and reach a level to better prepare them for their future.

The CCSSM and the NCTM's purpose for creating the new standards is to identify grade level curriculum focal points and connections to enable students to learn the content in the context of a focused and cohesive curriculum that implements problem

solving, reasoning, and critical thinking (NCTM, 2006). The Common Core proposes a set of *Mathematical Practices* that all teachers should develop in their students.

The characteristics of the new CCSSM reflect fewer and more rigorous standards per grade/topic; a goal for more clarity in standards taught; aligned with college and career expectations to prepare all students for success upon graduating from high school; internationally benchmarked, so that all students are prepared for succeeding in our global economy and society; includes rigorous content and application of higher order skills; builds upon strengths and lessons of current state standards; and they are research-based. The new CCSSM follow a certain format using domains, clusters, and standards. The domains are large groups of related standards. Standards from different domains may sometimes be closely related. Look for the name with the code number on it for a domain. Clusters are groups of related standards. Standards from different clusters may sometimes be closely related, because mathematics is a connected subject. Clusters appear inside domains. Standards define what students should be able to understand and be able to do as part of a cluster of related ideas. (From the *Common Core State Standards*—National Governors Association Center for Best Practices [NGA Center] and the Council of Chief State School Officers [CCSSO], [2010]).

The Common Core Format

Grades K–8	Grades 9–12 [High School]
Grade	Conceptual Category
Domain	Domain
Cluster	Cluster
Standards	Standards

The Standards by Domain for the CCSSM include:

- ❖ Counting and Cardinality
- ❖ Operations and Algebraic Thinking
- ❖ Number and Operations in Base Ten
- ❖ Number and Operations—Fractions
- ❖ Measurement and Data
- ❖ Geometry
- ❖ Ratios and Proportional Relationships
- ❖ The Number System
- ❖ Expressions and Equations
- ❖ Functions
- ❖ Statistics and Probability

The CCSSM and the NCTM believe that equity requires accommodating differences to help everyone learn mathematics (2000; 2010). Some students may need further assistance to meet high expectations. Students who are not native speakers of English may need special attention to allow them to participate fully in class discussions. Some of them may also need assessment accommodations. If understanding is assessed only in English, their mathematical proficiency may not be evaluated accurately (NCTM, 2000). The National Science Board (Selby, 2006) is concerned with increased achievement scores in mathematics and science; substantial performance gaps exist between some racial/ethnic subgroups. At each grade level tested (fourth, eighth, and twelfth), white and Asian/Pacific Islander students performed better than black, Hispanic, and American Indian/Alaska Native students in mathematics. Performance disparities in mathematics are evident among many student subgroups, such as the ELL population. In a high-tech globally competitive age, where knowledge of mathematics, science, and technology are critical, teachers must make sure

their math instruction is effective in reaching all students in their classroom. Special accommodations and strategies are essential for helping to increase achievement in mathematics for the ELL population, as they too need to compete for such high-tech jobs. Teachers must prevent causing math anxiety and work toward building students' confidence and understanding to do mathematics (Furner & Duffy, 2002).

Teachers must use a varied approach to assessment in mathematics to get a better picture of the learners' understanding. Teachers can assess mathematical understanding by using:

- ❖ Observation
- ❖ Questioning/interviews
- ❖ Performance tasks
- ❖ Portfolios
- ❖ Writings and work samples
- ❖ Written/achievement/standardized tests
- ❖ Self-assessments

Considering math test accommodations for students with limited English proficiency is important. Teachers need to consider things like the following when assessing mathematical understanding using written tests:

1. Using modified (simplified) English on tests
2. Providing a glossary with definitions with difficult nonmathematical terms
3. Allocating extra testing time for ESOL students

Providing such accommodations has shown significant increases in the performance levels of LEP students in mathematics (Abedi, 1999). Flores (1997) contended that if students read in their native language, but their level of English is weak, taking a test in English would not allow them to show what they know. Flores believes teachers need to provide native language translations of such assessments, as this is a fairer way of assessing the learner. Boaler (2008) contends that high stakes testing in the United States has had negative effects on students, mostly the low income and ELL populations. She has found that seventeen of the eighteen states that use high stakes testing found that student learning remained the same or went down. It also drove teachers from the profession and increased high school dropout rates. Boaler feels that the irony of the high stakes testing movement is that it has made inequality even worse.

Martiniello (2008) found how important language skills are for understanding and solving mathematical problems in large-scale assessments. Thus, the teaching of mathematics to ELLs can no longer be perceived as separate from the teaching of language. Research on teachers' perceptions has found some contradictions in the way teachers conceive of mathematics instruction (as free from language) and the kind of math assessments they use in their classrooms.

In a study by Abedi et al. (2006), their results indicated that, in general, ELL students reported less content coverage than their non-ELL peers, and they were in classes of overall lower math ability than their non-ELL peers. The assessments they took contained fewer linguistically modifiable items and demonstrated low reliability between items that were linguistically modified. Their study showed that all three class-level components of opportunities to learn (OTL) for ELL students were significantly related to math performance, after controlling for prior math ability at the individual student level. Class prior math ability had the strongest effect on math performance. Results also indicated that teacher content knowledge had a significant differential effect on the math performance of students grouped by a quick reading proficiency measure, but not by students' ELL status or by their reading achievement test percentile ranking.

Currently in math instruction there is more of a focus on process and problem solving as opposed to single answers and computation. Teachers can incorporate more problem-solving approaches into instruction as well as rubrics that grade based on the process rather than right answers only. Reys, Suydam, Lindquist, and Smith (2009) and NCTM (1989, 1995, 2000, 2006) suggested that teachers need to see that methods and tasks for assessing students' learning should be aligned with the curriculum's goals, math content, instructional approaches, and activities, including the use of calculators and manipulatives. Reys et al. (2009) and NCTM (1989, 1995, 2000, 2006) feel that assessment should allow for multiple sources of information with tasks that show different kinds of math thinking as well as present the same math concept or procedure in different contexts, formats, and problem situations. Flores (1997) feels that "the assessment of mathematics in other languages should include measures of high-level conceptual knowledge, high-level procedural knowledge, and higher-order-thinking skills" (p. 88). Also, appropriate assessment methods and uses need to be taken into consideration based on the type of information sought, how the information will be used, and the developmental level and maturity of each student. Schools really need to shift toward assessing students' full mathematical power by giving students multiple opportunities to demonstrate their full mathematical understanding, aligning assessment with curriculum and instruction, and regarding assessment as continual and recursive (NCTM, 1995). With less of an emphasis on right or wrong and more of an emphasis on process, teachers can thus help to create a population of students who can show competence in mathematics.

It is common for teachers to have ELL students in their classrooms who are very advanced mathematically. Oftentimes, students from other countries have been taught mathematics at a higher level in their homeland and excel compared with their U.S. counterparts. These students may seem advanced when doing most mathematical computations, but when confronted with word problems or complicated directions, they may not understand the language. It is frustrating for these students, who obviously know mathematics well, but the new language interferes with their mathematics success and often can wound their confidence. Again, here it is important that the teacher provide special accommodations for these students. Many teachers may say or use the excuse that because their ELL students cannot read English, they do not have the students do any problem solving. This, however, is unfair to the student who really needs experience with problem solving to learn how to read and understand English. When teaching mathematics, teachers are not only teaching about math, numbers, and geometry; they are also teaching communication skills such as reading, writing, and speaking/discussion.

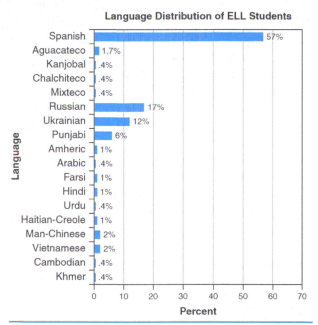

Language Distribution of ELL Students

Data Source: Ferndale School District, http://ferndalesd.org/?q=ell/home

In a book entitled *Best Practice: Bringing Standards to Life in America's Classrooms*, Zemelman, Daniels, and Hyde (2012) outlined the best practices for teaching mathematics, which include:

- ❖ Use of math manipulatives (concrete math)
- ❖ Cooperative group work
- ❖ Discussion of math
- ❖ Questioning and making conjectures

- ❖ Justification of thinking
- ❖ Writing in math: thinking, feelings, and problem solving
- ❖ Problem-solving approach to instruction as the central theme to teaching mathematics
- ❖ Content integration
- ❖ Use of calculators, computers, and all technology
- ❖ Being a facilitator of learning
- ❖ Assessing learning as a part of instruction

This chapter includes a list of ELL strategies teachers can use when teaching mathematics. It is critical that educators align their mathematics teaching approaches with NCTM's social goals for education. Teachers of LEP students may find the ELL strategies useful in their successes for mastering mathematics. Informed educators know that all students, whether LEP or not, must receive an equal education. Teachers must strive to prepare all students for a technologically advancing society. The standards developed by TESOL promote strategies (Crandall, 1987; Dale & Cuevas, 1992; FDOE, 1996; Moore, 1994) that build on and extend students' cultural background, knowledge, and experiences. Teachers can make learning comprehensible for the ELL by incorporating the following strategies into their teaching. These strategies do not need to be limited only to the teaching of math or to the teaching of ELL students; all students can benefit from such strategies. The Eastern Stream Center on Resources and Training (1998) in their teacher guide, *Help! They Don't Speak English Starter Kit for Primary Teachers: A Resource Guide for Educators of Limited English Proficient Migrant Students, Grades Pre-K–6* provides cultural assessment strategies for teaching LEP students.

Teachers are increasingly frustrated by the demands of teaching students from diverse backgrounds. Therefore, it is important for teachers to realize these strategies are really "best practice" for not only the LEP students, but for all students and for the teaching of all subjects. The Mathematics Education Leadership Training (MELT) Project at San Diego State University–Imperial Valley Campus works with bilingual teachers to provide sound math instruction for the emergent English speakers, especially the Latino population. MELT has incorporated the first four of NCTM's Process Standards to help students reach English language proficiency. The ESOL Endorsement Program at Florida Atlantic University in South Florida provides ESOL endorsement for elementary education majors going through the program by weaving ESOL theory and practice into each of the methods courses that a student must take as a preservice teacher. The following list provides mathematics teaching strategies along with examples and discussion for English speakers of other languages. Both are reflected in the two ESOL programs previously mentioned.

ESOL Math Strategies

✓ **Teaching ESOL Students While Creating Lesson Plans that Reach All**

garriphoto/Shutterstock.com

Teach Vocabulary Using Realia and Demonstration

Teachers can use real objects such as fruit, pattern blocks, beans, Popsicle sticks, marbles, buttons, and M&Ms as manipulatives in demonstrating math concepts. This can reinforce the number sentences visually. LEP students can also learn English and mathematics vocabularies. It is important to use concrete objects so students can be engaged in hands-on activities that not only make the comprehension of abstract math concepts easier, but are also enjoyable. It is critical that students understand the vocabulary of the math concepts they are learning.

Relate Math Problems and Vocabulary to Prior Knowledge and Background

Teachers can do research or ask students about the ways they learn math, especially for the teaching of students from diverse backgrounds. For example, Chinese students may be familiar with the use of an abacus to do their calculations. Teachers can perhaps ask these students to show their classmates how an abacus is used and can make cultural connections that make learning more meaningful for all students. Word problems about which ESOL students have no prior knowledge only serve to frustrate the students. Often this will be a barrier to their success in mathematics.

Honoring and recognizing students' ways of learning and experiences will boost their self-esteem by making them feel that they, too, have something to contribute to the learning process, despite their limited English abilities. In addition, teachers can

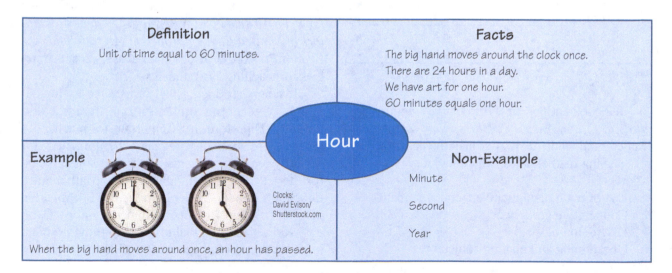

Definition	Facts
Unit of time equal to 60 minutes.	The big hand moves around the clock once. There are 24 hours in a day. We have art for one hour. 60 minutes equals one hour.

Hour

Example	Non-Example
Clocks: David Evison/ Shutterstock.com	Minute Second Year

When the big hand moves around once, an hour has passed.

prompt students to talk about their experience in learning some of the math concepts in their country of origin. By capitalizing on students' prior knowledge, teachers who are empathetic to their LEP students' situations bridge the new knowledge to the old, making learning new math concepts more manageable.

Too, creating "word walls" in the classroom is valuable for all students in the classroom, you can have the new words/vocabulary posted in English but have it also in other languages like Spanish or Creole and then all students are learning and/or retaining their mother tongue while learning words in other languages and seeing roots and patterns of words. This shows that you appreciate the variety of cultures in your classroom as well. Today in some school districts dual language programs are very popular helping students to learn a new language while retaining their own mother tongue so important for countries with large cultural diversities.

Apply the Math Problems to Daily Life Situations

Creative teachers can use a variety of methods to coach students in applying problems to daily life situations. For example, teachers can use restaurant take-out menus to teach students multiplication and division. Not only do such activities involve students with real life situations, but they also create a fun learning environment. Such an environment will also promote English language acquisition for nonnative English students. Krashen's (1985) metaphoric use of an affective filter reinforces the idea that teachers can lower the "affective filter" by fostering a spirit of mutual respect, high expectations, and cooperative learning. Moskowitz (1978) suggested that classrooms that offer techniques designed to relax students, increase the enjoyment of learning, raise self-esteem, and blend self-awareness will increase LEP students' proficiency in the target language. Arrowood (2004) provided a book with practical examples from everyday life in how we use mathematics. The book reviews how to teach most math topics for students whose first language is not English; measurement and the metric system are emphasized in the book, as many children from other countries use the metric system in their homelands.

Topics should not be limited to worksheets for three weeks and then forgotten. For example, in a unit on learning how to tell time, teachers can encourage students to tell time throughout the day as they participate in their daily schedule of school activities. As students progress in this skill, the activity can develop into a determination of the amount of time passed or time before a certain event occurs. Not only does this activity directly apply to students' own lives, but it also gives them a sense of control and understanding of their day. No longer do they ask, "When is lunch?" This competence is an important quality to develop in ELL students.

Use Manipulatives to Make Problems Concrete Instead of Abstract

Teachers can obtain commercial manipulatives, make their own, or help the students make their own. Examples of manipulatives are paper money, buttons, blocks, Cuisenaire rods, tangrams, geoboards, pattern blocks, algebra tiles, and base-ten blocks. The use of manipulatives provides teachers with a great potential to use their creativity to do further work on the math concepts instead of merely relying on worksheets. Consequently, students learn math in an enjoyable way, making connections between the concrete and the abstract. Piaget and Montessori philosophies are still alive and well received in today's math classroom. The CRA (Concrete-Representational-Abstract) Model for teaching mathematics is the main approach for teaching most math concepts for K–8 learners. When teaching mathematics, teachers always need to start with concrete manipulative materials to first teach for understanding, then transfer to representational models like pictures or diagrams, leading and bridging learning to the abstract level of understanding of symbols and operation signs so that students eventually do not need the manipulatives to do the mathematics.

David C. Rehner/Shutterstock.com

Shapiro Svetlana/Shutterstock.com

To understand the concept of money, teachers can have students "buy" items tagged for sale in the classroom. Students are given an opportunity to describe purchases they or an adult have made. Students select the proper combinations of coins to purchase the item. As each student participates, the class helps by showing the coins on the overhead. By handling the coins, students can correct mistakes and verify counting amounts of money.

Many studies over the years have demonstrated the benefits of using multiple modalities. ELL students, however, are disadvantaged in the one modality teachers seem to use the most: auditory. Claire and Haynes (1994) stated,

Of the three learning modes—auditory, visual, and kinesthetic—ESOL students will be weakest in auditory learning. It is unrealistic to expect them to listen to incomprehensible language for more than a few minutes before tuning out. But if you provide illustrations, dramatic gestures, actions, emotions, voice variety, blackboard sketches, photos, demonstrations, or hands-on materials, that same newcomer can direct his or her attention continuously. (p. 22)

Manipulatives and what they are used for in the teaching of Mathematics, manipulatives are powerful tools and can be used to teach many of the new *Common Core State Standards in Mathematics* as the following chart shows:

Manipulative	Common Core Math Standard Covered	Image of Manipulative (Photos courtesy of Joseph Furner)
Geoboards	CCSS.Math.Content.3.MD.C.5* Recognize area as an attribute of plane figures and understand concepts of area measurement.	
Pattern Blocks	CCSS.Math.Content.K.G.A.3* Identify shapes as two-dimensional (lying in a plane, "flat") or three-dimensional ("solid").	
Tangrams	CCSS.Math.Content.1.G.A.1* Distinguish between defining attributes (e.g., triangles are closed and three-sided) versus nondefining attributes (e.g., color, orientation, overall size); build and draw shapes to possess defining attributes.	

Manipulative	Common Core Math Standard Covered	Image of Manipulative (Photos courtesy of Joseph Furner)
Color Tiles	CCSS.Math.Content.2.G.A.2* Partition a rectangle into rows and columns of same size squares and count to find the total number of them.	
Unifix/Snap Cubes	CCSS.Math.Content.5.MD.C.3* Recognize volume as an attribute of solid figures and understand concepts of volume measurement.	
	CCSS.Math.Content.5.MD.C.3a* A cube with side length 1 unit, called a "unit cube," is said to have "one cubic unit" of volume, and can be used to measure volume.	
	CCSS.Math.Content.5.MD.C.3b* A solid figure which can be packed without gaps or overlaps using n unit cubes is said to have a volume of n cubic units.	
Triman Compass	CCSS.Math.Content.4.G.A.1* Draw points, lines, line segments, rays, angles (right, acute, obtuse), and perpendicular and parallel lines. Identify these in two-dimensional figures.	
Cuisenaire Rods	CCSS.Math.Content.7.RP.A.1* Compute unit rates associated with ratios of fractions, including ratios of lengths, areas and other quantities measured in like or different units. For example, if a person walks 1/2 mile in each 1/4 hour, compute the unit rate as the complex fraction 1/2/1/4 miles per hour, equivalently 2 miles per hour.	
Base-10 Blocks	CCSS.Math.Content.1.NBT.B.2* Understand that the two digits of a two-digit number represent amounts of tens and ones. Understand the following as special cases:	
	CCSS.Math.Content.1.NBT.B.2a* 10 can be thought of as a bundle of ten ones—called a "ten."	
	CCSS.Math.Content.1.NBT.B.2b* The numbers from 11 to 19 are composed of a ten and one, two, three, four, five, six, seven, eight, or nine ones.	
	CCSS.Math.Content.1.NBT.B.2c* The numbers 10, 20, 30, 40, 50, 60, 70, 80, 90 refer to one, two, three, four, five, six, seven, eight, or nine tens (and 0 ones).	
Number Tiles	CCSS.Math.Content.K.CC.A.3* Write numbers from 0 to 20. Represent a number of objects with a written numeral 0–20 (with 0 representing a count of no objects).	

(continued)

Manipulative	Common Core Math Standard Covered	Image of Manipulative (Photos courtesy of Joseph Furner)
TI Explorer Plus Calc.	CCSS.Math.Content.8.EE.A.4* Perform operations with numbers expressed in scientific notation, including problems where both decimal and scientific notation are used. Use scientific notation and choose units of appropriate size for measurements of very large or very small quantities (e.g., use millimeters per year for seafloor spreading). Interpret scientific notation that has been generated by technology.	
Two-Color Counters	CCSS.Math.Content.6.NS.C.5* Understand that positive and negative numbers are used together to describe quantities having opposite directions or values (e.g., temperature above/below zero, elevation above/below sea level, credits/debits, positive/negative electric charge); use positive and negative numbers to represent quantities in real world contexts, explaining the meaning of 0 in each situation.	
Judy Clock	CCSS.Math.Content.1.MD.B.3* Tell and write time in hours and half-hours using analog and digital clocks.	
Abacus	CCSS.Math.Content.1.NBT.C.4* Add within 100, including adding a two-digit number and a one-digit number, and adding a two-digit number and a multiple of 10, using concrete models or drawings and strategies based on place value, properties of operations, and/or the relationship between addition and subtraction; relate the strategy to a written method and explain the reasoning used. Understand that in adding two-digit numbers, one adds tens and tens, ones and ones; and sometimes it is necessary to compose a ten.	
Scale	CCSS.Math.Content.6.EE.A.4* Identify when two expressions are equivalent (i.e., when the two expressions name the same number regardless of which value is substituted into them). For example, the expressions y + y + y and 3y are equivalent because they name the same number regardless of which number y stands for.	

* © Copyright 2010. National Governors Association Center for Best Practices and Council of Chief State School Officers. All rights reserved.

Encourage Drawings to Translate and Visualize Word Problems

The natural approach (Krashen, 1985; Terrell, 1981) is used extensively for ELLs. One of the four principles of this approach is that the teacher understands that the student will need to have a silent period before being expected to speak English. One of the subsequent strategies of the natural approach is to allow students, especially those at the beginning level of their English language developmental stage, to use drawings and symbols in solving some of the math problems. In fact, as a comprehension check strategy, teachers can use students' drawings as testimony of their understanding of math concepts. This approach can alleviate frustrations for both teachers and students.

Use Wait Time to Encourage Understanding

There are two types of wait time: the time the teacher waits after asking a question before asking a student to respond and the time the teacher waits after the student has responded. During these two times, a teacher needs to preserve the wait time; this means that neither the teacher nor any of the students will speak. Allowing sufficient wait time permits ELLs the opportunity to process and, perhaps, translate the question before encountering interruptions or distractions from others attempting to answer the question. The wait time after the response allows the student time to monitor the response and do some "self-repair" if he or she feels the answer was incorrect. Both wait times are important because the student must not only listen to the teacher, but to the other students as well. Ignoring sufficient wait time can result in a student losing interest because the class continues at a pace that the student is unable to maintain. Thus, the student ceases to try.

Encourage Students to Follow the Four-Step Problem-Solving Process

Students should be encouraged to use Polya's (2004) four-step method when doing problem solving in mathematics. Students should be encouraged to write their thought processes as they go about solving problems. This is in alignment with NCTM's (1989, 2000, 2006) standards. As students solve math problems, they should:

Derrin Henry/Shutterstock.com

cherezoff/Shutterstock.com

1. Read and understand the problem. They write the problem in simpler terms.
2. Develop a strategy for solving the problem and discuss how they arrived at this strategy.
3. Carry out their plan and show all work justifying their answer.
4. Look back and check to see that their solution appears to be reasonable.

Teaching problem-solving strategies to students will provide them multiple methods to attack

(1) Draw the figure and label what you do know.	(2) List all information needed to solve and re-label if needed.
Time:	Time:
(3) Develop a plan to solve a problem.	(4) Solve for needed information and justify your answer.
Time:	Time:

problems. Examples of strategies include working backward, drawing a picture, making a simpler problem, looking for a pattern, trial and error, acting out, and using a table. These strategies can enrich and empower students mathematically as they problem solve.

Rewrite Word Problems in Simple Terms

Minority language students, especially those who are literate in their first language, often learn many mathematical concepts in their first language. The problems they have are language problems. Mathematics vocabulary can include words of a technical nature, such as denominator, quotient, and coefficient, or words defined by the content, such as rational, column, and table. Teachers can help students better understand math concepts in English by demonstrating to them what these terms mean through the use of visuals and hands-on activities. For example, in teaching fractions, teachers can use paper plates for imaginary pizzas and have students divide them into eight sections. The teacher can later demonstrate a lesson by introducing terms such as fraction, coefficient, and denominator using the student's manipulative. By having English language learners and mainstream students work collaboratively to write math problems, teachers perhaps will be able to see how technical terms might be used or even avoided when students express problems in their own words. Teachers can paraphrase and mod-

ify some of the more challenging questions by highlighting key terms. For example, in the problem "five times a number is two more than ten times the number," students must recognize that "a number" and "the number" refer to the same quantity. However, in the problem "the sum of two numbers is seventy-seven; if the first number is ten times the other, find the number," students need to know they are dealing with two numbers (Dale & Cuevas, 1992). Teachers can use pictures and symbols to illustrate the problem, and they can also emphasize that different articles such as *a* and *the* can add to the semantics of a problem.

Encourage Children to Think Aloud When Solving Word Problems and Have Students Give Oral Explanations of Their Thinking, Leading to Solutions

The think aloud protocol was a research tool originally used by psychologists. This research instrument is now popular with researchers in the language and reading fields. According to Chamot and O'Malley (1989), metacognitive knowledge includes awareness of task demands, of one's own approach to learning and experiences with similar tasks, and of appropriate strategies for the task. Encouraging children to think aloud when solving problems helps teachers to pinpoint students' difficulties in solving math problems. In addition, it can also help teachers instill in their students the metacognitive knowledge and strategies to learn math concepts. When students verbalize step by step how a math problem is solved, they often self-correct their mistakes. Similarly, this process allows peer corrections to occur.

Teachers should encourage higher level thinking skills in math by having students express their line of reasoning orally. Questions such as, "Why did you add in this problem?" help students to analyze and evaluate procedures undertaken in math. Higher level thinking is encouraged in many subject areas but is often neglected in math. Understanding the reasons for certain procedures in math will build competence and deeper understanding.

ZouZou/Shutterstock.com

Think Aloud

- ◆ I predict that . . .
- ◆ I can picture . . .
- ◆ A question I have is . . .
- ◆ This is like . . .
- ◆ This reminds me of . . .
- ◆ I am confused about . . .
- ◆ The big idea here is . . .
- ◆ I believe . . .

Have Students Write Original Word Problems to be Exchanged with Classmates

Having students write original word problems can be turned into competitive games among cooperative groups. Teachers can divide students into groups of three or four and have them write word problems collaboratively. For example, after the group has identified its math problems, the group members take turns in writing and adding to the word problems. The group that comes up with the most difficult word problem that is clear and well written wins. This activity can reinforce students' vocabulary, writing, and reading skills. The use of journal writing has also been shown to reinforce students' mathematics vocabulary and understanding. Writing allows students to elaborate on their thinking and problem-solving processes and strategies (Garrison, 1997). Radford, Netten, and Duquette (1997) suggested that students should be encouraged to cooperate and communicate in finding solutions to mathematics problems. We need to emphasize the importance of communications and cooperative problem solving in the learning of mathematics instruction; they contend that "language for communicative purposes is intricately linked with the development of other skills" (p. 95).

Explain Directions Clearly and Repeat Key Terms

Diaz-Rico and Weed (1995) asserted that "the difficulties that language minority students have with the language of mathematics lie in four major areas: vocabulary skills, syntax, semantics, and discourse features" (p. 137). Teachers who are sensitive to these students' language difficulties explain directions clearly and repeat key terms. There are several ways that teachers can do this. Common classroom directions such as "hand in your work" or "work quietly" should be written in bold letters and/or illustrated by drawings and diagrams and posted on the classroom wall. Teachers should repeat this direction every day or have students take turns repeating this direction daily so the language learners understand what they need to do. When teaching math formulae and symbols, teachers can assign group projects that elicit students' help to illustrate math concepts.

Realize That Not All Math Notations Are Necessarily Universal

Although math is considered by many as a universal language, students from South America and many European countries write a period instead of a comma in four-digit or larger numbers. Their decimal mark is a comma; ours is a period. For example, our number 4.547 is interpreted by these students as 4,547 or vice versa. Also, most of the world uses the metric system; therefore, math concepts based on feet, inches, miles, pounds, ounces, cups, pints, or quarts have to be converted. Math concepts that are based on money and time are not universal. American coins often confuse newcomers; one reason is that a relatively large nickel outweighs a coin of twice the value, and coin values are not written on the coins. Students from South America and the Caribbean display their work for division problems quite differently from the U.S. style:

Example: 25,000 divided by 5

U.S.: $5\overline{)25,000}$

Haiti: $25,000\overline{(}5$

Educators often mistakenly assume that the use of math symbols is culture-free and ideal for facilitating the transition of immigrant students into English instruction (California Department of Education, 1990). This is not true, and it is especially not true in the context-based math curriculum that stresses more communication and understanding (Lang, 1995).

Create Word Bank Charts and Display Them in the Classroom to Be Viewed— Emphasize Vocabulary

Teaching vocabulary in mathematics instruction is important (Diaz-Rico & Weed, 1995; Flores, 1997; Robison, 2006). Teachers can create a literate environment by filling the classroom with word-list charts or also known as "word walls." Teachers can keep word lists for each unit of study and add new words as they show up throughout a unit. Mathematics vocabulary can be represented graphically. Students can use the new vocabulary to do math journaling; for example, they can write about their reactions to mathematics or describe a math process like adding fractions with like denominators. Moschkovich (2000) discussed the importance of vocabulary and created the idea of a "mathematics register," where students have a set of meanings, words, and structures appropriate for learning mathematics. Students often need to know the equivalent meaning in their own language, and posting charts and word banks on classroom walls in both languages can help learners maintain and learn the new vocabulary in both languages while mapping and adding more vocabulary to their everyday register of words and meanings.

Pair Up ELLs with Non-ELL Students

According to Krashen (1985), language is acquired in an "amazingly simple way when we understand messages" (p. vii). He termed this understandable language as "comprehensible input." Peer interac-

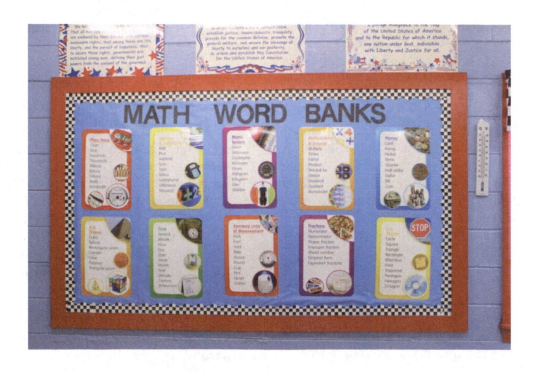

tion between native and nonnative speakers of English is one means of promoting "comprehensible input" or understandable language. Research by Diaz-Rico and Weed (1995) showed that in peer interaction, students use four communication strategies that contribute to the occurrence of comprehensible input: (a) embedding language within a meaningful context; (b) modifying language presented to nonnative peers; (c) using paraphrase and repetition judiciously; and (d) negotiating meaning consistently. When teachers pair ELLs and non-ELL students to accomplish content or language tasks' goals through the use of computers, collaborative work between the pair will promote ESOL students' acquisition of the English language through the learning of content areas such as math, science, and social studies. Students can be encouraged to take group "webquests" together or work on a piece of software in a cooperative fashion.

Computers are patient and never tire of correcting mistakes. They are nonjudgmental in their efforts to teach. By offering a nonthreatening environment, computers can encourage and motivate learning. It is important that teachers explain the computer program before allowing students access to the computer. Students get frustrated if they are uncertain about the procedures and are often unwilling to ask for assistance.

Group Students Heterogeneously during Cooperative Learning

Cooperative learning has positive results in the education of minority students (Cohen & Tellez, 1994; Kagan, 1989). According to Cazden (1988), classrooms may be "culturally incongruent" with the backgrounds of many groups if teachers emphasize individual performance, if the teacher is the controlling authority, and if there is little or no student control of participation. Cooperative learning not only restores a sense of comfort in a school setting where there are students from many cultural backgrounds, it also offers students psychological support for each other as they learn the content areas in English. This support provides all parties, teachers and students, a workable sociocultural compromise between the home culture and the culture of the

school. By grouping heterogeneously, students from diverse cultures can offer and enrich the mainstream students' learning process with their cultural experience and knowledge.

Cooperative learning encourages students of different backgrounds to work together. This type of learning integrates students socially and helps them to overcome biases against each other. Of significant importance for ELLs, cooperative learning develops communication skills and makes available a range of thinking, experiences, and help from others to increase comprehension of the content and other necessary skills. It is not uncommon to see a gifted ELL math student who is reluctant to work in a cooperative group setting. Although these students may prefer to work alone, cooperative learning is valuable for developing both social and language skills, and these students should be encouraged to work cooperatively.

Kagan (1997) believes that the structural bias hypothesis can explain why ELLs fall behind in achievement compared to non-ELL students. Traditional classroom structures rely heavily on competitive tasks and rewards. He stated, "Minority students, especially Hispanic students, are more cooperative in their social orientation than are majority students, and cooperative students achieve better and feel better about themselves and school in less competitive classrooms" (p. 2:7). He continued, "Whatever the reasons, the dramatic gains of low achievement students in cooperative learning is our best hope to respond successfully to the challenge provided by the progressive school achievement gap and the achievement crisis in general" (p. 2:8). Diaz (1989) confirmed this with research on the cognitive styles of Hispanics. He stated, "Hispanic students tend to be more field dependent (sensitive) than field independent. Field sensitive students tend to prefer cooperative learning activities which emphasize human interaction along with the transmission of academic content" (p. 1). Extensive research supports cooperative learning as a valuable learning tool for ELLs.

A think-pair-share activity only takes minutes. It helps students develop their own ideas as well as build on ideas that originated from co-learners. For example, the teacher poses a problem and students think alone about it for a certain amount of time. Students form pairs to discuss and revise their ideas, then share their answers with the class. This helps ELLs filter information and draw conclusions from the material before they are asked to speak.

Make Interdisciplinary Connections to What Students Are Learning in Math

By using themes in math lessons, teachers can draw interdisciplinary connections that will reinforce learning skills in different disciplines. For example, to teach students the difference between the metric system, which they are usually familiar with, and the U.S. customary system, teachers can utilize map skills from social studies class. Students can role-play as tourists who have just arrived in the United States. Given a map of the United States, they measure the distance between the airport and their destination using the scales provided. They then calculate the distance in miles and convert it to metric.

Themes or integrated curriculum can help ELLs by providing a link to connect knowledge in all content areas. Topics can be selected with the ELLs' backgrounds, interests, and strengths in mind. Themes motivate and involve students in the learning as they use their new language to read, write, and share ideas. Diaz (1989) stated, "The ability of a teacher to relate curriculum to elements of daily life with which students are familiar is a critical skill" (p. 3).

blinkblink/Shutterstock.com

This can be accomplished in such simple terms as using connections in the daily oral math problem. By tying math to another subject, students become more proficient in both areas. Lara-Alecio (1996), IDRA (1995), and McCloskey (1992) all advocate the use of interdisciplinary connections, especially teaching English in the content areas of mathematics, science, and computers when teaching to ELLs.

Make Cultural Connections for ELLs When Teaching Mathematics

Teachers can capitalize on the diverse cultural backgrounds of their students when teaching mathematics. For instance, a world study math center can be set up in the classroom in which students from multicultural backgrounds display the origins of math concepts from their cultures (e.g., algebra [Arabic], geometry [Greek], tangram [Chinese]). Math and art teachers can find common themes in which they can team-teach individual subject matter concepts in their classes. Buchanan and Helman (1993) advocated the importance of a math curriculum that is relevant to students' experiences. For example, teachers may want to show children how to use the Napier's bones/rods while sharing how they were widely used in Scotland and Europe several hundred years ago to do quick multiplications. As Furner (2008) suggests, when working with large populations, for example Mexicans and Guatemalans, here in the United States, it is nice to be able to explore some of the Mayan's contributions to mathematics to show these young learners the contributions of their ancestors to the field of mathematics. Wiest (2002) provided approaches and a list of resources for supporting multicultural mathematics instruction. Activities in Mathematics and Science (AIMS) also publishes many resources for integrating historical and cultural connections into the learning of mathematics.

Concretize Math Concepts with Total Physical Response (TPR)

TPR is an approach to second language acquisition that is based on the model of how children learn their first language (Asher, 1982). In the TPR approach, instructors issue commands while modeling actions. Math teachers can use TPR to illustrate problem-solving math questions. For example, in demonstrating the math concepts of equal to, more than, and less than ($=$, $>$, $<$), teachers can divide the class into two groups with equal numbers of students; for more than and less than, teachers can divide students into two groups with one group containing more students than the other. A more complex TPR activity would be to have students role-play a skit to demonstrate the concept of expansion: Students line up in a row as molecules in a rod; one student role-plays fire heating the rod. More students are added to the original row to signify expansion of the rod. Spectators measure the length of rod and record the difference. Many other creative activities can be made up using TPR. Students will have a lot of fun learning math using this approach, because teachers involve students in math concepts instead of solely talking about math concepts.

Total physical response involves students responding physically to commands or directions with their entire body. Physical response also involves manipulating objects or pictures. Students learn by doing and become more involved in the lesson. Students are not required to respond orally—only to follow the direction given by the teacher. To make a speech-print connection, the teacher should write the series of commands on the board for students to read. The teacher models while giving the commands; student volunteers model with the teacher; then other students act out as the teacher gives the command.

To demonstrate the commutative property for addition, students are selected in boy–girl combinations. The teacher creates a ticket booth and then sets the stage for a physical response by beginning a story about buying tickets. By lining up three boys followed by two girls, the students act out the number sentence: $3 + 2 = 5$. As the teacher continues the story, the girls buy the tickets first, students switching the order to show $2 + 3 = 5$. Students become very excited about "acting" and are more likely to recall concepts taught in this manner.

Take Internet Field Trips and Use Mathematics Websites/Software/ Technology

Today the Internet and computer software are being used as an instructional tool to explore, investigate, problem solve, interact, reflect, reason, communicate, and learn many concepts that are in U.S. school curricula. Students are able to take virtual tours of places like the Bronx Zoo, the White House, and the Louvre Museum, as well as to access information from NASA, the United Nations, and so on. The number of websites and educational software available designed for teachers and students with the intent to teach concepts is becoming endless. Websites like funschool.com or www.funbrain.com are ideal for both teachers and students to teach/learn a multitude of math and reading/language concepts. K–12 and software like *Math Blaster* or *TesselMania!* can really make the learning of mathematics dynamic.

Many websites are designed for teachers, students, and parents and keep track of student achievement and recordkeeping as well as being able to provide for learning in a very exciting and interactive way. Today more and more teachers can bring their students to sites to access information or interact and learn concepts on just about any topic under the sun. Teachers may want to group students in pairs at computers and bookmark the sites for the students in advance, creating a worksheet, treasure hunt, or activity sheet with the websites listed along with a guide of questions and activities to do as they visit various sites while taking their Internet Field Trip (Furner, Doan-Holbein, & Scullion-Jackson, 2000). Today many websites are designed for and include the actual pictures of the currently used math manipulatives that are used in classrooms across the country to help reinforce math concepts in a concrete way. Students can explore the geometrical math concept of a tessellation and actually create and interact to make their own while learning many geometry and spatial sense objectives. The possibilities are endless when one infuses the Internet into instruction.

Ameis and Ebenezer (2005) have recently written a book called *Mathematics on the Internet,* where they provide resources and suggestions for teaching mathematics via the Internet. The book connects many math concepts K–12 to many websites that can be used to help teach these concepts. Parents of homeschoolers can also greatly benefit from the use of the Internet as a means to learn via Internet field trips. The Internet has a definite role to play in the reform of traditional teaching. By using educational software and the Internet, students can now learn in ways that are more exciting and challenging. The Internet also provides students with the tools to use the computer to access information and become independent lifelong learners in an age that will increasingly depend on technology to survive in a complex multicultural world (Furner, Yahya, & Duffy, 2005).

Today a big technology that is used in schools for developing mathematics understanding and exploration it GeoGebra. GeoGebra is free and multi-platform dynamic mathematics software for all levels of education that joins geometry, algebra, tables, graphing, statistics, etc. in one easy-to-use package. GeoGebra is a free download at geogebra.org and is compatible with most platforms. Students can draw, measure, and explore math ideas using this software. Also, many teachers enjoy using the *National Library of Virtual Manipulatives* website to go a step away from concrete to representationl learning of math ideas. Students enjoy the virtual math manipulatives website with countless activities appropriate for all grade levels where teachers can illustrate many great concepts using the virtual manipulatives if they are concerned about classroom management and actual models. See the examples below of each emerging technology.

Students are better prepared for the STEM fields when the math curriculum is rich with technology use. Today students are immersed with technology surrounding them in all aspects of their lives especially with the smartphone and tablet explosion. Internet availability, data plans, and WiFi are everywhere and students have complete access to the information age we now live in. *Google* and *Wikipedia* provide instant access to knowledge. Memorizing in math is not as common any more, although important for fast recall and fluidity/automation.

Technology is playing a critical role today in all aspects of learning and using the Internet, interactive websites, virtual math manipulative sites, and exploratory software like GeoGebra are critical in this age of teaching mathematics to better reach all types of learners.

Use Children's Literature to Teach Mathematics and Develop the Language

Teachers can use children's literature to reach a child in a nonthreatening way by reading literature that can help to teach math concepts and really connect to the mathematical understanding of the learner and at the same time not intimidate, threaten, or turn off a child to mathematics like some traditional approaches may have in the past (Furner, Yahya, & Duffy, 2005). Children's and adolescent's literature can be a beneficial way of teaching mathematics.

Benefits of Using Literature in Mathematics

❖ Math concepts taught in the context of a story
❖ Incorporates integrated studies with reading, writing, speaking, listening, etc.
❖ Develops mathematical thinking
❖ Prevents math anxiety and creates a less math-anxious classroom environment
❖ Allows for a variety of responses
❖ Makes historical, cultural, and practical application connections
❖ May allow for the use of manipulatives as it relates to the story
❖ The teacher can assess a child's understanding by reading/questioning
❖ A range of books to use in teaching most math concepts K–8
❖ May lead to problem solving and active involvement from the context of the story
❖ Provides for a shared experience for students and the teacher

Teachers can address the NCTM's Communication Standard by incorporating literature in the teaching of mathematics (NCTM, 2000, 2006) as well as by having students discuss math from the stories and write about such concepts in mathematics to demonstrate their understanding of math concepts as well as their feelings toward math. Griffiths and Clyne (1991), in their book *Books You Can Count On: Linking Mathematics and Literature,* illustrate wonderfully many examples of how to connect children's literature into a math lesson. Jacobs, Bennett, and Bullock (2000) described a searchable database of appropriate children's literature books to teach mathematics, particularly for Spanish speakers.

Auditory, Visual, and Kinesthetic—Be Sure to Reach Different Learning Styles

Multimodal learning enables teachers to reach more students than the traditional direct instruction or paper-and-pencil/drill and practice forms of instruction. Some teachers use manipulatives, others allow verbal rehearsals, some may use the new series of math teaching videos by Math Vantage or make math visual using math software or the computer screen, whereas another option would be to consider kinesthetic learners. These learners learn best by doing. They complete the task by mounting a whole body effort. Sometimes the overwhelming energy put forth by this type of learner can lead to a loss of focus. Students get off the track and miss their objective. One way to meet the needs of these students would be to incorporate refocusing activities as part of the transition process. Moskowitz (1978) suggested that classrooms that offer techniques designed to relax students, increase the enjoyment of learning, raise self-esteem, and blend self-awareness will increase students' potential. For example, students may need a moment to stop and focus before beginning a group activity. This would involve the whole class or a small group taking a moment to close their eyes and think about what they need to do next. The students do not need words to project what they need to do, they think and hopefully think through the next step. Learners of varying modalities can focus and plan their next step. Teachers must take into consideration the modalities of their students and try to reach each child regardless of their learning style strength (Furner, Yahya, & Duffy, 2005).

Sample Lessons with Various Grades/Math Topics

Geometry
Activity #1 (Grades 3–5)

Use a paper bag with three-dimensional (3D) shapes in it to describe the characteristics of the shapes: sides, faces, corners, edges, etc. Place in a large paper bag items like a can of soup, a Rubik's cube, and some wooden 3D shapes (i.e., rectangular prism, triangular prism, pyramid, sphere, cube, etc.). Have a child in the class reach into the bag, feel a shape, and then describe the shape using as many characteristics as possible (i.e., shapes of faces, number of faces, corners, edges, smooth, etc.). Then ask the other students to listen to the descriptions and see if they can determine what shape the student is describing. Keep a word wall of all the descriptive characteristics of each 3D shape/item.

ESOL Strategy: Teach and emphasize vocabulary using realia and demonstration.

Activity #2 (Grades 6–8)

Use Geoboards to have students make a shape on their board. Construct the figures on your Geoboard or explain why you think it is impossible to do so.

1. a. A figure with just one right angle.
    b. A figure with two right angles.
    c. A figure with at least one right angle but no sides parallel to the edges of the Geoboard.
    d. A figure with six right angles.
2. A figure with exactly two congruent, adjacent sides.
3. Two figures with different shapes but the same area.
4. a. Find all possible squares that can be made on a 25-peg Geoboard.
    b. Make a quadrilateral with no parallel sides.
    c. Make a parallelogram with no sides parallel to the edge of the Geoboard.
    d. Make two shapes that have the same shape but are different sizes.
5. Make a regular and an irregular pentagon.

Teachers may also want to use geo-dot paper to have students copy their Geoboard work to dot paper to move from concrete to semi-concrete.

ESOL Strategy: Use manipulatives to make problems concrete instead of abstract.

Measurement
Activity #1 (Grades 3–5)

Use cups, pints, quarts, and gallon containers to compare either water or sand. Allow students to discover how many cups make a pint, how many pints make a quart, and how many quarts make a gallon. Allow students to explore and compare using the appropriate vocabulary.

ESOL Strategy: Apply problems to daily life situations.

Activity #1 (Grades K–2)

Make homemade analog Judy clocks and digital play clocks with slits for the hour and minute to slide through. Have students take turns making a time with the digital or analog clocks; then the other has to show how to do it with the other type of clock, and vice versa. Have students then use clock stamps to tell a story of their day as it relates to time and show different times in the day when they do certain things. It is important to encourage writing in the math classroom.

ESOL Strategy: Have students give oral explanations of their thinking, leading to solutions.

Algebraic Thinking
Activity #2 (Grades K–2)

Use actual fruits (or small plastic manipulatives), pattern blocks, and/or colors links to allow students to create a pattern. Students can arrange a pattern of days they will eat various fruit in a week or month on a calendar and then ask their partner to describe the pattern of fruits (i.e., banana, apple, orange, orange, banana, apple, orange, etc.).

The students can do the same with the pattern blocks by constructing sidewalks using the pattern blocks to create a sidewalk of shapes they would walk on (i.e., hexagon, square, square, hexagon, square, square, etc.). Or they can use the color links to create a pattern for a necklace or chain they create (i.e., red, blue, yellow, yellow, red, blue, yellow, yellow, etc.). Allow students to work in groups to share their patterns with others to see if they can figure out the patterns.

ESOL Strategy: Group students heterogeneously during cooperative learning and encourage group discussion.

Activity #2 (Grades 3–5)

Solve for unknowns using different shaped boxes (i.e., heart, square, hexagon, monkey in the barrel canisters, etc.). Create problems, like "There are one dozen monkeys in all, if five jumped out of the barrel, how many would be left in the barrel?" Encourage the students to write equations and then solve them (i.e., 5 + Barrel = 12; Barrel = 7). The same thing can be done using boxes of different shapes. For example, start with a heart-shaped box with twenty counters, show the student that there are six counters outside of the heart box and write the equation $6 + \heartsuit = 20$, so $\heartsuit = 14$; encourage students to use inverse operations to solve the unknowns. Encourage the students to write number sentences and use variables for unknowns and then work on solving them. Unifix cube manipulatives are also a great manipulative to model number sentences. Teachers can use three blue unifix cubes and then snap on seven red ones. Then allow students to create equations like 3 + Blue = 10, Blue = 7. It is important to mathematically model algebraic equations for the students.

ESOL Strategy: Have students write original word problems to be exchanged with classmates; encourage them to make drawings or use the manipulatives as well.

Number Sense Concepts and Operations
Activity #1 (Grades K–2)

Use unifix manipulatives in varying colors to allow students to randomly choose a few of two different colors, then allow them to snap them together by color and connect them. Have the students count how many of each color they have. Students then draw a picture of the two joined together, then from that write the number sentence with numbers and symbols to represent the equation as a whole.

ESOL Strategy: Be sure that all concepts are taught and understood concretely using the hands-on manipulatives.

Activity #2 (Grades 3–5)

Use pattern block manipulatives to represent fractions. Draw examples of the concrete fractions. For example, if the hexagon represents one whole, then the trapezoid represents one half. The blue parallelogram represents one third and the equilateral triangle represents one sixth. Students should be encouraged to draw the fractions and then create problems like $\frac{1}{2} + \frac{1}{3} + \frac{1}{6} = 1$ whole.

ESOL Strategy: Encourage drawings to translate and visualize word problems and to connect the concrete to the abstract.

Data Analysis and Probability
Activity #1 (Grades K–2)

Collect beverage containers from lunch, such as regular, low-fat, and chocolate milk; juices; etc. Have each student choose their preference. Then create a class pictograph showing all the choices and allow each student to place their beverage in the correct column. Ask questions like, "Which is the most preferred drink?" "Which is the least?" Allow students to now make a bar graph from their actual class pictograph, perhaps using Excel software or other technology graphing software.

ESOL Strategy: Use technology and computers in pairs with ELLs and non-ELL students to create graphs using software like Excel or other graphing software.

Activity #2 (Grades 6–8)

Place twelve color tile manipulatives into an envelope, use six yellow, three green, two blue, and one red. Then choose a student to come up to the board to keep track using tallies as the teacher walks around asking students to draw a tile from the bag.

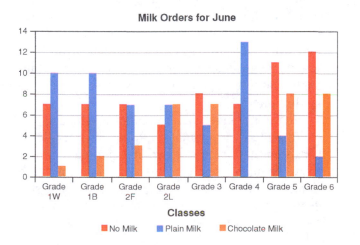

Suzanne Tucker/Shutterstock.com

Involving the entire class, have them observe each draw of the bag while returning the tiles after each draw; after twelve draws, have the class observe the tallies and predict how many of each color of the tiles is in the bag. Allow for twelve more draws, and then pool both sets of tallies. Have the students predict what is inside the bag. Students will be amazed at how close they will be to the actual number of color tiles in the bag.

ESOL Strategy: Use TPR; actively involve students while doing math.

Summary

The ESOL strategies for teaching mathematics for English speakers of other languages in this chapter are supported by several researchers (Crandall, 1987; Dale & Cuevas, 1992; FDOE, 1996; Garrison, 1997; Moore, 1994; O'Malley et al., 1985; Robison, 2006; Secada, 2000). Interestingly enough, the strategies appear to be in alignment with NCTM (1989, 2000, 2006) Standards for teaching mathematics as well as with Zemelman, Daniels, and Hyde (2012) best practices for teaching mathematics. Likewise, the Florida Department of Education has developed 25 performance standards for Teachers of English for Speakers of Other Languages, Inc. (TESOL, 1991). Four of these standards are more aligned to those of NCTM and reflect the ESOL strategies:

1. Select and develop appropriate ESOL content according to student levels of proficiency in listening, speaking, reading, and writing, taking into account: (a) basic interpersonal communicative skills (BICS), and (b) cognitive academic language proficiency skills (CALPS) as they apply to the ESOL curriculum.
2. Apply content-based ESOL approaches to instruction.
3. Evaluate, adapt, and employ appropriate instructional materials, media, and technology for ESOL in the content areas at elementary, middle, and high school levels.

4. Create a positive classroom environment to accommodate the various learning styles and cultural backgrounds of students.

Many preservice and in-service public school teachers have become anxious about the teaching of content areas to students from diverse backgrounds. They should be appeased with the notion that the ESOL mathematics strategies truly are "best practice" for all students, not only English speakers of other languages. Therefore, teachers are not shortchanging the education of the others in class by using ESOL strategies to meet the needs of only the LEP students. There are many teachers like the teacher in the opening vignette who feel frustrated by not knowing what to do to reach students whose first language is not English. Teachers in today's classrooms are confronted with the challenge of meeting the needs of students with diverse needs and backgrounds. If math teachers do something about helping their students to develop their confidence and ability to do math, they can impact these students' lives in a positive way forever. Students' careers, and ultimately, many of the decisions they will make in life, could rest on how mathematics is taught to them. Math teachers today must work hard to eliminate and prevent any math anxiety their students may develop or carry with them (Furner & Duffy, 2002). Also in light of all the new STEM initiatives, educators need to better prepare and excite young people for going into more career fields in the areas of mathematics, science, technology, and engineering. When students feel confident in their ability to "do the math" they are then more likely to choose careers using more mathematics in them. It is the job of all educators to make sure that when our young people graduate from high school, they can decide on any career choice, without hesitance ore apprehensiveness toward a particular discipline.

In light of current concerns for all students, including the ELL population, to achieve at a level consistent with or above national and international scores on math assessment tests, educators may need to take a more proactive role in encouraging students to become excited about math. When students see themselves as successful and confident, they are more likely to become mathematical problem solvers. In this global technological era and information age, all students require much knowledge related to mathematics and problem solving. As mathematics teachers, we need to be diligent in preparing our ELL population so they may possess mathematical expertise in our high-tech globally competitive world. Our children today are not only competing for jobs with others in the United States, but with young people from around the globe. Being confident in their ability to do mathematics in this competitively global society is critical. Teachers can make a difference in the futures of their students in an ever-growing, competitive global world that depends so heavily on mathematics. The new Common Core State Standards in Mathematics along with the NCTM Standards and the literature on diverse learners suggest an active and constructivist, hands-on approach that encourages all students to communicate mathematically. Teachers need to employ a variety of resources and innovative teaching strategies to make learning more meaningful. Students will become more interested in mathematics and will be able to communicate because they all speak the same languages (mathematics and English).

Points to Remember

- ❖ Teachers are guided by and must adhere to both state and national standards, more particularly, the new Common Core State Standards for teaching mathematics.

- ❖ ELLs can often excel mathematically; however, the language is a barrier to their success. Issues with verbal commands, word/text problems, and communicating with peers can lead to frustration necessitating accommodations.

- ❖ Teaching and emphasizing vocabulary is key in helping students make meaning of mathematics.

- ❖ Many math manipulatives can be employed to make the learning of mathematics more concrete for the learner. Teachers need to start with concrete manipulatives and then bridge learning to representational models in pictures and diagrams and then lastly to the abstract understanding of the concepts.

- ❖ Teaching strategies like cooperative learning; use of manipulatives; children's literature; writing/journaling; use of technology; and the use of a problem-solving approach are effective means of assisting ESOL students.

- ❖ Build on a child's prior knowledge and teach for understanding, allowing the child to communicate nonverbally and in writing.

- ❖ Special accommodations may be necessary for ESOL students in assessments or when learning mathematics. It is important to differentiate instruction for different types of learners.

- ❖ Teachers should use "wait time" and patience when asking questions and working with ELLs.

- ❖ We have become a more global society, and we need to make every effort to use "best practices" in the teaching of mathematics to reach all students.

- ❖ Preparing our young people for the STEM fields is now a big part of the U.S. push to have more young people doing these types of jobs for security sake.

Teaching and Learning through the Arts: Strategies for English Language Learners (ELLs)

KEY ISSUES

❖ The arts (dance, drama, music, visual art) encourage reading, writing, listening, speaking, and visually representing skills important in language development.

❖ Multiple avenues of expression are provided through the arts capitalizing on the strengths of diverse students.

❖ Each arts area has discipline specific content that must be taught with integrity and supports the inherent value of creativity, communication, and personal expression for all learners.

❖ Inquiry and open exploration of ideas in a safe and conducive learning community are necessary when teaching and learning through the arts.

❖ Culturally diverse arts forms connect all learners to the world around them providing unique experiences and opportunities for collaboration and reflection.

Mrs. Garcia shares the illustrated book *Flotsam* by David Wiesner (2006) with the fourth grade class before listening to *La Mer* by Claude Debussy (1905). Julio sits at his desk with his head down and eyes closed while in his mind's eye, he sees a vivid blue ocean sparkling in the sunlight like the glimmer of a thousand diamonds. Suddenly, porpoises break the surface spraying fine mist from their blow holes. He imagines the journey porpoises might take along their coastal migratory path. "Class, please open your eyes and begin to draw what you imagined," Mrs. Garcia announces after turning down the music volume. Julio draws a porpoise jumping from the sea using bold colors in the marker box.

After drawing time, Mrs. Garcia asks the class to share their artwork. Julio's hand immediately rises waving with enthusiasm. "Yes, Julio you can share first." Julio begins a tale of the porpoise's journey from the Caribbean islands to the coastline of Florida. Mrs. Garcia uses the map to indicate where Julio's porpoise travels. The geography clues help Julio to embellish the details of his tale. "Draw a line that shows the journey of the porpoise on the board, Julio," says Mrs. Garcia. Julio draws a wiggle line starting from the right bottom edge of the board toward the left side. "Class, let's show how the porpoise would move in the journey," states Mrs. Garcia, while playing an appropriate section of *La Mer*. The class uses their hands and arms to glide up and down from right to left.

"Julio, how does your porpoise feel when he is swimming on the journey?" "He is happy!" "What would he say or sing during this journey?" "I am happy. The ocean is blue and the sun is shining. Click, Click, Click," exclaims Julio imitating the chirps of a porpoise. "Wonderful use of descriptive words and sounds, Julio, can you write down your story of the porpoise's journey?" Julio gladly sits down and begins writing his narrative. When completed, he proudly displays his drawing and writing on the class bulletin board.

Mrs. Garcia has created a safe learning community where her students can express their creativity through the arts with confidence and enthusiasm. A space where students can create and communicate freely is a necessary place in any school. In the vignette, Julio's listening skills are strengthened through music. His visually representing skills are demonstrated through his drawing. Speaking skills are enhanced through storytelling, dramatic interpretation, and creative movement (dance), which also further guide his writing skills. Language development (listening, speaking, reading, writing, and visually representing) is supported throughout the arts experience in this classroom. The arts (dance, drama, music, and visual arts) are an expression of their lives and students value the chance to develop their ideas through a variety of media and forms. With an increasing number of English language learners (ELLs) in our American schools, innovative teaching and learning strategies must be integrated throughout the curriculum. The arts provide an avenue for ELLs to demonstrate their understanding in multiple ways by creating opportunities for interaction, collaboration, and communication with others.

Introduction

Twenty-first century skills demand effective use of visual literacy which led to the expansion of the four original language arts (reading, writing, speaking, and listening) to include viewing and visually representing (Kasten, Kristo, & McClure, 2005). Language development involves these aspects of communicating meaning. Experiences in the arts allow English language learners (ELLs) to communicate their comprehension through multiple avenues of expression (verbally and nonverbally). Visually representing includes production of something other than written or spoken language such as, a drawing, painting, sculpture, film, computer art/animation, drama, dance, or other nonprint media. According to DeVries (2012) listening, reading, and viewing support the receptive vocabulary development, while speaking, writing, and visually representing comprise the expressive vocabulary. An example of the importance of the arts in language development is that learning to draw is a necessary part and often

the first step of learning to write (Durkin, 1966; Gentry, 2010).

Another aspect of language development for ELLs is the creation of a visualization system, which is comprised of images and experiences organized in a person's memory. Activities in the arts provide a foundation for the visualization system formed in the brain because the arts require active engagement in unique and memorable ways. All experiences are stored in memory for later use when formulating words and sentences (verbally and written). The visualization system is used when associating new words with an existing memory, which in turn contributes to comprehension (Gentry, 2010). ELLs often communicate through the arts using their constructed visualization system, when learning a new language. Aliki's (1998) *Painted Words* and *Spoken Memories,* a children's book, illustrates how Marianthe, a young girl, uses visual art to communicate her life story to her new classmates. Once Marianthe learns English, she verbalizes her life story. The creation of visual images was easy for the young girl when communicating with others who did not speak the same language. Oral communication resulted after she learned the basics of the new language. Visually representing for ELLs often is demonstrated before speaking, reading, and writing in English occurs, due to the nature of this communication form and the ease of its use. (For more ideas about integrating *Painted Words* and *Spoken Memories* [Aliki, 1998] see the teacher's guide by Jane Claes found at https://www.teachervision.com/tv/printables/harpercollins/marianthes-story_sg.pdf.)

In this chapter, we identify key issues that support teaching and learning through the arts for all learners. Selected research that supports the integration of the arts as an important part of language development for ELLs is presented in order to provide a rationale for classroom practice. Specific content for each arts discipline is shared to support creativity, communication skills, and personal expression within a safe and conducive learning environment. Collaboration in various projects that include culturally diverse arts forms and reflection using all the language arts skills (reading, writing, speaking, listening, and visually representing) are emphasized in lesson examples.

Research Supporting Arts Learning for ELLs

The importance of the arts in language development is supported through current research studies (Catterall, 2009; Craig & Paraiso, 2008; Petitto, 2008; Stevenson, 2011). According to Craig and Paraiso (2008), ELLs realize the strong benefits of learning through the arts as their comfort and proficiency in speaking English grew along with their vocabulary when discussing artworks. The communication skills developed through art discussion helped the ELLs to succeed in all academic areas. Dramatic activities are also positively associated with literacy success by increasing a student's ability to read text accurately, fluently, and with more expression (Keehn, Harmon, & Shoho, 2008). Also concerning fluency, one study on musical training related it to stronger performance for ELLs in regard to expressive fluency and reading competency (Petitto, 2008). In overall support of learning through the arts, Cat-

terall (2009) found that ELLs and other underserved populations demonstrate the greatest relative improvement in academics due to participation in the arts. This research (Catterall, 2009) demonstrates that ELLs are significantly more likely to enter college if they attended "arts-rich" high schools. Their experiences in the arts built self-confidence which potentially led students to enroll in college.

For elementary aged students, research supports the use of dance, drama, music, and visual arts throughout the curriculum as leading to improved reading abilities and expression (Brouillette & Jennings, 2010; Cawthon, Dawson, & Ihom, 2011). Specifically beneficial for children is the use of puppetry in language-infused dramatic interactions which assisted ELLs in building confidence while speaking English. Another added benefit to arts learning is the fostering of cross-cultural understanding. Students who learn about cultural connections through the arts better understand the context of the art form and have an increased ability to explore their own and others' cultural values. Stevenson (2011) researched how a culturally diverse group of adolescents built cross-cultural understanding through collaborative performance of dance, drama, and music, which not only affected the participants, but also the audience for which they performed. Through the arts, the adolescents broke through barriers between cultural and ethnic groups which lead to a better understanding of each other's diversity demonstrated through collaboration and reflection.

ELLs are able to participate in the arts since the arts provide different avenues of demonstrating comprehension through reflection and interaction. Howard Gardner's (1999) multiple intelligences theory involves different processing systems to explain the importance of the different modes of expression. All learners understand and demonstrate information in a variety of ways: linguistic, logical-mathematical, spatial, musical, kinesthetic, interpersonal, intrapersonal, and naturalistic. Each person has their strengths and areas of improvement within these different intelligences as developed through personal and shared experiences within their environment. Identifying the strengths of a student can help teachers to better design lessons that meet individual needs. Most students benefit from learning environments that create an awareness of which intelligences can be used to help them succeed. Reaching diverse students is a common educational goal and teachers who implement Gardner's theory (1999) into their lessons build opportunities for student success. (For more information about Howard Gardner's theory of multiple intelligences see http://howardgardner.com/multiple-intelligences/).

Gardner continues to study how we think across different subject areas in creative ways. His Harvard University research entitled Project Zero and Arts PROPEL led to a better understanding of how we learn in and through the arts and the metacognitive processes involved in arts learning. The focus of Arts PROPEL included the creation of artworks, perception of artworks as connected to a student's own work, and reflection based upon personal goals and standards of excellence. Two major instruments were developed to support assessment and reinforce instruction, the domain project (open-ended problems for students to solve) and the process folio (student work that demonstrates the stages of the creative process). Both of these strategies work well with diverse students. (For more information about Arts PROPEL, see http://www.pz.gse.harvard.edu/arts_propel.php).

Another major researcher that has influenced the arts in education is Elliott Eisner (1992), who describes the arts as an essential part of the school curriculum. The arts provide a critically important means for students to express their ideas. Through the arts, all students make sense of their world and communicate their understanding to others in ways beyond words that reflect culture and personal experience. Eisner's theory (1992) emphasizes the importance of the arts as non-discursive forms of knowledge. The arts provide a unique avenue for expression of meaning and foster cultural and artistic development for diverse students.

> "Mind is a cultural achievement. The kinds of minds that children come to own are profoundly influenced by the kinds of experiences they are able to secure in the course of their lives (Eisner, 1992, p. 2).

The arts should be a part of these experiences. Eisner (1992) supports arts in education as it is through the arts that students express their unique ways of thinking and communicating. All students can learn through art making activities, artistic performances, critical and aesthetic discussions, creative writing, and historical research (arts forms from the past to the present). Through critical analysis and discussion of the arts, students perceive the world around them in greater detail and have more meaningful interactions with others while engaged in arts activities, which are worthy educational goals. Eisner (2002) argued for arts education based upon its inherent value and expression of understanding. (For more information about Eisner's support of the arts, see https://www.arteducators.org/advocacy/10-lessons-the-arts-teach).

Lev Vygotsky (1978) contends that students learn through social interaction, which leads to cognitive development. Vygotsky's (1978) sociocultural theory supports collaborative learning and peer modeling. Accordingly, social interaction allows students to internalize concepts, thus becoming a part of their individual development. Active engagement in a supportive learning environment promotes the understanding of diverse perspectives since students listen to peers and communicate ideas. When viewing language development as sociocultural practice, teachers should consider the relationship of personal narrative with language acquisition. Cultural heritage and personal history strengthen this interactive communication between students. Students create personally meaningful connections with each other through retold stories (personal narratives) of actual experiences. This strategy (personal narrative) works well with ELLs, since it allows each student to describe their point of view and learn from other's stories to gain unique perspectives on topics of study (Vygotsky, 1978).

All of the discussed research supports the concept that learning through the arts is a valuable tool for ELLs. There are a variety of research studies available to support arts education through professional organizations such as, the National Art Education Association (see https://www.arteducators.org/research/research), the National Association for

Music Education (see http://advocacy.nafme.org/all-research/), National Dance Education Association (see http://www.ndeo.org), and Educational Theatre Association (see http://schooltheatre.org/advocacy/national/researchandreports). Each of these professional organizations also designs educational standards of excellence for all age levels of students, pre-K–12, with the input of teachers across the nation. Most state level standards reflect the national standards in their construction and guiding principles. As you write lessons and unit plans for classroom use, consider the connections between the standards of all subject areas (arts, mathematics, science, language arts, social studies, and physical education) in order to strengthen the teaching and learning that occurs in your classroom.

FIGURE 25-1 Boy reading his illustrated journal.

Elements of the Arts: Expanding Vocabulary for Effective Discussions

In the arts field, each art form has basic elements providing a common vocabulary to support artistic performance. By understanding the basic vocabulary in each area, students can more effectively discuss a variety of artistic works. Comprehension of new vocabulary assists all students in production/performance, criticism, research about a variety of artists, and discussions that form a person's aesthetic likes and dislikes. In visual art, the creation of the artwork requires the manipulation of materials using line, shape, form, color, texture, value, and space as common elements (Dow, 1899). The elements of visual art are the pieces of the puzzle that a student puts together to create the image. Using these elements effectively lead to a successful composition. Understanding the basic vocabulary forms a foundation upon which students can critique and discuss various arts forms throughout history.

Music also has a set of elements that make up the basic of this artistic form. Some of the music elements include: melody (pitch and timbre), rhythm (basic beat), repetition, and contrast (Kratus, 1990). Students use their knowledge of the elements of music to describe, analyze, evaluate, compose, and perform. Some of the elements of dance involve movement, space, time, and energy. Dance performance is based upon movement in space. Students utilize their understanding of the basic elements of dance such as time and action, in order to critique, choreograph, and perform within this art form (Turner, 1963). Space, rhythm, movement, lighting, time, and character are a few of the elements of drama (Bailin, 1998). For every art form, connections are made between production/performance, criticism, historical/contemporary research or study, and philosophical discussion. Understanding the basic elements of each art form assists students in utilizing the art form more effectively and expands their vocabulary during discussions of the artistic work. To better understand new vocabulary, students can illustrate journals that include new words. Journal writing is an effective strategy for ELLs to practice using new words and construct sentences/paragraphs/essays, depending upon their skill level (Towell, 2013).

Comprehension in the Arts Disciplines

The "arts point to and help define meaning, truth, spirit, social values, religion, and other foundations of human culture" (Anderson, 1995, p. 10). Through lessons that integrate arts learning, we provide a chance for students to create artistic work, discuss their own work and the work of others, study historical and contemporary cultural connections, and consider conceptual and philosophical ideas about what was created. These four aspects of comprehension in the arts are summarized as **artistic production, criticism, historical/contemporary research, and aesthetics** (Hurwitz & Day, 2007).

The value of **artistic production/performance** is supported as it promotes expression, creativity, and reflection. Students are engaged through thoughtful discussion about the arts and these discussions support vocabulary development, comprehension, and fluency. **Criticism** focuses on meaning making (comprehension) through: (1) description (What do you see in the artistic work? Focusing on the elements); (2) analysis (How is the artistic work put together?); (3) interpretation (What is the artist/musician/dancer/actor communicating?); and (4) evaluation (Do you like the artistic work? Why or Why not?). This inquiry process of criticism helps students to use higher order thinking skills by applying criteria to their reasoning (Feldman, 1993). Students build a rationale based upon the communication of ideas within the art form. **Historical/contemporary research** includes information about the life of an artist/musician/dancer/actor and the time period of cultural influences for the artistic work. **Aesthetics** is the student's reaction while interacting with an artistic work. Our sense of wonder and beauty driven by delighted senses (sight, smell, touch, taste, and hearing) when engaged in the arts is our aesthetic response. Often understanding why we are experiencing awe and inspiration helps use to internalize the impact of the arts on our lives. *The capacity for aesthetics is a fundamental human characteristic* (Mayesky, 2009. P. 37). Appreciating and communicating ideas to others is a beneficial part of the arts. If teachers encourage reflection and sharing of thoughts in a safe conducive learning environment, students will respond through positive interaction and gain greater comprehension of its forms.

Developing Language Skills through Collaboration and Culturally Diverse Art Forms

Providing a balanced curriculum requires knowledge of the content area (arts, mathematics, language arts, science, social studies, physical education), which is the focus of the lesson. Since arts lesson plans include a broad base of media/materials and techniques, experience in creating/performing with the different media is necessary to imagine and plan unique lessons for students of all ages and abilities. This requires a commitment on the part of the teacher to experiment, create, perform, dance, sing, play an instrument, and participate in dramatic activities. Being aware of how and when to integrate the arts to support language development is an important part of lesson planning process. It works best when there is a relationship between the concepts that are being taught. Standards for each content area can assist the teacher in identifying the connecting concepts.

The artistic process leads to meaning making as we strive to communicate with others through our artistic work. We make connections that are personal and purposely anticipate that others are able to interpret the images/dance/drama/music. Through the arts, we better comprehend ourselves and others. This leads to understanding the human condition, which can be applied to the global community (Brown, 2013). The personal and social meanings of artistic work shed light on real world problems and help us to create solutions. An arts integrated curriculum focuses on topics that matter and are important to life beyond the classroom (Anderson & Milbrandt, 2005).

To begin conceptualizing what these concepts can look like in a classroom with ELLs, refer to Table 25.1, which provides brief starting points for lesson plans. Connections that are described can be mixed and matched in different rows and columns to suit individual classroom needs.

Table 25-1   **Classroom Connections for Integrating Language Arts Skills with Art Forms**

Art Form	Reading Connections	Writing Connections	Speaking Connections	Listening Connections	Visually Representing Connections
Dance	Viewing the performance and deriving meaning from the movement sequence; reading a poem with repetition and creating a ABAB movement sequence; read the emotions of each dancer	Choreographic notes of a scene or dance sequence; write a list of descriptive adjectives for each dancer; journal entry of their emotions during the performance; body shapes to become letters to spell words	Verbally sharing the meaning or interpretation behind the dance with others; share a list of words that are associated with the movements aloud; describe how the dance made you feel (emotions)	Analyze what others say about the dance and connect with their own ideas; identify onomatopoeia within the dance (words associated with the sounds of the dancers) i.e., swish, slide	Illustrating a movement sequence with line or color; draw or sculpt the dancers like Edgar Degas (French Impressionist); use textural items to depict the movement of the dancers
Drama	Read the script, character lines, scenery descriptions; watch the dramatic play and derive meaning and comprehension; compare the script with the performance	Write a script, character lines, and scenery descriptions; identify or list descriptive words that are associated with characters; change the cast of characters or scene and rewrite the script for an alternative ending	Read aloud character lines with expression and emotion; explain a scene, setting or character traits; use different voices to depict characters in a story or text; read quotes from newspaper articles	Listen to a play, movie, scene and imagine what will happen next (predict); listen to a story and pass along the information to another person; listen to a biography and identify facts about the person's character	Create puppets and perform the play; create a poster to advertise the play; create a diorama of a dramatic scene; sculpt or draw masks that depict the emotions of the actors/actresses; draw a storyline or story board that explains a historical event
Music	Read musical notation; listen to musical selection and explain the instruments used, the feelings and emotions depicted	Write notation; compose a musical piece or sound story using instruments in relation to characters, events, and settings; sing a poem or rhyme	Sing aloud alone and in a chorus; sing poetry; explain your likes and dislikes of a musical selection; Discuss with peers your favorite songs	Listen to a musical selection and create a list of colors and words that describe the music; Identify the genre of music; play name that tune	Paint, draw, sculpt to music, study artists that relate visual art and music such as Mondrian; notate music with icons, colors and lines
Visual Art	Read a visual image by describing the elements used; explain what is seen in the image (subject), interpret the meaning of the image	Draw images that illustrate words (adjective monsters or texture creatures); write about images, use a picture book and add words	Explain or interpret an image to friend; discuss your favorite artist/art work; critique an artwork; present information about an artist	Critique a work of art with peers; verbally teach how to create an artwork; present your artwork and explain how you made the work to a peer	Visually demonstrate how to draw, paint and sculpt an artwork without using words; create a step-by-step poster that explains how to cook favorite food

Adapted from Towell, P., and Brown (in-press). *Creative Literacy in Action: Birth To Age Nine* Cengage, Inc.

Lesson Starting Points for Integrating the Arts

An illustrated book can provide inspiration of utilizing various art forms in a classroom for ELLs. For example, *The Arrival* by Shaun Tan (2007) is a beautifully illustrated story about a man leaving his family to travel to a new imaginative world in order to find work. The man encounters many strange and wonderful contraptions, food items, animals, and people with which he interacts. In the story, he uses his drawing abilities to communicate to others who speak and write a different language. He meets interesting people who come from other distant lands and listens to their immigration story. The entire story is told through detailed value toned drawings (black, white, grays, and tans).

By visually representing the narrative, Shaun Tan (2007) creates a dynamic relationship between reading and writing through images. Shaun Tan invites students into his studio through a series of short videos that feature drawing lessons which can be an interesting way to introduce the concept of illustration (see YouTube video at http://www.youtube.com/watch?v=c9NCUydoJFk). Tan's *The Arrival* (2007) features illustrations telling an imaginary immigration story. Many ELLs have their own immigration stories or a story of their families' journey to the United States that can be related to the experiences within Tan's book. Sharing their own stories and reflecting upon the hardships that are often found in simple tasks is an important part of creating a classroom community. Students can create their own imaginary worlds with fantastical creatures and plants using air dry clay and found objects for dioramas (shoebox installations). Transportation issues can be resolved through inventions of various vehicles and machines that spring from a student's imagination. A short story or play provides an opportunity to write character lines in many different languages, which can lead to a dramatic performance, complete with costumes and masks. A sound story can accompany the play or students can create sounds using a variety of instruments for each illustration in *The Arrival* (Tan, 2007). The movement of the illustrations may inspire a dance sequence. In the book, the man creates an origami bird

FIGURE 25-2 Drawing of an African girl in traditional regional costume.

Courtesy of Susannah Brown.

before a flock of strange birds flies over his transportation ship. Origami is a wonderful start for ELLs to demonstrate knowledge of a step-by-step process. Another idea is to have students draw traditional costumes from various cultures and discuss events and celebrations that require specific clothes (see Figure 25.2). Cultural diversity can be experienced through the art forms and appreciation can be verbalized in short class presentations.

Other beautifully illustrated books can provide inspiration for lessons to support ELLs' language development and inspire through the arts. Brian Selznick's *Wonderstruck* (2011) is a blend of two stories, one written and one visual (see YouTube video at http://www.youtube.com/watch?v=9K2YaVxeTiM). Selznick's style of drawing is appealing to students wishing to incorporate black and white (value tones) in their work and focus on realistic style portraits. Drama sets the stage for Selznick's illustrations to tell the story. Students can act out scenes through movement (without words) using costumes and props to demonstrate their understanding of the book. Music that interprets the moment can be played during the dramatic performance. Single scenes can be connected to create a play focusing on movement. Sections of the written text can be read aloud during the dramatic play to demonstrate fluency and speaking skills. Drama, movement, music, and visual art combine to create a deeper understanding of the text and images in Selznick's book.

Another starting point for lesson planning can be the music of a cultural group such as, steel drum music from Barbados. Ann E. Barron (Ritzhaupt et al, 2013) relates an international cultural doll collection to short informational stories from different countries (see http://www.coedu.usf.edu/culture/about.htm for a complete list). In one example, a handmade figure playing a steel drum serves as an introduction to a twelve-year-old boy's short story of how he makes steel drums with his father on the island of Barbados. The pride of the boy's accomplishments shines through the story. After studying a variety of types of drums from around the world, ELLs can create their own drums, which leads to a musical and dance performance. Studying cultural examples of music, visual art, dance, and drama, such as steel drum music, can broaden ELLs' perspectives and enrich language use through reading, writing, speaking, listening, and visually representing their comprehension.

ELLs can engage in group discussions of art work from around the world. One way to begin the conversation is for students to create a "talking stick," inspired by Native American culture. Native American talking sticks are used during tribal meetings, councils, storytelling sessions, and other important ceremonies (see information about Traditional Talking Sticks at http://www.firstpeople.us/FP-Html-Legends/TraditionalTalkingStick-Unknown.html). Elementary students in Pinellas County School District, Florida, created talking sticks to represent themselves and their family (see YouTube video at http://www.youtube.com/watch?v=5bB27j83GHk). The elementary students discussed their work and interpreted the meaning behind the decorations added to their creative design. The talking stick project promotes a sense of community and respect by allowing each person to share their ideas. This lesson transfers to any lesson idea where students must discuss and brainstorm new ideas.

Celebrations can be an inspiration for students to engage in language. Discussion of family traditions can be another starting point to support ELLs. The artist, Carmen Lomas Garza paints scenes of her Mexican American life and traditions in Texas. Her illustrated book, *In My Family/En Mi Familia* (2000) provides a wonderful source of vocabulary to explore in both English and Spanish. She depicts Mexican American life such as, how her family prepares a meal, birthday celebrations, and dancing to the music of *conjuntos,* which play traditional Mexican music. Learning how different cultural groups celebrate strengthens the classroom community. ELLs can verbally present a celebration from their family sharing photographs, short videos, food, music, and dances. Comparisons can be made with celebrations throughout the world. Carmen Lomas Garza's paintings can be discussed through the art criticism process to gain a deeper understanding of her work. An example of how critique the painting, *Camas para Sueños,* is explained by Elizabeth Broun from the "Our America: The Latino Presence in American Art" exhibition at the Smithsonian American Art Museum (see YouTube video at http://www.youtube.com/watch?v=HTMvIEI2FHw). Learning about their family history can motivate ELLs to interview relatives, draw or paint family portraits, research and design a family tree, and create a video explaining an important family event such as a wedding or birthday. Our families are important and sharing family stories allow ELLs to produce evidence that strengthens their reading, writing, speaking, listening, and visually representing skills.

Technology often provides inspiration for ELLs to connect reading, writing, speaking, and listening skills to various arts forms (dance, drama, music, and visual art). Online reading and research is often referred to as new literacies (Leu et al., 2013). Reading comprehension through technology includes problem-based and inquiry-focused learning methods such as, formulating questions to be researched; identifying key words/vocabulary; using search engines to locate information; analyzing and summarizing information; and presenting information or conclusions (Leu et al., 2013). The arts and creativity come into play when ELLs communicate information through technology (i.e., blogs, Prezi, PowerPoint, iMovie, and YouTube videos) (Stegman, 2014). An example of integrating technology with language arts and the performing arts is a project where a group of students creates a YouTube video that interprets a poem utilizing creative dance and music (instrumental and vocal) while other students provide narration. This project can demonstrate reading fluency in a unique way. Also reading skills are honed through the use of technology in such a project. Poetry is an access point for blending creative inspiration between arts forms. The Creative Impact Michigan InsideOut Poetry program (2011) demonstrates the power of language and the impact that working with professional artists can have for students' work (see the YouTube video at http://www.youtube.com/watch?v=bLF380BLkbI). Another example of poetry inspiring dance, music, and dramatic activity is evidenced through the 2013 U.S. Presidential Scholars program. Robert Frost's poem *The Road Not Taken* (1920) provided a theme for the Salute to the 2013 U.S. Presidential Scholars, which demonstrates the power of the arts through expression and communication of meaning (see the YouTube video at http://www.youtube.com/watch?v=kfptREvh3xY).

When planning creative activities that support language development of ELLs, teachers can integrate games into a lesson. Interactive play or games provide avenues for the expression of understanding for ELLs. For younger children, music and dance can help them remember through repetition and pattern. For example, a vocabulary drumming circle is formed where each student wears a flash card of an English syllable as a necklace (you can easily hole punch cards and tie it with yarn). Using the traditions of African and Latin American music, the concept of call and response is set to the beat of the drum. The teacher selects vocabulary words, such as *elephant,* and phonetically breaks down the word, *el/e/phant*, by writing one syllable on a card. Other words are broken down phonetically so that each student has a syllable card necklace. As the drum beats out a rhythm, the teacher calls out the syllable "el." The students all answer with "el" and chant repeatedly until the student with the "el" card necklace comes to dance in the circle center. Next, the teacher calls out "e" and the class responds in chant

until that student dances next to the first. Finally, the teacher calls out "phant" and the class repeats until the third student joins the others to dance and create the word, "elephant." At this point the whole class repeats the word until the dancers return to their seated spots in the circle diameter. The process is repeated to include other vocabulary words giving each student a chance to dance in the center. Young children love the attention in the center of the circle and the repetition of new words is enhanced by involving music and dance (Garcia, 2004; Goldberg, 2004).

Another inspiration for a lesson that involves vocabulary acquisition is to create a pop-up book. Paper engineering or pop-ups are popular for children's books. Students can create their own pop-up pages using simple designs. A favorite is the pop-up mouth, where paper is folded inward forming two triangles which open and close once the page is folded. A character in a story is drawn around the pop-up mouth on the folded page. To make the pop-up mouth, first fold the paper in half like a card and cut a small slit on the folded edge. Using the slit as the open part of the mouth, fold the top edge of the paper and bottom edge of the paper into triangles. Unfold each triangle and open the page like a card. You should see a diamond shaped fold in the center surrounding the slit. The two triangle-shaped folds are pushed inward to create the mouth shape. When you open and close the page, the mouth also opens and closes, creating movement (Jackson, 1993). Students can use this simple pop-up to create a character in the story and speak the character's lines aloud while opening and closing the pop-up mouth. Young children love to illustrate animals and speak the sounds of the animals for each picture. For example, a drawing of a frog inspires croaking, "coqui, coqui," and "ribbit, ribbit."

Students can explore paper folding through Japanese origami and create many different creatures. These creatures form a class paper zoo. All the different creatures can also perform in a circus. The possibilities are limited only by the students' imaginations. A simple Japanese origami crane symbolizes people's hope for the future. Eleanor Coerr's (1977) *Sadako and the Thousand Cranes* can lead students to realize the importance of art in their lives and the meaningful connections art makes with emotions. The *Pinwheels for Peace* (Ayer & McMillan, 2011) program is another paper folding project for students to inspire them to make a difference in the world. In this program, students write about peace and what it means to them on a paper pinwheel. Drawings are included on the paper pinwheel. The pinwheels are installed around the school on International Day of Peace (September 21st) each year to remind everyone of the importance of peace. Ann Ayers and Ellen McMillan began *Pinwheels for Peace* in 2005 and the program continues around the world (see http://www.pinwheelsforpeace.com/pinwheelsforpeace/home.html).

After students participate in lessons such as the examples described previously, share what was learned with the school community. Communicating what was learned in school to parents and guardians is an important part of the learning process for students. Displaying artwork and performing music, dramatic works and dance in the classroom, school and community allows others to share the joy that the arts provide. Students enjoy the opportunity to view other artists' work through field trips to galleries, museums, local studios, performance auditoriums, and theaters. Don't forget to invite guest artists/musicians/dancers/actors to your classroom to discuss their work and share ideas with students. Rich sources of information are parents and other family members who either practice the arts or know a community member who is a performer/artist. When designing curriculum, include cultural arts forms that reflect the beauty and diversity found around the world. The benefits for students include a deeper cultural understanding that can engage and expand their perceptions in a global community.

Conclusion

The performance of teaching through the arts is a creative act requiring planning, concentration, and dedication. It is our commitment to sharing ideas with others that drives our desire and passion for teaching. Share this passion with your students and other teachers by integrating the arts into the curriculum. As teachers, you will encounter a variety of educational situations in which you must meet the needs of all students. Strategies and techniques discussed in this chapter can assist you throughout your professional teaching career and inspire unique solutions to specific situations for ELLs. Through an arts integrated curriculum, you are encouraging a lifelong interest in the arts for yourself and students. How can we better prepare generations of students to function in this age and the future? Training students to think independently and critically, to solve real world problems, and express their ideas creatively through the arts is a step in the right direction. The arts are a necessary part of the school curriculum and support learning for ELLs through active engagement and opportunities to express comprehension in unique ways (Bates, 2000; Brown, 2013; Eisner, 2002; Szekely & Bucknam, 2012).

Points to Remember

❖ English language learners are motivated through active engagement in the arts as integrated to support language skills.

❖ English language learners can demonstrate their learning through the arts and provide a more detailed representation for assessing their comprehension.

❖ The arts provide strong connections between language arts skills: reading, writing, speaking, listening, and visually representing.

❖ Creativity, communication, expression, inquiry, and reflection are enhanced through an arts curriculum taught with integrity within a safe learning environment.

❖ The arts support cultural diversity and represent ideas that occur throughout our global community.

Teaching Science to English Language Learners

chapter 26

KEY ISSUES
❖ Science for ALL students, as emphasized in the Next Generation Science Standards (NGSS) and National Science Education Standards (NSES)

❖ Scientific literacy: the goal of the science education community

❖ Importance of science learning for English Language Learners (ELLs)

a. ncreased academic learning and achievement

b. Development of critical thinking

❖ Strategies and techniques for teaching science to ELLs

❖ Benefits and considerations when using cooperative learning

❖ Importance of culturally responsive teaching

The Benefit of Science for All Students

Ms. Frank understands that science learning, when focused on the big ideas of science, will benefit students' cognitive development, lead toward the goal of scientific literacy, and improve their academic language or cognitive academic language proficiency. Maria is an English language learner (ELL) in Ms. Frank's fifth grade homeroom class who functions in the speech emergence phase of second language acquisition. Ms. Frank believes Maria would benefit from being in her class for science instead of being in an ESOL pullout for most of the day. Ms. Frank notes that she has three other ELLs in this class, and that she regularly employs strategies beneficial to ELLs. Ms. Frank feels strongly that not only do these strategies benefit her L2 students, but they also aid L1 students who are struggling with academic learning. She has therefore requested that Maria stay with her for science each day. Ms. Frank knows that inquiry-based science is interesting and important for all students and is willing to adjust her daily schedule to accommodate Maria's ESOL teacher, Ms. Ruiz. Both teachers meet regularly and have discussed the fact that academic language proficiency for ELLs often takes a much longer time to develop than their social language. Over time, they have seen Maria's social language improve markedly. She is now able to create sentences and communicate many of her ideas in English easily and clearly to others. Both teachers are aware that it is the development of academic language that is critical to future academic success for ELLs, and this development may best be accomplished in a content area class. When conferencing with Ms. Ruiz,

Ms. Frank explains that science is a wonderful subject for ELLs to develop their academic language because of the experiential nature of hands-on science. Concrete materials used in doing science make objects and events less foreign, and students better understand what they have personally observed and investigated. Ms. Ruiz agrees that Maria will benefit from science with Ms. Frank, and she appreciates Ms. Frank's willingness to adjust her schedule so that Maria can participate in science. Both teachers are eager to see what effect science learning will have on Maria's English language development. They plan to stay in close touch to assist in whatever way they can to ensure Maria's success in science and in her language proficiency. Both Ms. Ruiz and Ms. Frank feel comfortable asking for advice and assistance as Maria ventures into this arrangement.

The National Science Teachers Association (NSTA) released the following Position Statement, *Science for English Language Learners 2010*, emphasizing its agreement with the National Science Education Standards (NRC, 1996) and standards for TESOL (Teachers of English to Speakers of Other Languages, 2006).

> *The National Science Teachers Association (NSTA) asserts that all students, including those identified as ELLs (ELL), can and should have every opportunity to learn and succeed in science. Teachers play a critical and central role in this process and should receive necessary support. It is important that educators who teach science to students identified as ELLs be well versed in science content and pedagogy, and also skilled in pedagogical approaches for integrating language acquisition and science learning. Standards by TESOL supports this integration and promotes academic language proficiency—the language of school—in core content areas, including science (TESOL, 2006; The NSTA Board of Directors, December 2009).*

Since the release of the NSTA's position in 2010, new science standards, known as the Next Generation Science Standards (NGSS) (NGSS States, 2013), have been developed. The NGSS, developed to align to the *Framework for K–12 Science Education* (NRC, 2012), are conceptually different from the previous National Science Education Standards. These conceptual shifts (i.e., the focus on the interconnected nature of science as it is practiced; deeper understanding of content and application; integration of science and engineering practices; preparation of students for college, career, and citizenship; and the integration with the Common Core State Standards for English Language Arts and Mathematics [CCSS]) provide even more learning opportunities for English language learners (ELLs).

Demographics According to NGSS (NGSS State, 2013), more than one in five students speak a language other than English at home. The number of ELLs in our schools has been increasing rapidly, with about 5.5 million students now considered ELL (NSTA, 2010; NGSS, 2012). Although Spanish speakers make up the majority of the ELL population (73 percent), there are over 400 different languages spoken by U.S. students (U.S. Census Bureau, 2011). Urban areas have a greater percentage of ELLs—14 percent more than suburban and 8 percent more than rural areas (National Center Educational Statistics, 2009). ELLs consist of both foreign born and U.S. citizens with 80 percent of elementary school ELLs born in the United States (Newsroom, 2008).

Science Achievement The National Assessment of Educational Progress (NAEP) assesses a representative sample of U.S. students periodically in science, mathematics, reading, writing, and other subjects publishing findings in the Nation's Report Card (http://nationsreportcard.gov/).

Before 1996, NAEP did not offer accommodations for ELLs, and students who could not meaningfully participate in the assessment were excluded (National Center for Educational Statistics, 2013). The NAEP science assessments conducted in 1996, 2000, 2005, and 2009 included accommodations such as extended time, test items read aloud in English or Spanish, translated assessments, and bilingual dictionaries and glossaries. Unfortunately, the lack of consistent policy regarding the participation of ELLs produced wide variability in exclusion rates making it difficult to meaningfully assess ELL growth. In 2010, in an effort to be more inclusive, NAEP implemented a new policy that extended accommodations to all ELLs and enforced higher (85 percent) inclusion rates.

Despite the variability, NAEP science scores indicate ELLs' science achievement has fallen behind that of non-ELLs. For example, based on the 2009 NAEP science scores, only 3 percent of ELL eighth graders scored "proficient" on the science achievement assessment, compared to 34 percent of mainstream non-ELLs. In the same year, only 17 percent of eighth grade ELLs scored "basic" or above, compared to 68 percent of non-ELLs (NAEP, 2011). The science achievement gaps between ELL and non-ELLs widened considerably from 2005 to 2009 for fourth, eighth, and twelfth graders.

While the achievement of ELLs is not improving in relation to Caucasian English language speakers, it should be noted that our school population is becoming more ethnically and racially diverse; 36 percent of the U.S. population is made up of racial minorities. Statistically, Hispanics make up 16 percent of the population; African Americans, 13 percent; Asians, 5 percent; and American Indian or native Alaskan, 1 percent (U.S. Census Bureau, 2012). In 2010 minorities made up 45 percent of the school-age population and are forecasted to become the majority by 2022 (U.S. Census, 2010).

The terms *dominant* and *nondominant* groups, referring to categories of diversity in U.S. school age population, are used in the NGSS and its Appendix D "All Standards, All Students: Making the Next Generation Standards Accessible to All Students." Nondominant refers to students who have been traditionally underserved in our educational system (NGSS States, 2013). Student groups designated as nondominant are economically disadvantaged students, students from racial/ethnic groups, students with disabilities, and students with limited English proficiency. Three more categories have been added: girls, gifted/talented students, and students in alternative education programs. It is notable that ELLs could fall into three (or more) nondominant groups. For example they could be and often are within a racial/ethnic minority; they may be economically disadvantaged; and they could be students with limited English proficiency. The term *dominant* refers to students who have been well served in science teaching. Dominant students are frequently seen to have status in classrooms. However, the dominant group may not always represent the numerical majority population in a particular school, but may still be viewed as *privileged*.

It should be noted that American students in general do not achieve at the highest science levels in international rankings, and their performance on our National Assessment for Educational Progress (NAEP) in science has remained flat for quite some time. At the same time there is a significant achievement gap on the commonly used large-scale assessments between mainstream white students, a dominant group, and ELL (Silva et al., 2008). In 2006, NSF noted that the United States has strived, often quite unsuccessfully, to provide quality math and science instruction for nondominant groups such as ELLs. Schools serving ELLs often lack highly effective math and science teachers and have inadequate physical resources (i.e., computer equipment, laboratories, facilities) and ELL programs frequently lacking rigor (Rosebery & Ballenger, 2008, p. xi). This situation is also true for other nondominant groups.

"The Next Generation Science Standards (2013) are concerned about this situation and have included a comprehensive description identifying instructional strategies and behaviors shown in research to improve learning and assessment outcomes for ELLs in science (NGSS Appendix D)." These strategies will be discussed in more detail after a brief review of national efforts to reform science education and promote scientific literacy among Americans.

Why the Achievement Gap

Although an agenda of reform has been promoted for quite some time, American students have made only small gains in science achievement on the National Assessment of Educational Progress (NAEP) over the past few decades (Cambell, Hombo, & Mazzeo, 2000). However, ELL results have been worse. Rodriguez (2004) noted that the academic achievement in science of ELLs has lagged behind white students for the past thirty years with that gap increasing over time. There is a need to close the achievement gap that exists between ELLs and dominant groups, while increasing the science achievement of all students, dominants and nondominants.

In order to close the gap, it is necessary to review some of the reasons suggested in the literature for this achievement difference. First, ELLs are often placed in remedial classes where the focus is on learning and acquiring basic literacy skills, but where rigorous science instruction and content would be unlikely to occur (Garcia, 1988; Valdes, 2001). A common practice has been for ELLs to be taught English separately away from academic content (Silva et al., 2008; Stoddart, Pinal, Latzke, & Canady, 2002). The assumption has been that the English learners need to be proficient in English first before they would be able to understand academic content such as science. A critical reason for this assumption may be that learning an academic language takes as long as seven years to acquire the proficiency level of native speakers. Consequently, ELLs may fall behind in learning academic content as they concentrate on learning conversational standard English in remedial classes (Stoddart et al., 2002; Cummins, 2001).

Furthermore, many science teachers see themselves as content teachers of science with language and literacy outside their area of interest or competence or someone else's domain. On the other hand, literacy/diversity educators attend to sociocultural issues and language development, and do not attend to the teaching of subject matter or content such as science. Darling-Hammond (1996) has written of the need for an integration of research on content teaching (subject matter teaching) and research on diversity.

The de-contextualized language of science is also seen as a problem encountered by ELLs as they learn academic science. Spoken English, as found in a science lecture, may provide meaning in a formal and abstract manner, where the third person is often in use. When reading science text, ELLs may read language stripped of common phraseology, terms, or clues and written in an impersonal format, quite un-

like that to which he or she may have become accustomed to from reading and listening to standard English. This unusual use of language can present additional challenges for ELLs as they learn science, as ELLs commonly rely heavily on contextual clues.

Research Projects on Science Instruction and ELLs

The science education research community has been responding to this achievement problem, and a number of projects have found that culturally responsive teaching (Lee & Buxton, 2013), sheltered English instruction focusing on language and content objectives (Echevarria & Short, 2006; Echevarria & Vogt, 2008), guided inquiry and most recently *the language of science classroom* (Lee, Quinn, & Valdes, 2013) show promise for reducing the achievement gap. A few of these research and development projects are described below.

Two recent lines of research grounded in sociocultural and Vygotskian theory have shown promise as means of improving instruction for ELLs. One line of research was funded through the U.S. Department of Education-funded Center for Research on Education Diversity and Excellence (CREDE) (Doherty & Pinal, 2004; Estrada & Imhoff, 2001; Hilberg, Tharp, & DeGeest, 2000; Saunders & Goldenberg, 1999; Saunders, O'Brien, Lennon, & McLean, 1998; Tharp & Dalton, 2007). The CREDE Five Standards for Effective Practices (CFSEP) were predicted to improve learning and teaching of cultural and language minority students and include the following:

- ❖ Joint Productive Activity: Teacher and Students Producing Together
- ❖ Developing Language and Literacy Across the Curriculum
- ❖ Making Meaning: Connecting School to Students' Lives
- ❖ Teaching Complex Thinking
- ❖ Teaching Through Conversations

A series of research studies were conducted to examine the relationship between the CFSEP and student achievement. Results from the CREDE studies showed positive gains in reading, mathematics, as well as in motivation, perceptions, attitudes, and inclusions. Latino ELL students where CFSEP instructional practices were used perceived themselves as only slightly or moderately better readers, but having more cohesion in classroom experiences. Teachers' use of the practices were recorded with the Standards Performance Continuum (Doherty, Hilberg, Pinal, & Tharp, 2002), and student achievement gains were estimated from standardized test scores (SAT-9) for two consecutive years. Teachers using the practices regularly had better gains in terms of comprehension, language, reading, spelling and vocabulary than those who used them less reliably (Doherty et al., 2002). Students of teachers who used the practices extensively showed significantly greater achievement gains on all SAT-9 tests than students whose teachers had not used the practices as extensively. Overall, students whose teachers utilized the CREDE practices reliably and with greater adherence to the practices improved more than those who were less consistent or not as strongly attached to the practices. The CFSEP have not been used in science classes, but some teaching and instruction similarities in science have shown good results

The other line of research is a series of NSF-funded projects that have reported significant improvement in both science and literacy achievement of ELLs as a result of the interventions. Each of these research funded programs integrates science, language and literacy for ELLs. The projects are *Language Acquisition Through Science Education in Rural Schools* (Stoddart's LASERS project); *Seeds of Science*, *Roots of Reading*; the *Imperial Valley Project in Science*; *Science Instruction for All (SIFA);* and *Promoting Science among ELLs (P-SELL)* and *Effective Science Teaching for ELLs (ESTELL).*

Table 26.1 summarizes the NSF-funded research and development projects and instructional approaches that promoted gains in science and literacy achievement.

Table 26-1 **Summary of NSF-Funded Projects and Effective Instructional Approaches**

Projects	Participants/ Setting	Instructional Approach that Promoted Gains in Science and Literacy Achievement Implications for Teaching ELLs
Language Acquisition through Science Education in Rural Schools (LASERS)	Seven districts in central California	Inquiry science that integrates language and literacy development with an emphasis on cooperative learning, cultural and linguistic contextualization, and science talk. (Stoddart, 1999, 2005; Stoddart, Pinal, Latzke, & Canady, 2002)
Seeds of Science/Roots of Reading	Twenty second and third grade classes	Integrated literary-science curriculum (reading instruction including texts, routines for reading, word level skills, vocabulary, and comprehension instruction integrated into inquiry-based science) (Cervetti et al., 2007)
Imperial Valley Project in Science	Large school district in southern California with fourth and sixth grades	Hands-on investigations and journal writing (Amaral, Garrison, & Klentschy, 2002)
Science Instruction for All (SIFA)	Twenty-one third and fourth grade teaches at six schools in San Francisco Bay area	Curriculum units integrating science and literacy (Bravo & Garcia, 2004; Garcia & Baquedano-Lopez, 2007; Ku, Bravo, & Garcia, 2004)
Promoting Science Among ELLs (P-SELL)	Seven elementary schools in southeast U.S.	Curriculum units integrating science and literacy (Lee, 2004; Lee, Deaktor, Hart, Cuevas, & Enders, 2005; Cuevas, Lee, Hart, & Deaktor, 2005; Lee et al., 2007; & Lee, Deaktor, Enders, & Lambert, 2008)
Effective Science Teaching for ELLs (ESTELL)	Professional development of K–6 preservice teachers in California	Integration of science, language, and literacy development, scaffolding of English language development, engagement of students in scientific discourse, development of scientific understanding, collaborative inquiry, and contextualized science learning (Stoddart, Solis, Tolbert, & Bravo, 2010)

All of the studies focused on integrating science, language, and literacy instruction for ELLs. The interventions resulted in significant gains in ELL science and literacy achievement (Stoddart, Solis, Tolbert, & Bravo, 2010). A few highlights of the research are described below.

Stoddart et al. (2002) has referred to the *LASERS* project as a synergistic integration of science and language. They noted that effective science inquiry aids language development, and effective language teaching was able to aid in learning science ideas and processes. In *LASERS* there was an integration of contextualized science inquiry and discourse whereby teachers provided support with hands-on science activities and also "science talks." Students in *LASERS* classrooms exhibited significant achievement gains on both performance and standardized assessments where students' scientific understanding increased.

One noteworthy finding in the LASERS project is that teachers of science content were able to develop an understanding of the relationship between science and language, while the language teachers in this project were able to see how science processes and thought were fine vehicles for learning language. Both groups of teachers developed an understanding of the interconnectedness of each other's domains and how one enhanced the other. Teachers came to feel that all lessons were language lessons, not just for the learning of science, and science lessons were seen as vehicles for language development. They suggest that all science teaching should be integrated with language development, as the two are intertwined (Stoddart et al., 2002). Thomas and Collier noted in 2003 that the amount of time needed to acquire grade level proficiency in English can be reduced by integrating content and language.

Another large study directed toward increasing the science and literacy achievements of language minority and culturally diverse students has been the work of Okhee Lee (Lee, 2004; Lee, Deaktor, Hart, Cuevas, & Enders, 2005; Cuevas, Lee, Hart, & Deaktor, 2005; Lee et al., 2007; & Lee, Deaktor, Enders, & Lambert, 2008). Lee et al. (2005) noted a need to unite the areas of multicultural education/ESOL education where little attention is paid to the academic discipline of science, and science education, which is primarily focused on the teaching the science disciplines. In science education, there is not always sufficient concern for the cultural and linguistic diversity issues of so many of the students in our schools today (Lee et al., 2005). Their project combines the two areas to see if the achievement gap can be narrowed.

In their extensive work, teachers received professional development in the areas of science inquiry and literacy with a focus on how this might improve diverse students' language proficiency as well as their science understanding. An instructional congruence framework was part of the endeavor, meaning that there was an integration of science, English language/literacy, and the children's home language and culture. This cultural congruence component was included because language/racial minority students have been found to benefit achievement-wise when their cultural and linguistic backgrounds are taken into account (Lee, 2002).

The students in this study engaged in small group and whole group reading as well as expository writing on the science under discussion. Trade books were used, and experiments that students conducted were written as reports. Reading and writing from prompts, hands-on tasks, vignettes, and expository texts were utilized. The units developed for teaching used many means of communicating, including gestures and graphic representations. Student booklets were designed to connect with students' cultural backgrounds. An outcome of this intervention was that again there was a gap in achievement between ethnic/language minority students (ELLs) and L1 students at third grade with no growth rate differences between groups. However, at fourth grade, there was still an achievement gap, but the growth rate for the minority students was often larger, and the gap narrowed toward the end of the school year (Lee et al., 2005).

Effective science teaching for ELLs (ESTELL) has developed an instructional framework integrating two lines of research with documented positive results in science learning for ELLs, with examples of ESTELL pedagogy included in the framework (Stoddart, Solis, Tolbert, & Bravo, 2010).

Scientific Literacy and a Brief History of Science Education Reform

Though scientific literacy has been a goal of science education for the past few decades, it has not been clearly defined. The NSES (NRC, 1996) provided an indication of how scientific literacy might be evidenced. The NSES defines a scientifically literate student as leaving high school as an asker of questions with the ability to find answers to those questions. This young person should possess a curiosity about the natural world and be able to evaluate information based on evidence. The scientifically literate person should also be able to state a position on an issue and base their statements on the available evidence. As a result of school science, students should be able to make careful observations and record their observations into a written record. Predictions should be based on observations, and hypotheses should be in response to questions that have arisen. The scientifically literate person should use the tools of science for measuring and obtaining data. They should be able to organize their information into tables, graphs, or charts as documentation of finding. They should further be able to analyze data and results and draw conclusions from their findings. Developing such abilities or habits of mind would allow a person to make logical judgments on issues affecting their community, evaluate environmental concerns, and make informed decisions at the voting booth.

In the 1980s, the scientific community recognized that many American students were not scientifically literate, as described above, and often held negative feelings about school science. Furthermore, young people in the United States were exiting school with a weak knowledge of science and the scientific enterprise. This raised concern among scientists, science educators and science teachers, and expressed itself in an agenda of reform in science education (Bybee & Ben-Zvi, 1998; Lee & Fradd, 1998). The National Research Council (NRC, 1996) and Project 2061 of the American Association for the Advancement of Science (AAAS, 1989) produced three significant documents; the National Science Education Standards (NSES) (NRC, 1996), *Science for all Americans* (AAAS, 1989), and *Benchmarks for Science Literacy* (AAAS, 1993). With the publication of these reform documents, national science guidelines were now available to educators and the theme of *Science for All* was clear. The NSES stated that science should be active; that is, students should be doing science and school science should reflect real science. Stress was placed on standards of excellence for all students regardless of gender, race, religion, ethnicity, disability or language background (Lynch et al., 1996). Engaging in inquiry was recognized as the essence of science and should be reflected in the school curricula (NRC, 1996). The reform documents of the 1990s began the movement toward the full inclusion of science for ELLs just as the achievement gap for ELLs began to be recognized as significant, not improving, and with ELLs continuing to fall behind the dominant school population in their achievement performance on large scale assessments.

Following the reform of the 1990s, the NRC (2012) published the *Framework for K–12 Science Education* (hereby referred to as the Framework). The Framework has guided the writing of the *NGSS* (NGSS). The NGSS following the lead of the Framework took reform further than the previous national standards (NRC, 1996), and are more specific as to what needs to occur in science classrooms.

There are *three dimensions to the NGSS:*

1. **Disciplinary Core Ideas** in the physical, life, earth and space sciences, and engineering, technology, and applications of science
2. **Crosscutting Concepts** that have application across all domains of science Crosscutting concepts include patterns, similarity and diversity, cause and effect: mechanism and explanation, scale, proportion and quantity, energy and matter: flows cycles and conservation, structure and function, and stability and change. The NRC notes "students' understanding of crosscutting concepts should be reinforced by repeated use of them in the context of instruction in the disciplinary core ideas" (NRC 2012, p. 101).
3. **Scientific and Engineering Practices** that scientists and engineers engage in to investigate and build models and theories about the natural world.

The science and engineering practices further refine inquiry-based science and include "asking questions; developing and using models; planning and carrying out investigations; analyzing and interpreting data; using mathematics and computational thinking; constructing explanations and designing solutions(for engineering); engaging in argument from evidence; and obtaining, evaluating, and communicating information" (NRC, 2012).

The NGSS states that, by the end of twelfth grade, all students will have sufficient knowledge of the science and engineering practices to engage in public discussion on science-related issues NGSS (NGSS Lead States, 2013). Furthermore, the NGSS and its Appendix D are clear in their expectations that students such as ELLs should be able to master these new more cognitively challenging standards.

The NGSS Science and Engineering Practices and Language in the Science Classroom

Engineering was introduced in the NGSS because of its potential to recognize contributions of other cultures rather than just the traditions of western science. Engineering can also provide a relevant context for learning how to solve local issues and environmental problems in the lives of ELLs. Through this problem-based instruction, students should acquire knowledge of science and scientific practices (Rodriquez & Berryman, 2002). The practices support science learning for all students and offer both challenges and opportunities for ELLs. Special attention to these issues for ELL is found in NGSS Appendix D and Case Study 4 and describe how ELLs can benefit from high quality teaching and planning guided by and implemented under the NGSS.

The NGSS science and engineering practices rely heavily on language and offer many opportunities for teachers to assist ELLs in learning language as they teach science. All students, including ELLs need to be able to communicate through science discourse. Reading, writing, representing models and presenting explanations inferred from science investigations should occur regularly. Students would need to be able to argue from evidence as they interact with others to form shared conclusions. These important practices should be incorporated throughout science instruction and have connections to the Common Core State Standards (CCSS) for English language arts and mathematics (Lee, Quinn, & Valdés, 2013).

Lee, Quinn, and Valdes (2013) have written of the special features of language used in science and how that may affect the learning and understanding of science by ELLs. They note that the idea that language in science classrooms is often quite similar to language used in teaching and learning other disciplines, and many features are common across subject areas. There are, however, special forms of language and literacy specific to science. Teachers need to understand how oral and written science is used and help ELLs become aware of and use this science language, particularly as they engage in the *science and engineering practices*. These special ways of communicating in science are what is referred to as academic language and academic literacy, something that often takes quite some time for ELLs to acquire at the same level as native English speakers. They further note that they are introducing the term *language of the science classroom*. Their thesis is based on everyday language and moves closer as students advance in grade levels toward the language of disciplinary science, which is the language used by scientists. The language of the science classrooms initially is more like colloquial English and written materials may not resemble disciplinary science text to any great extent, but as students move through the grade levels, the language written in text becomes more like disciplinary science language.

Lee et al. (2013) have chosen four of the science and engineering practices to highlight their concern with the use of language in science teaching and chose these: *Develop and use models, develop explanations, engage in argumentation from evidence, and develop communicative scientific information.* They further note that as students perform analytical tasks, language is used to construct knowledge. Three elements of classroom language use are identified as: *modality* (various situations in which students may be required to perform such as in small groups or one on one conversations or whole class presentations or understanding lectures), then *registers* and examples of registers. (*Registers* refer to colloquial language or disciplinary science language or classroom language according to the specific situation.)

Strategies for Teaching Science to ELLs

The NGSS and research literature has indicated several approaches that teachers can use to support science and language for ELLs: (1) literacy strategies with all students, (2) language support strategies with ELLs, (3) discourse strategies with ELLs, (4) home language and cultural connections (Fathman & Crowther, 2006; Lee & Buxton, 2013; Warren & Rosebery, 2008), and (5) collaborative inquiry. These strategies can overlap and are discussed more broadly as strategies for supporting ELLs' English language and literacy development and integrating home language and culture into their science classroom and teaching.

Literacy Strategies

Learning opportunities that integrate all language skills—reading, writing, listening, and speaking—are important to ELLs (Echevarria et al., 2004). English language and literacy strategies involve more than just being able to speak, listen, read, and write but also learning to think, reason, and visually represent information via pictures, graphs, and tables in order to communicate ideas.

Effective teachers utilize reading and writing strategies in their teaching, such as activating prior knowledge regarding a science idea or principle, and using expository texts related to everyday happenings, or using trade books or literature to introduce science topics. Specific strategies that facilitate reading comprehension, while promoting academic language proficiency, include avoiding unnecessarily complex grammatical constructions and idiomatic usage, using graphic organizers and other visual aids in the presentation of content, explaining in simple language the meaning of unfamiliar terms, pre-teaching of content and providing a list of sci-

ence vocabulary words for each lesson (Echevarria, Vogt, & Short, 2004; Short, 1991).

Teachers should also have their students write narrative stories on science concepts, as well as expository paragraphs that describe processes or concepts under discussion. Specific types of writing for and in science, such as lab reports or posters as found at science conferences, might also be used, depending on the grade level.

Science process skills (i.e., observing, measuring, predicting, inferring, and communicating) might be brought forth at the same time as specific language functions like describing classifying, explaining, predicting, and interpreting might be developed. Science graphic organizers like concept maps Venn diagrams, and word walls can be used to integrate literacy and science concepts (Lee & Buxton, 2013).

In order to encourage literacy development (reading and writing), the NGSS Appendix D recommends that teachers activate students' prior knowledge; lead discussions where strategies for reading science are implemented; use science terms such as *describe, explain, predict, infer,* and *conclude* as part of their regular discussions; and have students keep science journals. Familiarizing students with graphic organizers such as concept maps and Venn diagrams, and utilizing word walls are also recommended as daily occurrences. Students should be encouraged and even required to read science trade books or other science related literature.

Language Support Strategies

The teaching of science is the focus of content-specific science teachers, but language development can be enhanced in science classrooms when science teachers provide hands-on learning opportunities as an integral part of their science instruction. With some additional teacher assistance, and the implementation of appropriate ESOL strategies, ELLs should be able to derive meaning from science. The experiential learning that should occur in the science classroom can aid students' scientific conceptual understanding as well as their academic language. In such a classroom, objects and materials should be labeled, demonstrations should be clearly linked to concepts under study, and labs or activities should illustrate scientific principles. Furthermore, all labs, demonstrations or inquiry activities should be discussed and written about so they will be meaningful to students. All of these strategies aid the conceptual understanding for ELLs.

Science, in many ways, is an ideal forum for language development. It is incumbent upon science teachers to make sure that their ELLs are actively engaged, and to regularly monitor their understanding. Teachers must reinforce new terms, and have ELLs repeat terms important to the lesson. Teachers should provide a variety of ways for ELLs to demonstrate their knowledge and understanding.

ESOL strategies, such as hands on inquiry-based strategies, are language support strategies. They are particularly beneficial to ELLs as they are less dependent on language mastery. Inquiry science promotes academic language development in an authentic manner allowing communication of understanding in many ways, such as gestural, oral pictorially, textually, and may rely on realia, modeling, and demonstration to explain science concepts.

Lee and Buxton suggest that teachers introduce and encourage students to understand and use a few key science words in context that are content specific (e.g., *condensation*) or discipline specific terms (e.g., *hypothesize*). They encourage teachers to introduce key terms in the beginning of each lesson and have students use these terms wherever possible.

To support English language development, the NGSS Appendix D recommends that teachers use language support strategies, such as real objects or events (realia), pictures, graphs, gestures, oral language, and especially hands-on activities as ways of connecting with and instructing ELLs. They would also help ELLs to understand important or critical science vocabulary in context.

A favorite strategy of Mr. Cooper, a sixth grade science teacher, is to create a learning packet for his ELLs that is only slightly different than that used by his native English speaking students. One packet on hurricanes consists of photographs of a hurricane striking the shoreline and another of coastal property and boats under siege as a hurricane moves ashore. He provides a space for writing and asks his ELLs to write words they know that are related to hurricanes, while the English speakers write what they know about hurricanes in paragraph form. He provides a space on another page for writing words that ELLs learn through the unit. Within the packet, he includes a map of the track of a recent hurricane and asks the students to trace the path with colored markers from the coast of Africa across the Atlantic and into the waters near and around the United States. He asks them to note places that they recognize. Another page of the packet lists the categories of hurricanes and the wind velocities for each category. The packet describes information on the terms storm watch versus storm warning, and how a tropical depression is different from a hurricane. Mr. Cooper also leaves space for students to add drawings, which provide insight for a teacher who is trying to find ways to assess what ELLs find meaningful. Mr. Cooper feels he gains insight into students' understanding through their drawings. He asks them to label their drawings. Although the science classroom experiences are meaningful to ELLs, they may not be able to express their understanding in traditional ways. Mr. Cooper is always ready to adapt his assessments and his teaching to accommodate his ELLs.*

In recent years, Mr. Cooper has been able to pair one ELL with a native speaker

and put them on the National Oceanographic and Atmospheric Administration (NOAA) website, which provides current information on storms and weather patterns. He may ask an English speaker to read and explain information on the website that an ELL might not be able to fully understand without assistance. The use of the Internet has been helpful now that Mr. Cooper has adequate computer technology for students to use in his classroom.

Discourse and Informal Conversations (Science Talks)

Effective discourse strategies facilitate classroom discussions for all students. To encourage and enhance the ability of ELLs to take part in discussions at the classroom level, the NGSS Appendix D recommends *discourse strategies* to aid ELLs in understanding academic content. Teachers should adapt the level of discussion and the means of communicating to bridge the language problems that may occur for ELLs while maintaining strong science content and appropriate use of science processes.

Strategies that effective teachers use are: clear enunciation and longer wait times; provide several explanations of the same concept by repeating and rephrasing main ideas; and extending or repeating with extensions students' talk or response (Lee & Buxton, 2013). These teachers operate at just slightly above their students' level of competence in language. Effective teachers help students learn *positional words* such as **on/in, above/below, inside/ outside,** and comparative terms **like hot/hotter/ hottest,** and other positional words like _**on top of, in front of, behind, above,** and **left/right**_.

Children who may struggle with academic tasks in writing, math, or, actually, any emerging learner of English, could have many questions and thoughts about the natural world. One form of verbal interaction and thought building in the science classroom is *Science Talks*, which have been shown to support learning in science as well as address the ideas that children have about science (Gallas, 1995; Rosebery & Ballenger, 2008; Rosebery & Hudicourt-Barnes, 2006). Science talks are more conversational forms of interaction between students, with the teacher behaving more like a facilitator and an important listener of the conversations, rather than the director of the conversation. Students discuss ideas, pose questions to each other and the group to consider, and explore, with no right or wrong answers. These talks are a time to think about an idea and how it may fit children's understanding of the world, as well as to hear what other children are thinking about this very same topic. (This type of activity would lend itself well to the use of a graphic organizer, such as a K-W-L chart.) Science talks aid children in making connections between what they know, what they have learned, and what they may be asked to learn in school. The children often come to terms with important ideas, learn how to present their ideas based on evidence, revise and clarify their thinking, and then come up with new questions. They have the chance to practice their developing English language skills in a comfortable, nonthreatening atmosphere related to science.

Science talks usually derive from students' questions and are part of the regular science instructional time. Teachers often set aside a block of time for such talks. Though the teacher may begin the science talk, the teacher may then remain quiet, taking notes on what is being said after initiating the talk, with the intention of building upon children's ideas. At times, the teacher may re-voice what students bring forth and request that a student elaborate on his or her idea. However, the teacher is there as an observer, listener, and facilitator (Rosebery & Ballenger, 2008). The researchers and teachers have found that all students, including ELLs, participate in science talks and note and emphasize that all children come to school with rich experiences of the natural world and with ways of explaining what they have seen, thought about, and reacted to. The researchers point out that teachers find that very quiet students will express ideas and new ways of looking at natural phenomena, with unusual ways of expressing what they feel and are thinking about science. Some suggestions for getting started with science talks include the following from Rosebery and Ballenger (2008, pp. 10–11).

❖ Engage children in a scientific event or with a scientific phenomenon and initiate an open discussion about what is occurring.

❖ Listen carefully to the children and support them in talking with each other in ways they find understandable, and allow them to express their thoughts as freely as possible.

❖ Assume the children understand each other, even if you (the teacher) do not quite get it.

❖ Then reflect on what children have said at the end of the science talk and revisit your notes on the talk.

❖ Later meet with other teachers to discuss and share how the ideas may influence what is taught and how to teach it so that children benefit and the teacher can improve upon her/his instruction.

Home Language and Cultural Connections

The idea of *instructional congruence*, proposed by Lee and Fradd (1998), implies that curriculum and instructional approaches should mediate academic content with students' linguistic and cultural experiences to make such content accessible, meaningful, and relevant. This notion emphasizes the need to develop congruence not only between students' cultural expectations and norms of classroom interaction, but also between academic disciplines and the knowledge students bring from their own cultural environments, referred to as *funds of knowledge*. Recognizing that students' cultural beliefs and practices are sometimes inconsistent with modern Western science, effective science instruction should enable students to cross cultural borders between their home cultures and the culture of science (Aikenhead & Jegede, 1999; Snively & Corsiglia, 2001). Thus, instructional congruence stresses the role of instruction (or instructional interventions) as teachers explore the relationship between academic disciplines and students' knowledge, devising ways to link the two.

García and Lee (2008) encourage teachers to consider what they refer to as creating **culturally responsive learning environments in the classroom**. By this they mean connecting instruction to what students bring to the classroom from their homes and cultural backgrounds. From a constructivist perspective on learning and teaching, we know that constructing knowledge is based on what students come to the learning situation already familiar with, and the new ideas that teachers want them to learn and understand. Accessing students' prior knowledge is important in making connections with the new ideas that students will encounter in school. We know that children are not "blank slates" but have ideas and understandings that will influence what they come to understand through instruction in the classroom. Teachers who can connect to the outside world of ELLs (what they are familiar with from their home and cultural community) will make what happens in the classroom more meaningful and easier to understand. Science in school settings tends to reflect Western science and Western habits of mind that may be less familiar to ELLs. Therefore, incorporating experiences that ELLs have with what they may be learning in school will be helpful as these students learn science. They may arrive with preconceived ideas that conflict with scientific beliefs found within the mainstream United States'

society. Great care and thoughtfulness should be given when trying to point out the differences.

Students behave, react, speak, and perform in a manner that reflects their home culture and their community. Connecting to ELLs' home culture has been determined to be valuable in learning science. Ways that this can be done is by connecting with the communication and interaction patterns of their home and community. Furthermore, it is important to retrieve and access ELLs "funds of knowledge" when it comes to science topics. Utilizing cultural artifacts and various community resources, including significant persons in the home culture, will be helpful to ELLs.

Science teachers must also recognize the difficulties ELLs may have with the attitudes of science. They need to understand that the values, dispositions, and habits of mind of a scientifically literate society do not necessarily correspond to the ways of thinking ELLs have experienced at home or through cultural interactions in their communities outside of school. It may require more effort on the part of science teachers to not only help ELLs develop their scientific language and science learning, but also to assist them in understanding the values, dispositions, and habits of mind related to scientific literacy.

Teachers can use home language effectively to build science learning in English. When possible, important or critical words could be introduced in both languages. Making students aware of cognates (and false cognates) between the two languages is helpful. Spanish and other Romance languages have countless words based on Latin roots, the primary language of science. Utilizing the skills and empathy of more proficient bilingual students in assisting ELLs is appropriate for ELLs in the earlier stages of language development (Lee & Buxton, 2013). Code switching (using the native word as well as English) would be acceptable.

Cooperative Learning via Complex Instruction

Learning science in collaborative or cooperative groups has long been recommended by the science education community (Lazarowitz & Hertz-Lazarowitz, 1998). Lazarowitz and Hertz-Lazarowitz note that cooperative learning is "the antithesis of the expository competitive classroom" and is based on a constructivist perspective toward teaching and learning. They further note that competitive methods have been unsuccessful with a large segment of the general population of students such as ELL and other nondominant groups. A well-researched and successful model of cooperative learning that was developed at Stanford University is called complex instruction. Elizabeth Cohen, Rachel Lotan, and a group of researchers at Stanford University developed a cooperative learning model called complex instruction. This program is designed for heterogeneous classrooms where students are of many nationalities and ethnicities, speaking many different languages, and at various levels of cognitive development and academic performance. An elementary program for fourth and fifth graders called *Finding Out/Descubrimiento*, focuses on science and math learning. Materials are in both English and Spanish. Students work in cooperative groups and adhere to the following norms of behavior (Cohen & DeAvila, 1983). An important aspect of the cooperative group work in complex instruction is based on the norm that everyone has some abilities, and none of us have all the abilities (Cohen, 1986).

Cooperative learning is linked with a constructivist perspective on learning that emphasizes collaboration, social interaction, sharing of ideas, and group efforts toward the solution of problems. Group efforts in doing projects are believed to enhance understanding and develop meaningful learning (Cohen, 1986). Cooperative group work allows for questions to come forth that might not be addressed in more formal and traditional classroom settings, encouraging students to question and challenge each other freely (Cohen, 1991).

Cooperative learning groups do pose some challenges, however. Groups may reinforce negative stereotypes and allow what are perceived as "high status" students to dominate talk and action. In such situations high status students' ideas may take precedence over the ideas of "low status" students (Cohen, 1984, 1991). High status students, because of their popularity or position, may be able to hold sway over more scientifically grounded ideas of lower status students. The fact that high status students may be considered "smart" by the group may allow them to dominate talk and materials. This is the very situation that a teacher would hope to avoid using cooperative learning groups. That is the unequal access to learning that can occur if some precautions are not taken (Cohen, 1984). It is therefore necessary for teachers to carefully monitor group work, especially if a teacher has a number of ELLs in the class and to form her cooperative groups with great care.

Teachers should consider the nature of the children with whom they place an English language learner, and know which partners and group members will be patient and understanding, and help the ELL to participate in the activity as fully as possible. Positive group interdependence can encourage students to express themselves in spite of limited academic language proficiency. One way to obtain successful group work that values all voices is to train the children for the roles that are going to be used in the cooperative groups and to establish norms, a set of expected behaviors that students will experience and be expected to exhibit (Cohen, 1986, 1991, 1994). This requires time at the beginning of the school year and further reinforcement of the roles and norms throughout the school year. The following norms of behavior are developed in complex instruction classrooms and adhered to throughout the program.

> No one has all of the abilities; all of us have some.
> It is your right to ask questions.
> It is your duty to answer a question.
> None of us is as smart as all of us together.

Under the complex instruction model, children are trained to take over many of the usual tasks of the teacher, freeing the teacher to monitor learning, and cooperative behavior. As the children take over these responsibilities, the teacher can observe students at work, probe students' thoughts and understandings, encourage cooperative behavior and higher level thinking, and suggest alternatives for the children as they work. The teacher takes the role of a guide and a resource. Children problem solve and investigate together as they interact in their groups. Cooperative grouping and "delegating authority" to learners provides time for teachers to assist ELLs. The model has also been developed for middle schools and is specifically designed for heterogeneous classes where students may be of various abilities, racial/ethnic groups, and language backgrounds. A key feature is that students work on challenging group projects where everyone's ability may be utilized (Cohen & Lotan, 1990).

A Sample Inquiry Lesson in a Cooperative Learning Environment

In Mr. Thomas's third grade classroom, each child has a diagram of an earthworm, but the class shares magnifying lenses and earthworms. The children do not mind. They are accustomed to sharing materials as they work in cooperative groups. In their groups, they will discuss the differences that they may see, and know that they may need to report their findings to the class. Because the children are accustomed to working in cooperative learning groups, they observe the norms of behavior and perform their roles well. This allows Mr. Thomas time to give special attention to Alejandro, a recent addition to Mr. Thomas's class.

Mr. Thomas realizes that Alejandro probably does not know what a magnifying lens is, nor has he had the experiences the other children in the class have had. Mr. Thomas sits by Alejandro's group, hands Alejandro a lens, and names this new tool for him, repeating the words "magnifying lens" for him clearly. He places a small clear plate containing salt crystals in front of Alejandro. Mr. Thomas knows that Alejandro knows what salt is and tells him it is salt. Alejandro has seen how the other children observe with the lenses. He begins to use his lens in the same way to observe the salt, as Mr. Thomas nods his head. Alejandro is very surprised by what he sees and becomes quite excited when he observes the tiny cubes of salt. He is amazed to see the enlargement and the detail of salt crystals. Mr. Thomas again repeats the words "magnifying lens." With gestures and careful speech he tells Alejandro that the lens magnifies and makes things seem bigger. Alejandro understands what Mr. Thomas is saying because he has observed the enlargement for himself. Mr. Thomas points to the other children and tells Alejandro to do as the other children are doing, to use his lens to observe the earthworm. Alejandro uses the lens to look at the earthworm. He understands that he too, should draw what he sees onto his earthworm diagram. Mr. Thomas asks the group to help Alejandro with any labeling that they decide is good to add to their drawings. The children have been trained to help each other and answer each other's questions before asking the teacher for help. Two of the children watch as Alejandro draws in great detail the tiny setae of the earthworm onto his diagram. After a while the group stops to look at his drawing. He has enhanced the simple drawing into a detailed reproduction of the earthworm. They are amazed at the complexity of the drawing that Alejandro has created. They realize that Alejandro has a special ability and is a careful observer. They praise his drawing. The group facilitator wants Mr. Thomas to see what Alejandro has created on his paper, and he asks him to come back to their group. Mr. Thomas is impressed and encourages Alejandro to continue and asks the children to help him label the earthworm parts. Pointing to the bulletin board, Mr. Thomas explains he is going to put Alejandro's drawing on the front board as display.

When Alejandro is finished drawing, the children show him their drawings and the labels. They explain that each label represents a part of the worm and point to the structure on the earthworm. They indicate that Alejandro, too, should label his drawing. He repeats each word after them and copies the word from their papers onto his. He too, notices that his drawing has greater detail and is more precise than the others in his group, and he feels quite proud of his work. He sees that he can contribute and succeed in science and that there is much positive feeling in his group and in Mr. Thomas's class.

Inquiry as Contextualized Science Instruction for ELLs

The context of language refers to the degree learners receive from meaningful cues (e.g., visual cues, concrete objects, and hands-on activities) that aid in their understanding of the content under study (Krashen, 1985). Research in science for ELLs indicates a need for the integration of science inquiry, discourse, and language learning in a contextualized program that is culturally socially and linguistically responsive (Amaral et al., 2002; Lee & Fradd, 1998; Lee, 2008; Rosebery et al.,1992; Stoddart, 1999; Ku et al., 2004). Contextualized, content-based instruction in second language is able to improve language proficiency of ELLs without harm to their academic learning (Cummins, 1981; Genesee, 1987; Met, 1994).

Inquiry science instruction relies on language where discourse and active thinking are in evidence, allowing students to demonstrate and communicate their understandings through graphs, charts, writing, diagrams, and oral communication, as the NGSS science and engineering practices advocate. In inquiry science students explore phenomena and scientific events in a hands-on manner, with language activities specifically tied to the processes, objects, experiments and naturally occurring events—they are contextualized (Baker & Saul, 1994; Lee & Fradd, 1998; Warren, Ogonowske, Ballenger, Rosebery, & Hudicourt-Barnes, 2001; Rosebery et al., 1992). When describing, hypothesizing, explaining, justifying, arguing, and summarizing, as in the practices of science and engineering, students use purposeful language and students may demonstrate their understanding in a variety of ways such as in writing, orally, and by drawing or creating tables and graphs (Lee & Fradd, 1998). The contextual nature of science language in inquiry instruction will aid ELLs in their understanding of science concepts as opposed to the de-contextualized lecture common in many science classrooms, particularly in the secondary science classroom (Rosebery et al., 1992).

Something that should be remembered in classroom teaching is that while hands on activities are critically important and beneficial to ELL learning, it is also extremely important that these same activities involve students in active thinking and discourse related to what is under investigation. Rosebery et al. (1992) used argumentation and inquiry as a means to guide language minority students in examining scientific claims and the nature of proof. Stoddart has called the relationship between science learning and language and literacy "reciprocal and synergistic." By using contextualized language func-

tions in description, explanation and discussion during science inquiry, students can practice and develop complex language forms, while improving their conceptual understanding.

Lee and Buxton (2013, p. 38) further write that "effective teachers model academic language functions in the context of science inquiry as students generate questions, formulate hypotheses, design experiments, collect data and interpret data, draw conclusions and communicate results."

Throughout an inquiry-based lesson, teachers help English learners "in moving from registers expressing their firsthand experience in oral language to those expressing academic knowledge in writing" (Gibbons, 2003, as cited in Dobb, 2004). Students can gain a deeper understanding of science when they write about their thinking, because the act of writing may cause new ideas and relationships to be integrated into their prior knowledge (Fellows, 1994).

Inquiry-based instruction is conducive to infusing content area goals with literacy objectives (Thier & Daviss, 2002). According to Carrier (2005), "these objectives are based on the specific content objectives of science lessons, and they include not only the vocabulary of science, but also strategies for effective reading, writing, listening, and note taking, as well as the academic language functions needed to participate in science learning" (p. 6).

Many inquiry-based instructional opportunities can strengthen students' English literacy skills. For instance, as teachers go over the procedures for experiments or other activities, they can take an opportunity to model a series of language structures for English learners, as well. Figures and tables also visually support concepts presented in the text.

To aid reading comprehension further, inquiry-based science lessons should follow a consistent format: introduction, science vocabulary, a list of materials, and an inquiry framework (e.g., 5-E instructional model). The 5-E Instructional model (Bybee, 1997) begins by assessing students' prior ideas and *engaging* them in the learning. Once engaged, students *explore* their ideas by participating in learning experiences. During the *explanation* phase, teachers and students exchange explanations of a particular concept or idea that they are now more familiar with due to the exploration phase. Students are then challenged to *elaborate* or extend their conceptual understanding to a new context. The fifth E is "*evaluation*," which is incorporated throughout inquiry-based lessons and at the end.

According to Short (Short & Echevarria, 2004), such routines help ELLs anticipate what is coming without relying solely on teacher's verbal cues. In each lesson, reading passages are divided into short sections followed by the corresponding step in the inquiry framework or questions to check comprehension. Such lesson structure allows for more frequent modeling of language by the teacher. This is a desirable situation because language forms are not targeted in isolation, but they are immediately applied in the science context. Science inquiry, therefore, can strengthen literacy skills by infusing them with meaning and purpose, while literacy skills can strengthen science knowledge by giving students a linguistic lens through which to focus and clarify their ideas, inferences, and conclusions (Thier & Daviss, 2002, p. 6).

Writing, which is frequently overlooked in science lessons, should be emphasized. Throughout an inquiry-based lesson, teachers help English learners "in moving from registers expressing their firsthand experience in oral language to those expressing academic knowledge in writing" (Gibbons, 2003, as cited in Dobb, 2004). Students can gain a deeper understanding of science when they write about their thinking, because the act of writing may cause new ideas and relationships to be integrated into their prior knowledge (Fellows, 1994). Text re-presentation encourages students to probe printed materials for deeper understanding. To improve student's writing skills and allow them to re-present what they have read, lesson activities may include recording observations in tables, constructing graphs, answering questions, and writing explanations for evidence.

The inclusion of *hands-on activities*, an essential component of the inquiry-based approach, depends less on formal mastery of the instruction language and offers better access to students with limited science experience than decontextualized textbook knowledge (Echevarria, et al., 2004; Lee, 2002; Lee & Fradd, 1998; Rosebery, Warren, & Conant, 1992; Short, 1991). By beginning a science lesson with concrete practical experiences, even recently arrived ELLs will develop some understanding of what the lesson is about. In addition, because comprehension precedes production (Krashen, 1982), ELLs can show their understanding by hands-on demonstrations rather than by providing detailed explanation.

Collaborative work, also a component of inquiry-based learning, provides ELLs with systematic opportunities to improve their English proficiency in the context of authentic peer communication. Group interactions with the focus on the task rather than the language provides a non-threatening opportunity for the second language learner to listen to other children's discourse, and, once confident, to contribute to the conversation (Amaral et al., 2002; Echevarria et al., 2004).

Strategies for Teaching Science to ELLs

❖ Use real objects or models (e.g., model of the relationship of the sun, moon, and earth), videos, Internet pictures and graphics or film, and picture books related to topics under study. When something can be seen, felt, or changed, it is more likely to be understood and remembered.

❖ Emergent speakers, fluent speakers, or the teacher can read a "picture book" related to the science topic to a child functioning in the silent stage of second language acquisition.

❖ Early-emergent speakers can write down all the words they can after reading from a picture book. Students in the silent stage may try to write down some words (if they have been pointed out to them). Spelling is not an issue under either set of circumstances.

❖ Use cooperative learning groups.

❖ Use hands-on science activities/investigations to engage students in active science learning (e.g., testing the hardness of rocks and minerals and using the Mohs scale to identify the category to which a sample belongs). A teacher-made outline of what to do and where the categories lie with pictorial representations can accompany the activity. Everyone in a group can participate in the classifying and testing activities.

- When most children are working alone, assign a buddy to the English language learner. The buddy should want to work with the ELL and talk aloud about a science assignment.

- Create word walls or word banks for topics under study that students can refer to for spelling and for memory jogs of particular concepts. These word walls can stay up for the entire unit and can be added to as the unit of study progresses.

- Native English speakers and fluent ELLs can write about what they know (e.g., Write all that you know about volcanoes and why you believe your ideas are correct. For ELLs: Write all the words you can think of related to volcanoes). The ELL could draw a volcano and label what he or she knows and possibly create phrases or short sentences about volcanoes. Use of words such as *magma, ash, molten,* and *pressure* can give the teacher an idea of what the student is learning and comprehending in science and give insight into the level of second language acquisition.

- Use writing by native English speakers from the class and fluent speakers as text for ELLs. Ask fluent speakers to write text that would aid students in the early emergent stage.

- Create a large, empty bubble diagram for early emergent students. Say words as you add them to the bubble. The ELL can also say them as well as in a choral reading. The student can keep a copy of the bubble diagram for personal reference.

- Have linguistically advanced and native speakers create concept maps. Have the less language proficient student try to create a simpler form of a concept map. Some students find it helpful to have a fluent speaker go over the concept map and explain ideas to them.

- Think-pair-share on days when the teacher does direct instruction, and engage in short "teacher talks." Have students listen to the teacher for five minutes. Then pair students and have them talk to each other about what they heard and learned. The more proficient student should explain his or her understanding first. As students develop proficiency with this technique, the time can be extended to ten minutes with two minutes of talk time together. All students will find that not everyone "hears" or understands the same thing from the teacher talk. This is sometimes called 10–2 in secondary school.

Science Language Usage and Adolescent Learners

There are additional problems for the older English language learner who is in a regular science class. Learning science content can be a challenge for L1 students because of the complexity of the material, the tasks performed in developing the necessary conceptual understanding, and the related problem of abstraction in learning some science content. This can pose an even greater problem for ELLs. If ELLs have had science instruction in their home country, they often fare better than students who have their science instruction in English or in ESOL classes. Science does not seem so abstract to these students. Second language learners who come from cultures where science is not a part of their schooling or where literacy and schooling are minimal are at a greater disadvantage and will probably need more assistance to be successful in science classes in secondary school than ELLs who have studied science in their home countries. Again, teachers should be cognizant of the fact that the acquisition of academic language may take several more years than the language exhibited by the second language learner in ordinary social conversational situations (Cummins, 2001; Teenant et al., 1995). Here the ideas of Stoddard et al. (2002) may prove useful; their teachers see themselves as not only teachers of science but also teachers of language development.

An adolescent ELL may seem quite proficient in the everyday use of English because of his or her strong *social* language ability. This may give the impression that the ELL fully comprehends all English. However, in context-reduced science language and teaching, they may not yet have developed sufficient proficiency to manage the science content at the same level as their social language would indicate. This may cause them to fall behind in science class. Teachers of adolescent students must be aware of this possibility and consider the following features of science language usage that may pose difficulties for ELL.

The lexical density of something read or discussed in science can be very high; that is, many concept words or content words may be found in a short passage:

❖ Science words with very different meanings than the same word with the same spelling in everyday English. For example, mass, matter, conductor, state (e.g., gas, not gasoline).
❖ Use of the passive voice, such as, *The temperature of the solution was taken.* Who actually did this is left unknown to the reader or to the listener.
❖ Interconnected definitions and relationships, and special expressions of science.

When science teachers are aware of these potential difficulties, they can explain or have L1 students explain meanings. They can switch an explanation from the passive to the active voice to make thoughts more in line with what is familiar to ELLs. Science teachers who make science language comprehensible to ELLs may also be aiding L1 students who are struggling to understand the text and terminology or having difficulty comprehending passages and comprehending definitions. In this way, science teachers may be assisting more than just ELL students.

In terms of lexical density (the density of content words in a passage) or where two definitions are interconnected, teachers can review words and any previously learned definitions and show how the ideas relate to each other. Creating word banks will aid students' scientific literacy. When observing ELLs in classrooms, one can notice them utilizing the word wall to locate words that they want to use in writing. Making concept maps in groups may also aid students, especially if word banks are referred to in creating the concept map. Concept maps should help students to see the connections between ideas. Demonstrations and labs that illustrate a concept or principle are very helpful and make the science class interesting for all students. However, demonstrations should be followed by discussions and description with emphasis on the concept or principle that was

demonstrated. Involvement of ELLs regarding what students saw and learned as a result of the demonstration is important. Teenant et al. (1995) recommend that teachers not dilute the science content for ELLs, and suggest some of the following strategies for teachers working with ELLs.

1. Recognize that students' knowledge of English might not be adequate to comfortably write about the science being taught. In such cases allow ELLs to write, phrase questions, and express themselves in their first or home language.
2. Another possibility is finding other students or aides who are proficient in English and fluent in the language of the ELL and letting them assist the ELL (Tobin, 1998).
3. Tobin (1998) further suggests that the learning of science could be a bilingual experience for ELLs. They can access and utilize all their knowledge and thought structures without being required to do so in English. ELLs should be able to express what they actually do know and understand in the language most comfortable for them while they acquire greater fluency in science academic English.
4. Another strategy for assisting older ELLs when learning science and developing literacy is for teachers to use sentence frames or sentence builders. According to Carrier (2005), sentence frames allow ELLs to develop the ability to use science vocabulary in a grammatically correct format within partially formed sentences. Such sentences are not complete but need words filled in to finish the meaning. The sentences are structured to be grammatically sound but lack all the vocabulary that would be needed to make the sentence complete in meaning. Students would then insert words they feel are appropriate to the content. These frames allow ELLs to develop fluency and communicate ideas without the stress of attempting to write grammatically correct English (Carrier, 2005). An example would be a frame used when investigating cells in an inquiry lesson: "Animal cells have different _____ than plant cells," or, "Animal cells are like plant cells because _____" (Carrier, 2005). Frames may

also be used to describe the methodology used in an experiment or how a hypothesis might be created or tested.

In Already Crowded Curricula, Why Teach Science to ELLs?

In this age of testing and accountability, science learning is not always viewed as important in elementary programs. Science teaching may be subordinated to language arts and mathematics, the two areas most commonly tested at the elementary level. This is more prevalent in schools that have been labeled "low achieving," often the very schools that ELLs attend. In such schools, teachers may be told to not teach science (or social studies) in order to focus on reading, writing, and mathematics, considered the critical areas, because of a belief among some administrators that a laserlike focus on skill development will bring up test scores. No one would argue the importance of language arts and math in all children's learning. These subjects should occupy a large percentage of time in the overall elementary program. However, to eliminate content learning is shortsighted. Aside from literature, what do we read about, if not the content areas? Furthermore, the children in these "low-achieving schools" will have less access and knowledge of important ideas in science, less exposure to scientific thinking, and have difficulty understanding and achieving in high school science. It is also argued that ELL academic language may be delayed, weak, or never fully developed when science is de-emphasized in K–8 settings (NGSS Lead States, 2013).

Science is an important subject in school and will most likely become even more important in the future. Science discoveries and events occupy the media, with daily news reports about new medical and health findings, about space exploration, and now with much incoming information regarding the impacts of climate change. Natural disasters capture the public's attention, with a growing concern for the environment and the consequences of the human impact on our planet. In order to understand and respond appropriately, citizens will need a degree of scientific literacy.

Selected principles endorsed by the NSTA Position Statement include:

❖ Lessons, instruction, and curriculum for ELL students should be grounded in the NGSS (2013), the National Science Education Standards (NSES) of 1996, The Benchmarks for Scientific Literacy (1993), and state standards, and should promote inquiry (NRC, 2006).
❖ Accessing students' prior knowledge and their science content, and beginning with guided inquiry leading to more open ended inquiry, will allow ELLs to learn the practice of science (Amaral, Garrison, & Klentschy, 2002; Fradd & Lee, 1999; Rosebery & Warren, 2008).
❖ Literacy skills of reading, writing, speaking, and listening should be incorporated into science instruction to develop academic language and science content
❖ Recognition and respect for the cultural and linguistic background of ELLs is critical and should be integrated into the teaching of science so that students from linguistically diverse backgrounds value that background. This will assist in the development of ELL students' identities as science learners (Garcia & Lee, 2008; Rosebery & Warren, 2008).

Further recommendations supported by the NSTA 2010 position statement include the following that are addressed in this chapter:

❖ Students from culturally and linguistically different backgrounds from their teachers should be able to express and demonstrate what they know in a manner that may be unfamiliar to their teachers.
❖ Teachers use strategies to benefit the science learning of ELLs **and also** enhance their English language proficiency. Teachers meet regularly to share, discuss activities, experiences, and resources found helpful to ELL learning science.
❖ Opportunities for ELLs to work cooperatively in small groups, as well as opportunities to work independently, and in whole class settings.

- ELLs should be allowed to use many means of expressing and representing their science ideas, such as through gestures, pictures, text, graphically, and orally.
- While instruction should be academically rigorous and cognitively demanding, it may be helpful to ELLs to use their home language in their academic learning as needed.

It is imperative that resources be allocated for instructing ELLs so that they can engage in rigorous science learning which will allow them to make sufficient academic growth so as to reduce and close the science achievement gap.

Points to Remember

- The science and engineering practices in the Next Generation Science Standards offer many opportunities for teachers to assist English language learners in developing literacy and language while learning science.

- The learning of science should promote science literacy and greater awareness of science in the everyday life of students.

- Learning science enhances English language learners' academic language, which is critical to success in secondary school.

- Research has shown that inquiry-based science instruction has a positive effect on literacy, language, and critical thinking development.

- Children have a natural curiosity for science and scientific events.

- Learning science has some special difficulties for many students, as well as English language learners (e.g., the lexical density of science passages and science reading, new and unfamiliar meaning for already familiar words when used in the context of science, and the use of the passive voice).

- Hands-on science in cooperative groups is effective in aiding student understanding and enjoyment of science but must be facilitated and monitored by the teacher to ensure that English language learners are included and are benefiting from the group, and that the group is truly cooperative.

- Crosscutting science topics, such as climate change or other environmental issues, may not only interest and help linguistically and culturally diverse students learn science, but also increase their literacy and language development.

Social Studies from a Global Perspective: Effective Pedagogy for English Language Learners

KEY ISSUES

❖ Preparing teachers to face the challenges in teaching social studies to English language learners from a global perspective

❖ Teaching abstract concepts and skill sets in elementary social studies instruction

❖ Employing second/new language acquisition techniques in teaching social studies

The primary goal of effective social studies instruction is to pose higher intellectual challenges to English language learners (ELLs) and to engage ELLs in the skill sets inherent in social studies that are critical for participating citizens in the United States.

The cognitive expectations inherent in effective social studies instruction demand the development of high levels of literacy skills embedded in the understanding of abstract concepts, social science terminology, and familiarity with social studies specific background knowledge. Further, essential elements of effective social studies instruction include higher order thinking skills: the ability of students to collect and interpret information, draw conclusions, make generalizations and inferences, determine cause-and-effect relationships, find alternative courses of action, form hypotheses and predictions, and represent text visually (Chapin, 2013; Beal et al, 2009). In addition, the social studies are increasingly taught from a global perspective. Students of the twenty-first century must be equipped with the attitudes, knowledge, and skill sets necessary to meet the challenges of a rapidly changing, increasingly interdependent world (Kirkwood-Tucker, 2014; Subedi, 2010; Tye, 2009). However, many immigrant and refugee students who have come to the United States have not received social studies instruction in their native country and, thus, lack requisite social studies knowledge, the ability to understand abstract concepts, and a global perspective of the world.

The Social Studies

The field of social studies is derived from the social science disciplines of anthropology, psychology, sociology, criminology, geography, economics, political science, and history. The existing social studies curriculum in American elementary schools generally follows the expanding communities organizational pattern (Chapin, 2013; Halvorsen, 2009; Hanna, 1963). This approach is based on the premise that during each academic year, the learner should be introduced to an increasingly extended social environment, moving from examining self to family, community, neighborhood, nation, and the world around them. Students learn the skills to observe, record, and analyze roles of institutions and the individuals who comprise them, draw conclusions about the principles that govern them, and utilize these generalizations to gain understanding of human nature and human interactions across space and time (Beal & Bolick, 2013).

According to the National Council for the Social Studies (NCSS, 1982, 1994), the largest and most prestigious professional organization of social studies educators in the United States, the primary purpose of the social studies is to "help young people develop the ability to make informed and reasoned decisions for the public good as citizens of a culturally diverse, democratic society in an interdependent world."

The National Curriculum Standards for Social Studies (Herczog, 2009) also produced by the National Council for the Social Studies, call for "the promotion of civic competence—the knowledge, intellectual processes, and democratic dispositions required of students to be active and engaged participants in public life" (p. 3).

Global Perspectives

The overarching purpose of integrating a global perspective in social studies content is to develop a well-informed, competent, humanistic, and participatory citizenry in the global age. Global perspectives are designed to "cultivate in young people a perspective of the world which emphasizes the interconnections among cultures, species, and the planet"

(NCSS, 2010). Beal, Bolick & Martorella (2009) suggested that advocates of global perspectives require us to consider, "the greatest good for the greatest number, or the concerns of all nations, including our own" (p. 49).

Social studies taught from a global perspective emphasizes (a) the human experience is an increasingly globalized phenomenon in which people are constantly being influenced by transnational, cross-cultural, multicultural, multiethnic interactions; (b) there is a variety of actors on the world stage; (c) humankind is an integral part of the world environment; (d) there are linkages among present social, political, and ecological realities and alternative futures; and (e) citizen participation in world affairs is important.

The national debate on the integration of a global perspective in American schools found expression in the publication of subject-specific standards by national professional organizations. For example, the National Council for the Accreditation of Teachers (NCATE), the American Association of Colleges for Teacher Education (AACTE), the International Global Education Commission of the Association for Supervision and Curriculum Development (ASCD), and the National Council for the Social Studies (NCSS) strongly recommended that global perspectives become an integral component in teacher education programs.

Pedagogy

Abstract social studies concepts such as citizenship, justice, freedom, democracy, and globalization are difficult concepts for children to grasp, regardless of their linguistic background. ELLs, however, face the dual problem of having to acquire the meaning of abstract concepts as well as the linguistic skills to comprehend these abstract concepts. Mehlinger (1981) in his classical discourse on hypothetical situations suggested several ideas that can be used to engage students in discussing their views on a given concept. For example, if students are asked about the concept of justice, they have no idea of its meaning. However, if they are asked what is fair and what is not fair, they are keenly aware of their respective meanings. To elementary students, the concept of justice is synonymous with fairness (Weisman & Hansen, 2007). Chapin (2013) also suggested that the concept of justice is synonymous with fairness and it is easily illustrated by using mock trials. This is true of native English speakers in mainstream classes. Additionally, be aware of background information that your student might have learned in the home country that differs from facts taught in the United States. For example, in South America students might be taught that there are five continents because they are grouped differently. Show students why schools in the United States teach facts as they do (Ariza, 2009).

But what about the ELLs who lack the linguistic skills that are necessary to comprehend the meaning of the concept? Cruz and Thorton (2012) suggested that visuals can "offer concrete representations of abstract concepts" (p. 100). If ELLs are provided with a visual of an example of "fair" and then provided with a visual of "not fair," then they are keenly aware of their respective meanings. The following three lessons provide selected examples of pedagogy that make social studies content, concepts, skills, and global perspectives comprehensible to the ELL.

Lesson One

Concept: Geography

The language of social studies content is a complex phenomenon. ELLs are expected to comprehend difficult terminology, an essential skill in comprehending social studies and global education instruction. Textbooks often fail to treat key terms adequately. Frequently, only ten words or fewer are explained for an entire chapter. Textbook glossaries only contain words highlighted in the chapters and in most instances, the vocabulary is specialized content vocabulary (Templeton et al., 2009; Chapin, 2013). Teachers cannot take for granted that ELLs possess an understanding of the meaning of key words and other difficult terminology used in social studies texts.

Materials

Globe, wall world map, large Styrofoam balls (or inflatable beach balls), string, glue, crayons, atlases, handouts of continents, enlarged continent pieces in proportion to Styrofoam or beach ball, construction paper, transparencies, CD: "We Are the World."

Teaching Episode 1: Latitudes and Longitudes

Mr. Seitz writes the content objectives of the lesson on the board with the key terminology underlined. For example, one content objective reads: Students will be able to demonstrate latitude and longitude on the world map. Mr. Seitz reads each content objective slowly and deliberately as he points to the objectives and circles each key term in different colors. Holding up a globe and turning it on its axis, Mr. Seitz informs students that the world is round. He then points to the large wall map, telling students that the world is also shown flat on maps. Geographers have created artificial lines called "latitude" and "longitude" that assist us in finding places on the world map. Mr. Seitz points out the latitudes and longitudes on the world map. He turns on the projector to show the latitude and longitude transparency.

Then Mr. Seitz explains that latitude lines extend horizontally from east to west. He demonstrates their direction by extending his arms in horizontal fashion, perpendicular to his body. The longitude lines are vertical lines, extending from north to south. He stretches one hand high into the air and the other hand toward the floor. Mr. Seitz asks a native and a nonnative speaker of English to come to the wall map and follow a latitude and longitude line with their finger.

Subsequently, Mr. Seitz places a blank transparency on the overhead with the heading "Geography Vocabulary." He slowly lists in printed letters the concepts of latitude and longitude. He asks students to write the terms on their vocabulary page under the heading "Geography Vocabulary."

Mr. Seitz continues his lesson by telling students that the most important latitude line is called the equator, which divides the world into two halves. He again places the latitude/longitude globe transparency on the overhead and prints "equator" on the central latitude line and thickens the existing equator line. Then he tells students that the most important longitude line, which divides the world vertically, is called the prime meridian. He prints "prime meridian" along the central longitude line on the same transparency and thickens the existing prime meridian line.

Then Mr. Seitz walks to the large wall map and moves his finger from east to west along the equator, slowly pronouncing the term "equator." He moves his finger slowly along the prime meridian from north to south, pronouncing the term "prime meridian." He points to zero degrees (0°) at each end of the two lines, showing his students that both the equator and the prime meridian hold a zero-degree position on the world map. Mr. Seitz then places the vocabulary transparency on the overhead and slowly adds "equator" and "prime meridian" to the vocabulary list. He asks students to add the two terms to their vocabulary list.

Then, Mr. Seitz asks a non-English speaker to come to the wall map to show the locations of the equator and the prime meridian. He asks, "What is the name of this latitude?" as he stretches out his arms in horizontal fashion. Mr. Seitz then reaches his right hand toward the ceiling and his left hand toward the floor, asking, "What is the name of the longitude that divides the world into two halves?"

Teaching Episode 2: Cardinal Directions

Mr. Seitz tells his students, "It is important for you to understand directions so you do not get lost when you go somewhere. There are four cardinal directions that help us find the right directions." He places the cardinal direction transparency on the overhead.

Mr. Seitz states, "The cardinal directions are located on the top, bottom, left, and right sides of the world map." As he shows each direction, he states, "North is located on the top of the map. South is located on the bottom of the map. East is located to the right of the map when you stand in front of the map. And west is located on your left." As he circles the cardinal directions of the content objectives, Mr. Seitz tells his students that the directions are generally abbreviated or shortened on the map by a capital letter. He adds *E* next to east, *W* next to west, *N* next to north, and *S* next to south. He places the four letters in their proper locations on the globe.

Mr. Seitz then points to each as he slowly and deliberately pronounces the terms again. He asks the class to recite the four cardinal directions as he points to them on the transparency. He then asks students to pronounce the four directions as he points to them on the wall map. He asks students to add the terms to their vocabulary list.

Mr. Seitz concludes by saying, "Here in the United States we call the four directions north, south, east, and west. In Germany, the German people call east 'Osten,' west 'Westen,' north 'Norden,' and south 'Sueden.' In Spanish-speaking countries east is called 'Este,' west is called 'Oeste,' north is called 'Norte,' and South is called 'Sur.' As you can see, people of different countries around the world use their own language in expressing the same concepts in geography."

Teaching Episode 3: Hemispheres

Mr. Seitz places the hemisphere transparency on the overhead.

He informs students, "Now we are going to learn that the world can be divided into four quarters or sections. The equator and prime meridian divide the world into four sections called 'hemispheres.'" He points to each hemisphere as he explains that the equator divides the world into the northern and southern hemispheres, and the prime meridian divides the world into the eastern and western hemispheres. Mr. Seitz circles the terms in the content objectives listed on the board. He then walks to the wall world map and points out the northern, southern, eastern, and western hemispheres on the wall map as he repeats each concept. Then Mr. Seitz places the vocabulary transparency on the overhead and slowly adds "hemisphere," "eastern," "western," "northern," and "southern" to the existing list of terms. He asks students to add the concepts to their own list. He invites several native and nonnative English speakers to come to the wall map to point out the northern, southern, eastern, and western hemispheres to the class.

Teaching Episode 4: Continents

Mr. Seitz continues the geography lesson by telling students that most people on earth live on land.

There are large pieces of land in the world that are called continents. They are named Africa, Antarctica, Australia, Eurasia, North America, and South America. (Social Studies in other nations might teach another way of looking at things, like the number of continents. Make sure students' prior knowledge corresponds to what you are teaching. For example, in South America they might teach that there are five continents.) He points out each continent on the world map as he simultaneously circles the name of each continent in the content objectives listed on the board. He then calls on several students to come up to the world map to point to each continent, asking them to state the name of each continent. Mr. Seitz asks yes/no questions as he asks students the correct name of each continent. For example, he points to Australia and asks, "Is this the continent of Africa?" The students respond, "No, it is Australia." Mr. Seitz points to North America and asks, "Is this the continent of Australia?" The students respond, "No, it is the continent of North America."

Then Mr. Seitz switches to either/or questions. For example, he asks, "Is this the continent of Antarctica or Eurasia?" as he points to Eurasia. The students respond, "Eurasia." He continues, "Is this the continent of South America or Australia?" as he points to the continent of Australia, and so on, until all continents are covered and he has received all correct answers. Then, Mr. Seitz turns on the overhead and writes "continent," "Africa," "Antarctica," "Australia," "Eurasia," "North America," and "South America" on the existing vocabulary transparency, asking students to do the same in their notebook.

Mr. Seitz asks students to form their preassigned groups of two native speakers and two English language learners. He places a transparency with individual continents on the overhead. (Europe and Asia are considered one continent referred to as Eurasia.)

Pointing to the individual continents, Mr. Seitz asks students to cut out the six continents from the handout distributed to them and label and color them. He calls on one group to attach the continents to the corresponding continents on the world map. He asks the remaining groups to paste the continents correctly into a round circle representing the globe on construction paper and place their world on the pre-assigned "geography wall."

Teaching Episode 5: Vocabulary

Mr. Seitz states, "Today, we have learned many geographic terms. Let's see if you have all of them written down in your vocabulary list." Mr. Seitz calls on several students to stand next to the overhead to read the terms while he indicates which ones to read. For example, the first student reads all the words that start with the letters "c" and "l." The second student will read all the continents; the third student will read the cardinal directions. Afterward, Mr. Seitz gives directions to the class for them to read those words.

geography	continent
latitude	Africa
longitude	Antarctica
cardinal directions	Australia
east (E)	Eurasia
west (W)	North America
north (N)	South America
south (S)	

Mr. Seitz tells students, "We are also going to add four more geography terms to our geography vocabulary list today." He challenges the class, "What part of the world have we left out?" (oceans) "What are the names of these oceans?" (Arctic Ocean, Atlantic Ocean, Indian Ocean, and Pacific Ocean). He points to each ocean on the wall world map and repeats the name of each ocean three times. He states, "Let's add the four major oceans to our vocabulary list." He walks to the overhead and writes the names of the four oceans on the transparency as students add them to their vocabulary list.

Teaching Episode 6: Create your World

Mr. Seitz tells his students, "The next activity will complete our geography lesson. Before we do that, I want to thank you for working so hard in learning new words in studying the geography of the world. Now, I want you to combine the geography terms learned into a final product. I want you to create your own world by using the enlarged continent pieces I have prepared for you and the Styrofoam (beach) balls. This is going to be cooperative learning experience—so pair up with your partner. You have thirty minutes to finish this activity. Let's read together the instruction sheet that I am distributing to you now."

Handout: Create Your Own World

Using the Styrofoam balls or inflated beach balls:

1. Draw and label the equator and prime meridian.
2. Place a zero degree (0°) at their proper locations.
3. Place the abbreviated letters of the four cardinal directions in their proper locations.
4. Draw lines to divide the world into four hemispheres.
5. Label the hemispheres.
6. Cut out, color, and label the continents.
7. Paste continents to their correct location on the Styrofoam ball or inflated globe.
8. Color and label the four largest oceans.
9. Write your names on a paper strip and glue it on the top of your world.
10. Attach a string and hang your world from our clothesline.

Mr. Seitz walks around the classroom assisting students with their work. He plays the CD: "We Are the World" as students construct "their world."

Reflections

In this activity, students learned new knowledge directly from their teacher rather than from written text. Mr. Seitz employs several techniques to make his teaching comprehensible to ELLS: (a) He writes the content objectives in simplified terms on the board, (b) he pronounces them orally, (3) he highlights visually the key terms embedded in the content objectives including the parentese/caregiver speech, making content comprehensible, and organizing instruction from simple to complex and scaffolding (Zainuddin et al, 2011).

As he demonstrates the key terms on the world map, (a) he underlines, colors, circles, and systematically points to them; (b) he reinforces key terms by demonstrating them directly on the wall map and in hands-on activities in group settings; (c) he demonstrates the new terms visually on the transparency, and (d) he requires students to practice the key terms orally and to write them in their notebooks. Mr. Seitz indirectly employs peer teaching, an often underestimated learning process in the classroom. Repetition, slow deliberate speech, reinforcement, visualization, and application in the acquisition of key social studies terminology are effective strategies in making new content comprehensible to English language learners. The pedagogy employed includes the methodology of content-based language learning where "teachers use instructional materials, learning tasks, and classroom techniques from academic content areas as vehicles for developing language" (Morales-Jones, 2011, p. 97).

Note: Teach the lesson over a two-day period as appropriate.

Lesson Two

Concept: Justice

This lesson illustrates how the social studies abstract concept of justice can be made comprehensible to ELLs. A strategy for ELLs to comprehend the concept of justice is to demonstrate the unequal or disproportionate distribution of the world's resources. The pedagogy employed includes the methodology of visualization and simplification of text. The pedagogy employed here includes the modification of elaboration.

For example, a visual representation of children and two slices of a pie, a smiling child holding a large piece of pie and a sad looking child holding a smaller piece of pie, provide children with a clear sense of unfairness.

The teaching of the concept of justice from a global perspective can be achieved if the teaching strategies follow the principles of global pedagogy. One element of global pedagogy is the discussion of global issues that affect other nations and their people. When the teacher moves from the concept of different pie sizes and two nameless children in an unidentified country to the unequal or disproportionate distribution of resources to people inhabiting the earth, the concept of justice acquires global properties. In the typical classroom of ELLs, a frequent methodology to demonstrate the worldwide, uneven distribution of resources is accomplished by having students extract specific information from text or teacher's brief lecture and demonstrations. For ELLs, the teacher makes the information comprehensible by using visuals such as graphs or charts representing the written text. This strategy simplifies length and complexity of text by reducing information to specific elements in the lesson to be learned.

Materials

Transparency or poster: children with unequal pie slices; examples of resources (books; pencils; backpacks); "baguette" (French bread); world wall map; chart of the world's population on continents and the world's distribution of resources per continent

Teaching Episode 1

Mrs. Romanova begins her lesson by showing students either a transparency or poster that gives a visual representation of two children with different pie sizes. She informs students, "Today's lesson addresses the concept of justice. This concept is synonymous with fairness." She writes justice = fairness in big letters on the board.

Teaching Episode 2

At this point in the lesson, ELLs must first possess an understanding of the concept of "resources" before engaging them in further concept development (Peregoy & Boyle, 2008). Mrs. Romanova writes "resources" in huge, colorful letters on the board. She states, "We have many resources in this classroom. For example, we have books. Books are resources you can use to find information. Pencils are resources. We use pencils as a resource to help us write. You have backpacks to put your school stuff in." Mrs. Romanova places a poster or a transparency on the overhead that shows books, pencils, backpacks representing the concept of resources. Mrs. Romanova uses "explicit" vocabulary in which she specifically targets a word for instruction, in this case "resources" (Taboda & Rutherford, 2011).

Teaching Episode 3

Mrs. Romanova divides her class into six groups of students representing the approximate population size of the continents of Africa, Asia, Europe, North America, South America, and Oceania listed on the world population chart. Then, she reads from the chart while pointing out on the graph the percentages of each resource (unequal) available to the population on each continent.

World Population per Continent in 2013		World Resources Distribution of Populations Living below US$2 a Day	
Continent	Population	Percentage	Percentage
Asia	4,302 billion	60.3	75.5
Africa	1,100 billion	15.4	22.0
North America	352 million	4.9	0
South America/ Caribbean	606 million	8.5	2.6
Europe	740 million	10.4	0
Oceania incl. Australia	38 million	0.5	0
World	7,137 billion	100.0	00.0

Source: Population Reference Bureau 2014
Source: World Bank 2014

Mrs. Romanova explains that 60.3 percent of the world's people live in Asia but three quarters or 75.5 percent of its population lives on less than US$2 a day; that Africans compose 15.4 percent of the world's people but almost one fifth of its population (22 percent) lives on less than US$2 a day; and that the South American/Caribbean people comprise 8.5 percent of the world's population but only receive 2.6 percent of the world's resources.

Teaching Episode 4

Mrs. Romanova asks students to sit on the floor. (Be certain that this practice is culturally acceptable to everyone. Some students may be uncomfortable sitting on the floor due to their particular family or cultural mores or beliefs. In that case, allow them to sit on an appropriate mat, chair, or stool [Ariza, 2009].)

She cuts the baguette according to the percentage of resources available to the population of each continent and hands it to each group representing Asia, Africa, and South America/Caribbean. Then she gives an entire baguette to each of the people of the European, North American, and Oceanian continent. She asks:

"Class, is this fair? Is this just? What happens when people do not get enough resources?" (Gives students time to think; waits for answers). Students should be upset! She slowly continues:

- ❖ What is another name for fair? (just)
- ❖ What is another name for fairness? (justice)
- ❖ What is another name for unfair? (unjust)
- ❖ What is another name for unfairness? (injustice)

Mrs. Romanova prints the concepts in large letters on the board and asks students to copy them into their notebook.

Note: This activity can also be implemented with using peanut M&Ms or cookies.

Lesson Three

Concept: Respect

The teaching of universal values is an essential element of a global education (Kirkwood-Tucker, 2014; Subedi, 2010). It is a critical aspect of social studies instruction that includes global issues such as ozone depletion, global warming, hunger, poverty, overpopulation, lack of education, child trafficking, and the spread of HIV/AIDS and are shared by all inhabitants of Earth. Universal values promote international understanding and empathy. They bond human families regardless of ability, age, class, culture, ethnicity, gender, race, or sexual orientation.

ELLs and their parents are immigrants from many countries around the world. They share many values with Americans, such as family, education, employment, opportunities, and quality of life.

One commonality among ELLs and their native language counterparts is respecting Mother Earth.

Despite advanced agricultural technology and scientific progress, the land areas of the world's continents are being increasingly depleted of precious nutrients. More and more land loses its fertility as the need for food increases with a growing world population. To respect Mother Earth is the responsibility of every individual living on earth. The concept is made comprehensible to ELLs with visual supports, gestures, guided practice, and role-play (Peregoy & Boyle, 2008; Zainuddin et al., 2011).

Teaching Episode 1

Materials

Cloth earth ball or regular globe; candle; pictures of nature; plastic knives; paper plates; napkins; handout showing flowers, bonsai tree, pine cones, rocks, sand, pictures of a waterfall and mountains with a blank line next to each item

Mrs. Chang forms students' desks into one large circle prior to students' arrival. In the middle of the circle, she places on a small table: flowers, a bonsai tree, pine cones, rocks, sand, and pictures of a waterfall and mountains. After students take their seats, she holds up the earth ball and informs them, "My students, today we are learning why it is important to respect Mother Earth." She hands the earth ball to the student nearest to her and asks the student to touch it gently and then hand it to the next student, and so on. After all students have touched the earth ball, Mrs. Chang places the ball amid the display on the table and lights a candle. The teacher then bows to the display. She walks to the board and prints "respect" in big, colorful letters.

Then, Mrs. Chang distributes a handout showing the items on the table (flowers, a bonsai tree, pine cones, rocks, sand, pictures of a waterfall and mountains) and asks students to write "respect" on the blank line next to each picture. Then she points to the board and asks, "What does this say?" The students respond with "respect." Then, she walks to the center of the circle, smiles and bows slowly before her students. She tells students, "I have respect for you." She smiles as she looks into each student's eyes, stating, "To respect others and their culture is a very important universal value."

Teaching Episode 2

Mrs. Chang asks a native English speaker and an ELL to sit on the floor in the circle. She asks students to take turns to hold up each item asking all other students to bow to the item. After the ritual, the teacher states, "We have respect for the flowers. We have respect for the bonsai tree," etc. until she has covered all items on the table. Then, Mrs. Chang asks the students to stand. She holds up the earth ball and asks students to show respect for the world by bowing to Mother Earth. Then Mrs. Chang asks, "What are we doing?" The students respond, "Showing respect."

Reflections

In this lesson, Mrs. Chang met four objectives that facilitated the acquisition of social studies content in comprehensible fashion for English language learners: (a) She conveyed to students that the globe simulates earth or Mother Earth; (b) she achieved concept attainment by multiple repetitions of the word respect; (c) she provided understanding why it is important to respect Mother Earth; and (d) she demonstrated a global perspective by showing that Mother Earth belongs to all people of the earth and must be respected. Mrs. Chang employed pedagogy that included gestures, repetition, deliberate speech, visualization, demonstration, and active student involvement to ensure content comprehension.

Points to Remember

❖ Identifying basic geographic concepts on the world map such as cardinal directions, continents, hemispheres, latitude, longitude, and oceans comprise essential skills in social studies instruction.

❖ Teaching abstract concepts to ELLs such as democracy, justice, respect, and universal values require examples and extensive visualization and repetition techniques to convey their intrinsic complexity.

❖ Integrating higher order thinking skills in social studies teaching includes collecting and interpreting information, drawing conclusions, making generalizations and inferences, determining cause-and-effect relationships, finding alternative courses of action, forming hypotheses, and making predictions.

❖ Infusing a global perspective to social studies content by integrating information and examples about the larger world and its people is a moral responsibility of teachers in the twenty-first century.

Special Education and the Linguistically Diverse Student

KEY ISSUES

❖ Identification and assessment of English language learners (ELLs) with disabilities

❖ Educational services for ELLs with disabilities

❖ Effective instruction for ELLs with disabilities

❖ Referral and assessment procedures for giftedness

❖ Identification of linguistically diverse gifted students

❖ Challenging the linguistically diverse gifted student

❖ Application of Common Core Standards to students with disabilities who are linguistically diverse students

Mrs. Killcoyne teaches in an inclusive third grade class. Her students' ability levels and learning needs are diverse. Of the twenty-nine children enrolled in her class, three students have been identified as having learning disabilities, one student has been identified as gifted, and five students are ELLs.

Maria, one of the ELLs in the class, has recently moved to Florida from her native country of Brazil. Mrs. Killcoyne has noticed that despite Maria's limited proficiency with the English language, her work is consistently creative and imaginative. Maria has an intense interest in science, particularly as it relates to animals; loves to read books (written in Portuguese); has demonstrated artistic talent; has excellent interpersonal skills; and learns most concepts rapidly. Maria's parents report that she spends most evenings doing her homework, reading, and writing or illustrating short stories in both English and Portuguese.

Based on Maria's learning characteristics and demonstrated ability, Mrs. Killcoyne has decided to challenge Maria by having her work in cooperative groups with high-ability learners, providing many opportunities for Maria to use high level thinking skills, and finding opportunities to nurture her artistic and creative abilities. In addition, Mrs. Killcoyne has decided to maintain an assessment portfolio of Maria's work (in both languages) that will be submitted, along with a nomination form to begin the process of identifying Maria as a gifted student.

Another of the ELLs, Juan, has been identified as having learning disabilities. Although Juan receives the majority of his instruction from Mrs. Killcoyne, the special education resource teacher comes into the general education classroom for thirty minutes a day during reading and works with Juan and the other students with learning disabilities on vocabulary and reading comprehension. Additionally, Juan leaves the general education classroom on Tuesdays and Thursdays during the language arts period to receive bilingual education services.

English language learners (ELLs) such as those in the vignette present unique challenges for educators. Teachers find it challenging to distinguish between the difficulty of acquiring a second language and a learning disability. Likewise, the complexity of acquiring a second language often masks gifts and talents that ELL students might possess. Thus, the placement of ELLs

> in special education is arguably a more complex issue than the placement of culturally and linguistically diverse students more generally, mainly because linguistic and immigration factors are added to the composite of cultural, social, and ethnic influences. These added factors force us to consider not only the problem of overrepresentation but also of underrepresentation in special education (Donovan & Cross, 2002, as cited in Klingner, Artiles, & Barletta, 2006, p. 109).

Identification and Assessment of ELLs with Disabilities

The population of ELLs attending schools in the United States continues to increase (U.S. Census Bureau, 2003), and it is estimated that by the year 2030, about 40 percent of the school population will speak English as a second language (USDOE & NICHD, 2003), representing the most rapidly growing segment of the U.S. student population.

Due to the complexities surrounding culture, language, and learning, ELLs are at a greater risk for being identified as having a disability (Artiles, Hary, Reschly, & Chinn, 2002). Even so, many districts do not have mechanisms in place for identifying ELLs with disabilities as a specific subgroup of students, and 75 percent of districts providing services for ELLs with disabilities do not provide programs de-

signed especially for these students (Zehler et al., 2003). The data about ELLs suggests that they are most likely to be identified as having a learning disability (56 percent), with the second most common category being speech and language impairments (24 percent) (USDOE, 2003). This is most likely due to the fact that characteristics of students acquiring a new language in many ways parallel those of students with language and learning disabilities, making it difficult to determine who actually has a disability (Ortiz, 1997).

Traditionally, students have most often been required to demonstrate a discrepancy between IQ and achievement (e.g., math or reading performance) to qualify for special education services due to a learning disability. Such discrepancy has been identified by determining their potential or ability, usually with an intelligence test, and comparing that with their achievement, as measured by reading or math tests. When English is a second or third language, it is difficult to determine if a learning disability exists because standardized intelligence and achievement testing procedures primarily assess language. Such tests are often biased against ELL students. "On many tests, being able to answer questions correctly too often depends on having specific culturally based information or knowledge. If students have not been exposed to that information, then they will not be able to answer certain questions at all or will answer them in a way that is considered 'incorrect' within the majority culture" (Waterman, 2000, p. 19). This can lead to misdiagnosis that can result in disproportionate representation of culturally and linguistically diverse (CLD) students (including ELLs) in special education.

When ELLs are evaluated for special education, examiners should proceed with extreme caution. Qualified professionals should be used to conduct the assessment. Such personnel "should have a good understanding of the first and second language acquisition theory, effective instructional practices for ELLs with disabilities, and the influence of culture and socioeconomic status on school performance" (Ortiz & Yates, 2001, as cited in Muller & Markowitz, 2004, p. 5).

The assessment process should be as free of cultural and linguistic bias as possible. Measurement devices used in the assessment process must not discriminate on the basis of race, culture, or language, and standardized tests should be validated for the purposes for which they are used (Muller & Markowitz, 2004). Before conducting any formal testing of an ELL, it is vital to determine the student's preferred language and to conduct a comprehensive language assessment in both English and the native language using equivalent instruments and procedures. This will permit the examiner to be able to compare what students know in each language and to be able to describe what students know cumulatively. When tests or evaluation materials are not available in the student's native language, examiners may find it necessary to use English language instruments. This must be done with extreme caution, as it is a practice fraught with the possibility of misinterpretation. Adaptations such as paraphrasing instructions, providing a demonstration of how test tasks are to be performed, reading test items to the student, allowing the student to respond verbally rather than in writing, or allowing the student to use a dictionary may be used. However, if any such adaptations are made, it is important that they be fully detailed in the report describing the student's test performance.

Other assessment procedures must also be an integral part of collecting information about the student such as thorough interviews and observations. It may be particularly useful to gather information from the home environment, which will help in the understanding of the student within his or her own culture. The information from these sources should be cross-validated with the results of the standardized tests. If the student's performance is low on both formal and informal assessments, it is more likely that the student has a disability (Muller & Markowitz, 2004).

Alternatively, the reauthorization of the Individuals with Disabilities Education Improvement Act (IDEIA, 2004) provides states with the option of discontinuing the use (though it does not require abandoning the use) of IQ achievement discrepancy criterion as the major determining factor for identifying the existence of a learning disability. Now states may use response to intervention (RTI) criteria as part of the special education identification process.

RTI is an intervention model consisting of evidence-based, multi-tiered interventions that increase in intensity (e.g., amount of instruction, group size) based on how well students are succeeding in a less intensive instructional format. The four key components of the RTI model are as follows: (1) high quality, research-based instruction matched to the needs of students, (2) monitor student's learning over time to determine their level and rate of performance, (3) provide interventions of increasing intensity when students continue to struggle, and (4) make educational decisions based on data. Though RTI models may be implemented in various ways and differ in the number of levels of support provided, the overall framework of the model is the same. Generally, the Tier 1 is high quality (evidence-based) appropriate classroom instruction, behavioral support, and ongoing progress monitoring (universal screening) within the general education classroom. The second tier is implemented for students who do not make progress in Tier 1 and is characterized by additional intensive instructional support (double dose) provided by the general education classroom teacher. It is in this second tier that ELLs can be assembled for additional small-group intensive instruction. Using scientifically based interventions in an RTI model with ELLs for prevention instruction can improve the early literacy skills and overall reading outcomes for these students (Linan-Thompson, Cirino, & Vaughn, 2007). Kamps et al. (2007) reported that a three-tiered RTI model, with Tier 2 addressing the needs of ELLs in small group instruction, resulted in higher gains than English as a second language (ESL) instruction alone. However, when students do not adequately respond to the second tier of intervention, they may qualify for special education or for referral for evaluation for possible placement in special education. Thus, Tier 3 is for students who need intensive individualized interventions either in small groups or one-on-one, which may be special education.

During the referral phase, general education teachers play an important role in ensuring that ELLs have had adequate evidence-based instruction as supported by the progress monitoring data, and in summarizing student progress for the multi-disciplinary team (MDT). Special educators, ELL teachers, and parents can serve as consultants to general educators on whether academic difficulties reflect poor English proficiency, a transition to academic language development, or a possible learning disability. The MDT must evaluate the results of the instruction and the status of language proficiency at each tier and decide if struggling ELL students received adequate instruction and intervention prior to referral for special education assessment (Rinaldi & Samson, 2008, pg. 7).

The notion that instructional practices at each tier of the RTI model are based on scientific evidence about what works is fundamental to the concept of RTI. For ELLs, this means instruction must be "culturally responsive" and validated with students like those for whom it is intended. RTI approaches that are culturally responsive consider the cultural and linguistic diversity of students and focus on understanding external or environmental factors that affect their opportunity to learn in addition to personal factors. For RTI to work, team members must have expertise in cultural and linguistic diversity and be knowledgeable about interventions that have been effective with CLD students with different needs. Second language acquisition, best practices for ELLs, and cultural variations should be considered when assessing student progress, designing interventions, and interpreting ELLs' responses to interventions. ELLs benefit from teachers who have the knowledge and skills to provide adequate instruction and who are highly interested in ensuring their ELL students make adequate progress.

Finally, schools using RTI models must inform and involve the families of ELL students in the pro-

cess. In keeping with the requirements of IDEA, families should be notified early (at least by the second tier) if their child appears to be struggling and the school intends to try specific interventions to help. Schools should (1) describe the RTI process, including the length of time (e.g., number of weeks, number of interventions per day) that will be allowed for the intervention to have a positive effect; (2) provide families with written intervention plans that are clearly explained, including a description of the intervention, who will be responsible for providing the intervention, and the location where the intervention will be provided (e.g., general education classroom); (3) provide families with a written description of the process monitoring approach, including regular updates about their child's progress, a progress monitoring schedule, and how frequently parents will receive reports; and (4) obtain families' consent (Vaughn, Boss, & Schumm, 2007).

Educational Services for ELLs with Disabilities

Decisions about appropriate services for students identified as both limited in English proficiency and disabled can be quite complex (McLoughlin & Lewis, 2001). Providing these students with some combination of multicultural, bilingual, and special education approaches can provide them with the unique education they need to achieve their potential. For example, students may receive "bilingual education with support from special education, special education with bilingual support services, special education with a bilingual teacher, or special education with a bilingual aide, volunteer, or peer tutor" (Plata, 1982; Yates & Ortiz, 1998, as cited in McLoughlin & Lewis, 2001, p. 490).

The four major partners involved in developing the curriculum for the ELL who is disabled are the parents, the general education teacher, the bilingual teacher, and the special education teacher. This team should undertake the following:

❖ Meet as a team to begin the planning process and outline the planning steps.
❖ Become familiar with the culture and language background of the child.

- Become familiar with the special learning style and educational needs of the child.
- Prepare an individualized education plan with short- and long-term goals (an IEP).
- Develop individualized lessons and materials appropriate to the child's exceptionality.
- Modify individualized lessons and materials using a "cultural screen" and sensitivity.
- Refer to resource people for assistance and cooperation in instruction; coordinate services.
- Evaluate the child's ongoing progress and develop a new IEP, materials, and so forth, as needed.
- Start the cycle over (Collier & Kalk, 1989, p. 207).

Effective Instruction for ELLs with Disabilities

Effective instruction for ELLs with disabilities must include an emphasis on language. In determining which language to use for instruction, special educators must consider the language used in the home, student's stage of development in the native and English languages, extent to which the student's disabilities affect language and literacy development, current and future needs for both languages, strength of each language for instructional purposes, and language preferences of the student and their parents (Cloud, 2002). Researchers have determined that ELLs with disabilities seem to benefit from dual language development (Bruck, 1982). That is, both instruction in the native language and *instruction in English language development are critical. According to Gersten and Baker (2000), effective instruction for ELLs includes five critical components:*

- Build vocabulary as an anchor to curriculum: Teach seven or fewer new words that convey key concepts of the academic content being learned.
- Use visuals: Develop visual aids (graphic organizers, concept and story maps, word banks) to help provide a concrete structure for thinking about new information.
- Implement cooperative learning and peer tutoring: Structure groups of students who question each other and provide feedback about content comprehension.
- Use the native language strategically: Use levels of English at which students are fluent, and introduce complexity in students' native language.
- Adjust language demands: Accept varying levels of language output as determined by the cognitive demands of the learning situation (pp. 93–94).

Teaching approaches that ELLs with disabilities appear to benefit from include multisensory teaching approaches, computer-assisted and other technology-supported approaches, learning style–based approaches, and whole language process approaches (Cloud, 2002). Additionally, instruction for ELLs with mild and moderate disabilities should emphasize content-based and cognitive learning strategies, whereas ELLs with more severe disabilities need life skills and vocationally related instruction.

Finally, classroom and school environments must be supportive of cultural and linguistic diversity and accommodating of individual differences. Schools must be caring communities that reflect the philosophy that all students can learn, that educators are responsible for helping all students to learn, and that parents from culturally and linguistically diverse (CLD) backgrounds are seen as partners in the education of their children (Cummins, 1989, 1994). CLD students represent a large segment of the school population. Teachers must be better prepared to work with these children, some of whom will have disabilities and others who will be gifted. The next part of this chapter explores linguistically diverse learners who are gifted.

The Linguistically Diverse Gifted Student

Gifted students can be found in every racial, ethnic, socioeconomic, and linguistic group; however, there is well-documented concern for the underrepresentation of CLD students in gifted programs throughout our country (Castellano, 2004; Ford, Trottman Scott, Moore, & Amos, 2013) Historically, CLD students have been overlooked for gifted programs; they remain unidentified and underserved in our schools and subsequently have no opportunity to have their gifts recognized or nurtured. The problem of underrepresentation is further compounded for students who have not acquired proficiency in the English language. As Castellano clearly stated, "One does not need to speak English in order to be gifted or academically talented" (2002, p. 96). Despite the fact that being able to speak two (or more) languages requires keen cognitive ability, bilingualism is frequently treated as a handicap in need of remedial efforts rather than a strength that requires enrichment (Angelelli, Enright, & Valdéz, 2002; Valdéz, 2003). Failure to identify and cultivate giftedness among our diverse student population is unfair to these students and to our society.

Several factors have contributed to the underrepresentation of linguistically diverse students in gifted and talented programs nationwide. Some of these factors include (a) teachers' perceptions of diverse students and lack of training in the identification of gifted students from diverse backgrounds (Ford & Milner, 2005; Kitano & Espinosa, 1995; Peterson & Margolin, 1997); (b) methodological problems affecting assessment of CLD children and test bias (Castellano, 2004; Joseph & Ford, 2006); and (c) reliance on a deficit-based paradigm that makes recognizing linguistically diverse students' strengths and talents less likely.

Teacher Perceptions and Initial Referrals

The identification of gifted learners typically begins with teacher recognition of a student's potential followed by a referral for assessment. This initial process should be nonbiased and result in a number of referrals for linguistically diverse learners in proportion to the demographics of the overall school population (Castellano, 2004). What happens when teachers have low academic expectations for CLD students or when teachers are unaware of what to look for and how to recognize gifted potential within their CLD student population? The result is selected referrals. In other words, teachers, as the gatekeepers for entrance into gifted programs, look for and refer students who possess the characteristics they perceive *reflect gifted potential. Teachers' percep-*

tions and expectations of low achievement can be a major contributor to the small numbers of CLD students in gifted programs (Joseph & Ford, 2005). A teacher's perception of a student's performance interacts with her/his own belief systems and biases and influence of the dominant culture. Research suggests that teachers often overlook students from linguistic and ethnic minority groups when making nominations for student participation in gifted and talented programs. According to Peterson and Margolin (1997), "Teachers use existing ideals and moralities of the dominant culture as their guide in assessing children's giftedness" (p. 82). In fact, the literature on teacher recognition of gifted students (from all *populations) suggests that without adequate training, general education teachers have difficulty identifying gifted students. When variations of linguistic and cultural backgrounds are added, the initial identification process becomes more problematic for untrained teachers.*

Teachers are encouraged to work with and consult gifted education experts in their school district, state department of education, and/or local universities. Teachers are also encouraged to request cross-discipline training and work collaboratively with other experts in the school and district to learn more about how CLD students can be academically challenged and have their strengths nurtured. Additionally, educators should investigate opportunities to obtain a teaching endorsement in gifted/talented education. Collaboration among all stakeholders in the school community can lead to significant change and advocacy for CLD students with gifted potential.

Referral Procedures and Assessment

One frequently discussed reason for the underrepresentation and limited participation of minority students and ELLs in gifted programs is related to assessment. The issue is extremely complex and centers on factors related to (a) misuse of identification instruments (Castellano, 2003), (b) test bias and lack of validity in many standardized instruments (Donovan & Cross, 2002), and (c) differences in test performance among racial, cultural, or ethnic groups and "effects of cultural, economic, and language differences or deprivations on the ability of minority students to achieve at levels associated with giftedness" (Frasier et al., 1995, p. 498).

Traditionally, once the gifted learner is identified by a knowledgeable adult (teacher, parent) familiar with the student, a referral is then made for assessment. Specific referral procedures, assessment protocol, and eligibility for gifted programs vary from state to state and frequently vary within the state's school districts. Typically, assessment of the student's potential involves collecting data such as the results of intelligence tests, achievement test scores, and creativity tests. Additionally, a student's work samples are reviewed along with rating scales and nomination forms completed by the student, parents, teachers, and/or peers. Once all the data are gathered and evaluated, a site-based team makes a determination regarding the student's identification as "gifted" and what kind of services will be provided (Kitano & Espinosa, 1995).

In an attempt to address identification problems and increase the participation of CLD students in gifted programs, states advocate the use of multiple criteria; however, problems remain. Despite good intentions, problems in identifying gifted minority students continue to challenge educators. Kitano and Espinosa posit that the multidimensional assessment of these students should include the following: (a) formal, informal, and dynamic assessment procedures that are objective and subjective, reliable, and valid for that population; (b) flexible criteria that promote inclusion versus exclusion; (c) assessment in the student's dominant language(s) by a qualified professional; and (d) a comprehensive measure of a student's abilities and performance across varied contexts. The use of portfolio and/or case study procedures has been recommended as another way to view a holistic measure of a student's performance (Robisheaux, 2002; Robisheaux & Banbury, 1994; Zappia, 1989). Zappia proposed that the identification and selection of gifted Hispanic students be conducted by an interdisciplinary team of professionals "committed to including greater numbers of minorities and accepting a multidimensional definition of giftedness. This team should include members who are knowledgeable in the areas of second language acquisition, bilingual education, cultural

differences, and issues related to minority assessment" (1989, p. 25).

The Parent–Family Connection: Members of the Team

Parents and family of potentially gifted CLD students need to be involved in all aspects of their child's education. The benefits of family involvement for CLD students are well documented and cannot be underestimated. According to Gallagher (2002), to increase the effectiveness of parent and family involvement, school efforts should be well planned, inclusive, and comprehensive. School districts are encouraged to reaffirm beliefs that parents are their child's first and best teacher, and they have a voice in their child's education. Schools are also encouraged to provide informal presentations about giftedness and address how to encourage individual strengths. Additionally, creating various parent support groups for parents of gifted CLD students can help form bonds between families and offer informal avenues to share information (Castellano, 2003). Family involvement can take many forms, including enriching the curriculum with information on unique cultural features and customs not ordinarily found in the literature (García, 2002). Parents can also serve as mentors for other students (Castellano, 2003).

Identification of Linguistically Diverse Gifted Students

The identification of gifted children from culturally diverse groups is affected by a restricted definition of giftedness. The individual student's cultural values, language, and ethnicity must be included and considered. Each culture brings a unique definition and value system of personality variables, cognitive attributes, and behavioral descriptions of what may be perceived as "giftedness" within the culture. Likewise, the level of English language proficiency or stage in second language acquisition must be considered. These factors may alter the ways in which a student can demonstrate her or his strengths. Several researchers have investigated gifted characteristics that may be common among certain CLD students.

For example, in an early study by Frasier and colleagues (1995), characteristics of giftedness in minority, language minority, and economically disadvantaged populations were explored. Ten core attributes associated with giftedness were identified to provide a better basis for establishing procedures to recognize, identify, and plan educational experiences for gifted students from minority or economically disadvantaged families and areas. Additionally, Aguirre (2003) identified characteristics of gifted CLD students in her work with the GOTCHA (Galaxies of Thinking and Creative Heights of Achievement) program, and Robisheaux (2002) created a sample checklist of behaviors to include in initial identification. Many of the characteristics identified by these researchers are presented in Table 28-1.

Table 28-1 Characteristics of Gifted Potential in CLD Student

Characteristic	Frasier et al. (1995)	Aguirre (2003)	Robisheaux (2002)
Motivation		Easily shares his/her native culture	Prefers to work independently or with students whose level of English proficiency is higher than his or hers Is independent and self-sufficient
Language, Communication, and Literacy Skills	Highly expressive and effective use of words, numbers, symbols, etc. Transmission and reception of signals or meanings through a system of symbols (codes, gestures, language, and numbers).	Shows strong desire to teach peers words from his/her native language Functions at language proficiency levels above that of his or her nongifted LEP peers Reads in the native language two grades above his or her grade level Is able to code switch Learns a second or third language at an accelerated pace (formal or informal) Eagerly translates for peers and adults Possesses strengths in the creative areas of fluency, elaboration, originality, and/or flexibility	Learns English quickly Takes risks in trying to communicate in English Practices English skills by him- or herself Initiates conversations with native English speakers Is curious about new words and phrases Questions word meanings Is able to modify his or her language for less-capable English speakers Uses English to demonstrate leadership skills, for example, uses English to resolve disagreements and to facilitate cooperative learning groups Looks for similarities between words in their native language and English Is able to express abstract verbal concepts with a limited English vocabulary
Interests and Leadership Skills	Intense (sometimes unusual) interests. Activities, avocations, objects, etc., that have special worth or significance and are given special attention	Demonstrates leadership abilities in nontraditional settings: playground, home, church, clubs, and so on	Demonstrates social maturity, especially in the home or community Has a great deal of curiosity Becomes absorbed with self-selected problems, topics, and issues Does not frustrate easily Becomes easily bored with routine tasks or drill work

Characteristic	Frasier et al. (1995)	Aguirre (2003)	Robisheaux (2002)
Imagination, Creativity, Curiosity, and Sensitivity	Produces many ideas; is highly original; process of forming mental images of objects, qualities, situations, or relationships, which are not immediately apparent to the senses; solves problems by pursuing nontraditional patterns of thinking	Possesses advanced knowledge of idioms and native dialects and ability to translate and explain meanings in English Possesses cross-cultural flexibility Has a sense of global community and an awareness of other cultures and languages	Is curious about American culture
Memory	Large storehouse of information on school or nonschool topics Exceptional ability to retain and retrieve information		Has a good, long attention span
Insight	Quickly grasps new concepts and makes connections; senses deeper meanings; sudden discovery of the correct solution following incorrect attempts based on primary trial and error	Balances appropriate behaviors expected of the native culture and the new culture	
Reasoning and Problem-Solving Abilities	Logical approaches to figuring out solutions Highly conscious, directed, controlled, active, intentional, forward-looking, goal-oriented thought Effective (often inventive) strategies for recognizing and solving problems Process of determining a correct sequence of alternatives leading to a desired goal or to successful completion or performance of task	Excels in math achievement tests	
Humor	Conveys and picks up on humor well. Ability to synthesize key ideas or problems in complex situations in a humorous way; exceptional sense of timing in words and gestures	Understands jokes and puns related to cultural differences	Is able to use English in a creative way (e.g., create puns, poems, jokes)

Moving Away from a Deficit-based Paradigm: Methods and Strategies for Challenging the Linguistically Diverse Gifted Student

Strategies for teaching gifted students are closely aligned with best practices in teaching English to speakers of other languages (TESOL) theory and practice (Robisheaux, 2002; Robisheaux & Banbury, 1994). "Learning activities that establish a learning environment that promotes creativity, integration and synthesis encourages cooperation and idea exchange. In turn, cooperation and idea exchange necessitate the natural usage of language in a grammatically unstructured setting" (Robisheaux, 2002, p. 171).

Curriculum and instruction for CLD gifted students should be developed around best practices in gifted education, multicultural education, and bilingual education (Granada, 2002) and provide opportunities for accelerated English language learning (Aguirre, 2003). Curriculum and instruction for gifted CLD learners should be qualitatively different. This includes providing experiences that develop critical and creative thinking skills and allowing students to use the language they are most comfortable with for speaking and writing (Castellano, 2004). Kaplan (1999) reminds us that when teaching gifted CLD students, the emphasis needs to be on the giftedness and not just the English language proficiency of the student. Kitano and Espinosa (1995, p. 246) recommended several general strategies for challenging the gifted ELL.

1. Incorporating instructional strategies appropriate for the gifted, irrespective of the language of instruction (e.g., strategies that promote higher level thinking, integration of subject matter areas using thematic approaches, and challenging context).
2. Taking advantage of student strengths such as problem solving, creativity, and primary language ability.
3. Demonstrating high expectations by providing a content-rich curriculum that promotes students' content mastery and provides opportunities for in-depth study.
4. Employing student-centered approaches that promote students' active involvement and engagement in learning.
5. Providing oral and written language development in English or native language throughout all aspects of instruction.
6. Valuing students' languages, cultures, and experiences and promoting their self-esteem.

Although most classroom teachers are familiar with the response to intervention (RTI) model as a way to provide services for students who are "struggling", gifted education scholars have recently begun exploring the use of a "strength-based" model of RTI as a means to provide services for gifted students, including gifted English learners (see Bianco, 2010, and Bianco & Harris, in press, for detailed description). Using a case study as an illustration, Bianco (2010) and Bianco and Harris (in press) proposed a *strength-based* model in which RTI was conceptualized as a multitiered system for developing *gifted potential with CLD students*. Rather than having a singular focus on students' deficits, a strength-based model encourages practitioners to capture and respond to students' strengths and learning styles. Bianco and Harris suggest that a strength-based RTI model *must* also provide culturally responsive curriculum with increasing levels of differentiation, enrichment, and acceleration. Thus, their model provides opportunities for students to investigate, develop, and demonstrate their interests, strengths, and talents while also attending to students' cultural needs.

The Ford-Harris matrix of multicultural gifted education (*see* Ford & Harris, 1999, and Ford, 2011, for detailed description) provides another example of how teachers can integrate higher level thinking skills with increasingly sophisticated levels of multicultural appreciation and social action. The Ford-Harris matrix combines Bloom's (1956) cognitive taxonomy (i.e., knowledge, comprehension, application, analysis, synthesis, and evaluation) with the four levels of Banks' (1995) multicultural infusion model (i.e., contributions, additive, transformation, and social action). The intersection of these frameworks results in a curricular model that is rigorous, culturally relevant (Ford, 2011) and can be adapted to meet the needs various learning needs of gifted English language learners. Table 28-2 provides an

Table 28-2 Example of a Thematic Unit Using the Ford-Harris Matrix Can Music Change The World? Musical Traditions, Styles, and Sociopolitical Influences

	Knowing	Comprehending	Applying	Analyzing	Evaluating	Creating
Contributions	The teacher presents information about a specific cultural music tradition to students.	The teacher presents information about a specific cultural music tradition (for example: blues, son, ranchera, mariachi, ragtime, bebop) to students. Assessment takes the form of fill-in-the-blank, multiple choice, or some other demonstration of concrete knowledge.	Students are asked to apply information acquired about a teacher-selected cultural music tradition to their own experiences with music or their own cultural music traditions.	Students read a biography of a historical musician in the tradition or origin of their choice and find all the things about where and when they grew up or began to perform that influenced them. They present their findings in the form of a short visual presentation. Students should be encouraged to narrate their presentation in two languages (heritage language and English).	Students interview a musician about their work (either in person or via email) and ask them about their influences, and what other styles of music they enjoy as a listener. Students summarize the interview into a short essay in both English and their heritage language.	Students create an imaginary "map" of similar and related musical styles as if they were physical locations and the areas where musical styles influence each other are borders. For instance, blues, jazz and ragtime might be neighboring countries because of their shared musical history. Students should be able to provide examples of what the music sounds like.
Additive	Students are taught about commonalities and cultural themes within specific musical traditions.	Students engage in discussion and debate about the themes, historical significance, and cultural underpinnings of specific musical traditions.	Students research and demonstrate how people usually dance to the style of music they have chosen to research.	Students draw comparisons between different cultural musical traditions, finding the commonalities and differences among them.	Students research what music or musicians inspired the contemporary performers of their chosen musical style. Students evaluate their findings and discuss influences that might be unusual or unexpected.	Students take a thematic element from one style of music and graft it onto a piece of music from another tradition. For example: what would corrida music sound like performed with synthesizers? What would blues sound like over a reggaeton beat?

Table *28-2* **Example of a Thematic Unit Using the Ford-Harris Matrix Can Music Change The World? Musical Traditions, Styles, and Sociopolitical Influences (continued)**

	Knowing	Comprehending	Applying	Analyzing	Evaluating	Creating
Transformation	Students are provided with information about themes, historical significance, and cultural underpinnings of specific musical traditions. They examine that musical tradition from the perspective of someone in the culture where the tradition originated, from a musician, from a music journalist, from an anthropologist/ ethnomusicologist, and from a newcomer to the music.	Students explore and discuss their own role and perspective on the musical tradition they have chosen, their place in the historical significance and the cultural underpinnings of the music. Students will compare their perspective to: that of someone in the culture where the tradition originated, b) from a musician, from a music journalist, from an anthropologist/ ethnomusicologist, and / or from a newcomer to the music.	Students are asked to identify reflections of cultural identity within the musical tradition they have chosen to study. Rather than study how society influenced the musical style, they look for expressions of society within the music itself.	Students analyze how music may reflect social change (both positive and negative) for multiple groups, and examine those perspectives on multiple musical traditions, including the one they have chosen to focus on.	Students find examples of elements taken from the musical tradition of their choice used in other contexts (commercials, cultural appropriation, hybrid musical forms). They are able to describe the significance to both the new audience and the originator.	Based on interviews or research into a previously unfamiliar musical tradition, students are able to present about the history, influence, stylistic elements and appeal of that musical tradition, using the language of the musical tradition they are most familiar with.

Table 28-2

Table 28-2 Example of a Thematic Unit Using the Ford-Harris Matrix Can Music Change The World? Musical Traditions, Styles, and Sociopolitical Influences (continued)

	Knowing	Comprehending	Applying	Analyzing	Evaluating	Creating
Social Action	Based on information obtained about a musical tradition or traditions, students explore, "How can music change the world?"	Students engage in a greater exploration of the role of music in effecting social change. They find examples of the role that their chosen musical genre has had in cultural change, and then make predictions and recommendations for how further social change can benefit from their chosen musical tradition.	Students apply their greater understanding of the way musical traditions reflect social conditions to a chosen social problem. How have musicians in their chosen musical tradition addressed social problems? Did they actually improve conditions? or have conditions remained the same? Students create an artistic product that reflects their chosen social problem through the unique lens of their chosen musical tradition.	Students will utilize the musical tradition they have chosen (even if it is only by writing lyrics or making a collage of imagery featured in the tradition) to address social issues common to the musical culture. For instance, if musicians of a specific style often sing about living in poverty—or racial struggles and discrimination, students would explore and respond to this this topic via visual collage, music lyrics, etc.	Sometimes music has "problematic" messages that are misinterpreted or might have a "bad reputation" for outside listeners. At this level, students critically examine their chosen musical culture, and evaluate both the potential positive and negative cultural force (from within or from the perspective of an outsider). Students will create a multimedia project using the music itself to highlight both the positive and negative aspects.	Students arrange work with musicians from their respective cultural traditions to create a cross-genre piece of music (either a performance or a recording) to draw attention to facilitate cross-cultural understanding through music.

example of a thematic unit of instruction using the Ford-Harris matrix of multicultural gifted education.

Another important consideration when planning curriculum and instruction for gifted CLD students is attention to the affective domain (Rance-Rooney, 2004). This is especially true for students who have recently arrived in the United States and feel the loneliness and frustration of leaving all they knew behind them (Rance-Rooney, 2004). By incorporating aspects of students' languages and cultures into educational planning, teachers will not only be strengthening their students' ethnic identities but also meet the affective needs of students by valuing their heritage, experiences, and memories.

Adopting broader and multidimensional perspectives of intelligence has a far-reaching impact on curriculum development and instructional strategies for all gifted learners, particularly for gifted learners who are learning English. Howard Gardner's theory of multiple intelligences (1993) provides an example of a broader perspective of this construct. Gardner has identified eight intelligences: verbal-linguistic, logical-mathematical, visual-spatial, musical-rhythmic, bodily-kinesthetic, naturalistic, interpersonal, and intrapersonal. There are many excellent print resources and websites available for classroom teachers that guide the use of multiple intelligences (MI) theory and transform it into practical classroom applications for thematic unit instruction (see Tables 28-3 and 28-4).

Differentiated Instruction for Linguistically Diverse Gifted Learners

Teachers can meet the needs of linguistically diverse gifted learners by differentiating curriculum and instruction. According to Tomlinson (2001), "In a differentiated classroom, the teacher proactively plans and carries out varied approaches to content, process, and product in anticipation of and response to student differences in readiness, interest, and learning needs" (p. 7). Differentiated instruction takes students' learning needs (including linguistic abilities), interests, and learning styles into account.

Teachers often mistakenly assume that differentiation for gifted learners means giving students *more* work. Differentiating instruction is more about making qualitative differences rather than quantitative. In a differentiated classroom, teachers modify curriculum and instruction by varying how students learn (process), what students learn (content), how students demonstrate their learning (products they produce), and the learning climate of the classroom as well as where students learn (environment). Figure 28-1 provides a series of questions teachers can ask themselves as they prepare to differentiate instruction for advanced linguistically diverse students.

Like their counterparts, linguistically diverse students will cover the spectrum in their abilities and performance. Some will be able to learn commensurate with their age and grade level, some will be below grade level, some will have disabilities, and yet others will be advanced beyond their grade levels. Special educators, general educators, bilingual educators, and gifted educators must work to develop and understand the complex interaction between language, culture, and disability and address these aspects in their instruction (Chamberlin, 2005).

Application of Common Core Standards to ELLs with Disabilities and ELLs Who Are Gifted

Common Core Standards identify the knowledge and skills students need in order to be successful in college and/or to be career ready. ELLs with disabilities, as well as ELLs who are gifted, must be challenged to excel within the general education curriculum and be prepared for success in their post-school lives. These common standards provide an opportunity to improve access to rigorous academic content for students with disabilities. For these students to meet high academic standards and to fully demonstrate their knowledge and skills in mathematics, reading, writing, speaking and listening (English language arts), their instruction must incorporate supports and accommodations, including:

FIGURE 28-1 Differentiation Planning Sheet for Linguistically Diverse Gifted Students

Differentiated Areas	Questions to Ask Yourself
Content	◆ How can I modify what and how I am teaching to include student's culture, language, interests, and advanced abilities?
	◆ How can I modify the pace of instruction so that the student can move through the curriculum quickly without missing key information?
	◆ What other texts and resources (e.g., films, DVDs, Internet, audiobooks, maps, etc.) are available that match the student's linguistic abilities and learning style?
	◆ How can I include advanced concepts and higher level thinking skills that match the student's linguistic abilities in one or more languages?
Process	◆ How can I include flexible grouping to maximize learning?
	◆ How can I redesign activities so they are more intellectually demanding?
	◆ How can I stimulate inquiry, active exploration, and discovery?
	◆ How can I include student choice in a range of activities to maximize interest and match ability and learning styles?
	◆ What strategies can I explore to help the student have a deeper understanding of content (e.g., graphic organizers, learning centers, choice boards, mind-mapping, etc.)?
	◆ How can I create a culturally responsive learning environment that meets the student's academic and social/emotional needs?
Product	◆ How can I replace or combine tests with other creative product assignments (e.g., building, creating, designing, developing, presenting, etc.) that maximize opportunities for the student to think about, apply, and demonstrate their learning?
	◆ How can I include product assignments that address authentic, real world problems?
	◆ How can I include student choice and a menu of product options?
	◆ How can I use both formative and summative assessment of the product?
Environment	◆ How can I create a learning environment that is student-centered and meets the student's academic and social/emotional needs?
	◆ How can I create a learning environment that addresses students' needs for independent learning while creating a learning community?
	◆ What other learning environments will meet the students' academic needs (e.g., museums, summer academies, college courses)?

❖ Supports and related services designed to meet the unique needs of these students and to enable their access to the general education curriculum (IDEA, 2004).

❖ An Individualized Education Program which includes annual goals aligned with and chosen to facilitate their attainment of appropriate academic standards including common core standards.

❖ Teachers and specialized instructional support personnel who are prepared and qualified to deliver high-quality, evidence-based, individualized instruction and support services (National Dissemination Center for Children with Disabilities, 2014).

Additional supports and services may be necessary so these students can participate successfully in the general education curriculum and meet the

Multiple Intelligence	Language Arrts	Social Atudies	Math/Science
Verbal-Linguistic	Research all you can about your native language. Illustrate and explain the alphabetic (or other) symbols used, number of and types of sounds produced that may be different from the English language. Read your favorite traditional folktale from your country of origin. Tell the story to your class using pictures of characters and/or illustrations you create. Invite a family member to come to class and read the story to the class in your native language and you translate (some or all) into English.	Select a social or political issue of interest to you. Investigate the various cultural and political perceptions of this issue. Write an article for a newspaper presenting two sides of the issue. Use diagrams and maps when possible.	Research mathematicians and/or scientists from your country of origin. Write or illustrate a biography of this individual and her/his accomplishments.
Logical-Mathematical	Create a political poster or a collage of a typical day in your country. Write a narrative to explain your work. Research the works of contemporary artists from your country. Use posters and/or postcards of artists' work and present your findings to the class (written or oral report).	Create a timeline of historical events of your country of origin. Identify significant people on this timeline.	Explain the monetary system of your country. Create a chart illustrating what coins and bills are used, what they look like, and their values. Compare this to the monetary system in the United States.
Visual-Spatial	Create a comic book of your life story. Share the comic book with the class. Create a PowerPoint presentation of the history of your life. Include information and photos about your culture, customs, and language.	Using a Venn diagram or other graphic organizer, compare and contrast the lives of women in your country of origin and the United States (or another country of your choice).	
Musical-Rhythmic	Research the music of your home country. If possible, bring some recordings in to share with the class. If you or any of your family members play a traditional instrument or are familiar with the music, invite them in to share their knowledge with the class.	Explore the use of music in your culture. How, when, and why is music used? Present your findings to the class in either a poster or multimedia presentation.	Diagram to scale several traditional instruments. Investigate the science behind the instrument (e.g., use of wind or breath, use of vibration, etc.)

Table 28-3   Example of MI Thematic Unit on Me, My Country, My Culture, My Language, My Story

Multiple Intelligence	Language Arrts	Social Atudies	Math/Science
Bodily-Kinesthetic	Act out one of the stories of a family member without using words. Use music and props to help you create the scene.	Using clay, sculpt a bust of a famous person from your country. Tell who they are and why you selected him/her.	
Naturalistic	Research the wildlife and natural resources of your country. Explain to the class what these animals are, where they are found, and what the natural resources are.	Using your research on the wildlife and natural resources of your country of origin, create a poster or visual presentation for the class.	Investigate which animals and natural resources have been affected by environmental pollution. Compare and contrast these findings with another country.
Interpersonal	Interview a classmate about his or her culture. Together, identify the similarities and differences of both cultures.	Interview a classmate about their perceptions of and cultural experiences with "elders." Share your experiences, compare, and contrast cultural perspectives on how community elders are perceived.	
Intrapersonal	Identify the accomplishments you are most proud of and explain what they are and why you are proud of yourself for these accomplishments. Make a list of your strengths and the things you can do best. Explain these to the class and share some of the ways you use your strengths.	What are the historical events of your country that you are most proud of and why? Share this with your classmates.	If you were a famous mathematician or scientist in your country, what would you be famous for and why?

requirements of the Common Core Standards. For example, instructional supports based on the principles of Universal Design for Learning (UDL) present information in multiple ways and provide flexibility in the ways in which students respond or demonstrate knowledge and skills. UDL also reduces barriers in instruction, and provides accommodations (changes in materials or procedures) and supports (assistive technology devices and services) which do not change the standards but allows students to learn within the framework of the Common Core.

Table 28-4 **Example of MI Thematic Unit on Hmong Voices** *(continued)*

Multiple Intelligence	Language Arrts	Social Atudies	Math/Science
Verbal-Linguistic	Read and research the works of a contemporary Hmong author. Illustrate or translate the work to share with the class. See: *Bamboo Among the Oaks: Contemporary Writing by Hmong Americans* by Mai Neng Moua (Author) Dust of Life: A True Ban Vinai Love Story by Dr. Gary Yia Lee	Until the end of the nineteenth century, the Hmong people had no written language. Create a five-minute narrated documentary or PowerPoint on the history of the Hmong language detailing how this culture was guided by oral tradition versus written language. (Why did they become an oral language society? There are reasons.)	List/display timelines and graphs illustrating the political shifts that have impacted the Hmong people. This presentation should go as far back as the Han Dynasty. Create a timeline/presentation of the Hmong language. This presentation should include the language profile and orthography of this oral language. See http://www.lmp.ucla.edu/Profile.aspx?LangID=195&menu=004
Logical-Mathematical	Research and report the demographics of the Hmong population including average family income, educational levels, etc. Compare this with the demographics of the United States.	Create an annotated outline or timeline explaining Hmong history in Southeast Asia and then in the United States.	Redesign the Southern Great Wall. Research the history of why the Great Wall of China was built and how the Southern Great Wall relates to the Hmong people. Calculate the amount of money and materials required to build this project (historically and what that translates into now). Translate this project to a current project around the world.
Visual-Spatial	Design a National Geographic Traveler magazine for Laos, Vietnam, or Thailand. Find, organize, and present these photos as a historical timeline of the country.	Create and sketch out a political cartoon for a newspaper of your choice. Using a Venn diagram or other graphic organizer, compare and contrast the lives of Hmong women in Laos versus Hmong women in the United States.	Investigate the topography of Southeast Asia. Draw a topo map of Southeast Asia.
Musical-Rhythmic	Create a presentation on Hmong language and how it is tied to song and music. Research an important Hmong ritual that would include poetry and song. See: *A Hmao (Hua Miao) Songs, Stories and Legends from China*, a new book collection edited by Nicholas Tapp and Mark Pfeifer and published by Lincom	Research historical music from Southeast Asia, specifically the Hmong people. Bring samples of the music to class and share your research of their life and musical influence (written or oral report).	Research the native language of the Hmong people. Find out how the language came to be what it is today. Also, present your findings on how Hmong people were able to learn English, as they were fully immersed in America's schools and communities.

Table 28-4 **Example of MI Thematic Unit on Hmong Voices** *(continued)*

Multiple Intelligence	Language Arrts	Social Atudies	Math/Science
Bodily-Kinesthetic	Re-enact the String-Tying tradition and explain the purpose of this ritual.	Using the Internet, create a photo display of typical Flower Hmong performances. Perform several typical Flower Hmong performances.	Explore the architecture of Southeast Asia. Create (draw or build) a structure using this style. See: http://www.comp.nus.edu.sg/~ngothanh/VN_ architecture.htm
Naturalistic		Create a diorama or develop a PowerPoint illustrating either Laos', Vietnam's, or Thailand's natural resources.	Design a collage depicting Southeast Asia's wildlife and natural habitat. Present your collage.
Interpersonal	Read: *The Spirit Catches You and You Fall Down: A Hmong Child, Her American Doctors, and the Collision of Two Cultures.* Write a reaction paper to the absence of multicultural representation in the American Medical System. Discuss the limitations that modern western medicine faces. See: "Portraits of Hmong Women" Ms. Vang and Ms. Xiong Join in a community premiere of short documentaries about the Hmong experience. Produce a short story of the Hmong experience. This can be in the form of prose, monologues, etc.	Create a dramatic play that is a snapshot from a day in the life of a Hmong immigrant. Become the voice of the Hmong people and pass along the civil concerns that remain. Write your own song, play, or news story covering what the Hmong students in the United States experience.	Design a menu of traditional Hmong dishes. Include cultural foods that are found in Southeast Asia. Bonus: Create a recipe book.

Table 28-4 **Example of MI Thematic Unit on Hmong Voices (continued)**

Multiple Intelligence	Language Arrts	Social Atudies	Math/Science
Intrapersonal	Write an essay sharing your personal feelings about the secret war. Write a "journal" of your imagined journey of refuge to the very different places you will land (Minneapolis, MN, or Fresno, CA).	Find a traditional myth or legend from the Hmong people. Write or illustrate your response as to the purpose and origin of the myth and how the myth or legend has been passed down from generation to generation. Create your own myth or legend using yourself as the main character.	

Created by Emily Pate Oldenburg, classroom teacher, Denver Public Schools, CO

Points to Remember

❖ Within the identified exceptional student population, there is well-documented concern for the under- or overrepresentation of certain racial, ethnic, and cultural minorities. ELLs tend to be underrepresented in programs for the gifted, but may be overrepresented in programs for students with disabilities.

❖ One of the most frequently discussed reasons for the underrepresentation or overrepresentation of culturally and linguistically diverse students in special education programs is related to assessment.

❖ Gifted students can be found in every racial, ethnic, socioeconomic, and linguistic group.

❖ The identification procedures of ELLs who may be gifted or have a disability should include the use of multiple criteria.

❖ The identification of gifted children from culturally diverse groups is affected by a restricted definition of giftedness. The individual student's cultural values, language, and ethnicity must be included and considered.

❖ Teachers need to be trained in the identification of and referral of students from culturally and linguistically diverse backgrounds.

❖ Differentiated curriculum and instruction is qualitatively different; it does not mean more of the same.

❖ A much broader and multidimensional perspective of intelligence has far-reaching impact on curriculum development and instructional strategies for all learners.

❖ Teachers should make culturally sensitive adaptations to their instruction and materials.

❖ Both ELLs with disabilities and those who are gifted must be challenged to excel within the general education curriculum including meeting the Common Core Standards.

Using Technology with English Learners

KEY ISSUES

- ❖ Using technology in second language instruction
- ❖ Technology for English language learners
- ❖ Technological vocabulary to use with English learners
- ❖ The teacher's role
- ❖ Language practice for communication
- ❖ Technology for primary grades
- ❖ Technology for intermediate grades
- ❖ Technology for secondary school
- ❖ Ideas for classroom activities using technology
- ❖ Problems to anticipate
- ❖ How do you know if your source is reliable?
- ❖ Professional organizations and journals
- ❖ Online discussion forums
- ❖ Techniques for teaching with technology
- ❖ Lesson plans, activities, and ideas—elementary school
- ❖ Lesson plans, activities, and ideas—middle school
- ❖ Lesson plans, activities, and ideas—high school
- ❖ Lesson plans, activities, and ideas—adult education
- ❖ Students Web sites K–12
- ❖ Resources for computer-assisted language learning (CALL)
- ❖ Sources for CALL software
- ❖ Reference materials

Ms. Rheinstein began her new teaching job with great enthusiasm. Her first position was to teach social studies in an urban middle school. Among the challenges she faces is the fact that she has students with various levels of English proficiency in her class. Her mission is to meet the needs of students who are native speakers of English, as well as those who are English language learners. She assessed the layout and environment of her classroom, and decided to introduce technology by using videos, CDs, computers, software, Internet, the Promethean board, DVDs, and television. The videos and CDs used to explain information were an excellent way to supplement understanding of the stories her students were reading. Ms. Rheinstein also planned to use her class-designed website as an interactive bulletin board to display additional information for students and provide them with an opportunity to add to their notes, questions, or sign up for focused instruction. To enhance literacy acquisition and scaffold comprehension, she placed visuals throughout her classroom that showed step-by-step modeling and "how-to" tools for the many devices, techniques, and strategies she employs. These ideas were a great beginning for Ms. Rheinstein, and she resolved to learn as much as she could about technology as a way to bridge the gap for her language learners.

Using Technology in Second Language Instruction

In the 21st century, technology is part of everything we do. The classroom is a place where students may receive instruction using technology, just as they are utilizing many of the ubiquitous electronic devices outside the classroom. Television, once thought of as a negative passive endeavor, can now be used creatively as technology infused learning. Many students have iPads, smartphones, tablets, and other mobile devices which allow them immediate access to the Internet at home or in public locations. Moreover, by using Web based applications, or Web 2.0 tools, students have the opportunity to become very active creators of information as opposed to merely consumers of prepackaged information. Social networking has taken the world by storm and students can communicate interactively and spontaneously (synchronously) at the touch of a keystroke. Facebook, Twitter, Instagram, Snapchat, and Tumblr, to name a few, are sites where learners can practice language by posting text messages, images, their own videos, bookmarked information, YouTube videos, blogs, photos, and graphics. Wikipedia, an online user generated encyclopedia, dictionaries, and thesauruses are available in seconds, and creating one's own website is easier than ever. A teacher's only limitation to implementing these applications educationally would be his or her own imagination, and students can be taught how to use all these resources.

As Ms. Rheinstein surmised, when used judiciously, these electronic modes and devices can provide scaffolding for students with limited English proficiency to demonstrate concepts, connect meaning, and add relevance, depth, and texture to a topic of study.

Literature lesson example: Students may read a selection of text and then observe a DVD or video that amplifies and clarifies what they have read. Their understanding of the content can be demonstrated through classroom activities using realia. Ms. Rheinstein uses YouTube, CDs or DVDs for classroom viewing, which satisfies the need to provide language scaffolding for the English language learner (ELL), while engaging the native speaker. It also permits the teacher to focus on one aspect of a book at a time. With some guidance and appropriate prompts, students may create a reflective journal of their reading experiences. Some activities that English language learners may include: response journals in a blog or an online discussion posting. They may craft mini videos or audio recordings and upload them to a class site, or may use presentation software to demonstrate their comprehension. By using text with characters and situations they most relate to, students can reflect and write about their own experiences in real life situations. To enhance the experience, students may use props such as hats, vests constructed of colored paper, or other visual character identifiers to support their narration of the character's role and their purpose in the plot of the story. As an extended activity, students may build a "word wall" with vocabulary from the book or create and share a circle of stories they extract or relate to from the main story. Students may wish to include visual objects to support their vocabulary development which can be downloaded from ClipArt or some other online site. Often students enjoy bringing cultural objects from home to demonstrate their understanding or artifacts that support their experience related to the story; this activity can be carried out by any age group, and the students will enjoy sharing what their possessions mean to them. Older students may enjoy using pictures or real objects to demonstrate their understanding of the story and its symbols. Students may practice their writing skills by participating in wiki-writing activities. During wiki writing, students collaboratively author projects that include multilayered documents, images, videos, slide presentations, and more. This is especially appealing due to the ability to maintain a cutting edge of recently emerging materials. The Wiki format allows students to alter the content. Wikis may be shared within student dyads, groups, classes inside or outside the school and beyond. All these activities provide scaffolding for the English language learner, which assists them to interact with native-speaking peers during content instruction (Echevarria, Vogt, & Short, 2004; Gibbons, 2002; Plaut, 2009).

Technology for English Language Learners

Many strategies can be incorporated to enhance the English learners' language proficiency. Technology can simplify content delivery. DVDs, audio, film, and photography are standard tools, but teachers may use specialized technology as well. Word card readers, *Leap Frog*, *TextAloud*, Dragon Dictation and other programs read text, email, Web pages, and documents using a choice of voices. A teacher also can insert voice comments into students' word documents or make podcasts to support directed instruc-

tion. The student may repeatedly review this type of instruction and therefore receive support for listening and comprehension. This allows the student to use technology and reinforces the content of the lesson. Additionally parents, tutors, or anyone who is helping the student may review the instruction to validate the students' interpretation and assist in their production of activity or artifact to substantiate their learning. By browsing the Internet, one can find actual translators within online dictionaries that give definitions and audio files and often include a thesaurus such as www.m-w.com, http://translation2.paralink.com/, and http://www.languageguide.org/english/index.jsp.

The Teacher's Role

As a first step the teacher will want to assess students' previous exposure to technology. Today's classrooms are commonly equipped with a desktop PC for the teacher, some projection device, an overhead projector, the ability to project a DVD or other movie image device as well as an audio MP3 player with amplification, and a media player. Certainly, there are some classrooms that are still lacking such equipment, but the new norm typically includes some of these.

Each device should have a simple assessment tool in which the student is asked to identify working parts and perform simple tasks. A PC readiness tool would be a line drawing of a similar device with a word bank of terms that refer to significant parts. The diagram should allow the student to choose from the word bank and label the parts in place on the drawing. These assessments can be readily constructed with ten or less terms. They are useful for establishing a baseline to begin instruction (Roblyer & Doering, 2010, p. 55). New devices are so user friendly that they may be implemented into a lesson plan easily. They add life and texture to content and help students learn by approaching several modes of intellectual intake, such as hearing, sight, touch, and other sensations. Students receive multifaceted input when lessons are supported with technological content. Implementing technology has proved that students will grasp the material with greater ease and perform at measurably higher levels (Heinich, et al, 2002; Bersin, 2004).

The basic categories of media are:

1. **Audio:** Students have learned from listening to the teacher and recorded sound, and now taped, digital, and handheld devices such as the iPad and iPod Touch are available to augment lessons and modes of delivery.

2. **Visual:** Teachers have used visual demonstrations since recorded history of teaching. Chalkboards and blackboards held words, figures, or diagrams that accompanied classroom discussion and learning. Today's visuals may include whiteboards, smartboards, posters, decorative areas of the classroom or common areas of the school, photographs, graphics, film, TV, CD, DVD, and much more.

    The Internet is both audio and visual and employs text and skill; its applications are limitless. This chapter offers suggestions for inclusion of the Internet in the classroom, including an e-text where students read online text, and blogs where students publish their responses to the literature, or content matter.

3. **Manipulatives** include models, or materials students may touch and examine. These may be puppets, lifelike models, blocks, rods, or any artifact associated with the content.

This list is by no means inclusive of what is available; a teacher is only limited by his or her comfort level in exploring these materials and methods that add substance, texture, and depth to content instruction.

What you need to know before you begin using technology:

❖ Students' issues or characteristics
❖ The classroom setting and environment
❖ Physical resources available such as:
  ◆ Black, white, bulletin boards
  ◆ TVs /videos
  ◆ DVDs/CDs
  ◆ Mobile devices (iPads and tablets)
  ◆ Computers/laptops
  ◆ Internet

◆ Presentation software
◆ Other software

Once you know your population, setting, and resources:

❖ Make plan to deliver content.
❖ Determine objectives.
❖ Prepare for implementation.
❖ Decide what devices you will implement.
  ◆ What portion of the lesson might be delivered by the appropriate mode or method, such as DVD, Internet, mobile devices, etc.?
  ◆ Find out how your school supports technology use in the classroom. Do you have to requisition or sign out materials?
  ◆ Knowing the process for your school will help you make a smooth transition into using technology to support content.

Ideas for Language Communication Practice

Reading: Students may enjoy eBooks, online stories, and Internet information search activities that require reading. Scaffolding tools such as online dictionaries or translators increase ELLs' ability to read and participate with native English-speaking peers.

Writing: Instant messaging, email or online journaling such as blogging will motivate students' interests in writing tasks and increase their technological skills while enhancing their writing competencies.

Listening: Students may listen to stories or content material from the Internet in an audio format, CDs, DVDs, film, audiotape, podcasts, or digital recording. This material may be a good foundation for a concept map to study, write about, or research later. Students may listen to musical performances to determine the theme, message, and overall meaning of music in a story or play.

Speaking: Students may learn correct word pronunciation, have audio discussions, and create scripts for plays and other venues for conversational practice.

Activities: Students may use photographs, cutouts, news articles, realia, models, and more to support their verbal presentation of content knowledge. Teachers help students create graphic organizers such as *k/w/l* charts, whereas older or more proficient students may add complexities such as identifying central ideas, characters, and ideas that reflect the relationship of story lines to character and symbols. As a group activity, classes may work together to form the concept map or eco-gram of the main elements of the content being taught.

Technology for Primary Grades

Young children are engaged by traditional instruction methods augmented by the use of the full range of technology. Instruction for younger children needs to have interactive active, hands-on facets for each portion of content instruction. Heeding Vygotsky's (1987) ideas of transporting children from their zone of actual development (what they are already able to do) to their zone of proximal development (what they need from other's assistance or props to complete), we use functions and activities to solidify and demonstrate the acquisition of these new skills. In other words, the actions used by a child in creating cutouts of characters to demonstrate understanding of that role in a story actually increases the child's depth of knowledge acquired from the reading or viewing of a DVD/CD/video or film.

Bean (2011) recommended that teachers enhance the writing process by offering the students a path to learning through active practice. Children will enjoy creating a role-play or skit to act out a story they learned. They can craft costumes, bring appropriate food, and take photographs to stimulate their creative side and then use audio- or videotape to write and record their work. Students delight in seeing themselves on film, and even a beginning language learner can join the others in a skit by memorizing a short script.

The writing that occurs following the inclusion of the cognitively active learning through technology will reveal that the students have acquired a more advanced lexicon, and verbal usage will have greater acuity. As a result, students will have a better sense of academic accomplishment (Vygotsky & Hillocks, 1999; Gore, 2004).

Introducing technology will require you to first determine the level of the student you are instructing as well as to establish appropriate instructional strategies for the most effective instruction.

Beginner students need rudimentary vocabulary, which can be illustrated by large colorful charts depicting function and action. English learners will benefit from reinforced instruction by the use of repetition and recurring demonstrations and gain the vocabulary along with the actual skills.

Intermediate students will have a working knowledge of functional basic vocabulary. Vocabulary is needed for most common and repetitive actions to operate the keyboard of a computer. Students need to be able to follow directions with little support; therefore, the technological language and terminology should be clear and easily understood.

Some students with advanced proficiency in language or in computer usage may have had plentiful access to computers and other technological devices such as computer games or even home-based learning. These students will readily adapt to the infusion of technology with little guidance and will move quickly through the required steps to complete tasks assigned. Advanced learners will benefit from instruction in responsible search techniques and should be aware of personal safety protocols when using email or chat rooms. Remember to address the cultural and cognitive learning style of your students.

Technology for Intermediate Grades

Middle schoolers are kinesthetically active and respond to socially cooperative activities (Slavin, 1990; Willis & Willis 2009). An interactive approach to teaching could include the use of a tactile map, models, or collaborative projects that require participation of each student. Students can be taught to brainstorm, work collectively to choose a topic they have been researching on the Internet, and later decide to invite a speaker from the community to address the class. A number of extension activities can result from student-generated ideas. Choosing to include technology allows the teacher to manipulate student configurations for study purposes by targeting students into clusters or groups within the class as a whole. Depending on the objectives of the teacher, students may learn the same content at their own pace by using the Internet, viewing DVDs or CDs, or using a tape player or disk player for audio programming. Students can return to the assignments again and again to check understanding, clarify instructions, and fill in any gaps they missed the first time.

Another wonderful use of technology for English learners to increase literacy comprehension is through recorded stories. Listening to recorded stories through headphones allows the student to hear the text while reading the book. The student hears a native speaker's voice, and the pronunciation, stress, pitch, and rhythm of English are internalized as the reader's eyes become accustomed to the outline of letters and word formations. Depending on the instructional objectives, teachers can capitalize on a broadcast shown on educational television channels such as PBS or A&E. Peruse the Internet, newspapers, and international magazines for articles that complement the lesson content. Students may make Internet searches or the instructor can arrange e-pen pals or blogs for the students to communicate with and share their writing, thoughts, opinions, and comments. It is a great thrill when a student's writing is published, and it can be shared with and responded to with the blog reading public (Leverett, 2005).

Beginners will need active and very clear instructions delivered by a format, such as a video or PowerPoint presentation with visuals. They need to learn vocabulary and basic functions of the computer and know whatever is expected of them. Be very clear and offer materials that offer unambiguous preparation for the intended activity.

Instructors often like to use handouts with terminology in the form of a game, such as word search or crossword, which may be of limited help for the new language learner. Caution is urged when this type of activity is implemented. If a word is shown, make sure an illustration accompanies the word. Arrows pointing to the subject will ensure the reader knows which label pertains to the correct object.

Peruse the following site for activities of this nature, but use the activity judiciously. Beware that the early language learner might have to do cognitive gymnastics to decipher words, and this type of activity might only further word recognition as opposed to lexical understanding. Activities are available at http://www.languageguide.org/english/.

Intermediate students who have a basic familiarity with computers will know the main vocabulary and functions for using computers, printers, scanners, and audio devices, but they may only know it in their native language. Meaning is quickly transferred if it is connected to obvious cognitive clues. These students may complete simple assignments using word processing or data storage programs with specified instruction. Intermediate students will need to learn the skills of maneuvering search engines through library portals using databases and other educational supports. Prepare instructional notes that remind students of basic functions and technological jargon that they can keep in their notebooks for easy reference.

Advanced middle school students will be able to incorporate computer usage in many areas of academic function. They may create their own Web pages or a class blog or use etexts (electronic texts) for completion of content activities. Students may have expertise with digital cameras and other devices that will enrich their production of work artifacts. Students will still need supervision for responsible searching, as well as for instructions about how to safely peruse the Internet and interact in areas such as chat rooms and other public venues.

Technology for High School

High school students use a plethora of technological devices outside the classroom. In the past, ELLs of this age bracket needed technological instruction the most but have felt the least included. Infusing technology can be an egalitarian tool of inclusion. In this arena, the ground shifts so the least-accomplished student may achieve complex projects and content goals through the implementation of technological sources and venues for student expression. After being properly instructed, ELLs may offer sophisticated reports and may interact with others who have native language skills on a higher level through tools such as blogs (Leverett, 2005).

Beginners will need functional vocabulary and hands-on instruction. Students who have not been exposed to computers or the Internet will need to be introduced with how-to handouts and step-by-step directions to support computer use. Diagrams and common vocabulary should be clear for the English learner. With practice, students learn computer functions quickly and will be able to move into the intermediate level after mastering the basics of turning on the machine, using a keyboard or control panel, and observing the proper sequence of keystrokes or command prompts to deliver their chosen program.

Intermediate learners have had some exposure to computers and the Internet and will probably know the basic vocabulary and keyboard or command panel usage in their native language or in English. They will need instruction in the use of search functions, database exploration, and program-specific instruction based on the software chosen by the school. Intermediate learners may know how to access and use parallel devices such as fax machines or printers. Intermediate learners will benefit from the teacher-directed addition of devices such as digital camera, video recorder, smart board, and sophisticated software for presentation.

Advanced students will have Internet use background and may have knowledge of many potential applications for the computer and its portal to support content. Students who are advanced will benefit from use of library portals and specialized search training to support their focused needs. These students will be able to incorporate high-level functions such as the creation of their own Web pages and blogs (Smaldino et al., 2002). They may use or may be ready to use additional software applications to create graphs, charts, spreadsheets, artistic renderings, and combinations of all of these.

Classroom Resources
- ❖ Bulletin boards
- ❖ Audiocassettes/recorders
- ❖ TVs/videos
- ❖ DVDs/CDs

- ❖ Computers
- ❖ Internet
- ❖ Presentation software
- ❖ Other software

Ideas for Classroom Activities Using Technology

Blogs

What is a blog?

A blog is a Web publishing tool that allows people to self-publish text, artwork, links to other blogs or websites, and much more.

Blogs are set up as conventions through websites, with navigation links, and other website features. Blog postings are text entries, similar to a diary or journal, that include a posting date and comments made by people other than the author.

Postings are often short and frequently updated. They appear in reverse chronological order and can include archived entries.

Blogs work well for students because they can be worked on any time and in any place with Internet access. Hence, they can be used by teachers to create a classroom that extends beyond the boundaries of the school.

Presentation Software

English language learning students, from Kindergarten forward, use presentation software to deliver assignments. These are in the form of slides created on the classroom computer with color, animation, sound, embedded video, and audio. These various attributes diversify the ELL's choices for communication. These types of software are commonly available in K–12 settings as part of their software resources and often offered as free downloads. English learners are able to use presentation software to expand their expression and accuracy in response to assignment (Roblyer & Doering, 2010, p. 186). Some types that have free user-friendly applications for the classroom are:

www.prezi.com
www.openoffice.org
www.powerbullet.com

Email Pen Pals

EPALS Classroom Exchange is internationally recognized as the leading provider of school-safe email and collaborative technology. Used in classrooms in 191 countries, ePALS's multilingual network has made it possible for more than six million students and educators to employ the Internet as the ultimate communication and cross-cultural learning tool.

Teachers can use ePALS to broaden students' cultural outlook by introducing them to other students around the world while they practice writing and communication skills. It can be accessed at http://www.epals.com.

Web Quest

A Web Quest is an online inquiry-oriented activity in which some or all of the information that students include comes from resources on the Internet. Creating Web Quests is a strategy for integrating the Web with instructional goals. Web Quests are designed to make the best use of students' time and allow them to surf with a clear task in mind.

A Web Quest has six critical attributes:

1. Introduction
2. Tasks
3. Description of the process
4. Set of information sources
5. Evaluation
6. Conclusion.

Go to this website and view the online presentation that describes what is needed to put in a Web Quest: http://school.discovery.com/schrockguide/webquest/wqsL1.html.

Online Portfolio

Online portfolios are collections of work that students have created and have been published online. Putting the students' work online provides a way for parents, teachers, students, and relatives to view the progress and growth of the student work over time. Students can choose what material they wish to include in their portfolio. Portfolios can consist of stories, reports, poems, math, science, and social studies work. Online portfolios help English language learners to participate in the use of software to offer creative outlets for academic efforts.

These websites give ideas on how to use portfolios, benefits of use, how to set them up, and how you can find resources to help with portfolios in the classroom.

http://electricteacher.com/onlineportfolio/
http://teaching-strategies-mentorship.suite101.
    com/...cfm/how_to_use_portfolios_in_the_
    classroom
http://www.ncrel.org/sdrs/areas/issues/students/
    earlycld/ea5L143.htm
https://www.msu.edu/user/pdickson/cep813/
    portfoliosclassroom.htm

Problems to Anticipate

When using technological devices, always have a plan B. Whatever can go wrong very often does. When planning lessons using technology, something as simple as a power failure can alter the best laid plans. BE PREPARED. Make a hard copy of your presentation and be ready to substitute ancillary devices. Example of a backup plan: If you plan to show a movie and the VCR fails, you could still deliver the story content and have the students interact and participate if you have copies of the book. Perhaps the school librarian or the media specialist might have posters or visual story aids that may augment the telling of the story. With the available copies, teach the students how to do a "jigsaw" activity. Place the students in groups and assign each group a section of the book. Each group then becomes an "expert" on the assigned chapter and teaches the rest of the class about their assigned chapter. This strategy makes it possible for English learners to tackle more challenging literary pieces.

How Do You Know If the Website Is a Reliable Source?

Teach your students about the dangers inherent when using social networks and Web applications. Phishing, slamming, and identity theft are real problems that users need to be aware of. Before using websites with your students, you need to evaluate the worthiness and authenticity of the Web page. The following sites offer information on guidelines for determining the value, authenticity, trustworthiness, and educational accuracy of Web pages. After several visits to the following websites, you will become adept at evaluating interesting websites and will be able to make choices based on the needs of your population.

University of California, Berkeley http://www.lib.berkeley.edu/TeachingLib/Guides/Internet/Evaluate.html

University of the State of Colorado
http://lib.colostate.edu/howto/evalweb.html

New Mexico State University Library
http://lib.nmsu.edu/instruction/evalcrit.html

Cornell University in New York State
http://guides.library.cornell.edu/evaluating_Web_pages

World Wide Web Virtual Library
http://www.vuw.ac.nz/staff/alastair_smith/evaln/evaln.htm

Professional Organizations and Journals

AAIEP—The American Association of Intensive English Programs
http://www.aaiep.org/

CAL—Center for Applied Linguistics
http://www.cal.org

CREDE—Center for Research on Education, Diversity and Excellence
http://www.cal.org/crede

EFL Web—English as a Foreign Language Magazine Great resources with jobs, activities, links, and worldwide connections
http://www.eflWeb.com/

Humanizing Language Teaching Online magazine for teachers of English
http://www.hltmag.co.uk/

The Internet TESL Journal
Teaching techniques, resources, activities, etc.
http://iteslj.org/

Language Learning & Technology
http://LLT.msu.edu/

The Language Teacher Online
http://www.jalt-publications.org/tlt/

The Modern Language Journal
http://polyglot.lss.wisc.edu/mlj/

Multicultural Pavilion
http://www.edchange.org/multicultural/

NABE—National Association for Bilingual Education
http://www.nabe.org/

TESL-EJ Master Page
http://www-writing.berkeley.edu/TESL-EJ/

TESOL, Inc. Home Page
http://www.tesol.org/s_tesol/index.asp

UCIEP—University and College Intensive English Programs
http://www.uciep.org/index.php

Online Discussion Forums

Aardvarks English Forum.com
http://www.englishforum.com/00/

ESLCafe.Com—Discussion Forums (Dave Sperling)
http://www.esLcafe.com

TESL Electronic Discussion Lists and Newsgroups
http://www.linguistic-funland.com/tesllist.html

How to Teach Technology—Teaching Techniques

Consortium for School Networking provides you with timely resources, materials, publications, and information on technology and learning issues
http://www.cosn.org/

ICYouSee, A Guide to the World Wide Web A Guide to Critical Thinking about What You See on the Web
http://www.ithaca.edu/library/training/think.html

International Society for Technology in Education
http://www.iste.org/template.cfm

Internet 4 Classrooms
Step-by-step tutorials for learning programs: Word, Excel, Hyper Studio, Web Quest, Internet explorer, PowerPoint, Inspiration, and many others
http://www.internet4classrooms.com/on-line.htm

ITESLJ's Articles on Teaching Techniques
http://iteslj.org/Techniques/

Learn to use the mouse
http://www.instruction.greenriver.edu/avery/activities/mouse/MouseSkills.htm

Lesson Plans, Activities, and Ideas
Elementary

The Amazing Picture Machine
This site offers an extensive collection of pictures for use by teachers or students and sample lesson plans geared toward K–12, which can be adapted for adults
http://www.ncrtec.org/picture.htm

The EFL Playhouse for teachers and young children
Games, discussion boards, recommended books, and learning center ideas
www.esL4Kids.net

ESL Lesson Plans and Resources
This is a list of many lesson plans and resources
http://www.csun.edu/~hcedu013/eslplans.html

Guide to Grammar and Writing
http://grammar.ccc.commnet.edu/grammar/

Internet 4 Classrooms Links for K–12 teachers
http://www.internet4classrooms.com/

Internet Treasure Hunts for ESL Students
A project of the Internet TESL journal
http://www.aitech.ac.jp/~iteslj/th/

Kathy Schrock's Guide for Educators Comprehensive list of Web sites full of information content, method, personal interest, and lesson plans
http://school.discovery.com/schrockguide/indexa-b.html

Kristina Pfaff's Linguistic Funland
This site is a resource for teachers and students and offers books, lessons, activities, and much more
http://www.linguistic-funland.com/

Online ESL Grammar Exercises and Quizzes
http://eslcafe.com/quiz
http://eslgo.com/quizzes.html
http://eslpartyland.com/quiz-center/quiz.htm
http://eflnet.com/grammar/index.php
http://rong-chang.com/quiz.htm
http://a4esl.org

The PuzzleMaker
Puzzles for teachers and students to make. Word search, cryptograms, criss-cross puzzles; text is entered and a puzzle is printed
http://puzzlemaker.school.discovery.com/

Scholastic
Teachers, kids, parents, administrators, and librarians
http://www.scholastic.com

Teacher guides and activities K–12
http://www.sdcoe.k12.ca.us/score/cyberguide.html

Teachersfirst.com
Classroom, professional, and site references K–12
http://www.teachersfirst.com/index.cfm

Lesson Plans, Activities, and Ideas
Middle School

The Amazing Picture Machine
This site offers an extensive collection of pictures for use by teachers or students and sample lesson plans geared toward K–12, which can be adapted for adults
http://www.ncrtec.org/picture.htm

Daily Lesson Plan for English Teachers published by the New York Times.
6–12
http://www.nytimes.com/learning/teachers/lessons/archive.html

ESL Lesson Plans and Resources
This is a list of many lesson plans and resources
http://www.csun.edu/~hcedu013/eslplans.html

Guide to Grammar and Writing
http://grammar.ccc.commnet.edu/grammar/

Internet 4 Classrooms Links for K–12 teachers
http://www.internet4classrooms.com/

Internet Treasure Hunts for ESL Students
A project of the Internet TESL journal
http://www.aitech.ac.jp/~iteslj/th/

Kathy Schrock's Guide for Educators
Extremely comprehensive list of websites full of information content, method, personal interest, lesson plans, and so on.
http://school.discovery.com/schrockguide/indexa-b.html

Kristina Pfaff's Linguistic Funland
This site is a resource for teachers and students and offers books, lessons, activities, and much more
http://www.linguistic-funland.com/

Online ESL Grammar Exercises and Quizzes
http://eslcafe.com/quiz
http://eslgo.com/quizzes.html
http://eslpartyland.com/quiz-center/quiz.htm
http://eflnet.com/grammar/index.php
http://rong-chang.com/quiz.htm
http://a4esl.org

The PuzzleMaker
Puzzles for teachers and students to make. Word search, cryptograms, criss-cross puzzles; enter your text and print out a puzzle for the classroom
http://puzzlemaker.school.discovery.com/

Scholastic
Teachers, Kids, Parents, administrators, and librarians
http://www.scholastic.com

Teacher guides and activities K–12
http://www.sdcoe.k12.ca.us/score/cyberguide.html

Teachersfirst.com
Classroom, professional, and site references K–12
http://www.teachersfirst.com/index.cfm

Lesson Plans, Activities, and Ideas
High School

The Amazing Picture Machine
This site offers an extensive collection of pictures for use by teachers or students and sample lesson plans geared toward K–12, which can be adapted for adults
http://www.ncrtec.org/picture.htm

Daily Lesson Plan for English Teachers published by the *New York Times*
6–12
http://www.nytimes.com/learning/teachers/lessons/archive.html

ESL Lesson Plans and Resources
This is a list of many lesson plans and resources
http://www.csun.edu/~hcedu013/eslplans.html

Guide to Grammar and Writing
http://grammar.ccc.commnet.edu/grammar/

Internet 4 Classrooms Links for K–12 teachers
http://www.internet4classrooms.com/

Internet Treasure Hunts for ESL Students
A project of the Internet TESL journal
http://www.aitech.ac.jp/~iteslj/th/

Kathy Schrock's Guide for Educators
Extremely comprehensive list of Web sites full of information content, method, personal interest, lesson plans, and so on
http://school.discovery.com/schrockguide/indexa-b.html

Kristina Pfaff's Linguistic Funland
This site is a resource for teachers and students and offers books, lessons, activities, and much more
http://www.linguistic-funland.com/

Online ESL Grammar Exercises and Quizzes
http://eslcafe.com/quiz
http://eslgo.com/quizzes.html
http://eslpartyland.com/quiz-center/quiz.htm
http://eflnet.com/grammar/index.php
http://rong-chang.com/quiz.htm
http://a4esl.org

The PuzzleMaker
Puzzles for teachers and students to make. Word search, cryptograms, criss-cross puzzles; enter your text and print out a puzzle for the classroom
http://puzzlemaker.school.discovery.com/

Scholastic
Teachers, kids, parents, administrators, and librarians
http://www.scholastic.com

Teacher guides and activities K–12
http://www.sdcoe.k12.ca.us/score/cyberguide.html

Teachersfirst.com
Classroom, professional, and site references K–12
http://www.teachersfirst.com/index.cfm

Lesson Plans, Activities, and Ideas
Adult Education

Aardvark English Forum.com
Comprehensive Web with numerous resources for students and teachers of English (ESL/EFL). Inter-active Exercises, Message Boards, ELT Book Cata-logue, Good School Guide, Web Directory, World News, Learning and Teaching Links, Useful Tools, and more . . .
http://www.englishforum.com/

Accents in English with eViews
Advanced listening comprehension; listen to native English speakers for accent and pronunciation practice.
http://www.eviews.net/

The Adult education teacher's annotated webliogra-phy reviews of websites for adult education and ESL
http://alri.org/pubs/webliography.html

The Amazing Picture Machine
This site offers an extensive collection of pictures for use by teachers or students and sample lesson plans geared toward K–12, which can be adapted for adults.
http://www.ncrtec.org/picture.htm

Dave's ESL Cafe
Site with a huge number of links for teachers of English language learners
http://eslcafe.com/

EFL/ESL Lessons Using Websites
 http://iteslj.org/t/ws/

E.L. Easton Business English
http://eleaston.com/biz/home.html

ESL Lesson Plans and Resources
This is a list of many lesson plans and resources
http://www.csun.edu/~hcedu013/eslplans.html

ESLoop
A variety of sites for English language teaching and learning
http://www.linguistic-funland.com/esloop/

The ESL Quiz Center
Tests students' knowledge of verbs, prepositions, clauses, punctuation, etc.
Multilevel; particularly good for lower levels
http://www.pacificnet.net/~spelling/quiz

Guide to Grammar and Writing
http://grammar.ccc.commnet.edu/grammar/

Internet Treasure Hunts for ESL Students A project of the Internet TESL journal
http://www.aitech.ac.jp/~iteslj/th/

John's Activities for English Learners Especially for adult English language learners
http://www.csun.edu/~hcedu013/eslplans.html

Kathy Schrock's Guide for Educators
Extremely comprehensive list of Web sites full of information content, method, personal interest, les-son plans, and etc.
http://school.discovery.com/schrockguide/indexa-b.html

Kristina Pfaff's Linguistic Funland
This site is a resource for teachers and students and offers books, lessons, activities, and much more
http://www.linguistic-funland.com/

Online ESL Grammar Exercises and Quizzes
http://eslcafe.com/quiz
http://eslgo.com/quizzes.html
http://eslpartyland.com/quiz-center/quiz.htm
http://eflnet.com/grammar/index.php
http://rong-chang.com/quiz.htm
http://a4esl.org

The PuzzleMaker
Puzzles for teachers and students to make. Word search, cryptograms, criss-cross puzzles; enter your text and print out a puzzle for the classroom
http://puzzlemaker.school.discovery.com/

Students Websites K–12

Scholastic is for teachers, kids, parents, administrators, and librarians
http://www.scholastic.com

Kristina Pfaff's Linguistic Funland
This site is a resource for teachers and students and offers books, lessons, activities, and much more
http://www.linguistic-funland.com/

Resources for Computer-assisted Language Learning (CALL)
Sources for CALL Software

TESOL CALL-IS website is maintained by webmaster Leslie Opp-Beckman and is the best place to start when looking for CALL resources, including CALL software.
http://legacy.Lclark.edu/~Krauss/Tesol98/call.html/
Links at the site include:

- ❖ ESOL Internet Resources
- ❖ CALL-IS Software Database
- ❖ CALL-IS Software Fair
- ❖ Tech Tips Monthly Column
- ❖ CALL Presentation Handouts Online
- ❖ Register Your Presentation
- ❖ TESOL CALL-IS Events

Vocabulary for Technology Use with English Learners

Antivirus software—A program that will find and destroy viruses in a computer.

Backup—A copy on a removable storage disk or tape of files from a computer's hard disk. A backup is used in case the hard disk files are damaged.

Bit/bytes—A bit is the smallest piece of information that computers use. These bits are in groups of 8 called bytes (8 bits = 1 byte).

Blog—A meeting place on the World Wide Web (WWW) where people share their feelings or ideas.

Boot/boot up/boot disk—You boot (or boot up) your computer when you turn it on and wait while it comes to attention. Startup information is given to the computer from a boot disk.

Browser/to browse—A browser is a program such as Internet Explorer/Netscape/Mozilla. You use it to look at pages on the Internet.

Bug—A glitch or defect or fault in a program.

Cache—A place inside the hard drive where information may be stored and memory used to make a computer work faster.

CD—A disk for storing information.

Chat—A function of communication through the computer in real time (right now) usually a group who is friendly and based on some common interest.

Chat room—A place on the WWW to chat (safety instruction should be provided before chat room use is taught).

CPU—Central Processing Unit. This is the computer's brains.

Desktop—The image you see when your computer is turned on.

Disk drive—The device used to run a floppy disk (usually drive A).

DOS—Disk Operating System. Original system used for computers.

Driver—A small program that may "drive" a device, such as a printer.

Electronic mail (e-mail)—Short notes sent from one computer to another.

Folder (directory)—A place to store files on your hard drive.

Font—A particular typeface of lettering such as the following: Times New Roman.

Format—Getting the computer area inside the computer ready for use, the process is called formatting. Hard disks are often preformatted by the computer maker.

Graphics card—This is a card in your computer's CPU that makes images visible.

Hard disk—This is the main disk inside a computer. It stores programs and information.

Icon—A small image or picture you see on the desktop or screen is a symbol for folders, or programs.

IM—Instant messaging—a way to talk to one other person, different than chatting, which often includes a group, IM is one to one and live.

Internet—**Inter**national **net**work of computers currently connected by telephone line.

Kb, Mb, Gb—Kilobytes, megabytes, gigabytes. Units of measure of computer memory and storage.

Keyboard—Device with letters of the alphabet and numbers, attached to the computer's CPU, allowing typing of commands and words.

Memory—Memory is for the temporary storage of information while a computer is being used.

MHz—Megahertz. This describes a speed of some computer equipment.

Modem—Equipment connected to a computer for sending/receiving digital information by telephone line. You need a modem or wireless router to connect to the Internet.

Monitor—Looks like a TV screen, for viewing the images stored in the computer CPU.

Mouse—Small device attached to the computer guiding a small, on-screen arrow so you may "click" on areas of the image displayed. Mouses or mice can be connected to the CPU by wire or may be wireless.

Parallel port—A plug or socket on the back of a computer for connecting external equipment such as printers, speakers, and much more.

Peripheral—Any equipment that is connected externally to a computer—speakers, printers, and scanners are peripherals.

Phishing—Scamming as a result of Internet fraud.

Pixel—The image that you see on the screen is made of many hundreds of little dots called pixels.

Program—This is the information framework that operates a function or more than one function in the computer's brain.

RAM, ROM—RAM (Random Access Memory) is the main memory used as the computer is working. RAM is temporary. ROM (Read Only Memory) is for information the computer keeps permanently.

Resolution—The number of dots/pixels in each inch used to create the image that you see.

Scanner—Device for converting documents to electronic documents that can be stored by computer.

Serial port—Plug/socket on the back of a computer for connecting peripheral devices.

Social networks—Facebook and MySpace are examples of social networks where people can interact with each other.

Start button—The start button, in the bottom left corner of your desktop image, is for opening new programs.

Taskbar—The taskbar, at the bottom of the screen, shows the programs in use and the time and date when you scan them with your mouse.

Virus—Unwelcome unauthorized program that can damage a computer; sometimes they come in email or attached to advertising.

Wikipedia—A user generated encyclopedia; not a reliable bibliographic resource.

Windows—An operating system used by the majority of computers.

World Wide Web, WWW, the Web—WWW are the letters that stand for World Wide Web.

Points to Remember

- ❖ Internet use can promote learner autonomy after initial training.

- ❖ Make sure your students are knowledgeable about appropriate vocabulary, technological jargon, and commands before using computers.

- ❖ Students must learn to evaluate websites and understand that any quality of material can be published on the Internet.

- ❖ Students should be taught and must understand what plagiarism is and that copyright laws must be obeyed.

- ❖ Consideration of the expense of keeping a service provider up and running must be a priority for the school.

- ❖ Teachers must be willing to shift the paradigm from the old lecture and textbook style to include the new technologies.

- ❖ Students need to be aware of the inherent dangers in social networking and online "phishing."

- ❖ Students need to be taught how to recognize phishing and scams to avoid identity theft.

Tying It All Together: Tools for the Teacher

Center Schedules

The document I created which includes the center checklists for my small group center rotations. You will find the first checklist in Chapter 30.

Centers

1. Meet with Teacher
2. Work with Words (Spelling)
3. Computer Center (Follow Schedule)
4. Phonics Center (Graphing—Wednesday Only)
5. Reading Comprehension Center (Passages and Questions and Task Cards)
6. Writing Center

Meet with Teacher Schedule

Monday—L1, L2, M1, M2, H (Fluency First Read)

Tuesday—L1, L2, M1, M2

Wednesday—L1, L2, M1, M2

Thursday—No Centers

Friday—L1 + L2, M1 + M2, H (Spelling Assessment and Fluency)

Future Permanent Schedule

Monday—L1, L2, M1

Tuesday—L1, L2, M2

Wednesday—L1, L2, H

Thursday—No Centers

Friday—L1 + L2, M1 + M2, H (Spelling Assessment and Fluency)

Center Rotation Daily Schedule

Monday

L1	L2	M1	M2	H
Teacher	Vocabulary	RC	Writing	Work with Words
Work with Words	Teacher	Vocabulary	RC	Writing
Writing	Work with Words	Teacher	Vocabulary	RC
RC	Writing	Work with Words	Teacher	Vocabulary
Vocabulary	RC	Writing	Work with Words	Teacher

Tuesday

L1	L2	M1	M2	H
Teacher	Computers	RC	Writing	Work with Words
Work with Words	Teacher	Computers	RC	Writing
Writing	Work with Words	Teacher	Computers	RC
RC	Writing	Work with Words	Teacher	Computers
Computers	RC	Writing	Work with Words	Vocabulary

Wednesday

L1	L2	M1	M2	H
Teacher	Vocabulary	RC Selection Test	Phonics	Work with Words
Work with Words	Teacher	Vocabulary	RC Selection Test	Phonics
Phonics	Work with Words	Teacher	Vocabulary	RC Selection Test
RC Selection Test	Phonics	Work with Words	Teacher	Vocabulary
Vocabulary	RC Selection Test	Phonics	Work with Words	Writing

Friday

L1	L2	M1	M2	H
Teacher	Teacher	Computers	Writing	Vocabulary
Teacher	Teacher	Writing	Computers	RC Cold Reads
RC Cold Reads	Writing	Teacher	Teacher	Computers
Computers	RC Cold Reads	Teacher	Teacher	Writing
Writing	Computers	RC Cold Reads	RC Cold Reads	Teacher

Centers Schedule by Group

Highs: Purple Chameleons

Monday	Tuesday	Wednesday	Thursday	Friday
Work with Words (2 Task Cards from 1–9)	Work with Words (2 Task Cards from 1–9)	Work with Words (2 Task Cards from 1–9)	NO CENTERS	Vocabulary Center (Adventures in Vocabulary)
Writing Center	Writing Center	Phonics Center	NO CENTERS	Reading Comprehension (Cold Reads)
Reading Comprehension	Reading Comprehension	Reading Comprehension (Selection Test)	NO CENTERS	Computer Center in Pairs
Vocabulary Center (Index Cards)	Computer Center in Pairs	Vocabulary Center (Adventures in Vocabulary)	NO CENTERS	Writing Center
Meet with Teacher	Vocabulary Center (Adventures in Vocabulary)	Writing Center	NO CENTERS	Meet with Teacher

Mids 2: Pink Chameleons

Monday	Tuesday	Wednesday	Thursday	Friday
Writing Center	Writing Center	Phonics Center	NO CENTERS	Writing Center
Reading Comprehension	Reading Comprehension	Reading Comprehension (Selection Test)	NO CENTERS	Computer Center in Pairs
Vocabulary Center (Index Cards)	Computer Center in Pairs	Vocabulary Center (Adventures in Vocabulary)	NO CENTERS	Meet with Teacher
Meet with Teacher	Meet with Teacher	Meet with Teacher	NO CENTERS	Meet with Teacher
Work with Words (2 Task Cards from 1–9)	Work with Words (2 Task Cards from 1–9)	Work with Words (2 Task Cards from 1–9)	NO CENTERS	Reading Comprehension (Cold Reads)

Mids 1: Blue Chameleons

Monday	Tuesday	Wednesday	Thursday	Friday
Reading Comprehension	Reading Comprehension	Reading Comprehension (Selection Test)	NO CENTERS	Computer Center in Pairs
Vocabulary Center (Index Cards)	Computer Center in Pairs	Vocabulary Center (Adventures in Vocabulary)	NO CENTERS	Writing Center
Meet with Teacher	Meet with Teacher	Meet with Teacher	NO CENTERS	Meet with Teacher
Work with Words (2 Task Cards from 1–9)	Word with Words (2 Task Cards from 1–9)	Work with Words (2 Task Cards from 1–9)	NO CENTERS	Meet with Teacher
Writing Center	Writing Center	Phonics Center	NO CENTERS	Reading Comprehension (Cold Reads)

Low 2: Yellow Chameleons

Monday	Tuesday	Wednesday	Thursday	Friday
Vocabulary Center (Index Cards)	Computer Center in Pairs	Vocabulary Center (Adventures in Vocabulary)	NO CENTERS	Meet with Teacher
Meet with Teacher	Meet with Teacher	Meet with Teacher	NO CENTERS	Meet with Teacher
Work with Words (2 Task Cards from 1–9)	Work with Words (2 Task Cards from 1–9)	Work with Words (2 Task Cards from 1–9)	NO CENTERS	Writing Center
Writing Center	Writing Center	Phonics Center	NO CENTERS	Reading Comprehension (Cold Reads)
Reading Comprehension	Reading Comprehension	Reading Comprehension (Selection Test)	NO CENTERS	Computer Center in Pairs

Low 1: Orange Chameleons

Monday	Tuesday	Wednesday	Thursday	Friday
Meet with Teacher	Meet with Teacher	Meet with Teacher	NO CENTERS	Meet with Teacher
Work with Words (2 Task Cards from 1–9)	Work with Words (2 Task Cards from 1–9)	Work with Words (2 Task Cards from 1–9)	NO CENTERS	Meet with Teacher
Writing Center	Writing Center	Phonics Center	NO CENTERS	Reading Comprehension (Cold Reads)
Reading Comprehension	Reading Comprehension	Reading Comprehension (Selection Test)	NO CENTERS	Computer Center in Pairs
Vocabulary Center (Index Cards)	Computer Center in Pairs	Vocabulary Center (Adventures in Vocabulary)	NO CENTERS	Writing Center

Purple Chameleons' Centers Checklist

THIS MENU MUST BE COMPLETED BY THE END OF READING ON TUESDAY.

MAKE SURE ALL OF YOUR WORK IS PLACED IN YOUR CENTERS FOLDER.

Directions:

Write the task card number of the activities you have completed in the boxes.

If the activity has no task card number, place a check (✔) in the box.

Remember to keep all of your work in your centers folder!

Tuesday	Task Card Number
Work with Words 1. You MUST complete 2 task cards from numbers 1–9. 2. You MAY complete any task card.	
Reading Comprehension 1. You MUST complete 1 reading comprehension passage and answer ALL questions. 2. You MAY complete a second reading comprehension passage and answer ALL questions.	
Vocabulary Center 1. You MUST complete an index card for each of the vocabulary words. Include the word, definition, a sentence, and picture. 2. You MAY complete a word study sheet.	
Writing Center 1. You MUST complete 2 activities from the Writing Menu. 2. You MAY complete any other activity.	

Teacher Note:

_____

_____

_____

_____

Total Dojo Points: _____

Purple Chameleons' Centers Checklist

THIS MENU MUST BE COMPLETED BY THE END OF READING ON WEDNESDAY.

MAKE SURE ALL OF YOUR WORK IS PLACED IN YOUR CENTERS FOLDER.

Directions:

Write the task card number of the activities you have completed in the boxes.

If the activity has no task card number, place a check (✔) in the box.

Remember to keep all of your work in your centers folder!

Wednesday	Task Card Number
Vocabulary Center 1. You MUST complete 2 activities from the vocabulary menu. Make sure to COLOR THE SQUARES. 2. You MAY complete any other activity from the menu.	
Phonics Center 1. You MUST complete the Phonics Graphing Sheet. 2. You MAY complete phonics task cards.	
Reading Comprehension 1. You MUST complete the Selection Test. 2. You MAY complete a reading comprehension passage and answer ALL questions.	
Writing Center 1. You MUST complete 2 activities from the Writing Menu. 2. You MAY complete any other activity.	

Teacher Note:

_____

_____

_____

_____

Total Dojo Points: _____

Purple Chameleons' Centers Checklist

THIS MENU MUST BE COMPLETED BY THE END OF READING ON THURSDAY.

MAKE SURE ALL OF YOUR WORK IS PLACED IN YOUR CENTERS FOLDER.

Directions:

Write the task card number of the activities you have completed in the boxes.

If the activity has no task card number, place a check (✔) in the box.

Remember to keep all of your work in your centers folder!

Thursday	Task Card Number
Writing Center 1. You MUST complete 2 activities from the Writing Menu. 2. You MAY complete any other activity.	▢ ▢ ▢ ▢
Vocabulary Center 1. You MUST complete 2 activities from the vocabulary menu. Make sure to COLOR THE SQUARES. 2. You MAY complete any other activity from the menu.	▢ ▢ ▢ ▢
Reading Comprehension 1. You MUST complete the Cold Read and answer ALL questions. 2. You MAY complete a reading comprehension passage and answer ALL questions.	▢ ▢
Meet with Teacher	▢

Teacher Note:

_____

_____

_____

Total Dojo Points: _____

Name: _____

Purple Chameleons' Centers Checklist

THIS MENU MUST BE COMPLETED BY THE END OF READING ON FRIDAY.

MAKE SURE ALL OF YOUR WORK IS PLACED IN YOUR CENTERS FOLDER.

Directions:

Write the task card number of the activities you have completed in the boxes.

If the activity has no task card number, place a check (✔) in the box.

Remember to keep all of your work in your centers folder!

Friday	Task Card Number
Phonics Center	
1. You MUST complete the Phonics Worksheets.	
2. You MAY complete phonics task cards.	
Reading Comprehension	
1. You MUST complete the reading comprehension passage and answer ALL questions.	
2. You MAY complete a reading comprehension passage and answer ALL questions.	
Meet with Teacher	

Teacher Note:

_____

_____

_____

_____

Total Dojo Points: _____

Pink Chameleons' Centers Checklist

THIS MENU MUST BE COMPLETED BY THE END OF READING ON TUESDAY.

MAKE SURE ALL OF YOUR WORK IS PLACED IN YOUR CENTERS FOLDER.

Directions:

Write the task card number of the activities you have completed in the boxes.

If the activity has no task card number, place a check (✔) in the box.

Remember to keep all of your work in your centers folder!

Tuesday	Task Card Number
Reading Comprehension	
1. You MUST complete 1 reading comprehension passage and answer ALL questions.	☐
2. You MAY complete a second reading comprehension passage and answer ALL questions.	☐
Vocabulary Center	
1. You MUST complete an index card for each of the vocabulary words. Include the word, definition, a sentence, and picture.	☐
2. YYou MAY complete a word study sheet.	☐
Meet with Teacher	☐
Work with Words	☐ ☐
1. You MUST complete 2 task cards from numbers 1–9.	
2. You MAY complete any task card.	☐ ☐

Teacher Note:

_____

_____

_____

Total Dojo Points: _____

Pink Chameleons' Centers Checklist

THIS MENU MUST BE COMPLETED BY THE END OF READING ON WEDNESDAY.

MAKE SURE ALL OF YOUR WORK IS PLACED IN YOUR CENTERS FOLDER.

Directions:

Write the task card number of the activities you have completed in the boxes.

If the activity has no task card number, place a check (✔) in the box.

Remember to keep all of your work in your centers folder!

Wednesday	Task Card Number
Phonics Center 1. You MUST complete the Phonics Graphing Sheet. 2. You MAY complete phonics task cards.	
Reading Comprehension 1. You MUST complete the Selection Test. 2. You MAY complete a reading comprehension passage and answer ALL questions.	
Meet with Teacher	
Vocabulary Center 1. You MUST complete 2 activities from the vocabulary menu. Make sure to COLOR THE SQUARES. 2. You MAY complete any other activity from the menu.	

Teacher Note:

_____

_____

_____

Total Dojo Points: _____

Thursday　　　Name: _____

Pink Chameleons' Centers Checklist

THIS MENU MUST BE COMPLETED BY THE END OF READING ON THURSDAY.

MAKE SURE ALL OF YOUR WORK IS PLACED IN YOUR CENTERS FOLDER.

Directions:

Write the task card number of the activities you have completed in the boxes.

If the activity has no task card number, place a check (✔) in the box.

Remember to keep all of your work in your centers folder!

Thursday	Task Card Number
Vocabulary Center 1. You MUST complete 2 activities from the vocabulary menu. Make sure to COLOR THE SQUARES. 2. You MAY complete any other activity from the menu.	
Writing Center 1. You MUST complete 2 activities from the Writing Menu. 2. You MAY complete any other activity.	
Meet with Teacher	
Reading Comprehension 1. You MUST complete the Cold Read and answer ALL questions. 2. You MAY complete a reading comprehension passage and answer ALL questions.	

Teacher Note:

_____

_____

_____

Total Dojo Points: _____

Pink Chameleons' Centers Checklist

THIS MENU MUST BE COMPLETED BY THE END OF READING ON FRIDAY.

MAKE SURE ALL OF YOUR WORK IS PLACED IN YOUR CENTERS FOLDER.

Directions:

Write the task card number of the activities you have completed in the boxes.

If the activity has no task card number, place a check (✔) in the box.

Remember to keep all of your work in your centers folder!

Friday	Task Card Number
Reading Comprehension 1. You MUST complete the reading comprehension passage and answer ALL questions. 2. You MAY complete a reading comprehension passage and answer ALL questions.	☐ ☐
Meet with Teacher	☐
Phonics Center 1. You MUST complete the Phonics Worksheets. 2. You MAY complete phonics task cards.	☐☐ ☐☐

Teacher Note:

_____

_____

_____

_____

Total Dojo Points: _____

Blue Chameleons' Centers Checklist

THIS MENU MUST BE COMPLETED BY THE END OF READING ON TUESDAY.

MAKE SURE ALL OF YOUR WORK IS PLACED IN YOUR CENTERS FOLDER.

Directions:

Write the task card number of the activities you have completed in the boxes.

If the activity has no task card number, place a check (✔) in the box.

Remember to keep all of your work in your centers folder!

Tuesday	Task Card Number
Vocabulary Center 1. You MUST complete an index card for each of the vocabulary words. Include the word, definition, a sentence, and picture. 2. You MAY complete a word study sheet.	☐ ☐
Meet with Teacher	☐
Work with Words 1. You MUST complete 2 task cards from numbers 1–9. 2. You MAY complete any task card.	☐☐ ☐☐
Reading Comprehension 1. You MUST complete 1 reading comprehension passage and answer ALL questions. 2. You MAY complete a second reading comprehension passage and answer ALL questions.	☐ ☐

Teacher Note:

_____

_____

_____

Total Dojo Points: _____

Blue Chameleons' Centers Checklist

THIS MENU MUST BE COMPLETED BY THE END OF READING ON WEDNESDAY.

MAKE SURE ALL OF YOUR WORK IS PLACED IN YOUR CENTERS FOLDER.

Directions:

Write the task card number of the activities you have completed in the boxes.

If the activity has no task card number, place a check (✔) in the box.

Remember to keep all of your work in your centers folder!

Wednesday	Task Card Number
Reading Comprehension 1. You MUST complete the Selection Test. 2. You MAY complete a reading comprehension passage and answer ALL questions.	▢ ▢
Meet with Teacher	▢
Vocabulary Center 1. You MUST complete 2 activities from the vocabulary menu. Make sure to COLOR THE SQUARES. 2. You MAY complete any other activity from the menu.	▢▢ ▢▢
Phonics Center 1. You MUST complete the Phonics Graphing Sheet. 2. You MAY complete phonics task cards.	▢▢ ▢▢

Teacher Note:

_____

_____

_____

Total Dojo Points: _____

Blue Chameleons' Centers Checklist

THIS MENU MUST BE COMPLETED BY THE END OF READING ON THURSDAY.

MAKE SURE ALL OF YOUR WORK IS PLACED IN YOUR CENTERS FOLDER.

Directions:

Write the task card number of the activities you have completed in the boxes.

If the activity has no task card number, place a check (✔) in the box.

Remember to keep all of your work in your centers folder!

Thursday	Task Card Number
Reading Comprehension 1. You MUST complete the Cold Read and answer ALL questions. 2. You MAY complete a reading comprehension passage and answer ALL questions.	☐ ☐
Meet with Teacher	☐
Writing Center 1. You MUST complete 2 activities from the Writing Menu. 2. You MAY complete any other activity.	☐ ☐ ☐ ☐
Vocabulary Center 1. You MUST complete 2 activities from the vocabulary menu. Make sure to COLOR THE SQUARES. 2. You MAY complete any other activity from the menu.	☐ ☐ ☐ ☐

Teacher Note:

_____

_____

_____

Total Dojo Points: _____

Name: _____

Blue Chameleons' Centers Checklist

THIS MENU MUST BE COMPLETED BY THE END OF READING ON FRIDAY.

MAKE SURE ALL OF YOUR WORK IS PLACED IN YOUR CENTERS FOLDER.

Directions:

Write the task card number of the activities you have completed in the boxes.

If the activity has no task card number, place a check (✔) in the box.

Remember to keep all of your work in your centers folder!

Friday	Task Card Number
Reading Comprehension 1. You MUST complete the reading comprehension passage and answer ALL questions. 2. You MAY complete a reading comprehension passage and answer ALL questions.	☐ ☐
Meet with Teacher	☐
Phonics Center 1. You MUST complete the Phonics Worksheets. 2. You MAY complete phonics task cards.	☐☐ ☐☐

Teacher Note:

_____

_____

_____

_____

Total Dojo Points: _____

Yellow Chameleons' Centers Checklist

THIS MENU MUST BE COMPLETED BY THE END OF READING ON TUESDAY.

MAKE SURE ALL OF YOUR WORK IS PLACED IN YOUR CENTERS FOLDER.

Directions:

Write the task card number of the activities you have completed in the boxes.

If the activity has no task card number, place a check (✔) in the box.

Remember to keep all of your work in your centers folder!

Tuesday	Task Card Number
Meet with Teacher	☐
Work with Words 1. You MUST complete 2 task cards from numbers 1–9. 2. You MAY complete any task card.	☐ ☐ ☐
Reading Comprehension 1. You MUST complete 1 reading comprehension passage and answer ALL questions. 2. You MAY complete a second reading comprehension passage and answer ALL questions.	☐ ☐
Vocabulary Center 1. You MUST complete an index card for each of the vocabulary words. Include the word, definition, a sentence, and picture. 2. You MAY complete a word study sheet.	☐ ☐

Teacher Note:

_____

_____

_____

Total Dojo Points: _____

Yellow Chameleons' Centers Checklist

THIS MENU MUST BE COMPLETED BY THE END OF READING ON WEDNESDAY.

MAKE SURE ALL OF YOUR WORK IS PLACED IN YOUR CENTERS FOLDER.

Directions:

Write the task card number of the activities you have completed in the boxes.

If the activity has no task card number, place a check (✔) in the box.

Remember to keep all of your work in your centers folder!

Wednesday	Task Card Number
Meet with Teacher	☐
Work with Words 1. You MUST complete 2 task cards from numbers 1–9. 2. You MAY complete any task card.	☐ ☐ ☐
Phonics Center 1. You MUST complete a phonics task card. 2. You MAY complete a phonics task card.	☐ ☐
Reading Comprehension 1. You MUST complete the Selection Test. 2. You MAY complete a reading comprehension passage and answer ALL questions.	☐ ☐

Teacher Note:

_____

_____

_____

Total Dojo Points: _____

Yellow Chameleons' Centers Checklist

THIS MENU MUST BE COMPLETED BY THE END OF READING ON THURSDAY.

MAKE SURE ALL OF YOUR WORK IS PLACED IN YOUR CENTERS FOLDER.

Directions:

Write the task card number of the activities you have completed in the boxes.

If the activity has no task card number, place a check (✔) in the box.

Remember to keep all of your work in your centers folder!

Thursday	Task Card Number
Meet with Teacher	
Phonics Center 1. You MUST complete the Phonics Graphing Sheet. 2. You MAY complete phonics task cards.	
Reading Comprehension 1. You MUST complete the Cold Read and answer ALL questions. 2. You MAY complete a reading comprehension passage and answer ALL questions.	
Writing Center 1. You MUST complete 1 activity from the Writing Menu. 2. You MAY complete any other activity.	

Teacher Note:

_____

_____

_____

Total Dojo Points: _____

Yellow Chameleons' Centers Checklist

THIS MENU MUST BE COMPLETED BY THE END OF READING ON FRIDAY.

MAKE SURE ALL OF YOUR WORK IS PLACED IN YOUR CENTERS FOLDER.

Directions:

Write the task card number of the activities you have completed in the boxes.

If the activity has no task card number, place a check (✔) in the box.

Remember to keep all of your work in your centers folder!

Friday	Task Card Number
Meet with Teacher	
Phonics Center 1. You MUST complete the Phonics Worksheets. 2. You MAY complete phonics task cards.	
Reading Comprehension 1. You MUST complete 1 reading comprehension passage and answer ALL questions. 2. You MAY complete a second reading comprehension passage and answer ALL questions.	

Teacher Note:

_____

_____

_____

_____

Total Dojo Points: _____

Name: _____

Orange Chameleons' Centers Checklist

THIS MENU MUST BE COMPLETED BY THE END OF READING ON TUESDAY.

MAKE SURE ALL OF YOUR WORK IS PLACED IN YOUR CENTERS FOLDER.

Directions:

Write the task card number of the activities you have completed in the boxes.

If the activity has no task card number, place a check (✔) in the box.

Remember to keep all of your work in your centers folder!

Tuesday	Task Card Number
Meet with Teacher	☐
Work with Words 1. You MUST complete 2 task cards from numbers 1–9. 2. You MAY complete any task card.	☐ ☐ ☐
Reading Comprehension 1. You MUST complete 1 reading comprehension passage and answer ALL questions. 2. You MAY complete a second reading comprehension passage and answer ALL questions.	☐ ☐
Vocabulary Center 1. You MUST complete an index card for each of the vocabulary words. Include the word, definition, a sentence, and picture. 2. You MAY complete a word study sheet.	☐ ☐

Teacher Note:

_____

_____

_____

Total Dojo Points: _____

Name: _____

Orange Chameleons' Centers Checklist

THIS MENU MUST BE COMPLETED BY THE END OF READING ON WEDNESDAY.

MAKE SURE ALL OF YOUR WORK IS PLACED IN YOUR CENTERS FOLDER.

Directions:

Write the task card number of the activities you have completed in the boxes.

If the activity has no task card number, place a check (✔) in the box.

Remember to keep all of your work in your centers folder!

Wednesday	Task Card Number
Meet with Teacher	☐
Work with Words 1. You MUST complete 2 task cards from numbers 1–9. 2. You MAY complete any task card.	☐ ☐ ☐
Phonics Center 1. You MUST complete a phonics task card. 2. You MAY complete a second phonics task card.	☐ ☐
Reading Comprehension 1. You MUST complete the Selection Test. 2. You MAY complete a reading comprehension passage and answer ALL questions.	☐ ☐

Teacher Note:

_____

_____

_____

Total Dojo Points: _____

Name: _____

Orange Chameleons' Centers Checklist

THIS MENU MUST BE COMPLETED BY THE END OF READING ON THURSDAY.

MAKE SURE ALL OF YOUR WORK IS PLACED IN YOUR CENTERS FOLDER.

Directions:

Write the task card number of the activities you have completed in the boxes.

If the activity has no task card number, place a check (✔) in the box.

Remember to keep all of your work in your centers folder!

Thursday	Task Card Number
Meet with Teacher	☐
Phonics Center 1. You MUST complete the Phonics Graphing Sheet. 2. You MAY complete phonics task cards.	☐ ☐☐
Reading Comprehension 1. You MUST complete the Cold Read and answer ALL questions. 2. You MAY complete a reading comprehension passage and answer ALL questions.	☐ ☐
Writing Center 1. You MUST complete 1 activity from the Writing Menu. 2. You MAY complete any other activity.	☐ ☐

Teacher Note:

_____

_____

_____

Total Dojo Points: _____

Orange Chameleons' Centers Checklist

THIS MENU MUST BE COMPLETED BY THE END OF READING ON FRIDAY.

MAKE SURE ALL OF YOUR WORK IS PLACED IN YOUR CENTERS FOLDER.

Directions:

Write the task card number of the activities you have completed in the boxes.

If the activity has no task card number, place a check (✔) in the box.

Remember to keep all of your work in your centers folder!

Friday	Task Card Number
Meet with Teacher	☐
Phonics Center 1. You MUST complete the Phonics Worksheets. 2. You MAY complete phonics task cards.	☐ ☐ ☐
Reading Comprehension 1. You MUST complete 1 reading comprehension passage and answer ALL questions. 2. You MAY complete a second reading comprehension passage and answer ALL questions.	☐ ☐

Teacher Note:

_____

_____

_____

_____

Total Dojo Points: _____

ESOL Instructional Strategies Matrix

Appendix B

Accommodations	B Clear Communication	C Assessments	D Vocabulary	E Collaboration & Conversation	F Metacognitive & Metalinguistic
A1 Heritage Dictionary MA, NC, MK, FM, FNR, NS, GV	B1 Concise Language	C1 Rubrics	D1 Etymology/Cognates	Grouping Configurations:	F1 L1 Transfer
A2 Heritage Language (L1) Support MA, EB, LAC, NC, RJCO, AC, CLG, JBQJ, MM, FM, AR, FNR, NS, GV, APV, KV, LV	B2 Clear Directions	C2 Presentation	D2 Semantic Feature Analysis	E1 Heterogeneous Grouping (Language/Content Readiness; Learner Profiles; Interests) MA, IA, EB, LAC, NC, CC, EC,RJCO, AC, CLG, TJ, JBQJ, MK, MM, NM, NM, FM, AR, FNR, NS, GV, APV, KV, LV	F2 Mnemonic Devices
	B3 Enunciation	C3 Portfolio	D3 Context Clues		F3 Dialogue Journals
	B4 Pauses & Pacing	C4 Checklist	D4 Tier II/Tier III Analysis	E2 Homogeneous Grouping (Language/Content Readiness; Learner Profiles; Interests)	F4 Self-Correction
	B5 Pointing MA, IA, EB, LAC, NC, CC, EC,RJCO, AC, CLG, TJ, JBQJ, MK, MM, NM, FM, AR, FNR, NS, GV, APV, KV, LV	C5 Labeling	D5 Interactive Word Walls	E3 Jigsaw	F5 Self-Evaluation
A3 Flexible Scheduling MA, IA, EB, LAC, NC, CC, EC,RJCO, AC, CLG, TJ, JBQJ, MK, MM, NM, FM, AR, FNR, NS, GV, APV, KV, LV		C6 Interview	D6 Vocabulary Games	E4 Peer Pair	F6 Self-Monitor
	B6 Repeating/ Paraphrasing	C7 Response Cards	D7 Multiple Meanings	E5 Reader's Theater	F7 Peer Editing
	B7 Gestures	C8 Oral Assessment	D8 Phonology	E6 Think/Pair/Share	F8 Associations
	B8 Show Examples & Non-Examples	C9 Observation MA, IA, EB, LAC, NC, CC, EC,RJCO, AC, CLG, TJ, JBQJ, MK, MM, NM, FM, AR, FNR, NS, GV, APV, KV, LV	D9 Vocabulary Banks	E7 Academic Games	
A4 Flexible Setting MA, IA, EB, LAC, NC, CC, EC,RJCO, AC, CLG, TJ, JBQJ, MK, MM, NM, FM, AR, FNR, NS, GV, APV, KV, LV	B9 Demonstrations	C10 Context-Embedded Text		E8 Group Presentations/ Projects	
	B10 Anecdote/ Storytelling	C11 Voting Devices		E9 Socratic Seminar	
A5 Flexible Timing MA, IA, EB, LAC, NC, CC, EC,RJCO, AC, CLG, TJ, JBQJ, MK, MM, NM, FM, AR, FNR, NS, GV, APV, KV, LV		C12 Cloze Test		E10 Panel Discussion	
		C13 Visual Representations		E11 Debate/Defend with Evidence	
		C14 Self /Peer Assessment			
		C15 Samples			
		C16 Sentence Frames			

ESOL Instructional Strategies Matrix (How We Teach is as Important as What We Teach) *(continued)*

G Context Embedded Supports & Close Reading	H Multimodal & Multimedia	I Advance Organizers	J Additional Resources
G1 Activating and/or Building Prior Knowledge G2 Chunking Text G3 Annotations & Symbols G4 Ask Inferential & HOT Questions G5 Ask Clarifying Questions G6 Modeling G7 Read Aloud G8 Think Aloud G9 Multimodal Texts G10 Visualization/Illustrations G11 Summarizing G12 Dramatic Enactments/Role Play G13 Identify Key Concepts G14 Similarities & Differences G15 Language Experience Approach	G16 Note-Taking/Outline Notes G17 Question–Answer–Relationship (QAR) G18 Reading with Specific Purpose G19 Reread Text MA, IA, EB, LAC, NC, CC, EC, RJCO, AC, CLG, TJ, JBQJ, MK, MM, NM, FM, AR, FNR, NS, GV, APV, KV, LV G20 Text Features & Structural Analysis G21 Survey, Question, Read, Recite, Review (SQ3R) G22 Text Connections G23 Total Physical Response (TPR) G24 Vary Complexity of Assignment G25 Realia/Manipulatives G26 Captioning	H1 Audio-Visual Applications H2 Digital Books H3 Computer Software H4 Document Camera H5 Interactive White Board MA, IA, EB, LAC, NC, CC, EC, RJCO, AC, CLG, TJ, JBQJ, MK, MM, NM, FM, AR, FNR, NS, GV, APV, KV, LV H6 Tablet/Interactive Devices H7 Language Master H8 Video/Film/CD/MP3 H9 Digital Simulations H10 Translation Device	I1 Charts (Flowcharts, T-Charts, etc.) I2 Anticipation Guide I3 Cornell Notes I4 Digital Tools/Software I5 Foldables I6 Graphs/Diagrams MA, IA, EB, LAC, NC, CC, EC, RJCO, AC, CLG, TJ, JBQJ, MK, MM, NM, FM, AR, FNR, NS, GV, APV, KV, LV I7 K-W-L I8 Reading and Analyzing Non-Fiction (RAN) I9 Notes TM I10 Webbing/Mapping I11 Story Maps I12 Timelines I13 Venn Diagrams I14 Vocabulary Improvement Strategy (VIS)	J1 Art Integration J2 Community Resources J3 Cultural Sharing J4 Celebrations J5 Field Trips J6 Guest Speakers J7 Holiday Programs J8 Multicultural Resources J9 Music/Songs/Jazz Chants

Broward County Public Schools, Bilingual/ESOL Department

09/2014

ESOL Matrix

http://www.broward.k12.fl.us/esol/eng/ESOL/PDF/Handbook/Appendices/AppendixM_Matrix.pdf

Explanation: Broward County's most recent list of ESOL strategies to be used in mainstream classrooms. Each week I align my lesson plan with a number of strategies I will use for my ESOL students. The red font are the initials of the students, strategies A1–A5 always remain the same, and the highlighted strategies change weekly depending on the lesson and activity. During our programmatic audit, the auditors saw this and absolutely loved the idea of placing student initials under each strategy.

Appendix C

Lesson Plan:
The Water Cycle

This is a fifth grade lesson plan based on the water cycle and includes an experiment and assessment. The assessment questions are comprised of a table of specifications with the breakdown of Bloom's taxonomy. Each question targets a specific higher order thinking skill. Under "Content" is a description of the lesson plan.

Grade: 5th   75 Minutes
Unit: Weather

The Water Cycle

I. Content

In this lesson students will learn about the water cycle, also known as the hydrologic cycle, and the continuous flow it undergoes as it changes form. Students will build upon prior knowledge, understand the basic concepts of evaporation and condensation, and the basic properties of solids, liquids, and gas. The teacher will conduct a brief lecture and distribute a water cycle flow map to each student. The students will discuss and define each processes of the cycle. Students will create a small-scale replica of the water cycle, and observe their experiment over the course of a few hours. The replica will demonstrate evaporation and condensation. Through this experiment, students will understand the importance of water to biological systems. By the end of this lesson, students will be able to define, identify, and summarize the seven key processes of the water cycle, and describe the relationship between the water cycle and the Earth. Lastly, students will be able to generalize the new concepts and key processes to other and/or new situations.

Students will learn about global awareness through this lesson, because they will understand that the water cycle is of profound importance to life on earth. This lesson will integrate knowledge of global dynamics, because the water cycle is part of the world's interconnected systems of complex mechanisms. Students will learn and become conscious of the global changes that occur in biological systems due to their dependence on the water cycle, and the impact of the water cycle on the Earth. Integration strategies like cooperative learning and United Nations observances (World Water Day) will infuse global awareness dimensions into the science content area and instruction of the lesson.

In this lesson, the teacher will emphasize and encourage the use of several skills. Students will use their listening skills to understand the content knowledge, important facts, and processes of the water cycle. Listening skills will be necessary for students to participate in the lesson and complete the necessary tasks of the lesson correctly. Students will engage in cooperative learning, because they will exchange ideas and information through the lesson, and work in teams to complete an experiment for the lesson. Students will reflect on what they've learned about the water cycle and apply it to real world problems or circumstances.

Florida State Standards

SC.5.E.7.1 Create a model to explain the parts of the water cycle. Water can be a gas, a liquid, or a solid and can go back and forth from one state to another.*

SC.5.P.9.1 Investigate and describe that many physical and chemical changes are affected by temperature.*

SC.5.P.8.1 Compare and contrast the basic properties of solids, liquids, and gases, such as mass, volume, color, texture, and temperature.*

ESE and ESOL Accommodations

❖ Use a blank card or tool to focus attention on the questions.
❖ Respond to answers directly on the test.
❖ Extend the time in the testing session to complete the test.
❖ Take the test alone or in a small group.

II. Objectives

After completing this unit, the student should be able to:

1. Identify the seven key processes of the water cycle.
2. Define the seven key processes of the water cycle.
3. Identify the three forms of matter.
4. Differentiate between the basic properties of solids, liquids, and gases.
5. Apply the key processes to new and other situations.
6. Distinguish between the key processes of the water cycle.

---

* Courtesy of Florida Department of Education accessed through www.cpalms.org.

7. Create a small-scale replica of the water cycle.
8. Describe the relationship between the water cycle and the Earth.
9. Summarize the processes of the water cycle.
10. Explain the importance of water as a resource on Earth.
11. Recommend ways to protect and conserve water.

III. Concepts

❖ **The Water/Hydrologic Cycle:** The cycle of evaporation and condensation that controls the distribution of the Earth's water as it evaporates from bodies of water, condenses, precipitates, and returns to those bodies of water. Also called *hydrologic cycle*.

❖ **Precipitation:** Water that falls from the air to Earth in the form of rain, snow, hail, sleet, and/or dew.

❖ **Condensation:** The change of a gas or vapor to a liquid. When water vapor cools in the atmosphere, for example, it condenses into tiny drops of water, which form clouds.

❖ **Infiltration:** The flow of water from the ground surface into the ground. Once infiltrated, the water becomes groundwater.

❖ **Ground Water:** Water that soaks into the Earth and fills the spaces or pores between the rocks and soil.

❖ **Evaporation:** The process of a liquid changing into a gas.

❖ **Transpiration:** The release of water vapor from plants and soil into the air.

❖ **Surface Runoff:** The water flow that occurs when the soil is infiltrated to full capacity and excess water from rain, meltwater, or other sources flows over the land.

❖ **Water Vapor:** The gas form of water, which is invisible in the air.

*Underlined concepts are part of the seven key processes of the water cycle.

IV. Resources

Education Resource—Water Cycle. (n.d.). *National Weather Service Southern Region homepage*. Retrieved February 24, 2013, from http://www.srh.noaa.gov/crp/?n=education-watercycle

Worksheets/Handouts:

❖ PD#1 The Water Cycle
❖ PD#2 Creating Your Own Mini Water Cycle
❖ PD#3 Record Your Data

Handouts are teacher originals.

V. Instructional Procedure

1. Learning Initiating Activity (Springboard)

The topic will be introduced through observation. A week before this lesson is scheduled, the teacher will fill two bottles with water. One bottle will be capped and the other will be uncapped. Every day, for one week, the teacher will ask students to observe and write a sentence for each bottle in their science journals. On the day of the lesson, the teacher will ask the students the following questions:

❖ Think about this for a moment before you answer, where does water in an open container go when it disappears?
❖ Think about this for a moment before you answer, why doesn't it disappear in a closed container?
❖ Remember what we learned, what are the three forms of matter?

The teacher will provide appropriate feedback to student responses.

Next, the teacher will briefly review the three forms of matter in terms of water. The teacher will half-fill a glass with water, put a few ice cubes in a dish, and place a wet paper towel in a separate dish. One item at a time will be presented to students, in the order mentioned above. Students will be asked the following questions.

For the half-filled glass:

❖ Is the water a liquid, solid, or gas?
❖ Where can you find water?
❖ Where does it come from?

Teacher will guide students in establishing that water is a liquid that falls from the sky in the form of rain and can be found in oceans, lakes, streams, and underground. Teacher will explain the properties of liquids: take the shape of its container and has a fixed volume. The teacher will provide appropriate feedback to student responses.

For the dish with ice cubes:

❖ Is the ice a liquid, solid, or gas?
❖ What is ice made of?
❖ How is it made?

Teacher will guide students in establishing that ice is water that has been frozen into a solid due to its exposure to very low temperatures. Emphasize that when ice warms up, it returns to liquid water. Teacher will explain the properties of solids: does not change shape and has a fixed volume. The teacher will provide appropriate feedback to student responses.

For the paper towel dish:

❖ What would happen if I left it out for a few hours?
❖ Why would it dry out?
❖ What are other examples of wet things that dry out over time?
❖ What if I put this wet paper towel outside during the winter? What might happen to it? Why?

Teacher will explain the properties of gases: hard to contain because it has no shape and has no volume. By discussing the differences and properties of the three forms of matter, this activity will allow the teacher to formatively assess students' understanding. At this point, students will understand that when water is exposed to warm temperatures, it disappears or evaporates, becoming a gas, while under colder temperatures it freezes into ice, becoming a solid. Emphasize that the three samples of

water represent the three states that water takes on as temperature and other conditions change. The teacher will provide appropriate feedback to student responses.

2. Core Activities (2.a and 2.b—two required by FPMS)

2.a Brief Lecture

Teacher will conduct a brief lecture by handing out a water cycle flow chart (PD#1) to each student, in which the seven key processes of the water cycle will be illustrated. Teacher will load an enlarged version of the chart on the SMART board. The lecture will include the vocabulary words and definitions listed under "concepts" above, and explanations and important facts about each key processes, beginning with precipitation, followed by surface runoff, infiltration, ground water, evaporation, condensation, transpiration, and water vapor. Teacher will write the definitions and important facts on the board for students to copy into their notebooks. At the end of the lecture, the teacher will formatively assess students by asking the following questions:

❖ Name the scientific name for the water cycle.
❖ Fill in the missing key process, _____ is the flow of water from the ground surface into the ground. (Answer: Infiltration)
❖ Give a definition of precipitation in your own words.
❖ When swimmers get out of the pool and sit in the sun, their wet skin dries quickly. What happens to the water?
❖ Give examples of how the water cycle affects the Earth.
❖ How are plants and the water cycle interconnected?
❖ As a group, let's summarize the water cycle.

The teacher will provide appropriate feedback to student questions and responses.

2.b Creating Your Own Mini Water Cycle

Students will be placed into teams of four. Students will follow the instructions on the "Creating Your Own Mini Water Cycle" handout (PD#2), and use the "Record Your Data" handout (PD#3) to analyze and record their observations. Each group will receive the following materials:

- A large, clear bowl
- A ruler
- Plastic wrap
- A weight
- A smaller container
- A rubber band

Students will be instructed to place the small container in the middle of the large, clear bowl, and to fill the bowl with a little water, and then use the ruler to measure 2 inches of water. Teacher and students will make sure that the small container inside does not have any water in it. Students will cover the bowl with plastic wrap, and fasten the plastic wrap around the rim of the bowl with the rubber band. The weight will be placed on top of the plastic wrap in the center. Each group will place their bowl on the windowsill where the sun will hit it. After lunch, students will continue answering the questions on the "Record Your Data" handout (PD#3). Students will observe that the heat of the sun will evaporate the water, and it will rise, and condense on the cool plastic wrap. The condensed water will fall into the smaller container. This serves as a small-scale replica of the water cycle that occurs on Earth every day. Teacher will assess by collecting both handouts at the end of class. The teacher will provide appropriate feedback to student questions and responses.

3. Application of Global Awareness Questions

Knowledge of Global Awareness

- Give examples of how the water cycle affects the Earth.
- How are plants and the water cycle interconnected?
- What if the sun disappeared entirely, what would happen to the water cycle?

State-of-the-Planet Awareness

- Explain how this particular body of water helps the environment.
- What if this body of water disappeared, what changes would occur to the environment around it?
- Describe the importance of water as a resource.
- Recommend two ways to protect and save water.

VI. Closure

In closing, the teacher will review the objectives covered by asking the students the following question:

- What have we learned today?

The teacher will provide appropriate feedback to student questions and responses. Teacher will augment the students' reporting, and ask the following follow-up questions:

- Name the seven key processes of the water cycle.
- Define the seven key processes of the water cycle.
- What is the difference between evaporation and condensation? Precipitation and transpiration?
- What are the three forms of matter? Give examples.
- What is the difference between the basic properties of a solid, liquid, and gas?
- Explain the water cycle.
- What did we see in the experiment?
- Describe the relationship between the water cycle and the Earth.
- Explain the importance of water as a resource on Earth.
- Recommend ways to protect and conserve water.

Teacher and students will ask and answer questions. Teacher will formatively assess that students have learned all objectives, by ensuring that all students respond to questions and participate in the closing discussion.

VII. Assessment

Students will be assessed based on class discussions, class participation, the group experiment handouts (PD#2–3), and homework.

VIII. Homework

The name of the homework assignment is the "My Life As A Drop" story. Students will imagine he/she is a drop of water, and write a creative short story about their journey through the water cycle. The students' "journey" may begin at any point of the water cycle, but the entire cycle must be completed at the end of the story. Students may be as creative as they'd like, but the parts of the water cycle must remain factual. Illustrations will be allowed.

IX. Follow-Up Activities/Extra Credit

In observance of United Nations World Water Day, on or around the day, the teacher will take students on a mini excursion to a local river, lake, or reservoir. Students will answer the following question in a few paragraphs their science journals:

❖ Explain how this particular body of water helps the environment.
❖ What if this body of water disappeared, what changes would occur to the environment around it?
❖ Describe the importance of water as a resource.
❖ Recommend two ways to protect and save water.

The teacher will provide appropriate feedback to student questions and responses.

The Hydrologic Cycle

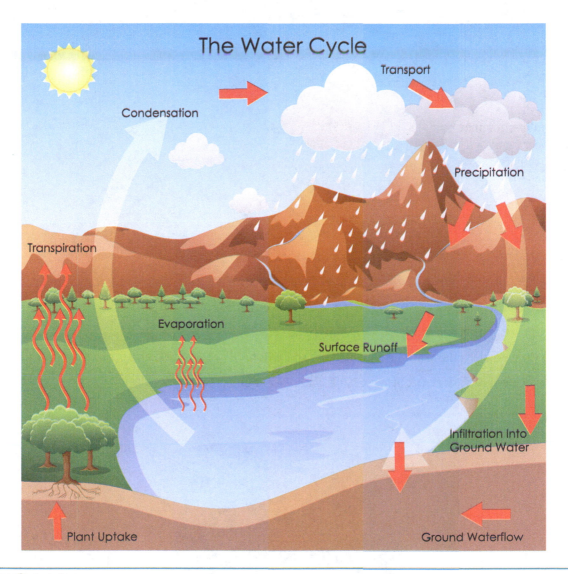

stockshoppe/Shutterstock.com

Creating Your Own Mini Water Cycle

Materials:
* A large, clear bowl
* A ruler
* Plastic wrap
* A weight
* A smaller container
* A rubber band
* Piece of paper
* Pen/pencil

Procedure:
1. Place the small container in the middle of the large, clear bowl.

2. Using the ruler, fill the bowl with 2 inches of water. Make sure there is no water in the small container.

3. Cover the bowl with plastic wrap and place the rubber band around the rim of the bowl.

4. Place the weight on top of the plastic wrap in the center.

5. Place your bowl on the windowsill where the sun will hit it.

6. On a piece of paper, write your team name and place it under your bowl.

Example:

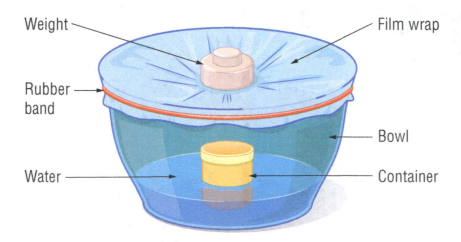

Weight — — Film wrap

Rubber band —

Water —

Bowl

Container

PD#3

Record Your Data

1. What do you think will happen to the water?

Hypothesis: _____

_____

2. List observations of the bowl before it sits in the sun. Include the water phases.

_____

_____

3. List observations of the bowl after it sits in the sun. Include the water phases.

_____

_____

4. Draw a picture of the bowl after it sits in the sun.

5. Identify the heat source that fuels the water cycle. _____

6. What if the heat source disappeared entirely, what would happen to the water cycle?

_____

_____

_____

Weather Unit

Table of Specification
Summative Assessment for The Water Cycle

Content Outline		Knowledge		Comprehension		Application		Analysis		Synthesis		Evaluation	
I. Multiple Choice		Identify the three forms of matter.								Distinguish between the key processes of the water cycle.			
25%	10	40%	4							60%	6		
II. True/False				Differentiate between the basic properties of solids, liquids, and gases.		Apply the key processes to new and other situations.							
25%	10			50%	5	50%	5						
III. Matching		Define the key processes of the water cycle.											
20%	8	100%	8										
IV. Labeling		Identify the key processes of the water cycle.											
20%	8	100%	8										
V. Short Answer				Summarize the processes of the water cycle.		Illustrate a small-scale replica of the water cycle.		Explain the relationship between the water cycle and the Earth.				Explain the importance of water and recommend ways to protect water.	
10%	4			25%	1		1		1			25%	1

The Water Cycle Exam

Multiple Choice

Directions: Circle the best answer for each question. Make sure the answer is clearly marked.

1. Liquids, solids, and gases are.
   A. Invisible
   B. Forms of matter
   C. Only found in water
   D. Water vapor

2. An example of a solid is.
   A. Oxygen
   B. Water
   C. Orange juice
   D. Ice cubes

3. Where does ground water come from?
   A. Underground rivers
   B. Oceans and streams
   C. Rainfall and melting snow
   D. Landfills.

4. The part of the water cycle when a liquid dissolves to a gas is called:
   A. Precipitation
   B. Evaporation
   C. Transpiration
   D. Condensation

5. An example of a liquid is.
   A. Sand
   B. Water vapor
   C. Hair
   D. Orange juice

6. Water vapor rises into the sky, it is cooled, and forms into a cloud. What is this called?
   A. Evaporation
   B. Infiltration
   C. Condensation
   D. Transpiration

7. An example of a gas is.
   A. Water vapor
   B. Perfume
   C. Orange juice
   D. Water

8. Which of the following is an example of *runoff?*
   A. Water flowing down a mountainside.
   B. Lake water evaporating during a drought.
   C. Ground water being absorbed by the roots of trees.
   D. Water evaporation to form clouds.

9. During which part of the water cycle is it easiest to see water?
   A. Evaporation
   B. Infiltration
   C. Precipitation
   D. Transpiration

10. When condensation occurs, water changes from:
   A. Solid to liquid
   B. Liquid to vapor
   C. Vapor to liquid
   D. Vapor to solid

True/False

Directions: Answer TRUE or FALSE for questions 16 to 25. DO NOT WRITE (T) OR (F).

16. _____ Liquids do not take the shape of its container and do not have a fixed volume.

17. _____ If all evaporation of water stopped, then there would be no more precipitation.

18. _____ Solids and liquids have fixed volume .

19. _____ When swimmers get out of the pool and sit in the sun, their wet skin dries quickly, because it becomes part of the water on the ground.

20. _____ Gases contain shape and have fixed volume.

21. _____ A boiling tea kettle filled with water is an example of condensation.

22. _____ Solids do not change shape.

23. _____ Plants affect the water cycle because they draw water up from the ground.

24. _____ Breathing on a mirror is an example of evaporation.

25. _____ Gases contain shape and have no volume.

Matching Columns

Directions: Match terms in Column B to definitions in Column A. Write the letter of the corresponding term in the blank space provided. Each term may only be used ONCE.

Column A	Column B
_____ 26. Water that falls from the air to Earth in the form of rain, snow, hail, sleet, and/or dew.	A. Infiltration
_____ 27. The change of a gas or vapor to a liquid. When water vapor cools in the atmosphere, for example, it condenses into tiny drops of water, which form clouds.	B. Evaporation C. Precipitation
_____ 28. The flow of water from the ground surface into the ground.	D. Transpiration
_____ 29. Water that soaks into the Earth and fills the spaces or pores between the rocks and soil.	E. Surface Runoff F. Ground Water
_____ 30. The process of a liquid changing into a gas.	G. Condensation
_____ 31. The release of water vapor from plants and soil into the air.	H. The Hydrologic Cycle
_____ 32. The water flow that occurs when the soil is penetrated to full capacity and excess water from rain, meltwater, or other sources flows over the land.	
_____ 33. The transfer of water that controls the distribution of the earth's water.	

Label the Diagram

Directions: Label 1 to 7 with the appropriate water cycle processes. Processes may be used more than once.

The Water Cycle
(The Hydrologic Cycle)

Merkushev Vasily/Shutterstock.com

1 _____

2 _____

3 _____

4 _____

5 _____

6 _____

7 _____

Short Answer

Directions: Answer questions 1 to 4. Be sure to use full sentences and proper grammar.

1. Illustrate a small-scale replica of the water cycle. Be sure to label the materials used in the illustration.

2. Explain what happens to the water in this experiment.

_____

_____

_____

_____

3. Explain the importance of water to as a resource to Earth. Recommend two ways to protect and conserve water.

_____

_____

_____

_____

4. In a short paragraph, summarize the water cycle. **BEGIN** with precipitation. Be sure to include all **SEVEN** key processes.

_____

_____

_____

_____

_____

_____

_____

Weather Unit

The Water Cycle Exam Answer Key

Multiple Choice

1.	B	Knowledge
2.	D	Knowledge
3.	C	Synthesis
4.	B	Synthesis
5.	D	Knowledge
6.	C	Synthesis
7.	A	Knowledge
8.	A	Synthesis
9.	C	Synthesis
10.	C	Synthesis

True/False

16.	FALSE	Comprehension
17.	TRUE	Application
18	TRUE	Comprehension
19.	FALSE	Application
20.	FALSE	Comprehension
21.	FALSE	Application
22.	TRUE	Comprehension
23.	TRUE	Application
24.	FALSE	Application
25.	FALSE	Comprehension

Matching Columns

26.	C	Knowledge
27.	G	Knowledge
28	A	Knowledge
29.	F	Knowledge
30.	B	Knowledge
31.	D	Knowledge
32.	E	Knowledge
33.	H	Knowledge

Label the Diagram

1.	Precipitation	Knowledge
2.	Snowmelt Runoff	Knowledge
3	Surface Runoff	Knowledge
4.	Infiltration	Knowledge
5.	Evaporation	Knowledge
6.	Transpiration	Knowledge
7.	Condensation	Knowledge

Short Answer

1. Illustrate a small-scale replica of the water cycle. Be sure to label the materials used in the illustration. (**Application**)

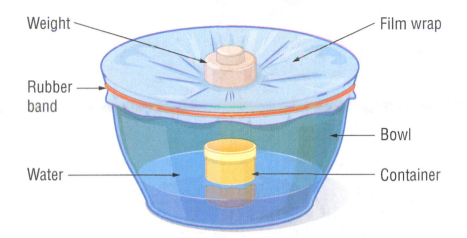

Weight

Film wrap

Rubber band

Bowl

Water

Container

2. Explain what happens to the water in this experiment. (**Analysis**)

The heat of the sun will evaporate the water, and it will rise, and condense on the cool plastic wrap. The condensed water will fall into the smaller container.

3. Explain the importance of water as a resource to Earth. Recommend two ways to protect and conserve water. (**Evaluation**)

Water is an important resource to Earth because it is a nutrient for all living things. Plants need it to grow, underwater creatures need it to live, and humans need it to consume. Some ways to protect and conserve water are to not use more lawn chemicals than necessary, and to dispose of hazardous and household chemicals properly.

4. In a short paragraph, summarize the water cycle. **BEGIN** with precipitation. Be sure to include all **SEVEN** key processes. (**Comprehension**)

The water cycle is the movement of water on Earth. It begins with precipitation. Precipitation falls from the sky in the form of rain, snow, hail, sleet, or dew. Then, surface runoff occurs, where the precipitation flows over the ground and back into the bodies of water or land. The runoff that does not flow back into water and stays on land seeps into the soil through infiltration; this water is called ground water. Plants help the water cycle because they soak up ground water from the soil, and some of the water turns into vapor and is released into the air. Some of the water, including water from large bodies, evaporates as vapor into the air. This water condenses and helps form clouds. When clouds form, precipitation occurs again and the water cycle continues.

Student Data Tracking and Graphing

Name _____

Go Math Assessment Student Data Tracking and Graphing

Domain: Number and Operation in Base Ten

Understand that the four digits of a four-digit number represent amounts of thousands, hundreds, tens, and ones.

"I can"

I know that four-digit numbers are made up of thousands, hundreds, tens, and ones.

Big Idea 1

Score	
100	_____
95	_____
90	_____
85	_____
80	_____
75	_____
70	_____
65	_____
60	_____
55	_____
50	_____
45	_____
40	_____
35	_____
30	_____
25	_____
20	_____
15	_____
10	_____
5	_____
0	_____

Numbers in Base Ten

Rate Yourself

1. I don't understand.
2. I can do this with help. Not by myself.
3. I understand. I can do this alone.
4. I can teach this!

Name _____

Go Math Assessment Student Data Tracking and Graphing

MAFS NBT.1.1

Understand that the four digits of a four-digit number represent amounts of thousands, hundreds, tens, and ones.

"I can"

I know that three-digit numbers are made up of hundreds, tens, a

Chapter 3

Score	
100	_____
95	_____
90	_____
85	_____
80	_____
75	_____
70	_____
65	_____
60	_____
55	_____
50	_____
45	_____
40	_____
35	_____
30	_____
25	_____
20	_____
15	_____
10	_____
5	_____
0	_____

NBT.1.1

Rate Yourself

1. I don't understand.
2. I can do this with help. Not by myself.
3. I understand. I can do this alone.
4. I can teach this!

Did you meet your goal?

Yes   No

Next Week's Goal _____%

Name _____

Go Math Assessment Student Data Tracking and Graphing

MAFS NBT.1.1

Understand that the three digits of a three-digit number represent amounts of hundreds, tens, and ones.

"I can"

I know that three-digit numbers are made up of hundreds, tens, and ones.

Chapter 2

Score

100	_____
95	_____
90	_____
85	_____
80	_____
75	_____
70	_____
65	_____
60	_____
55	_____
50	_____
45	_____
40	_____
35	_____
30	_____
25	_____
20	_____
15	_____
10	_____
5	_____
0	_____

NBT.1.1

Rate Yourself

1. I don't understand.
2. I can do this with help. Not by myself.
3. I understand. I can do this alone.
4. I can teach this!

Did you meet your goal?

Yes   No

Next Week's Goal _____ %

Name _____

Go Math Assessment Student Data Tracking and Graphing

MAFS NBT.1.1

Understand that the three digits of a three-digit number represent amounts of hundreds, tens, and ones.

"I can"

I know that three-digit numbers are made up of hundreds, tens, and ones.

Chapter 1

Score
100 _____
95 _____
90 _____
85 _____
80 _____
75 _____
70 _____
65 _____
60 _____
55 _____
50 _____
45 _____
40 _____
35 _____
30 _____
25 _____
20 _____
15 _____
10 _____
5 _____
0 _____

NBT.1.1

Rate Yourself

1. I don't understand.
2. I can do this with help. Not by myself.
3. I understand. I can do this alone.
4. I can teach this!

Did you meet your goal?

Yes   No

Next Week's Goal _____%

Name _____

Weekly Assessment Student Data Tracking and Graphing

LAFS RI.1.3

Describe the connection between a series of historical events, scientific ideas or concepts, or steps in technical procedures in a text.

"I can"

I can describe how details in a text are connected.

Unit 2 Week 5

Score

Score
100 _____
90 _____
80 _____
70 _____
60 _____
50 _____
40 _____
30 _____
20 _____
10 _____
0 _____

RI.1.3

Reading Comprehension
❖ Compare and Contrast ___/2

Short Answer
❖ Compare and Contrats ___/3

Vocabulary Strategies
❖ Suffixes; Context Clues ___/3

Grammar, Mechanics, and Usage
❖ Plurals and Possessive Apostrophes ___/3

Phonics
❖ Long u; Inflectional Endings -ing ___/3

Rate Yourself

5. I don't understand.

6. I can do this with help. Not by myself.

7. I understand. I can do this alone.

8. I can teach this!

Did you meet your goal?

Yes   No

Next Week's Goal _____%

Name _____

Weekly Assessment Student Data Tracking and Graphing

LAFS RI.1.2

Identify the main topic of multiparagraph text as well as the focus of specific paragraphs within the text.

"I can"

I can describe the events of a story and their purposes.

Unit 2 Week 5

Score

100	_____
90	_____
80	_____
70	_____
60	_____
50	_____
40	_____
30	_____
20	_____
10	_____
0	_____

RI.1.3

Reading Comprehension
❖ Compare and Contrast ___/2

Short Answer
❖ Compare and Contrast ___/3

Vocabulary Strategies
❖ Suffixes; Context Clues ___/3

Grammar, Mechanics, and Usage
❖ Plurals and Possessives; Apostrophes ___/3

Phonics
❖ Long u; Inflectional Ending -ing ___/3

Rate Yourself

5. I don't understand.

6. I can do this with help. Not by myself.

7. I understand. I can do this alone.

8. I can teach this!

Did you meet your goal?

Yes   No

Next Week's Goal _____%

Weekly Assessment Student Data Tracking and Graphing

LAFS K12.R.1.3

Analyze how and why individuals, events, and ideas develop and interact over the course of a text.

"I can"

I can use identify causes and effects in a stories.

Unit 2 Week 2

Score

100	_____
90	_____
80	_____
70	_____
60	_____
50	_____
40	_____
30	_____
20	_____
10	_____
0	_____

K12.R.1.3

Reading Comprehension
❖ Cause and Effect ___/2

Short Answer
❖ Cause and Effect ___/3

Vocabulary Strategies
❖ Context Clues; Multiple-Meaning Words ___/3

Grammar, Mechanics, and Usage
❖ Plural Nouns; Capitalization and Commas ___/3

Phonics
❖ Long e (e, ee, ea, y, ey, ie); Prefixes ___/3

Rate Yourself
1. I don't understand.
2. I can do this with help. Not by myself.
3. I understand. I can do this alone.
4. I can teach this!

Did you meet your goal?

Yes   No

Next Week's Goal _____%

Weekly Assessment Student Data Tracking and Graphing

LAFS RL.3.7

Use information gained from the illustrations and words in a print or digital text to demonstrate understanding of its characters, setting, or plot.

"I can"

I can use pictures and words to figure out the parts of a story.

Unit 2 Week 1

Score

100	_____
90	_____
80	_____
70	_____
60	_____
50	_____
40	_____
30	_____
20	_____
10	_____
0	_____

RL.3.7

Reading Comprehension
❖ Character, Setting, Plot ____/2

Short Answer
❖ Character, Setting, Plot ____/3

Vocabulary Strategies
❖ Context Clues ____/3

Grammar, Mechanics, and Usage
❖ Nouns; Commas in a Series ____/3

Phonics
❖ Long a (a, ai, ay, ea, ei) ____/3

Rate Yourself

1. I don't understand.
2. I can do this with help. Not by myself.
3. I understand. I can do this alone.
4. I can teach this!

Did you meet your goal?

Yes   No

Next Week's Goal _____%

Weekly Assessment Student Data Tracking and Graphing

LAFS RI.1.1

Ask and answer such questions as *who, what, where, when, why,* and *how* to demonstrate understanding of key details in a text.

"I can"

I can ask and answer questions about the text to show my understanding.

Unit 1 Week 5

Score

100 _____
90 _____
80 _____
70 _____
60 _____
50 _____
40 _____
30 _____
20 _____
10 _____
0 _____

RI.1.1

Listening Comprehension
❖ Character; Plot ___/3

Reading Comprehension
❖ Character; Plot; Main Idea and Details ___/4

Short Answer
❖ Make/Confirm Predictions; Main Idea and Details ___/6

Vocabulary Strategies
❖ Words ending in –ed; Prefixes; Dictionary/ABC Order ___/5

Literary Elements
❖ Rhyme; Rhythmic Patterns ___/2

Text Features and Study Skills
❖ Photos and Captions; Using Parts of a Book; Bar Graphs ___/4
❖ Grammar, Mechanics, and Usage: ___/4

Phonics
❖ Short *o, a,* e; Long o; Soft *c*; Consonant Diagraph *sh st* ___/6

Rate Yourself

1. I don't understand.

2. I can do this with help. Not by myself.

3. I understand. I can do this alone.

4. I can teach this!

Name _____

Weekly Assessment Student Data Tracking and Graphing

LAFS RI.1.2

Identify the main topic of multiparagraph text as well as the focus of specific paragraphs within the text.

"I can"

I can describe the events of a story and their purposes.

Unit 1 Week 4

Score	
100	_____
90	_____
80	_____
70	_____
60	_____
50	_____
40	_____
30	_____
20	_____
10	_____
0	_____

RI.1.2

Reading Comprehension
❖ Main Idea and Details ____/2

Short Answer
❖ Main Idea and Details ____/3

Vocabulary Strategies
❖ Context Clues; Dictionary ____/3

Grammar, Mechanics, and Usage
❖ Predicates; Commas ____/3

Phonics
❖ Short *i*, Long *i*; Soft *c* and *g* ____/3

Rate Yourself

1. I don't understand.
2. I can do this with help. Not by myself.
3. I understand. I can do this alone.
4. I can teach this!

Did you meet your goal?

Yes   No

Next Week's Goal _____%

Name _____

Weekly Assessment Student Data Tracking and Graphing

LAFS RL.2.5

Describe the overall structure of a story, including describing how the beginning introduces the story and the ending concludes the action.

"I can"

I can describe the events of a story and their purposes.

Unit 1 Week 3

Score

100 _____

90 _____

80 _____

70 _____

60 _____

50 _____

40 _____

30 _____

20 _____

10 _____

0 _____

RL.2.5

Reading Comprehension
❖ Main Idea and Details ___/2

Short Answer
❖ Main Idea and Details ___/3

Vocabulary Strategies
❖ Context Clues; Word Parts: *Prefixes* ___/3

Grammar, Mechanics, and Usage
❖ Letter Punctuation and Subjects ___/3

Phonics
❖ Short *a*, Long a; Consonant Blends: *sl, dr, sk, sp, st* ___/3

Rate Yourself

1. I don't understand.

2. I can do this with help. Not by myself.

3. I understand. I can do this alone.

4. I can teach this!

Did you meet your goal?

Yes   No

Next Week's Goal _____%

Charlie and the Chocolate Factory

Explanation:

Following is an example of fourth grade unit study of Roald Dahl's *Charlie and the Chocolate Factory*, including center activities for the book and examples. The unit study is arts integrated and includes specific ESOL standards.

Charlie and the Chocolate Factory Unit Study

Subject: Language Arts/Visual Arts   **Grade:** 4   **Length of Lesson:** 70 Minutes

I. Instructional Objectives/ Outcomes:

Specific Learning Objectives

The learner will . . .

❖ Illustrate a drawing of their own factory. (Visually Representing)

❖ Engage in a class discussion about their illustration, and tell the class what item their factory produces, what machines produce such items, and the size of the rooms of the factory. (Speaking/Thinking)

❖ Define the vocabulary words and identify them by putting their hands on their shoulders every time they hear a vocabulary word during the read aloud. (Listening/Viewing)

❖ Listen to the story, *Charlie and the Chocolate Factory*. (Chapters 1–4) (Listening/Viewing/ Speaking) Verbally retell the story by summarizing the chapters, identifying characters, plot, setting, and genre. (Thinking/Speaking)

❖ Create a book report, which includes the following information for Chapters 1–4. (Writing)

   ◆ Title of the book, author, illustrator, and a picture.
   ◆ The publisher, year of publication, and genre.
   ◆ Description of the setting using at least two vocabulary words.

   ◆ Provide character analysis for the main characters using at least five vocabulary words.
   ◆ Description of the plot using the applicable elements; exposition, foreshadowing, inflicting force, conflict, rising action, crisis, climax, falling action, and resolution.
   ◆ Identify the themes of the story.

Florida Sunshine State Standards

LA.4.1.6.1 The student will use new vocabulary that is introduced and taught directly;*

LA.4.2.1.1 The student will read and distinguish among the genres and sub-genres of fiction, nonfiction, poetry, drama, and media;*

LA.4.2.1.2: The student will identify and explain the elements of plot structure, including exposition, setting, character development, problem/resolution, and theme in a variety of fiction;*

VA.4.C.1.1 Integrate ideas during the art-making process to convey meaning in personal works of art.*

Florida Goal 3 Standards

Standard 3.1: **Information Managers.** *Florida students locate, comprehend, interpret, evaluate, maintain, and apply information, concepts, and ideas found in literature, the arts, symbols, recordings, video and other graphic displays, and com-*

---

* Courtesy of Florida Department of Education accessed through www.cpalms.org.

puter files in order to perform tasks and/or for enjoyment.*

Standard 3.2: Effective Communicators. *Florida students communicate in English and other languages using information, concepts, prose, symbols, reports, audio and video recordings, speeches, graphic displays, and computer-based programs.**

Standard 3.8: Cooperative Workers. *Florida students work cooperatively to successfully complete a project or activity.**

ESOL Standards

Standard 5: Determine and use appropriate instructional methods and strategies for individuals and groups, using knowledge of first and second language acquisition processes.

Standard 6: Apply current and effective ESOL teaching methodologies in planning and delivering instruction to LEP students.

Standard 12: Apply content-based ESOL approaches to instruction.

Standard 18: Create a positive classroom environment to accommodate the various learning styles and cultural backgrounds of students.

II. Subject Matter Content:

❖ Cognitive Knowledge
  ◆ Define, identify, and use vocabulary words.
  ◆ Comprehend the read aloud.
  ◆ Create a book report and apply key story elements. (Book information, setting, plot, genre, character analysis, theme, etc.)
❖ Behavioral Knowledge
  ◆ Engage in class discussions.
  ◆ Actively listen to read aloud without fidgeting.
  ◆ Follow teacher directions and complete tasks on time.
❖ Affective Knowledge
  ◆ Show enthusiasm about learning.

III. Instructional Procedures:

Lesson Initiating Activities

Schema Activation: Before introducing the book *Charlie and the Chocolate Factory* by Roald Dahl, students are asked to draw their own dream factory with their own imaginations. The following prompt will be used to activate the children's schema:

❖ Imagine you are given a factory and allowed to produce anything you wanted. Draw a picture of what you would want to produce a tremendous amount of and sell to the world. Think about how large and how many rooms your factory will have. What machines will you need?

Students will be given construction paper, colored pencils, and markers. This activity will give them the opportunity to create their own world of fantasy, and will easily connect this experience with the fantasy fiction. This activity will stimulate students' imagination, let them draw without concrete boundaries or clear guidelines, and associate art with the key literature. Once students complete their illustrations, the teacher will ask the students to briefly talk about their works, as a class. I will repeat the children's responses, and make sure I give them encouragement and praise for their participation. If children are attempting to express their thoughts and ideas, but are having trouble putting them together, then I will assist them in voicing those thoughts and ideas. I want to have a conversation with the students, not an interrogation. I will follow the children's responses with questions, like the ones below.

❖ Why did you choose to produce (the item) in your factory?
❖ Would your factory be open all day and all night?
❖ Who would work in your factory?

Book Introduction: I will gather the class and have them sit around me in our "Read Aloud Center" in the classroom. The read aloud book for this

---

* Courtesy of Florida Department of Education accessed through www.cpalms.org.

Appendix E   485

lesson is called, *Charlie and the Chocolate Factory* by Roald Dahl.

Predictions: The read aloud book will be revealed, and I will indicate where the spine, cover, and title page of the book are located. I will ask the children the following questions:

- ❖ Can anybody tell me what he or she thinks this story is going to be about?
- ❖ What can you tell me about this story from the cover and the title of the book?

I will repeat the children's responses, and make sure I give them encouragement and praise for their participation. If children are attempting to express their thoughts and ideas, but are having trouble putting them together, then I will assist them in voicing those thoughts and ideas. I will follow the children's responses with questions, like the ones below.

- ❖ Why do you think that is going to happen in this book?
- ❖ What makes you think that is going to happen in this book?
- ❖ What else can anybody share with us about the cover and title of the book?

Pre-Read, Pre-Teach Concepts, and Vocabulary: Before the read aloud, I will conduct a mini lesson on the following vocabulary words and their definitions to help the children understand the reading. All the vocabulary words appear somewhere in the text, and will be pointed out to the class when they are read during the read aloud. The vocabulary words will help the children explore the important concepts of the book. The words and their definitions will be posted on a large chart near the "Read Aloud Center" in the classroom. I will write and say the word, and have the children repeat the word with me. I will attach an easy-to-understand definition to the word, and provide examples of the word in contexts. Students will engage in thinking about the word and its definition by participating in this exercise. I will ask, "When do I use this word? Do I turn on my *furnace* on a hot summer day?" (NO!) And I will continue by asking, "Would I turn on my *furnace* in the middle of a snowstorm?" (YES!) This exercise allows me to

assess their knowledge of the word. The children will repeat the word again for phonological reinforcement. I will repeat this procedure for each vocabulary word.

- ❖ Draft: A current of air.
  - ◆ Example: Amy was cold, because a cold *draft* was coming in through the open door.
- ❖ Desperately: Intensely.
  - ◆ Example: The little boy cried *desperately*, because he lost his mom in the supermarket.
- ❖ Inventor: A person who invents.
  - ◆ Example: Thomas Edison is the *inventor* of the light bulb.
- ❖ Absurd: Ridiculous.
  - ◆ Example: Asking people on the Internet how to do your homework seems *absurd*.
- ❖ Clever: Mentally quick; smart.
  - ◆ Example: The fox was *clever* and did not let the deer get away.
- ❖ Furnace: An enclosure where heat is formed.
- ❖ Example: Every winter we turn on the *furnace*, so we can stay warm during the snowstorms.
- ❖ Nibble: To take small bites out of.
  - ◆ Example: The baby *nibbled* on the cracker, since it was the first time eating food.
- ❖ Colossal: Enormous; very large; huge.
  - ◆ Example: The *colossal* sculpture is much larger than life size; I have to walk away just so I can see the face.
- ❖ Proper: Suitable; fitting.
  - ◆ Example: At the dinosaur themed birthday party, the *proper* attire was a T-Rex costume.
- ❖ Nightcap: A cap worn at night.
  - ◆ Example: Grandma Anne puts on her *nightcap* before going to bed every night.
- ❖ Stammer: To repeat the same sound without meaning.
  - ◆ Example: When I have to speak in front of a big crowd I *stammer*, because I'm nervous.
- ❖ Torture: To afflict with physical or mental pain.
  - ◆ Example: The dog was so hungry. Watching all the people around him eat was like *torture*.

- ❖ Marvelous: Causing wonder or amazement.
  - ◆ Example: Watching the tight rope walker walk between buildings, thousands of feet in the air was *marvelous*.
- ❖ Deserted: Abandoned.
  - ◆ Example: The puppy's mom was nowhere to be found. He was *deserted*.
- ❖ Greedily: Selfish.
  - ◆ Example: Robbie *greedily* ate all the chocolate, and did not share one piece with his sisters.

Before we begin our read aloud, I will explain to the children that this story is a fantasy-fiction novel. I will ask the students that while I'm reading, I would like them to think about the real aspects of the book and the fantasy aspects of the book.

We will briefly review what are the plot, setting, and genre of a book. Students will have prior knowledge of these story elements from previous lessons.

Set Listening Goal for Reading: I will tell the students that I want them to put their hands on their shoulders every time they hear a vocabulary word.

Core Activities (During Reading: Guided Instruction)

Dramatic Reading:
This read aloud will cover Chapters 1–4.

- ❖ I will hold the book up in front of me, so that all the children can see the cover before we begin. I will verbally print reference by asking, "Where is the title of the book?" Once the children respond, I will state the author and illustrator. The title is, *Charlie and the Chocolate Factory* by Roald Dahl and illustrated by Quentin Blake. I will flip to the title page and read, "*Charlie and the Chocolate Factory* by Roald Dahl and illustrated by Quentin Blake."
- ❖ On page five, I will comment about print by verbally print referencing, and stating, "There are our vocabulary words, draft and proper!" In order to check comprehension of the word and text, I will ask, "What did Mr. Bucket do for a living? What kinds of meals could the Buckets afford?"
- ❖ On page six, I will comment about print by verbally print referencing, and stating, "There are

our vocabulary words, nibble, greedily, desperately, and tortured!" In order to check comprehension of the word and text, I will ask, "How often did Charlie Bucket get to eat chocolate? How long would the chocolate bar last him?"
- ❖ On page seven, I will comment about print by verbally print referencing, and stating, "There's our vocabulary word, inventor!" In order to check comprehension of the word and text, I will ask, "What have we learned about Mr. Wonka? Who is he?"
- ❖ On page nine, I will comment about print by verbally print referencing, and stating, "There are our vocabulary words, clever and nightcap!"
- ❖ On page eleven, I will comment about print by verbally print referencing, and stating, "There are our vocabulary words, absurd and colossal!" In order to check comprehension of the word and text, I will ask, "What did Mr. Wonka invent? What kinds of sweets can you find at Mr. Wonka's chocolate factory?"
- ❖ On page fourteen, I will comment about print by verbally print referencing, and stating, "There's our vocabulary word, stammer!" In order to check comprehension of the word and text, I will ask, "Who do you think works in the chocolate factory? How does Charlie react to what Grandpa Joe tells him?"
- ❖ On page sixteen, I will comment about print by verbally print referencing, and stating, "There are our vocabulary words, marvelous, furnace, and deserted!" In order to check comprehension of the word and text, I will ask, "Why did Mr. Wonka shut the factory gates? Why were people surprised that the furnaces were lit? Does anyone want to predict what will happen next?"
- ❖ On page nineteen, I will print reference nonverbally, by tracking print. The text reads, "*Wonka Factory to be opened at last to lucky few!*" I will track my finger under the words of this sentence, because it explains a key point in the story.

Children Retell Story: After the read aloud, the children will be assessed for listening comprehension skills by retelling the story. I will ask the students the following questions.

- ❖ What do we know about the plot?
- ❖ What do we know about the setting?
- ❖ What is the genre?
- ❖ Who are the main characters of the story so far?
- ❖ What do we know about them?
- ❖ Describe what the Buckets' house is like.
- ❖ What are some of the mysteries about the chocolate factory?
- ❖ What do you think will happen next?
- ❖ What are some real events of the story and what are some fantasy events?

In our read loud center, we will sit in a circle and begin retelling the story. I will begin and the student to my left will continue, and everyone will have a chance to retell a part of the story at least once. As we retell the story, the events must occur in chronological order.

Closure Activities (After Reading: Concluding Set)

Students will create a book report about the story using the vocabulary words and key elements of the story. Teacher will distribute one sheet of construction paper and five sheets of copy paper and a copy of the book to each student. The teacher will demonstrate the instructions once, and repeat them a second time with the students. The students will line up the edges of all six pieces of paper, and fold them in half like a book. The students will title the pages and complete the necessary information as indicated below.

For this lesson, students will only be responsible for filling out information that pertains to Chapters 1–4 only. Students will be allowed to work in groups.

- ❖ Page 1: Title of the book, author, and illustrator. Draw a picture that reflects the title of the book.
- ❖ Page 2: The publisher, year of publication, and genre. The genre is the type of book. Fiction, nonfiction, fantasy, autobiography, historical fiction, romance, comedy, drama, fantasy, mystery, science fiction, etc.

- ❖ Page 3: Write "Setting" on the top left corner. The time (when), the place (where), and the environment in which the story takes place. It sets the scene for the events in the story. Use at least two vocabulary words when describing the setting.
- ❖ Pages 4–8: Write "Character Analysis" on the top left corner. The cast of the story. Describe the characters of the story. Use at least five vocabulary words when describing the characters.
- ❖ Pages 9–10: Write "Plot" on the top left corner. Underneath write "Chapters 1–4" Summary of the chapters. Describe the elements of the plot: exposition, foreshadowing, inflicting force, conflict, rising action, crisis, climax, falling action, and resolution.
- ❖ Page 11: Write "Themes" on the top left corner. The moral of the story. There may be more than one. Themes may include, nature, coming of age, discovering, life lesson, etc., if applicable.

As we continue reading the story, students will be responsible for completing the rest of the information in their book. Teacher will allot specific times for students to complete the information after readings.

Accommodations for Diverse Learners (ESOL, ESE, Gifted Strategies)

Allow sufficient time for completion of the project. Use visuals and demonstrate steps of creating the artwork using simplified directions. Have peers assist students who are having difficulty.

Classroom Management

The teacher will ask the students to pay close attention to the read aloud. The teacher will ask students to discontinue any side conversations, and join the "Read Aloud Center." The teacher will implement positive reinforcement in the classroom by giving checks to the students who participate. The teacher will ask for volunteers to pass out supplies. The teacher will also use the light as a way to quiet the class, if necessary.

IV. Materials and Equipment:

- *Charlie and the Chocolate Factory* by Roald Dahl. A teacher copy and a copy for each student in the class.
- Construction Paper
- Crayons, Markers, and Colored Pencils
- Glue
- Stapler

V. Assessment/Evaluation:

Students will be assessed based on the following:

- Visually Representing: Creates a drawing of their own factory.
- Speaking/Thinking: Participates in class discussion about their illustration at least once. Tells the class about the item their factory produces, what machines produce the items, and the size of the rooms in the factory.
- Listening/Viewing: Defines the vocabulary words, and identifies them by putting their hands on their shoulders every time they hear a vocabulary word.
- Listening/Viewing/Speaking/Thinking: Can verbally retell the story by summarizing the chapters, identifying characters, plot, setting, and genre.
- Writing: Creates a book report for Chapters 1–4. *See attached rubric.*

VI. Follow-up Activities:

- Teacher will assign Chapters 5–9 for homework.
- Students will read the chapters, and list at least eight words they are unfamiliar with.
- Students will write down the definition of each word.
- Students will continue filling out the book report. The words they defined will be the vocabulary words they must use.

VII. Self-Assessment (to be completed after the lesson is presented):

- How did my students respond to what I did in class?
- What are my reactions to what I did in class?
- How would I change the lesson if I were to teach it again?

REFERENCES

Florida Department of Education. (2005). Next Generation Sunshine State Standards. Retrieved March 4, 2012, from http://www.fldoe.org/bii/curriculum/sss/.

Book Report: Charlie and the Chocolate Factory Rubric

Teacher Name: Ms. Mittone   **Student Name:** _____

Category	4	3	2	1	Points Earned
Front Cover	Includes an illustration, title of the book, author name, and illustrator name. The graphic illustrates some scene from the book.	Includes an illustration, title of the book, author name, and illustrator name.	Includes an illustration. Missing one: the title of the book, author name, or illustrator name.	Does not include illustration, title, author name, and illustrator name.	
Inside Left Flap	Includes the publisher, year of publication, and genre.	Missing one: the publisher, year of publication, or genre.	Missing two: the publisher, year of publication, or genre.	Does not include the publisher, year of publication, and genre.	
Setting	Includes the time, the place, and the environment in which the story takes place. Uses at least two vocabulary words.	Missing one: The time, the place, or a vocabulary word.	Missing two: The time, the place, or vocabulary words.	Does not include the time, the place, or two vocabulary words.	
Character Analysis	Includes descriptions of at least four characters in the story. Uses at least five vocabulary words.	Missing one: Description of a character or a vocabulary word.	Missing two or three: Description of characters or vocabulary words.	Does not include descriptions of characters and does not use vocabulary words.	
Plot	Summary is well-written and includes all aspects of the story. Paragraphs are well formed. It is clear the student read the book and understood it. Includes an element of the plot.	Summary includes all aspects of the story, but at least one paragraph is not well formed. It is clear the student read the book. Includes an element of the plot.	Includes a description of some of the things that happened in the story. It appears the student read most of the book, but might not understand it. Does not include an element of the plot.	Summary is too vague. Does not appear the student read or understood the book. Does not include an element of the plot.	
Themes	Includes at least four themes. MAY NOT BE APPLICABLE UNTIL LATER ON IN BOOK.	Includes at least three themes. MAY NOT BE APPLICABLE UNTIL LATER ON IN BOOK.	Includes at least two themes. MAY NOT BE APPLICABLE UNTIL LATER ON IN BOOK.	Includes one or no themes. MAY NOT BE APPLICABLE UNTIL LATER ON IN BOOK.	
Grammar	There are no grammatical mistakes in the book report.	There is one grammatical mistake in the book report.	There are two to three grammatical mistakes in the book report.	There are more than three grammatical mistakes in the book report.	

Comments:

Charlie and the Chocolate Factory Unit Plan

DAY 1:

Read Aloud: Teacher will read Chapters 1–4 in the "Read Aloud Center."

Objective

Students will illustrate a drawing of their own factory, and engage in a class discussion. They will tell the class about their illustrations, what item their factory produces, what machines produce such items, and the size of the rooms of the factory. Students will be able to define the vocabulary words and identify them by putting their hands on their shoulders every time they hear a vocabulary word during the read aloud. Students will listen to the story. Students will verbally retell the story by summarizing the chapters, identifying characters, plot, setting, and genre. Students will create a book report, in which they will apply the elements of a story to the book. *(See attached rubric for book report.)*

Procedure

Teacher will begin by asking students to draw their own dream factory, and follow with a class discussion about their drawing. Teacher will conduct a mini lesson on vocabulary words and review the elements of a story. Teacher will introduce the book and read Chapters 1–4. Teacher will lead a class discussion, where students will verbally retell the story by summarizing the chapters, identifying characters, plot, setting, and genre.

Extension Activity

Students will create a book report about the story using the vocabulary words and key elements of the story. Teacher will distribute one sheet of construction paper and five sheets of copy paper and a copy of the book to each student. The students will line up the edges of all six pieces of paper, and fold them in half like a book. The students will title the pages and complete the necessary information as indicated below.

For this lesson, students will only be responsible for filling out information that pertains to Chapters 1–4 only. Students will be allowed to work in groups.

❖ Page 1: Title of the book, author, and illustrator. Draw a picture that reflects the title of the book.
❖ Page 2: The publisher, year of publication, and genre. The genre is the type of book. Fiction, nonfiction, fantasy, autobiography, historical fiction, romance, comedy, drama, fantasy, mystery, science fiction, etc.
❖ Page 3: Write "Setting" on the top left corner. The time (when), the place (where), and the environment in which the story takes place. It sets the scene for the events in the story. Use at least two vocabulary words when describing the setting.
❖ Pages 4–8: Write "Character Analysis" on the top left corner. The cast of the story. Describe the characters of the story. Use at least five vocabulary words when describing the characters.

- ❖ Pages 9–10: Write "Plot" on the top left corner. Underneath write "Chapters 1–4, Summary of the chapters." Describe the elements of the plot: exposition, foreshadowing, inflicting force, conflict, rising action, crisis, climax, falling action, and resolution.
- ❖ Page 11: Write "Themes" on the top left corner. The moral of the story. There may be more than one. Themes may include, nature, coming of age, discovering, life lesson, etc., if applicable.

Day 2

Shared Reading #1: The teacher will project Chapters 10–12 of the book onto the board, so the class may read together. Additionally, teacher will allow students to use their copies of the book, so the class may read together.

Objective

Students will participate in a shared reading session for Chapters 10–12. Students will participate in a class discussion. Students will demonstrate literary comprehension of the text by answering the questions on the worksheet labeled, "Chapters 10–12." Students will identify the multiple meanings and the differences between "want" and "desire" or "crave." Students will work in pairs and come up with two scenarios; one that shows "want" and one that shows "desire" or "crave." Students will act out both scenarios for the class.

Procedure

The teacher will briefly review Chapters 5–9, which were assigned for homework the night before. The teacher will conduct a class discussion about each of the four ticket holders "wants." The students will share their opinions about the difference between "want" and "desire" or "crave." The teacher will ask a volunteer to give each student a copy of the worksheet labeled, "Chapters 10–12." The teacher will project Chapters 10–12 of the book onto the board, and ask students to take out their copies of the book, if they feel more comfortable reading from it. The class will read Chapters 10–12 together. Students will independently complete the worksheet. They

may use dictionaries, if necessary. Upon completion, students will share their answers during a class discussion. Then, students will work in pairs and come up with two scenarios; one that shows "want" and one that shows "desire" or "crave." Students will act out both scenarios for the class.

Extension Activity

Students will independently complete the worksheet labeled, "Chapters 10–12." They will use dictionaries, if necessary. Students will share their answers during a class discussion. Next, students will work in pairs and come up with two scenarios; one that shows "want" and one that shows "desire" or "crave." Students will act out both scenarios for the class.

Follow-up Activity

For homework, students will continue filling out the book report for Chapters 10–12.

Day 3

Shared Reading #2: The teacher will project Chapters 13–15 of the book onto the board, so the class may read together. Additionally, teacher will allow students to use their copies of the book, so the class may read together.

Objective

Students will participate in a shared reading session for Chapters 13–15. Students will identify analogies in the text while reading. Students will demonstrate literary comprehension of the text by participating in a class discussion. Students will be able to define the vocabulary words and identify them by putting their hands on their shoulders every time they read an analogy during the shared reading. Students will complete analogies using the vocabulary words. Students will create their own analogies.

Procedure

Teacher will conduct a mini lesson on vocabulary words and analogies. The vocabulary words are:

Stencil, goatee, alight, enraptured, muffled, bustled, warren, churning, whirlpool, aiders, mauve, flabbergasted, dumfounded, delectable. The teacher will project Chapters 13–15 of the book onto the board, and ask students to take out their copies of the book, if they feel more comfortable reading from it. The class will read Chapters 13–15 together. The teacher will ask the students to put their hands on their shoulders every time we read an analogy during the shared reading. In a circle, each student will summarize a part of the shared reading in sequential order. The teacher will proceed by writing three analogies on the board and asking students to complete them with the missing vocabulary word. The teacher will then divide students into groups of four, and ask them to create their own analogies.

Extension Activity

Teacher will write the three analogies below on the board. Students will select the vocabulary word that corresponds.

1. Beard is to **goatee** as hair is to braid.
2. **Stenciled** is to t-shirt as paint is to poster.
3. Darkened is to anger as **mauve** is to laughter.

The teacher will divide students into groups of four, and ask them to create at least four analogies. The use of the vocabulary words is not necessary, but encouraged. Students may use dictionaries, if necessary.

Follow-up Activity:

For homework, students will continue filling out the book report for Chapters 13–15.

Day 4

Shared Reading #3: The teacher will project Chapters 16–18 of the book onto the board, so the class may read together. Additionally, teacher will allow students to use their copies of the book, so the class may read together.

Objective

Students will participate in a shared reading session for Chapters 16–18. Students will participate in a class discussion. Students will demonstrate literary comprehension of the text by answering the questions on the worksheet labeled, "Chapters 16–18." Students will engage in a creative writing exercise. They will work in groups of four, and write a letter to Mr. Wonka about a "new" room they've created chocolate factory, being as descriptive as possible in their writing. Students must write at least one page. Students will create an illustration of the new room.

Procedure

Teacher will conduct a mini lesson on vocabulary words and descriptive words. The vocabulary words are: Cacao, wretched, suction, torpedo, brigade, peals, infantile, gall. The teacher will project Chapters 16–18 of the book onto the board, and ask students to take out their copies of the book, if they feel more comfortable reading from it. The class will read Chapters 16–18 together. The teacher will ask the students to put their hands on their shoulders every time we read a vocabulary word during the shared reading. In a circle, each student will summarize a part of the shared reading in sequential order using as many descriptive words as possible.. The teacher will proceed by dividing students into groups of four, and asking students to write a letter to Mr. Wonka about a "new" room they've created for the chocolate factory. Students must write at least one page, and be as descriptive as possible in their writing. Students will create an illustration of their new room.

Extension Activity

Teacher will divide the students in groups of four, and inform students that this is a creative writing exercise. Teacher will provide students with the following prompt.

❖ *Mr. Wonka would like to build a new room in the factory. Remember, the factory already has a Chocolate Room, a Fudge Room, an Inventing Room, a Nut Sorting Room, a Spotty Power*

Mixing Room, and a Television Room, so be creative! He must leave to recruit some more Oompa-Loompas for the new room, so he is leaving you in charge of creating the new room. Write a one-page letter to Mr. Wonka describing the new room you've created, and draw a picture of the room. Make Mr. Wonka proud!

Once completed, each group will present their letter and illustration to the class. Each student will have to speak during the presentation. Peers in the audience will be responsible for writing each group a note with a comment based on the presentation.

Follow-up Activity

For homework, students will continue filling out the book report for Chapters 16–18.

Day 5

Read Aloud: Teacher will read Chapters 19–21 in the "Read Aloud Center."

Objective

Students will listen to the teacher read Chapters 22–25 aloud in the "Read Aloud Center." Students will demonstrate literary comprehension of the text by participating in a class discussion. Students will solve mathematical word problems relating to *Charlie and the Chocolate Factory*. Students will work independently. Students will write their solutions on the board, and explain to the class how they arrived to their answer.

Procedure

Teacher will read *Charlie and the Chocolate Factory* Chapters 22–25 aloud in the "Read Aloud Center." Teacher will lead a class discussion, where students will verbally retell the story by summarizing the chapters. The teacher will place a word problem face down on each student's desk; each word problem will be different. The teacher will explain to the students that they will have one minute to complete the word problem, and show all their work. Teacher will ask the students to turn over the word

problem, and begin. Once the minute is over each student will pass their word problem back face down to the next student, and they will flip the problem over when the teacher allows them to, and continue the same procedure.

Extension Activity

The teacher will place a word problem face down on each student's desk; each word problem will be different. The teacher will explain to the students that they will have one minute to complete the word problem, and show all their work. Teacher will ask the students to turn over the word problem, and begin. Once the minute is over each student will pass their word problem back face down to the next student, and they will flip the problem over when the teacher allows them to, and continue the same procedure. Once completed, each student will write their solutions to at least one of the problems on the board, and explain to the class how they arrived to their answer.

Follow-up Activity

For homework, students will continue filling out the book report for Chapters 19–21.

Day 6

Guided Reading: Teacher will aid students in small, homogenous groups (students reading at the same level) using guided reading techniques using Roald Dahls' book, *Charlie and the Chocolate Factory*. Students will read Chapters 21–23.

Objective:

To focus closer on reading ability of individual students, they will read Chapters 21–23 aloud in their assigned guided reading groups. Students will demonstrate literary comprehension of the text by discussing the chapters, and acting out a scene from the chapters read in the reader theater for the class.

Procedure

Teacher will sit with each group, but work closely with each individual reading level, as they perform reading sentences from *Charlie and the Chocolate Factory* in unison reading. Teacher will make sure students emphasize words properly, pronounce words correctly, and assist them in reading more fluently. Once the reading is completed, students will discuss their favorite scene from the chapters read. Each group will recreate the scene they choose, and perform it for the class in the reader theater.

Extension Activity

Students will discuss their favorite scene from Chapters 21–23, and assign each other a character. Each group will re-create the scene they choose, and perform it for the class in the reader theater.

Follow-up Activity

For homework, students will continue filling out the book report for Chapters 21–23.

Day 7

Independent Reading: Students will individually read Chapters 24–27.

Objective

Students will read Chapters 24–27 of *Charlie and the Chocolate Factory* independently. Using arts and crafts materials, students will create their own candy bar. Students will discuss their candy bars with the class.

Procedure

Teacher will ask students to take out their copies of the book, and read Chapters 24–27 quietly to themselves. Once completed, the teacher will distribute a variety of arts and crafts materials and allow the students to create their own candy bar.

Extension Activity

Students will design their own candy bar using a variety of art and crafts materials. Students will be encouraged to use their imaginations, mix ingredients, and be creative! Students will present their candy bars to the class.

Follow-up Activity

For homework, students will continue filling out the book report for Chapters 24–27.

Day 8

Literature Circle: The class will be split into heterogeneous reading groups (students reading at different levels) and read Chapters 28–30.

Objective

Students will read Chapters 28–30 of *Charlie and the Chocolate Factory* in a literature circle. Students will identify and understand the author's purpose for writing, and summarize the main ideas and supporting details of the book. Students will create their own lyrics to the Oompa-Loompa Song.

Procedure

The teacher will divide the students up into groups combined with all different reading levels together, and the will read Chapters 28–30. The students will discuss with the teacher and class their own ideas as to why they think the author wrote this book, and how they feel about the overall ending of the book. The teacher will show several clips from the motion picture version of the book, and with a partner, students will create their own lyrics to the Oompa-Loompa Song.

Extension Activity

The teacher will show several clips from the motion picture version of the book, and with a partner, students will create their own lyrics to the Oompa-Loompa Song.

Follow-up Activity

For homework, students will continue filling out the book report for Chapters 24–27.

Literature Unit: *Charlie and the Chocolate Factory* by Roald Dahl
Shared Reading #1

Read Chapters 10–12.
Multiple Meanings:

Want. We looked at what each ticket-holding jerk *wanted*. There, "want" means "desire" or "crave". In Chapter 10, Charlie has a very different kind of *want*. Explain the meaning of Charlie's want. (You can use a dictionary.) Then write a sentence about him that uses *want* in this way.

_____

_____

List **two** ways Charlie tries to save his strength before he finds the dollar.

_____

_____

Briefly describe the appearance of the man who sells Charlie the Wonka Bar in Chapter 11. What is the most probable reason he looks this way?

_____

_____

How does Charlie feel the instant he discovers the Golden Ticket?

_____

_____

How does Grandpa Joe take the news of the discovery of the ticket?

_____

_____

Stephen Clarke/Shutterstock.com

Stencil	Muffled	Whirlpool	Dumfounded
Goatee	Bustled	Aiders	Delectable
Alight	Warren	Mauve	
Enraptured	Churning	Flabbergasted	

1. <u>Beard</u> is to **goatee** as <u>hair</u> is to <u>braid</u>.

2. **Stencil** is to <u>t-shirt</u> as <u>paint</u> is to <u>poster</u>.

3. <u>Darkened</u> is to <u>anger</u> as **mauve** is to <u>laughter</u>.

_____

_____

_____

Mr. Wonka would like to build a new room in the factory. Remember, the factory already has a Chocolate Room, a Fudge Room, an Inventing Room, a Nut Sorting Room, a Spotty Powder Mixing Room, and a Television Room, so be creative! He must leave to recruit some more Oompa-Loompas for the new room, so he is leaving you in charge of creating the new room. Write a one-page letter to Mr. Wonka describing the new room you've created, and draw a picture of the room. Use as many descriptive words as possible. Make Mr. Wonka proud!

Dear Mr. Wonka,

    I hope you are doing well and recruiting many Oompa-Loompas for our new room in the factory. We have created a Cotton Candy Room. The Cotton Candy Room will transform any type of food into cotton candy. For example, you are able to make delicious fettuccine alfredo flavored cotton candy. You may create heavenly cotton candy flavored anything in this room! In this room there is a laboratory on the second floor, which is fully equipped with top of the line icandyapple computers and oversees the first floor. The computers are programmed to take the user through a step-by-step process, in which the user is allowed to mix, add, or create any flavor cotton candy.

    On the first floor you will see a huge blender, larger than any blender you've ever seen before, in which you are able to blend and mix any type of food into. Above the blender there is a cotton ball maker, which makes cotton balls all day. A string hangs from the cotton ball-maker, when you pull the string; it releases cotton balls into the blender. You may add as many cotton balls, as you'd like to create fluffier or denser texture to your cotton candy. Once blended, the cotton candy will funnel through a large clear pipe, and enter a whirlpool. Next to the whirlpool there is a machine that creates paper cylinders. When you are ready to serve yourself cotton candy, you simply grab a paper cylinder, and dip three-quarters of it into the whirlpool, and take it out when you are satisfied with the size of your cotton candy.

    Mr. Wonka, I hope you are pleased with our new room. We hope to see you soon!

Sincerely,

Ms. Mittone

If a chocolate bar costs 10¢ (as mentioned in the book!), list four different ways (combinations of coins) to pay exactly 10¢ for the Wonka bar.

List all the coin combinations you could use to pay the exact price of two Wonka bars—one for Charlie and one for Grandpa Joe, if each bar costs 20¢. How many ways did you find?

If there is no sales tax on the chocolate bars above, how many bars can Charlie buy if he finds a quarter on the street?

Will he get any change back? If so, how much?

If the money Charlie finds in the street is a dollar bill, how many 10¢ candy bars could he buy then?

If Charlie uses the dollar he finds to buy a 40¢ loaf of bread for his family, and two of the Wonka bars above, how much money will he have left to give his parents?

If eight squares of chocolate make up a Wonka bar, and Charlie eats two squares, what fraction of the bar did he eat?

Four of Charlie's classmates pool their change to buy three Wonka bars. Since each bar is marked into eight squares, how many squares will each child get to eat?

As Charlie walks home from school, he stops to stare through the locked gate of the Wonka factory at 3:23pm. If he spends five minutes talking to a strange poetry-spouting tinker, and then forty minutes more staring at the factory windows for signs of the workers who never go in and never come out, what time will it be when Charlie starts for home again?

If Charlie reaches home at 4:54 pm, how many minutes' walk does he live from the factory? How many minutes' walk from home to school?

If Verruca wears a mink coat that cost $345 total, and has three others like it at home, what is the total amount spent on mink coats?

If Augustus Gloop goes on an all-chocolate diet, and can eat only 1,500 calories a day, how many 250-calorie Wonka bars can he eat each day?

As Charlie takes the first Wonka bar from a display box of them on the store shelf, he can see that the box had five stacks of four bars. How many bars fill a display box?

If each display box arrives in a case containing five rows of five display boxes, how many Wonka bars are in a case?

If a store orders fifteen cases, how many Wonka bars would that be?

If Mr. Salt's nut factory has 120 employees, and each employee can shuck the wrappers off three Wonka bars per minute, how many bars will be unwrapped in an hour? How many bars would be unwrapped in an 8-hour work day?

About how many cases would that be?

If Mr. Beauregarde earns a 10% commission on the cars he sells, how much commission did he earn on the day he sold a $1,200 car, a $1,350 car, a $2,600 car, and a $4,500 station wagon?

If Mr. Beauregarde's commission is 10% on the first $5,000 worth, and 20% thereafter, what would he earn then?

If a Wonka bar is 250 calories, what percentage of the daily 1,500 calories would that one bar be?

An Oompa-Loompa has six candies in his pocket: a gobstopper, a caramel, a hair toffee, a luminous lolly, a rainbow drop, and a mint jujube. He decides to eat three and give three to his best friend. How many different combinations of candies could he eat?

One Scrumdiddlyumptious bar costs twice as much as a Nutty Crunch Surprise bar. If Mike Teavee spends $13 buying ten Scrumdidlyumptious bars and five Nutty Crunch bars, what is the price of each Wonka bar?

Assume that Oompa-Loompas work for six days a week, and that they all work at the same rate. If a team of three Oompa-Loompas takes three weeks and two days to de-juice a giant blueberry, how long would it take a team of four Oompa-Loompas to do the same job?

The Oompa-Loompas pack 350 pounds of cavity-filling caramels into boxes that hold 1¾ pounds of caramel each. If each box sells for $1.75, what is the total selling price of all the caramel?

Every Everlasting Gobstopper weighs the same. The weight of a glass jar and the gobstoppers inside is fifty ounces. If the number of gobstoppers in the jar doubles, the total weight of jar and gobstoppers becomes ninety-two ounces. What is the weight of the jar?

A jar full of chocolate sauce weighs ten pounds. When one-half of the sauce is poured out, the jar and remaining sauce weigh 5¾ pounds. How much does the jar weigh?

Draw a perfect square of chocolate, then divide it in half with a vertical line. Next draw two horizontal lines across the square to divide it into six congruent rectangles. If this square of chocolate has an area of 144 square inches, what is the perimeter of one of the rectangles?

Mr. Wonka has prepared a huge square of chocolate to send by Wonkavision. Draw the square, and draw two lines dividing the square into three congruent rectangles. If each of the three rectangles has a perimeter of sixteen meters, how many meters are in the perimeter of the entire square?

What is the volume of the Great Glass Elevator, if it is 81 inches deep, 55 inches wide, and 85 inches high? (The front, with door, is 55 in x 85 in.) If Mr. Wonka decides to coat the entire exterior with chocolate sauce, what area needs to be covered?

If the floor and the door of the elevator do not have buttons, but every other square inch of the elevator contains a button, how many buttons total are inside?

OOMPA LOOMPA SONG

Oompa Loompa, do-ba-dee doo,

I've got a perfect puzzle for you.

Oompa Loompa, do-ba-dee-dee,

If you are wise you'll listen to me.

_____

_____

_____

_____

_____

References

Abedi, J. (1999, April). *NAEP math test accommodations for students with limited English proficiency.* Paper presented at the Annual Meeting of the American Educational Research Association. Montreal, Quebec, Canada. (ERIC Document Reproduction Service No. ED 431787).

Abedi, J., Courtney, M., Leon, S., Kao, J., & Azzam, T. (2006). *English language learners and math achievement: A study of opportunity to learn and language accommodation.* National Center for Research on Evaluation, Standards, and Student Testing (CRESST) Center for Study of Evaluation (CSE) Graduate School of Education & Information Studies University of California, Los Angeles: Authors.

Ada, A. F. (1993). *Mother-tongue, literacy as a bridge between home and school cultures: The power of two languages.* New York: McGraw-Hill School Publishing.

Ada, A. F., Harris, V. J., & Hopkins, L. B. (1993). *A chorus of cultures: Developing literacy through multicultural poetry.* Carmel, CA: Hampton-Brown Books.

Adams, M. J. (1990). *Beginning to read: Thinking and learning about print.* Cambridge, MA: MIT Press.

Adkins, M., Birman, D., & Sample, B. (1999). *Cultural adjustment, mental health and ESL: The refugee experience, the role of the teacher and ESL activities.* ELT Technical Assistance Project.

Agar, M. (1994). *Language shock*: *Understanding the culture of conversation.* New York: Morrow.

Aguirre, N. (2003). ESL students in gifted education. In J. A. Castellano (Ed.), *Special populations in gifted education* (pp. 17–27). Boston: Allyn & Bacon.

Aikenhead, G. S., & Jegede, O. J. (1999). Cross-cultural science education: A cognitive explanation of a cultural phenomenon. *Journal of Research in Science Teaching, 36*(3), 269–287.

Akhavan, N. (2006). *Help! My kids don't all speak English: How to set up a language workshop in your linguistically diverse classroom.* Portsmouth, NH: Heinemann.

Alderson, J. (1984). Reading in a foreign language: A reading problem or a language problem? In J. Alderson & A. Urquhart (Eds.), *Reading in a foreign language* (pp. 1–27). London: Longman.

Aliki. (1998). *Marianthe's story: Painted words and spoken memories.* New York: Green- Willow Books

Allen, V. G. (1994). Selecting materials for the reading instruction of ESL children. In K. Spangenberg-Urbschat & R. Pritchard (Eds.), *Kids come in all languages: Reading instruction for ESL children.* Newark, DE: International Reading Association.

Amaral, O. M., Garrison, L., & Klentschy, M. (2002). Helping English learners increase achievement through inquiry-based science instruction. *Bilingual Research Journal, 26*(2), 213–239.

Ameis, J. A., & Ebenezer, J. V. (2005). *Mathematics on the internet: A resource for K–12 teachers* (3rd ed.). Upper Saddle River, NJ: Merrill/Prentice-Hall.

American Association for the Advancement of Science (AAAS). (1989). *Science for all Americans.* Washington, DC: Author.

American Association for the Advancement of Science (AAAS). (1993). *Benchmarks for Science Literacy.* Oxford University Press, NY.

Andersen, P.A. (1989) The cultural dimensions of non-verbal communication. *Handbook of International and Intercultural Communication,* 163–185.

Andersen, P.A. (1999). *Nonverbal communication: Forms and functions.* Mountain View, CA: Mayfield.

Anderson, A., & Lynch, T. (1988). *Listening.* Oxford, England: Oxford University Press.

Anderson, J. W. (1991). A comparison of Arab and American conceptions of effective persuasion. In L. A. Samovar & R. E. Porter (Eds.), *Intercultural communication: A reader* (pp. 96–106). Belmont, CA: Wadsworth.

Anderson, L. F. (1990). A rationale for global education. In K. A. Tye (Ed.), *Global education from thought to action* (pp. 13–34). Alexandria, VA: Association for Curriculum and Supervision Development (ASCD).

Anderson, J. (2010). *Cognitive psychology and its implications.* New York, Worth Publishers.

Anderson, L. W., & Krathwohl, D. R. (Eds.) (2001). *A Taxonomy for Learning, Teaching, and Assessing: A Revision of Bloom's Taxonomy of Educational Objectives.* New York: Longman.

Anderson, N. J. (1994). Developing active readers: a pedagogical framework for the second language reading class. *System, 22,* 177–194.

Anderson, R. C., & Pearson, P. R. (1988). A schema-theoretic view of basic processes in reading comprehension. In P. L. Carrell, J. Devine, & D. E. Eskey (Eds.), *Interactive approaches to second language reading* (pp. 37–56). Cambridge, England: Cambridge University Press.

Anderson, R. C., Reynolds, R. E., Schallert, D. L. & Goetz, G. T. (1977). Frameworks for comprehending discourse. *American Educational Research Journal, 14*(4), 367–381.

Anderson, T. (1995). Rediscovering the connection between the arts: Introduction to the symposium on interdisciplinary arts education. *Arts Education Policy Review, 96*(4), 10–12.

Anderson, T. & Milbrandt, M. (2005). *Art for life: Authentic instruction in art.* New York: McGraw-Hill.

Angelelli, C., Enright, K., & Valdés, G. (2002). *Developing the talents and abilities of linguistically gifted bilingual students: Guidelines for developing curriculum at the high school level* (RM02156). Storrs, CT: The National Research Center on the Gifted and Talented, University of Connecticut.

Angelou, M. (2004). Human family. In A. Schifini, D. Short & J. V. Tinajero. *High point* (pp. 88–89). Teacher's Edition. Carmel, CA: Hampton Brown.

Ariza, E. (2002). Cultural considerations: Immigrant parent involvement. *Kappa Delta Pi Record, 38* (3), 134–137.

Ariza, E.N. (2009) *Not for ESOL teachers: What every classroom teacher needs to know about the linguistically, culturally, and ethnically diverse student.* (2nd Ed). Boston, MA: Allyn and Bacon Publishing (Division of Pearson).

Ariza, E. N. & Lapp, S. I. (2012). *Literacy, Language, and Culture, Methods and Strategies for Mainstream Teachers with Not-So-Mainstream Learners.* Charlotte, North Carolina: Kona Publishing and Media Group.

Arrowood, J. C. (2004). *Mathematics for ESL learners.* Lanham, MD: Rowman & Littlefield.

Artiles, A. J., Harry, B., Reschly, D. J., & Chinn, P. C. (2002). Over-identification of students of color in special education: A critical overview. *Multicultural Perspectives, 4*(1), 3–10.

Asher, J. J. (1972). Children's first language as a model for second language learning. *The Modern Language Journal, 56,* 133–139.

Asher, J. J. (1977). *Learning Another Language through Actions: The Complete Teacher's Guidebook.*

Asher, J. J. (1982). *Learning Another Language through Actions: The complete teachers' guidebook.* Los Gatos, CA: Sky Oaks.

Atkinson, D. (2003). L2 writing in the post-process era: Introduction. *Journal of Second Language Writing, 12,* 3–15.

Atwater, M. M. (1994). Research on cultural diversity in the classroom. In D. L. Gabel (Ed.), *Handbook of research on science teaching and learning* (pp. 558–576).

August, D., & Hakuta, K. (Eds.). (1997). *Improving schooling for language-minority children: A research agenda.* Washington, DC: National Academy Press.

August, D., & Hakuta, K. (Eds.). (1998). *Educating language-minority children.* Washington, DC: National Academy Press.

August, D., & Shanahan, T. (Eds.). (2006). *Executive summary. Developing literacy in second-language learners: Report of the National Literacy Panel on Language—Minority Children and Youth.* Mahwah, NJ: Lawrence Erlbaum. Available: http:www.cal.org/projects/archive/nlpreports/Executive_Summary.pdf

Ayer, A. & McMillan, E. (2011). Whirled peace: The evolution of pinwheels for peace. *SchoolArts, 111*(1), 50.

Bachman, L. F. (1990). *Fundamental considerations in language testing.* New York: Oxford University Press.

Bacon, S. M. & Finnemann, M. D. (1990), A Study of the Attitudes, Motives, and Strategies of University Foreign Language Students and Their Disposition to Authentic Oral and Written Input. *The Modern Language Journal, 74:* 459–473. doi: 10.1111/j.1540-4781.1990.tb05338.x

Badger, R.G. & Yan, X. (2009) 'The use of tactics and strategies by Chinese students in the Listening component of IELTS' *in IELTS Research Reports Volume 11,* ed P Thompson, IELTS Australia,

Canberra and British Council, London, pp 43–64.

Bailin, S. (1998). Critical thinking and drama education. *Research in Drama Education: The Journal of Applied Theatre and Performance 3*(2), 145–153.

Baker, C. (2007). *A parent's and teacher's guide to bilingualism* (3rd ed.). Bristol, UK: Multilingual Matters.

Baker, C. (2006). *Foundations of bilingual education and bilingualism* (4th ed.). Bristol, UK: Multilingual Matters.

Baker, C. (2011). *Foundations of Bilingual Education and Bilingualism.* Clevedon, UK: Multilingual Matters.

Baker, C., & Hornberger, N. (2001). *An introductory reader to the writings of Jim Cummins.* Clevedon, UK: Multilingual Matters.

Baker and Saul (1994)

Bandouin, E. M., Bober, E. S., Clarke, M. A., Dobson, B. K., & Silberstein, S. (1977). *Reader's choice: A reading skills textbook for students of English as a second language.* Ann Arbor: University of Michigan Press.

Banks, C. A. M. (1997). Parents and teachers: Partners in school reform. In J. A. Banks & C. A. M. Banks (Eds.), *Multicultural education: Issues and perspectives* (3rd ed.) (pp. 408–426). Boston: Allyn & Bacon.

Banks, J. A., & Banks, C. A. M. (Eds.). (1995). *Handbook of research on multicultural education.* New York: Macmillan.

Banks, J. A., & Banks, C. A. M. (2009). *Multicultural education: Issues and perspectives.* John Wiley & Sons.

Bartholomae, D. (1985). Inventing the university. In M. Rose (Ed.), *When a writer can't write: Studies in writer's block and other composing problems* (pp. 134–165). New York: Guilford Press.

Barufaldi, J., & Swift, J. (1977). Children learning to read should experience science. *Reading Teacher*, 388–393.

Baruth, L. G., & Manning, M. L. (1992). *Multicultural education of children and adolescents.* Needham Heights, MA: Allyn & Bacon.

Baruth, L. G., & Manning, M. L. (2002). *Multicultural counseling and psychotherapy; A lifespan perspective* (2nd ed.). New York: Merrill.

Batalova, J., Mittelstadt, M., Mather, M., & Lee, M. (2008). *Immigration: Data matters.* Washington DC: Migration Policy Institute and Population Reference Bureau. Retrieved on January 31, 2010, from http://www.migrationpolicy.org/pubs/2008DataGuide.pdf

Bates, J. (2000). *Becoming an art teacher.* Stamford, CT: Wadsworth/Thompson Learning.

Beal, C. M., Bolick, C., & Martorella, P. H. (2009). *Teaching social studies in middle and secondary schools.* Boston, MA: Pearson Education, Inc.

Bean, J. C. (2011). *Engaging ideas: The professor's guide to integrating writing, critical thinking, and active learning in the classroom.* John Wiley & Sons.

Been, S. (1975). Reading in the foreign language teaching program. *TESOL Quarterly, 9,* 233–242.

Belisle, R. (1996, December). E-mail activities in the ESL writing class. *The Internet TESL Journal, II*(12).

Bennett, C. I. (Ed.). (1990). *Comprehensive multicultural education: Theory and practice.* Needham Heights, MA: Allyn & Bacon.

Bennett, M. J. (1993). Towards ethnorelativism: A developmental approach to training for intercultural sensitivity. In R. Michael Paige (Ed.), *Education for the intercultural experience* (pp. 21–71). Yarmouth, ME: Intercultural Press.

Berman, P., McLaughlin, B., McLeod, B., Minicucci, C., Nelson, B., & Woodworth, K. (1995). School reform and student diversity. In From risk to excellence: Principles of practice. *ERIC Digest* (Online), Available: http//www.cal.org/ericcll/digest/Crede/001.htm

Bernat, E. (2004). *Attending to adult learners: Affective domain in the ESL classroom, humanizing language teaching* (Online), Available: http://www.hltmag.co.uk/sept04/mart2.htm

Bersin, J. (2004). *The blended learning book: Best practices, proven methodologies, and lessons learned.* John Wiley & Sons.

Beyer, B. K. (2008). How to teach thinking skills in social studies and history. *The Social Studies*, 99(5), 196–201.

Bialystok, E. (1982). On the relationship between knowing and using linguistic forms. *Applied Linguistics, 3*, 181–206.

Bialystok, E. (Ed.). (1991). *Language processing in bilingual children*. Cambridge: Cambridge University Press.

Bialystok, E. (1992). *Selective attention in cognitive processing: The bilingual edge*. In R.J. Harris (Ed.), Cognitive processing in bilinguals (pp. 501–513). Amsterdam: North Holland.

Bialystok, E. (2001). *Bilingualism in development: Language, literacy, and cognition*. Cambridge: Cambridge University Press.

Bianco, M. (2010). Strength-based RTI: Conceptualizing a multi-tiered system for developing gifted potential. *Theory Into Practice, 49*(4), 323-330.

Bianco, M., & Harris, B. (2014). Strength-Based RTI Developing Gifted Potential in Spanish-Speaking English Language Learners. *Gifted Child Today, 37*(3), 169–176.

Birman, D. (2002). Spring Institute for Intercultural Learning. Mental Health of Refugee Children. A Guide for the ESL Teacher.

Blau, E. K. (1990). The effects of syntax, speed and pauses on listening comprehension. *TESOL Quarterly, 24*, 746–753.

Blaz, D. (1999). *Foreign language teachers guide to active learning*. New York: Eye on Education. Bloom, B. S. (Ed.). (1984). *Taxonomy of educational objectives book 1, Cognitive domain*. White Plains, NY: Longman.

Blaz, D. (2002). *Bringing the standards for foreign language learning to life*. Eye on Education.

Bloom, B. S. (1956). *Taxonomy of educational objectives*. New York: David McKay, 356, 1998-1999.

Boaler, J. (2008). *What's math got to do with it? Helping children learn to love their least favorite subject—and why it's important for America*. New York, NY: Penguin.

Boseker, B. J. (1991). Successful solutions for preventing Native American dropouts. *International Third World Studies Journal and Review, 3*, 33–40.

Boseker, B. J., & Gordon, S. L. (1983). What Native Americans have taught us as teacher educators. *Journal of American Indian Education, 22*, 20–24.

Bradley, J., & Thalgott, M. (1987). Reducing reading anxiety. *Academic Therapy, 22*(4), 349–358.

Brand, D. (1987a, August 31). The new whiz kids. *Time, 130*, 42–51. EJ 358–595.

Brand, D. (1987b, August 3). Why Asians are going to the head of the class: Some fear colleges use quotas to limit admissions. *New York Times*, sec 12, pp. 18–23.

Brouillette, L., & Jennings, L. (2010). Helping children cross cultural boundaries in the borderlands: Arts program at Freese Elementary in San Diego creates cultural bridge. *Journal for Learning Through the Arts*, 6(1).

Brown, C. L. (2007). Strategies for making social studies texts more comprehensible for English-language learners. *The Social Studies, 98*(5), 185–188.

Brown, J. D., & Bailey, K. M. (1984). A categorical instrument for scoring second language writing skills. *Language Learning, 34*(4), 21–38.

Brown, G. (1986). Investigating listening comprehension in context. *Applied Linguistics, 71*(3), 284–306.

Brown, J. D. (1990). Where do tests fit into language programs? *JALT Journal, 12*(1), 121–140.

Brown, G. D. A., & Hulme, C. (1992). Cognitive processing and second language processing: The role of short term memory. In R. J. Harris (Ed.), *Cognitive processing in bilinguals* (pp. 105–121). New York: Elsevier.

Brown, G. D. A., & Yule, G. (1983). *Teaching the spoken language*. Cambridge, England: Cambridge University Press.

Brown, H. (1994). *Teaching by principles: An interactive approach language pedagogy* (3rd ed.). Englewood Cliffs, NJ: Prentice Hall.

Brown, S. (2013). *Art integration in the schools*. Mason, Ohio: Cengage Learning.

Bruck, M. (1982). Language disabled children: Performance in an additive bilingual education program. *Applied Psycholinguistics, 3*, 45–60.

Buchanan, K., & Helman, M. (1993). *Reforming mathematics instruction for ESL literacy students*. Washington, DC: National Clearinghouse for Bilingual Education.

Burns, A., & Joyce, H. (1997). *Focus on speaking*. Sydney, Australia: National Center for English Language Teaching and Research.

Bybee, R. (1997). Achieving scientific literacy: From purposes to practices. Portsmouth, NH: Heinemann.

Bybee, R. & Ben Zvi, N. (1998). Curriculum change in science: Transforming goals to practice. In B. Fraser & K. Tobin (Eds.) *International handbook of science education*. Kluwer Academic Publishers.

Byrnes, H. (1984). The role of listening comprehension: a theoretical base. *Foreign Language Annals, 17*(4), 317–329.

California Department of Education. (1990). *Bilingual education handbook*. Sacramento: California Department of Education.

Cambell, J. R., Hombo, C. M., & Mazzeo, J. (2000). *NAEP 1999 trends in academic programs; Three decades of student performance* (NCES 2000-469). Washington, DC: U.S. Department of Education, National Center for Education Statistics.

Canale, M. (1983). From communicative competence to communicative language pedagogy. In J. C. Richards & R. Schmidt (Eds.), *Language and communication*. London: Longman Group Limited.

Canale, M., & Swain, M. (1980). Theoretical bases of communicative approaches to second language teaching and testing. *Applied Linguistics, 1*, 1–47.

Carrasquillo, A. (1991). *Hispanic children and youth in the United States: A resource guide*. New York: Garland.

Carrell, P. L. (1988). Some causes of text-boundedness and schema interference in ESL reading. In P. L. Carrell, J. Devine, & D. Eskey (Eds.), *Interactive approaches to second language reading* (pp. 101–113). New York: Cambridge University Press.

Carrell, P. L. (1992). Awareness of Text Structure: Effects on Recall*. *Language Learning, 42*(1), 1–18.

Carrell, P. L., Devine, J. & Eskey, D. E. (Eds.) (1988). *Interactive Approaches to Second Language Reading*. Cambridge: CUP.

Carrell, P. L., & Eisterhold, J. C. (1983). Schema theory and ESL reading pedagogy. *TESOL Quarterly, 17*(4), 553–573.

Carrier, K. A. (2005). Supporting science learning through science literary objectives for English language learners. *Science Activities, 42*(2), 5–11.

Carter, R., & McCarthy, M. (1995). Grammar and spoken language. *Applied Linguistics, 16*(2), 141–158.

Castellano, J. A. (2002). Renavigating the waters. The identification and assessment of culturally and linguistically diverse students for gifted and talented education. In J. A. Castellano & E. I. Diaz (Eds.), *Reaching new horizons* (pp. 94–116). Boston: Allyn & Bacon.

Castellano, J. A. (2003). *Special populations in gifted education*. Boston: Allyn & Bacon.

Castellano, J. A. (2004). Empowering and serving Hispanic students in gifted programs. In D. Boothe & J. C. Stanley (Eds.), *Critical issues for diversity in gifted education* (pp. 1–14). Waco, TX: Prufrock Press.

Catterall, J. S. (2009). *Doing well and doing good by doing art: The effects of education in the visual and performing arts on the achievements and values of young adults.* Los Angeles/London: Imagination Group/I-Group Books.

Cawthon, S., Dawson, K., & Ihom, S. (2011). Activating student engagement through drama- based instruction. *Journal for Learning through the Arts, 7*(1).

Cazden, C. (1988). *Classroom discourse.* Portsmouth, NH: Heinemann.

Cervetti, G. N., Pearson, P. D., Barber, J., Hiebert, E., & Bravo, M.A. (2007). Integrating literacy and science: The research we have, the research we need. In M. Pressley, A. K. Billman, K. Perry, K. Refitt & J. Reynolds (Eds.), *Shaping literacy achievement.* New York: Guilford.

Chaika, E. (1989). *Language, the social mirror* (2nd ed.). Rowley, MA: Newbury House.

Chamberlin, S. P. (2005). Recognizing and responding to cultural difference in education of culturally and linguistically diverse learners. *Intervention in School and Clinic, 40*(4), 195–211.

Chamot, A. U. (2001). The role of learning strategies in second language acquisition. In M. P. Breen (Ed.), *Learner contributions to language learning: New directions in research* (pp. 25-43). London: Longman.

Chamot, A. U., Cummins, J., Kessler, C., O'Malley, J. M., & Fillmore, L. W. (2001). *ESL: Accelerating English language learning* (Teacher's Ed.). New York: Longman.

Chamot, A. U., & O'Malley, J. M. (1989). The cognitive academic language learning approach. In P. Rigg & V. Allen (Eds.), *When they don't all speak English.* Urbana, IL: National Council of Teachers of English.

Chamot, A. U., & O'Malley, J. M. (1994). *The CALLA handbook: How to implement the cognitive academic language learning approach.* Reading, MA: Addison-Wesley.

Chamot, A. U., & O'Malley, J. M. (1996). The cognitive academic language learning approach: A model for linguistically diverse classrooms. *Elementary School Journal 96*(3), 259–273.

Chapelle, C., & Roberts, C. (1986). Ambiguity tolerance and field independence as predictors in English as a second language. *Language Learning, 36*(1), 27–45.

Chapin, J.R. (2013) *Elementary Social Studies: A Practical Guide* (8th Edition). Boston: Pearson.

Chapin, J. R., & Messick, R. G. (2009). *Elementary social studies: A practical guide* (5th ed.). Boston: Allyn & Bacon.

Chitravelu, N., Sithamparam, S., & The, S. C. (1995). *ELT methodology: Principles and practice.* Shah Alam, Malaysia: Penerbit Fajar Bakti Sdn. Bhd.

Chomsky, N. (1957). *Syntactic structures.* The Hague, the Netherlands: Mouton.

Chomsky, N. (1959). A review of Skinner's verbal behavior. *Language, 35*, 26–58.

Chomsky, N. (1969). Linguistics and philosophy. In S. Hook (Ed.), *Language and philosophy.* New York: New York University Press.

Christison, M. (1996, Autumn). Teaching and learning languages through multiple intelligences. *TESOL Journal*, 10–14.

Chun, D. M., & Plass, J. L. (1996). Effects of multimedia annotations on vocabulary acquisition. *Modern Language Journal, 80*, 183–198.

Claire, E., & Haynes J. (1994). *Classroom teacher's ESL survival kit #1.* Englewood Cliffs, NJ: Alemany Press.

Clair, N., Snow, C., & Fillmore, L. (2001). *Why reading is hard.* VHS. DELTA Publishing.

Clarkson, P. C. (1992). Language and mathematics: A comparison of bilingual and monolingual students of mathematics. *Educational Studies in Mathematics, 23, 329–417.*

Clay, M. (1975). *What did I write?* Auckland: Heinemann Educational Books.

Clay, M. (1982). *Observing young readers: Selected papers.* Portsmouth, NH: Heinemann.

Clay, M. (1993). The early detection of reading difficulties. In S. F. Peregoy & O. F. Boyle, *Reading, writing, and learning in ESL: A resource book for K–12 teachers.* New York: Addison Wesley Longman.

Cloud, N. (2002). Culturally and linguistically responsive instructional planning. In A. J. Artiles, & A.A. Ortiz (Eds.), *English language learners with special needs: Identification, placement, and instruction* (pp. 107–132). Washington DC: Center for Applied Linguistics.

Coady, J. (1997). L2 vocabulary through extensive reading. In J. Coady & T. Huckin (Eds.), *Second language vocabulary acquisition* (pp. 225–237). Cambridge: Cambridge University Press.

Coady, M. (2009). "*Solamente libros importantes:*" Literacy practies and ideologies of migrant farmworking families in north central Florida. In G. Li (Ed.) *Multicutural families, home literacies, and mainstream schooling* (pp. 113–128). Charlotte, NC: New Age.

Coady M. & Ariza, E. (2010). Struggling for meaning and identity (and a passing grade): High stakes writing in English as a second language. *MEXTESOL, 34*(1) 11–27.

Coady, M. & Escamilla, K. (2005). Audible voices, visible tongues: Exploring social realities in Spanish-speaking students' writing. *Language Arts, 82*(6), 462–471.

Coady, M. & Moore, C. (2010). Using Libros: The emergent bi-literacy development of Spanish-speaking children. *TESOL Journal, 2*, 91–108.

Coady, M., Nelson, A. & Coady, T. (2014, in press). Assessing the needs of immigrant, Latino families and teachers in rural settings: Building home-school partnerships. *NABE Journal of Research and Practice,* 6.

Coerr, E. (1977). *Sadako and the thousand cranes.* New York: The Putnam & Grosset Group.

Cohen, A. (1990). *Language learning: Insights for learners, teachers, and researchers.* Boston: Hienle & Hienle.

Cohen, A. (1996). Developing the ability to perform speech acts. *Studies in Second Language Acquisition, 18*(2), 253–267.

Cohen, A., Glasman, H., Rosenbaum-Cohen, P. R., Ferrara, J., & Fine, J. (1979). Reading for specialized purposes: Discourse analysis and the use of student informants. *TESOL Quarterly, 13*, 551–564.

Cohen, E. G. (1984). Talking and working together: Status interaction and learning. In P. Peterson & L. C. Wilkinson (Eds.), *The social context of instruction: Group organization and group processes* (pp. 171–187). New York: Academic Press.

Cohen, E. G. (1986). *Designing group work: Strategies for heterogeneous classrooms.* New York: Teachers College Press, Columbia University.

Cohen, E. G. (1991). From theory to practice: The development of an applied research program. In J. Berger & M. Zelditch (Eds.), *Theoretical research programs* (pp. 1–56). Stanford, CA: Stanford University Press.

Cohen, E. G., & DeAvila, E. (1983). *Learning to think in math and science: Improving local education for minority children.* Stanford, CA: Stanford University Press.

Cohen, E. G., & Lotan, R. A. (1990). *Untracking the middle school: Curriculum, instructional strategies, and access.* Proposal to the Carnegie Corporation, New York.

Cohen, M. D., & Tellez, K. (1994). Implementing cooperative learning for language minority students. *Bilingual Education, 18*, 1–19.

Coleman, C. (2003). Simple steps to successful revision in L2 writing. *The Internet TESL Journal, IX*(5). Retrieved July 10, 2009, from http://iteslj.org/

Collier, C., & Kalk, M. (1989). Bilingual special education curriculum development. In L. M. Baca & H. T. Cervantes (Eds.), *The bilingual special education interface* (pp. 257–290). Columbus, OH: Merrill.

Collier, V. P., & Thomas, W. (1999/2000). Making U.S. schools effective for English language learners, Part 3. *TESOL Matters, 9*(6). Available: http://www.tesol.org/s_document.asp?CID=196&DID= 826

Collier, V. P., & Thomas, W. P. (2009). *Educating English learners for a transformed world.* Albuquerque, NM: Fuente Press.

Common Core State Standards (CCSS). (2014). Retrieved on June, 2014 from http://www.corestandards. org/

Condon, J. C., & Yousef, F. S. (1974). *An introduction to intercultural communication.* Bobbs-Merrill.

Condon, J. C., & Saito, M. (Eds.) (1976). *Communication across cultures for what? A symposium on humane responsibility in intercultural communication.* Tokyo: Simul Press.

Connor, U. (1987). Argumentative patterns in student essays; Cross-cultural differences. In U. Connor & R. B. Kaplan (Eds.), *Writing across languages: Analysis of L2 text.* Reading, MA: Addison-Wesley.

Cook, V. D. (1991). *Second language learning and language teaching.* London: Edward Arnold.

Coombe, C., Folse, K., & Hubley, N. (2007). *A Practical Guide to Assessing English Language Learners.* Ann Arbor, MI: University of Michigan Press.

Cornet, C. E. (1983). *What you should know about teaching and learning styles.* Bloomington, IN: Phi Delta Kappa Education Foundation.

Cotterell, S., & Cohen, R. (2003). Scaffolding for second language writers: Producing an academic essay. *ELT Journal, 57*(2), 158–166.

Cox, B. G., & Ramirez, M. (1981). Cognitive styles: Implications for multiethnic education. In J. Banks (Ed.), *Education in the 80's: Implications for multiethnic education.* Washington, DC: National Education Association.

Cox, C. (1999). *Teaching language arts: A student- and response-centered classroom.* Boston: Allyn & Bacon.

Cox, C., & Many, J. E. (1992). Towards an understanding of the aesthetic stance towards literature. *Language Arts, 66*, 287–294.

Craig, D.V. & *Paraiso*, J. (2008). Dual diaspora and barrio art. *Journal of Learning Through the Arts, 4*(1), 120–169.

Crandall, J. A. (1987). *ESL through content-area instruction.* Englewood Cliffs, NJ: Prentice Hall.

Crandall, J. A (1994, January). Content-centered language learning. *ERIC Digest* (Online), Available: http://www.cal.org/ericcll/digest/crede/001.html

Crandall, J. A. (1987). *ESL through content-area instruction: Mathematics, science, social studies.* Englewood Cliffs, NJ: Prentice Hall.

Crew, A. (1977). *Experiential learning: Theory and practical applications in secondary schools.* Tuscaloosa, AL: University of Alabama, College of Education. (ERIC Document Reproduction Services No. ED256523).

Crowther, D. T., Vila, J. S., & Fathman, A. K. (2006). Learners, programs and teaching practices. In: A. K. Fathman & D. T. Crowther (Eds.), *Science for English language learners: K–12 classroom strategies* (pp. 9–20). Arlington, VA: NSTA Press.

Cruz, B. C. (1998, November). Global education in the middle school curriculum: An interdisciplinary perspective. *Middle School Journal, 30*(2), 26–31.

Cruz, B. C., & Thornton, S. J. (2012). Visualizing social studies literacy: Teaching content and skills to English language learners. *Social Studies Research & Practice, 7*(3), 98–111.

Cuevas, P., Lee, O., Hart, J., & Deaktor, R. (2005). Improving science inquiry with elementary students of diverse backgrounds. *Journal of Research in Science Teaching, 42*(3), 337–357.

Cummins, J. (1979). Linguistic interdependence and the educational development of bilingual children. *Review of Educational Research, 49*, 222–251.

Cummins, J. (1980). The construct of language proficiency in bilingual education. In J. E. Alatis (Ed.), *Georgetown University roundtable on language and linguistics* (pp. 76–93). Washington DC: Georgetown University Press.

Cummins, J. (1981). The role of primary language development in promoting educational success for language minority students. *Schooling and language minority students: A theoretical framework.* Sacramento: California State Department of Education.

Cummins, J. (1984). Implications of bilingual proficiency for the education of minority language students. In P. Allen and M. Swain (Eds.), *Language issues and education policies* (pp. 21–34). Oxford: Pergamon Press. ELT Documents 119.

Cummins, J. (1989a). *Empowering minority students.* Sacramento, CA: CABE.

Cummins, J. (1989b). A theoretical framework for bilingual special education. *Exceptional Children, 56*, 111–119.

Cummins, J. (1994). Knowledge, power, and identity in teaching English as a second language. In F. Genesee (Ed.), *Educating second language children: The whole child, the whole curriculum, the whole community* (pp. 103–125). Cambridge, England: Cambridge University Press.

Cummins, J. (1996). *Negotiating identities: Education for empowerment in a diverse society.* Ontario, CA: California Association for Bilingual Education.

Cummins, J. (2001a). Linguistic interdependence and the educational development of bilingual children. In C. Baker & N. Hornberger (Eds), *An introductory reader to the writings of Jim Cummins* (pp. 63–95). Buffalo, NY: Multilingual Matters Ltd.

Cummins, J. (2001b). The entry and exit fallacy. In C. Baker and N. Hornberger (Eds). *An introductory reader to the writings of Jim Cummins* (pp. 110–138). Buffalo, NY: Multilingual Matters Ltd.

Cummins, J. (2001c). *Language, power, and pedagogy: Bilingual children in the crossfire.* Clevedon, UK: Multilingual Matters.

Cummins, J. (2007). Promoting literacy in multilingual contexts. *Ontario: What works? Research into Practice.* Ontario, Canada: Literacy and Numeracy Secretariat and Ontario Association of Deans of Education.

Curtain, H., & Dahlberg, C. A. (2004). *Languages and children, making the match: New languages for young learners.* New York: Longman.

Cziko, G. A. (1980). Language competence and reading strategies: A comparison of first and second language oral reading errors. *Language Learning, 30,* 101–116.

Dale, T., & Cuevas, G. (1992). Integrating mathematics and language learning. In P. Richard-Amato & M. Snow (Eds.), *The multicultural classroom*. White Plains, NY: Longman.

Dalton, S. (1989). *Teachers as assessors and assisters: Institutional constraints on interpersonal relationships*. Paper presented at the meeting of the American Educational Research Association, San Francisco, CA.

Darling-Hammond, L. (1996). The quiet revolution: Rethinking teacher development. *Educational Leadership, 53*(6), 4–10.

Day, R. R., Omura, C. C., & Hiramatsu, M. (1991). Incidental EFL vocabulary learning and reading. *Reading in a Foreign Language, 7,* 541–551.

Debussy, C. (1905). *La Mer.* Musical Composition.

Deshler, D. D., & Hock, M. F. (2006). *Shaping Literacy Achievement*. Guilford Press: New York. (http:// www.adliktlorg/article/19750) All About Adolescent Literacy; Resources for parents and educators (grade 4–12) website www.adlit.org

DeVries, B. (2012). Vocabulary assessment as predictor of literacy skills. *New England Reading Association Journal, 47*(2), 4–9.

Dewey, J. (1934). The supreme intellectual obligation. *Science Education, 18,* 1–4.

Dias, P. (1990). A literacy-response respective on teaching reading comprehension. In D. Bogdan & S. B. Straw (Eds.), *Beyond communication: Reading comprehension and criticism* (pp. 283–299).

Diaz, C. F. (1989). Hispanic cultures and cognitive styles: Implications for teachers. *Multicultural Leader, 2*(4), 1–4.

Diaz, C. F., Massialas, B. G., & Xanthopoulos, J. A. (1999). *Global perspectives for educators*. Boston: Allyn & Bacon.

Diaz-Rico, L. T., & Weed, K. Z. (1995). *The crosscultural, language, and academic development handbook: A complete K–12 reference guide*. Boston: Allyn & Bacon.

Dickinson, D. K., & Tabors, P. O. (2001). *Beginning literacy with language: young children learning at home and school*. Baltimore: Paul H. Brookes.

Doherty, R.W. & Pinal, A. (2004). Joint productive activity and cognitive reading strategy use. *TESOL.*

Doherty, R.W., Hilberg, R., Pinal, A., & Tharp, R. (2002). *Transformed pedagogy, organization, and student achievement*. Paper presented at the annual conference of the American Education Research Association. New Orleans, LA.

Donovan, M. S., & Cross, C. T. (Eds.). (2002). *Minority students in special and gifted education*. Washington, DC: National Academy Press.

Douglas, D. (1988). Testing listening comprehension in the context of ACTFL. Proficiency guidelines. *Studies in Second Language Acquisition, 10,* 245–361.

Dow, A. (1899). *Composition*. Berkley and Los Angeles, CA: University of California Press.

Dulay, H., Burt, M., & Krashen, S. (1982). *Language two*. Oxford, England: Oxford University.

Dumont, R. (1972). Learning English and how to be silent: Studies in Sioux and Cherokee classrooms. In C. Cazden, V. John, & D. Hymes (Eds.), *Functions of language in the classroom*. New York: Teachers College Press.

Dunkel, P. (1986). Developing listening fluency in L2: Theoretical principles and pedagogical considerations. *The Modern Language Journal, 70*(2), 99–106.

Dunkel, P. (1991). Listening in the native and second/foreign language: Toward an integration of research and practice. *Tesol Quarterly, 25*(3), 431–457.

Dunn, R. S., & Dunn, K. J. (1979). Learning styles/teaching styles: Should they . . . can they . . . be matched? *Educational Leadership, 36*, 238–244.

Dunn, R. S., & Griggs, S. A. (1995). *Multiculturalism and learning styles: Teaching and counseling adolescents*. Westport, CT: Praeger.

Duquette, G., Dunnett, S. Papalia, A. The effect of authentic materials in acquiring a second language. *Canadian Modern Language Review, 43* (3) (1987), pp. 479–492.

Durkin, D. (1966). *Children Who Read Early*. New York: Teachers. College Press.

Eastern Stream Center on Resources and Training (ESCORT). (1998). *Help! They don't speak English starter kit for primary teachers: A resource guide for educators of limited English proficient migrant students, grades pre-K–6* (3rd ed.). Oneonta, NY: Authors.

Echevarria, J., & Graves, A. (2003). *Sheltered content instruction: Teaching English to English language learners with diverse abilities* (2nd ed.). Boston: Allyn & Bacon.

Echevarria, J., & Graves, A. (2007). *Sheltered content instruction: Teaching English learners with diverse abilities*. Boston: Allyn & Bacon.

Echevarria, J., & Short, D. (2002). *Using multiple perspectives in observations of diverse classrooms: The sheltered instruction observation protocol (SIOP)*. Santa Cruz, CA: Center for Research on Education, Diversity, and Excellence.

Echevarria, J., & Short, D. (2007). Academic uses of English: A focus on science. Presented at the CREATE Conference, Available: www.cal.org/create

Echevarria, J., Vogt, M., & Short, D. (2004). *Making content comprehensible for English learners: The SIOP model*. Boston: Allyn and Bacon.

Echevarria, J., Short, D., & Powers, K. (2006). School reform and standards-based education: A model for English-language learners. *The Journal of Educational Research, 99*(4), 195–211.

Echevarria, J., Vogt, M., & Short, D. (2004). *Making content comprehensible for English language learners* (2nd ed.). Boston: Pearson/Allyn & Bacon.

Echevarria, J., Vogt, M., & Short, D. J. (2008). *Making content comprehensible for English language learners* (3rd ed.). Boston: Pearson Education.

Ehrman, M. E., & Oxford R. (1988). *Ants and grasshoppers, badgers and butterflies: Qualitative and quantitative exploration of adult language learning styles and strategies*. Paper presented at the Symposium on Research Perspectives on Adult Language Learning and Acquisition, Ohio State University, Columbus, OH.

Ehrman, M. E., & Oxford, R. (1989). Effects of sex differences, career choice, and psychological type on adults' language learning strategies. *Modern Language Journal, 73*, 1–13.

Ehrman, M. E., & Oxford, R. (1995). Cognition plus: Correlates of language learning success. *Modern Language Journal, 79*(1), 67–89.

Eisner, E. (1992). Educational reform and ecology of schooling. *Teachers College Record, 93*(4), 610–628.

Eisner, E. (2002). *The Arts and the Creation of Mind*, In Chapter 4, What the Arts Teach and How It Shows (pp. 70–92). Yale University Press. Available from NAEA Publications.

Elbow, P. (1973) *Writing without teachers*. London: Macmillan Education.

Elias, M., & Tobias, D. (1996). *Social problem solving inventions in the schools*. Guilford Publications.

Elley, W. B. (1989). Vocabulary acquisition from listening to stories. *Reading Research Quarterly*, 24(2), 174–189.

Elliott, J. (1985). A Class Divided. Online available: http://www.pbs.org/wgbh/pages/frontline/shows/divided/

Ellis, R. (1993). The structural syllabus and second language acquisition. *TESOL Quarterly*, 27, 91–113.

Ellis, R. (2006). Current issues in the teaching of grammar: An SLA perspective. *TESOL Quarterly*, 40(1), 83–107.

Ellis, R. (2008). Principles of instructed second language acquisition. *CAL Digest*, 1–6.

Elster, A. (2001). Learning through the arts: Program goals, features, and pilot results. *International Journal of Education and the Arts*, 2(7).

Emig, J. (1977). Writing as a mode of learning. *College composition and communication*, 28, 122–128.

Enright, D., & McCloskey, M. (1988). *Integrating English: Developing English language and literacy in the multilingual classroom*. Reading, MA: Addison-Wesley.

Ericson, L., & Juliebo, M. (1988). *The phonological awareness handbook for kindergarten and primary teachers*. Newark, DE: International Reading Association.

Ersoz, A. (2000). Six games for the EFL/ESL classroom. *The Internet TESL Journal*, VI(6). Retrieved February 15, 2010, from http://iteslj.org/

Escamilla, K., Hopewell, S., & Butvilofsky, S. (2013). *Biliteracy from the start: Literacy squared in action*. Caslon.

Eskey, D. E. (1973). A model program for teaching advanced reading to students of English as a second language. *Language Learning*, 23(4), 169–184.

Eskey, D., & Grabe, W. (1995). Interactive models for second language reading: Perspectives on instruction. In P. Carrell, J. Devine & D. Devine, (Eds.), *Interactive approaches to second language reading* (pp. 223–238). Cambridge: Cambridge University Press.

Esler, W. K. (1977). *Teaching elementary school science*. Belmont, CA: Wadsworth.

Estrada, P., & Imhoff, B. D. (2001). *Patterns of language arts instructional activity: Excellence, inclusion, fairness, and harmony in six first grade classrooms*. Paper presented at the annual meeting of the American Educations Research Association. Seattle, WA.

Fang, Z., & Schleppegrell, M. J. (2008). *Reading in Secondary Content Areas: A Language-Based Pedagogy*. University of Michigan Press.

Fathman, A. K., & Crowther, D. T. (Eds.). (2006). *Science for English language learners: K–12 classroom strategies* (pp. 9–20). Arlington, VA: National Science Teachers Association.

Fawcett, S. (2007). *Evergreen: A guide to writing* (7th ed.). Florence, KY: Centage.

Felder, R. M., & Henriques, E. R. (1995). Learning and teaching styles in foreign and second language acquisition. *Foreign Language Annals*, 28(1), 21–31.

Feldman, E. (1993). *Practical art criticism*. Upper Saddle River, NJ: Prentice-Hall.

Fellows, N. J. (1994). A window into thinking: Using student writing to understand conceptual change in science learning. *Journal of Research in Science Teaching*, 31.

Feng, J. (1994). Asian-American children: What teachers should know. *ERIC Digest*, Champaign, IL: Clearinghouse on Elementary and Early Childhood Education (Online). Available: http://ericps.ed.uiuc.edu/eecepubs

Ferreiro, E., & Teberosky, A. (1982). *Literacy before schooling* (K. Castro, Trans.). Exeter, NH: Heinemann.

Ferris, D. R. (2011). *Treatment of Error in Second Language Student Writing*. Second Edition. Ann Arbor: University Michigan Press.

Ferris, D. R. (2012). Written corrective feedback in second language acquisition and writing studies. *Language Teaching, 45*, 446–459.

Field, J. (2002). The changing face of listening. In J. Richards & W. Renandya (Eds.), *Methodology in language teaching: An anthology of current practice* (pp. 242–247). Cambridge: Cambridge University Press.

Field, J. (2008). Emergent and divergent: A view of second language listening research. *System, 36*, 2–9.

Fillmore, L. W. (2001). *Scott Foresman ESL: Accelerating English language learning.* White Plains, NY: Pearson ESL, Sunshine Edition.

Finocchiaro, M., & Brumfit, C. (1983). *The functional-notional approach: From theory to practice.* New York: Oxford University Press.

Fishman, M. (1980). We all make the same mistakes: A comparative study of native and non-native errors in taking dictation. In J. W. Oller, Jr., & K. Perkins (Eds.), *Research in language testing.* Rowley, MA: Newbury House.

Flores, A. (1997). Si se puede, "It can be done:" Quality mathematics in more than one language. In National Council of Teachers of Mathematics (Ed.), *Multicultural and gender equity in the mathematics classroom: The gift of diversity.* Reston, VA: Author.

Florida Department of Education. (1996). *Performance standards for teachers of English for speakers of other languages.* Tallahassee: Florida Department of Education.

Florida Department of Education, Office of Multicultural Student Language Education. (2003). *Language arts through ESOL: A guide for teachers and administrators.* Tallahassee: Florida State Department of Education.

Flower, L. (1979). *Writer-based prose: A cognitive basis for problems in writing college English, 41*, 1, pp. 19–37.

Flower, L., & Hayes, J. (1980). A cognitive process theory of writing. *College composition and communication, 31*(4), 365–387.

Folse, K. (2004a). *Vocabulary myths: Applying second language research to classroom teaching.* Ann Arbor: University of Michigan Press.

Folse, K. (2004b, Fall). How lack of ELL grammar knowledge affects K–12 teachers and their ELLs. *Essential Teacher*.

Folse, K. (2009a). *Keys to teaching grammar to English language learners: A practical handbook.* Ann Arbor: University of Michigan Press

Folse, K. (2009b) How lack of ELL grammar knowledge affects K-12 teachers and their ELLs. *Essential Teacher*, Fall 2009. TESOL: DC.

Ford, D. Y., & Milner, R. (2005). *Teaching culturally diverse gifted students.* Waco, TX: Prufrock Press.

Ford, D. Y., Scott, M. T., Moore, J. L., & Amos, S. O. (2013). Gifted Education and Culturally Different Students Examining Prejudice and Discrimination via Microaggressions. *Gifted Child Today, 36*(3), 205–208.

Ford, D. Y., & Harris, J. J. (1999). *Multicultural gifted education.* Teachers College Press.

Forhand, M. (2005). Bloom's taxonomy: Original and revised. In M. Orey (Ed.), Emerging perspectives on learning, teaching, and technology. Retrieved (March 2010) from http://projects.coe.uga.edu/epltt/index.php?title=Bloom%27sTaxonomy

Fox, G. (1998, September). The Internet: Making it work in the ESL classroom. *The Internet TESL Journal, IV*(9). http://www.aitech.ac.jp/~iteslj/Articles/Fox-Internet.html

Fradd, S. H., & Lee, O. (1999). Teachers' roles in promoting science inquiry with students from diverse language backgrounds. *Educational Researcher, 14*–42.

Fraser Gupta, A. (2012). Grammar teaching and standards. In L. Alsagoff, S. L. McKay, G. Hu, and W. A. Renandya (Eds.), *Principles and practices for teaching English as an international language.* (pp. 244–260). New York: Routledge.

Frasier, M., Hunsaker, S. L., Lee, J., Mitchell, S., Cramond, B., Krisel, S., Garcia, J. H., Martin, D., Frank, E., & Finley, V. S. (1995). *Core attributes of giftedness: A foundation for recognizing the gifted potential of minority and economically disadvantaged students (*Report No. RM-95210) Storrs, CT: National Research Center on the Gifted and Talented. (ERIC Document Reproduction Service No. ED 402 703).

Freeman, Y. S., & Freeman, D. E. (1998). *ESL/EFL teaching principles for success.* Portsmouth, NH: Heinemann.

Freire, P. (1970). *Pedagogy of the oppressed.* New York: Continuum.

Friedman, T. L. (1999). *The lexus and the olive tree.* New York: Farrar, Strauss and Giroux.

Frodesen, J., & Holten, C. (2003). Grammar in the ESL writing class. In B. Kroll (Ed.), *Exploring the dynamics of second language writing* (pp. 141–161). Cambridge: Cambridge University Press.

Frost, R. (1920). *The road not taken: Mountain interval.* New York: Henry Holt and Company.

Fuller, B. (Autumn, 1987). What school factors raise achievement in the third world? *Review of Educational Research, 57*(3), 255–292.

Furner, J. M. (2008). Connecting students to their culture by exploring Mayan mathematics. *Essential Teacher, 5*(1), 26–28.

Furner, J. M., Doan-Holbein, M. F., & Scullion-Jackson, K. (2000). Taking an Internet field trip: Promoting cultural and historical diversity through Mayan mathematics. *TechTrends, 44*(6), 18–22.

Furner, J. M., & Duffy, M. L. (2002). Equity for all students in the new millennium: Disabling math anxiety. *Intervention in School and Clinic, 38*(2), 67–74.

Furner, J. M., Yahya, N., & Duffy, M. L. (2005). 20 ways to teach mathematics: Strategies to reach all students. *Intervention in School and Clinic, 41*(1), 16–23.

Furnham, A., & Bochner, S. (1986). *Culture shock: Psychological reactions to unfamiliar environments.* London: Methuen.

Gallagher, R. M. (2002). A parent-family involvement model to serve gifted Hispanic English-language learners in urban public school settings. In J. A. Castellano & E. I. Diaz (Eds.), *Reaching new horizons* (pp. 250–264). Boston: Allyn & Bacon.

Gallas, K. (1995). *Talking their way into science.* New York, NY: Teachers College Press.

Gambrell, L. B., & Koskinen, P. S. (2002). Imagery: A strategy for enhancing comprehension. In C. C. Block & M. Pressley (Eds.), *Comprehension instruction: Research-based best practices* (pp. 305–318). New York: The Guilford Press.

Garcia (1988). Bilingualism: Theory practice and schooling. In S. Fradd and O. Lee, *Creating Florida's Multilingual Workforce.* Miami, Florida: Florida State Department of Education, 196–217.

Garcia, E. (2004). *The many languages of art*. In M. Goldberg (Ed.), *Teaching English language learners through the arts: A suave experience*. (pp. 43–54). New York: Pearson Education, Inc.

Garcia, E. E., & Baquedano-López, P. (2007). Science instruction for all: An approach to equity and access in science education. *Language Magazine, 6*(6), 24–31.

García, J. H. (2002). Research directions for bilingual gifted education. In J. A. Castellano & E. I. Diaz (Eds.), *Reaching new horizons* (pp. 282–289). Boston: Allyn & Bacon.

García, E., & Lee, O. (2008). Creating culturally responsive learning communities. In A. Rosebery & B. Warren (Eds.), *Teaching science to English language learners* (pp. 147–150). Arlington, VA: NSTA Press.

Gardner, H. (1983). *Frames of mind: The theory of multiple intelligences*. New York: Basic Books.

Gardner, H. (1993). *Multiple intelligences: The theory in practice*. New York: Basic Books.

Gardner, H. (1999). *Intelligences reframed: Multiple intelligences for the 21st century*. New York: Basic Books.

Gardner, H. (2005). Intelligence in seven steps. *New horizons for learning* (Online) Available: http://www.newhorizons.org

Gardner, H., & Hatch, T. (1989). "Multiple intelligences go to school. Educational implications of the theory of multiple intelligences." *Educational Research, 18*(8), 4–9.

Gardner, H., & Lambert, W. (1972). *Attitudes and motivation in second-language learning*. Newbury House Publishers.

Garrison, L. (1997). Making the NCTM's standards work for emergent English speakers. *Teaching Children Mathematics, 4*(3), 132–138.

Gass, S., & Selinker, L. (1995). *SLA: An introduction*. Mahwah, NJ: Lawrence Erlbaum.

Gee, J. P. (2008). Essay: What is academic literacy? In A. Rosebery & B. Warren (Eds.), *Teaching science to English language learners* (pp. 57–70). Arlington, VA: NSTA Press.

Genesee, F. (1987). *Learning through two languages: Studies of immersion and bilingual education* (Vol. 163). Cambridge, MA: Newbury House.

Genesee, F. (1995, December). Integrating language and content: Lessons from immersion. *ERIC Digest* (Online), Available: http://www.cal.org/ericcll/digest/ncrcds05.html

Genesee, F., & Christian, D. (2008). Programs for teaching English language learners. In A. Rosebery & B. Warren (Eds.), *Teaching science to English language learners* (pp. 129–146). Arlington, VA: NSTA Press.

Gentry, J.R. (2010). *Raising confident readers: How to teach your child to read and write—from baby to age 7*. Cambridge, MA: Da Capo Lifelong Books.gf

Gerena, L. (2009a). Understanding and supporting ELL writing in college level classes. In D. Swoboda (Ed.), *DisCover* (Vol. 2.1). The Center for Excellence in Teaching and Learning (CETL), by the Division of Academic Affairs, York College of the City University of New York.

Gerena, L. (2009b, November). Writing and grammar in culturally explicit rhetorical discourse. Presentation at TESOL, France: *28th Annual Colloquium*, Paris, France.

Gerena, L. (2010a, January). Written discourse in college classes: How can faculty guide and support their ELL students? Presentation at *The Hawaii International Conference on Education,* Honolulu, HI.

Gerena, L. (2010b, March). Teaching grammar across the grades: Can grammar be fun? Presentation at *TESOL, Building Bridges: New Competencies in the EFL Classroom,* Lleida, Spain.

Gersten, R., & Baker, S. (2000). What we know about effective instructional practices for English-language learners. *Exceptional Children*, *66*(4), 454–470.

Gibbons, P. (2003). Mediating language learning: Teacher interactions with ESL students in a content-based classroom. *TESOL Quarterly, 37*(2), 247–272.

Glazer, S. M., and Brown, C. S. (1993). *Portfolios and beyond: Collaborative assessment in reading and writing*. Norwood, MA: Christopher-Gordon.

Glicksberg, D. H. (1963). *A study of the span of immediate memory among adult students of English as a foreign language*. Unpublished doctoral dissertation. University of Michigan.

Goh, C. (2000). A cognitive perspective on language learners' listening comprehension problems. *System, 28*, 55–75

Goh, C. (2002). *Teaching listening in the language classroom*. Singapore: SEAMEO Regional Language Center.

Goh, C. (2005). Second language listening expertise. In: K. Johnson (Ed.), *Expertise in second language learning and teaching*. New York: Palgrave Macmillan.

Goh, C. (2008). Metacognitive instruction for second language listening development: theory, practice and research implications. *RELC, 39*, 188–213.

Goh, C. & Hu, G. (2013). Exploring the relationship between metacognitive awareness and listening performance with questionnaire data. *Language Awareness*

Goldberg, M. (2004). *Teaching English language learners through the arts: A SUAVE experience, MyLabSchool Edition*. Boston: Allyn & Bacon.

Goldenberg, C. (2008). Teaching English language learners: What the research does—and does not—say. *American Educator, 32*(2), 42–44.

Goldenberg, C. (2013). *Unlocking the Research on English Learners: What We Know and Don't Yet Know about Effective Instruction*. American Educator, Summer 2013.

Gollnick, D. M., & Chin, P. C. (1998). *Multicultural education in a pluralistic society* (5th ed.). Upper Saddle River, NJ: Prentice Hall.

Gonzalez, F. (1978). *Mexican American culture in the bilingual education classroom*. Unpublished doctoral dissertation. The University of Texas, Austin.

Goodenough, W. H. (1981). *Language, culture, and society*. New York: Cambridge University Press.

Goodman, K. (1988). 1 The reading process. *Interactive approaches to second language reading, 11*.

Goodman, K. S. (1988). The reading process. In P. L. Carrell, J. Devine, & D. E. Eskey (Eds.), *Interactive approaches to second language reading* (pp. 11–21). Cambridge, England: Cambridge University Press.

Goodman, K. S., Goodman, Y., & Flores, B. (1979). *Reading in the bilingual classroom: Literacy and biliteracy*. Rosslyn, VA: National Clearinghouse for Bilingual Education.

Goodman, Y. (1994). One among many: A multicultural, multilingual perspective. In A. D. Flurkey and R. J. Meyher (Eds.), *Under the whole language umbrella many cultures, many voices* (pp. 267–277). Urbana, IL: National Council of Teachers of English.

Gordon, A. (2001). *How to cope with culture shock*. Unpublished manuscript.

Gordon, S. L., & Boseker, B. J. (1984). Enriching education for Indian and non-Indian students. *Journal of Thought, 19*, 143–148.

Gore, C. (2004). *The ultimate film festival survival guide*. Lone Eagle Publishing Company.

Gottlieb, A. (2005). *Evidence-based teaching strategies for achieving academic English and content. The theory behind the research.* Presentation at OELA. Retrieved from: http://reviewing.co.uk.research/experiential.learning.htm

Grabe, W. (1991). Current developments in second language reading. *TESOL Quarterly, 25*(3), 375–405.

Grabe, W. (2000). Reading research and its implications for reading assessment. In A. Kunnan (Ed.), Fairness and validation in language assessment. *Studies in Language Testing, 9*, 226-262. Cambridge, UK: Cambridge University Press.

Grabe, W. (2003). Reading and writing relations: Second language perspectives on research and practice. In B. Kroll (Ed.), *Exploring the dynamics of second language writing* (pp. 242–262). Cambridge: Cambridge University Press.

Grabe, W. (2009). *Reading in a second language: Moving from theory to practice.* Cambridge, UK: Cambridge University Press.

Grabe, W., & Kaplan, R. B. (1996). *Theory and practice of writing.* London: Longman.

Grabe, W., & Stoller, F. (2013). *Teaching and researching: Reading* (Applied Linguistics in Action). (2nd Ed.) Routledge.

Graham, S. & Macari, E. (2008). Strategy instruction in listening for lower-intermediate learners of French. *Language Learning, 58,* 747–783.

Granada, A. J. (2002). Addressing the curriculum, instruction and assessment needs of the gifted bilingual/bicultural student. In J. A. Castellano & E. I. Diaz (Eds.), *Reaching new horizons* (pp. 133–153). Boston: Allyn & Bacon.

Griffiths, C. (2003). Patterns of language learning strategy use. *System, 31*(3), 367–383.

Griffiths, R., & Clyne, M. (1991). *Books you can count on: Linking mathematics and literature.* Portsmouth, NH: Heinemann.

Gunning, T. G. (2000). *Creating literacy instruction for all children* (3rd ed.). Boston, MA: Allyn & Bacon.

Gunning, T. G. (2001). *Building words: A resource manual for teaching word analysis and spelling strategies.* Allyn & Bacon.

Gunning, T. G. (2012). *Creating literacy instruction for all students* (8th ed.). Upper Saddle River, NJ: Pearson.

Hall, E. T. (1959). *The silent language.* NY: Doubleday & Company, Inc.

Hall, E. T. (1966). *The hidden dimension.* New York: Doubleday.

Hall, E. T. (1976). *Beyond culture.* New York: Anchor Press/Doubleday.

Hall, E. T. (1982). Making oneself misunderstood: Languages no one listens to. *Speaking of Japan, 3*(17), 20–22 (Tokyo: Keizai Koho Center).

Hall, E. T. (1983). *The dance of life: The other dimension of time.* Garden City, NJ: Anchor Press/Doubleday.

Hall, E. T. (1966). *The hidden dimension.* New York: Doubleday.

Halvorsen, A. (2009, May–June). Back to the future: The expanding communities curriculum in geography education. *Social Studies, 100*(3), 115–119.

Hancock, M. (1997). Behind classroom code-switching: layering and language choice in L2 learner interaction. *TESOL Quarterly, 31*(2), 217–235.

Hancock, J., Turbill, J., & Cambourne, B. (1994). Assessment and evaluation of literacy learning. In S. Valencia, E. Hiebert, & P. Afflerbach (Eds.), *Authentic reading assessment: Practices and possibilities* (pp. 46–70). Newark, DE: International Reading Association.

Hancock, S., Ariza, E., (2002, May). *A panel of TESOL professors and preservice students discuss ESOL integrated teacher education programs*. The 26th Sunshine State TESOL Conference, West Palm Beach, FL.

Hancock, S., & Ariza, E. (2007). Critical thinking about learning styles: Challenging literature reviews. *ABAC Journal, 27*. Assumption University: Bangkok, Thailand.

Hanna, P. R. (1963). Revising the social studies: What is needed? *Social Education, 27*, 190–196.

Harkins, A. (2004). *Alternative futures for experiential and service learning*. Minneapolis: University of Minnesota Press.

Harmer, J. (1991). *The practice of English language teaching*. Harlow, UK: Longman.

Harmer, J. (1998). *How to teach English*. Harlow, UK: Longman.

Harste, J., Woodward, V., & Burke, C. (1984). *Language stories and literacy lessons*. Portsmouth, NH: Heinemann.

Harste, J. C., Short, K. G., & Burke, C. (1988). *The authoring cycle: A theoretical and practical overview*. Portsmouth, NH: Heinemann Educational Books.

Hasan, A. (2000). Learners' perceptions of listening comprehension problems. *Language, Culture and Curriculum, 13*, 137–153.

Haynes, J. (2007). *Getting started with English language learners: How educators can meet the challenge*. Alexandria, VA: Association for Supervision and Curriculum Development.

Heald-Taylor, G. (1991). *Whole language strategies for ESL students*. San Diego, CA: Dormac.

Hegelsen, M. (1993). *Find the mistakes in new ways in teaching reading* (R. R. Day, Ed.). Bloomington, IL: Pantagraph Printing.

Heinich, R., Molenda, M., Russel, J. D., & Smaldino, S. E. (2002). *Instructional Media and Technologies for Learning*, Merrill Prentice Hall. ISBN 0-13-030536-7.

Herczog, M. (2010). Using the NCSS national curriculum standards for social studies: A framework for teaching, learning, and assessment to meet state social studies standards. *Social Education, 74*(4), 217–224.

Herrell, A. & Jordan, M. (2011). *50 strategies for teaching English language learners*. Pearson.

Herrera, S. (2010). *Biography-driven culturally responsive teaching*. New York: Teachers College Press.

Herron, C., Cole, S., York, H., & Linden, P. (1998). A comparison study of student retention of foreign language video: Declarative versus interrogative advance organizers. *Modern Language Journal, 82*, 237–247.

Hickson, M., III, Stacks, D. W., & Moore, N. J. (2004). *Nonverbal communication: Studies and applications* (4th ed.). Los Angeles, CA: Roxbury.

Hilberg, R. S., Tharp, R.G., & DeGeest, L. (2000). Efficacy of CREDE's standards-based instruction in American Indian mathematics classes. *Equity and Excellence in Education, 33*(2), 32–40.

Himmel, J., Short, D. J., Richards, C., & Echevarria, J. (2009). Using the SIOP Model to Improve Middle School Science Instruction. CREATE Brief. *Center for Research on the Educational Achievement and Teaching of English Language Learners*.

Hinkel, E. (2010). What Research on Second Language Writing Tells Us and What it Doesn't. In E. Hinkel (Ed.), *Handbook of research in second language teaching*, Vol 2. New York: Routlage.

Hofstede, G. (1991). *Cultures and organisations-software of the mind: intercultural cooperation and its importance for survival*. McGraw-Hill.

Holdren, J., Lander, E., & Varmus, H. (2010). Prepare and inspire:k-12 education in science, technology, engineering and math education for America's future. The President's Council of Advisors on Science and Technology, Office of Science and Technology Policy. Retrieved January 6, 2014 at: http://www.whitehouse.gov/administration/eop/ostp/pcast/docsreports.

Hornberger, N. (1989). Continua of biliteracy. *Review of Educational Research, 59*(3), 271–296.

Hornberger, N. (2003). *Continuua of biliteracy: An ecological framework*. Clevedon, UK: Multilingual Matters.

Hornberger, N. H. (2004). The continua of biliteracy and the bilingual educator: Educational linguistics in practice. *Bilingual Education and Bilingualism, 7*(2 & 3), 155–171.

Hornsby, D., Sukarna, D., & Parry, J. (1986). *Read on: A conference approach to reading*. Portsmouth, NH: Heinemann.

Horowitz, D. (1988). To see our text as others see it: Toward a social sense of coherence. *JALT Journal, 10*(2), 91–100.

Hosenfeld, C. (1984). Case studies of ninth grade readers. In J. C. Alderson & A. H. Urquhart (Eds.), *Reading in a foreign language* (pp. 231–244). New York: Longman.

Huckin, T., & Bloch, J. (1993). Strategies for inferring word meaning in context: A cognitive model. In T. Huckin, M. Haynnes, & J. Coady (Eds.), *Second language reading and vocabulary acquisition* (pp. 153–178). Norwood, NJ: Ablex.

Hudelson, S. (1984). Kan yu ret an rayt en ingles: Children become literate in English as a second language. *TESOL Quarterly, 18*, 221–238.

Hudelson, S. (1986). ESL children's writing: What we've learned, what we're learning. In P. Rigg & D. S. Enright (Eds.), *Children and ESL: Integrating perspectives* (pp. 23–54). Washington, DC: Teachers of English to speakers of other languages.

Hudelson, S. (1989a). "Teaching" English through content-area activities. In P. Rigg & V. G. Allen (Eds.), *When they don't all speak English: Integrating the ESL student into the regular classroom*. Urbana, IL: National Council for Teachers of English.

Hudelson, S. (1989b). *Write on. Children writing in ESL*. Englewood Cliffs, NJ: Prentice Hall.

Hudelson, S. (1991). Write on: Children writing in ESL. *The Modern Language Journal, 75*(4), 518.

Hudelson, S. (1994). Literacy development of second language children. In F. Genesee (Ed.), *Educating second language children* (pp. 129–158). New York: Cambridge University Press.

Hulstijn, J. H. (1992). Retention of inferred and given word meanings: experiments in incidental vocabulary learning. In P. J. L. Arnaud & H. Bejoint (Eds.), *Vocabulary and applied linguistics* (pp. 113–125). London: MacMillan.

Hulstijn, J., Hollander, M., & Greidanus, T. (1996). Incidental vocabulary learning by advanced language students: The influence of marginal glosses, dictionary use, and reoccurrence of unknown words. *The Modern Language Journal, 80*, 327–339.

Hunt, A., & Beglar, D. (1998). Current research and practice in teaching vocabulary. *The Language Teacher, 22*, 7–11.

Hurwitz, A. & Day, M. (2007). *Children and their art: Methods for the elementary school.* Belmont, CA: Thomson Wadsworth.

Hymes, D. (1972). On communicative competence. *sociolinguistics, 269293,* 269–293.

Imhof, M. (2010). What is Going on in the Mind of a Listener? The Cognitive Psychology of Listening. In: Wolvin, A. (ed.) *Listening and Human Communication in the 21st Century.* Oxford: Wiley-Blackwell

Individuals with Disabilities Education Act of 1990, (Pub.L. No. 101-476), 20 U.S.C. Chapter 33, §1400–1485.

Individuals with Disabilities Education Act of 2004. 20 U. S. C. §1400 *et seq.* (2004).

Individuals with Education Improvement Act of 2004, Pub. L. 108-466.

Intercultural Development Research Association (IDRA). (1995). Math and science. IDRA Focus. *IDRA Newsletter, 22*(2). San Antonio, Texas: Author.

Jackson, E. (1994). *Cinder Edna.* New York, NY: HarperCollins.

Jackson, P. (1993). *The pop-up book.* New York: Owl Books, Henry Holt and Company, L.L.C.

Jacobs, V. R., Bennett, T., & Bullock, C. (2000). Selecting books in Spanish to teach mathematics. *Teaching Children Mathematics, 6*(9), 582–587.

James, M. (1996). *Improving second language reading comprehension: A computer assisted vocabulary development approach.* Unpublished doctoral dissertation. University of Hawaii, Manoa.

Jarvis J., & Robinson, M. (1997). Analyzing educational discourse: An exploratory study of teacher response and support to pupils' learning. *Applied Linguistics, 18*(2), 212–228.

Jensen, L. (2001). Planning lessons. In M. Celce-Murcia (Ed.), *Teaching English as a second or foreign language* (3rd ed.). Boston: Heinle & Heinle.

Jiang, N. (2004). Semantic transfer and its implication for vocabulary teaching in a second language. *The Modern Language Journal, 88*(iii), 416–432.

Johns, A. M. (1991). *Insights into the reading-writing relationship.* Paper presented at the California TESOL Conference (CATESOL), Santa Clara.

Johnson, D. W., & Johnson, R. T. (1992). Encouraging thinking through constructive controversy. In N. Davidson & T. Worsham (Eds.), *Enhancing thinking through cooperative thinking* (pp. 120–137). New York: Teachers College Press.

Joiner, E. (1986). Listening in the foreign language. In B. H. Wing (Ed.), *Listening, reading and writing: Analysis and application* (pp. 43–70). Middlebury, VT: Northeast Conference on Teaching of Foreign Languages.

Jones, L., & Plass, J. (2002). Supporting listening comprehension and vocabulary acquistion in French with multimedia annotations. *The Modern Language Journal, 86,* 546–561.

Joseph, L .M., & Ford, D. Y. (2005). Nondiscriminatory assessment: Considerations for gifted education. *Gifted Child Quarterly, 50*(1), 42–51.

Juffer, K. A. (1984). State of the art research on culture shock. *ISECSI, Bulletin of International Interchanges, 21,* 16–28.

Kagan, S. (1989). *Cooperative learning: Resources for teachers.* San Juan Capistrano, CA: Resources for Teachers.

Kagan, S. (1995). We can talk: Cooperative learning in the elementary ESL classroom. *Eric Digest* (Online), Available at eric@cal.org

Kagan, S. (1997). *Cooperative learning.* San Clemente, CA: Kagan Cooperative Learning.

Kamps, D., Abbott, M., Greenwood, C., Arreaga-Mayer, C., Willis, H., & Lonstaff, J. (2007). Use of evidence-based, small group reading instruction for English language learners in elementary grades: Secondary-tier intervention. *Learning Disabilities Quarterly, 30*, 163–168.

Kaplan, R. B. (1988). Contrastive rhetoric and second language learning: Notes towards a theory of contrastive rhetoric. In A. Purves (Ed.), *Writing across languages and cultures: Issues in contrastive rhetoric* (pp. 275–304). Newbury Park, CA: Sage Publication.

Kaplan, R. B. (1990). Writing in a multilingual/multicultural context: What's contrastive rhetoric all about? *Writing instructor, 10*(1), 7–17.

Kaplan, S. (1999). Teaching up to the needs of the gifted English language learner. *Tempo, 19*(2), 1, 20–21, 25.

Kasten, W., Kristo, J. V., & McClure, A. (2005). *Living literature: Using children's literature to support reading and language arts*. Upper Saddle River, NJ: Pearson Merrill Prentice Hall.

Keehn, S., Harmon, J., & Shoho, A. (2008). A study of readers theater in eighth grade: Issues of fluency, comprehension, and vocabulary. *Reading & Writing Quarterly, 24*(4), 335–362.

Keene, E., & Zimmermann, S. (1997). *Mosaic of thought*. Portsmouth, NH: Heinemann.

Kelch, K. (1985). Modified input as an aid to comprehend. *Studies in Second Language Acquisition, 7*, 81–89.

Kessler, C., & Quinn, M. E. (1987). ESL and science learning. In J. Crandall (Ed.), *ESL through content-area instruction: Mathematics, science, social studies* (pp. 55–88). Englewood Cliffs, NJ: Prentice Hall.

Kienbaum, B. E. (1986). *Communicative Competence in Foreign Language Learning with Authentic Materials*. Final Project Report.

King, P. E., & Behnke, R. R. (1989). The effect of time-compressed speech on comprehensive, interpretive, and short-term listening. *Human Communication Research, 15*, 428–441.

Kirkwood, T. F. (1995). Teaching from a global perspective: A case study of three high school social studies teachers. *International Dissertation Abstracts*. Miami, FL: Florida International University.

Kirkwood, T. F. (2001a). Our global age requires global education: Clarifying definitional ambiguities. *The Social Studies, 92*(1), 10–15.

Kirkwood, T. F. (2001b). Preparing teachers to teach from a global perspective. *The Delta Kappa Gamma Bulletin, 67*(2), 5–12.

Kirkwood-Tucker, T. F. (2014). From Miami to Moscow: Critical Dialogue in Global Education. *Journal of International Social Studies, 4*(1), 81–91.

Kirsch, G. (1990). Experienced writer's sense of audience and authority: Three case studies. In Kirsch, G. & Roen, D. H. *A sense of audience in written communication*. Newbury Park, CA: Sage Publications.

Kitano M., & Espinosa, R. (1995). Language diversity and giftedness: Working with gifted English language learners. *Journal of the Education for the Gifted, 18*(3), 234–254.

Klingner, J. K., Artiles, A. J., & Barletta, L. M. (2006). English language learners who struggle with reading: Language acquisition or LD? *Journal of Learning Disabilities, 39*, 108–128.

Klingner, J. K., Vaughn, S., Boardman, A., & Swanson, E. (2012). *Now we get it!: Boosting comprehension with collaborative strategic reading*. John Wiley & Sons.

Knerr, J. L., & James, C. J. (1991). Partner work and small-group work for cooperative and communicative learning. *Focus on the foreign language learner: Priorities and strategies*. Lincolnwood, IL: National Textbook.

Knight, S. (1994). Dictionary use while reading: The effects of comprehension and vocabulary acquisition for students of different verbal abilities. *Modern Language Journal, 78,* 285–299.

Knopp, C. (1994). Workshop handout. In H. Curtain & C. A. Pesola (Eds.), *Language and children, Making the match.* New York: Longman.

Kohls, R. (1984). *Survival kit for overseas living.* Chicago: Intercultural Press.

Kohls, L. R. (2001). *Survival kit for overseas living* (4th ed.). Yarmouth, ME: Intercultural Press.

Kojic-Sabo, I., & Lightbown, P. (1999). Students' approaches to vocabulary learning and their relationship success. *The Modern Language Journal, 83*(2), 176–192.

Kramsch, C. J. (1993). *Content and culture in language teaching.* Oxford: Oxford University Press.

Kramsch, C. J. (1998). Language and culture. In *Oxford introductions to language study.* Oxford: Oxford University Press.

Krashen, S. (1981a). Bilingual education and second language acquisition theory. In California State Department of Education (Ed.), *Schooling and language minority students: A theoretical framework.* Los Angeles: Evaluation.

Krashen, S. (1981b). *Second language acquisition and second language learning.* Oxford: Pergamon Press.

Krashen, S. (1982). *Principles and practices in second language acquisition.* Oxford: Pergamon Press.

Krashen, S. (1985). *The input hypothesis: Issues and implications.* New York: Longman.

Krashen, S. (2004a). *Applying the comprehension hypothesis: Some suggestions.* Presented at the 13th International Symposium and Book Fair on language teaching (English Teachers' Association of the Republic of China). Retrieved from http://www.sdkrshen.com/articles/eta_paper/01.html.oct.2005

Krashen, S. (2004b). *The power of reading insights from research* (2nd ed.). Westport: Heinemann.

Krashen, S. (2009a). *Principles and practices in second language acquisition.* First online ed. http://www.sdkrashen.com

Krashen, S. (2009b). *What is academic language proficiency? In press STETS Language & Communication Review.* (Online), Available: http://www.sdkrashen.com/articles/Krashen_Brown_ALP.pdf

Krashen, S., & Terrell, T. (1983). *The natural approach: Language acquisition in the classroom.* New York: Pergamon Press.

Krashen, S. D. (2011). *Free voluntary reading.* Santa Barbara, CA: Greenwood Publishing.

Krashen, S. D., Long, M. A., & Scarcella, R. C. (1979). Age, rate and eventual attainment in second language acquisition. *TESOL Quarterly, 13,* 575–582.

Kratus, J. (1990). Structuring the music curriculum for creative learning. *Music Educators Journal, 77*(33), 33–37.

Kratwohl, D. R., Bloom, B. S., & Masia, B. B. (1964). *Taxonomy of educational goals, Handbook 2, Affective domain.* New York: David McKay.

Kroll, B. (1985). Social-cognitive ability and writing performance: How are they related? *Written Communication, 2*(3), 293–305.

Ku, Y. M., Bravo, M., & Garcia, E. E. (2004). Science instruction for all. *ABE Journal of Research and Practice, 21*(1), 20–44.

Lafond, S. (2012). *Common Core and ELLs: Key Shifts in Language Arts and Literacy (Part II).* Retrieved on June 1, 2014 from www.Colorincolorado.org

Lang, F. K. (1995). Math power for all students? Toward equity issues for students of color. In A. Darder (Ed.), *Culture and difference: Critical perspectives on the bicultural experience in the United States* (pp. 106–126). Westport, CT: Bergin and Garvey.

Language Files: Materials for an Introduction to Language and Linguistics (1994). In S. Jennedy, R. Poletto, & Tracey L. Weldon, (Eds.). Columbus: Ohio State University Press.

Lapp, D., & Flood, J. (1992). *Teaching reading to every child.* New York: Macmillan.

Lapp, S. (2001). Using e-mail dialogue to generate communication in an English as a second language classroom. *The Australian Journal of Language and Literacy, 23*(1), 50–62.

Lara-Alecio, R. (1996, April). *A three year study of a new pedagogical theory/model in a bilingual education program using mathematics as a vehicle of instruction.* Paper presented at the Annual Meeting of the American Educational Research Association. (ERIC Document Reproduction Service Nol ED 398735).

Larsen-Freeman, D. (1997). Grammar and its teaching: Challenging the myths. *ERIC Digest* (Online), Available: http://www.cal.org/ericcll/digest/larsen01.html

Laudin, T. (Ed.). (1991). *ESL, English as a second language—Methodology and curriculum development in second language instruction. No. 1, Second language acquisition* (video-recording). Louisiana Public Broadcasting, Lincoln, NE: GPN Distributor.

Laufer, B. (1992). How much lexis is necessary for reading comprehension? In P. Arnaud, & H. Bejoint (Eds.), *Vocabulary and applied linguistics* (pp. 126–131). London: Macmillan Academic and Professional Limited.

Laufer, B. (1997). The lexical plight in second language reading: Words you don't know, words you think you know and words you can't guess. In J. Coady & T. Huckin (Eds.), *Second language vocabulary acquisition* (pp. 20–34). New York: Cambridge University Press.

Laufer, B., & Hadar, L. (1997). Assessing the effectiveness of monolingual, bilingual and "bilingualized" dictionaries in the comprehension and production of new words. *Modern Language Journal, 81,* 189–196.

Laufer, B., & Sim, D. D. (1983). *To what extent is L2 reading comprehension a function of L2 competence rather than reading strategies?* Haifa, Israel: Department of English, Haifa University.

Laufer, B. (2003). Vocabulary acquisition in a second language: Do learners really acquire most vocabulary by reading? Some empirical evidence. *Canadian modern language review, 59*(4), 567–587.

Lazarowitz, R., & Hertz-Lazarowitz, R. (1998). Cooperative learning in the science curriculum. In B. J. Fraser & K. G. Tobin (Eds.), *International handbook of science education* (pp. 449–469). Boston: Kluwer Academic.

Lazear, D. (2000). *The intelligent curriculum.* Tucson, AZ: Zephyr Press.

Lee, O. (2002). Science inquiry for elementary students from diverse backgrounds. In W. G. Secada (Ed.), *Review of research in education* (Vol. 26, pp. 23–69). Washington, DC: American Educational Research Association.

Lee, O. (2004). Teacher change in belief and practices in science and literacy instruction with English language learners. *Journal of Research in Science Teaching, 41,* 65–93.

Lee, O., & Buxton, C. (2013). Teacher professional development to improve science and literacy achievement of English language learners. *Theory into Practice 52,* 110-117.

Lee, O., & Buxton, C. (2013). Integrating science and English proficiency for English language learners. *Theory into Practice 52,* 36-42.

Lee, O., Deaktor, R., Enders, C., & Lambert, J. (2008). Impact of a multi-year professional development intervention on science achievement of culturally and linguistically diverse elementary students. *Journal of Research on Science Teaching, 45*(6), 726–747.

Lee, O., Deaktor, R. A., Hart, J. E., Cuevos, P., & Enders, C. (2005). An instructional intervention's impact on the science and literacy achievement of culturally and linguistically diverse elementary students. *Journal of Research in Science Teaching, 42,* 857–887.

Lee, O., & Fradd, S. H. (1998). Science for all, including students from non-English-language backgrounds. *Educational Researcher, 27,* 12–20.

Lee, O., Lewis, S., Adamson, K., Maerten-Rivera, J., & Secada, W. (2007). Urban science teachers' knowledge and practices in teaching science to English language learners. *Science Education,* 733–758.

Lee, O., Maerten-Rivera, J., Penfield, D., LeRoy, K., & Secada, W. G. (2008). Science achievement of English language learners in urban elementary schools: Results of a first-year professional development intervention. *Journal of Research in Science Teaching, 45,* 31–52.

Lee, O., Quinn, H. & Valdes, G. (2013). Science and language for English language learners in relation to Next Generation Science Standards and with implications for Common Core State Standards for English language arts and mathematics. Educational Researcher DOI: 10.3102/0013189X13480524.

Lee, S. K. (1995). Creative games for the language class. *English Teaching Forum, 33*(1), 35–36.

Lengeling, M. M., & Malarcher, C. (1997). Index cards: A natural resource for teachers. *English Teaching Forum, 35*(4), 42.

Lenneberg, E. (1967). *Biological foundations of language.* New York: Wiley.

Leu, D.J., Kinzer, C.K., Coiro, J., Castek, J., & Henry, L.A. (2013). New literacies: A dual-level theory of the changing nature of literacy, instruction, and assessment. In D.E. Alvermann, J.J. Unrau, & R.B. Rundell (Eds.), *Theoretical models and processes of reading* (6th ed., pp. 1150–1181). Newark, DE: International Reading Association.

Leverett, T. (2005, March). *Daring to enter the blogosphere.* Paper presented at the annual meeting TESOL—Daring to Lead 40th Annual Conference, Tampa, FL.

Lewis, G., & Bedson, G. (1999). *Games for children.* Oxford: Oxford University Press.

Lewis, M. (1997). *Implementing the lexical approach.* Hove: Language Teaching Publications.

Linan-Thompson, S., Cirino, P. T., & Vaughn, S. (2007). Determining English language learners' response to intervention: Questions and some answers. *Learning Disabilities Quarterly, 30,* 185–195.

Lines drawn over census result. (2010). Retrieved March 1, 2010 from http://topics.edition.cnn.com/topics/u_s_census_bureau

Lip, E. (1985). *Chinese beliefs and superstitions.* Singapore: Graham Brash.

Louie, A. (1982). *Yeh-Shen: A Cinderella story from China.* New York: Philomel.

Little, D., Devitt, S., & Singleton, D. (1994). The communicative approach and authentic texts. *Teaching Modern Languages,* 43–47.

Lomas Garza, C. (2000). *In my family/En mi familia.* San Francisco, CA: Children's Book Press.

Long, M. H., & Porter, P. A. (1985). Group work, interlanguage talk, and second language acquisition. *TESOL quarterly, 19*(2), 207–228.

Lozanov, G. (1982). *Suggestology and outline of suggestopedy.* New York: Gordon & Breach Science Publishers.

Lund, R. J. (1990). A taxonomy for teaching second language listening. *Foreign Language Annals, 23*(2), 105–115.

Luppescu, S., & Day, R. (1993). Reading, dictionaries, and vocabulary learning. *Language Learning, 43*, 262–287.

Lynch, S., Atwater, M., Cawley, J., Eccles, J., Lee, O., Marrett, C., Rojas-Medlin, D., Secada, W. Stefanivh, G., & Willetto, A. (1996). *An equity blueprint for Project 2061*. Washington, DC: AAAS.

Lynch, T. (2002). Listening: Questions of level. In R. B. Kaplan (Ed.), *Oxford handbook of applied linguistics* (pp. 39–48). Oxford: Oxford University Press.

Lynch, T. (2006). Academic listening: marrying top and bottom. In Uso-Juan, E. & Martinez-Flor, A. (Eds.) *Current trends in the development and teaching of the four language skills.* Berlin: Mouton de Gruyter.

Lynch, T. (2009). *Teaching Second Language Listening.* Oxford: Oxford University Press.

Macaro, E. (2010). The relationship between strategic behaviour and language learning success. In E. Macaro (Ed.), *The Continuum Companion to Second Language Acquisition.* London: Continuum.

Macceca, S. (2007). *Reading strategies for social studies, grades 1–8.* Shell Education Pub. Teacher Created Materials.

Mangelsdorf, K., Roen, D., and Taylor, V. (1990). ESL students' use of audience. In G. Kirsch & D. H. Roen (Eds.), *A sense of audience in written communication* (pp. 231–247). Newbury Park, CA: Sage.

Maple, E. (1971). *Superstition and the superstitious.* New York: A. S. Barnes.

Mareschal, C. (2002). *A cognitive perspective on the listening comprehension strategies of second language learners in the intermediate grades.* Unpublished MA thesis, University of Ottawa.

Markham, P. L. (1988). Gender differences and the perceived expertness of the speaker as factors in ESL listening recall. *TESOL Quarterly, 22*, 397–406.

Markham, P. L., Peter, L., & McCarthy, T. (2001). The effects of native language vs. target language captions on foreign language students' DVD video comprehension. *Foreign Language Annals, 34*, 439–445.

Marshall, C. (1991). Teachers' learning styles: How they affect student learning. *The Clearing House, 64*(4), 225–226.

Martiniello, M. (2008). Language and the performance of English-language learners in math word problems. *Harvard Educational Review, 78*(2), 333–368.

Mathis, W. J. (2010). The "Common Core" Standards Initiative: An Effective Reform Tool? Boulder and Tempe: Education and the Public Interest Center & Education Policy Research Unit. Retrieved [date] from http://epicpolicy.org/publication/common-core-standards

Mauranen, A. (1994). Two discourse worlds. *Finlance, 13*, 1–40.

May, F. (1998). *Reading as communication: To help children read and write.* Upper Saddle River, NJ: Merrill/Prentice Hall.

Mayesky, M. (2009). *Creative activities for young children.* Clifton Park, NY: Delmar Cengage Learning.

McCallum, M. E. (1999). *Strategies and activities to stimulate adequate ESOL instruction in content area courses and increase honest effort and motivation among ESOL students.* Decatur, GA: DeKalb County School System. (ERIC Document Reproduction Service No. ED 436 969).

McCloskey, M. L. (1992). Turn on units: English as a second language content area curriculum in math, science, and computer science for grades K–6. *Teaching Guides.* Georgia State Board of Education, Atlanta, GA. (ERIC Document Reproduction Service No. ED 347090)

McDonald, D. (1975) Music and reading readiness. *Language Arts,* September 1975 52, 872–876. Mills, A. *Old MacDonald had a farm.*

McLaughlin, B. (1987). Reading in a second language. Studies of adult and child learners. In S. R. Goldman, & H. T. Trueba (Eds.), *Becoming literate in English as a second language* (pp. 57–70). Norwood, NJ: Ablex.

McLaughlin & McLeod (1996). *Educating all our students: Improving education for children from culturally and linguistically diverse backgrounds.* Retrieved from http://www.edtechpolicy.org/ ArchivedWebsites/edall.htm#Introduction:#Introduction

McLoughlin, J. A., & Lewis, R. B. (2001). *Assessing students with special needs* (3rd ed.). Upper Saddle River, NJ: Merrill/Prentice Hall.

McNeil, J. (1992). *Reading comprehension* (3rd ed.). New York: HarperCollins.

McShane, D. A., & Plas, J. M. (1982). Wechsler scale performance patterns of American Indian children. *Psychology in the Schools, 19,* 8–17.

McTighe, J. (1992). Graphic organizers: Collaborative links to better thinking. In N. Davison & T. Worsham (Eds.), *Enhancing thinking through collaborative learning* (pp. 182–197). New York: Teachers College Press of Columbia University.

Mehlinger, H. D. (Ed.). (1981). *UNESCO handbook for the teaching of social studies.* New York: UNESCO.

Mendelson, D. (1995). Applying learning strategies in the second/foreign language listening comprehension lesson. In D. Mendelson & J. Rubin (Eds.). *A guide for the teaching of second language listening* (pp. 132–150). San Diego: Dominie Press.

Merryfield, M. M. (1990). *Teaching about the world: Teacher education programs with a global perspective.* Columbus, OH: Mershon Center, The Ohio State University.

Merryfield, M. M. (1997). *A framework for teacher education. Preparing teachers to teach global perspectives: A handbook for teacher educators* (M. M. Merryfield, E. Jarchow, & S. Pickert, Eds.). Thousand Oaks, CA: Corwin Press.

Met, M. (1994). Teaching content through a second language. *Educating second language children: The whole child, the whole curriculum, the whole community,* 159–182.

Meyer, B. J. F., Brandt, D. M., & Bluth, G. J. (1980). Use of top-level structure in text: Key for reading comprehension of ninth grade students. *Reading Research Quarterly, 16,* 72–103.

Miranda, A. O., Bilot, J. M., Peluso, P. R., Berman, K., & Van Meek, L. G. (2006). Latino families: The relevance of the connection among acculturation, family dynamics, and health for family counseling research and practice. *Family Journal: Counseling and Therapy for Couples and Families, 14,* 268–273.

Moll, L., Amanti, C., Neff, D., & González, N. (1992). Funds of knowledge for teaching: Using a qualitative approach to connect homes and classrooms. *Theory Into Practice, 31,* 132-141.

Montrul, S. (2011). Morphological errors in Spanish second language learners and heritage speakers. *Studies in Second Language Acquisition, 33*(02), 163–192.

Moore, C. G. (1994). Research in Native American mathematics education. *For the Learning of Mathematics, 14*(2), 9–14.

Morales-Jones, C. A. (2000). "Teachers facing the challenges of linguistically diverse classrooms" *Trends and Issues. The Publication of the Florida Council for the Social Studies XII*(2), 25–27.

Morales-Jones, C. A. (2011). Methods/Approaches of Teaching ESOL: A Historical Overview. H. Zainuddin, N, Yahya, C.A. Morales-Jones & E.N. Whelan Ariza (Eds.), *Fundamentals of Teaching English to Speakers of Other Languages in K–12 Mainstream* Classrooms, 63–74.

Morley, J. (1999). Current perspectives on improving aural comprehension. Retrieved from http://www.eslmag.com/Morleyauralstory.htm

Morrow, R. D., & McBride, H. J. (1988). *Considerations for Educators in Working with Southeast Asian Children and Their Families.*

Morrow, L. M. (1983). Home and school correlates of early interest in literature. *Journal of Educational Research, 76,* 24–30.

Morrow, L. M. (1993). *Literacy development in the early years: Helping children read and write* (2nd ed.). Boston: Allyn & Bacon.

Morrow, L. M. (2001). *Literacy development in the early years.* Boston: Allyn & Bacon.

Morrow, R. (1989). Southeast Asian parent involvement: Can it be a reality? *Elementary School Guidance of Counseling, 23,* 289–297.

Morrow, R. D., & McBride, H. J. (1988). *Considerations for Educators in Working with Southeast Asian Children and Their Families.*

Moschkovich, J. (2000). Learning mathematics in two languages: Moving from obstacles to resources. In W. G. Secada (Ed.), *Changing the faces of mathematics: Perspectives on multiculturalism and gender equity.* Reston, VA: National Council of Teachers of Mathematics.

Moskowitz, G. (1978). *Caring and sharing in the foreign language class.* Cambridge, MA: Newbury House.

Muller, E., & Markowitz, J. (2004). *English language learners with disabilities.* Alexandria, VA: Project FORUM.

Murray, D. M. (2004). *Write to learn.* New York: Cengage.

Nagel, P. S. (1999). E-mail in the virtual ESL/EFL classroom. *The Internet TESL Journal.* (Online), Available: http://www.aitech.ac.jp/!iteslj/Articles/Nagel-Email.htm

Nagy, W. E., Herman, P. A., & Anderson, R. C. (1985). Learning words from context. *Reading Research Quarterly, 20*(2), 233–253.

Nathenson-Mejia, S., & Escamilla, K. (2003). Connecting with Latino children: Bridging gaps with children's literature. *Bilingual Research Journal, 27*(1), 101–116.

Nation, P. (Ed.) (1994). *New ways in teaching vocabulary.* Alexandria, VA: Teachers of English to Speakers of Other Languages.

National Council for the Social Studies (NCSS). (1982). *Position statement on global education.* Washington, DC: Author.

National Council for the Social Studies (NCSS). (1994a). *Curriculum standards for social studies: Expectations of excellence.* Washington, DC: Author.

National Council for the Social Studies (NCSS). (1994b). *Expectations of excellence: Curriculum standards.* Washington, DC: Author.

National Council of Teachers of Mathematics (NCTM). (1989). *Curriculum and evaluation standards for school mathematics.* Reston, VA: Author.

National Council of Teachers of Mathematics (NCTM). (1995). *Professional assessment standards for teaching mathematics.* Reston, VA: Author.

National Council of Teachers of Mathematics (NCTM). (2000). *Principles and standards for school mathematics.* Reston, VA: Author.

National Council of Teachers of Mathematics. (2006). *Curriculum focal points for prekindergarten through grade 8 mathematics: A quest for coherence.* Reston, VA: NCTM.

National Governors Association Center for Best Practices (NGA Center) and the Council of Chief State School Officers (CCSSO) (2010). *Common core state standards initiative.* Washington, DC. Authors. The Common Core State Standards may be accessed and/or retrieved on January 6, 2014 from http://www.corestandards.org.

National Reading Panel. (2000). *National Reading Panel: Teaching children to read.* Washington, DC: National Institutes of Health.

National Research Council. (1996). *National science education standards.* Washington, DC: National Academy Press.

National Research Council. (2012). *A framework for K–12 science education: Practices, cross cutting concepts and core ideas.* Washington, DC: The National Academies Press.

National Science Foundation, (2006). *Science and engineering indicators,* 2006. Arlington, VA: National Science Foundation.

Nattinger, J. R., & DeCarrico, J. S. (1992). *Lexical phrases and language teaching.* Oxford: Oxford University Press.

Nguyen, T., & Khuat, T. (2003). Learning vocabulary through games: The effectiveness of learning vocabulary through games. *Asian EFL Journal, 5*(4).

NGSS Lead States. (2013). *Next generation science standards: For states, by states.* Washington, DC: The National Academies Press.

Nilson, L. & Zimmerman, B. J. (2013). *Creating self-regulated learners: Strategies to strengthen students' self-awareness and learning skills.* Stylus Publishing.

Noddings, N. (Ed.). (2005). *Educating citizens for global awareness.* New York: Teachers College Press. Nolan, R. W. (1990). Culture shock and cross-cultural adaptation or I was ok until I got here. *Practicing Anthropology, 12*(4), 2–20.

Nolan, R. W., & Patterson, R. (2000). Curtains, lights: Using skits to teach English to Spanish-speaking adolescents and adults. *Journal of Adolescent & Adult Literacy, 44*(1), 6–14.

Norton, D. (1992). *The impact of literature-based reading.* New York: Merrill.

Nunan, D. (1989). *Understanding language classrooms.* A guide for teacher-initiated action. Englewood Cliffs, NJ: Prentice Hall.

Nunan, D. (1991). *Language teaching methodology: A textbook for teachers.* Prentice Hall.

Nunan, D., & Miller, L. (Eds.). (1995). *New ways in teaching listening.* Alexandria, VA: Teachers of English to Speakers of Other Languages. (ERIC Document Reproduction Service No. ED 388 054).

Nutall, C. (1982). *Teaching reading skills in a foreign language.* London: Heinemann.

Oberg, K. (1960). Cultural shock: Adjustment to new cultural environments. *Practical Anthropology, 7,* 177–182.

Ogbu, J. (1988). Cultural diversity and human development. In D. T. Slaughter (Ed.), *Black children and poverty. A developmental perspective* (pp. 11–28). San Francisco: Jossey-Boss.

Ohata, K. (2006). Auditory short-term memory in L2 listening comprehension process. *Journal of Language Learning, 5*(1), 21–28.

Olszewski-Kubilius, P., & Clarenbach, J. (2014). Closing the Opportunity Gap Program Factors Contributing to Academic Success in Culturally Different Youth. *Gifted Child Today, 37*(2), 103–110.

O'Malley, J. M., Chamot, A. U., & Küpper, L. (1989). Listening comprehension strategies in second language acquisition. *Applied Linguistics, 10*(4), 418-437.

O'Malley, J. M., Chamot, A. U., Stewner-Manzanares, G., Kupper, L., & Russo, R. P. (1985). Learning strategies used by beginning and intermediate ESL students. *Language Learning, 35*(1), 21–46.

O'Malley, J. M., & Chamot, A. U. (1990). *Learning strategies in second language acquisition.* New York: Cambridge University Press.

O'Malley, J. M., & Pierce, L. V. (1996). *Authentic assessment for English language learners: Practical approaches for teachers.* Reading, MA: Addison-Wesley.

Ortega, L. (2009). *Understanding Second Language Acquisition,* London: Hodder Education.

Ortiz, T. (1997). Characteristics of limited English proficient Hispanic students served in programs for the learning disabled: Implications for policy and practice (Part II). *Bilingual Special Education Newsletter,* University of Texas at Austin, Vol. IV.

Ortiz, A., & Yates, J. R. (2001). A framework for serving English language learners with disabilities. *Journal of Special Education Leadership, 14*(2), 72–80.

Osada, N. (2001). What strategy do less proficient learners employ in listening comprehension? A reappraisal of bottom-up and top-down processing. *Journal of the Pan-Pacific Association of Applied Linguistics, 5,* 73–90.

Ovando, C., & Collier, V. (1985). *Bilingual and ESL classrooms: Teaching in multicultural contexts.* New York: McGraw-Hill.

Oxford, R. L. (1990). *Language learning strategies: What every teacher should know.* Boston: Heinle & Heinle.

Oxford, R., & Ehrman, M. (1988). Psychological type and adult language learning strategies: A pilot study. *Journal of Psychological Type, 16,* 22–32.

Oxford, R., & Erhman, M. E. (1995). Adults' language learning strategies in an intensive foreign language program in the United States. *System, 23*(3), 359–386.

Oxford, R., Ehrman, M. E., & Lavine, R. Z. (1991). Style wars: Teacher-student style conflicts in the language classroom. In S. Magnan (Ed.), *Challenges in the 1990's for College Foreign Language Programs* (pp. 1–25). Boston: Heinle & Heinle.

Padilla, A. M. (1980). The role of cultural awareness and ethnic loyalty in acculturation. In A. M. Padilla (Ed.), *Acculturation: Theory, models, and some new findings* (pp. 47–84). Boulder, CO: Westview Press.

Paige, R. M. (1993). On the nature of intercultural experiences and intercultural education. In R. M. Paige (Ed.), *Education for the intercultural experience* (pp. 169–199). Yarmouth, MA: Intercultural Press.

Pajares, F. M. (1992). Teacher's beliefs and educational research: Cleaning up a messy construct. *Review of Educational Research, 62*(3), 307–322.

Pang, V. O. (1990, Fall). Asian-American children: A diverse population. *The Education Forum, 55*(1), 49–66.

Paribakht, T., & Wesche, M. (1999). Reading and "incidental" L2 vocabulary acquisition. *Studies in Second Language Acquisition, 21,* 195–224.

Park-Oh, Y. Y. (1994). *Self-regulated strategy training in second-language reading: Its effects on reading comprehension, strategy use, reading attitudes, and learning styles of college ESL students.* Unpublished dissertation, University of Alabama, Tuscaloosa, AL.

Paulenich, (1992). Teaching literature using real world materials. Paper presented at the Literacy Conference at Indiana University, Bloomington, IN.

Pawan, F., & Sietman, G. B. (2007). *Helping English language learners succeed in middle and high schools.* F. Pawan, G. B. Sietman (Eds.).. Alexandra, VA: TESOL Inc.

Pepper, F. C. (1976). Teaching the American Indian child in mainstream settings. In R. L. Jones (Ed.), *Mainstreaming and the minority child* (pp. 133–158). Reston, VA: Council for Exceptional Children.

Peregoy, S., & Boyle, O. F. (1990). Kindergartners write! Emergent literacy of Mexican American children in a two-way Spanish immersion program. *Journal of the Association of Mexican American Educators,* 6–18.

Peregoy, S. F., and Boyle, O. F. (2000). *Reading, writing, and learning in ESL* (3rd Ed.). Boston: Pearson Addison Wesley.

Peregoy, S. F., & Boyle, O. F. (2008). *Reading, writing, & learning in ESL: A resource book for K–12 teachers* (5th ed.). New York: Allyn Bacon.

Peregoy, S. F. & Boyle, O. F. (2012). *Reading, writing, and learning in ESL: A resource book* (6th Ed.). Pearson.

Pérez, B., & Torres-Guzmán, M. (1992). *Learning in two worlds: An integrated Spanish/English biliteracy approach.* New York: Longman.

Perkins, D. N. (1992). *Smart schools.* New York: Free Press.

Peters, M. (1999). The listening comprehension strategies of students in a French immersion program. Unpublished Ph.D. dissertation. University of Ottawa.

Peterson, B. (1992). Selecting books for beginning readers. In D. E. DeFord, G. S. Pinnell, & C. Lyons (Eds.), *Bridges to literacy.* Portsmouth, NH: Heinemann.

Peterson, J. S., & Margolin, L. (1997). Naming gifted children: An example of unintended "reproduction." *Journal for the Education of the Gifted, 21*(1), 82–100.

Petitto, L.A. (2008). Arts Education, the Brain, and Language. In the *Arts and Cognition Monograph: The Dana Consortium Report on Arts and Cognition.* New York: Dana Press, pp. 93-104.

Philips, S. U. (1972). Participant structures and communicative competence: Warm Springs children in community and classroom. In C. Cazden, V. John, & D. Hymes (Eds.), *Functions of language in the classroom.* New York: Teachers College Press.

Philips, S. U. (1983). *The invisible culture: Communication in classroom and community on the Warm Springs Indian Reservation.* White Plains, NY: Longman.

Piche, G. L., & Roen, D. (1987). Social cognition and writing: Interpersonal cognitive complexity and abstractness and the quality of students' persuasive writing. *Written Communication, 4*(1), 68–89.

Piper, W. (1976). *The little engine that could.* New York: Putman.

Poelmans, P. (2003). Developing second language listening comprehension: Effects of training lower-order skills versus higher-order strategy. Unpublished Ph.D. dissertation, University of Amsterdam.

Polacco, P. (1988). *The keeping quilt.* New York, NY: Aladdin Paperbacks.

Polya, G. (2004). *How to solve it: A new aspect of mathematical methods.* Princeton, NJ: Princeton University Press.

Population Reference Bureau. (2009). *Data by geography: Multiple geographic regions*. Retrieved February 9, 2010, from http://www.prb.org/Datafinder/Geography/MultiCompareBar.aspx?variables=130%2c133%2c134%2c2%2c20%2c17&sort=v&order=a&regions=6%2c70%2c101%2c115%2c172%2c222

Porter, R. E., & Samovar, L. A. (Eds.) (1988). *Intercultural communication: A reader* (5th ed.). Belmont: Wadsworth Publishing Company.

Portes, A., & Rumbaut, R. G. (1996). *Immigrant America* (2nd ed.). Berkeley: University of California Press.

Portes, A., & Zhou, M. (1993). The new second generation: Segmented assimilation and its variants among post-1965 immigrant youth. *Annals of the American Academy of Political and Social Science, 53*, 74–98.

Prince, P. (1996). Second language vocabulary learning: The role of context versus translations as a function of proficiency. *The Modern Language Journal, 80*, 478–493.

Radford, L., Netten, J., & Duquette, G. (1997). Developing target second language skills through problem-solving activities in mathematics. *NYSABE Journal, 12*(1), 84–97.

Raines, S., & Isbell, R. (1994). *Stories: Children's literature in early education*. Albany, NY: Delmar.

Ramirez, M., & Castañeda, A. (1974). *Cultural democracy, bicognitive development and education*. New York: Academic Press.

Ramirez, A. G., & Politzer, R. L. (1976). The acquisition of English and maintenance of Spanish in a bilingual education program. In J. E. Alatis & K. Twaddell (Eds), *English as a second language in a bilingual education*. Washington, DC: TESOL.

Rance-Rooney, J. A. (2004). The affective dimension of second culture/second language acquisition in gifted adolecents. In D. Boothe & J. C. Stanley (Eds.), *Critical issues for diversity in gifted education* (pp. 73–86). Waco, TX: Prufrock Press.

Rasekh, Z., & Ranjbary, R. (2003). Metacognitive strategy training for vocabulary learning. *TESL-EJ, 7*(2), 1–15.

Read, C. (1971). Pre-school children's knowledge of English phonology. *Harvard Educational Review, 41*, 1–34.

Region V Academic Center for Educational Excellence, 2000. Chicago, IL.

Reid, J. M. (1987). The perceptual learning style preferences of ESL students. *TESOL Quarterly, 21*(1), 87–111.

Reid, J. M. (1993). *Teaching ESL writing*. Englewood Cliffs, NJ: Prentice Hall.

Reid, J. M. (1995). Preface. In J. Reid (Ed.), *Learning styles in the ESL/EFL classroom* (pp. ix–xvii). Boston: Heinle & Heinle.

Reiss, J. (2008). *102 content strategies for English language learners: Teaching for academic success in grades 3–12*. Pearson: Merrill/Prentice Hall.

Remland, M. S., & Jones, T. S. (1995). Interpersonal distance, body orientation, and touch: Effects of culture, gender, and age. *Journal of Social Psychology, 135*(3), 281–297.

Reyes, M. (1992). Challenging venerable assumptions: Literacy instruction for linguistically different students. *Harvard Educational Review, 62*(4), 427–446.

Reys, R E., Lindquist, M. M., Lambdin, D. V., Smith, N.L., & Suydam, M. N. (2012). *Helping children learn mathematics* (10th Ed.). Boston, MA: John Wiley & Sons Publishing, Inc.

Reys, R. E., Suydam, M. N., Lindquist, M. N., & Smith, N. L. (2009). *Helping children learn mathematics* (9th Ed.). Boston: John Wiley & Sons.

Rhodes, L., & Dudley-Marling, C. (1988). *Readers and writers with a difference: A holistic approach to teaching learning disabled and remedial students*. Portsmouth, NH: Heinemann.

Richards, J., & Rodgers, T. (1986). *Approaches and methods in language teaching: A description and analysis*. New York: Cambridge University Press.

Rief, L. (1990). Finding the value of evaluation: Self-assessment in a middle school classroom. *Educational Leadership, 47*(6), 24–29.

Rinaldi, C., & Samson, J. (2008). English language learners and response to intervention: Referral considerations. *Teaching Exceptional Children, 40*(5), 6.

Ritzhaupt, A. D., Liu, F., Dawson, K., & Barron, A. E. (2013). Differences in student information and communication technology literacy based on socio-economic status, ethnicity, and gender: Evidence of a digital divide in Florida schools. *Journal of Research on Technology in Education, 45*(4), 291–307.

Rivers, W. M. (1981). *Teaching foreign language skills* (2nd ed.). Chicago: University of Chicago Press.

Rivers, W. M., & Temperly, M. S. (1978). *A practical guide to the teaching of English as a second or foreign language*. New York: Oxford University Press.

Robb, L. (1999). *Easy mini-lessons for building vocabulary: Practical strategies that boost work knowledge and reading comprehension*. New York: Scholastic Professional Books.

Roberts, P. L., Kellough, R. D., & Moore, K. (2005). *A Resource Guide for Elementary School Teaching*. Prentice Hall.

Roberts, P. L., & Kellough, R. D. (2008). *A guide for developing interdisciplinary thematic units* (4th ed.). Upper Saddle River, NJ: Pearson Education, Allyn & Bacon.

Robisheaux, J. A. (2002). The intersection of language, high potential, and culture in gifted English as a second language students. *Reaching new horizons: Gifted and talented education for culturally and linguistically diverse students,* 154–174.

Robisheaux, J. A., & Banbury, M. M. (1994, September–October). Students who don't fit the mold. *Gifted Child Today Magazine, 17*(4), 28–31.

Robison, S. (2006). Teaching math to English learners—Myths and methods. In E. N. Whelan Ariza (Ed.), *Not for ESOL teachers: What every classroom teacher needs to know about the linguistically, culturally, and ethnically diverse students*. Boston: Pearson.

Roblyer, M. D., & Doering, A. H. (2010). *Integrating educational technology into teaching.* (5th ed.). Boston: Allyn and Bacon.

Rodriguez, A. J. (2004). Turnign despondency into hope: Charting new paths to improve students' acheivement and participation in science education. Southeast Eisenhower Regional Consortium for Mathematics and Science Education @ SERVE. Tallahassee, FL.

Rodgriquez, A. J. & Berryman, C. (2002). Using sociotransformative constructivism to teach for understanding in diverse classrooms: A beginning teacher's journey. *American Educational Research Journal. 39*(4), 1017–1045.

Rosebery, A. S., & Ballenger, C. (2008). Creating a foundation through student conversation. In A. S. Rosebery & B. Warren (Eds.), *Teaching science to English language learners: Building on students' strengths*. Arlington, VA: NSTA Press.

Rosebery, A., & Hudicourt-Barnes, J. (2006). Using diversity as a strength in the science classroom: The benefits of science talk. *Linking science & literacy in the K–8 classroom,* 305–320.

Rosebery, A. S., Warren, B., & Conant, F. R. (1992). Appropriating scientific discourse: Findings from language minority classrooms. *Journal of the Learning Sciences, 21*, 61–94.

Rosenblatt, L. M. (1978). *The reader, the text, the poem.* Carbondale: Southern Illinois University Press. Rosenblatt, L. M. (1988). *Writing and reading: The transactional theory.* Berkeley, CA: University of California, Center for the Study of Writing.

Rosenblatt, L. M. (1988). *Writing and Reading: The Transactional Theory.* Technical Report No. 416.

Rosenblatt, L. M. (1991). Literature—S.O.S.! *Language Arts, 68*, 444–448.

Rosenblatt, L. M. (1994). The traditional theory of reading and writing. In R. B. Ruddell, M. R.

Rosenblatt, L. M. (1994). *The reader, the text, the poem: The transactional theory of the literary work.* SIU Press.

Rosenblatt, L. M. (2005). *Making meaning with texts: Selected essays.* Heinemann Educational Books.

Rost, M. (2002). *Teaching and researching listening.* London: Logman.

Routman, R. (1991). *Invitations.* Portsmouth, NH: Heinemann.

Rubin, J. (1994). A review of second language listening comprehension research. *Modern Language Journal, 78*, 199–221.

Rubin, J. (1995). The contribution of video to the development of competence in listening. In D. Mendelsohn & J. Rubin (Eds.), *A guide for the teaching of listening* (pp. 151–165). San Diego, CA: Dominie Press.

Rudell, & H. Singer (Eds.), *Theoretical models and processes of reading* (4th ed., pp. 1057–1092). Newark, DE: International Reading Association.

Samson, M., Allen, R., & Sampson, M. (1990). *Pathways to literacy.* Chicago: Holt, Rinehart, & Winston.

Samuels, S. J. (1994). Toward a theory of automatic information processing in reading revisited. In R. B. Ruddell, M. R. Rudell, & H. Singer (Eds.), *Theoretical models and processes of reading* (4th ed., pp. 816–837). Newark, DE: International Reading Association.

Samuels, S. J., & Kamil, M. L. (1988). Models of the reading process. In P. L. Carrell, J. Devine, & D. E. Eskey (Eds.), *Interactive approaches to second language reading* (pp. 22–37). Cambridge: Cambridge University Press.

Sanaoui, R. (1995). Adult learners' approaches to learning vocabulary in second languages. *Modern Language Journal, 79*(1), 15–28.

Sano, F. (1999). Strategy instruction for writing in ESL/EFL. In R. Oxford (Ed.), *Language learning strategies in the context of autonomy: Strategy research compendium: Proceedings of the first annual strategy research symposium,* Teachers College (pp. 70–72). NY: Columbia University.

Saravia-Shore, M., & Arvizu, S. F. (1992). Introduction to cross-cultural literacy: An anthropological approach to dealing with diversity. In M. Saravia-Shore & S. F. Arvizu (Eds.), *Cross-cultural literacy: Ethnographies of communication in multiethnic classrooms* (pp. xv–xxxviii). New York: Garland.

Saunders, W., Claude Goldenberg, C., & David Marcelletti, D. (2013) *English Language Development: Guidelines for Instruction.* American Educator, Summer 2013.

Saunders, W. O., O'Brien, G., Lennon, D., & McLean, J. (1998). Making the transition to English literacy successful: Effective strategies for studying literature with transition students. In R. G. R. Jimenez (Ed.), *Promoting learning for culturally and linguistically diverse students.* Monterey, CA: Brooks Cole Publishers.

Sauvignon, S. J. (2002). Communicative curriculum design for the 21st century. Retrieved from http:// iteslj.rog/links/search.cgl?query=communicative

Saville-Troike, M. (1973). Reading and the audiolingual method. *TESOL Quarterly, 7*(4), 395–405.

Saville-Troike, M. (1978). *A guide to culture in the classroom.* Rosslyn, VA: National Clearinghouse for Bilingual Education.

Savingon, S. (1983). *Communicative competence: Theory and practice.* Reading, MA: Addison-Wesley.

Scafe, M., & Kontas, G. (1982). Classroom implication of culturally defined organizational patterns in speeches by Native Americans. In F. Barkin, E. Brandt, & J. Orstein-Galicia (Eds.), *Bilingualism and language contact: Spanish, English, and Native American languages.* New York: Teachers College Press.

Schifini, A., Short, D., & Tinajero, J. V. (2005a). *High point.* Teacher's Edition. Carmel, CA: Hampton Brown.

Schifini, A., Short, D. & Tinajero, J. V. (2005b). *The Basics Student Textbook (High Point: Success in Language, Literature, Content).* Carmel, CA: Hampton-Brown.

Schifini, A., Short, D., & Tinajero, J. V. (2005c). *The reading basics teacher scripts to teach phonics and model decoding strategies.* Carmel, CA: Hampton Brown.

Schleppegrell, M. (2001). Linguistic features of the language of schooling. *Linguistics and Education, 12,* 431–459.

Schleppegrell, M. J. (2004). *The Language of Schooling: A functional linguistics perspective.* Mahwah, NJ: Erlbaum.

Secada, W. G. (2000). *Changing the faces of mathematics: Perspectives on multiculturalism and gender equity.* Reston, VA: National Council of Teachers of Mathematics.

Segalowitz, N., & Segalowitz, S. (1993). Skilled performance practice and the differentiation of speed-up from automatization effects: Evidence from second language word recognition. *Applied Psycholinguistics, 19,* 53–67.

Selby, C. C. (2006). What makes it science. *Journal of College Science Teaching, 35*(7), 8–11.

Selinker, L. (1972). Interlanguage. *IRAL-International Review of Applied Linguistics in Language Teaching, 10*(1-4), 209–232.

Selznick, B. (2011). *Wonderstruck.* New York: Scholastic Press.

Senior, R (2005) Authentic Responses to Authentic Materials. *English Teaching Professional 38,* pp7.

Shohamy, E., & Inbar, O. (1991). Validation of listening comprehension tests: The effect of text and question type. *Language Testing, 8,* 23–40.

Short, D., & Echevarria, J. (2004). Teacher skills to support English language learners. *Educational Leadership, 62*(4), 8-13.

Short, D. J. (1994). *Integrating language and culture in middle school American History classes* (Educational practice Rep. No.*). Santa Cruz, CA, and Washington, DC: National Center for Research on Culture Diversity and Second Language Learning.

Short, D., Fidelman, C., & Louguit, M. (2009). The effects of SIOP Model instruction on the academic language development of English language learners. *Manuscript submitted for publication.*

Silva, C., Weinburgh, M., Smith, M. H., Barreto, G., & Gabel, J. (2008/2009, Winter). Partnering to develop academic language for English language learners through mathematics and science. *Childhood Education,* 107–112.

Silverstein, S. (1974). *Where the sidewalk ends.* New York: Harper Collins.

Skinner, B. F. (1957). *Verbal behavior.* New York: Appleton-Century-Crofts.

Skutnabb-Kangas, T., & Toukomaa, P. (1976). *Teaching migrant children's mother tongue and learning the language of the host country in the context of the socio-cultural situation of the migrant family.* Helsinki: The Finnish National Commission for UNESCO.

Slavin, R. E. (1989–1990). Research on cooperative learning: Consensus and controversy. *Educational Leadership, 47*(4), 52–54.

Slavin, R. E., Lake, C., Chambers, B., Cheung, A., & Davis, S. (2009, February). *Effective beginning reading programs: A best-evidence synthesis.* Baltimore, MD: Johns Hopkins University, Center for Research and Reform in Education.

Slowinski, J. (2000, January). Breaking the language barrier: How technology can enhance multilingual communication. *Electronic School* (Online), Available: http://www.electronicschool.com/2000/01/0100f3.html

Smalley, R. L., & Hank, M. R. (1992). College teachers. In A. K. Koshi (Ed.), *Discoveries: Reading, thinking, writing* (pp. 125–127). Boston: Heinle & Heinle.

Smalley, W. A. (1963). Culture shock, language shock and the shock of self-discovery. *Practical Anthropology, 10,* 45–56.

Smith, D. D. (2006). *Introduction to special education: Teaching in an age of opportunity* (5th ed.). Boston, MA: Pearson Allyn & Bacon.

Smith, F. (1988). *Understanding reading: A psycholinguistic analysis of reading and learning to read.* Hillsdale, NJ: Lawrence Erlbaum.

Snively, G., & Corsiglia, J. (2001). Discovering indigenous science: Implications for science education. *Science Education, 85*(1), 6–34.

Snow, C. (2008). What is the vocabulary of science? In A. Rosebery & B. Warren (Eds.), *Teaching science to English language learners* (pp. 71–84). Arlington, VA: NSTA Press.

Snyder, T. D., & Dillow, S. A. (2012). *Digest of education statistics 2011.* National Center for Education Statistics.

Solomon, I. D. (1996). Workshops on a multicultural curriculum: Issues and caveats. *Education, 117*(1), 81–84.

Soto, G. (2005). In A. Schifini, D. Short, & J. V. Tinajero (Eds.). *High point.* Teacher's Edition. Carmel, CA: Hampton Brown.

Spanos, G., Rhodes, N., Dale, T., & Crandall, J. (1998). Linguistic features of mathematical problem-solving: Insights and applications. In J. P. Mestre & R. R. Cocking (Eds.), *Linguistic and culture influences on learning mathematics* (pp. 221–240). Hillsdale, NJ: Lawrence Erlbaum.

Speidel, G. E. (1987). Language differences in the classroom: Two approaches for developing language skills in dialect-speaking children. In E. Okaar (Ed.), *Socioculture perspectives of language acquisition and multi-legalism.* Tubingen, Germany: Gunter Narr.

Sperling, D. (1999). *Dave Sperling's Internet guide for English language teachers.* Burlingame, CA: Alta.

Stanovich (1980). Toward an interactive-compensatory model of individual differences in the development of reading fluency. *Reading Research Quarterly, 16,* 32–71.

The State of New Jersey Curriculum Frameworks for World Language. (2006). Online document: www. state.nj.us/njded/frameworks/worldlanguages/appendc.pdf

Stegman, B. (2014). Inquiry, new literacies, and the common core. *Kappa Delta Pi Record, 50*(1), 31–36.

Stevens, V. (2006, February 23). *ESL_Home a web resource for CALL lab managers.* Retrieved February 9, 2006, from http://www.geocities.com/vance_stevens/esl_home.htm

Stevenson, L. M. (2011). Creating destiny: Youth, arts and social change. (Unpublished doctoral dissertation). Stanford University, Stanford, CA. Available at: http://www.artsedsearch.org/summaries/creating-destiny-youth-arts-and-social-change#sthash.y70qXcWv.dpuf

Stewig, J. (1981). Choral speaking. Who has the time? Why take the time? *Childhood Education, 58*(1), 25–29.

Stoddart, T. (1999). *Language Acquisition Through Science Inquiry.* Paper presented at the annual meeting of the American Educational Research Association, Montreal.

Stoddart, T. (2005). Improving student achievement with the CREDE Five Standards Pedagogy. Technical Report No. (J1). Santa Cruz, CA: University of California, Center for Research on Education, Diversity and Excellence.

Stoddard, T., Pinal, A., Latzke, M., & Canady, D. (2002). Integrating inquiry science and language development. *Journal of Research in Science Teaching, 39,* 664–687.

Stoddart, T., Solis, J., Tolbert, S. & Bravo, M. (2010). A framework for the effective science teaching of English language learners in elementary schools. In *Teaching Science with Hispanic ELLs in K–16 Classrooms.* Information Age Publishing.

Subedi, B. (2010). *Critical global perspectives: Rethinking knowledge about global societies.* IAP.

Sulzby, E. (1985). Children's emergent reading of favorite storybooks. *Reading Research Quarterly, 20,* 458–481.

Swaffar, J. K., & Bacon, S. M. (1993). Reading and listening comprehension: Perspectives on research and implications for practice. In A. H. Omaggio (Ed.), *Research in language learning: Principles, processes, and prospects* (pp. 124–155). Lincolnwood, IL: National Textbook.

Swain, M. (1978, May). French immersion: Early, late or partial? In S.T. Carey (Ed.), *The Canadian Modern Language Review, 34,* 557–585.

Swisher, K., & Deyhle, D. (1989, August). The styles of learning are different, but teaching is just the same: Suggestions for teachers of American Indian youth. *Journal of American Indian Education,* 1–14.

Sysoyer, P. V. (2000, March). Developing an English for specific purposes course using a learner centered approach: A Russian experience. *The Internet TESL Journal, VI*(3) (Online), Available: http://www.aitech.ac.jp/~iteslj/techniques/sysoyev-ESP.htm

Szekely, G. & Bucknam, J. (2012). *Art teaching: Elementary through middle school.* New York: Routledge, Taylor & Francis.

Szpara, Y., & Ahmad, I. (2007). Supporting English-language learners in social studies class: Results from a study of high school teachers. *The Social Studies, 98*(5), 189–194.

Taboada, A., & Rutherford, V. (2011). Developing reading comprehension and academic vocabulary for English language learners through science content: A formative experiment. *Reading Psychology, 32*(2), 113–157.

Tan, G., Gallo, P. B., Jacobs, G. M., & Kim-Eng Lee, C. (1999, August). Using cooperative learning to integrate thinking and information technology in a content-based writing lesson. *The Internet TESL Journal, V*(8) (Online), Available: http://www.aitech.ac.jp/~iteslj/techniques/Tan-Cooperative.htm

Tan, S. (2006). *The arrival.* New York: Arthur A. Levine Books, Scholastic, Inc.

Tannen, D. (1990). *You just don't understand: Women and men in conversations.* New York: Morrow.

Tarkington, K. (1996). The rationale for experiential/participatory learning. *Working Papers in Early Childhood Development, 16.* Available from the Bernard von Leer Foundation, Communications Section, P.O. Box 92334, 2508 EH The Hague, The Netherlands.

Tauroza, S., & Allison, D. (1990). Speech rates in British English. *Applied Linguistics, 11*, 90–105.

Taylor, B. M. (1980). Children's memory for expository text after reading. *Reading Research Quarterly, 15*, 399–411.

Taylor, D., & Dorsey-Gaines, C. (1988). *Growing up literate: Learning from inner city families.* Portsmouth, NH: Heinemann.

Teachers of English to Speakers of Other Languages, Inc. (TESOL). (1991). *ESL standards for pre-K–12* [Brochure]. Alexandria, VA: Author.

Teenant, A., Bernhardt, E. B., Rodriquez-Munoz, M., & Aiello, M. (1995). *Bringing science & second language learning together: What every teacher needs to know.* Columbus, OH: National Center for Science Teaching & Learning.

Templeton, S., Johnston, F., Bear, D. R., & Invernizzi, M. (2009). *Vocabulary their way: Word study with middle and secondary students.* Boston, MA: Pearson Publications.

Terrell, T. D. (1977). A natural approach to second language acquisition and learning. *The Modern Language Journal, 66*, 121–132.

Terrell, T. D. (1981). The natural approach in bilingual education. In *Schooling and language minority students: A theoretical framework* (pp. 117–146). Los Angeles: Evaluation, Dissemination and Assessment Center, California State University, Los Angeles.

Terrell, T. D. (1991). The role of grammar instruction in a communicative approach. *The Modern Language Journal, 75*, 52–63.

TESOL. (2005). *PreK–12 English language proficiency standards in the core content areas.* Alexandria, VA: TESOL Quarterly.

Tharp, R. (1989a). Culturally compatible education: A formula for designing effective classrooms. In H. Trueba, G. Spindler, & L. Spindler (Eds.), *What do anthropologists have to say about dropouts?* New York: Falmer Press.

Tharp, R. (1989b, February). Psychocultural variables and constants: Effects on teaching and learning in schools. *American Psychologist, 44*(2), 349–359.

Tharp, R. G. (1997). *From at-risk to excellence: Research, theory, and principles for practice* (Research Report 1). Santa Cruz, CA: Center for Research on Education, Diversity & Excellence.

Tharp, R. G., & Dalton, S. S. (2007). Orthodoxy, culture compatibility, and universals in education. *Comparative Education, 43*(1), 53–70.

Thewlis, S. H. (2000). *Grammar dimension book 3: Form, meaning, and use.* Boston, MA: Heinle & Heinle.

Thier, M., & Daviss, B. (2002). *The new science literacy: Using language skills to help students learn science.* Portsmouth, NH: Heinemann.

Thomas, W. P. & Collier, V. P. (2003). The multiple benefits of dual language. *Educational Leadership, 61*(2), 61–64.

Thornton, S. J. (2005). *Teaching social studies that matters: Curriculum for active learning.* New York: Teachers College Press.

Tiedt, P. L., & Tiedt I. M. (1998). *Multicultural teaching: A handbook of activities, information, and resources* (5th ed.). Boston: Allyn & Bacon.

Tierney, R. J., Carter, M. A., & Desai, L. E. (1991). *Portfolio assessment in the reading-writing classroom.* Norwood, MA: Christopher-Gordon.

Tierney, R. J., & Gee, M. (1990). Reading comprehension. In D. Bogdan & S. B. Straw (Eds.), *Beyond communication: Reading comprehension and criticism* (pp. 167–196). Portsmouth, NH: Boynton/Cook and Heinemann.

Tinajero, J., & Calderon, M. (1988). Language experience approach plus. *Journal of Educational Issues of Language Minority Students, 2*, 31–45.

Tobin, K. (1998). Issues and trends in the teaching of science. In B. J. Fraser, & K. Tobin (Eds.), *International handbook of science education* (pp. 129–151). Great Britain: Kluwer Academic Publishers.

Tomkins, G. (2013). *Literacy for the 21st Century: A Balanced Approach* (6th ed.). Upper Saddle River, NJ: Pearson.

Tomlinson, C. A. (2001). *How to differentiate instruction in mixed-ability classrooms* (2nd ed.). Alexandria, VA: ASCD.

Towell, J. (2013). *Hooked on books: Language and literature in elementary classrooms.* Dubuque, IA: Kendal Hunt.

Towell, J., Powell, K., & Brown, S. (in press). *Creative literacy in action: Birth to age nine.* Mason, OH: Cengage Learning.

Trueba, H. T., & Cheng, L. (1993). *Myth or reality: Adaptive strategies of Asian Americans in California.* Bristol, PA: Palmer Press.

Tudor, I. (1996). *Learner-centeredness as language education.* Cambridge: Cambridge University Press.

Turner, M. (1963). A study of modern dance in relations to communication, choreographic structure, and elements of composition. *Research Quarterly. American Association for Health, Physical Education and Recreation. 34*(2), 219–227.

Tye, B. B., & Tye, K. A. (1992). *Global education: A study of school change.* Albany: State University of New York Press.

Tye, K. A. (1999). *Global education: A worldwide movement.* Orange, CA: Independence Press.

Tye, K. A. (2009). A history of the global education movement in the United States. *Visions in global education: The globalization of curriculum and pedagogy in teacher education and schools, 3*–24.

U.S. Census Bureau. (2001, April 2). *U.S. Census Bureau Population Division.* Retrieved March 26, 2003, from http://www.census.gov/population/www/cen2000/phc-tl.html

U.S. Census Bureau. (2003, April 2). *U.S. Census Bureau Population Division.* Retrieved March 26, 2003, from http://www.census.gov/population/www/cen2000/phc-tl.html

U.S. Department of Education. (2003, June). Key indicators of Hispanic student achievement: National goals and benchmarks for the next decade. Retrieved June 27, 2003, from http://www.ed.gov/pubs/hispaincindicators/

U.S. Department of Education & National Institute of Child Health and Human Development. (2003). *National symposium on learning disabilities in English language learners. Symposium summary.* Washington, DC: Authors.

United States Hispanic Chamber of Commerce pushes "return on investment" regarding education reform for Hispanics at White House summit. (2008). Retrieved March 5, 2010, from http://www.ushcc.com/index.cfm?fuseaction=feature.showFeature&FeatureID=32&varuniqueuserid=59749160244

Ur, P. (1996). *A course in language teaching: Practice and theory.* Cambridge: Cambridge University Press.

Valdés, G. (2003). *Expanding definitions of giftedness.* Mahwah, NJ: Lawrence Erlbaum Associates.

Valdez, P. S. (2001). Alternative assessment. *The Science Teacher, 68*(8), 41.

Valdez-Pierce, L. (2003). *Assessing English language learners.* Washington, DC: National Education Association.

Valenza, J. (2001, December 31). *Evaluating web pages: A webquest.* Retrieved January 2, 2006, from Montgomery County Pennsylvania Public Schools, http://mciunix.mciu.k12.pa.us/~spjvweb/ evalwebteach.html

Vandergrift, L. (2002). "It was nice to see that our predictions were right": Developing metacognition in L2 listening comprehension. *Canadian Modern Language Review, 58,* 555–575.

Vandergrift, L. (2003). Orchestrating strategy use: Toward a model of the skilled second language listener. *Language Learning, 53,* 463–496.

Vandergrift, L. (2004). Listening to learn or learning to listen? *Annual Review of Applied Linguistic, 24,* 3–25.

Vandergrift L. (2006). Second language listening: listening ability or language proficiency? *The Modern Language Journal, 90*(1), 6–18.

Vandergrift, L., & Goh, C. (2012). *Teaching and Learning Second Language Listening: Metacognition in Action.* Oxon: Routledge.

VanPatten, B., & Cadierno, T. (1993). Explicit instruction and input processing. *Studies in second language acquisition, 15*(02), 225–243.

Vaisentein, A. (2008). A teacher's perspective: Creating culturally responsive learning communities. In A. Rosebery & B. Warren (eds.), *Teaching science to English language learners* (pp. 163–167). Arlington, VA: NSTA Press.

Vaughn, S., Boss, C. S., & Schumm, J. S. (2007). *Teaching students who are exceptional, diverse, and at risk in the general education classroom.* Boston: Pearson.

Vaughn, S., Wanzek, J., Murray, C.S., Scammacca, N., Linan-Thompson, S., & Woodruff, A. (2009). Response to early reading intervention: Examining higher and lower responders. *Exceptional Children, 75*(2), 165–183.

Verplaetse, L. S. (1998). How content teachers interact with English language learners. *TESOL Journal Autumn,* 24–28.

Voss, B. (1979). Hesitation phenomena as sources of perceptual errors for non-native speakers. *Language and Speech, 22,* 129–144.

Vygotsky, L. S. (1934/1986). *Thought and Language,* trans. A. Kozulin. Cambridge, MA: Harvard University Press.

Vygotsky, L. S. (1962). *Thought and language.* Cambridge, MA: MIT Press.

Vygotsky, L. S. (1978). *Mind in society: The development of higher psychological process.* Cambridge, MA: Harvard University Press.

Vygotski, L. S. (1987). The Collected Works of LS Vygotsky.

Vygostky, L. S. (1987). The development of scientific concepts in childhood. In R. W. Rieber & A. S. Carton (Eds.), *The collected works of L. S. Vygostky* (Vol. 1, pp. 167–241) (N. Mink, Trans.). New York: Plenum.

Walter, T. (1995). *English learner achievement project (ELAP) training handbook.* San Diego, CA: San Diego City Schools.

Walter, T. (1996). *Amazing English!* Reading, MA: Addison-Wesley.

Warren, B., & Rosebery, A. (2008). Using everyday experience to teach science. *Teaching science to English language learners*, 39–50.

Warren, B., Ballenger, C., Ogonowski, M., Rosebery, A. S., & Hudicourt-Barnes, J. (2001). Rethinking diversity in learning science: The logic of everyday sense-making. *Journal of research in science teaching, 38*(5), 529–552.

Waterman, B. (2000). Assessing children for the presence of a disability. *National Information Center for Children and Youth with Disabilities News Digest, 14*. Retrieved March 26, 2001, http://www.ldonline. org/ld_indepth/assessment/assess-nichcy.html

Wax, R. H. (1976). Ogala Sioux Dropouts and their problems with educators. In J. I. Roberts & S. K. Akinsanya (Eds.), *Schooling in the cultural context* (pp. 216–226). New York: David McKay.

Weisman, E., & Hansen, L. (2007). Strategies for teaching social studies to English-language learners at the elementary level. *The Social Studies, 98*(5), 180–184.

Weisner, D. (2006). *Flotsam*. New York: Clarion Books.

Wells, G. (1986). *The meaning makers: Children learning language and using language to learn*. Portsmouth, NH: Heinemann.

Whorf, B. L. (1956). *Language, thought and reality*. Cambridge, MA: The MIT Press.

WIDA Consortium. (2004). *English language proficiency standards for English language learners in kindergarten through Grade 12*. Retrieved February 25, 2010, from http://www.wida.us/standards/elpoverview.pdf

WIDA Consortium. (2006). English language proficiency standards and resource guide, 2007 edition, prekindergarten through Grade 12. Madison, WI: *Board of Regents of the University of Wisconsin System*.

Widdowson, H. G. (1983). *Learning purpose and language use*. London, Oxford: Oxford University Press.

Widdowson, H. G. (1990). *Aspects of language teaching*. Oxford University Press.

Wiest, L. R. (2002). Multicultural mathematics instruction: Approaches and resources. *Teaching Children Mathematics, 9*(1), 49–54.

Willis, J. (1981). *Teaching English through English* (Vol. 8). Harlow: Longman.

Willis, D., & Willis, J. (2008). *Doing task-based teaching*. Oxford University Press.

Worth, K. (2006). Introduction. In R. Douglas, M. P. Klentschy, & K. Worth (Eds.), *Linking sicence and literacy in the K–8 classroom*. Arlington, VA: NSTA Press.

Wright, A. (1999). *Pictures for language learning* (8th ed.). Cambridge, England: Cambridge University Press.

Wright, A., Betteridge, D., & Buckby, M. (2006). *Games for language learning* (3rd ed.). New York: Cambridge University Press.

Wright, W. (2010). *Foundations for teaching English language learners*. Caslon.

Yamada, K. (2003). What prevents ESL/EFL writers from avoiding plagiarism? Analyses of 10 north American college websites. *System 31*(2), 247–258.

Yin-Young, M., & Jang, Y. (2000). *Using games in EFL classess for children*. Retrieved February 15, 2010, from http://english.daejin.ac.kr/~rtyson/fall2000/eltgames.html

Zainuddin, H., & Moore, R. (2003). Enhancing critical thinking with structured controversial dialogues. *The Internet TESL Journal, IX*(6), http://iteslj.org/

Zainuddin, H., Yahya, N., Morales-Jones, C., & Ariza, E. (2011). *Fundamentals of teaching English to speakers of other languages in K-12 mainstream classrooms*. (3rd ed.) Dubuque, IA: Kendall/Hunt Publishing.

Zappia, I. A. (1989). Identification of gifted Hispanic students: A multidimensional view. In C. J. Maker & S. W. Schiever (Eds.), *Critical issues in gifted education* (pp. 19–26). Austin, TX: PRO-ED.

Zehler, A. M., Fleischman, H. L., Hopstock, P. J., Stephenson, T. G., Pendzick, M. L., & Sapru, S. (2003). *Descriptive study of services to LEP students and LEP students with disabilities, Vol 1A: Research report*. Development Associates, Inc. (Online), Available: http://www.devassoc.comlLEPdoclist.html

Zeigler, L., & Johns, J. (2005). *Visualization: Using mental images to strengthen comprehension*. Dubuque, IA: Kendall Hunt.

Zemelman, S., Daniels, H., & Hyde, A. (1998). *Best practice: New standards for teaching and learning in America's school* (2nd ed.). Portsmouth, NH: Heinemann.

Zemelman, S, Daniels, H., Hyde, H. (2012). *Best practice: Bringing standards to life in America's classrooms* (4th ed.). Portsmouth, NH: Heinemann.

Zero Population Growth Bureau, Inc. (2000). *Facts and statistics*. Washington, DC: Author.

Ziefert, H. (1995). *The three little pigs*. New York: Penguin.

Zimmerman, C. B. (1997). Does reading and interactive vocabulary instruction make a difference? An empirical study. *TESOL Quarterly, 31,* 121–140.

Index

A

AAAS. *See* American Association for Advancement of Science

AAIEP-American Association of Intensive English Programs, 413

Aardvark English Forum.com, 413, 416

Academic language, 53

Accents in English with eViews, 416

Acculturation, 25–29. *See also* Culture

Achievement gap, scientific, 357–358

Acquisition *vs.* learning hypothesis, 86–89

Action, as cultural value, 23

Adolescent science learners, 371–373

The Adult Educating Teacher's Annotated Webliography, 416

Aesthetics, 348

Affective filter hypothesis, 88, 90

Algebraic thinking, sample lesson, 338–339

ALM. *See* Audio-lingual method

Alphabetic writing, 238
   development of, 265–270

Alternative assessment, 146–147

The Amazing Picture Machine, 414–416

American Association for Advancement of Science, 361

American values, 21–24
   as cultural value, 23
   term "American," 21
   traits, 23

Analytical scoring, writing, 287–288

Anecdotal observations, 252
   checklists, 197

Antivirus software, defined, 417

Application, 130

Arab culture, cultural characteristics, 61–65

Articles, 296

Artistic production, 348

Arts, 343–354
   collaborative work, 348–349
   comprehension, 347–348
   elements, 347
   forms, integrating language skills, 349
   integration lessons, 350–353

Asher, James, 96

Asian culture, cultural characteristics, 70–75

Asylees, 50

Attribute wheel, 246

Audio-lingual method, 93–94
   communicative language teaching, compared, 110–111
   mainstream classroom use, 94

Auditory discrimination, 264

Auditory learning style, 337

Authenticity, language, 111–112

B

Background of multicultural education, 4–5

Backup, defined, 417

Barton, Byron, 250

Base-10 blocks, 327

Beginning readers
   characteristics of, 238
   choral speaking, 241–242
   language experience approach, 240–241
   literature circles, 242–243

read alouds, 241

shared reading, 243–244

strategies, 240–245

thematic units, 244

Beginning vocabulary learning, 209–210, 220

Beginning writers, 272–274

Behavior, culturally appropriate, 52

Behaviorist theory, 84–85
   scenario, 85

Berlitz language schools, 93

Biliteracy development, assessment, 289–291

Birthright inheritance, as cultural value, 23

Block programming, teacher schedules, 53

Blogging, 411
   defined, 417

Bloom's taxonomy, revised, 141–143, 231–233

Blues Clues, 170

Bodily-kinesthetic intelligence, 151, 155

Boot disk, defined, 417

Bottom-up processing, 164

Brown, Marc, 250

Browser to browse, defined, 417

Buddy journal, writing, 270

Buddy system, 115

Bug, defined, 417

Bureau of Citizenship and Immigrations Services, 50

Bureau of Population, Refugees, and Migration, 50

Business letters, writing, 270

Bytes, defined, 417

C

Cache, defined, 417
CAL-Center for Applied Linguistics, 413
CALL. *See* Computer-assisted language learning
Captions, writing, 270
CCSS. *See* Common Core State Standards
CD, defined, 417
CD-ROMs, 191
Center for Research on Education, Diversity and Excellence, 413
Central processing unit, defined, 417
Change, as cultural value, 23
Character map, 246
Character trait chart, 313
Characteristics of cultures, 55–78. *See also* Cultural characteristics
Charlie and the Chocolate Factory, 483–503
Charlotte's Web, 312
Chat room, defined, 417
Chats
  defined, 417
  as spoken language source, 169
Checks, writing, 270
Children's literature, with math lesson, 336–337
Chomsky, Noam, 85
Choral reading, 191
Chronemics, defined, 40
Class differences, cultural value, 23
Clause reduction, 299
Close reading, 311
Coerr, Eleanor, 352
Cognitive complexity, 137
Cognitive domain, Bloom's taxonomy, revised, 141–143, 231–233
Cohesive ties, in reading, 228
Collaboration, 5, 348–349, 370
Collaborative arts, 348–349
Color tiles, 327
Colors, cultural significance of, 80
Common Core State Standards, 309, 312–315
  domains, 321–324
Common underlying proficiency model, 168, 234
Communication, 83–90
  acquisition *vs.* learning hypothesis, 86–89
  affective filter hypothesis, 88, 90
  behaviorist theory, 84–85
  comprehension hypothesis, 88–90

grammar, 107–123
innatist theory, 85–86
interactionist theory, 86
Krashen hypotheses, 86–90
language, defined, 84
language acquisition theories, 84–87
monitor hypothesis, 87–89
natural order hypothesis, 87, 89
nonverbal, 37–42
  eye contact, 40–41
  gestures, 39–40
  proxemics, 39
verbal, 31–36
  high-context culture, 33–34
  left hemisphere societies, 33–34
  low-context culture, 33–34
  right hemisphere societies, 33–34
Communicative language teaching, 102–103
  audio-lingual method, compared, 110–111
  mainstream classroom use, 103
Comprehension hypothesis, 88–90
Computer-assisted language learning, 417
  software sources, 417
Confirming meanings, in reading, 248
Consortium for School Networking, 413
Contemporary research, 348
Content, language integration, 127–133
  content-based language learning, 129–130, 133
  experiential learning, 129, 133
  language experience approach, 131–133
  models, 129
  sheltered instruction, 130, 133
  sheltered instruction observation protocol model, 130–131, 133
  specially designed academic instruction in English, 130, 133
  treat making, tasting, 131–132
Content area instruction, 191–195
Content areas
  arts, 343–354
    art forms, 348–349
    comprehension, 347–348
    elements, 347
    integrating, 350–353
  mathematics, 317–341
    sample lessons, 337–340
    strategies, 324–337
  science, 355–374
    achievement gap, 357–358
    adolescent learners, 371–373

contextualized instruction, 368–370
engineering practices, 362–363
Next Generation Science Standards, 355–358, 361–364, 369, 373
research projects, 358–360
science education reform, 361–362
science language usage, 371–373
scientific literacy, 361–362
standards, core state standards, 312–315
teaching strategies, 363–368, 370–371
social studies, 375–383
  global perspectives, 376
  pedagogy, 376–377
special education, 385–404
  disabilities, students with, 386–389, 398–404
  gifted students, 389–398
  initial referrals, 390
  parent-family connection, 391
  referral, 390–391
  teacher perceptions, 390
standards, 307–315
  incorporating, unpacking approach, 310–311
  lesson planning, 311–312
  teaching strategies, 312–315
technology, 405–419
  activities using, 411–412
  high school, 410–411
  intermediate grades, 409–410
  primary grades, 409
  problems, 412
  strategies, 408–409
  teacher's role, 407–408
  vocabulary for, 417–418
  website reliability, 412–417
website reliability, 412–417
Content-based learning, 53, 129–130, 133
Content of language, 53
Contextualized instruction, 368–370
Control over environment, as cultural value, 23
Control over time, as cultural value, 23
Cooperative learning, 333–334, 366–368
  benefits of, 114
Cornell University in New York State, 413
Count/noncount nouns, 296, 299
CPU, central processing unit, 417

CREDE. *See* Center for Research on Education, Diversity and Excellence
Critical period hypothesis, 184
Criticism, 348
Cuisenaire rods, 327
Cultural characteristics, 55–78
    Arab culture, 61–65
    Asian culture, 70–75
    classroom strategies, 76–78
    cultural awareness, 75
    cultural knowledge, 56
    Haitian culture, 67–69
    Islamic culture, 61–66
    Native American culture, 73–75
    Spanish-speaking culture, 57–60
Cultural significance of colors, 80
Cultural significance of numbers, 80
Cultural values, contrasts in, 23
Culturally reflected learning styles, 47
Culture, 13–16
    ethnocentrism, 14–15
    historical overview, 14
    language in, 17–20
        deep culture, 18–20
        surface culture, 18–20
    role of culture, 15
Culture shock, 25–29
    acculturation, 28
    defined, 26
    recovery from, 28
CUP model. *See* Common underlying proficiency model
Curriculum
    assessment, 145–147
        alternative assessment, 146–147
        performance assessment, 147
        portfolio assessment, 147
        purpose, 146–147
    contextualizing teaching, 137
    creating, 5
    design, 135–158
        Bloom's taxonomy, revised, 141–143, 231–233
        bodily-kinesthetic intelligence, 151, 155
        content, conceptualizing, 143–144
        existential intelligence, 157
        Gardner's eight intelligences, 148
        goals, 139–140
        interdisciplinary, content-based thematic units, 137–139
        interpersonal intelligence, 148, 151–152, 156
        intrapersonal intelligence, 148, 152–153, 156

kinesthetic intelligence, 148
linguistic intelligence, 148–149, 154
logical-mathematical intelligence, 148–150, 155
materials, 145
musical intelligence, 148, 150–151, 154
naturalistic intelligence, 148, 153, 157
objectives, 139–140
planning activities, 148–157
principles of, 136–137
procedures, instructional, 144–145
teacher reflection, 147
theme phrases, sample, 138
theme web, sample, 139
theme words, sample, 138
verbal intelligence, 154
visual-spatial intelligence, 148, 150, 155
web of theme, sample, 140
interdisciplinary, content-based thematic units
    theme, choice of, 137–139
    topics, choice of, 139
multiple intelligences
    inventory of, 154–157
    learning styles, 147–148
objectives, classifying, 140–141

D

Daily Lesson Plan for English Teachers, 414–415
Daily rotation center schedule, 422–423
Data analysis, sample lesson, 339–340
Decision-making model, 246
Deep culture, 18–20
Defining intelligences, 147
Defining multicultural education, 5
Depression, 26
Designing curriculum, 135–158
Desktop, defined, 417
Determiners, 299
Dialogue, 137
Dictionary use, 2
Direct teaching method, 93
Directions, giving, 331
Directness, as cultural value, 23
Directory, defined, 417
Disabilities, students with, 386–388
    Common Core Standards, 398–404
    educational services, 388–389
    instruction, 389
Discourse competence, 109

Disk drive, defined, 417
Disk operating system, defined, 417
Displaced persons, 50
DOS, disk operating system, 417
Drafting, 277
Drawings, 328
Driver, defined, 417

E

Editing, 278–279
Effective Science Teaching for ELLs, project, 359
EFL/ESL Lessons Using Website, 416
The EFL Playhouse, 414
EFL Web-English as Foreign Language Magazine, 413
Egalitarianism, as cultural value, 23
E.L. Easton Business English, 416
Elementary grades, vocabulary teaching, 220
email, 412, 417
Enabling skills, 162
Enrichment packets, 211
Enumeration, writing, 270
ESL Lesson Plans and Resources, 414–416
The ESL Quiz Center, 416
ESLCafe.Com-Discussion Forums, 413
ESLoop, 416
Essay forms, 270
ESTELL. *See* Effective Science Teaching for ELLs
Ethnocentrism, 14–15
Evacuees, 50
Existential intelligence, 157
Experiential learning, 129, 133
Explicit instruction, vocabulary, 205–206
Eye contact, 40–41

F

Face-to-face interactions, as spoken language source, 169
Fantastic fiction game, 303
Fate, as cultural value, 23
Field-independent behavior, field-sensitive behavior, contrasted, 46
Fine motor coordination, 141
Flash cards, 211
    native language flash cards, 211
    picture flash cards, 211
Fluency *versus* accuracy, 109
Folder, defined, 417
Folse, Keith, 204

Font, defined, 417
Ford-Harris matrix of multicultural gifted education, 394–398
Formal education, interrupted, 52–53
Formality, as cultural value, 23
Format, defined, 417
Four-step problem solving, 329–330
Future orientation, as cultural value, 23
Future tense, 121

G

Games, 212, 302–304
Gardner's eight intelligences, 148
Gattegno, Caleb, 95
Gender-based groups, 115
Geoboards, 326
Geography lesson, 377–380
    handout, 380
Geometry, sample lesson, 337–338
Gerund, verbs followed by, 299
Gestures, 39–40
Gifted potential, characteristics, 392–393
Gifted students, 389–390
    challenging, 394–398
    Common Core Standards, 398–404
    differentiated instruction, 398
    differentiation planning sheet, 399
    identification of, 391–393
Gigabytes, defined, 418
Goals, multicultural curriculum, 5
Gouin series, 100–101
    benefits of, 100–101
Grammar, 295–304
    competence in, 109
    discourse competence, 109
    future tense, 121
    goals, 112
    grammar teaching, role, 116–119
        misconceptions, 116–119
    imperative structure, 120
    impersonal pronouns, 121
    integrated grammar, reading activities, 122–123
    language authenticity, 111–112
    past perfect tense, 122
    plural nouns, 123
    present perfect tense, 122
    present progressive, 121
    present progressive verb, use of, 120
    question, answer, 121
    role of learner, 113
    role of teacher, 113
    role-play, 120–121
    settings, 114–116

simple present verb, use of, 120
singular nouns, 123
sociolinguistic competence, 109
strategic competence, 109–111
teaching, 116–120
    strategies for, 120
verb tenses, 299
Grammar round up game, 303
Grammar translation method, 92–93
    mainstream classroom use, 92–93
Grammatical errors, 299
Graphic organizers, 246–247
    attribute wheel, 246
    character map, 246
    decision-making model, 246
    main idea table, 247
    sequence chain, 247
    story map, 247
    Venn diagram, 246
    web, 247
Graphics card, defined, 417
Graphing student assessments, 471–482
Gross motor coordination, psychomotor domain, 141
Group orientation, as cultural value, 23
Grouping learners, 114–116
Guide to Grammar and Writing, 414–416

H

Haitian culture, cultural characteristics, 67–69
Hall, Edward, 14, 33, 38–39
Haptics, 39
Hard disk, defined, 418
HC communication. See High-context communication
Helplessness, feeling of, 26
The Hidden Dimension, 38–39
Hierarchy, as cultural value, 23
High-considerateness pattern, 32
High-context communication, 33
High-context culture, 33–34
High-involvement conversational patterns, 32
Higher order thinking skills, 231–233
Historical methodology, 91–105
    audio-lingual teaching method, 93–94
        mainstream classroom use, 94
    Berlitz language schools, 93
    communicative teaching approach, 102–103
        mainstream classroom use, 103
    direct teaching method, 93
    Gouin series, 100–101

grammar translation teaching method, 92–93
    mainstream classroom use, 92–93
natural teaching approach, 101–102
    Krashen's monitor model, 87–89, 101
    mainstream classroom use, 102
silent way, 95–96
    mainstream classroom use, 95–96
suggestopedia, 94–95
    mainstream classroom use, 95
total physical response, 96–101
    mainstream classroom use, 97
Historical overview, culture, 14
Historical research, 348
Holistic scoring, writing, 287–288
Honeymoon stage, 27
Hostile stage, 27
Human trafficking, victims of, 50
Humanizing Language Teaching Online magazine for teachers of English, 413
Hypotheses, language, Krashen's, 86–90, 184

I

Icon, defined, 418
ICYouSee, A Guide to World Wide Web, 413
Idiomatic usage, 296
Immigrants, 49–53
    Bureau of Citizenship and Immigrations Services, 50
    culturally appropriate behavior, 52
    defined, 50
    interrupted formal education, 52–53
    life before U.S., 51
    Newcomer Programs, 52
    Office of Refugee Resettlement, 50–51
    Refugee Children School Impact Grant Program, 51
Imperative structure, 120
Imperial Valley Project in Science, project, 359
Impersonal pronouns, 121
Incidental learning, vocabulary, 205
Independent strategy development, vocabulary learning, 206–207
Indirectness as cultural value, 23
Individualism, as cultural value, 23
Inferences, in reading, 248
Infinitive, verbs followed by, 299
Informal conversations, 364–365
Informal reading inventory, 253

Informality, as cultural value, 23
Innatist theory, 85–86
Instant messaging, defined, 418
Instruction, 159–304
  grammar, 295–304
  listening, 161–180
    comprehension assessment,
      179–180
    difficulties, 170
    process, 163–169
    skills, TESOL standards, 171
    tasks, 170
    techniques, 170
  oral development, 181–202
    content area instruction, 191–195
    language arts, 191–195
    models, 184
    oral language assessment, 195–200
    research, 182–184
    speaking difficulties, 184–187
    speech error correcting, 200–201
    tools, 187–191
  reading, 223–260
    beginning readers, 240–245
    critical thinking, 230–231
    difficulties in reading, 235–239
    effective instruction, 239–240
    higher order thinking skills,
      231–233
    interactive perspective, 229–230
    intermediate learners, 244–248
    literature selection, 248–251
    psycholinguistic perspective,
      226–227
    questioning techniques, 231–233
    reading assessments, 251–252
    research, 224–226
    Rosenblatt's transactional theory,
      228–229
    schema theory, 227
    sheltered instruction, 239–240
    social interactionist perspective,
      230
  vocabulary, 203–222
    assessment, 221
    content areas, 216–222
    defining, 204–207
    strategies, 207–209
    teaching techniques, 209–216
  writing, 261–293
    alphabetic writing, 265–270
    assessment, 286–289
    beginning writers, 272–274
    biliteracy, 289–291
    intermediate writers, 274–275,
      281–286

    linguistic errors, 272
    research, 262
    samples, 264–265
    strategies, 276–281
    writing skills, 270–272
Integrated grammar, reading activities,
  122–123
Integrated language assessment, 286
Integration of language, content,
  127–133
  content-based language learning,
    129–130, 133
  experiential learning, 129, 133
  language experience approach,
    131–133
  models, 129
  sheltered instruction, 130, 133
  sheltered instruction observation
    protocol model, 130–131, 133
  specially designed academic
    instruction in English, 130, 133
  treat making, tasting, 131–132
Intellectual pursuits, as cultural value,
  23
Interactionist theory, 86
Interactive journal, writing, 270
Interactive perspective, 229–230
Interactive process, reading as, 225
Interdisciplinary, content-based
    thematic units, 137–139
  theme, choice of, 137–139
  topics, choice of, 139
Interest groups, grouping by, 115
Interlocutor characteristics, in listening
    comprehension, 163
Intermediate learners, 244–248
  directed reading-thinking activity,
    244–245
  graphic organizers, 245
  learning logs, 245, 247–248
  vocabulary, 213
Intermediate readers, characteristics of,
  238–239
Intermediate writers, 274–275, 281–286
International Society for Technology in
    Education, 413
Internet, defined, 418
Internet 4 Classrooms, 414
  Links for K-12 teachers, 414–415
Internet field trips, 335–336
The Internet TESL Journal, 413
Internet Treasure Hunts for ESL
    Students, 414–416
Interpersonal intelligence, 148,
  151–152, 156
Interrupted formal education, 52–53

Intrapersonal intelligence, 148,
  152–153, 156
IRI. See Informal reading inventory
Islamic culture, cultural characteristics,
  61–66
ITESLJ's Articles on Teaching
    Techniques, 414

J

John's Activities for English Learners,
  416
Joint activity, among teachers, students,
  136
Jokes, 190
Journal log, 248
Journals, 281, 413
Justice lesson, 380–382

K

Kathy Schrock's Guide for Educators,
  414–416
The Keeping Quilt, 7
Keyboard, defined, 418
Kilobytes, defined, 418
Kinesics, 38
Kinesthetic intelligence, 148
Kinesthetic learning style, 337
Krashen, Stephen, 86
Krashen's language hypotheses, 86–90
Krensky, Stephen, 250
Kristina Pfaff's Linguistic Funland,
  414–417

L

Language, 17–20
  deep culture, 18–20
  defined, 84
  innatist theory, 84–86
  surface culture, 18–20
Language acquisition theories, 84–87
Language Acquisition Through Science
    Education in Rural Schools,
    project, 359
Language arts, 139, 191–195
Language experience approach,
  131–133, 240–241
Language Learning and Technology,
  413
Language shock, 26
The Language Teacher Online, 413
Language teaching principles, 81–124
  communication goal, 83–90
    acquisition vs. learning hypothesis,
      86–87

affective filter hypothesis, 88
behaviorist theory, 84–85
comprehension hypothesis, 88
first language acquisition theories, 84
innatist theory, 85–86
interactionist theory, 86
Krashen's hypotheses for classroom teacher, 88–90
language, defined, 84
monitor hypothesis, 87–88
natural order hypothesis, 87
second/new language acquisition, 86
communicative language teaching, 107–123
future tense, 121
grammar, 116–120
language authenticity, 111–112
role of learner, 113
role of teacher, 113
settings, 114–116
strategies, 120
ESOL
audio-lingual method, 93–94
communicative approach, 102–103
direct method, 93
grammar translation method, 92–93
historical overview, 91–105
natural approach, 101–102
silent way, 95–96
suggestopedia, 94–95
total physical response, 96–101
Language transfer, 272
LASERS. See Language Acquisition through Science Education in Rural Schools
Lau v. Nichols, 308
LC communication. See Low-context communication
LEA. See Language experience approach
Learning hypotheses, 86–89
Learning styles, 43–48
cultural differences, 46–47
field-independent behavior, field-sensitive behavior, contrasted, 46
teacher strategies, 47
Lectures, as spoken language source, 169
Ledgers, writing, 270
Left hemisphere societies, communication in, 33–34

Lesson preparation, 130
Life before coming to U.S., 51
Linguistic error, 272
Linguistic intelligence, 148–149, 154
Linguistic interdependence, overlapping skills, 235
Listener characteristics, 163
Listening comprehension, 163
Listening development, 165–168
advanced organizers, 169
bottom-up skills, 169
comprehension assessment, 179–180
DVDs with captions, 169
listening activities, TESOL standards, 174–175
listening difficulties, 170
listening instruction, 168–169
listening lesson, 171
listening skills, TESOL standards, 171
listening tasks, 170
metacognitive strategies, 169
multiple levels of language proficiency, listening activities, 173–174
selecting listening techniques, 170
stages in language proficiency, 174
standards 1-5, 171
strategy-based approach, 168–169
types of spoken language, 169
casual chats, 169
face-to-face interactions, 169
formal lectures, 169
native speakers' speech, 169
radio, TV presentations, 169
telephone messages, 169
Lists, writing, 270
Literacy instruction, critical reading, 230–231
Literacy perspective, 264
Literacy reporter sheet, 243
Literature in math, 336–337
Literature selection, 248–251
concept books, 250
materials, 249–250
pattern books, 250
poems, 250
real world materials, 249–250
text sets, 251
Logical-mathematical intelligence, 148–150, 155
Loss of appetite, 26
Low-context communication, 33
Low-context culture, 33–34
Lozanov, Georgi, 94–95

M

Maestro, Betsy, 251
Magic School Bus, 170
Main idea table, 247
Malam, John, 250
Manipulatives, math teaching, 325–328
Marking code, writing, 278
Materialism, as cultural value, 23
Mathematics, 317–341
algebraic thinking, sample lesson, 338–339
auditory learning style, 337
children's literature, 336–337
Common Core State Standards, domains, 321–324
cooperative learning, 333–334
cultural connections, 334
daily life situations, 325
data analysis, probability, sample lesson, 339–340
demonstration, 324
directions, giving, 331
drawings, 328
four-step problem solving, 329–330
geometry, sample lesson, 337–338
interdisciplinary connections, 334
Internet field trips, 335–336
kinesthetic learning style, 337
literature in, 336–337
manipulatives, 325–328
measurement, sample lesson, 338
notations, 331–332
number sense concepts, operations, sample lesson, 339
pairing up, 332–333
prior knowledge, 324–325
sample lessons, 337–340
strategies, 324–337
thinking aloud, 330
Third International Mathematics and Science Study, 319
total physical response, 334–335
visual learning style, 337
wait time, 329
word bank charts, 332
word problems, 331
rewriting, 330
Mathematics websites, 335–336
Matrix, instructional strategies, 449–451
Maynard, Christopher, 250
Measurement, sample lesson, 338
Megabytes, defined, 418
Megahertz, defined, 418
Memory, defined, 418
Metacognitive teaching strategies, 169

Microskills in listening, 162
Miscues
    analysis, 254
    interpreting, 254–256
    marking, 256
Mnemonic associations, 210–211
Models of integrated approaches, 133
The Modern Language Journal, 413
Monitor, defined, 418
Monitor hypothesis, 87–89
Monochronics, 41
Motor skills, 264
Mouse, defined, 418
*Multicultural Education in Pluralistic
    Society,* 45
Multicultural issues, 1–80
    American values, 21–24
        concept of "American," 21
    cultural facts, 79–80
        colors, 80
        numbers, 80
    culture, 13–16
        ethnocentrism, 14–15
        historical overview, 14
        role of, 15
    culture characteristics, 55–78
        Asian cultures, 72
        cultural awareness, 75
        cultural classroom activities, 76–78
        Haitian students, 68–69
        Islamic cultures, 62–66
        Native Americans, 74–75
        Spanish-speaking cultures, 58–60
        speakers of Arabic, 62–66
    culture shock, 25–29
        acculturation, 28
        recovering from, 28
    immigrants, 49–53
        culturally appropriate behavior, 52
        life before United States, 51
        Students with Interrupted Formal
            Education, 52–53
    language, 17–20
        deep culture, 18–20
        surface culture, 18–20
    learning styles, 43–48
        cultural differences, 46–47
        strategies, 47
    multicultural education, 3–11
        background, 4–5
        curriculum, 5
        defining, 5
        parental involvement, 5
        sample activities, 7–11
    nonverbal communication, 37–42
        eye contact, 40–41

    gestures, 39–40
    proxemics, 39
    refugees, 49–53
        culturally appropriate behavior, 52
        defined, 50–51
        life before United States, 51
        Students with Interrupted Formal
            Education, 52–53
    verbal communication, 31–36
        high-context culture, 33
        low-context culture, 33
Multicultural Pavilion, 413
Multiple intelligences
    inventory of, 154–157
    learning styles, 147–148
Multiple levels of language proficiency,
    listening activities, 173–174
Music, 139
Musical intelligence, 148, 150–151, 154

N
NABE-National Association for
    Bilingual Education, 413
NAEP. *See* National Assessment of
    Educational Progress
Narratives, writing, 270
National Assessment of Educational
    Progress, 357
National Science Education Standards,
    355, 361, 373
Native American culture, cultural
    characteristics, 73–75
Native language flash cards, 211
Native speech as spoken language
    source, 169
Natural order hypothesis, 87, 89
Natural teaching approach, 101–102
    Krashen's monitor model, 87–89, 101
    mainstream classroom use, 102
Naturalistic intelligence, 148, 153, 157
New Mexico State University Library,
    413
Newcomer Programs, 52
Next Generation Science Standards,
    355–358, 361–364, 369, 373
NGSS. *See* Next Generation Science
    Standards
Nine-Curt, Carmen Judith, 33–34
Nonverbal communication, 37–42
    eye contact, 40–41
    gestures, 39–40
    proxemics, 39
Notations, mathematic, 331–332
Notes, writing, 270

Nouns
    count/noncount, 296, 299
    plural, 123
    singular, 123
NSES. *See* National Science Education
    Standards
Number sense concepts, operations,
    sample lesson, 339
Number tiles, 327
Numbers, cultural significance of, 80

O
Oberg, Kalvero, 14
Objectives of language, 53
Observation chart, 199
Observation matrix, 195–196
Office of English Language Learning
    and Migrant Education, 53
Office of Refugee Resettlement, 50–51
Online discussion forums, 413
Online ESL Grammar Exercises and
    Quizzes, 414–416
Online portfolio, 412
Oral, written language, contrasted,
    269–270
Oral development, 181–202
    advanced speaking activity, 193
    anecdotal observations, checklists,
        197
    assessment, 195–200
    beginning speaking activities,
        192–193
    CD-ROMs, 191
    choral reading, 191
    content area instruction, 191–195
    games, 189
    intermediate speaking activities, 193
    jokes, 190
    language arts, 191–195
    math, 193–194
    observation chart, 199
    observation matrix, 195–196
    poetry, 188–189
    pronunciation skills, 188
    recording studio, 190
    research, 182–184
    riddles, 190
    science, 194
    show-and-tell, 189–190
    social studies, 194–195
    songs, 189
    speaking difficulties, 184–187
    speech errors, correcting, 200–201
    spoken language models, 184

Student Oral Language Observation Matrix, 195
television, 191
tools, 187–191
videotapes, 191
Order forms, writing, 270
ORR. *See* Office of Refugee Resettlement
Oxford Picture Dictionary for Content Areas, 216–218

P

P-SELL. *See* Promoting Science Among ELLs
Paragraph organization, 284–285
Paragraph pyramid, 285–286
Paragraph structure, 286
Paralinguistics, 39
Parallel port, defined, 418
Parent-family connection, 391
Parental involvement, 5
Partnership for Assessment of Readiness for College and Careers, 309
Past orientation, as cultural value, 23
Past perfect tense, 122
Pattern blocks, 326
Pattern writing, 281–282
Pedagogy, 376–377
Peer buddies, 315
Performance assessment, 147
Peripheral, defined, 418
Personal journals, writing, 270
Personal letters, writing, 270
Personality types, grouping by, 115–116
Phishing, defined, 418
Phrasal verbs, 299
Piaget, Jean, 86
Picture flash cards, 211
Pixel, defined, 418
Planning instruction, 125–158
  content, language integration, 127–133
    models, 129
  curriculum, 135–158
    alternative assessment, 146–147
    assessment, 145–146
    Bloom's taxonomy, revised, 141–143
    classifying objectives, 140–141
    content, 143–144
    goals, 139–140
    instructional objectives, 139–140
    instructional procedures, 144–145
    interdisciplinary, content-based thematic units, 137–139

materials, 145
multiple intelligences, 147–157
principles, 136–137
teacher reflection, 147
Plural nouns, 123
Poetry, 188–189
Polacco, Patricia, 7
Polychronic individuals, 41
Portfolio assessment, 147
Posttraumatic stress disorder, 52
Practice, 130
Prepositions, 296, 299
Present participle verbs, 92
Present perfect tense, 122
Present progressive verb, 121
  use of, 120
Presentation software, 411
Prewriting, 276–277
Primary trait scoring, writing, 287
Probability, sample lesson, 339–340
Process characteristics, in listening comprehension, 163
Process writing, 262–263, 276–277
Professional organizations, 413
Program, defined, 418
Programs for Students with Interrupted Formal Education, 52–53
Progressiveness, as cultural value, 23
Promoting Science Among ELLs, project, 359
Promotion of own benefit, as cultural value, 23
Pronouncing words, 211
Pronouns, impersonal, 121
Pronunciation skills, 188
Providing comprehensible input, 130
Proxemics, 38–39
Psycholinguistic perspective, 226–227
Psychomotor domain, 140–141
PTSD. *See* Posttraumatic stress disorder
Publishing writing, 279
Pull out models, 53
Push in models, 53
The PuzzleMaker, 414–416

Q

Qualifiers, 299
Question dial, 277
Questions game, 302–303

R

Radio presentations, as spoken language source, 169
RAM, defined, 418
Reactions to culture shock, 26

Reader's theater, 270
Reading activities, integrated grammar, 122–123
Reading development, 223–260
  alphabetic writing system, 238
  beginning readers
    characteristics of, 238
    choral speaking, 241–242
    language experience approach, 240–241
    literature circles, 242–243
    read alouds, 241
    shared reading, 243–244
    strategies, 240–245
    thematic units, 244
  Bloom's taxonomy, revised, 141–143, 231–233
  cohesive ties, 228
  confirming meanings, 248
  ESL reading rubric, 257
  graphic organizers, 246–247
    attribute wheel, 246
    character map, 246
    decision-making model, 246
    main idea table, 247
    sequence chain, 247
    story map, 247
    Venn diagram, 246
    web, 247
  higher order thinking skills, 231–233
  inference, 248
  interactive perspective, 229–230
  interactive process, 225
  intermediate learners, 244–248
    directed reading-thinking activity, 244–245
    graphic organizers, 245
    learning logs, 245, 247–248
  intermediate readers, characteristics of, 238–239
  journal log, 248
  learning objectives, 231–233
  literacy instruction, critical reading, 230–231
  literacy reporter sheet, 243
  literature selection, 248–251
    concept books, 250
    materials, 249–250
    pattern books, 250
    poems, 250
    real world materials, 249–250
    text sets, 251
  logographic writing system, 238
  miscues
    interpreting, 254–256
    marking, 256

psycholinguistic perspective, 226–227

questioning techniques, 231–233

reading assessments, 251–252
   anecdotal records of classroom observation, 251–252
   informal reading inventory, 253
   miscue analysis, 254
   running records, 257
   self-assessment, 256–257

reading difficulties, 235–239

reading logs, 258

research, 224–226

Rosenblatt's transactional theory of reading, 228–229

schema theory, 227

sheltered, effective instruction contrasts, 239
   shared features, 240
   unique features, 240

social interactionist perspective, 230

social process, 225

syllabic writing system, 238

theories, 225–226

think-aloud checklist, 253

transactional theory of reading, 228–229

Reading logs, 258

Reading rubric, 257

Record-keeping journal, writing, 270

Recording studio, 190

Recording thoughts, 139

Recovering from culture shock, 28

Red Riding Hood, 214

Reform in science education, 361–362

Refugee Children School Impact Grant Program, 51

Refugees, 49–53
   Bureau of Citizenship and Immigrations Services, 50
   culturally appropriate behavior, 52
   defined, 50–51
   interrupted formal education, 52–53
   life before U.S., 51
   Newcomer Programs, 52
   Office of Refugee Resettlement, 50–51
   Refugee Children School Impact Grant Program, 51

Reinforcement, 84

Reliability of websites, 412–417

Resolution, 418

Respect lesson, 382–383

Response to intervention model, 387

Review of material, 130

Revision, 277–279

Riddles, 190

Right hemisphere societies, communication in, 33–34

Role of culture, 15

Role playing, 120–121

ROM, defined, 418

Rosenblatt's transactional theory of reading, 228–229

RTI. *See* Response to intervention

Running records, 257

S

Sample lesson plan, water cycle, 453–469

Sample theme web, 140

Sample unit study, 483–503

Samples of writing, 264–265

Saving face, as cultural value, 23

Scale, 328

Scanner, defined, 418

Schedule for center by group, 424–448

Schema theory, reading, 227

Scholastic, 414–415

School community involvement, 5

Science, 355–374
   achievement gap, 357–358
   adolescent learners, 371–373
   contextualized instruction, 368–370
   cooperative learning, 366–368
   discourse, 364–365
   education reform, 361–362
   home language, 365–366
   informal conversations, 364–365
   language support strategies, 363–364
   literacy strategies, 363
   National Assessment of Educational Progress, 357
   National Science Education Standards, 355, 361, 373
   Next Generation Science Standards, 355–358, 361–364, 369, 373
   research projects, 358–360
   science language usage, 371–373
   scientific literacy, 361–362
   teaching strategies, 363–368, 370–371, 373–374

Science Instruction for All, project, 359

Scoring writing, 287–288
   analytical scoring, 287–288
   holistic scoring, 287
   primary trait scoring, 287

Scripting strategies, 266–268
   developmental, 266

Scripts, 270
   writing, 270

SDAIE. *See* Specially designed academic instruction in English

Seeds of Science/Roots of Reading, project, 359

Self-assessment, 256–257

Self-help, as cultural value, 23

Semantic feature analysis, 214

Semantic maps, 211

Sentence combining, 296

Sentence construction, 299

Sequence chain, 247

Serial port, defined, 418

Sesame Street, 170

Shared writing, 279–281

Sheltered instruction, 53, 130, 133, 239–240

Sheltered instruction observation protocol model, 130–131, 133

Shiritori word game, 303

Shock, culture, 25–29
   acculturation, 28
   recovery from, 28

Show-and-tell, 189–190

SIFA. *See* Science Instruction for All

SIFE. *See* Programs for Students with Interrupted Formal Education

Silent way, 95–96
   mainstream classroom use, 95–96

Simple present verb, use of, 120

Singular nouns, 123

SIOP model. *See* Sheltered instruction observation protocol model

Skinner, B.F., 84

Sleep pattern, 26

Slobin, Dan, 86

Smarter Balanced Assessments, 309

Snap cubes, 327

Social language, 53

Social nature of writing, 263–264

Social network, defined, 418

Social process, reading as, 225

Social studies, 194–195, 375–383
   geography lesson, 377–380
      handout, 380
   global perspectives, 376
   justice lesson, 380–382
   pedagogy, 376–377
   respect lesson, 382–383

Sociolinguistic competence, 109

Software, presentation, 411

SOLOM. *See* Student Oral Language Observation Matrix

Songs, 189, 212

Spanish-speaking culture, cultural characteristics, 57–60

Speaking activities
  advanced, 193
  beginning, 192–193
  intermediate, 193
Speaking difficulties, 184–187
Special education, 385–404
  disabilities, students with, 386–388
    Common Core Standards, 398–404
    educational services, 388–389
    instruction, 389
  Ford-Harris matrix of multicultural
    gifted education, 394–398
  gifted potential characteristics,
    392–393
  gifted students, 389–390
    challenging, 394–398
    differentiated instruction, 398
    differentiation planning sheet, 399
    identification of, 391–393
  initial referrals, 390
  parent-family connection, 391
  referral procedures, 390–391
  response to intervention model, 387
  teacher perceptions, 390
Specially designed academic instruction
  in English, 130, 133, 239
Speech errors, correcting, 200–201
Spiritualism, as cultural value, 23
Spoken language models, 184
Spoken language types, 169
Stages in language proficiency, 174
Stages of culture shock, 27–28
Standards, 307–315
  character trait chart, 313
  Common Core State Standards, 309,
    312–315
    by domain, 321–324
  defined, 309–310
  gifted students, Common Core,
    398–404
  incorporation, unpacking approach,
    310–311
  Lau v. Nichols case, 308
  National Science Education
    Standards, 355, 361, 373
  Next Generation Science Standards,
    355–358, 361–364, 369, 373
  planning lessons, 311–312
  strategies, 312–315
  students with disabilities, Common
    Core, 398–404
  teaching, 307–315
  TESOL, 171, 174–175
Start button, defined, 418
Status, cultural value, 23

Stimulus, 84
Story map, 247
Strategic competence, 109–111
Structural analysis, vocabulary, 213
Structured controversial dialogues,
  writing, 283–284
Structured controversies, writing,
  282–283
Student Oral Language Observation
  Matrix, 195
Student-selected groups, grouping by,
  116
Styles of learning, 43–48
  cultural differences, 46–47
  field-independent behavior, field-
    sensitive behavior, contrasted,
    46
  teacher strategies, 47
Subject, verb agreement, 296
Suggestopedia, 94–95
  mainstream classroom use, 95
Surface culture, 18–20
Syllabic writing system, 238

T

Tangrams, 326
Tannen, Deborah, 32
Task-based approach, 197
Task characteristics, in listening
  comprehension, 163
Taskbar, defined, 418
Teacher guides and activities K–12,
  414–416
Teacher schedules, block programming,
  53
Teachers of English to Speakers of
  Other Languages. See TESOL
Teachersfirst.com, 414–416
Team topple game, 304
Technology, 405–419
  activities using, 411–412
  adult education, 416
  blogs, 411
  computer-assisted language learning,
    417
    software sources, 417
  elementary school, 414
  email, 412
  high school, 415–416
  for high school, 410–411
  for intermediate grades, 409–410
  language communication practice,
    408–409
  lesson plans, 414

  for middle school, 414–415
  online discussion forums, 413
  online portfolio, 412
  presentation software, 411
  for primary grades, 409
  problems, 412
  professional organizations, journals,
    413
  reliability of websites, 412–417
  role of teacher, 407–408
  students websites K–12, 417
  technology-teaching techniques,
    413–414
  vocabulary, 417–418
  web pages, 413–417
  Web Quest, 412
Telephone messages, as spoken
  language source, 169
Television presentations, 169, 191
Tense
  future tense, 121
  past perfect tense, 122
  present perfect tense, 122
  verb tenses, 299
Terminology, "American," 21
Terrell, Tracy, 101
TESL-EJ Master Page, 413
TESL Electronic Discussion Lists and
  Newsgroups, 413
TESOL, 171, 174–175, 179–180, 413,
  417
TESOL CALL-IS software, 417
TESOL Inc. Home Page, 413
Text characteristics, in listening
  comprehension, 163
Theater, reader's, 270
Theme phrases, sample, 138
Theme web, sample, 139
Theme words, sample, 138
Theory of multiple intelligences,
  147–148
Thesis, writing, 270
Think-aloud checklist, 253
Thinking aloud, 330
Third International Mathematics and
  Science Study, 319
Thoughts, recording, 139
Time, as cultural value, 23
Time line, 285
TIMSS. See Third International
  Mathematics and Science Study
Top down processing, 164
Torture, victims of, 50
Total physical response, 96–101, 109,
  165, 334–335

mainstream classroom use, 97
vocabulary, 212–213, 220
TPR. *See* Total physical response
Tracking student assessments, 471–482
Tradition, as cultural value, 23
Transactional theory, reading, 228–229
Treats, making, tasting, 131–132
Triman compass, 327
Twenty questions game, 304
Two-color counters, 328
Two-dimensional works of art, 139
Types of spoken language, 169
casual chats, 169
face-to-face interactions, 169
formal lectures, 169
native speakers' speech, 169
radio presentations, 169
telephone messages, 169
TV presentations, 169

U

UCIEP-University and College
Intensive English Programs, 413
Unaccompanied minors, 50
Unfamiliar environment. *See* Culture
shock
Unfamiliar vocabulary, 208
Unifix cubes, 327
Unit study sample, 483–503
University of California, 413
University of State of Colorado, 413
Unpacking approach, standards,
310–311

V

Values, cultural, contrasts in, 23
Vandergrift, Larry, 164
Venn diagram, 246
Verbal communication, 31–36
high-context culture, 33–34
left hemisphere societies, 33–34
low-context culture, 33–34
right hemisphere societies, 33–34
Verbal frequency types, 216
Verbal intelligence, 154
Verbs
followed by gerund, 299
followed by infinitive, 299
forms, 299
present progressive, 121
simple present, use of, 120
subject agreement, 296
tenses, 296, 299

Victims of human trafficking, 50
Victims of torture, 50
Videotapes, 191
Virus, defined, 418
Visual discrimination, 264
Visual learning style, 337
Visual map, 276
Visual-spatial intelligence, 148, 150,
155
Visualizing words, 211
Vocabulary development, 203–222
assessment, 221
beginning level, 209–210
content areas, 216–222
beginning vocabulary activity, 220
elementary grades, 220
total physical response, teaching
vocabulary, 220
Word Wall, 216
dictionary use, 2
difficulty with, 204–205
difficulty with vocabulary, 204–205
enrichment packets, 211
explicit instruction, 205–206
flash cards, 211
native language, 211
picture, 211
games, 212
incidental learning, 205
independent strategy development,
206–207
intermediate learners, 213
mnemonic associations, 210–211
research, 205
semantic feature analysis, 214
semantic maps, 211
skills, 207–209
songs, 212
strategies, 206–209
structural analysis, 213
techniques, 209–216
total physical response, 212–213
vocabulary learning, defined,
204–207
Vygotsky, L.S., 230

W

Wait time, 329
Water cycle lesson plan, 453–469
Web, as graphic organizer, 247
sample, 140
Web pages, 413–417
Web Quest, 412
Websites, reliability of, 412–417

Wikipedia, defined, 418
Windows, defined, 418
Wood, Audrey, 242
Word bank charts, 332
Word choice, 296, 299
Word endings, 296
Word problems, 331
rewriting, 330
Word Wall, 216
Word webs, 211
Work orientation, as cultural value, 23
World Wide Web, defined, 418
World Wide Web Virtual Library, 413
Writing development, 261–293
alphabetic writing, development of,
265–270
assessment, 286–289
beginning writers, 272–274
biliteracy development, assessment,
289–291
drafting, 277
editing, 278–279
holistic scoring rubric, 288
integrated language assessment, 286
intermediate writers, 274–275,
281–286
journal writing, 281
language transfer, 272
linguistic error, 272
literacy perspective, 264
marking code, 278
oral, written language, contrasted,
269–270
paragraph organization, 284–285
paragraph pyramid, 285–286
paragraph structure, 286
pattern writing, 281–282
prewriting, 276–277
process writing, 262–263, 276–277
publishing, 279
question dial, 277
research, 262
revising, 277–279
samples, 264–265, 273
scoring, 287–288
analytical scoring, 287–288
holistic scoring, 287
primary trait scoring, 287
scripting strategies, 266–268
developmental, 266
self-assessment, 288–289
shared writing, 279–281
skills, 270–272
social nature, 263–264
strategies, 276–281

structured controversial dialogues, 283–284
structured controversies, 282–283
subskills, 264
    auditory discrimination, 264
    motor skills, 264
    visual discrimination, 264

tasks, 286–287
time line, 285
types of classroom writing, 270
visual map, 276
Writing samples, 273
Writing skills, 139
Writing tasks, 286–287
Writing words, 211

Y

You Just Don't Understand, 32

Z

Zones of comfort, 190
Zones of proximal development, 137